THE ILLUSTRATED ENCYCLOPEDIA OF WORLD BOXING

Peter Arnold

GALLERY BOOKS
An Imprint of W. H. Smith Publishers Inc.
112 Madison Avenue
New York City 10016

Foreword

Every now and then there are stories in the newspapers about people who would like to see boxing banned. Most of them want to prevent boxers coming to harm. It does them no good, they say. Well, all I can say is that it never did me any harm, and I'm sure my life now is a lot better than it would have been had I taken some other less strenuous job. And I've enjoyed every minute of it . . . well, almost.

Despite the do-gooders, boxing seems to be as popular as ever it was. People still talk of the Hagler–Leonard fight two years afterwards. Everybody likes to talk of the heroes of the old days, but there are plenty of good new boxers still coming along. We've got a few in Britain and I hope some of them win world titles and get their names in books like this one.

Of course a lot of the boxing news in the second half of 1988 was about Mike Tyson and what has been happening to him outside the ring. Boxers' private lives were always good for the papers — and that's another thing you can say for boxing. The papers wouldn't be full of stories about Mike Tyson if he were the heavyweight champion of tiddleywinks, would they?

I can sympathize a bit with Tyson because I had my troubles with managers and contracts and the like and got plenty of publicity I didn't much care for. At the time I'm writing Tyson has just fought Frank Bruno, and the papers had been saying he was fat and out of shape. Of course, when he stepped into the ring he was 100 per cent fit. Because in boxing you should never take a chance. Never underestimate your opponent. When you climb in the ring there's only you and him up there. You don't want to be feeling one degree under. The talking has stopped by then. You've got no friends to help, and nowhere to hide. It's down to the basics, and all you've got to rely on is your own skill, strength and guts, and pray for a bit of luck, perhaps. That's why the public will always watch boxing. And when the fight's over, the discussion starts — and that's why they'll always read books like this, too.

John Conteh

***Left:** John Conteh was one of Britain's best post-war champions. He was WBC light-heavyweight champion for about three years, and suffered only four defeats, at the end of his career.*

House Editor: Pat Pierce
Editor: Donna Wood
Art Editor: Chris Walker
Production: Craig Chubb
Picture Research: Moira McIlroy

Published by
GALLERY BOOKS
An imprint of W.H. Smith Publishers Inc.
112 Madison Avenue, New York
New York 10016

ISBN 0-8317-2789-6

Typeset in 10/11pt Times by Quadraset Limited

Printed and bound in Hong Kong

Contents

Beginnings and Prize Ring Days	6
The Heavyweights and Cruiserweights	28
The Light-Heavyweights and Super-Middleweights	78
The Middleweights and Light-Middleweights	90
The Welterweights and Light-Welterweights	112
The Lightweights and Junior Lightweights	128
The Featherweights and Light-Featherweights	140
The Bantamweights and Light-Bantamweights	152
The Flyweights and the Smaller Men	162
The Great Boxers	172
The Big Fights	208
Records	218
Bibliography	252
Index	253
Acknowledgements	256

***Left:** Mike Tyson began his fighting career in March 1985, since when he has built up an awesome reputation for deadly punching power.*

ΝΙΚΟΣΘΕΝΕΣ ΕΠΟΙΕΣΕΝ

Beginnings and Prize Ring Days

Although boxing can be traced back to the ancient Greeks and Romans, there was a long hiatus in its history, and the sport as we know it today has its ancestry in the growing popularity of bare-knuckle fighting in England in the 17th century. James Figg became the first acknowledged champion of the prize ring, as it became called, and was succeeded by famous men who became in turn the toast of the 'Fancy' — the aristocracy, including royalty, the politicians, the poets, novelists and the men-about-town who flocked to the fights. Sailors took the sport to America, where John L. Sullivan became a national hero. But by the end of the 19th century the prize-ring had been replaced by the more formal boxing to the new rules devised by the Marquess of Queensberry.

Left: *Naked Greek boxers shown on a vase by Nikosthenes in the British Museum. They are wearing oxhide binding laced around their hands to form a kind of glove. The date is around 525 B.C., about 150 years after boxing became an event in the ancient Olympic Games.*

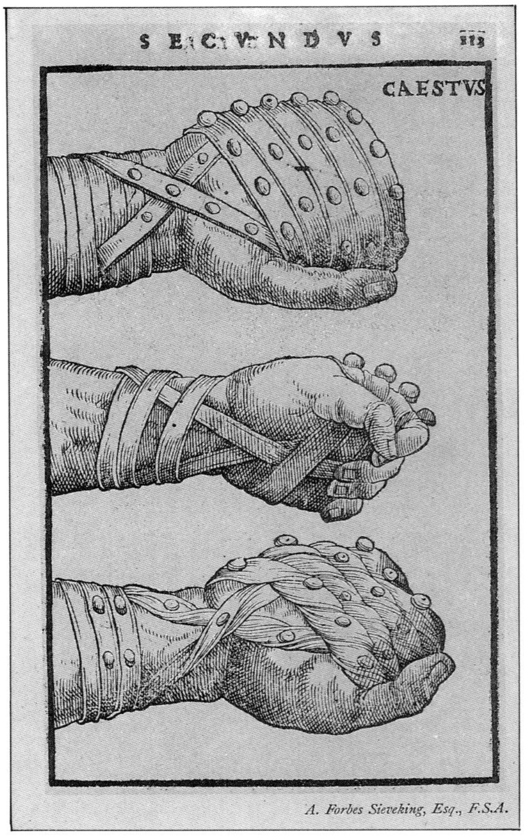

A. Forbes Sieveking, Esq., F.S.A.

Right: *Examples of the* caestus, *introduced into boxing by the Romans. The* caestus *was a gauntlet made of thongs studded with iron, which could cause the death of a boxer.*

Fighting with the fists is a natural activity that must have been invented as soon as the first man on earth was threatened by his neighbour and found there was no handy stick or stone nearby. When men began to feel pride in their ability with their fists, and tested themselves against their neighbours without the need of a threat or an argument, and when perhaps other men realized the pleasure of watching such scraps, then boxing as a sport was born.

Slabs found in a temple at Khafaje, near Baghdad in Mesopotamia, show Sumerians fighting with fists tied in leather thongs perhaps 5,000 years ago. Egyptian hieroglyphics of a little later also suggest soldiers fought each other in fistic combat with thongs tied round their fists.

The Greeks and Romans practised man-to-man combat. The word 'pugilism' (the practice of fighting with the fists) comes from the Latin *pugil* (a boxer), from *pugnus* (a fist), and *pugnare* (to fight). The first blossoming of pugilism as a spectator sport came in about 900 B.C., and it proved a brutal practice. Theseus, the son of the Greek monarch Aegeus, devised a bloodthirsty show. The young warriors of the monarch, fit and strong men, were made to fight for the entertainment of the crowds at the many holidays and festivals. They sat facing each other on flat stones in the arena, fists enclosed in leather thongs. On a signal they would pummel each other, and manpower being cheap, the fights were usually to the death. When one man had been knocked unconscious, the other continued to punch until he was awarded the victory on his opponent's death.

Of course, this took a long time, and the sight of one man battering an opponent insensible was not particularly thrilling, so a means was needed to speed up the contests. The thongs were studded with metal, and the device was called a *caestus*. Only a few blows were required to render a man senseless, when his complete despatch would be reasonably quick. The studs became spikes called *myrmekes*, and, clearly, the winner would be almost always the first man to get in a good, face-smashing blow. One champion, Theagenes of Thásos, is reckoned to have destroyed over 1,000 opponents.

THE HEROES OF THE FANCY

Records were kept of the Olympic Games from 760 B.C., so it is known that pugilism came on the programme of events in 688 B.C., with a fighter called Onamastus being the first Olympic champion. The bouts were not to the death, and the contestants even wore ear guards as protection. The more cruel, gladiatorial shows continued, however, and even in the Olympic Games a battle called the *pancratium* (a complete contest) was introduced — complete in the sense that practically everything was legal.

The gladiatorial battles to the death remained a feature of the big public feast days and of the funeral games of famous Greeks and Romans. The great exponents were honoured in song and speech and were the heroes of the day. Winners were given exotic prizes, such as captive maidens. When the Romans conquered Greece, they devised more and more efficient forms of *caestus* and eliminated the Greek warriors.

Eventually, it began to dawn on the Roman emperors that killing off some of their best warriors for the entertainment of the public was not the best way to build an army, so the *caestus* was banned, but this, of course, took away much of the appeal of the combat as a spectator sport. Even fighting without the *caestus* began to decline in the years before Christ was born. The Olympic Games themselves were terminated in A.D. 393 by the Roman Emperor, Theodosius I, and, eventually, pugilism, as a pastime and spectacle, died out.

The big mystery concerning the history of boxing is why there should be no further records of pugilism until the 17th century. It seems as if the brutality of the *caestus* had killed the sport entirely.

Boxing's revival in England

Boxing resurfaced again in England, where it was closely associated with fencing and the use of the backsword and quarterstaff. It became common for men to settle grudges with their fists, and even to box for fun or for small bets. The masters who taught the 'noble science of defence' began to teach the use of the fists, and to give exhibitions of boxing when giving demonstrations of swordplay.

Fist-fighting became a popular form of entertainment and those who fancied their proficiency started to make a spectacle of it and to make money. Roaming the countryside, they would issue challenges at towns and villages, inviting anybody to do battle to a knockdown or a fall for, say, a guinea. The usual practice was to travel in a party of two or three to fairs or carnivals. The boxers would attract a crowd, which was invited to hold a rope and form a ring, announce one of their number as the champion of this or that village, and issue the challenge. The practice for a local youth accepting the challenge was to 'throw his cap into the ring', a phrase which is still used to denote a challenge of any sort. Should nobody be brave enough to challenge, two of the boxers would provide an exhibition match. Whoever fought, the onlookers would be asked to show their appreciation by contributing to a collection for the combatants. At the end of the fair, the party would move on to another village.

There were few rules, if any, and the contests were what might be called a 'rough and tumble'. Anything was allowed provided the spectators would stand for it, and in those early days in England the spectators were really the referees as well. The British instinct for fair play was what allowed the bare-knuckle boxing to flourish. Gradually, kicking, biting, eye-gouging and hitting a man when he was down came to be outlawed. Wrestling was an essential part of the battle, but grabbing and hitting below the waist were frowned upon. The boxers were stripped to the waist, so 'above and below the waist' were easily appreciated concepts. Bear-hugs were allowed, and a boxer could pick his opponent up and dash him to the ground. Grabbing by the hair (and punching with the other hand) was legal, as was gripping round the neck and strangling. A popular move was the cross-buttock, by which a boxer rammed his buttock into his opponent's crotch while grabbing his arm and tossing him over his shoulder.

The object was to put the opponent on the ground, either by a throw or a blow. At first that would terminate the fight, but later, when the concept of 'rounds' developed, that would end the round, and the boxer downed would be allowed 30 seconds' rest before coming back into the fray. A boxer downing a man was then allowed to reap full reward for his efforts by falling on him as heavily as possible. Gradually, men would become so proficient that they would acquire some local fame, and their friends and acquaintances would support them in putting up money to challenge other local champions. The money for the winner would be kept in a 'purse', which is still the term used for prize-money in many sports. The sport became known as the 'prize ring'.

Naturally, the nobility and squirearchy became proud of outstanding boxers in their locality, and began to patronize them. Outstanding performers would be taken onto the staff of the local member of the aristocracy. (These days companies, universities and even governments find posts for outstanding amateur sportsmen.) It is as a result of one such arrangement that we have the first report of a boxing match in England. *The Protestant Mercury* of January 1681 reported:

> Yesterday, a match of Boxing was performed before his Grace the Duke of Albemarle between the Duke's footman and a butcher. The latter won the prize, as he had done many times before, being accounted, though but a little man, the best at that exercise in England.

Boxing enriches the language

As boxing became more formalized and popular, so it gave more expressions to the language. The ring, for instance, became square because surging spectators holding the rope became unmanageable, so stakes were driven into the ground and the rope wound around them. The purse was attached to one of the stakes so that it was in view at all times to the boxers and their supporters. The money became 'stake money', a term used today in all forms of gambling, or methods of contributing to a prize — indeed, the most famous of all horse-races is the Derby Stakes.

A line was scratched across the centre of the ring, and it was to this line that the boxers had to make their way at the start of each round (at first, their seconds could help them). A boxer, therefore, had to 'toe the line', but if he could not, then he 'failed to

Left: *Roman boxers wearing the* caestus. *In the days of classical Rome boxing matches were frequently to the death, one blow to the temple with the iron-studded glove often being sufficient to kill the recipient.*

come up to scratch' — two expressions which are still widely used to signify an obligation in the first instance, and failure to meet it in the second.

As boxing became more and more a hobby of the aristocracy and the upper class (who called themselves 'The Fancy'), so a second ring was built outside the first to give these important people (who were possibly the patrons or sponsors of the boxers) an unhindered view, free of the ordinary spectators. For important matches this ring also included umpires (to see fair play — there was no such thing as a points decision), 'seconds', 'timekeepers' and 'whips'. Whips were men who held short whips to dissuade the crowd from trying to interfere with the fight. They were also used afterwards to persuade the public to contribute to collections for the boxers, and the 'whip-round' is still used for a collection of money for any purpose.

The seconds were so-called because they were second-line boxers, who might be called upon to provide a second bout if the first finished quickly. One second bent a knee for his man to rest upon between rounds, while the other was the 'bottle-man', who provided his boxer with a mouthwash.

The timekeeper would begin proceedings with a whistle or gong, and when a man went down, thus ending a round, he would start calculating the 30-second interval before he would blow his whistle or strike his gong for the next round. A boxer was given eight seconds from then to come up to scratch, and if he failed, was counted out of time, and lost. At first, it was permissible for the seconds to help a stricken man back, when he could immediately fall again, thus ending another round before it could begin and earning another rest. These apparently pointless conventions remained in force until the London Prize Ring Rules amended them in 1838.

The first champion

England was called 'The Cradle of Pugilism'. The man whose name has gone into the annals as the first Champion of England, which meant in those days Champion of the World, is James Figg, or Fig, of Thame in Oxfordshire. A master of the backsword and quarterstaff, he opened, in 1719, an academy in Tottenham Court Road, London called 'Figg's Amphitheatre'. He soon moved to Oxford Road (now Oxford Street) and the famous artist, William Hogarth, drew a business card for him, calling him the 'Master of ye Noble Science of Defence'.

Figg's fame is partly due to one of his clients, Captain Godfrey, who wrote about him and pressed his claim to be the champion of England. He was, in fact, far more adept as a cudgeller and fencer, but beat all who challenged him. Hogarth's famous picture of Southwark Fair, where all from kings to beggars disported, shows Figg challenging all-comers 'for money, for love, or a bellyful'.

Figg was challenged in 1727 by Ned Sutton the Pipe-maker, from Gravesend, who had fought Figg before, each man winning once. The decider was to be with bare fists and then cudgels, on the Bowling Green at Southwark. Sutton was winning, and odds of 4-1 were offered against Figg, when Figg forced Sutton to yield with an arm-lock. Figg easily won the match with the cudgels.

One of the battles in Figg's Amphitheatre featured a Venetian gondolier named Carini, a fearsome man who challenged all-comers. Bob Whitaker was deputed to see off the foreigner and, after being nearly overcome, did so with a blow of tremendous force to the stomach which winded the gondolier, who then retired.

Figg died, probably in 1734, and there were soon plenty of pretenders to his title. He had named one of his pupils, George Taylor the Barber, as his successor, and Taylor built his own booth in Tottenham Court Road, and listed the Prince of Wales among his patrons. However, Tom Pipes and Bill Gretting also claimed the title, and Pipes defeated Gretting on three occasions.

Another of Figg's pupils, Jack Broughton, also had ambitions. He had been a waterman at Bristol where Figg, attending the Fair with his fighters, had seen Broughton beat a bully and had invited him to return to London. Broughton now beat Pipes, Gretting and Taylor, and he was generally acknowledged as the new champion. He, too, opened a new amphitheatre at Oxford Road, backing on to the late Figg's, and advertised a great display including a 'battle royal' between 'the noted Buckhorse and seven or eight more' — a battle royal was a fight in which all the men enter the ring at once, the last remaining being the winner. The 'noted Buckhorse' was an ugly, misshapen boxer whose real name was John Smith. He appeared in many of Broughton's promotions, and was very tough and talented. This display of Broughton's was scheduled for the same day as a fight of Taylor's and the incensed Taylor immediately issued a challenge to Broughton. But Taylor finally decided on discretion, gave up his own booth and became the principal performer at Broughton's, to where his own performers followed him.

Broughton's most famous battle was with George Stevenson the Coachman, at Taylor's booth on 24 April 1741. Famed for his skill all over Yorkshire, Stevenson was persuaded to come to London to challenge Broughton, and was backed by none other than the Prince of Wales, largely because his brother, the Duke of Cumberland, was Broughton's patron. The young Stevenson (he was barely 20) fought bravely and well, but took a terrible beating which ended after 39 minutes with him unconscious and with broken ribs. Alas, he did not recover to return to Yorkshire, dying a month later — a month during which he and the dismayed Broughton ironically became friends.

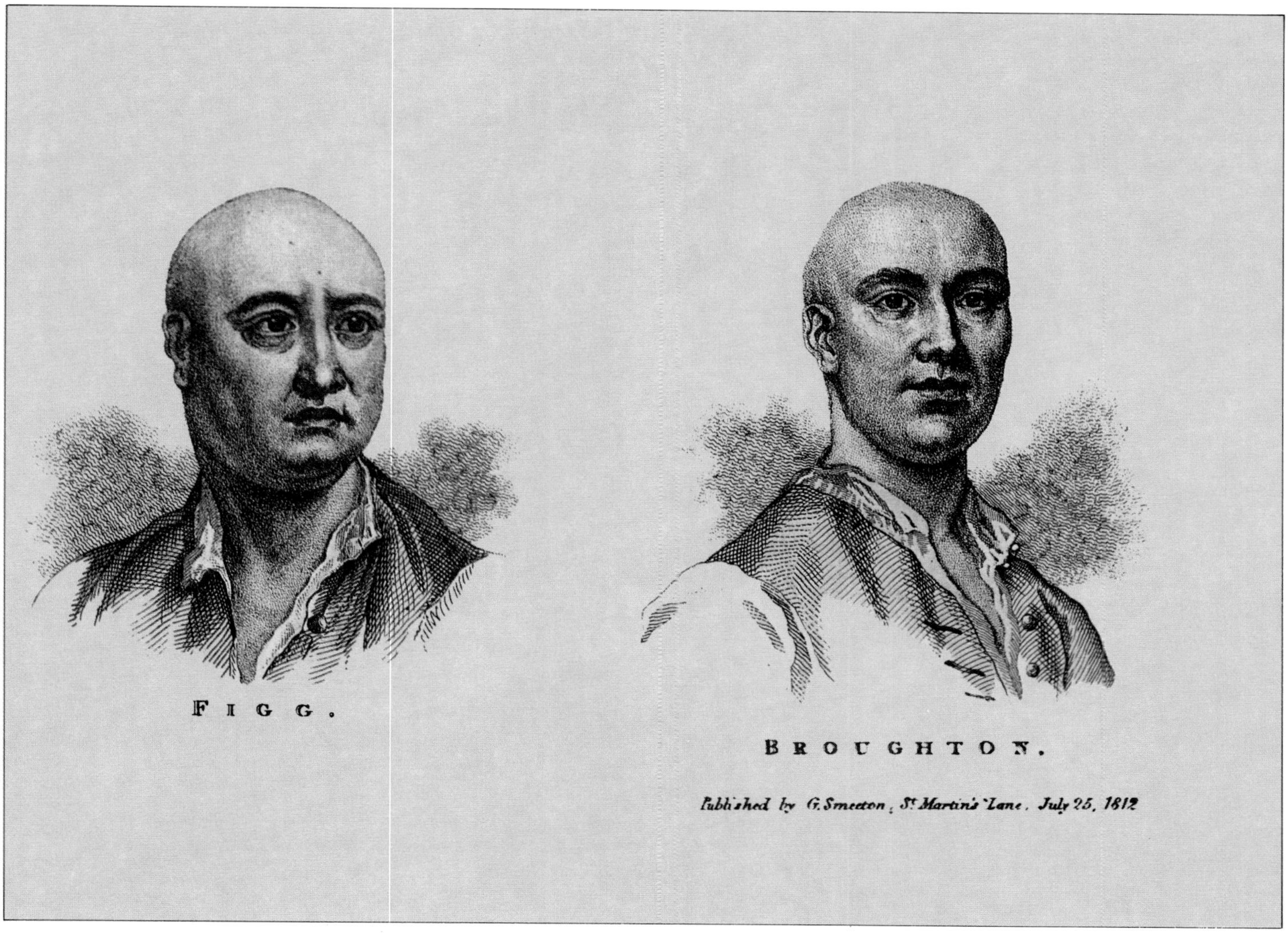

Above: *James Figg (left) and Jack Broughton, the first two generally acknowledged bare-knuckle champions of England. Figg opened the first boxing academy in London's Tottenham Court Road, in 1719, and Broughton drew up the first formal rules, in 1743.*

Broughton's Rules

To try to prevent such a tragedy happening again, Broughton drew up a set of rules, which were published on 16 August 1743. They were the first published boxing rules and, while meant for contests on his own premises, they received acceptance elsewhere, being used for many fights until modified in 1838. They read:

1. That a square of a yard be chalked in the middle of the stage; and every fresh set-to after a fall, or being parted from the rails, each second is to bring his man to the side of the square, and place him opposite to the other, and till they are fairly set to at the lines, it shall not be lawful for one to strike the other.

2. That, in order to prevent any disputes, the time a man lies after a fall, if the second does not bring his man to the side of the square within the space of half a minute, he shall be deemed a beaten man.

3. That in every main battle, no person whatever shall be upon the stage except the principals and their seconds; the same rule to be observed in by-battles, except that in the latter, Mr Broughton is allowed to be upon the stage to keep decorum, and to assist gentlemen in getting to their places, provided always he does not interfere in the battle; and whoever pretends to infringe these rules to be turned immediately out of the house. Everybody is to quit the stage as soon as the champions are stripped, before set-to.

4. That no champion be deemed beaten unless he fails coming up to the line in the limited time; or, that his own second declares him beaten. No second is to be allowed to ask his man's adversary any questions, or advise him to give out.

5. That in by-battles, the winning man to have two-thirds of the money given, which shall be publicly divided upon the stage notwithstanding any private agreements to the contrary.

6. That to prevent disputes in every main battle, the principals shall, on the coming on the stage, choose from among the gentlemen present, two umpires, who shall absolutely decide all disputes that may arise about the battle; and if the two umpires cannot agree, the said umpires to choose a third, who is to determine it.

7. That no person is to hit his adversary when he is down, or seize him by the hair, the breeches, or any part below the waist; a man on his knees to be reckoned down.

Broughton has been called 'The Father of British Boxing' for his work in bringing order to the sport, plus the fact that he was a great champion, who studied the art and brought a higher degree of skill to boxing than it had previously seen. He improved the technique

Right: *The first written rules of the prize ring as drawn up by Jack Broughton in 1743. Broughton wanted to prevent the kind of tragedy in which his opponent of two years earlier, George Stevenson, had died through taking excessive punishment.*

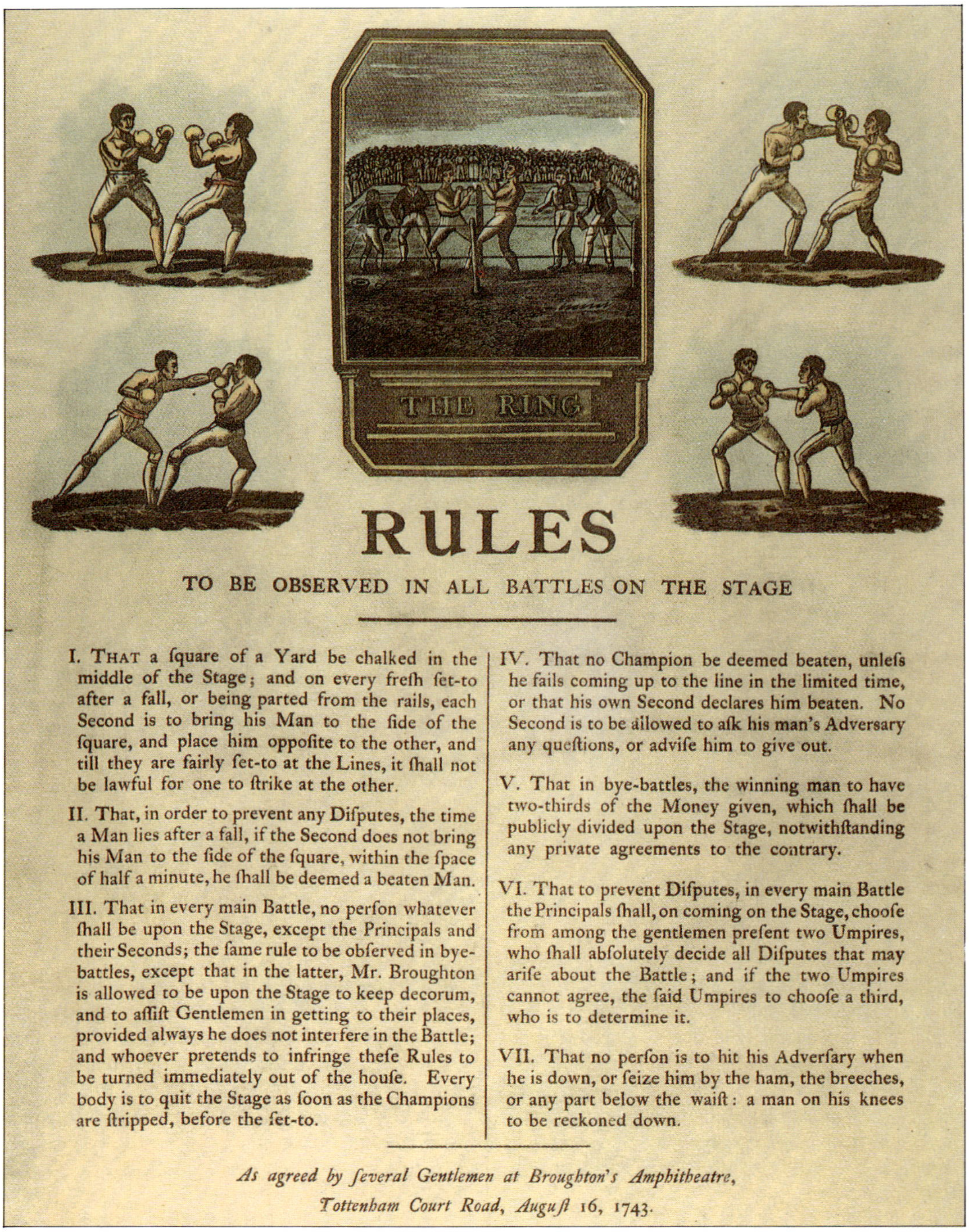

THE RING

RULES

TO BE OBSERVED IN ALL BATTLES ON THE STAGE

I. THAT a ſquare of a Yard be chalked in the middle of the Stage; and on every freſh ſet-to after a fall, or being parted from the rails, each Second is to bring his Man to the ſide of the ſquare, and place him oppoſite to the other, and till they are fairly ſet-to at the Lines, it ſhall not be lawful for one to ſtrike at the other.

II. That, in order to prevent any Diſputes, the time a Man lies after a fall, if the Second does not bring his Man to the ſide of the ſquare, within the ſpace of half a minute, he ſhall be deemed a beaten Man.

III. That in every main Battle, no perſon whatever ſhall be upon the Stage, except the Principals and their Seconds; the ſame rule to be obſerved in bye-battles, except that in the latter, Mr. Broughton is allowed to be upon the Stage to keep decorum, and to aſſiſt Gentlemen in getting to their places, provided always he does not interfere in the Battle; and whoever pretends to infringe theſe Rules to be turned immediately out of the houſe. Every body is to quit the Stage as ſoon as the Champions are ſtripped, before the ſet-to.

IV. That no Champion be deemed beaten, unleſs he fails coming up to the line in the limited time, or that his own Second declares him beaten. No Second is to be allowed to aſk his man's Adverſary any queſtions, or adviſe him to give out.

V. That in bye-battles, the winning man to have two-thirds of the Money given, which ſhall be publicly divided upon the Stage, notwithſtanding any private agreements to the contrary.

VI. That to prevent Diſputes, in every main Battle the Principals ſhall, on coming on the Stage, chooſe from among the gentlemen preſent two Umpires, who ſhall abſolutely decide all Diſputes that may ariſe about the Battle; and if the two Umpires cannot agree, the ſaid Umpires to chooſe a third, who is to determine it.

VII. That no perſon is to hit his Adverſary when he is down, or ſeize him by the ham, the breeches, or any part below the waiſt: a man on his knees to be reckoned down.

As agreed by ſeveral Gentlemen at Broughton's Amphitheatre, Tottenham Court Road, Auguſt 16, 1743.

of striking with the fist, which he realized could be a more potent weapon than the wrestling, throwing and mauling which made up much of the tactics of the day.

He lost his title in 1750 after a splendid career of at least ten years, during which he beat all-comers. Jack Slack, a butcher from Norwich, was a rough and ready fighter who was not suited by Broughton's rules. He was known as 'The First Knight of the Cleaver'. Slack met Broughton at Hounslow Races, insulted him, and on being threatened with a horsewhipping, challenged Broughton to a fight in the ring, which the champion accepted.

The fight was scheduled for 10 April 1750, but Broughton feared that Slack would not appear, and did not train. In fact, he felt obliged to send Slack ten guineas to ensure his presence, not wishing to disappoint his patrons. Slack did turn up, but Broughton's superiority was so obvious that the odds were soon 10-1 on him. However, after ten minutes or so Slack jumped forward and caught Broughton a downward chopper blow between the eyes, which closed them up and made him temporarily blind. Not realizing what had happened, and seeing Broughton groping about for his adversary, his patron, the Duke of Cumberland, who had wagered £10,000 on his man, exclaimed: 'What are you about, Broughton? You can't fight — you're beat.' To which Broughton replied: 'I can't see my man, your Highness. I am blind but not beat. Only let me be placed before my antagonist, and he shall not gain the day yet.' However, Slack flattened Broughton and his seconds threw in the sponge.

The disgusted Duke of Cumberland, convinced Broughton had sold the fight, turned his back on him and had his amphitheatre shut by law.

It was inevitable that the standards set by two such great champions as Figg and Broughton could not be maintained, and the next few years of prize fighting were unsavoury, full of suspected betting swindles and with even the championship bought and sold. Perhaps the best thing Slack did during his ten years as champion was to beat off another foreign challenge. This came from a 6ft 3in (1.91m) Frenchman known in England as simply Monsieur Pettit. At Hailston, in Norfolk, Pettit began by almost strangling Slack, who released himself with a kick. Several times Slack was hurled from the stage and pushed back by spectators, but Slack's powerful blows were the deciding factor. They became so famous that a knock-out punch became known as a 'Slack 'un'. After 25 minutes, with one eye closed and his face a bloody pulp, Monsieur Pettit bolted, and who can blame him?

Slack's style depended on kicking, gouging and throttling as much as punching, but he met his match on 17 June 1760, when he took on Bill Stevens the Nailer, at the tennis courts in the Haymarket, London. The fight was a hard one until Stevens tripped Slack, who was knocked out when his head struck the ring boards. The Duke of Cumberland, who had lost a fortune on Broughton's defeat by Slack, and was now Slack's backer, vowed he had again been sold out and turned his back on boxing for good.

Slack now returned to his butcher's business in Covent Garden, but exercised an influence on the prize ring by fixing fights. He trained George Meggs the Collier to beat Stevens, realized he couldn't, and so paid Stevens to lose. Although Stevens' patron was the Duke of York, he willingly admitted his duplicity, which he thought was more common sense than wickedness.

Meggs lost the title to George Millson the Baker, who was beaten by Tom Juchau the Paviour. He was beaten by Bill Darts the Dyer at Guildford, and Darts lost to Tom Lyons the Waterman at Kingston in a gruelling battle. Lyons thought so little of the title that he retired immediately and went back to ferrying passengers across the Thames, so Darts reclaimed the title.

An Irishman, Colonel Dennis O'Kelly, now came into the picture. He was a man of the turf, who owned one of the most famous racehorses of all time, Eclipse — he was also a great gambler. O'Kelly met a countryman, Peter Corcoran from Athoye, County Carlow, a strong man who was a coal-heaver and then a sailor, before he became a successful pugilist. O'Kelly arranged a championship match between Corcoran and Darts for Derby Day, 18 May 1771, on Epsom Downs. He paid Darts £100 to lose, and Darts, who had fought so bravely and well against Lyons, lost in one round. O'Kelly collected several thousand pounds in bets and Corcoran became the first of many Irish boxing champions.

Corcoran himself lost the title four years later in a match assumed to be fixed, although it lasted 30 rounds. It was fought at the Crown Inn, Staines, and Sellers won after Corcoran had put him down and appeared set to win. Sellers was champion for four years and he built up a reputation for bravery. When he lost to another Irishman, Duggan Fearns, after one and a half minutes and one blow, whereupon he declined to continue, it was generally regarded as a 'cross', or swindle, particularly as a lot of gambling money had changed hands.

Tom Johnson's honourable role

The whole concept of a champion was now thoroughly discredited, but luckily the prize ring was saved by a man who began to beat everybody he fought, and who, becoming champion by common consent, fought with integrity and brought honour back to the sport.

Tom Johnson, whose real name was Jackling, travelled to London when young and worked as a corn porter. He built up his strength by lifting and carrying sacks one-handed, and his strength was noted by all when he did a sick friend's work as well, carrying two sacks instead of one. Johnson was acknowledged champion from about 1783, his most famous battle coming in 1789. This was against Isaac Perrins, a giant coppersmith from Birmingham. Perrins, who had beaten all the pugilists from the Midlands, issued a challenge to all England for 500 guineas and was accepted by Johnson.

The fight took place at Banbury, Oxfordshire, and Perrins was favourite, largely because at 6ft 2in (1.88m) and around 240lb (109kg), he had advantages of about 5in (2cm) and 40lb (18kg). It was a tremendous battle, with Johnson undeterred and attacking the body instead of the head, his more usual target. After weakening Perrins, he launched an attack to the head, until Perrins' friends prevented him from going on — Perrins himself refusing to capitulate. The contest lasted 80 minutes, divided into 62 rounds.

Johnson finally lost his title to another big man, Benjamin Brain, who was known as 'Big Ben', although his actual height and weight has not been established. He was a collier in Bristol, where he had his first bare-knuckle battles before moving to London, because of lack of work, to become a coal porter. His first big fight was with a well-known pugilist, John Boone, who was known as the Fighting Grenadier. Brain, although practically blinded, just won. He continued to win his fights, mostly because of his 'bottom', which was the Fancy's name for raw courage and durability. He could only draw in a notorious contest with Bill Hooper the Tinman, because Hooper went down at every opportunity, and the match was finally declared a draw after three and a half hours and 80 rounds, when darkness fell. Otherwise, Brain had won all his fights when he met the champion, also unbeaten, at Wrotham,

Kent, in 1791. Although both men were good, scientific boxers, the match after a few rounds became one of passion and ferocity, with both men taking punishment. Johnson eventually broke his finger, and in desperation abandoned the sportsmanship he had exercised throughout his career, several times grabbing Brain's hair and delivering blows to his face. After 18 minutes Brain won the 500-guineas stake for his patron, the Duke of Hamilton, with a crippling blow to the ribs and another which split Johnson's lip in two.

Neither boxer fought again, both claiming that the punishment taken in this match hastened their end. Johnson died six years later, aged 47, and Brain only three years later, aged 41, his liver damaged by the blows he had taken.

Mendoza the Jew

The next fighter to make a big impression was Daniel Mendoza, a Jew from London's East End, and a scientific boxer who later became an excellent teacher of the art. He was also one of the first to realize the commercial prospects of prize-fighting, and promoted his own fights. Not tall or heavy, but muscular, he stood only 5ft 7in (1.70m) and weighed 160lb (73kg). After several wins, he beat a proven man called Martin, known as the Bath Butcher.

Another prominent pugilist was Richard Humphries, known as the 'Gentleman Boxer' because of his upbringing and style. He took a dislike to Mendoza and regularly insulted him, on one occasion having Mendoza detained by the police for a while over an alleged unpaid debt. Humphries, too, had beaten the Bath Butcher, and then had been his second when Mendoza beat him. Finally, after Humphries and Mendoza had had a fierce row in an inn at Epping near London, they were matched at Odiham in Hampshire for 400 guineas a side. The battled swayed both ways in a rain-soaked ring, but Mendoza seemed to be getting ahead, having felled Humphries six times, when he himself was knocked down by blows to the groin and neck, falling awkwardly and twisting an ankle. Dragged to his corner, he found he could not stand, and was forced to retire. Mendoza's supporters, who had lost thousands of pounds in wagers, released a black pigeon to take the news back to the East End of London, while Humphries sent a note to his backer which read: 'Sir, I have done the Jew and am in good health.'

Mendoza immediately issued a further challenge to Humphries, and the two met again in May 1789, in the grounds of a private park at Stilton, famous for its cheeses. The betting was even, but Mendoza gradually gained the upper hand, impressing the spectators by his clever blocking of Humphries' blows, and quick counter-punching. In the 22nd round Humphries appeared to fall without a blow, which meant defeat. Mendoza's seconds and supporters immediately shouted 'foul' and claimed the prize, but Humphries and his supporters vehemently asserted that he had taken a blow before falling and was entitled to come up to scratch for further rounds. The two umpires could not agree, and blows and threats were exchanged between seconds and spectators. Finally, Mendoza agreed to continue, and punished Humphries further, who was always the man knocked down to end the round. After a further eight minutes of milling, Humphries again went down to avoid follow-up blows by Mendoza, and this time did not argue with the decision that he was beaten.

The Fancy, however, did not like the idea of the Jew beating their favourite Gentleman Boxer, and a third meeting was held at an inn at Doncaster, selected because the River Don flowed on one side, and unruly gatecrashers could be kept out. The plan failed as the 500 paying spectators (half-a-guinea each) were joined by more who rowed across the river and broke down the fencing. Mendoza was now the betting favourite at 4-1, if not the favourite of the spectators, and stamped his authority on a brave opponent. Both men were marked by blows, but it was Humphries who was forced to give up, and was taken to hospital after the fight.

Mendoza, who gained respect by the sporting manner in which he fought Humphries, claimed the championship of England, but there were other claimants. Before Big Ben died in 1794, he had been forced to pull out of a fight with William Wood the Coachman, who thereupon claimed the crown. Then Wood was beaten by William Hooper the Tinman, who had fought the infamous draw with Big Ben Brain, so Hooper thus regarded himself as champion.

Below: The deciding third match between Daniel Mendoza, on the right, and Richard Humphries at Doncaster in 1790. Mendoza won and established his claim to be champion of England.

Mendoza, however, was generally accepted as the best, particularly after beating Bill Ward, or Warr, another of the many famous fighters coming from Bristol at the time. Ward also claimed to be champion, and was matched with Mendoza first of all at Stoken Church, Oxfordshire, in 1791. But prize fighting had been illegal since 1750, and it became known that the magistrates intended to visit this battle and make arrests, so it was postponed for three months, and again put off for the same reason. In May 1792, the fight was arranged for Smitham Bottom, near Croydon, Surrey, and despite the fact that fights, naturally, could not be advertised, the roads from London to Croydon saw many pedestrians and vehicles in the days leading up to the big event.

Ward was favourite, there still being a reluctance to accept a Jew (with Spanish connections at that) as champion of England. Ward started well, and in the 14th round appeared to be about to win, with Mendoza knocked off his feet by a tremendous blow to the jaw, but Mendoza fought back well and gradually got on top, finally winning in the 23rd round when he knocked down Ward and fell on him, knocking the breath from the exhausted man's body.

Mendoza toured Ireland, beating the well-known sportsman Squire Fitzgerald, and was acknowledged as champion of Ireland. He beat Ward again in only 15 minutes at Bexley Common, Kent, in another fight postponed because the magistrates in Hounslow, where it was originally planned, heard about it.

The influence of Gentleman John

Mendoza, the 'Star of the East', finally met his match in John Jackson. Jackson, an outstanding all-round sportsman, had turned professional at 19, taking as his first opponent William Fewterell, a giant from Birmingham. Although Jackson was 5ft 11in (1.80m), 195lb (88kg) and of such physique as to make the lady spectators stare in admiration, he was dwarfed by Fewterell, the Birmingham giant of 230lb (104kg). Fewterell, moreover, was a seasoned campaigner with many victories, and was much favoured in the betting. The fight was at Smitham Bottom, Croydon, in June 1788 and Jackson won with a sustained exhibition of scientific hitting, reducing Fewterell to helplessness in one hour and seven minutes. The Prince of Wales (later King George IV) was a fascinated spectator and gave Jackson a present, believed to be a snuff box, at the ringside.

Fewterell became the publisher of an early boxing paper, but Jackson continued his career with a bout the following year with George Inglestone the Brewer at Ingatestone. He seemed on the point of winning when he slipped on the rain-sodden boards and broke a bone in his leg. Forced to retire, he gave up pugilism for six years. During this time Jackson mixed with society, and his dress and manners earned him the nickname of 'Gentleman John' Jackson.

Daniel Mendoza, meanwhile, who had also lost a fight because of an injury, became champion. Although Mendoza was popular with the Fancy, he was, as has been noted, a Jew, and Jackson's high-born friends persuaded him to attempt to 'win back' the crown. Jackson agreed, and the two men met at Hornchurch, Essex, in April 1795, for 200 guineas a side. Mendoza was favourite, because of his impressive record; Jackson was a novice, but his physical advantages gave him the upper hand early on. In the fifth round, Jackson belied his 'Gentleman' image by grabbing Mendoza by his long black curly hair and pummelling his face with his free hand. Mendoza had always been proud of his hair, refusing to cut it short in the fashion of the prize fighters — it now proved his undoing. His corner cried 'foul' but the umpires allowed the fight to continue, and Mendoza could not recover. He sank to defeat in only 11 minutes.

Now Jackson was champion of England after only three fights — fights which constituted his whole career, for he retired. He opened an academy at 13 Bond Street, London; among his friends and pupils were the Dukes of York and Clarence and Lord Byron, the poet, who was addicted to the prize ring and made a screen covered with drawings of the battles and the pugilists of the

__Below:__ Gentleman John Jackson, who became champion after only three fights, as painted by Ben Marshall in 1810. His academy was patronized by royalty, and Byron wrote that 'men unpractised in exchanging knocks must go to Jackson ere they dare box'.

Right: *Bob Gregson, the Lancashire Giant, was one of the leading pugilists of the early 19th century. He twice fought John Gully for the title, and was beaten by Tom Cribb only by twisting his knee at the climax of a terrific battle which otherwise he looked like winning.*

day. Jackson formed the Pugilistic Club in 1814, to which belonged the leading patrons of prize fighting. This club was formed to bring some order to the ring, to provide purses and to eliminate fixing. It had a good influence while it lasted, but it did not become the ruling body, as the Jockey Club did in horse-racing. Despite this club, and Jackson's friendship with the Prince of Wales and the Royal Dukes, and their support of the ring, prize fighting remained strictly illegal.

There were several good pugilists around in the 1790s, among them two men who weighed less than 145lb (66kg), yet mixed it with many a battler of 40lb (18kg) or so more. One was Caleb Baldwin, sometimes called the lightweight champion of 1792–6, and the other Samuel Elias, or Dutch Sam the Terrible Jew, who inflicted on Baldwin his only defeat.

The one-eyed Belcher

The man who became top of the heavyweight pile was another from Bristol, Jem Belcher. By the time he was 17 he had beaten Jack Britton, the 'Star of the West', and went to London to seek his fortune. He beat Paddington Jones, one of the best fighters of the day, and, in 1800, Jack Bartholomew for 300 guineas and the 'Championship of England'. He won a return contest but then was matched with the Irish champion, Andrew Gamble, the Fancy not yet convinced that Belcher was the true champion. He proved he was by disposing of Gamble in less than ten minutes, Gamble's kidneys swelling greatly after the blows Belcher delivered.

Belcher was only 19 and clearly the champion. He beat Joe Berk three times, dealing out tremendous punishment. A smart dresser, Belcher introduced the Ascot tie, and with the habit of pinning his 'colours' to the ring post, these became known as 'Belchers'. He continued his destructive way by reducing to impotence a big strong fighter called Jack Fearby, the Young Ruffian. Tragedy then overtook Belcher, for he was struck in the eye playing rackets, and lost the sight of it. He retired, and the unbeaten Henry Pearce claimed the championship. Belcher took the Two Brewers Inn in Wardour Street, London, but in December 1805 he challenged Pearce. Still only 24, Belcher's condition had sunk since his eye injury, and he was well beaten by Pearce, who took care not to damage Belcher's good eye.

Pearce, from Bristol, had his first name shortened to Hen by his friends, and on showing great bravery in the ring he became known as 'The Game Chicken'. His career lasted only seven fights, when he retired as undefeated champion. He died suddenly in 1809, aged only 32. His friend Belcher claimed the title again on Pearce's retirement, but was twice beaten by Tom Cribb. Belcher, too, soon died, in 1811, aged only 30.

One of Pearce's wins had been against John Gully, whose life story was remarkable. He had been in a debtor's prison after failing in business when Pearce, who had heard of his prowess with his fists, paid his debt and fought him for the title. Gully put up a great show, losing in 64 rounds, and when Pearce retired he named Gully as his successor. When Gully twice beat Bob Gregson, the Lancashire Giant, his claims were acknowledged by all. Gully, however, immediately announced his retirement and proceeded to make a fortune, not altogether honestly, in horse-racing, twice winning the Derby. He owned coal-mines, became an MP and died a very wealthy old man.

Tom Cribb beats the Blacks

Tom Cribb was the next great champion of the prize ring. When only 13 he went from his birthplace, Hanham in Gloucestershire, to London to become a stevedore. He survived two serious accidents, joined the navy, and, being a big strong man, earned a reputation at fisticuffs. His first professional fight was against George Maddox the Coster-monger, an outstanding fighter, but now 50 years old. Cribb won a terrific battle in 75 rounds, lasting two hours and ten minutes. He then suffered his only defeat, a 52-round beating by George Nicholls in 1805.

Meanwhile, the first black boxer had made a mark in a British ring. Bill Richmond was born in Staten Island, New York, in 1763, the son of a slave. He was noticed looking after himself in a brawl with three British soldiers (the army then held New York), by General Earl Percy, later the Duke of Northumberland, who brought him to England. Although beaten by George Maddox, Richmond beat many other leading fighters, and challenged Cribb, after Cribb's defeat by Nicholls. It was a mismatch and Cribb knocked him out. Richmond retired for a while, but then made a comeback and fought successfully until he was 55. He died in London, aged 66, a well-respected fighter.

When Belcher reclaimed the title on Pearce's retirement, Cribb's backer, Captain Barclay, challenged him for 200 guineas. The fight took place at Moulsey Hirst, and one-eyed Belcher fought brilliantly, so much so that after 18 rounds the odds were 5-1 on him. But he hurt his hand and received a blow over his good eye; he was forced to retire after 40 rounds, when Cribb himself was practically exhausted.

Cribb was acknowledged champion, and beat Dick Horton the Baker before having another tremendous battle, this time with Bob Gregson, again at Moulsey Hirst. The stakes were £500 a side, and again Cribb appeared to be beaten. In the 23rd round, with both men hardly able to stand, they clinched and fell awkwardly to the ground, Gregson twisting a knee. They were dragged to their corners, but only Cribb was able to totter to the mark when time was called. He was declared the winner, and immediately fell unconscious to the ground.

Cribb again beat the gallant Belcher, whose handicap now proved too much, although he resisted for 31 rounds. Cribb, after this fight, was presented with a large silver cup, and shortly afterwards announced his retirement.

However, it was not the end of Cribb, for another black ex-slave had arrived from America, and challenged him. He was Tom Molyneaux, from Virginia. Helped by Bill Richmond, he had begun beating the best boxers on his arrival in England. Bill Burrows, the 'Bristol Unknown' and a protégé of Cribb, was outclassed, as was Tom Blake, whom Cribb expected to beat Molyneaux.

Molyneaux announced that if Cribb would not fight him, he would regard himself as champion of England, a claim which gave the Fancy apoplexy. Cribb was persuaded by the nobility to come out of retirement and beat the upstart; he bowed to the pressure.

A crowd of 20,000 watched the first international title fight between a white man and a black man. The bout was on 18 December 1810 at Copthall Common, Grinstead, Sussex.

There was a little skulduggery in this fight. It was evenly fought on a bitterly cold morning, with rain falling, conditions which did not favour Molyneaux. However, he fought well, and the 28th round should have been conclusive. He staggered Cribb with body blows, and then put him down with a fierce right to the face. Cribb was dragged to his corner, and when time was called he could not toe the line. Molyneaux was about to be declared the winner when Cribb's second accused him of having weights in his hand. This was, of course, untrue, but in the uproar Cribb was revived, and given some brandy. When the ring was cleared, the referee allowed the fight to continue. The break had enabled the cold to get to Molyneaux and finding Cribb apparently completely recovered, he became dispirited. After five more rounds it was Cribb who delivered the decisive blow to the face. The unconscious Molyneaux was taken from the scene. He should have been champion, but, of course, he wasn't. Cribb was, and the hero of the Fancy again announced his retirement.

Molyneaux, meanwhile, resumed his winning way, challenged Cribb again, and on being refused, styled himself the champion. Once more Cribb had to take up the cudgels for England. Molyneaux faced tremendous odds in this second encounter, at Thistleton Gap, on the borders of Leicestershire and Rutland. It took place on 28 September 1911, attended by the nobility and 25,000 fans. Cribb, aware of his task, had trained to perfection under the patronage of Captain Barclay. Molyneaux, on the other hand, had had to fend for himself, and his unpopularity was made manifest. Molyneaux was not in quite as fine condition as the year before. Cribb got in first with a blow to the throat which ended the first round. Molyneaux fought back to get on top briefly, but Cribb seized Molyneaux's head under his arm in the eighth (called a chancery suit) and pummelled him until he collapsed. Three rounds later it was over; Molyneaux was unconscious, with a fractured jaw. Cribb was again a national hero, and was fêted all the way back to London.

With Cribb once more inactive, a championship battle was arranged between Bill Neat, the 'Bristol Bull', and Tom Hickman, the 'Gas-light Man'. The fight was at Hungerford Downs, some half-way between Bristol and London, on 11 December 1821 and the previous weekend the carriages of the Fancy

Left: *The slave from Virginia, Tom Molyneaux, who twice fought Cribb and was unlucky to lose on the first occasion, only quick-witted gamesmanship by Cribb's second preventing the title being won by a foreigner for the first time.*

were to be seen beginning the two-day journey from London. Neat was the younger man, and the bigger at around 200lb (91kg), but Hickman, some 30lb (14kg) lighter, was more experienced and had an excellent record. The betting was close, and the fight was a tremendous one, described by William Hazlitt in a famous essay called *The Fight*. Neat's strength proved the decisive factor after 18 rounds and the brave Gas was put out — for good, shortly afterwards, as he was killed when the chaise he was driving overturned and he fell under the wheels.

Cribb, meanwhile, had opened a sporting parlour, and was impressed by a young boxer called Tom Winter, who changed his name to Spring when he fought. Cribb coached him towards the championship, and Spring was in the Gas-light Man's corner when he was beaten by Neat. Spring beat several good men, including Joshua Hudson, the 'John Bull Fighter', and, in 1821, Tom Oliver, at which Cribb announced his retirement as champion and handed the mantle on to Spring. Of course, this did not please Bill Neat, who considered himself champion, and immediately issued a challenge to Spring to settle matters.

Spring beat Neat in eight rounds lasting thirty-seven minutes at Hinckley Downs in 1823. He was a scientific boxer, well taught by Cribb, and was beaten only once in his career, by Ned Painter, whom he had previously beaten. Spring suffered an eye injury in the first round of that fight, but resisted stoutly for 42 rounds before giving best. The climax of his career was two battles with Jack Langan.

***Below:** The silver cup presented to Tom Cribb, the champion of England. It was given to him after his victory over Jem Belcher in 1809, so the black boxer shown in the engraving must be Bill Richmond and not Tom Molyneaux, over whom Cribb had his greatest victories.*

The Spring–Langan battles

The first Spring–Langan contest took place on Worcester racecourse on 7 January 1824, and for the first time in boxing a grandstand was erected for spectators. Thirty thousand arrived from all over England to see the encounter (despite magistrates becoming firmer in their attempts to stop the illegal prize fighting). One stand collapsed just before the fight, killing one person and injuring others, and another collapsed in the ninth round, causing a pause in the proceedings.

With the crowd frequently surging forward, it was difficult to keep order in the ring, but the two prize fighters ignored everything and gave a sterling display. Spring finally dispatched a tottering Langan with a blow in the 77th round. The fight lasted a minute short of two and a half hours.

Such was the excitement caused by this fight that five months later, on 8 June, at Birdham Bridge, near Chichester, the two met again. Spring, at 190lb (86kg) was 14lb (6kg) heavier than Langan, but Langan's backers put up 500 guineas for the return, so confident were they of reversing the result. But Spring again won a hard struggle, lasting an hour and 49 minutes, this time covering 76 rounds. Spring damaged his hands so badly in winning that he never fought again. He became the prosperous landlord of the Castle Tavern, Holborn, while Langan also took an inn, in Liverpool.

After Spring retired there was a period of comparative mediocrity. Josh Hudson beat Jem Ward to establish a claim to the title, but he was soon twice beaten by Tom Cannon, the son of a Windsor bargee, and known as 'the Great Gun of Windsor'. These wins gained Cannon recognition, but in 1825 he was well beaten by the clever Jem Ward in only ten minutes. Ward, who worked in a coal yard, was known as the 'Black Diamond'. He was known to have 'thrown' two fights, and boxing was not proud of its new champion. On 2 January 1827 Ward was beaten in 11 rounds by Peter Crawley, the son of a butcher, who was known as 'Young Rump Steak'. Crawley had suffered only one defeat in an excellent career, but as soon as he won the championship he retired from boxing to go into business.

Ward, who had been carried insensible from the ring after his battle with Crawley, claimed the title again, and after he had beaten Jack Carter and Simon Byrne, the Irish Champion, he was duly accepted as champion, and in fact given a champion's belt, the second fighter so honoured, Cribb having been given a belt by George III after beating Tom Molyneaux. In 1832 he announced his retirement.

James Burke, the 'Deaf 'Un', now claimed the crown, and was acknowledged champion when he defeated his first challenger, Harry Macone. Burke was a Londoner of Irish parents, and it was an Irishman who next challenged him, Simon Byrne. This battle was one of the most savage ever, with both men on several occasions brought up to the mark by their seconds in a state of helplessness, only to be given another debilitating blow. The fight was at St Albans and lasted for 98 rounds spread over three hours and 16 minutes, the longest of all championship fights. Burke won, and Byrne ended the fight in a coma, from which he never regained consciousness, dying three days later. Ironically, Byrne had himself been acquitted of manslaughter when Sandy McKay had died after a fearful battering three years earlier.

Burke, although exonerated from blame, fled to America, where he found an enemy, Samuel O'Rourke. O'Rourke had once claimed the Irish championship and was anxious to avenge his countryman Byrne's death. He was running a boxing school and styling himself 'world champion'. He antagonized Burke, and a match was arranged at New Orleans. O'Rourke was a gangster who stood no chance in even contest with Burke, but the plan was for his mob to interrupt the fight and murder Burke. In the third round they duly cut the ropes and invaded the ring. Despite their guns, Burke escaped to New York, where he beat Paddy O'Connell before he returned to England.

Another ring fatality in 1838 caused an examination of the rules. In March, Bill Phelps, a lightweight boxer known as Brighton Bill, died after a beating by Owen Swift. The London Prize Ring rules came into force and received general acceptance anywhere in the world where boxing was practised. The principal change from the rules as followed before was that a boxer could not be carried by his seconds to the scratch line at the beginning of a round. In other words a boxer unable to toe the line, unaided, was beaten.

Bad Bold Bendigo

In Burke's absence another great bare-knuckle boxer had come to the fore: Bold Bendigo. His real name was William Thompson, and he was one of triplets, born to a Nottingham family of 21. The triplets were nicknamed Shadrach, Meshach and Abednego, from the Bible. 'Abednego', who was taught to fight by his mother (a violent woman who frequently fought men), became known to the public as Bold Bendigo. He built up a string of victories and a big reputation.

Bendigo's closest rival was Ben Caunt, a gamekeeper from Hucknall Torkard, only five miles from Nottingham. Jealous of his fame, Caunt challenged Bendigo. Bendigo was reluctant to accept the challenge, because Caunt, four years older and with an impressive string of victories himself, stood some 6ft 2½in (1.89m) and weighed 210lb (95kg). Bendigo was only 5ft 9¼in (1.76m) and 165lb (75kg). However, he was forced to agree and the two met at Appleby House, Nottingham, on 21 July 1835.

Above: William Thompson, a southpaw, who fought under the name 'Bold Bendigo'. Egged on by his mother, who despite having 21 children enjoyed a fight herself, and a gang of supporting ruffians known as the 'Nottingham Lambs', he enjoyed a long and successful career as a champion prize fighter.

Bendigo had talents which 130 years later might have been admired by Muhammad Ali. He was a master of psychological warfare, and before the contest enraged Caunt with his taunts and insults. He was also a master acrobat, and his verbal assaults and general antics in the ring exasperated poor Caunt. After 22 rounds of a brawling contest, Caunt dashed across the ring during the interval, asked Bendigo why he couldn't fight like a man, then gave him a blow which knocked him from his second's knee. Bendigo was immediately awarded the fight, and claimed to be champion of England.

Bendigo won more fights by strange means. In one he picked up Bill Looney by the waist after they had fought for two and a half hours and turned him upside down, driving his head into the ground until he was unconscious (and temporarily blinded). Bendigo then faced Caunt again, in another dirty fight in which their feud was apparent. This time Bendigo was disqualified for going down in the 75th round without being hit, a decision which so incensed Bendigo's supporters that a riot broke out and Caunt was lucky to escape without serious injury. His coach was overturned, and he had to grab a horse and flee on bareback.

On James 'Deaf' Burke's return to England, he pointed out that he was still the legitimate champion, and he was immediately challenged by Bendigo. A proposed meeting in 1838 fell through, but on 12 February 1839 the two met at Heather, in Leicestershire. This was the first championship battle to be fought under the new London Prize Ring Rules. Bendigo won on a foul in 10 rounds and 24 minutes, when Burke was adjudged guilty of deliberate butting. Jem Ward, who had been presented with a championship belt, now awarded it to Bendigo, but it did not become a 'badge of office' because it was never seen again after Bendigo took it. Bold Bendigo, after this win, injured his knee while somersaulting for children, and decided to retire, taking an inn in London, whose wares he proceeded to enjoy.

The two main claimants to the title now were Ben Caunt and Nick Ward, the brother of Jem, who had beaten Burke in 1840. The two men faced each other to settle the issue on 2 February 1841 at Crookham Common. Ward won after seven rounds on a foul blow, but on 11 May at Long Marsden, Caunt knocked out Ward in 33 rounds.

As the champion, Caunt went to America to cash in by challenging all-comers. Few were forthcoming but Caunt gave exhibitions and generally did well financially.

On returning to England, Caunt was anxious to teach a lesson to his hated rival Bendigo. He continually challenged and insulted him but Bendigo would not be tempted into battle, although his knee was now back to normal. Eventually, however, Bendigo's belligerent mother persuaded him to accept the match, and the two agreed to meet at Stony Stratford. The law enforcement officers were determined this grudge battle would not take place. Three attempts were made to stage it, and finally it took place at Lillington Level, near Sutfield Green, Oxfordshire. A crowd of 10,000 was present at the fight, although the police were apparently unaware of the venue.

It was another bitter fight. Caunt was clearly the stronger and frequently threw Bendigo, but Bendigo was quicker and got in many telling blows. His supporters also got in a blow or two when Caunt was close enough. The fight ended in great controversy, despite the presence of the famous sportsman, Squire Osbaldeston, as referee. After two hours ten minutes of brawling, spread over 93 rounds, Caunt was disqualified for going down without a blow. Caunt protested he was resting on one knee, believing that Bendigo had fouled him. The decision stood, and further riots ensued.

Bendigo was champion again, but of course retired once more. It was not for good, however. After another five years he was challenged by Tom Paddock, a muscular farmworker who had won a few fights and wanted the championship. Once again Bendigo's mother urged him to the scratch line, and after a few weeks training he faced Paddock for £200 a side at Mildenham, Staffordshire.

Bendigo, by now 31, used all his guile in this fight, constantly going down when in danger of punishment. In the 49th round, coming up to an hour's fighting, Paddock appeared to be on the point of victory as he held and pummelled Bendigo, who finally fell into a sitting position. The enthusiastic Paddock then delivered two punches to flatten Bendigo, and was promptly disqualified. The enraged Paddock then flattened Bendigo, who had risen, again, and another riot ensued, but Bendigo had kept his crown again. His retirement this time proved final.

William Perry, the Tipton Slasher, claimed to be champion but was immediately challenged by Paddock. Perry, who came from Tipton, in Staffordshire, was a man of just over 6ft (1.83m) and 185lb (84kg); he had beaten some good men, but had lost to Charles Freeman, an American brought back to England by Ben Caunt. The giant Freeman stood 6ft 10½in (2.10m) and scaled 276lb (125kg). He died of tuberculosis soon after beating Perry. Perry fought Paddock at Woking Common, Surrey, on 17 December 1850, and was confirmed as champion when Paddock was disqualified for a foul blow after 27 savage rounds, lasting 42 minutes. Perry was challenged by another title claimant, Harry Broome, from Birmingham, and was himself disqualified for a foul blow in the 15th round.

Paddock, meanwhile, also claimed the championship, on the grounds that both Perry and Broome had declined to fight him. Broome, in fact, twice accepted challenges from Paddock and each time paid a forfeit rather than face him. Paddock continued to have gruelling fights, losing once and winning twice against a tough Nottinghamshire railway worker, Harry Poulson. After 80 rounds of the second contest, the police and magistrates arrived, but were prevented by spectators from stopping the fight. Afterwards, however, both pugilists were arrested and sentenced to ten months' imprisonment, the most meted out to boxers so far.

Paddock persuaded the editor of *Bell's Life*, later to combine with the *Sporting Life*, to support his claims, and a match between him and Aaron Jones on 26 June 1855 at Mildenhall was put forward for the championship. Jones collapsed after 61 rounds and 90 minutes of bruising action, and Paddock claimed the championship.

Broome, who had defended against Harry Orme in 1853 but then retired, had second thoughts about his retirement, having fallen on hard times, so he now challenged Paddock for £200 a side and the undisputed championship. They met on 18 May 1856 near Bentley, Suffolk, and battled for over an hour, Broome being unable to come up to scratch after 51 rounds.

The great Tom Sayers

Unfortunately for Paddock, who had worked so hard to become undisputed champion, he now fell ill. During his illness another great bare-knuckle fighter took the centre of the stage. He was Tom Sayers, known as the 'Napoleon of the Ring'. Born in Brighton, he was a bricklayer. Showing skill at scrapping, he was sent to London, and began a successful career as a prize fighter. Sayers was remarkable in that he never weighed more than 152lb (69kg), and in his younger days was only a welterweight by today's standards. He fought and beat men weighing 40 to 50lb (18 to 23kg) more.

After many good wins, including one over Aaron Jones, Sayers challenged William Perry, the Tipton Slasher, for the title. Paddock was ill and to all intents and purposes retired, and Sayers and Perry had claims to be his successor. Nobody gave Sayers much chance, as he was conceding four inches (10cm) and some 40lb (18kg). The fight was on 16 June 1857, and the first ring built was abandoned when word came that a police raid was imminent. All fled a few miles down the Kent coast and a new ring was built on the Isle of Grain. Sayers demonstrated how he beat the big men by evading the Slasher's rushes, landing some quick blows and going down whenever caught by the big man. After six rounds, Perry began to tire, and Sayers began punishing him. Perry's seconds finally retired their man after ten rounds, representing one hour 42 minutes of frustration and pain for him.

With Sayers now recognized by most as champion, he was challenged by Paddock, who had run into financial difficulties. Paddock, of course, was still 'officially' champion. Unfortunately, he was not quite fit when facing Sayers, and took a fearful battering for 21 rounds. The brave Paddock stood up to Sayers for one hour and 20 minutes, by which time he was practically blinded, and did not demur when Sayers compassionately led him back to his corner.

The Prize Ring in America

Sayers was now undisputed champion, and disposed of Bill Bainge before being challenged by John C. Heenan, the Champion of America. Sayers accepted the challenge, and the fight aroused more interest than any other until that date. To set the scene for the big international battle, we must go back a few years to trace the development of prize fighting in America, and to see how Heenan came to represent his countrymen in England.

Prize fighting in America grew with the immigration of many English and Irish in the early 19th century. Previously, fights had been seen around the ports, where seamen would indulge in fisticuffs after celebrating in the bars. Gradually, the sport spread inland.

The first fight in America where the rules as developed in England were applied, and where there was an audience, is generally held to be that between Jacob Hyer and Tom Beasley in New York in 1816. Hyer won and later was given the title of 'The Father of the American Ring'.

Standing 6ft 2in (1.88m) and weighing 182lb (83kg), Jacob Hyer was a fine figure, a New Yorker of strong Dutch ancestry. But he fought only once and did not begin a tradition — there was a long hiatus in

__Above:__ The great Tom Sayers must be, pound for pound, one of the greatest of all the prize fighters. Although rarely topping 150lb (68kg), he was beaten only once, and was overall champion of England for three years, retiring after his drawn battle with the American John C. Heenan.

Right: An illustration and poem published after the battle between Tom Sayers and John C. Heenan, the Benicia Boy. The last verse turned out not to be an accurate forecast, for the two did not meet again in the ring, and indeed both were dead within 13 years.

SAYERS' & HEENAN'S GREAT FIGHT
FOR THE CHAMPIONSHIP.

Upon the seventeenth day of April,
All in the morning soon,
The Yankee and the champion Sayers
Prepared to meet their doom.
The train it ran along like wind,
Coaches and cabs did fly,
Both men appeared determined
To conquer or to die.

They fought like lions in the ring,
Both men did boldly stand,
They two hours and six minutes fought,
And neither beat his man.

Tom hit at the Benicia boy
Right well you may suppose,
Heenan returned the compliment
Upon the champion's nose.
Like two game cocks they stood the test,
And each to win did try,
Erin-go-bragh, cried Heenan,
I will conquer, lads, or die.

Cried Sayers, I will not give in,
Nor to a Yankee yield,
The belt I mean to keep my boys,
Or die upon the field.
They together stood it manfully,
Surprised all in the ring,
There was never such a battle, since
Jack Langham tackled Spring.

Such fibbing and such up and down
Lor, how the swells did shout,
Their ribs did nicely rattle,
And their daylight near knocked out,
Tom Sayers let into Heenan,
Heenan let into Tom,
While the Fancy bawled and shouted,
Lads, my jolly lads, go on.

Two long hours and six minutes
They fought, and the claret flew,
Sayers proved himself a brick, so did
Yankee doodle doo.
The bets did fly about, my boys,
And numbers looked with joy
On Sayers, the British champion,
And the bold Benicia boy.

They both had pluck and courage,
Each proved himself a man,
None better since the days of Spring
In the British ring did stand.
Erin-go-bragh, cried Heenan,
I want the English belt,
When Tom let fly, saying, I will die,
Or keep the belt myself.

At length bounced in the peelers,
And around the ring did jog,
So those heroes were surrounded
By a lot of Hampshire hogs,
Who caused them to cut their stick,
And from the fight refrain,
That they were both determined
In the ring to meet again.

We admit Tom Sayers had his match
One who did him annoy,
With lots of pluck and courage,
Was the bold Benicia boy.
And when two heroes fight again,
For honour and for wealth,
He that's the best man in the ring,
Shall carry off the belt.

H. Disley, Printer, 57, High Street, St. Giles, London.

boxing's development thereafter. Richmond and Molyneaux, of course, were Americans who had already fought in England.

William Fuller, a British boxer, opened an academy in America and tried to get accepted as champion, but without success, as did Samuel O'Rourke, who fought James 'Deaf' Burke, as related already.

Irish immigrants were particularly active in getting prize fighting established in the United States, and many of the interesting encounters were between the native Americans and the newly arrived Irish (in the 20th century the Jewish population were also to become prominent in the sport). Ben Caunt, the British champion, visited the USA in 1840 without being able to find a legitimate challenger.

On 9 September 1841 Jacob Hyer's son, Tom Hyer, fought George McChester, known as 'Country McCluskey', at Caldwell's Landing, New York. Hyer won in 101 rounds, lasting two hours and 55 minutes. Hyer was then picked on by Yankee Sullivan, an Irishman born as John Ambrose. Convicted of larceny in Britain, he had been sentenced to 20 years in the penal colony of Australia, and then paroled provided he emigrated to America. Sullivan heaped abuse on Hyer, and eventually the two met in the ring to settle their differences. There was a $5,000 side-stake, and the two men met at Rock Point, Maryland, on 7 February 1849. There was a layer of snow on the ground but plenty of heat in the ring. Hyer won in 16 rounds and was generally regarded as the first champion of America.

Hyer, born on 1 January 1819, stood over 6ft (1.83m) and weighed 185lb (84kg). He invited William Perry, the Tipton Slasher, to fight him but the Slasher would not cross the Atlantic to New York. Hyer retired, and died in 1864.

On Hyer's retirement, the Irish took the fighting honours in America. John Morrissey was the next to come to the fore. He was born in Templemore, County Tipperary, in 1831, and became a gambling proprietor, Congressman and Senator. His first impact on boxing was to fix a fight for a friend, John Willis, on whom he won a lot of money. He tried to arrange a title fight between Willis and Hyer, and then accepted a challenge himself from Yankee Sullivan to fight for the vacant crown. Morrissey beat Sullivan in 37 rounds at Boston Corners, New York, in 1853. Sullivan, disgusted at losing to his rival Tammany Hall politician, went to California where, apparently, he was murdered.

Morrissey's main asset was his durability. He found another bitter opponent in John C. Heenan, a fellow New Yorker. Heenan was born in West Troy, where Morrissey's parents had settled. He was known as the 'Benicia Boy', having built a reputation as a pugilist while working for the Pacific Mail Steamship Company in Benicia, San Francisco. Heenan, like Morrissey, was of Irish descent, and the two men, having insulted each other freely, settled their differences at Long Point, Canada, on 20 October 1858. Heenan was handicapped when a punch struck one of the stakes of the ring and he lost the use of his right hand. Morrissey won in 11 rounds, and then retired, devoting himself to his gambling and politics, but dying aged only 47.

Morrissey refused all pleas to give Heenan a return, and Heenan was recognized as champion. There were no serious challengers in America, so Heenan's future wife and George Wilkes, editor of the *Spirit of the Times* in New York, decided to challenge the British champion, Tom Sayers, for the championship of the world. Sayers accepted, and Heenan sailed for England for the great fight.

The Sayers–Heenan championship

The fight, which took place on 17 April 1860, caused such interest that for the first time there was an international press present, with the *Police Gazette*, *Leslie's Illustrated Weekly*, the *Spirit of the Times* and others sending reporters and artists from America. All the British papers covered the fight, and *The Times* brought out a special edition next day which had to be reprinted several times. The fight was illegal, of course, and the two principals had to make their way to the venue in disguise. Fans boarded the special trains in London not knowing where they would stop. The venue was actually Farnborough, 25 miles outside London. The novelists Dickens and Thackeray and the Prime Minister, Lord Palmerston, were among the spectators.

Heenan was nearly six inches (15cm) taller than Sayers and 43lb (19.5kg) heavier. Sayers, of course, was the more experienced warrior. The pair put on a tremendous exhibition, in which Sayers' punching made a mess of Heenan's face, gradually closing up his eyes, while Heenan continually threw Sayers, knocking the wind from his body.

It was an even battle, but the 37th round might have seen the end, for Heenan grabbed Sayers round the neck and, with the back of Sayers' neck on the upper rope, began to strangle him. Some partisan spectators now cut the rope, ending the round and causing the referee to flee. Heenan wanted a new site found, but the two parties decided to continue without a referee. After five more rounds, however, the police intervened, and everybody fled. A draw was given as the result. The two protagonists had fought for two hours and 20 minutes.

If the result itself was unsatisfactory, the sequel was excellent. Both boxers were given championship belts and they became the best of friends, making an exhibition tour together. Sayers did not fight again, and died five years later.

On Sayers' retirement, the backers of a wrestler, Sam Hurst, known as the 'Stalybridge Infant', decided to claim the British title. Hurst was a 6ft 3in (1.91m) foundry worker who had developed a muscular physique by hammering nails. He weighed well over 200lb (91kg) and was immensely strong. However, he was not a prize fighter, and when a challenge was issued to Heenan for £50 a side, Heenan ignored it. One man who needed a fight, though, was ex-champion Tom Paddock, still ill and still in debt. He scraped together £200 and challenged Hurst for the title. Poor Paddock had left hospital only two weeks when he was stabbed by a coffee-house keeper, and was very unfit when he took on the Stalybridge Infant on 5 November 1860 on the Berkshire Downs. He did well for two rounds, then took a huge blow to the ribs, which broke three. He could not continue, and the Stalybridge Infant claimed to be champion after one fight.

Above: *The match between Sayers and Heenan in 1860. The difference in size between the two men is apparent. This fight caused more interest than any other up to then.*

The Swaffham Gypsy

Hurst was not champion for long. In 1861 Jem Mace challenged him for a stake of £200 a side.

Mace, the 'Swaffham Gypsy', learned his boxing in the boxing booths, and preferred to fight with the new gloves, which were becoming popular. Mace was a small man by heavyweight standards, never weighing more than 160lb (73kg), but he was a classy fighter, one who brought boxing to its highest scientific level yet. He had no trouble with the Stalybridge Infant, despite being outweighed by at least 50lb (23kg). Eight rounds lasting 40 minutes were enough to see Mace the new champion.

Mace had one rival in England worthy of his talent. Tom King, a London dockyard worker, who under the tutelage of ex-champion Jem Ward had won a number of contests, challenged Mace for £200 a side; they fought at Godstone, Surrey, on 28 January 1862. King, at 6ft 2in (1.88m) was 16lb (7kg) heavier than Mace, and at 27 four years younger, but Mace's skill and experience told and King was defeated in 68 minutes. When the two met again, at Medway, Kent, the following November, the fight seemed to be going the same way until King, practically exhausted, caught Mace with a desperate wild swing. Although Mace seemed to recover, he collapsed two rounds later, and King was champion after 38 minutes.

King then decided to retire, and Mace reclaimed the championship in September 1863 by beating Joe Goss in 19 rounds that lasted nearly two hours. However, John C. Heenan issued a challenge to King for the crown, and with £1,000 a side resting on the challenge, King decided to accept. The American had his friend Tom Sayers in his corner when he fought King at Wadhurst, Kent, in December 1863. The 30-year-old Heenan, although heavier and stronger than King, was not the force he had been against Sayers, and the superior boxing of King saw him win in 24 rounds, lasting 35 minutes. It was Heenan's last fight and ten years later he died in Wyoming. It was also King's last fight. He made a fortune on the turf and died a very rich man in 1888.

Mace and King were the last two real bare-knuckle champions of England. Mace twice more beat Joe Goss, but prize fighting was becoming increasingly difficult in Victorian England, with the clergy, the judiciary and the police becoming more determined to wipe it out. Soon the best fighters were going to America to practise there, and the domination of boxing gradually passed from England to the United States.

Mace was a very influential figure in the spread of the 'noble art'. He travelled to South Africa, Australia and New Zealand, finding and coaching boxers — his biggest discovery was the Cornishman Bob Fitzsimmons, whom he found in New Zealand. Fitzsimmons was to become the first boxer to win world titles at three weights. Mace then went on to the United States, where also had landed several other prominent British fighters including Joe Goss, Ned Baldwin, Joe Wormwald and Tom Allen.

Below: Jem Mace was champion during the time in which prize fighting was finally suppressed by the forces of the law and the new Queensberry Rules boxing was establishing itself. He did much to bring science to boxing, teaching and spreading the noble art in South Africa, Australia, New Zealand and the United States.

The American succession

In America, after the retirement of John C. Heenan, the title had been assumed by Joe Coburn, who beat Mick McCoole in one hour ten minutes at Charlesworth, Maryland on 5 May 1863. Coburn was born at Middletown, Co Armagh, in 1835. He was only 5ft 9in (1.75m) but weighed 190lb (86kg). After winning the title he challenged Mace for the world crown, the two to meet in Ireland. Mace agreed for £500 a side, Coburn getting £100 expenses to come from the USA, and the contest took place near Dublin on 4 October 1864. Unfortunately, Coburn would not accept any referee except his friend, James Bowler, to which Mace could not agree, so the two fought a harmless exhibition without a referee, termed a draw.

Coburn retired temporarily, and Mick McCoole, another Irish immigrant, claimed the American championship by beating Bill

Davis in 35 minutes near St Louis on 19 September 1866. On 10 May 1867, backers of Jimmy Elliott, who had served a prison term for assault and robbery, claimed the title for him on the grounds of a knock-out of Bill Davis in Canada and the refusal of Coburn to meet him, but his claim was not generally accepted. He was a rough fighter, who in 1879 soaked his hands in turpentine to blind his opponent Johnny Dwyer, who was giving him a beating. Dwyer's seconds restored him with careful washing with water, and Dwyer systematically continued the beating. Elliott was finally shot dead in a tavern brawl.

McCoole, a riverman from Cincinnati, was the first American champion for a long time not based in New York. Having lost to Coburn in 1863, he was scheduled to meet him again in Indiana in 1868, but Coburn was arrested. On 15 June 1869 he fought Tom Allen from Birmingham, one of the English boxers who had gone to the States, and despite taking a beating finally came through to win after nine rounds, at Foster's Island, Mississippi.

Jem Mace now arrived in America and began to take on the best men. He beat Tom Allen in ten rounds at Kennerville, Louisiana, and then fought Joe Coburn in a strange fight in Canada, but after 77 rounds in which Coburn appeared unwilling to fight, the authorities stepped in and stopped it. Six months later the two met in St Louis, and the 40-year-old Mace was winning easily when the crowd got out of hand and the referee called it a draw. Mace departed from the USA in disgust.

In 1873 Tom Allen and Mick McCoole fought a return of their title fight, and this time Allen won easily in 20 minutes near St Louis.

So an Englishman was champion of America, and he was challenged by another, Joe Goss. Goss came from Northampton, and was another small man at 5ft 8½in (1.74m) and only 150lb (68kg), a welterweight by today's standards. Nevertheless, Goss won on a foul after 21 rounds fought in two rings in Kenton and Boone counties, Kentucky, in 1876. Allen appeared to have the fight won easily, but the crowd was behind Goss, by now a naturalized American, and Allen, having rendered Goss helpless and kneeling, gave him two quick punches to the head to earn disqualification but save himself from something perhaps worse. It was the same partiality that Mace had met with Coburn. It is a measure of the greatness of Mace that neither Allen nor Goss could beat him.

However, Mace was by now 45, and there were no more outstanding Englishmen coming along. The superiority of the country called the 'cradle of boxing' passed for ever with the arrival of a handsome Tipperary-born Irishman, Paddy Ryan, who had arrived in Troy, the fighting quarter of New York, when a boy. He was a real heavyweight, being 5ft 11in (1.80m) and 200lb (91kg), and he challenged Joe Goss for the American championship at Collier Station, West Vancouver, on 30 May 1880. Ryan did not possess anything like the skill of Goss, but he was much younger, bigger and stronger, and took everything the 42-year-old veteran could hand him. After 87 rounds he threw Goss heavily to the ground and jumped on him and, when Goss could not toe the line for the 88th round, became the new champion.

Above: *Paddy Ryan defeating Joe Goss for the championship of America at Collier's Station, West Virginia, in 1880. The battle lasted 87 rounds, and was the first formal fight for the young and strong 'Trojan Giant'.*

Enter John L. Sullivan

Ryan, known as the 'Trojan Giant', was a charismatic champion, but not a long-lasting one, for he lost the title in his next fight, on 7 February 1882, to one of the most famous champions of all, John L. Sullivan.

Sullivan was known as 'The Boston Strong Boy', and his Irish swagger and charisma built for him a huge following. He beat Ryan at Mississippi City for $2,500 a side in just over ten minutes.

Sullivan was really the last of the bare-knuckle world champions. For nearly 200 years to Mace, the English champions were in effect the world champions, but when Sullivan became American champion Mace had retired from serious combat, and while there was little correspondence between the best in America and the best of those remaining in England, Sullivan was so outstanding as to be accepted as the best in the world.

Sullivan and Mace were the bridges between bare-knuckle fighting and fighting with gloves. Both preferred to fight under the Queensberry Rules with gloves.

The Queensberry Rules

John Sholto Douglas, the eighth Marquess of Queensberry, was a sportsman who liked riding horses and boxing, at which he was an amateur champion. He was an aggressive man, famous later in life for his part in the downfall of Oscar Wilde. Queensberry drew

Right: *John L. Sullivan, the first great name in American boxing. Sullivan was a brave man with no science but with great strength and a tremendous punch. He became probably the most popular fighter in the whole of US ring history.*

Far right: *Richard Kyle Fox was the editor and publisher of the* Police Gazette, *subtitled* The Leading Illustrated Sporting Journal of America. *It began publication in 1873 and ended in 1932. Features of early editions were the imaginative drawings of the big fights. The feud between Fox and Sullivan led to Sullivan being given a famous belt by his supporters.*

up his boxing rules with the help of John Graham Chambers, who had been a student with him at Cambridge University. In fact it is likely that Chambers did all the work, and Queensberry was his patron who allowed his name to be used. The rules were published in 1867 and were as follows:

1. To be a fair stand-up boxing match in a twenty-four foot ring, or as near that size as practicable.

2. No wrestling or hugging allowed.

3. The rounds to be of three minutes' duration, and one minute's time between rounds.

4. If either man fall through weakness or otherwise, he must get up unassisted, ten seconds to be allowed him to do so; the other man meanwhile to return to his corner, and when the fallen man is on his legs the round is to be resumed, and continued till the three minutes have expired. If one man fails to come to the scratch in the ten seconds allowed, it shall be in the power of the referee to give his award in favour of the other man.

5. A man hanging on the ropes in a helpless state, with his toes off the ground, shall be considered down.

6. No seconds or any other person to be allowed in the ring during the rounds.

7. Should the contest be stopped by any unavoidable interference, the referee to name the time and place as soon as possible for finishing the contest; so that the match must be won and lost, unless the backers of both men agree to draw the stakes.

8. The gloves to be fair-sized boxing gloves of the best quality and new.

9. Should a glove burst, or come off, it must be replaced to the referee's satisfaction.

10. A man on one knee is considered down, and if struck is entitled to the stakes.

11. No shoes or boots with springs allowed.

12. The contest in all other respects to be governed by revised rules of the London Prize Ring.

The main differences to the old order were the use of gloves, the three-minute round and no wrestling. There was still not a time limit to a contest, which was fought to a finish. When, later, the concept of a time limit to a fight was incorporated, and decisions were rendered 'on points', boxing had taken the shape it retains to this day.

For 25 years or so, gloved fights under the Queensberry Rules were fought side by side with prize ring contests. There were still a few men who built big reputations fighting with bare knuckles. Jem Smith claimed the British championship in 1885 in one of the last bare-knuckle fights in England, and fought Jake Kilrain, of Quincey, Massachusetts, on the Isle des Souverains, in the River Seine, Paris, in 1887. By then fighting in England was difficult, forcing the two to go to France, but after two and a half hours and 106 rounds the match was declared a draw when it became too dark to continue.

Sullivan also fought with bare knuckles in France. A great rival was Charlie Mitchell, from Birmingham, who was little more than a middleweight but fancied his chances against Sullivan. He downed Sullivan in an 1883 exhibition at Madison Square Garden but was knocked out of the ring for his pains. However, the two met at Chantilly on 10 March 1888 for the world championship. The match took place behind the racing stables of Baron Rothschild. It had rained for 36 hours and the ground was muddy. The cunning Mitchell took the corner with his back to the wind, and Sullivan throughout the fight faced a wind and a cold drizzle.

The immensely strong Sullivan did his best to finish Mitchell with his heavy blows, but Mitchell kept dancing around and going down if in difficulties, and as Sullivan slowed in the conditions Mitchell began to score handsomely with blows of his own. Unfortunately, the gendarmerie stopped the fight after 39 rounds, lasting over three hours, at a stage where both men could claim they would have won. It was declared a draw, and both men were arrested.

This was not quite the last big bare-knuckle fight in Europe, for in the following year Jem Smith drew with Frank Slavin, an Australian claiming to be the Empire champion, in Bruges, Belgium. This fight ended the bare-knuckle era on a sour note, for there were many English bets on Smith, and when Slavin was about to win in the 14th round, ruffians entered the ring and the referee was forced to declare a draw.

The last important bare-knuckle fight in America featured John L. Sullivan and Jake Kilrain and it took place at Richburg, Mississippi, on 8 July 1889, for $10,000 a side. Kilrain had the backing of Richard K. Fox, the proprietor of the American boxing paper, the *Police Gazette*. He had declared Kilrain champion and given him a belt when Sullivan refused to meet him. After being almost humiliated by the lighter Mitchell, Sullivan now accepted a challenge from Kilrain, and the two fought a blazing fight. Charlie Mitchell was in Kilrain's corner.

The battle ran to 75 rounds in the hot sun, lasting two hours and 16 minutes. Towards the end Sullivan got on top, and the brave Kilrain was in danger of permanent injury when his seconds finally retired him.

It was the end of the prize ring. Kilrain later fought Slavin wearing gloves under Queensberry Rules, and Sullivan, after a stage career in which he gave boxing exhibitions and appeared in a melodrama, *Honest Hearts and Willing Hands*, was to take part in what became the first fight for the world heavyweight championship, wearing gloves.

***Below:** An illustration of the last great bare-knuckle fight in America, in which John L. Sullivan defeated Jake Kilrain, the* Police Gazette *champion, at Richburg, Mississippi, in 1889. Kilrain was forced to retire after two hours and 16 minutes of a bitter battle.*

EVERLAST

The Heavyweights and Cruiserweights

Because, as they say in boxing, 'a good big 'un will always beat a good little 'un', the heavyweight champion of the world is *the* champion; the man who can lick anybody else alive. Over the years it is the heavyweight champion who has attracted the most attention, the most money, the most spectators and the most fame. Muhammad Ali was regarded for a while in the 1970s as the most famous man in the world. There was intense excitement when crowds flocked to New Orleans in 1892 to see Jim Corbett become the first champion, there was hysteria in 1908 when Jack Johnson became the first black champion and provoked race riots, there was gold when Jack Dempsey and Georges Carpentier persuaded the public for the first time to part with over $1 million for the privilege of watching them fight in 1921. Enthusiasm had waned little by 1988, when Mike Tyson earned himself over $20 million for spending 91 seconds knocking out Michael Spinks for the 'richest prize in sport'.

Left: *Cassius Clay and Sonny Liston compete for the heavyweight championship of the world at Miami Beach, Florida, in 1964.*

THE RICHEST PRIZE IN SPORT

Most ring historians regard the fight promoted by the Olympic Club at New Orleans on 7 September 1892 as the first for the heavyweight championship of the world, a championship which can be traced from this battle to 1988 when Mike Tyson became the undisputed champion.

However, this would deny the title to John L. Sullivan, who lost this particular contest, and perhaps partly because John L. was probably the most idolized fighter in the history of boxing, some experts prefer to go back a little earlier to claim that John L. Sullivan was the first world heavyweight champion. This view rests largely on two premises. First is that Sullivan became world champion when he beat Tommy Ryan, who had beaten Joe Goss, who had beaten Tom Allen, who had claimed the world title when Jem Mace, generally regarded as the champion, had relinquished it. But neither Goss nor Allen could beat Mace, and others in Britain claimed the title, notably Jem Smith, and later Charlie Mitchell, who actually beat Mace in 1890 when Mace was 58 years old. So there was no clear-cut line of succession which made Sullivan world champion at all, although there is no doubt that for the first half of the 1880s at least, he was capable of beating anybody in the world. However, bare-knuckle contests are separated in the archives from matches made under the Marquess of Queensberry rules, and in all weight divisions the listings of modern world champions begin with the advent of gloves.

This gives much more credence to the second strand on which Sullivan's claim to the title is based. It has recently been rediscovered that a gloved contest between Sullivan and Dominic McCaffrey held in Chester Park, Cincinnati, on 29 August 1885 was advertised as being 'to decide the Marquess of Queensberry glove contest for the championship of the world'. The fight was held under Queensberry Rules, and if Sullivan is accepted as being the world's best, then it could be argued that this fight has as good a claim as that with Corbett to being regarded as the first world title fight. It is so regarded in some quarters, and *The Ring* Record Book recognized it as such. However, the fight was over only six rounds, and referee Billy Tate did not render a verdict, and gave Sullivan as the winner only when asked for his decision two days later, when he was in Toledo. So it does not seem an auspicious bout to be accepted as a focal point in boxing history. The Sullivan-Corbett contest in 1892 was a different matter altogether.

Sullivan led a dissipated life in the latter half of the 1880s, particularly after beating Jake Kilrain in 1889, and was being challenged on all sides. In 1891 he issued a challenge himself, in which he named his preferred opponents: Frank Slavin of Australia, Charlie Mitchell of England, who he said he 'would sooner whip than any man in the world', and James J. Corbett of California, who had done 'his share of bombast'. His condition was a $10,000 side-bet.

Corbett, a promising boxer, had been a warehouse clerk and teller in a bank, where he became interested in physical culture and boxing; he studied boxing scientifically, particularly the art of avoiding the opponent's punches. Where the practice of the bare-knuckle days had led to boxing becoming a trial of strength, with the winner being the man who could land the heavier blows and withstand the replies of his opponent better, Corbett developed the theory that the usual round-arm swings could be evaded by a boxer quick on his feet, and that an accumulation of straight left jabs, while not having the same spectacular effects, could so wear down and demoralize a man that he would be ripe for the kill.

Corbett's style had been given polish by

***Right:** James J. Corbett was regarded as a handsome man in his day. He also dressed well, was educated, and was a good boxer. But he was never popular because he dethroned the heroic John L. Sullivan.*

Left: Peter Jackson was a black boxer who around 1890 was probably as good as anybody in the world. Sullivan drew the 'colour line' and would not fight him. He fought Corbett (illustrated) in 1891, and the draw Corbett earned after 61 rounds convinced fans he was a suitable challenger to Sullivan.

William Watson, an English boxing instructor at the Olympic Club in New Orleans, and he was managed by the theatrical impressario William A. Brady, who had already employed the good-looking young boxer in a play he had taken on tour. Brady billed Corbett as 'the next heavyweight champion of the world' and consequently was delighted to accept Sullivan's challenge and put up the first instalment of the stake money. Corbett had met Sullivan on the stage at the Royal Opera House, San Francisco, when Sullivan was on tour, and the two had boxed a four-round exhibition, Corbett being of the opinion that he had learned enough from this to work out a way of beating Sullivan. He had already stopped Joe Choynski and Jake Kilrain, and fought a 61-round draw with Peter Jackson, a very talented black boxer whom Sullivan had declined to fight, drawing the colour line.

The Olympic Club secured the contest, making it the climax of a three-day Carnival of Champions, on the first two days of which George Dixon and Jack McAuliffe kept their world feather and lightweight crowns. Sullivan was a 4-1 on favourite to follow suit. Although, at nearly 34, he was eight years older than Corbett, he had a weight advantage of 34lb (15kg) at 212lb (96kg) to 178lb (81kg), and was considered invincible.

Corbett becomes champion

The battle commenced in an open-air arena soon after 9 o'clock, and it became clear early on to the 7000 or so spectators that Sullivan's usual superiority over his opponents was lacking. He could not connect on the wily Corbett and was forced to look clumsy as he missed with swing after swing. The crowd did not like the 'new' boxing and jeered the cool and confident Corbett as he dodged and retaliated with his more accurate jabs. Eventually, the out-of-condition Sullivan was confused, demoralized and exhausted by his unsuccessful efforts, and, as Corbett had planned, he was ready for dethronement.

Switching to all-out attack in the 21st round, Corbett overwhelmed Sullivan with rapid punches that sank the veteran battler to his knees. A little later a barrage ending with a left to the jaw had Sullivan face down and out in the centre of the ring, and the story of boxing had opened a new chapter: the old bare-knuckle champion had been superseded by the first heavyweight champion of the world.

Corbett successfully defended his title against veteran Charlie Mitchell of England, knocking him out in three rounds, and then announced his retirement, naming the winner of a fight between Steve O'Donnell, in whom he had an interest, and Peter Maher, an Irish heavyweight, as his successor. Unfortunately for Corbett, Maher won, but nobody, least of all Maher, took the view that Maher was the new champion. Nobody either should take seriously another of Corbett's ideas, the first-ever fight film, in which the champion knocked out Peter Courtney in the sixth round, two years to the day after winning the title. The fight was staged in a Kinetographic theatre at the Edison Laboratory, Oregon, New Jersey. Known as 'Black Maria', the theatre was only 15ft (4.57m) wide and padded to a height of 6ft (1.83m), the walls marking the boundaries of the 'ring' on opposite sides, and ropes being used on the other two sides. The Kinetoscope needed strong sunlight, so the theatre was on a circular track, so that it could move around and follow the sun. The rounds were scheduled to last two minutes, but since the film lasted only 90 seconds or so, time was called as soon as the film ran out. The intervals between rounds were longer than the rounds. The film was never shown.

Bob Fitzsimmons, an Englishman, had already knocked out Maher, and beat him again in 95 seconds on 21 February 1896. This fight was also scheduled to be filmed, but Fitzsimmons, not being party to the film rights, knocked out his man before the cameras began rolling. Fitzsimmons was the middleweight champion, having taken the title from 'Nonpareil' Jack Dempsey in 1891. His spindly legs and receding hair-line made him look most unlike a fighter, but work as a blacksmith in New Zealand had developed his upper body and he was capable of hitting as hard as anybody. Moreover, he was an experienced campaigner. Corbett scorned Fitzsimmons as a mere middleweight, and Fitzsimmons hated Corbett, whom he considered had avoided giving him a chance at the title for many years. Three attempts to stage a meeting fell through before the two finally climbed into the ring together at Carson City on 17 March 1897, with the championship at stake.

The solar plexus punch

Fitzsimmons, at 167lb (76kg), was 16lb (7kg) lighter than Corbett, and Corbett appeared to have matters well in hand when he dropped Fitzsimmons in the sixth, causing the challenger to hang on to survive. But Fitzsimmons fought back with body punches, and in the 14th round sank a left to Corbett's solar plexus which completely knocked the breath from the champion. Although in command of his senses, he sank to the floor with a grey face and could not rise before being counted out.

Fitzsimmons, known as 'Ruby Robert' because of his sandy-red hair and freckles,

Below: Bob Fitzsimmons in 1891 when he was the world middleweight champion. He does not look like a heavyweight, but in 1897 he knocked out Corbett to win the top prize in boxing.

was a fighting freak who never weighed more than a super-middleweight. Like Sullivan and Corbett before him he went on the stage, touring with his own show.

One man unimpressed with the new champion was a former sparring partner of Corbett's, James J. Jeffries. He began to climb the heavyweight ladder and registered wins against Tom Sharkey, an Irishman who was a leading contender of the period, and Peter Jackson, who had boxed a draw with Corbett. Jeffries was managed by William A. Brady, who also managed Corbett, and one of Brady's gimmicks to get attention for his challenger for the title was to bring Jeffries to New York and have him fight two men on the same night, Bob Armstrong and Steve O'Donnell. Unfortunately, Jeffries hurt his hand early in the first fight, which he won on points, and had to back out of the second.

This probably worked to Jeffries' advantage because Fitzsimmons was persuaded that he could safely put his title on the line in a contest with him. Jeffries, of Dutch and Scottish ancestry, was 24 years old at the time, 6ft 2½in (1.89m) and weighed around 205lb (93kg). He was 12 years younger than Fitzsimmons and seemed to have all the advantages, but Fitzsimmons reckoned he was safer against a young, raw fighter than against one with the skill of Corbett. Jeffries might have had a suspicion this was true, as he bet on Fitzsimmons to win, as an insurance policy.

If the knowledge of Jeffries' bet gave Fitzsimmons confidence, then the bear-hug with which Jeffries greeted Fitzsimmons in the dressing rooms beforehand dissipated it. Jeffries, known as 'The Boilermaker' because of his earlier profession, was immensely strong, and his 38lb (17kg) advantage in weight proved all too much for the champion. The fight took place on 9 June 1899 in New York City. Fitzsimmons was down in the second round, and although he rose and continued to take the fight to his opponent, he was repeatedly set back with heavy swinging lefts and rights to his face and body. Finally, in the tenth round, he was knocked down twice more, and had not recovered when in the 11th a left hook put him out for the count.

Jeffries' first defence of his title followed in five months — a distinct speeding-up on the two or three years that had separated title fights in this division previously. It was one of the most savage fights that ever took place. Jeffries' challenger was the ex-sailor Tom Sharkey, a man who looked every inch a heavyweight boxer, his most noticeable features being a large tattoo of a sailing ship under a five-pointed star, sailing on the hairs of his chest, and a pronounced cauliflower ear. Sharkey held decisions over Fitzsimmons and Corbett, though both were disqualifications, the former aided by a 'fix'.

The gallant Tom Sharkey

The two men met at New York City on 3 November 1899. The contest was the first to be filmed indoors, which meant the hanging of 400 arc lights of 200 candlepower each over the ring. The heat was so tremendous that the referee, George Siler, had to wear a hat. The heads of Sharkey and Jeffries were burned, but the two men kept dealing each other severe blows for the whole of the 25 rounds. At the end of his exertions Jeffries had lost 20lb (9kg) in weight. Sharkey, however, took the more material punishment. Although knocked down in the second round, he fought on for 23 more, suffering two broken ribs and horrific facial cuts. Jeffries, who dislocated an elbow, won the decision, although he too was utterly exhausted at the end of the bout. Sharkey was taken to hospital and Jeffries held for a while in case Sharkey died and charges might be preferred. Later in life the two men became the firmest of friends, and Sharkey went to stay with Jeffries and they talked over the old fights again.

After he had knocked out Jack Finnegan in one round in Detroit, Jeffries next took part in another gruelling affair, against his old 'master' James J. Corbett, who was never happy about the way he lost the title to Fitzsimmons. The contest was on 11 May 1900 in New York City, and was the classic 'boxer *v.* slugger' encounter. Corbett had trained hard for a year and outclassed his 37lb (17kg) heavier opponent, dancing around him as he had Sullivan and making his face a mess with his persistent jabs. It was obvious that Jeffries could keep his title only by a knockout, and in the 23rd of the 25 rounds, he got his chance at last. Corbett confessed afterwards that he was already anticipating the headlines and dreaming of his name in lights again when Jeffries caught him with two left hooks to the jaw, and that was that for the 33-year-old ex-champion.

Jeffries defended once a year for the next four years. His next defence was against Gus Ruhlin, who retired in the fifth, then on 25 July 1902 Bob Fitzsimmons was given another chance. The amazing Ruby Robert

***Above:** Champion Fitzsimmons shakes hands with challenger James J. Jeffries before their title fight in 1899. The younger, stronger Jeffries knocked out 'Ruby Robert' in the 11th round. The referee is Ed Graney.*

was now in his 40th year, but still a formidable fighter. He had knocked out Ruhlin and Sharkey, among others, since losing the title. This time he did not take Jeffries lightly, and instead of trying to swap punches with him he adopted Corbett's tactics, moving around and sneaking out his punches, and retiring before Jeffries could counter with his bombs. Within three or four rounds the champion's nose was broken and he was bleeding profusely from cuts all over his face. However, in the eighth round Jeffries at last thudded a huge right to Fitzsimmons' stomach. Fitzsimmons dropped his hands and tried to make light of the blow by smiling and talking to Jeffries, but it did not save him from a left hook to the jaw which knocked him clean out.

Fitzsimmons' brave show encouraged Corbett to try again, but this time, although he again outboxed his younger opponent, retribution came earlier and he was counted out in the 10th. Jeffries then knocked out Jack Munroe in the second round on 26 August 1904 and, having run out of logical contenders, and having reigned for over five years, he announced his retirement, reserving the right to decide his successor.

Jeffries fancied Marvin Hart, a 28-year-old from Jefferson County, Kentucky, who had a points win over Jack Johnson, a black heavyweight who was looming threateningly over the scene. He matched Hart with Jack Root, an Austrian-born fighter who, two years earlier, had been the first world light-heavyweight champion, a division invented for him by his manager, since he was of an awkward weight between middleweight and heavyweight. Jeffries refereed the bout in Reno, Nevada, and although Root knocked down Hart in the seventh, Hart won by a 12th-round knockout to become the new champion.

Burns clears the air

Jeffries presented Hart with the belt, and Hart has his name in the records, but the public were unconvinced, and so were many of the other heavyweight battlers of the day. Among these was a man born in Canada as Noah Brusso, who boxed as Tommy Burns. Burns was an unlikely heavyweight as he stood only 5ft 7in (1.70m) tall. He weighed around 175lb (79kg), and at the time of Hart's reign had suffered only three defeats, on points, in 38 contests. He obtained a match with Hart on 23 February 1906 and won an easy decision to assume the title.

Burns was a very shrewd businessman who knew how to cash in on the title (not that he was recognized by the public much more than Hart. Jeffries was still the 'people's champion'). Burns made more defences (12) than anybody until Joe Louis arrived in the

Right: Canadian Tommy Burns was the shortest heavyweight champion. He was also one of the busiest, and not until Ali did another champion travel so much. He defended in England, France, and Australia, and made the most of his title in financial terms.

***Left:** Burns was no match for Jack Johnson, when the challenger at last caught up with him in a ring near Sydney, Australia. Johnson was the first black champion, and his victory, and its manner, provoked race hatred in America.*

1930s. What's more he travelled the world to make them, which none of his predecessors was prepared to do. He fought some ordinary men among his challengers, but Fireman Jim Flynn and Philadelphia Jack O'Brien, the light-heavyweight champion, were worthy opponents. Bill Squires, a previously unbeaten Australian, followed Burns around and was knocked out in Los Angeles, Paris and Sydney. Part of the reason for Burns' wanderings might have been the threatening behaviour of Jack Johnson. Johnson, too, decided to follow Burns abroad, first to London and then to Sydney.

Jack Johnson was one of several excellent US black boxers of the period who could not get a title fight in the USA. Sullivan had drawn the colour line with Peter Jackson in the 1890s. Before World War I, Sam Langford, Sam McVey and Joe Jeannette were all worthy of a title shot, but were forced on the whole to fight each other. Some black boxers were forced by economic pressure to drop decisions purposely to up-and-coming white boxers to keep the promoters happy with them. Some fought in 'battles-royal', in which half-a-dozen were put into the ring together and eliminated each other until one was left. Johnson in particular declined these undignified procedures and went after a championship fight with great singleness of purpose.

Burns' flight to Australia can be interpreted as fear of Johnson, but Burns might well have fostered this idea to ensure a big pay day. If he did, it worked, for he persuaded an Australian promoter, Hugh D. McIntosh, to pay him a guaranteed £6,000 (then worth $30,000) to defend. McIntosh (known as 'Huge Deal' McIntosh) built an open-air arena on waste-ground at Rushcutter's Bay, on the outskirts of Sydney. He made a huge profit, as 16,000 fans paid over four times Burns' fee to see the fight, hyped as the great 'Black *v.* White' battle.

Johnson was far too good for Burns, being around 6in (15cm) taller and 12lb (5.5kg) heavier, and he toyed with the game champion. The police finally ended the fight in the 14th round, and the world had its first black heavyweight champion.

Right: *Johnson at the races in England with Etta Terry Duryea, a married woman who eloped with him and later became his wife. She soon committed suicide, blaming Johnson for her desperation, and within months Johnson had married a 19-year-old white girl whom he was charged with abducting. Johnson's associations with white women eventually led to his downfall.*

The dreaded Jack Johnson

Johnson was the most hated of all champions, because he was the sort of black man that American whites could not stand — opinionated and not at all servile. Further, he had a liking for white women (three of whom he was to marry). Stories of his contemptuous behaviour during the title fight in Australia were enough to initiate a series of violent race riots and lynchings in many states of the USA.

Johnson seemed so superior to the rest that challengers were not forthcoming, and he was forced to cash in by boxing exhibitions, among his opponents being Victor McLagen, who was to achieve fame as a Hollywood film star. His first title challenger was the middleweight champion Stanley Ketchel, although their fight at Los Angeles on 16 October 1909 is generally regarded as a 'fix'. Ketchel was one of the greatest of all middleweights and had a tremendous punch, and, as 'Sunny Jim' Coffroth, the promoter at the Colma Arena, anticipated, many thought the eight-years-younger Ketchel might surprise Johnson. Ketchel did surprise Johnson, but not in the way the 12,000 crowd anticipated. It is thought now that the two boxers had an arrangement by which Johnson would 'carry' Ketchel to the 12th round, making the fight look good for the cameras. Ketchel, it appeared, tried too hard, and in the 12th actually landed a good right on Johnson's ear which floored the champion. Johnson recognized an attempt to double-cross him, pretended to be hurt more than he was, and as Ketchel leapt in for the kill caught him with such a right that not only was Stanley knocked cold but some of his teeth remained embedded in Johnson's glove.

Johnson naturally became more disliked than ever, and there was a desperate search to find a white boxer to beat him. It seemed there might be one who could — Jim Jeffries, who had retired unbeaten in 1904. Jeffries, after all, was only three years older than Johnson, and was taller and heavier. Eventually, Jeffries was persuaded back into the ring, and the two men met at Reno on 4 July 1910. The promoter was Tex Rickard, the greatest of all promoters, who had made an impact with a lightweight title promotion at Goldfield in 1906, and was to make an even bigger impression later with Jack Dempsey. He bid $101,000 for the fight, plus under-the-table bonuses.

The Johnson–Jeffries riots

This was the most eagerly awaited fight in boxing history at that date, and the crowds poured into Reno. There was so much hype that not only was Jeffries regarded as having a chance, he was actually installed as a 10-6 favourite. In retrospect it is easy to see that the 35-year-old, overweight, out-of-training Jeffries would be no match for the super-fit Johnson, and so it proved to be. It was as humiliating a spectacle as the Burns fight, as Johnson taunted and toyed with Jeffries, before the fight was stopped in the 15th, with the former champion helpless on the floor, and suffering his first defeat.

If the defeat of the Canadian Burns in Australia had inspired race riots, think of the reaction of white America to the humiliation of their own hero in their own backyard. There were fights, lynchings and other murders, and general violence and destruction all over America. Nobody dared show the film for fear of further riots.

The next 'white hope' to try to beat Johnson was Fireman Jim Flynn, who had already failed to beat Tommy Burns. Johnson had no difficulty in knocking out Flynn in New Mexico two years to the day after he had defeated Jeffries.

Johnson's private life was now the target of his ill-wishers, and he was convicted of a contravention of the Mann Act, which prohibited taking women across state lines for immoral purposes. Johnson, who had abandoned his black wife, had travelled with numerous white prostitutes, and the testimony of one, Belle Schreiber, was enough to earn him a year's imprisonment. On bail, Johnson fled to Paris, where he drew over ten rounds with Jim Johnson (the first all-black heavyweight title fight) and outpointed a former Pittsburgh dentist, Frank Moran, over 20 rounds.

In his absence, the 'white hope' search was intensified. Moran was only one of a number of hopefuls from the USA, Britain, France and Australia who were fondly put forward as possibles. One of the most promising, Luther McCarty, who styled himself the 'white champion', sadly died after a contest with another, Arthur Pelkey, although an earlier accident with a horse was thought to be the main reason for the tragedy. The most convincing evidence of Johnson's mastery was the public recognition of the 'white heavyweight championship', a reversal of the days when Johnson and others were forced to call themselves 'the black champions'. By knocking out Pelkey, Gunboat Smith claimed this title in 1914. Georges Carpentier took it from him, and it virtually ceased with World War I, during which Johnson was at last defeated.

***Below:** The* San Francisco Chronicle *profiled the two contestants in the big fight of 1910, when unbeaten ex-champion Jeffries came out of retirement in an attempt to stop the progress of the unpopular champion Johnson. Johnson's easy victory caused terrible race riots.*

Johnson had become homesick, and was anyway forced to flee Europe when war broke out. He went to Buenos Aires and was persuaded to accept a challenge from Jess Willard, a 6ft 6¼in (1.99m) giant, who did not begin boxing until he was 29, when he had been picked as an obvious 'white hope'. The contest took place at Havana, Cuba, and was scheduled for 45 rounds. In blistering heat Johnson survived 25 rounds, being comfortably the more accomplished craftsman, but his 37-year-old frame succumbed to a knock-out blow in the 26th. At least, that is how the records have it. Johnson later claimed to have lost deliberately both for money and because the promoter, Jack Curley, had promised him his prison sentence would be cancelled if he were no longer champion. While this version has been accepted by many, it has always been the subject of speculation, and nobody will know for sure.

Willard held the title for over four years, during which he did not defend it, unless one counts a 'no-decision' contest with Frank Moran. 'No decision' bouts were those held in New York State under the Frawley Law from 1911 until it was replaced by the Walker Law in 1920. Under the Frawley Law boxing was allowed in public, but the bouts were classed as 'exhibitions'. No decision could be rendered officially. Newspaper reporters pronounced verdicts, but these had not the weight to deprive a champion of his title, of course, so the only way a title could change hands was by a knock-out.

During this time a real fighting man was learning his trade: Jack Dempsey. After some initial setbacks, he had been taken over by an astute manager, Jack 'Doc' Kearns, and had lately been demolishing many of the former 'white hopes' and others in double-quick time (e.g. five consecutive one-round knock-outs). Kearns, whose nickname 'Doc' was due to the black bag in which he always carried his equipment for cuts, etc, persuaded Tex Rickard to match Dempsey with Willard. Rickard did, and the resulting hype led to another big crowd at Bay View Park, Toledo, Ohio, on 4 July 1919.

Dempsey destroys Willard

Willard was by now 37, the age Johnson had been when Willard took his title. His physical advantages were immense: 5¼in (13.3cm) in height and 58lb (26kg). But he was a lumbering giant when compared to the fast and ruthless Dempsey, who proceeded to knock him down seven times in the first round. Willard was actually counted out at the end of it, but the referee had not appreciated that the round had ended. Dempsey, who had a big bet on a first-round win, hurriedly left the ring, but was recalled by Kearns and forced to deal out more pain for two more rounds, by when the brave Willard was forced to retire, being unable to stand with two ribs smashed.

Dempsey's career marks a turning point in the history of boxing, for although he made only five successful defences, four of his contests were huge moneymakers, and with his manager Kearns and promoter Rickard he can claim to have advanced the public consciousness of boxing to a marked degree. Unpopular at one point of his career, he became immensely popular by the end of it.

His first defence was against a former sparring partner, Billy Miske, who had given

Below: *Jack Dempsey (right) ducking and weaving while he searches for an opening for his destructive punches to knock out Jess Willard, who suffered more injuries in three rounds than any heavyweight champion until Schmeling was destroyed by Louis nearly 20 years later.*

him two hard fights in his up-and-coming days, but who now was seriously ill with Bright's Disease. Miske earned $25,000 for his family, and Dempsey considerately knocked him out in the third round. Dempsey then despatched Bill Brennan in 12 in New York, but was unimpressive.

A wartime publicity photograph now rebounded on Dempsey. It was meant to show him helping the war effort, by hammering in rivets in a shipyard, but a newspaper now published the picture again and pointed out his patent leather shoes. It was enough to earn Dempsey the reputation of a draft dodger.

The million-dollar fight

It was now that Rickard showed his flair for promotion. A handsome, decorated French war hero, Georges Carpentier, was brought to America, won the world light-heavyweight title by knocking out Battling Levinsky, and was matched with Dempsey for the title at Boyle's Thirty Acres, Jersey City. The contrast between the two men, as hyped by Rickard, was almost as clear-cut as the Black *v.* White of Johnson and Burns 13 years earlier. This time it was good *v.* bad, war hero *v.* slacker, the Orchid Man against the Manassa Mauler. Rickard built an open-air arena and 91,000 turned up to see the confrontation on 2 July 1921. Never before had a million dollars been paid at the gate of a boxing match, but the receipts for this one soared to $1,789,238. Dempsey himself was guaranteed $300,000. Even the Americans began by supporting Carpentier, but if it really was good *v.* bad, then it was a night that bad triumphed. Carpentier was hardly a heavyweight, and although Dempsey, too, was light for the division at 188lb (85kg), he had a 16lb (7kg) advantage. In the event, Carpentier could not resist the strength of Dempsey, and was knocked out in the fourth round.

Dempsey's next defence, two years later, led to financial disaster for the town of Shelby, Montana, persuaded by the receipts of the Carpentier fight to guarantee Dempsey $300,000 to meet Tommy Gibbons. The plan was to put Shelby on the map, but it nearly did the reverse. Only 7,000 turned up to watch and all four of the town's banks went bankrupt. The fight itself was an uninteresting one, Dempsey being foxed by Gibbons and winning unimpressively on points. His popularity remained low.

Above: *The end of Carpentier's challenge to Dempsey. The French war hero broke his thumb on Dempsey's head in the second round and could not keep out the Manassa Mauler, finishing draped over the rope in the fourth round.*

Below: Gene Tunney, the ex-Marine, whose career followed an exemplary upward path to the heavyweight championship, from which he retired unbeaten to become successful in business.

Rickard, meanwhile, was looking for another bonanza pay day and his main requirement was another big, strong, destructive puncher. He found the man he wanted in Luis Firpo, of the Argentine. He was 6ft 3in (1.90m), crude, and had won 11 of 12 fights inside the distance, including a victory over a 41-year-old Jess Willard. He was known as 'The Wild Bull of the Pampas' and Rickard's publicity drew 125,000 to the Polo Grounds, New York, to see the encounter with the million-dollar gate.

The first round was one of the most savage ever, with Dempsey down first, then Firpo down seven times, and finally Dempsey was knocked clean out of the ring. He was helped back (illegally) and saved from a probable knock-out by the bell. In the second round Dempsey had more know-how than Firpo, and floored the challenger twice more before knocking him out. Never has a fight seen more action in less than four minutes.

Dempsey now went to Hollywood for a film career and married the star Estelle Taylor, a union which meant the break-up of another, for Miss Taylor and Doc Kearns found themselves incompatible. Rickard, with Gene Normile, took over Dempsey's affairs from then on.

A prominent black boxer of the time was Harry Wills, who at 6ft 4in (1.93m) and 220lb (100kg) and possessing exceptional boxing skill, would have been a formidable opponent for anybody. He was six years older than Dempsey, and the public wanted to see them matched. The New York State Athletic Commission proposed the match, and it was more than once signed and agreed, even to the extent that tickets were printed for a match on 6 September 1924. Eventually, Rickard refused to allow Dempsey to fight Wills, despite being appealed to by the Boxing Board, and Dempsey was barred from fighting in New York.

Dempsey was out of the ring for three years, and the Hollywood life might well have softened up the 31-year-old when he next stepped through the ropes to fight Gene Tunney on 23 September 1926. Rickard wanted the fight in the Yankee Stadium, but the unrelenting Boxing Board forced him away from New York, and the Sesquicentennial Stadium at Philadelphia was the one that made history. Its claim to fame is the biggest live attendance at a boxing match: 120,757. Needless to say it was another million-dollar gate.

Tunney takes the title

Tunney was a clean-cut ex-Marine of intelligence who had studied boxing and scientific defence much as Corbett had done, and he used it to the same effect as Corbett had when defeating Sullivan 34 years earlier. The rain poured throughout the ten rounds (the maximum distance allowed in Philadelphia), and Tunney kept his feet better and cleverly outboxed Dempsey, who hardly got in an effective blow. At the end there was only one possible decision, and it was a win for Tunney.

The large crowd was not in favour of the new champion's style, however, and like Corbett he was never forgiven for having replaced the excitement of a champion who went all out to wreak damage or be destroyed himself with the less stirring appeal of a boxing lesson. Dempsey's consolation on being dethroned came from the opposite feeling: from now on he was the hero whose style the public wanted to see triumph.

Above: The end of the most discussed 14 seconds in boxing history. Tunney is down in his return fight with Dempsey, but referee Dave Barry did not begin to count until Dempsey had gone to a neutral corner. Tunney is about to rise at Barry's count of 'nine', but the timekeeper in the foreground has beat out at least 14 seconds. Dempsey is beginning to rush in to attempt to finish the job, but he couldn't. Fight fans have argued ever since about how much his failure was due to Tunney's extra five seconds rest.

A return between the two men would be an obvious crowd-puller, but Dempsey first had to re-establish his reputation. This he did by taking on Jack Sharkey, an up-and-coming boxer who had removed some of the arguments from the heavyweight ranks by defeating the veteran Wills (albeit on a foul). Sharkey, like his earlier heavyweight namesake an ex-sailor, had a penchant for hitting low, but was dealt with by Dempsey who himself hit Sharkey low in the seventh round (or at least Sharkey alleged so). While Sharkey grasped his midriff in agony, Dempsey knocked him out with a left.

The return championship match was at Soldiers Field, Chicago, on 22 September 1927, a year but a day after the title had changed hands. The fight was boxing's first two-million dollar gate ($2,658,660), which remained a record for 49 years until Muhammad Ali fought Ken Norton. Because of the interest in boxing at the time, this fight is probably the most controversial in history. The controversy centred on an incident in the seventh round when Dempsey, who was mostly on the receiving end, floored Tunney with a powerful barrage of punches. Dempsey failed to go to a neutral corner, and referee Dave Barry delayed his count and forced Dempsey to move away. Tunney remained down for what has been estimated as 14 seconds, and then rose to continue his dominance of the ex-champion. Would Dempsey have won had the count not been delayed? The question provided fight scribes of the day (and since) with a controversial story which ran and ran. Whatever the answer, it marked the end of Dempsey as a championship force.

Tunney defended his title once more. On 26 July 1928 he took on a New Zealander, Tom Heeney, who had come through an elimination tournament organized by Tex Rickard and had drawn in the final with Jack Sharkey. As Sharkey had already been beaten by Dempsey, Heeney was matched with Tunney, but the 'Hard Rock', as he was called, was outclassed and stopped in the 11th. Tunney then retired — the first of the (so far only two) heavyweight champions to retire while still champion and not to make a come-back.

With Tunney's retirement another eliminating competition was required — not to find a contender this time, but a new champion. Rickard, who had lost money for the first time as a promoter with the Tunney *v.* Heeney fight, went to Miami to match Sharkey with Young Stribling in the first stages, but while he was there he was forced to have an appendix operation and died shortly afterwards. Dempsey, who still had connections with Rickard, took over the promotion with the Madison Square Garden Corporation, and Sharkey won the decision.

Meanwhile, a young German, Max Schmeling, was entering the lists. He knocked out Johnny Risko and beat Paolino Uzcudun. Sharkey beat a British contender, 'Phainting'

Right: *The only heavyweight champion to win his title on a disqualification, Max Schmeling. The fact that he became a propaganda weapon of Nazism, and that Louis symbolically beat him savagely in one round just before World War II has disguised the fact that Schmeling was a good boxer with a devastating right-hand punch.*

Phil Scott, in a peculiar bout in which Scott outboxed Sharkey until the third, when he was floored, as he claimed, with a blow below the belt. This happened twice more and referee Lou Magnolia insisted he either get on with the fight or quit. Scott continued but once again was struck low, and was counted out.

This fight has an echo in what happened when Sharkey and Schmeling were matched for the vacant title. On 12 June 1930, 79,222 fans attended proceedings at the Yankee Stadium, and paid $749,935 for the privilege. The million-dollar gate seemed to have ended with the defeat of Dempsey and the death of Rickard. The 1920s was the Golden Era of boxing, and the 1930s was to prove an era of mediocrity until the arrival of Joe Louis.

The Sharkey *v.* Schmeling encounter seemed to get the 1930s off on the wrong foot. Neither boxer had established an advantage when, in the fourth round, Sharkey drove a hard punch into Schmeling's midriff, which doubled up the German and left him writhing on the floor. His manager, Joe Jacobs, leapt into the ring to insist to the referee, Jim Crowley, that the punch was low. The referee and one of the judges claimed not to have seen the blow, but a Hearst newspaper editor in the ringside seats then threatened Crowley that should Sharkey not be disqualified the powerful newspaper chain would ensure that the Walker Law, which permitted public boxing in New York, would be repealed. The second judge agreed the blow was low and Schmeling was given the verdict on a disqualification, the only heavyweight champion to win his crown in this way.

The New York Commission wanted an immediate return match and declined to recognize Schmeling when one was not forthcoming. A year after winning the crown Schmeling decided instead to accept a challenge from Young Stribling. Schmeling won comfortably in Cleveland, the referee stopping the contest with only a minute left of the last round.

Schmeling and Sharkey met again on 21 June 1932, at the Long Island Bowl. It was an uninspired fight between two cagey men. The sporting press seemed to think that at the end of the 15 rounds Schmeling had done enough to keep his crown, but the official verdict went the other way, and Sharkey had brought the title back to America. Schmeling protested bitterly, but could do nothing.

Primo Carnera, the Italian giant

The man proposed as Sharkey's first challenger was a freakish Italian, Primo Carnera. A huge man of 6ft 5¾in (1.98m) and 260lb (118kg), he was not a natural fighter, and was indeed amiable, but he was chosen by the boxing rulers, official and unofficial, to be the man to bring back appeal to the sport. His record was not impressive. Sharkey had beaten him, as had Young Stribling and Larry Gains, a Canadian who currently rejoiced in the 'black heavyweight champion' title. Gains, incidentally, had previously knocked out Schmeling, so hereabouts was possibly the best heavyweight in the world.

Among Carnera's 'handlers' were many shady characters from the underworld, perhaps the best known being Owney Madden. He fought an amazing number of times in the early 1930s — 18 times in the last six months of 1932. Before tackling Sharkey, Carnera fought Sharkey's pal Eddie Schaaf, and knocked him out in the 13th round with a fairly soft punch. Schaaf did not recover consciousness and died two days later, a tragedy which had an effect not only on Carnera but on Sharkey, who was in Schaaf's corner.

The title fight at Woodside, Long Island, was a peculiar affair. For five rounds Sharkey controlled the lumbering giant, and in the fifth actually seemed on the point of finishing it. But in the sixth Carnera landed a couple of heavy blows and swung the fight. A right uppercut and a left as Sharkey pitched forward left the champion flat on his face to be counted out.

So the 'Ambling Alp', many of whose fights it is generally assumed were 'fixed', was the new world champion. He made his first defence in Italy — the first heavyweight title fight outside the USA since Johnson lost in Cuba 18 years earlier. The champion repeated a points win over Paolino Uzcudun in Rome. In March 1934 he outpointed Tommy Loughran, the former light-heavyweight champion, who was forced to concede no less than 86lb (39kg). Carnera took size 18 shoes and was known as 'Satchel-feet', and one of Loughran's complaints was: 'The bum kept standing on my feet'.

The bum's next challenger was a playboy, Max Baer. Baer was a big man of 6ft 2½in (1.89m) and 220lb (100kg), and had a happy outgoing personality. His strength as a boxer was a tremendous right with which he could knock out anybody. In 1930 he had beaten Frankie Campbell severely in five rounds in San Francisco, and Campbell died. The State Athletic Commission suspended Baer for six months. He had been apprehensive on his return, and had been outpointed by Ernie Schaaf, but later had also given Schaaf a bad beating, and it is assumed that this contributed more to Schaaf's death than Carnera's blows. One of Baer's best wins was a tenth-round knock-out of Max Schmeling in 1933, and on 14 June 1934 he stepped into the ring with the champion at the Long Island Bowl.

Baer was favourite to win, even it seemed with Carnera, whose retiring nature had fallen under the spell of the challenger's personality. It was called the 'Comedy Battle', because of its stumblings and jokes. Once when Baer tripped in putting Carnera down and joined him on the canvas he quipped: 'Last one up is a cissy'. Carnera was down 11 times in all, before the referee, Arthur Donovan, stepped in, in the 11th round.

Below: *Primo Carnera was the biggest heavyweight champion at around 260lb (118kg). His physique matched his weight (he was once a circus strongman) but he was not a natural fighter, although he won 88 of his 103 contests, 69 inside the distance.*

Above: Carnera and Max Baer weigh in before their title fight in June 1934. Baer, on the scales, looks happy and confident, while Carnera, the champion, has a slightly bemused expression. This summarizes the title fight, and much of their careers.

Baer should have been heavyweight king for a long time, but he lost the title on his first defence to a man with none of his charisma or advantages. James J. Braddock, a one-time light-heavyweight challenger, had all but retired by 1933 when he was 27. After 20 or so defeats he had gone back to dock labouring and even been forced to accept state benefits. His career took a sudden upward leap with a third-round knock-out of an up-and-coming prospect, Corn Griffin, for whom he was meant to be a stepping-stone. This was on the Carnera-Baer bill, and he followed with a win against John Henry Lewis, another promising fighter. One more win and he was matched with Baer at the Long Island Bowl.

Happy-go-lucky Max did not train properly for this fight, expecting Braddock to buckle quickly — he was not alone for Braddock was quoted in the betting at 10-1, astonishing odds for a world title fight. But Braddock surprised Baer by taking the fight to him, and as the rounds went by and Baer's right failed to connect, so the out-of-condition champion wilted, and at the end Braddock was a clear points winner and the new champion.

Meanwhile, a young boxer was shaping a career which would soon put an end to all this off-hand treatment of the richest prize in sport. He was born Joseph Louis Barrow, but he had dropped his last name when he began fighting as a professional in 1934, less than a year before Braddock won the title. He won his 12 contests in his first year, and then in June 1934, when Braddock beat Baer, he knocked out ex-champ Primo Carnera, after giving him a beating for six rounds. Three months later he demolished an apprehensive Baer in four rounds.

Louis gets a shock from Schmeling

Louis' policy of destroying the ex-champions suffered an upset on 20 June 1936 at the Yankee Stadium, New York. Max Schmeling, brought over as another stepping-stone for Louis to stride to the title, found he could cross his right comfortably over Louis' jabs, and he dumped the would-be champion on the canvas in the fourth. In the 12th he went one better and knocked Louis out. Louis suffered no more such setbacks, and he next beat Jack Sharkey, another former champion, in three rounds.

During this time, Louis had brought excitement back into the heavyweight ranks. He was clearly an outstanding boxer and fighter, and although he was patronized by the white population of America in the way that blacks were at that time, his demeanour (carefully coached by his trainer, Jack Blackburn) led to popularity rather than fear, and there was none of the hatred inspired by Jack Johnson. Mike Jacobs, his manager, was now a very powerful man in boxing — he 'owned' its star attraction and also controlled the Madison Square Garden Corporation, for whom the champion Braddock had an obligation to make his defences. Louis was now ready for a title fight, and nothing seemed more natural, then, that it should follow and that Louis would be the new champion.

There was one drawback to the plan: Max Schmeling. Schmeling, it will be recalled, had lost his title to Sharkey on a dubious decision, and had knocked out the young Louis. Ever since Braddock had won the title, Schmeling had been agitating for a title shot, and his manager, Joe Jacobs (not to be confused with Louis' manager, Mike Jacobs) took him to New York and persuaded the Boxing Commission to announce that Schmeling was the logical contender and that Braddock must defend first against the German.

Mike Jacobs had to act swiftly. Realizing that Schmeling might well beat Braddock, and that if he did the heavyweight championship would suddenly become outside his (Jacobs') control, and moreover, that with the possibility of Germany becoming involved with war in Europe, he might well lose his meal-ticket for several years, Jacobs made a unique deal with Braddock and his manager,

Joe Gould. The terms of this deal were that Braddock should ignore the Boxing Commission and put his title at stake against Louis for nearly $300,000, with the additional inducement that should he lose he would receive ten per cent of the profits made by Jacobs from heavyweight championship promotions for the next ten years. It was a deal impossible to refuse, particularly by a heavyweight on the wrong side of 30 who had once been almost retired and knew what it was to stand in a breadline. The fight was signed for 22 June 1937.

Thus, poor Schmeling, who generally received a bad deal from boxing, was sidetracked. That he was potentially a trump card for Nazi propaganda led the public to overlook the injustice of the situation. The New York Boxing Commission did fix a date for him to fight Braddock, and Schmeling duly weighed in for what was called the Phantom Fight, earning the Commission's recognition as world champion. But nobody else took this seriously and Schmeling has not gone into the record books as the first man to regain the title (it would have been a remarkable double if he had, since his first win was on a disqualification).

Comiskey Park, Chicago, was the venue for the Braddock-Louis fight, and those who expected the champion to take the money and depart with as little bother as possible to himself or Louis were quickly robbed of their opinion. In fact, Braddock, as if to disprove the view that he was the softest champion of all, fought like a real champion, and went after his young challenger from the first bell. Soon a right over Louis' head dumped 'The Brown Bomber', as he was called, on to the canvas. But Louis recovered well, and in succeeding rounds his jabbing began not only to halt Braddock's attacks but to cut up his

***Left:** One of the biggest upsets in boxing. The upwardly mobile Joe Louis, considered unbeatable, is knocked out by ex-champion Max Schmeling in 1936. It was Louis' only defeat until he retired and made a comeback after the war.*

face. Gould was ready to throw in the towel, but Braddock insisted on giving his all, and only relinquished the title when one of Louis' hardest punches, a right to his chin, knocked him out completely. His face needed 23 stitches afterwards but his pride was whole and his bank balance was about to multiply.

Having 'won' the title, and with two 'champions' on his promotional payroll, Jacobs quickly looked round for some fights which would bring in revenue without much pain to his gladiator. It so happened that a boxer from Britain, Welshman Tommy Farr, was building up just the reputation to appeal to Jacobs. He was British and Empire champion, having outpointed Ben Foord in 1937, and in the next couple of months he defeated Max Baer and knocked out Walter Neusel, a very tough German fighter. Despite this knock-out, Farr was not a heavy puncher, and it seemed inconceivable that he could withstand the blazing fists of Louis for 15 rounds.

The choice of Farr for Louis' first defence was hastened when Jacobs heard of a move to match Farr with Schmeling for the New York version of the title and Farr was rapidly signed to meet Louis at the Yankee Stadium on 30 August 1937, only nine weeks after Louis had won the title.

Farr put up a much better battle than any in America, in particular, expected. Farr took the fight to the champion and was still battling away hard at the end of the 15th round. The superior weight of Louis' punching was all that separated the two men and this won Louis the decision.

Louis was to prove one of the most active of all champions, and he clocked up two quick knock-out victories in 1938 when disposing of Nathan Mann and Harry Thomas. Meanwhile, Schmeling also continued winning, including Harry Thomas among his victims, too. There was a demand in America that the two should meet. Schmeling badly wanted the contest — it would be his last chance to regain the crown and he was con-

***Right:** The first challenger for Louis' title was the British champion, Tommy Farr (facing camera) who gave Louis one of his hardest fights. At the end Louis took the verdict on points, but it was a close one.*

fident he could do to Louis what he had achieved in 1936. Louis, too, wanted the contest to remove the only blot on his otherwise outstanding record. Mike Jacobs certainly wanted the contest because it would be a money-spinner. Shamelessly, he exploited the political situation. Schmeling was portrayed as the representative of Hitler's 'master race'. All that Hitler stood for — the extolment of the Caucasian race and the suppression of the black and Jewish races — was personified in the hype of Schmeling. All that was good and democratic as understood in 'the American way of life' was personified in Louis. It all led to gate receipts topping the million dollars as 70,000 packed into Yankee Stadium to see virtue triumph.

That virtue would triumph there was little doubt in Jacobs' mind or anybody else's. It was exactly a year since Louis had won the title and two years and two days since Schmeling had knocked him out. Louis was now 24, and a much better fighter than two years earlier, while Schmeling was now approaching 33 and presumably on the wane.

The Brown Bomber's revenge

Louis put on the best display of his career in what became his most famous fight. If he had any lingering doubts about the power of the German's right hand he did not give them time to affect his performance. Schmeling was floored with a right to the jaw almost as soon as the fight had started. Several times in the following minute or so Louis powered punches into the helpless German, who twisted and turned as he clung to the top rope. This led Schmeling to take some tremendous blows in the region of his kidneys and back, and his scream of pain when two vertebrae were broken was heard by the millions in Germany around their radio sets. Twice more Schmeling sank to the canvas, and on the third occasion his corner threw in the towel, but this was ignored and referee Arthur Donovan counted him out. The contest had lasted only 124 seconds, and Schmeling was still on a stretcher when he embarked for home. The revenge for Louis was complete, and he had shown in those two minutes that he was the most destructive boxer the division had seen for many years.

Louis kept himself busy during 1939 and 1940, taking four fights in each year. Only one of the fights, against the Chilean Arturo Godoy, went the distance. He knocked out his friend, John Henry Lewis, the light-heavyweight champion, in the first round — to save him punishment, he claimed. This was the second all-black world heavyweight title fight. Lewis had trouble with his eyes, and failed a medical in England to defend his title against Len Harvey, and sadly he was to go blind.

One of the most colourful of Louis' challengers was a very fat New Jersey bar owner known as 'Two-Ton' Tony Galento, who allegedly trained in the bar and consumed much of its beer and cigars himself. He strutted around promising to 'moider da bum', but was, in fact, a serious if crude fighter who actually floored Louis in the first round. Louis, however, gave him a fearful beating during the rest of the four rounds the contest lasted.

From December 1940 to June 1941, Louis speeded up and fought one opponent in each month, and was said by the press to be on a 'bum-of-the-month' campaign. All of these fights were won inside the distance, but Louis seemed to take longer against the really big men. Abe Simon, who stood 6ft 4in (1.93m) and weighed 255lb (116kg), lasted into the 13th round. There was nearly a big upset when another big man, Buddy Baer, the brother of the former champion, Max, knocked Louis through the ropes and onto the apron of the ring in the first round of their bout in Washington in May 1941. Louis clambered back and won the fight in a peculiar manner. Baer claimed that Louis had struck him after the bell had ended for the sixth round and that he should have been disqualified. When Baer refused to come out for the seventh, the referee disqualified *him* and awarded the fight to Louis.

Above: *'Two-Ton' Tony Galento in his bar before fighting Joe Louis for the title. The roly-poly Galento was a rough fighter who surprised Louis by flooring him, but Louis was too good and knocked him out in the fourth round.*

Conn spurns fame

Louis' seventh fight in seven months turned out to be a classic. His challenger was Billy Conn, who had recently relinquished the light-heavyweight championship in order to campaign among the heavyweights. Having knocked out Bob Paster, who had lasted 11 rounds with Louis, he fancied his chances against the champion. They met at the New York Polo Grounds on 18 June 1941, and Conn, as well as giving away height and reach, was the lighter by 24lb (11kg). But he boxed brilliantly and dazzled Louis with his skill and speed. From the 11th onwards the confident Conn went on the offensive and began to slug it out with Louis, effectively beating the confused champion at his own game.

Alas, it proved his downfall. Examination of the judges' and referee's cards afterwards showed that Conn was well ahead entering the 13th and needed only to revert to his boxing to win the title comfortably. His Irish blood did not allow him to stand-off when his man was beaten however, and in that round Louis at last landed a hard left hook to the jaw followed by a solid right and the roles were suddenly reversed. A previously bewildered Louis now punched away at a suddenly drained Conn, and just before the end of the round a final right knocked out the challenger. It was the champion's hardest defence to date.

Louis now took three months off before stopping Lou Nova, who had ended the career of Max Baer with a bad beating. Nova was stopped in the sixth round.

This ended 1941's boxing activity for Louis, who now enlisted in the US Army. In January 1942 he gave a return to Buddy Baer, knocking him out in the first round. He donated his entire purse to the Naval Relief Fund, with his manager Jacobs and Baer also making contributions. In March Louis gave a return to Abe Simon, and knocked him out in six rounds. This purse was donated to the Army Relief Fund. The champion then spent four years in uniform, giving exhibitions with a sparring partner, George Nicholson, and visiting troops at home and abroad. It was a programme which earned him great respect among the public (and contrasted with the reputation Dempsey was saddled with after World War I).

Once out of the Army, Louis was matched by Jacobs with Billy Conn again. Conn, too, had served for four years in the Army. Their 1941 contest had been one of the best of the period before America entered the war, and 45,266 spectators were happy to make their way to the Yankee Stadium in New York and pay almost two million dollars to see if the two men could put up as good a display. The date was 19 June 1946, five years and one day since their previous encounter.

Although he was three years the younger, Conn appeared to have gone back the more in the interim. He was no more the smiling, arrogant fighter who had all but beaten Louis. He elected to use completely different tactics, and fought entirely on the retreat. Louis was so rusty he could not time his punches to catch him. The fight was a dull one until in the eighth Louis at last caught Conn with a right and left and Conn was dumped on the canvas where he was counted out shading his eyes from the hot overhead lights.

Tami Mauriello came next, and had the satisfaction of staggering the champion with the first punch of their fight, but that was all he achieved, for after two minutes and nine seconds Mauriello was out, knocked clean off his feet by the final punch of a crushing onslaught. It looked as if Louis had recovered his old destructive powers, but the next fight was to prove otherwise.

Having run out of worthy opponents, Louis was inactive except for a series of exhibitions, for 15 months. On 5 December 1947 another exhibition was arranged at Madison Square Garden with Jersey Joe Walcott, a boxer even older than Louis, and moreover one with an undistinguished record who had retired in 1944 aged 30. He had returned to the ring to help a local promoter. Louis was by now experiencing financial problems after some ill-advised spending and investment, and as the crowds were not flocking to the exhibitions, he and Jacobs persuaded the New York Boxing Commission to recognize the fight as being for the title. This improved the gate, 18,194 paying $216,407 to watch, but few expected Walcott to offer any real opposition.

To everybody's surprise, Walcott dropped Louis in the first round and then proceeded to outbox him, dumping him on the canvas again in the fourth. Louis' efforts at retaliation were clumsy, and his only success came when he cornered Jersey Joe for a spell in the ninth. But Walcott stayed on his feet, avoided Louis for the rest of the fight, and in the opinion of most of the onlookers had won the match. The referee agreed with this view, but the two judges did not, and Louis was given the split decision. Louis certainly thought he had lost and was almost out of the ring in disappointment when the verdict was announced in his favour. In fact, it is said he apologized to Walcott. Walcott probably lost the decision through being over-awed by the champion. After Louis' flurry in the ninth Walcott did little but throw round-arm haymakers as he dodged Louis' attacks, and no doubt lost points through his tactics.

Clearly there had to be a return, and six months later more than twice as many fans went to the Yankee Stadium, New York, to see if Walcott could repeat his performance and take the title. For ten rounds it looked as if he could, as he baffled Louis with his crafty hit-and-run tactics, putting him down again in the third round, but in the 11th Louis put in a sustained barrage and Walcott began to weaken. He desperately tried to fight back but under the non-stop assault he finally sank to the canvas, and was still crawling forwards in an attempt to rise when the referee reached the count of ten.

Louis then embarked on a nation-wide series of exhibition bouts, during which he announced his retirement as unbeaten champion. He had been the heavyweight champion of the world for just short of 12 years, and had made 25 successful defences, a record in any division. It was a great career, with the defeat by Schmeling in his up-and-coming days the only blot on it. Some still say Louis was the best of all.

Louis announced his retirement on 1 March 1949 during an exhibition in Nassau, but did not relinquish his interest in the title. As part of an agreement to quit, he signed the two leading contenders, Walcott and Ezzard Charles, and sold the rights to the fight for the vacant title to James D. Norris, a promoter who formed the International Boxing Club with an associate, Arthur Wirtz. With John Reed Kilpatrick, chairman of the Madison Square Garden Corporation, these men took control of the heavyweight division from the now sick Mike Jacobs, and between them brought boxing into the television age.

The National Boxing Association agreed to recognize as champion the winner of the Ezzard Charles – Joe Walcott bout, which took place at Comiskey Park, Chicago, on 22 June 1949. It was not a display of fireworks between two cagey old warriors. Charles had been an outstanding light-heavyweight, who, although not fighting for the title, had beaten three times each Archie Moore and Joey Maxim, both men who later won the championship. He was one of the lightest of heavyweights, but had a devastating punch, although after Sam Baroudi had died after being knocked out by him, he was reluctant to use it to its full advantage. He had the upper hand throughout most of the fight with Walcott and took a comfortable decision to become the new champion.

He was the new champion, that is, as far as the National Boxing Association was concerned. This body was formed in 1921 to challenge the monopoly of world championships which had been assumed by the New York State Athletic Commission, through its boxing section. The promoters in states in which boxing took place outside New York always resented the favouritism shown to New York-based boxers in recognition for title challenges, and from 1921, there were frequent disagreements between the NBA and the New York Commission as to who was champion. In fact, there were often two champions at one weight, a state of affairs which was irritating then, but which, nowadays, fans would almost welcome a return to, since, with the WBA, WBC and IBF, there are usually three men now claiming each crown.

There had not been a disagreement before 1949 in the heavyweight ranks, but now the New York authorities decided not to recognize the winner of this Chicago bout as champion, giving their approval to a bout between Lee Savold and the British champion, Bruce Woodcock, which was arranged to take place in London by promoter Jack Solomons. This fight was also recognized by the BBBC and the EBU. Unfortunately, the match was delayed for a year because Woodcock was involved in a car accident.

Below: *London promoter Jack Solomons (centre, with buttonhole) with a collection of boxing champions, among them world middleweight champions Randolph Turpin (left at rear) and Terry Downes (second from left, crouching), world flyweight champion Rinty Monaghan (left arm raised) and world light-heavyweight champion Gus Lesnevich (centre, crouching). On the extreme right is British heavyweight champion Don Cockell, who fought Rocky Marciano for the world title.*

Right: *Ezzard Charles succeeded Joe Louis, and was the first new heavyweight champion for exactly 12 years. He beat Louis when Louis made a comeback and later gave Marciano two of his hardest fights.*

Meanwhile, Charles proved a busy fighter, and defended his crown twice before the end of 1949. He first took on the former light-heavyweight champion Gus Lesnevich, and convincingly knocked him out in the seventh round in a Jim Norris International Boxing Club promotion. Then he stopped Pat Valentino in the eighth round at San Francisco.

The year's delay to the Savold–Woodcock bout had reduced its interest somewhat, specially with Charles building up a few good victories. However, when Savold beat Woodcock, who was forced to retire with a badly cut eye in the fourth, he was officially recognized in Britain and Europe. This recognition was withdrawn, however, with the news that Louis was to make a comeback. In August 1949 Louis signed to meet Charles the following month, and those associations which had refused to recognize Charles now agreed that the winner would be the undisputed champion. Charles meanwhile disposed of Freddie Bershore in Buffalo, the referee stopping the contest in the 14th round. Louis was forced into a comeback because of financial difficulties, particularly with the income tax authorities, to whom he owed $500,000. Although during the war he had given purses to aid the war effort, there were no concessions granted him by the Internal Revenue Service and the only way Louis could attempt to pay his taxes was to stage a comeback. So the old warrior had to climb back into the ring to face Charles, who was not himself too pleased with the idea because as a young man Louis had been his idol. However, it gave him the opportunity of universal recognition as champion.

Charles gets his recognition

The 22,375 in the Yankee Stadium did not, on the whole, wish for this outcome — they were hoping that the veteran could regain his crown. Louis was a much bigger man than Charles in every respect and outweighed him by no less than 34lb (15kg). But there was one statistic which over-ruled all the others: Louis was 36 years old, and Charles only 29. Although he briefly threatened in the fourth round, Louis was outspeeded, outpunched and comfortably outpointed by Charles, who at last was recognized by all as the worthy heavyweight champion of the world.

Charles continued to fight frequently, taking on five more opponents in eight months from December 1950. First he knocked out Nick Barrone in the 11th round in Cincinnati, then he returned to New York and Madison Square Garden to give a chance to Lee Oma, and stopped him in the tenth. The most obvious challenger now was the old war-horse Jersey Joe Walcott again and the two put on their usual professional display at the Olympia Stadium, Detroit, with the same result as in their first encounter: Walcott did his best, fought hard, but was clearly outpointed by the fast-moving, crisp-hitting Charles. Joey Maxim, the light-heavyweight champion, now put in a challenge, but went the way of all previous light-heavyweight champions who had attempted to take the top crown. Maxim, was, in fact, barely lighter than Charles, but he had already been beaten three times as a light-heavyweight and again he had to be satisfied with going the distance — he was clearly outpointed.

Charles was making his ninth defence in less than two years when he stepped into the ring at the Forbes Field Stadium at Pittsburgh on 18 July 1951 and his opponent was once again the man whom he had beaten to take the title: Jersey Joe Walcott. It was Walcott's fifth attempt to win the crown, he having fought Louis and Charles twice each previously, and it must be said the public were getting tired of his unsuccessful challenges.

As if realizing that this was his last chance, Walcott fought far more aggressively than on his previous title attempts, and consistently beat Charles to the punch. His blows were the heavier, and for six rounds he had the edge on the champion. In the seventh Walcott flung over a left hook which caught Charles flush on the chin, and the title disappeared as the holder slid down, trying to steady himself on Walcott's legs. There was never a chance he would beat the count, and Walcott had the reward for his persistence. At 37 years and five months he was now the oldest-ever heavyweight champion of the world. His boxing record actually went back to 1930, and some said his 'official' age was three or four years short of his real one.

Time was clearly not on Walcott's side, but he waited nearly 11 months before cashing in with a defence, giving Ezzard Charles a return and beating him on points at Philadelphia. Less than four months later, however, he was in the ring again in Philadelphia, and this time his challenger was something not seen on the heavyweight scene since Dempsey — an all-action, no-science, rough throwback to prize-fighting days: Rocky Marciano.

Marciano had been far from outstanding in a brief career as an amateur and was none too promising a professional until he came under the wing of Al Weill, to whom he was recommended. Weill was the matchmaker for the IBC, so his son became Marciano's official manager, to avoid a conflict of interest. Charley Goldman, a former bantamweight, was Marciano's trainer, but found it impossible to iron out his crudities — all he could do was to try to help Marciano use his assets to the best advantage. These assets were strength, courage and a powerful punch, which could knock out anybody. He could easily be outboxed, but he could take a punch and his heart propelled him forward so relentlessly that it was difficult to keep him at a distance for more than a few rounds.

By 1952 Marciano had built up an impressive record of quick victories. His first big test was against Carmine Vingo, almost as rugged as himself, and the two had put on a tremendous show in Madison Square Garden, with no quarter asked, and Marciano's reputation grew as Vingo was finally taken unconscious to hospital, where he remained in a coma for a week before recovering. It was an unhappy time for Marciano, who outside the ring was nothing like the savage he was inside. His defeat of Roland La Starza, unbeaten in 37 fights, was as close as it could be, the judges being unable to separate them and only a supplementary points system giving the decision to Rocky.

After other good wins, Marciano fought Louis, still on the come-back trail, but not diminishing his tax debt by much. Louis had won eight contests since being beaten by Charles, including a battering of Lee Savold, one-time holder of the disputed crown. However, he was far too old to keep away the blazing Marciano, and was knocked through the ropes onto the ring apron in the eighth, soon after which the referee stopped the contest. After more wins, including one over Savold and a two-round destruction of a contender in Harry Matthews, Marciano had only one more step to take, the meeting with champion Walcott at Philadelphia as previously mentioned.

Below: Jersey Joe Walcott (right) won the heavyweight title on his fifth attempt when a left in the seventh round sank Ezzard Charles to the floor. At over 37, Walcott remains the oldest man to be world heavyweight champion.

Rocky the Champ

Marciano's drawing power by now was such that over 40,000 fans wanted to be at the Municipal Stadium to see the action live, and they were not disappointed. Walcott astounded everybody by putting Marciano on the deck in the first round, and from then on matched Marciano's bludgeoning blows with his own more carefully selected shots. Marciano then had trouble with a substance in his eye from the seventh onwards, and Walcott piled up a lead which would surely have won him the decision had it not been for the 13th. In this round Marciano at last caught Walcott with a perfectly timed right hook and Walcott slowly slid down the ropes to pitch face down on the canvas. It was an irresistible punch, but referee Charles Daggert completed the count before the stricken Walcott's seconds rushed to his aid. Marciano, unbeaten in 43 fights, was the new champion.

The power of Marciano's winning punch and his durability made fight fans realize that a new champion as exciting as Dempsey might have arisen, although he clearly lacked the skill to be compared to Louis. The return with Walcott was eagerly awaited, as likely to provide further information of his stature. It did not, in fact, provide much.

The contest came eight months later at the Chicago Stadium and was a disappointment. In a pattern which Louis had established and Marciano would continue, having once extended the champion an opponent folded much quicker the second time around. In fact, Walcott lasted only 2 minutes 25 seconds of the first round. Marciano tore into him at the bell and a left and right knocked him on his back, legs in the air. Walcott was, by now, in his fortieth year and cynics assumed that he had not tried too hard to prolong the fight, but of course few men ever stood up to a barrage from Marciano, and Jersey Joe, after the first fight, would have clearly fancied his chances of winning. Walcott announced his retirement.

The public wanted to see Marciano given a hard test, and the obvious man to supply this was Roland LaStarza, who had lost to him earlier only on a very close decision. LaStarza was a classy boxer, and was durable. Younger than Marciano, the decision which Marciano held over him was not only close, but, like all such, resented and disputed. The Polo Grounds, New York, was the venue and 44,562 piled in to see if the bludgeon could overcome the rapier.

For six rounds LaStarza made Marciano look as crude as ever, but, unfortunately for him, he did not possess a knock-out punch. Marciano was never particular where or how he hit his opponents and in this bout was frequently warned by referee Ruby Goldstein, who penalized him in the sixth round. This provoked Marciano, who from the seventh onwards redoubled his ferocity. LaStarza had been winning the title comfortably, but although he took on his arms many of the blows which Marciano now rained upon him, he could not withstand the assault forever. The end came in the 11th, when he was battered through the ropes onto the ring apron. He forced himself back, but the referee did not allow it to go any further. LaStarza was found afterwards to have broken blood vessels in his arms where he had been blocking Marciano's ferocious blows.

Marciano had by now clearly established that he was a fighter out of the ordinary and the question was whether anybody had the skill and endurance to tame him. He could easily be outboxed, but could his attacks be withstood long enough? And how well could he take a really hard punch himself?

The champion had nine months' rest and manager Weill found what he thought would not be too challenging a task for his next defence. Since losing his title to Walcott in two contests, Ezzard Charles had won 11 of 14 fights, being outpointed on three occasions by promising young boxers. Nino Valdes, a huge Cuban heavyweight, and Harold Johnson, a light-heavyweight, had both recently outpointed him, so he should have been relatively easy for the 'Rock'.

This battle was far from easy, and answered one or two of the questions posed above. The 33-year-old Charles fought gamely and skilfully, and the Yankee Stadium crowd were prepared for an upset when, in the fourth round, a Charles blow gave Marciano a deep gash by his left eye. It was a cut that might well have stopped a lesser man, but Marciano fought on relentlessly and, in the eighth, cut Charles over the right eye. From now onwards the strength of Marciano began to overcome the veteran's boxing, but could not stop him, and Charles even fought back bravely at times. In the last round Marciano did his best to land a knock-out blow on Charles, but although Charles was exhausted, so was Marciano. The champion had won a clear points decision, but Charles had given him the toughest fight of his career so far.

The 47,585 who had seen it, and the boxing public at large, demanded a return, and on 17 September 1954 the two men climbed into the same ring at the Yankee Stadium to continue the argument. Surprisingly, the live attendance was smaller.

The return match took an entirely different course. Charles began confidently, but was floored in the second. However, he kept in the fight, and in the sixth opened a cut on Marciano's left nostril which began to spout blood. It was the worst injury of Marciano's career, and as the blood covered both contestants there was every likelihood that the fight would have to be stopped. At the end of the round Marciano's corner pleaded with the doctor and referee Al Berl to allow him another round, and were granted it. Marciano showed his greatness in the seventh, going all out for victory. He knew the fight could not

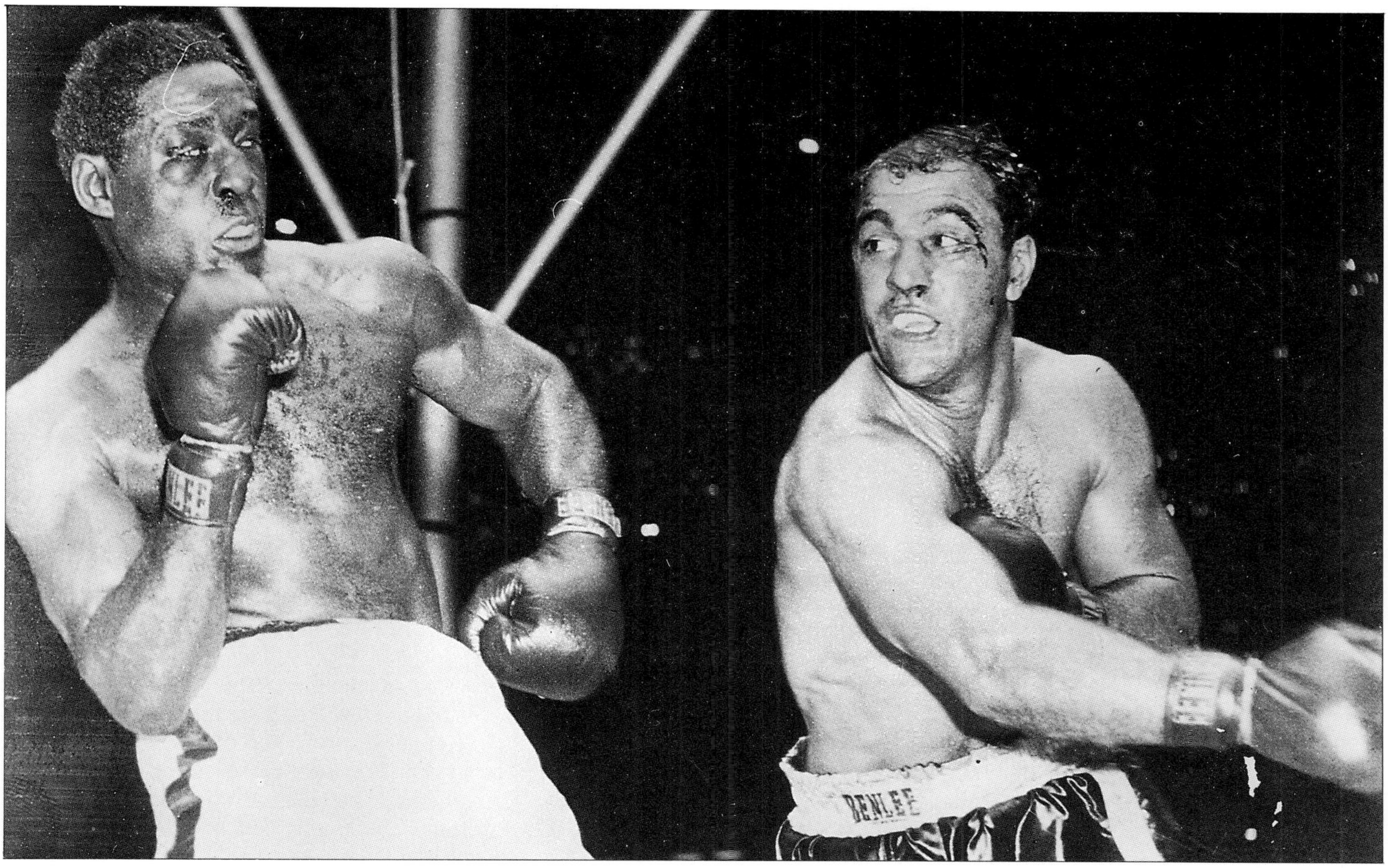

go the distance and poured everything into a final assault. Charles was rocked but game, and at the end of the round still on his feet. The doctor could hardly stop the fight now with Marciano pressing for the knockout, so allowed the fight to continue. At the beginning of the next round Rocky took a right which opened a cut on his eye. Still he crashed on with his fury and finally Charles was down, rose, staggered, was dropped again and then counted out on one knee.

It was a courageous win by the champion, gained against tremendous adversity. Marciano once again needed an easier opponent against whom to reassert himself, and, as often happens, the choice fell upon the British champion, Don Cockell who was, in any case, the only logical contender remaining. Cockell had been an excellent British light-heavyweight champion, but after ill-health had thickened round the middle, putting on around 30lb (14kg). He surprised everybody by doing well as a heavyweight and beat Harry Matthews on two visits to the States to establish his claim to fight Marciano. Unfortunately, it was a fight which confirmed a lot of prejudices in the view of some British fight fans. The match was in San Francisco, and the referee the highly-rated Frankie Brown.

Marciano had, throughout his career, been careless of the rules. He fought like the prize-fighters, and most of the time his faults were due to over-enthusiasm or over-anxiety, as when LaStarza was outboxing him. But against Cockell he was permitted every foul in the book, including butting, hitting low, hitting after the bell and even hitting an opponent who was down. The brave Cockell took it all stoically while the referee did not even caution the champion. In the end the weight of the blows, legal and illegal, told on Cockell and his resistance ended when he was trapped on the ropes and stopped in the ninth.

Rocky Marciano had now fought 48 times, winning all of his contests and was now approaching 32. He was challenged by Archie Moore, the outstanding light-heavyweight champion. 'Ancient Archie' was by now 38 or 41, according to whether you believed him or his mother, was unchallenged in his own division, and had recently beaten the heavyweight Nino Valdes. Moore waged a publicity campaign to get himself a fight with Marciano, and eventually took him on at the Yankee Stadium.

This fight, postponed for a day because of a threatening hurricane, drew the biggest crowd and highest receipts of Marciano's career: 61,574 paying $2,248,147; receipts second only to the second Tunney–Dempsey battle. Moore was a very knowledgeable campaigner, who despite his age seemed to have the armoury to upset the champion if all went his way, and all did in the second round. He beat Marciano to the punch, and a perfect right sent Rocky to his knees where he pitched forward onto his arms. He was up groggily at 'two', whereupon referee Harry Kessler mistakenly continued the count. In New York the rule was that a boxer knocked down was given a mandatory count of 'eight' before the fight could recommence, but Kessler forgot that

***Above:** The second title fight between Charles and Marciano was one of the most punishing ever seen. In the later stages Charles had an eye rapidly closing, while Marciano had a nose ready to spurt blood and a cut over the eye. Marciano's strength finally prevailed.*

this rule did not apply in a title fight. Moore frequently claimed later that the mistake and his own furious reaction to it, which led him not to capitalize coolly on his advantage, cost him the title. It is not a generally held view, because Ancient Archie had trouble keeping Marciano at a distance from the third round onwards, and he was down twice himself in the sixth. But he fought hard, and it was not until the ninth that he was finally counted out, leaning peacefully against the lower rope.

Marciano was now 32, and had suffered knockdowns and bad injuries in the last 15 months of his career, and he now decided to agree with his wife that he should retire. He is the only heavyweight champion never to be beaten, either before or after winning the title, and he is usually included among those discussed as the best of all time.

Just before Marciano's retirement, the US government had moved against the IBC and its virtual monopoly of world championship contests. The USA's anti-trust laws are designed to prevent an organization cornering a market to this extent. This government activity, coupled with the success of a young heavyweight building up an impressive record, virtually meant an end to the power the IBC and Jim Norris had wielded since the retirement of Louis.

PATTERSON BECOMES YOUNGEST CHAMPION

The young heavyweight was Floyd Patterson, who had won the Olympic middleweight title in 1952. His manager, Cus d'Amato, had brought him along a successful career path which had nothing to do with the IBC, and he had grown into a heavyweight contender with only a narrow defeat by the former light-heavyweight champion Joey Maxim to spoil his record. Patterson was chosen to fight Tommy 'Hurricane' Jackson in an eliminating contest, the winner to meet Archie Moore for the vacant title.

Jackson was an extremely game and durable fighter who attacked with the intensity of Marciano, but unfortunately without his destructive power. This meant that he could be picked off by a good boxer and made to suffer. Patterson's punches made a mess of Jackson's face, and it was a surprise when the verdict in his favour was only a split one.

Patterson and Moore met for the vacant title on 30 November 1956 at the Chicago Stadium. It was very much a battle of youth versus experience, for Patterson was not yet 22 while Moore was almost twice his age at practically 40 (at least). In fact Moore had begun his professional career in the year that Patterson was born.

The old-stager was the favourite. He had, after all, floored Marciano on his last fight, while Patterson had not beaten anybody whose name was known to the public at large. For four rounds Moore tried to outbox his rival but was missing badly with his punches, while Patterson showed a good defence. Patterson, who fought with a strange style, hiding behind a high guard and delivering hooks at a bound, then landed one of his hooks in the fifth that floored Moore for a count of nine. He rose, but a two-fisted attack saw him sink down again for the count.

Patterson thus became the new heavyweight champion of the world, and at the time he was the youngest. This was the first of two distinguished records he was to set in his career.

His opponents, however, were hardly distinguished. The IBC were still controlling a number of leading heavyweights and Cus d'Amato refused to have anything to do with this organization. His choice of opponents was therefore limited, as were some of the opponents. He began by giving a return to Tommy Jackson, which was the correct decision since Patterson's victory had been on a split decision, but Jackson was not one to win the title. Jackson was floored in the first and second rounds and halted in the tenth, when some thought referee Ruby Goldstein hasty in stopping the fight, but Jackson was later to have his licence suspended to save him from taking too much punishment. This heavyweight title fight was the first not promoted by the IBC for years, and sadly it lost money.

Next on the list, a month later, was Peter Rademacher, the 1956 Olympic heavyweight champion, who was making his debut as a professional. There were appeals from all over the world to the Washington Commission to stop this apparently unequal fight, but it went on in Sick's Stadium, Seattle on 22 August 1957. Surprisingly Rademacher began well, and Patterson was floored in the second round. From the third onwards, however, the fight was as one-sided as predicted, and Rademacher was knocked out just before the end of the sixth round.

Gates for these fights had not been good, and neither was that for the next, against Roy Harris, whose main claims to fame as a title challenger, so far as the history books are concerned, seem to be that he was a schoolteacher and came from a Texas town called Cut and Shoot. He had the distinction, which was becoming less and less rare, of flooring Patterson in the second round before being so badly beaten that he could not come out for the 12th.

On 1 May 1959 Brian London was imported from Britain to provide the opposition at Indianapolis. London had briefly been British champion, but the British Boxing

Board of Control would not sanction the match. London defied them, and, in fact, put up a better show than expected in reaching the 11th round before being knocked out. He earned his £20,000 pay that night, into which the subsequent BBBC fine made only a small dent.

Patterson's next imported 'victim' was another European about whom there were conflicting form lines. He was a Swede, Ingemar Johansson, who first gained the notice of the world outside Scandinavia when he was disqualified in the final of the 1952 Olympic Games' heavyweight competition. The French referee had seen enough after two rounds, and Johansson was ruled out for not trying. His opponent had been a huge, fearsome American, Ed Sanders, and Johansson, winner of 80 out of 89 amateur contests, was reported to be scared for his life. Sadly it was Sanders who died prematurely, of a brain haemorrhage after he had turned professional.

Johansson's professional record was impressive, however. He was the European champion, with a knock-out over challenger Henry Cooper to his credit; he had won 22 contests, 14 by the short route; he had a

***Below:** Ingemar Johansson's powerful left hook brings champion Floyd Patterson to a shuddering halt in the first round of their championship bout at Miami Beach in 1961.*

tremendous right-hand punch; and he had knocked out in one round Eddie Machen, who was ranked second to Patterson in the United States. With Patterson's known weakness of being knocked down by boxers not in his class Cus d'Amato was taking a chance with the big, handsome Swede.

Johansson's arrival in America caused something of a stir, because he appeared to train in a manner completely new to the boxing press. Boxers had travelled with an entourage before, and surrounded themselves with hangers-on, but Johansson's party consisted mostly of his family and his striking fiancée, Birgit, and his first object seemed to be to preserve the comforts of home life. Publicity pictures of the challenger and fiancée dancing and lazing by the pool did not impress the fight fans, and Patterson was a 4-1 favourite to keep his crown.

The fight marked a big advance on television's role in boxing. The paying public, despite Birgit, were apathetic, only 18,125 fans turning up on a rainy evening at the Yankee Stadium, over 3,000 fewer than those who saw the Harris fight. This would have meant a loss for promoter William Rosensohn, but for the first time the receipts from the closed circuit television screenings grossed over a million dollars.

The Hammer of Thor

The fight was ordinary for two rounds, with Patterson apparently controlling affairs, but early in the third a left hook from Johansson was followed by the right that he had been telling everybody about: 'The Hammer of Thor' he called it. It thundered onto Patterson's mouth and Patterson not only went down for nine, but when he arose he did not know where he was. He was a simple standing target for Johansson to knock him down again, and this he did, six more times in the third round, equalling the heavyweight title record set in the Dempsey-Firpo fight. Referee Ruby Goldstein then stopped the slaughter, and Sweden owned her first and only professional boxing champion.

Patterson, a complex, private man, seemed so ashamed by his defeat that he slunk about in disguise and finally went into seclusion to train, and get his mind fixed on regaining the title. Some wondered if he had retired for good. There was nothing retiring about Johansson, of course. His training methods had been fully vindicated, and he could not wait to put them into operation again.

He waited six days short of a year before stepping into the ring again with Patterson for the obligatory return match, and he found a different Patterson. In the first fight, Patterson, at 182lb (83kg) was 14lb (6kg) the lighter man. In the second, at the Polo Grounds, he weighed 190lb (86kg) and the difference was a mere 4lb (1.8kg). He appeared to have lost none of his speed, and he boxed more confidently and aggressively from the start. By keeping his jab in the champion's face and constantly keeping busy with fast flurries of punches, he did not give Johansson time to get set to throw his dangerous right.

Patterson's left hook was the destroyer in what was probably his best performance, both in terms of ringcraft and the controlled way in which he crushed his man. Less than a minute into the sixth round, a tremendous leaping left hook to the jaw sent Johansson to the canvas for a count of nine. It was the killer blow. The Swede rose, fought back, but could not resist a barrage of blows that Patterson threw at him with both fists. Finally, it was the left hook again which sent the champion crashing to the floor, leg twitching. Patterson feared at first that he might have done permanent harm, but luckily Johansson recovered quickly enough. Patterson, ironically, was never able to recreate the ferocity which caused him such anxiety.

This time the crowd was nearly 32,000 and the closed circuit television receipts were over two million dollars. What the watchers saw, of course, was history being made, for never before had an ex-champion been able to regain the heavyweight championship. Patterson was the ninth to try, and he now had two records; the youngest champion and the first to come back.

There had to be a rubber match, and this took place at the Convention Hall, Miami Beach, on 13 March 1961. Both men knew the other's capabilities, and the general opinion was that either could win. Much would depend on which landed cleanly first: the champion's left hook or the right-handed 'Hammer of Thor'. This time both men were at their heaviest: at 206½lb (94kg), Johansson was nearly 12lb (5.5kg) the heavier.

The exchanges were not as skilful as in the earlier contests, both men appearing clumsy, and both attempting to land a big blow. Johansson succeeded first, and Patterson was twice on the canvas in the first round from swinging blows, but Patterson showed more resolution in this fight than he had before, and far from becoming a punchbag, he fought back so well that Johansson was also decked before the end of the round. The two exchanged blows in a brawling sort of contest until the sixth, when Patterson got in another left hook to the chin which dropped Johansson. He started to rise but pitched forward as he was about to stand up and just failed to beat the count.

Patterson had thus lost and regained the title in three fights with the Swede, in the last two of which he had been very impressive, showing strength as well as resilience.

It was back to the more straightforward and useful fare for the next challenge. Tom McNeeley was strong, game, unbeaten, but still a novice, and he was thoroughly outclassed and knocked out in the fourth round before a very small audience in the Maple Leaf Gardens, Toronto. He did, however, floor the champion. Cus D'Amato's choice of opponent for Patterson was not based on picking easy options so much as his refusal to have anything to do with the IBC contenders.

One man that Patterson could not continue to ignore for ever was Sonny Liston, whose press suggested that he was virtually unbeatable. He, too, like Johansson, had beaten Machen, but on points, and he also had a victory over Zora Folley, another top contender. The brooding Liston had been the obvious challenger for a couple of years, but was easily dodged by Patterson because of his well-publicized criminal background.

Below: ***Below:** Floyd Patterson sits down hard in the first round of the 1961 championship, but later rallies to regain his heavyweight title, knocking out Johansson in the sixth round.*

The brooding Liston

Liston came from a desperately poor, large family and had received little education. For a man of his strength and upbringing a shady start to life was almost mandatory. He had been in numerous scrapes, had underworld associations, was a strike-breaker and had convictions for assaulting the police. The boxing world did not want Liston as champion, and Cus d'Amato did not want Patterson to fight him. But here Patterson's strange, fatalistic streak took over. He knew he could hardly regard himself as champion until he had beaten Liston. His heart forced him to accept the challenge. Yet his mind told him he had little chance, and seldom can a man have entered a world heavyweight title contest with less confidence.

The New York Boxing Commission did not want anything to do with a Liston title fight, and the contest was taken to Comiskey Park, Chicago, where Liston's capabilities were well known.

Liston was a much bigger man than Patterson in every way, and outweighed him by 25lb (11kg). He had a long reach and huge fists. The most menacing thing about him however was his stare. He was the master of the weigh-in and the period of pre-fight instruction from the referee, because he would stare with big malevolent eyes from a stony face at his opponents, striking fear into them. It was too much for Patterson, who took a disguise, including a false beard, with him to the stadium so that he could slink away unrecognized after his expected humiliation. His pride had forced him to take the match, but could not persuade him that he could win.

The contest, on 25 September 1962, was something of a farce. Patterson shot out his fast jabs but Liston ignored them and moved in to hook thunderously to the body. Patterson clinched but Liston shrugged him off and sank in more shattering blows. Patterson protected his body and a punch to his chin knocked him clean off his feet to the canvas, where he stayed. It was all over in 126 seconds, two seconds longer than it had taken Louis to defeat Schmeling.

Few thought Patterson would want to exercize his option on the rematch, but he did, although his private thoughts about his chances are not known. He faced the icy stare and the huge fists again in the Convention Hall, Las Vegas, ten months after his first humiliation. He did little better: four seconds better to be precise, being counted out in 130 seconds of the first round.

Liston had lived up to all the pre-fight ballyhoo and looked unbeatable. His birthday was a little uncertain, but he was thought to be past 31 when winning the second of his contests with Patterson, and this seemed the only consolation for any aspiring challenger.

Right: *Sonny Liston, because of his cold and sullen demeanour, his baleful stare, his physique and huge fists, his underworld connections and two one-round destructions of Floyd Patterson, seemed the most impregnable of all champions until he met Cassius Clay.*

The Louisville Lip

The challenger who was emerging fastest was not one who, superficially at least, seemed likely to lack confidence. He was Cassius Clay, a gregarious, talkative boxer from Louisville, only 20 years old when Liston took the title. He had won the light-heavyweight gold medal at the 1960 Rome Olympics, and had embarked on a professional career of continuous success. He was also his own publicity machine, quickly attracting the attention of the newspapers with his assertion that he was 'The Greatest' and his liking for predicting in which round he would win his fights. The whole idea was borrowed from a wrestling acquaintance, but Clay was so loquacious that he would have needed little encouragement to talk to the masses. At the Rome Olympics he had been noticed more for being the friendliest, most enthusiastic competitor than for his boxing, undoubtedly classy though it was.

One of Clay's tricks was to predict the outcome in rhyme — not very good verse, but catchy enough to make the papers notice, especially when he was confident enough to make his predictions work. He had a perfect physique for a heavyweight fighter. He weighed over 200lb (91kg) but stood 6ft 3in (1.91m), and the poundage was distributed where he needed it, and not around the waist as with some others. Furthermore, he was extremely light on his feet, and his dancing style made him a very difficult opponent to pin down. Angelo Dundee, a man experienced in many aspects of the fight game, was hired by the syndicate who backed him to introduce some devil into his punches. He was never to be a big puncher, but he was destructive enough with his well-directed blows and he mastered the whole repertoire of punches.

His bragging, of course, made him unpopular with the masses, and Archie Moore, his 18th opponent, was confidently expected to put 'The Louisville Lip' in his place. Moore had at one time helped to coach Clay, but the two had fallen out. Clay now predicted that Moore, naturally, would 'go in four' but few agreed, although Archie was by now 46. Clay was right — the old warrior was stopped in the fourth round, and his career virtually came to an end.

Everybody now took the upstart seriously, and although Doug Jones took him the full distance at a packed Madison Square Garden, thus ruining his poetry, he was regarded as the next challenger to whoever emerged from the Liston–Patterson series. Meanwhile, he took on the British champion Henry Cooper at Wembley Stadium, London, and predicted 'five'. He was right, but this was the bout which nearly upset the whole plan.

Cooper was a dedicated boxer with a famous left hook ('Enery's 'Ammer), who might have improved on an already excellent career had he not been prone to cuts, which bled profusely every time he took a punch around his eyebrows. The confident Clay opened some cuts in the first couple of rounds, and to some it appeared as if he were merely dancing around Cooper in the third and fourth, waiting for the predicted fifth to cut loose. But towards the end of the fourth round, Cooper manoeuvred him into position for the hook, it was perfectly delivered, and Clay went down with a glazed look in his eyes, his arm hooked over the rope. He rose at 'four' but was dazed and ready for the knock-out when the bell rang. Fortuitously for Clay, a split in his glove was enough for Angelo Dundee to make a fuss about to referee Tommy Little, and the subsequent delay was enough for Clay to recover fully and to inflict more cuts on Cooper in the fifth round, forcing the referee to stop the contest.

Above: *Cassius Clay, later to be Muhammad Ali, became probably the most famous boxer of all time. His record was amazing. After being an exceptional world champion he was out of action for over three years while in dispute with the US government, and then returned for a second incredible career.*

Clay's next stop was the challenge to Liston, and he predicted eight rounds would be sufficient as he left London. To say that nobody believed he could beat the formidable champion is not quite true. Three of 46 experts polled in the United States gave Clay the vote. But the majority saw an easy victory for the champion, who was 7-1 favourite in the betting.

Clay, who called Liston 'The Ugly Bear', stepped up his campaign of gaining publicity and confusing his opponent. It reached its climax at the weigh-in ceremony for the fight, scheduled to take place at the Convention Hall at Miami Beach on 25 February 1964. Clay acted like a madman, and indeed the Miami Commission doctor claimed that he was out of his mind with fright. The challenger shouted abuse at Liston, he dashed around quite uncontrollably, caused havoc with the ceremony, and was eventually fined $2,500 for his behaviour.

If it were a ploy, it worked brilliantly, for the slower-witted Liston was clearly confused by the contrast between this scared, hyperactive youngster and the boxer he faced in the ring. It is more likely that Clay's antics were real, as his blood pressure rose alarmingly during the whole performance, and there was even a suggestion that he was unfit to fight. He was to show a trace of the same panic in the fight itself.

Although the contest was televised, the live attendance was still very low at 8,297. One explanation might be that neither boxer was popular with the public, who cared little who won, another that Liston was assumed to have an easy task.

Clay, however, was of a calibre Liston was unused to — he was his equal physically, and was younger and stronger. Furthermore, scared or not, it was impossible to cow him into submission, as perhaps Patterson had been. Clay attacked from the bell, scoring with quick, light jabs, although keeping at a respectful distance, while Liston plodded after him attempting to land the big punch. Clay's hit-and-run tactics opened a cut below Liston's left eye in the third, but Liston was delivering enough to keep the fight even until the fifth. In the previous round, medication from Liston's corner found its way into Clay's eye, and between rounds the challenger insisted he could not see. He wanted to quit there and then, pleading with Dundee to cut off his gloves, but Angelo sent him out for the fifth.

In a curious way, this round decided the contest, and it was to epitomize Clay's future greatness. He improvised. He ran away from Liston, at the same time keeping his left extended towards Liston's face like a sort of sign post. He attempted no aggression himself, but demonstrated that even half-blind he could keep the champion at bay. It was tactics born of quick intelligence — a true boxer's awareness of how to act in any situation. It utterly demoralized Liston.

Clay was even reluctant to come out for the sixth, but he did, and as his vision cleared, so he began to mix some punches of his own with his dancing avoidance of Liston's. He looked as if he might be about to gain control.

He had no need. At the end of the round, Liston suddenly looked old as he sat on his stool, and to everybody's surprise he retired, claiming a shoulder injury and facial cuts.

While Liston sat dejected, the new champion, Clay, went berserk, dashing around the ring, mouth agape and screaming 'I told you so'. He was certainly not acting now. Liston was subsequently proved to have a shoulder injury, but champions continue with far more serious problems and the truth is that for the third title fight in succession, the issue was settled as much in the mind as anywhere else.

The new champion was only just turned 22, hardly older than Patterson when he won the title. He caused a second sensation the day after his win by calling a press conference and announcing that he had joined the Black Muslim movement, led by Malcolm X. He himself was renouncing his 'slave' name, Cassius Clay (derived from a slave ancestor who, as was the custom, took the name of his 'owner') and would be known as Cassius X

Below: *Ali on the scales in London for his world title fight with British champion Henry Cooper in 1966. Cooper had come nearer to beating Ali than anybody when flooring him in their encounter three years earlier. But Cooper, 13½lb (6kg) lighter, lost the title fight through his old bugbear — cut eyebrows.*

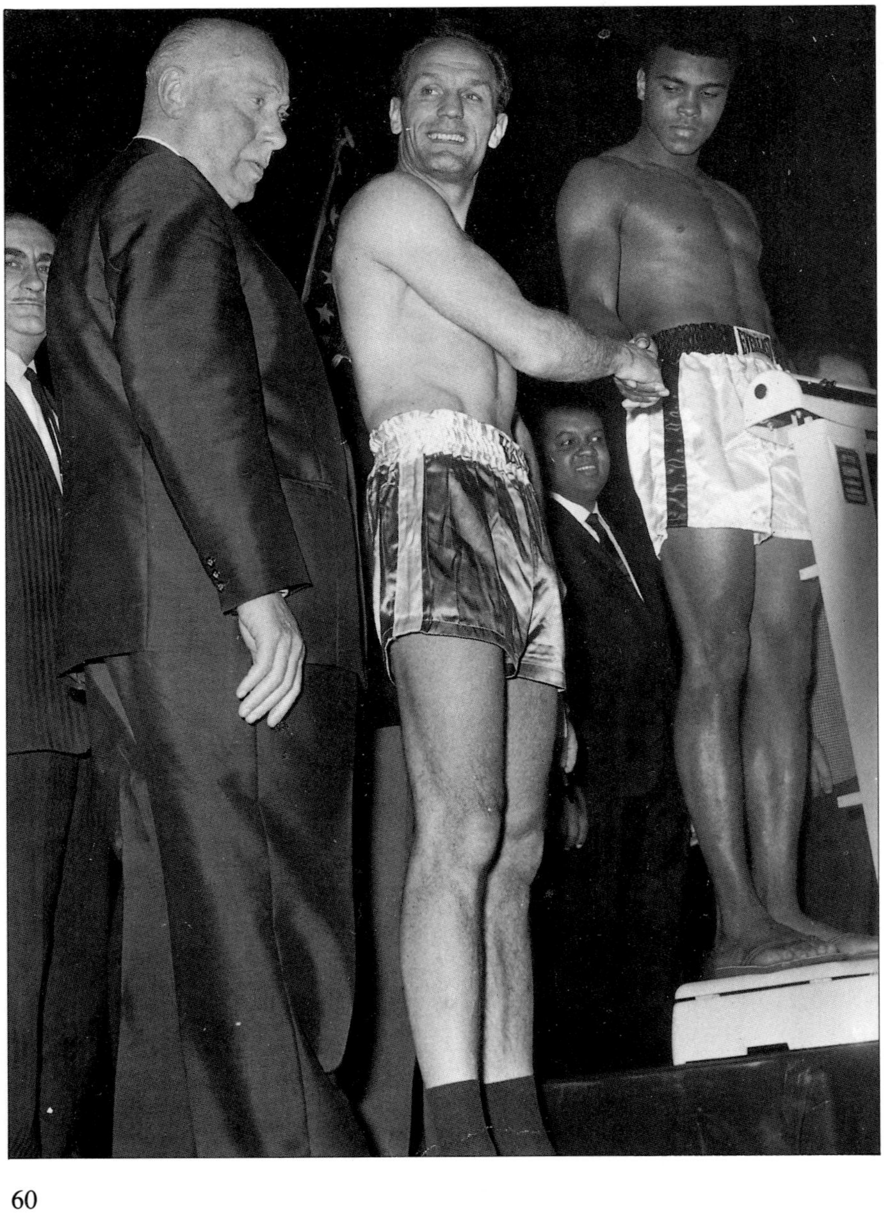

until he could assume a Muslim name.

This move angered white America, for whom the Black Muslims represented a dangerous and aggressive movement for disruption. It also angered the boxing fraternity, who saw the supreme championship being used for political purposes, rather than representing the pinnacle of the sport. Many boxing writers and boxers themselves refused to acknowledge Clay's, or X's, change of name. Before the return fight with Liston, written into the contract, X had assumed a name which he was to make even more famous than his first: Muhammad Ali.

The anger of the boxing establishment led to a childish decision by the World Boxing Association. The WBA came into being in August 1962, although only as a name change of the National Boxing Association of 1920. The NBA itself had come about when an Englishman, William A. Gavin, had attempted to set up an organization in New York based on London's National Sporting Club, which was an official ruling body deciding British championships. In 1927 the NBA started recognizing world champions of its own in opposition to the Boxing Department of the New York State Athletic Commission, which until then had assumed a monopoly of championship contest and decisions. In 1963, the World Boxing Council was set up as a rival body to the WBA, the Council comprising boxing authorities all over the world, including those of American states not affiliated to the WBA. The WBC had strong support from the boxing authorities.

Above: *Ali was not a friend of Floyd Patterson, who would not recognize Ali's new Black Muslim name, and Ali tortured the ex-champion by giving him a severe beating over 12 rounds in 1965.*

Right: *Ali outpointed the tough Canadian, George Chuvalo, who challenged him in 1966. In this contest Ali gave an early indication of his willingness to adopt new and seemingly eccentric tactics by allowing Chuvalo to wear himself out by pounding him around the body.*

Ali is stripped

The WBA's reaction to Ali's joining the Black Muslims was to strip him of the title. Although in other divisions the old NBA and New York authorities (not to mention the British and European) had often been in conflict, so that there was more than one champion at a given weight, there had never been any dispute until now about the heavyweight title, except for the brief Lee Savold episode in 1950. The WBA's decision was based ostensibly on Ali having signed a contract giving Liston an automatic return fight should he lose. This now was adjudged to be against their rule, although it was a rule honoured more in the breach than the observance.

The WBA decided that the vacant title would be awarded to the winner of a match between Eddie Machen, the victim both of Johansson and Liston, and Ernie Terrell, a boxer suspected of underworld connections and singled out in quiz books because his sister happened to become one of a well-known pop group called The Supremes.

Terrell outpointed Machen in Chicago on 5 March 1965, two months before the Ali and Liston return. Thus, the world had two heavyweight champions, and although Ali did reunify matters later, his eventual defeat later sparked off a situation in the 1980s when there were, for a time, three heavyweight champions.

The second Ali–Liston encounter, which took place at Dominic's Hall, Lewiston, Maine, on 25 May 1965 is one of the most unsatisfactory and mysterious of fights. The basic facts are simple. After a minute or so of sparring similar to the first contest, with Ali dancing and Liston lumbering, Liston suddenly went down to a punch which many were convinced was actually thrown only after watching the film. Even so, it hardly looked hard enough to knock down Liston. Ali stood over Liston, threatening or taunting him, and the referee, ex-champion Jersey Joe Walcott, eventually forced him to a neutral corner before deciding to take up a count. However, by this time Liston had risen, and the two boxers resumed their sparring. Walcott, meantime, had been called over by the timekeeper, who informed him that the count had reached 22, and that Liston was out. The inexperienced Walcott thereupon stopped the fight, declaring that Liston had been knocked out.

The first controversy was over the punch. Most onlookers agreed that it could not possibly have knocked out Liston. Was Liston, therefore, making a final gesture to the authorities and public who had rejected him for so long by making a gesture of contempt for their set of rules? Ali insisted that the punch was his new 'corkscrew' secret weapon, but Ali-watchers would not be surprised at that claim, or that it might have been invented on the spot. The second mystery is why Liston should have been counted out

before the referee had made a count to ten over him. The editor of the *The Ring*, the late Nat Fleischer, claimed to have told Walcott that Liston had been counted out, but only the referee can count out a boxer, not the timekeeper. Jack Dempsey must have wished he had such a timekeeper in 1927. Liston said, reasonably, that he was staying down until the referee had taken Ali to a neutral corner, at which he rose — how can he then be counted out 'in retrospect'?

The man who knew most of what had occurred was Liston, but he was not talking even after he retired, and as he is now dead the whole affair will remain a mystery. The confusion was added to by the official time being given as one minute, whereas the film shows Liston to have gone down at 1 minute 42 seconds, and Walcott to have stopped the fight 30 seconds later.

Ali and Ernie Terrell proceeded to defend their respective halves of the heavyweight title, although the world at large regarded Ali as the true champion, and Terrell, who would not acknowledge Ali's new name, as the pretender. Both men defended in November 1965, Terrell in Toronto against the durable Canadian tough guy, George Chuvalo, whom he outpointed, and Ali against Floyd Patterson, another who insisted on calling him Cassius Clay. Patterson was brave, but no match for Ali who showed a vengeful side of his nature by inflicting tremendous punish-

ment for 12 rounds before the referee, mercifully, stopped it.

Ali then began to emulate Joe Louis. He defended five times in 1966, and for the first time since Burns took the title on the road, boxing in Toronto, London and Frankfurt before returning to Houston. First of all he outpointed Chuvalo over 15 rounds, and fought a strange fight, allowing the Canadian to batter him about the body almost as if testing out how much he could take. He handed back a worse beating in return, clearly outclassing the brave Canadian.

In London, at Highbury Football Ground, Ali gave a return to Henry Cooper, treating his left hook with great respect, but winning in six rounds when Cooper's eyebrow was again pouring blood all down his face. The referee was forced to intervene. Ali then moved to the Earls Court Exhibition Hall to take on Brian London, who had previously challenged Patterson. London was knocked out in the third.

Ali then went to Frankfurt to tackle the awkward southpaw Karl Mildenberger, the German champion. He proved durable, but the referee was forced to come to his assistance in the 12th round. It was then back to Houston, Texas, to stop the giant Cleveland Williams in the third round, a scintillating performance against a man many thought would give him trouble.

In the meantime Ernie Terrell had made one further defence, outpointing Doug Jones at Houston. Attempts to bring Ali and Terrell together to unify the championship had failed, partly because New York had refused the fight because of Terrell's background and Chicago because of Ali's declared views in opposition to the war in Vietnam. The fight was at last arranged for the Houston Astrodome on 6 February 1967.

Terrell was a lanky 6ft 6in (1.98m) boxer from Chicago, more than 3in (7.6cm) taller than Ali, but at around 213lb (97kg) only a matter of ounces heavier. The fight was one of the nastiest of Ali's career. At this stage he was in his prime and capable of doing almost what he liked with any other boxer in the world. He decided to give Terrell the beating of his life for refusing to acknowledge his name. Terrell's left eye was closed in the fifth and a gash was cut over the right shortly afterwards, so for the second half of the fight the brave WBA champion was boxing with limited vision. Ali appeared able to hit him at will, yet seemed reluctant to land a knock-out blow. Instead, Terrell was continually jolted with punches to his bloody face, after many of which Ali would ask: 'What's my name?' The fight went the distance, many thought on Ali's disinclination to put Terrell out of his misery.

Zora Folley, who was denied a chance to fight Patterson, whom he might have beaten, at last got a chance at the title, but it was too late for the 34-year-old and he succumbed to a seventh round knock-out at Madison Square Garden. It was now March 1967, and Ali's ninth defence in the three years since he won the title, but he was now to go into boxing exile.

Ali's troubles had begun with his association with the Black Muslims. Then he was classified IY by his Army Draft Board, showing a deficiency of intelligence which was clearly absurd. In February 1966 he was reclassified 1A, but claimed exemption on conscientious grounds as a minister of the Islam religion. He also claimed to have no quarrel with the Vietcong. During all this time Ali split American opinion almost as Jack Johnson had done. There were those to whom he was a hero, but to the majority of white Americans he was a draft dodger, who should go to war or go to prison.

In April 1967 he reported to the Houston induction board but refused the draft; in May he was indicted; in June he was tried, found guilty and sentenced to five years' imprisonment. He immediately appealed, and began long litigation. Meanwhile, at the end of April, the WBA and the New York authorities stripped Ali of his title, the WBA banning him fighting under their banner in America. The WBC held aloof.

The WBA promptly decided on a competition to find a new champion among its top eight ranked boxers: Joe Frazier, Thad Spencer, Ernie Terrell, Oscar Bonavena, Karl Mildenberger, Jimmy Ellis, Floyd Patterson and Jerry Quarry. However, Frazier, the 1964 Tokyo Olympic gold medalist, knocked out George Chuvalo in Madison Square Garden and refused to join the eliminators. He was dropped in the WBA ranking list to number nine, and Leotis Martin took his place in the quest for the title. The New York Boxing Commission then stated it would not recognize any WBA champion that emerged until that champion had beaten Frazier.

In August 1967 the WBA competition got under way. Thad Spencer outpointed Ernie Terrell, Jimmy Ellis stopped Leotis Martin, Oscar Bonavena outpointed Karl Mildenberger and Jerry Quarry outpointed Floyd Patterson on a split decision. In the semi-final Jimmy Ellis outpointed Oscar Bonavena and Jerry Quarry caused a surprise by stopping Thad Spencer in the 12th and last round. On 27 April 1968 Ellis outpointed Quarry at Oakland, California, to become the WBA champion.

A month earlier, Joe Frazier had been recognized as the New York champion when he beat Buster Mathis, who had beaten him twice as an amateur in the Olympic trials but then had broken his hand, giving Frazier the chance to become Olympic champion. Frazier, a stubby, seemingly indestructible, two-fisted slugger, outlasted his opponent. He was called the 'Black Marciano' because of his style of fighting.

The public (those few who did not regard Ali as the true champion anyway) now wanted a unifying battle between Ellis and Frazier, but it was a long time in coming, and the two boxers defended their respective claims to the title, Frazier being the busier. In 1968 he stopped Manuel Ramos in two rounds and outpointed Oscar Bonavena and in 1969 he knocked out Dave Zyglewicz in the first and stopped Jerry Quarry in the seventh. Ellis, meanwhile, made only the one defence, giving Floyd Patterson his last chance to regain the crown, and outpointed the 33-year-old over 15 rounds. On 16 February 1970 Frazier and Ellis met at Madison Square Garden, and Frazier, the overwhelming favourite, had no difficulty in powering his way past the ring-rusty defences of Ellis to have him in such a bad way at the end of the fourth that he was unable to come out for the fifth. Frazier was now the undisputed champion, because in March 1969 the WBC had declared the title vacant because of Ali's inability to defend owing to his continuing legal problems. With other world bodies who had not recognized either Frazier or Ellis, they had agreed to declare as champion the winner of this bout.

Frazier, then, became undisputed heavyweight champion two weeks after Ali had publicly announced his retirement. It seemed

__Below:__ The contest advertised as the 'Fight of the Century', when the undefeated champion Ali made a comeback and challenged the new undefeated champion Joe Frazier. Frazier (left) won the fight on points, a victory made certain when Ali was toppled by a left in the last round. It was Frazier's only victory over Ali in three fights.

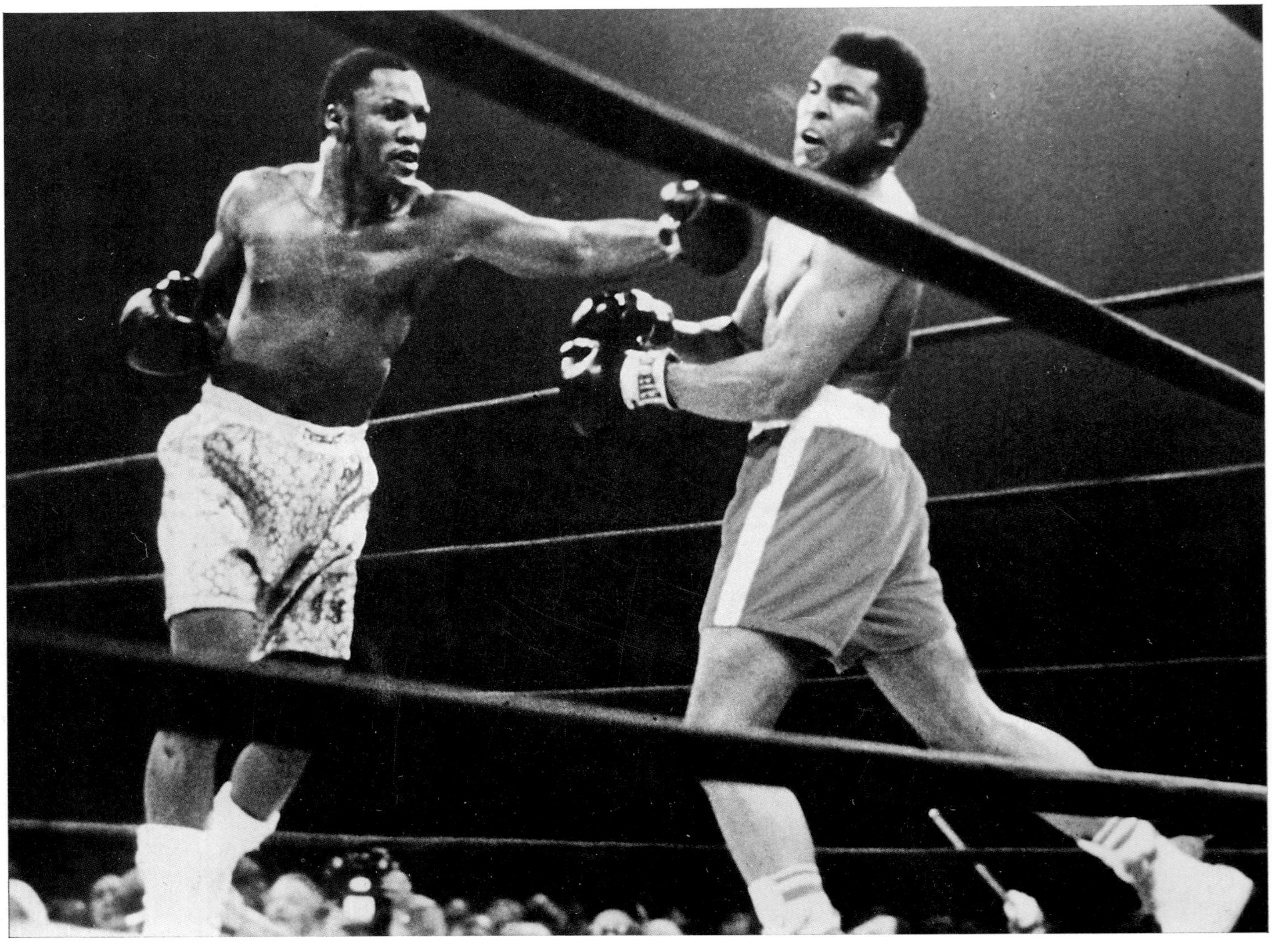

that the whole messy business was over, but now Ali, still the 'people's champion', changed his mind and announced he would like to make a comeback. Surprisingly, the state of Georgia gave him a licence, and on 26 October 1970 he returned after three and a half years' inactivity to stop Jerry Quarry in the third round. Hardened boxing reporters were amazed at how little the enforced rest had apparently affected the dancing master.

The match everybody wanted now, of course, was Ali *v.* Frazier, a unique meeting of two unbeaten heavyweight champions. They remained that way as Frazier disposed of the light-heavyweight champion, Bob Foster, attempting to become the first to step up and take the top crown but, like those before him, failing. Frazier was much too strong and knocked him out in two rounds. Ali won a small battle in his war with the state when a Federal Court judge ruled that the New York refusal to give Ali a licence was unreasonable. On 7 December 1970 Ali took on Oscar Bonavena, the tough Argentinian, at Madison Square Garden, New York, and knocked him out in the 15th round, a feat Frazier had failed to achieve two years earlier. Soon afterwards the big fight was announced: for Madison Square Garden on 8 March 1971.

The Fight of the Century

With a live audience of over 20,000 plus an audience of 1.3 million watching on closed circuit television and with over 300 million all over the world awaiting the televised recording, the fight was a huge financial bonanza, for once justifying the tag 'Fight of the Century'. Ali was by no means the unpopular character he had been four years earlier. Opinion in America about the Vietnam War had swung considerably, and his long fight for his principles against the US government was seen as more of a brave struggle than a selfish refusal to acknowledge his responsibilities. He was supported by blacks and liberals, while Frazier had the backing of the whites and the establishment. Opinion as to the outcome was, equally, evenly divided, with old-stagers favouring Frazier on the grounds that 'they never come back' (particularly after four years) and the young favouring the charismatic Ali. In the event, Ali proved to be not quite ready.

It was a tremendous battle, fulfilling all hopes, with the plodding, relentless Frazier persistently boring in like a bull and the tall, more athletic Ali continually dodging and spearing in his shafts like a matador. First one, then the other, seemed to have an advantage, but towards the end it was Frazier who stayed the course better. If there were any doubts when the last round began they were dispelled when a left hook from Frazier sent Ali tumbling to the canvas as his leg buckled beneath him. He rose at three and remained upright to the bell, but Frazier won the unanimous decision. Both men had suffered physical punishment, but Ali took his defeat gracefully. Frazier was now undisputed champion in every respect. Ali had a big victory to come in the courts. On 28 June 1971 the Supreme Court decided unanimously in his favour, his prison sentence was quashed, and he was free to continue his comeback unhindered.

In 1972 Frazier 'rested' from the extremely punishing fight with Ali with two easier defences, both ending by the referee's intervention in the fourth round: he beat two comparative unknowns, Terry Daniels at New Orleans and Ron Stander at Omaha. Ali was much busier, becoming a champion of sorts by beating Jimmy Ellis, the former WBA champion and earlier still his humble sparring partner, for the title of a newly-formed body called the North American Boxing Federation. He defended this against Buster Mathis, and, in 1972, George Chuvalo, Jerry Quarry, Floyd Patterson and Bob Foster.

***Above:** The second Ali–Frazier fight in 1974 was the only one of the three in which the world title was not at stake, but it nevertheless aroused worldwide interest. This poster shows the cinemas around London where British fight fans could see the contest live from Madison Square Garden. Doors opened at 1am.*

Another Olympic boxing champion then appeared on the scene as a threat to Frazier. He was the 1968 champion, George Foreman, and a much bigger man than Frazier, standing 6ft 3in (1.91m) and weighing some 217lb (98kg). He gained his chance of the title on 22 January 1973 at Kingston, Jamaica, by which time he had won his first 37 professional contests, an amazing 34 of them inside the scheduled distance, a ratio as high as any heavyweight before or since. However, Frazier was expected to beat him and was the 3-1 favourite.

The progress of the fight surprised everybody. Frazier came boring in as usual, but it seemed as if Foreman had the strength to push him away or to take the punches on his powerful arms. Suddenly, he launched a right to the champion's chin that put him on the canvas. Given an enforced count of eight, Frazier resumed his two-fisted attack, but appeared unable to shake Foreman. It was a different story when Foreman replied. His power pushed Frazier back onto the ropes, and a few cracking rights sent him to the floor again, where this time he was pleased to stay for the count of eight. Resuming in the only way he knew how, he was met with another right that put him back on the floor as the bell sounded.

It was a similar story in the second round: the blow which knocked the champion down for the third time lifted him clean off his feet, and persuaded referee Arthur Mercante that he had seen enough. A new and impressive champion was on the throne, and Frazier had suffered his first defeat. He might have regretted some of his activities since becoming champion, which had centred round a pop group he had formed rather than his boxing training.

Ali, too, his main rival during his reign, suffered a reverse in 1973. He fought Ken Norton, another boxer with an impressive physique, and suffered a broken jaw early in the fight. But he clung on to the end of the 12th round to lose a split decision. In the circumstances Ali had taken a tremendous risk boxing on with his jaw in such a state, and in some respects it was one of his bravest performances. This defeat cost Ali the NABF title, but he regained it by beating Norton in a return bout, which was also a close points decision. Although Frazier no longer held the world title, Ali was prepared to put his title up against Frazier in a return of their epic encounter. Frazier had made a come-back by outpointing the European champion, Joe Bugner, who had also suffered a points defeat at the hands of Ali, on his come-back trail.

The second Ali–Frazier battle took place at Madison Square Garden on 28 January 1974. The arena was packed, and with closed-circuit TV and world film rights the gross revenue was around $25 million, of which each boxer had been guaranteed $3 million.

Ali was much fitter this time than he had been for the previous meeting, and Frazier had since then suffered a crushing defeat, so the balance was different. The tactics were much the same with the shorter Frazier boring in to the body and throwing an occasional hook to the head, while Ali danced and countered fluently with blows almost entirely aimed at Frazier's head. Although not so exciting as their first match, it was another hard and very strength-sapping struggle. A strange incident occurred in the second round when the referee, Tony Perez, stopped the fight thinking the bell had rung. Frazier was thus given a 20-second break at a point when Ali was mounting a strong attack and Frazier was hurt. Frazier came back in the second half of the fight but Ali was a good points winner at the end of the 12 rounds.

Ali had now emerged as the obvious challenger to Foreman, who had made two successful defences, knocking out José Roman, from Puerto Rico, with the third of three crushing knock-down rights in the first round. He then took on Ken Norton in Caracas, Venezuela, and overwhelmed him. Norton fought tentatively, and when he was smashed to the canvas in the second round his trainer leapt in to try to stop it, and the referee saw he was beaten and did so.

Left: *The amazing climax to the title fight in the 20th of May Stadium in Kinshasa, Zaire, on 30 October 1974. Ali, the challenger, soaked up the heavy punches of George Foreman and then dispatched him face down in the eighth with a perfect combination. Ali had regained the title.*

Ali returns

Ali now challenged Foreman, who had begun his champion's career with three title wins in less than five rounds. It was, to opponents, as frightening a start as that of Liston, whom Ali deposed ten years earlier. The difference from Ali's point of view was those ten years. He was not now the young challenger of an old man, he was the 32-year-old challenger of a man six years younger than himself, whom some thought was the hardest puncher of all time. Indeed, there were critics who feared for Ali's safety.

The fight had all the ingredients of box-office success, and it was taken to Africa, the first heavyweight title fight to be staged on that continent. The 20th of May Stadium in Kinshasa, Zaire, was packed with 62,000 fans on the fight night, 30 October 1974. The promoter was a man who was to take over the heavyweight title as had others before him: Don King, whose grey hair, which stood straight upwards in an exorbitant style, typified his larger-than-life personality.

Once again Ali showed how a fighting intelligence can overcome apparently impossible physical odds. From the beginning Foreman seemed to be in control as he hammered away at Ali, frequently pinning him to the ropes and belting him about the body. Ali appeared to comply with Foreman's fight pattern, often seeming to take the blows rather than dodge. A confused Foreman, who expected the dancing Ali, found a static opponent who allowed him to punch him about the body. After five rounds the champion began to get tired, and Ali began to score with a few telling counters. Foreman became demoralized, just as Liston had done, and when Ali caught him with a perfect left and right in the eighth he pitched forward and was unable to rise before being counted out. It was a remarkable performance by a remarkable champion, who became the second in history to regain the heavyweight crown.

As if making up for lost time, Ali now embarked on his second busy spell as champion. Four times he defended in 1975. Chuck Wepner, a 6ft 5in (1.96m), 225lb (102kg) journeyman with a number of defeats on his record, was not likely to present any problems, and he did not, being stopped 19 seconds from the end of the fight at the Cleveland Coliseum.

Ron Lyle, like Ali 33 years old, had a better record than Wepner, with only two points defeats on his record. The two met at the Convention Hall, Las Vegas, and after dancing round his man for ten rounds, Ali decided to end it in the 11th, and did so by forcing the referee to intervene after a flurry of punches.

Joe Bugner, the former British champion, was potentially a bigger threat than either of these two when given the chance of the title. He was eight years younger than Ali, was slightly taller and heavier, and had an equally powerful physique. He had already gone the distance with both Ali and Frazier. Don King, whose policy was to maximize the television revenue, put this fight on at Kuala Lumpur, Malaysia. Unfortunately, Bugner, never a natural fighter, was in introspective mood and content to be comfortably outpointed again.

All this led up to what was billed as 'The Thrilla in Manila', the third Ali–Frazier meeting. The two had built up a special rivalry since the 'Fight of the Century' four and a half years earlier, and the public was anxious to see the rubber match between them, despite the fact that each had now suffered two defeats. The ultimate television audience was reckoned to be about 700 million in 68 countries. Frazier had stopped Jerry Quarry and Jimmy Ellis since losing to Ali, and the two men looked to be the best heavyweights in the business with the possible exception of Foreman, whose future ambitions were uncertain.

Ali predicted an early knock-out for the bout, in the Philippine Coliseum, Manila, and in the opening four rounds appeared to attempt to satisfy this prophecy, buckling Frazier's legs in the first and continually jerking his head back in the third. But his fight strategy had to be revised when the challenger fought back hard in the fifth and sixth, having Ali in trouble. After ten rounds the contest was level, but with both men down to their last reserves of strength, Ali's long distance pummelling of Frazier's face began to make the decisive difference, as Frazier's eyes puffed up. By the end of the 14th Frazier could hardly see, and his manager Eddie Futch would not allow him to go out for the last round. Both men were utterly exhausted and spoke of retiring, and neither was quite as good again.

Ali, however, was champion, and there were challenges to meet and turn aside. He rested for over four months and then took on a Belgian, Jean-Pierre Coopman, in San Juan, Puerto Rico, knocking him out in the fifth. Jimmy Young, an American contender, put up a good resistance before losing the decision at Landover, then Ali went to Munich in West Germany to face the European champion, Richard Dunn of Britain, and forced the referee to stop it in the fifth. He indulged in an exhibition bout with a wrestler, Antonio Inoki, in Tokyo, and then gave a chance to Ken Norton, who stood 1-1 with him after two exciting bouts. Norton had appeared to have lost some confidence after his heavy defeat by Foreman two and a half years earlier, but always fought well against Ali, and took him the distance again at Madison Square Garden in another good battle.

Alfredo Evangelista, of Italy, who later was to be European champion, was well outpointed over 15 rounds at the Capital Centre, Landover, but Earnie Shavers, a shaven-headed puncher from Warren, Ohio, gave him a sterner test. Shavers had won 52 of his 60 contests inside the distance, but Ali kept him well in control to take the decision.

Ali was now 36, and heavier and slower than in his early championship years, and he now took on a man who could exploit the slowness, if nothing else. He was Leon Spinks, the 1976 Olympic light-heavyweight champion. Spinks was 27lb (12kg) the lighter and 12 years the younger, but his professional career consisted of seven fights only, in one of which he had been held to a draw.

Ali and Spinks met at the Hilton Pavilion, Las Vegas, on 15 February 1978. Ali fought a very lethargic, careless fight. He allowed Spinks, a 10-1 underdog in the betting, to punch away at him at will, allowing himself to be backed into the ropes, just as he had performed against Foreman. But Spinks did not wilt. He was a much lighter puncher and looked as if he could buzz around the champion all night. In fact, Spinks looked hyped up, and kept up a tremendous feverish pace, accentuated by Ali's sluggishness. Occasionally Ali fought back and looked the more dangerous when he did, but the points were being piled up by Spinks. Only in the last round did Ali stage a fight-back, when he hurt Spinks and drove him all around the ring. It was too late. Although it earned him the verdict of one judge, the title changed hands on a split decision.

There were those who wondered whether Ali's commitment had been subconsciously less than total, in view of the fact that he now had an excellent chance, with a return-fight clause, to win the title for an unprecedented third time.

The World Boxing Council were having none of this, and called upon Spinks to defend against Ken Norton. Since his defeat by Ali, Norton had beaten Duane Berbick and Jimmy Young in an eliminator to make himself the top challenger. Spinks had to refuse to meet Norton and was thus stripped by the WBC, and Norton was named as champion, on the grounds of his having won the eliminator.

Holmes assumes the title

Norton proved to be a champion who never won a title fight, and on the strength of this his name is not usually included in lists of champions. He was 'crowned' in March 1978 and was matched to 'defend' against Larry Holmes on 9 June 1978 at Caesars Palace, Las Vegas. Holmes was another big heavyweight

***Above left:** Ali defended against Britain's Joe Bugner in Kuala Lumpur in 1975. Both men looked good, but Bugner was a cautious boxer and there was little to excite the spectators as Ali took the decision.*

***Above:** An official magazine issued for a world title fight week at the Las Vegas Hilton in February 1978. The raw Leon Spinks appeared to have the least chance of upsetting the reigning champion, but in the event he was the only challenger to win.*

***Left:** The Ali–Spinks return fight in 1978 was a very different affair to the first. This time a rejuvenated Ali took the fight to Spinks and won easily to become the first to win the heavyweight title three times. By now, however, the ruling bodies had split, and this was the WBA version only.*

of 6ft 4in (1.93m) and 210lb (95kg). He was 29 years old and had an unbeaten record stretching back over 27 professional fights. He had waited a long time for his chance, but it paid off when his experience helped him to outpoint Norton in an exciting bout.

Nobody but the WBC believed Holmes was the true champion with Ali and Spinks about to do battle again. The Superdrome in New Orleans was the venue for a Carnival of Boxing, four world titles being decided. The date was 15 September 1978 — over 14 years after Ali first won the title — and he made ring history by becoming heavyweight champion for the third time. In this contest he did not allow Spinks any chance to dictate the pace. Instead of leaning on the ropes he gave Spinks a lesson in the art of moving in and out with stiff blows and using the ring to bewilder an opponent. This time Spinks did tire, probably because he was always fighting a losing battle, and Ali in the late stages ripped into him with the intention of knocking him out. He failed to do so but won a very convincing decision. He was now approaching 37 years old. He did not defend for a year, and then decided to retire, leaving Holmes as the outstanding claimant to the title.

The heavyweight situation was now in greater confusion than it had ever been. Holmes was, indeed, promising to be a worthy WBC champion, and had knocked out Alfredo Evangelista in seven rounds, and had stopped Osvaldo Ocasio (Puerto Rico) and Mike Weaver and Earnie Shavers (both USA) before the WBA had a replacement title-holder. That body agreed to recognize the winner of a bout between John Tate, at 6ft

Above: Ali challenged new WBC champion Larry Holmes in 1980. Holmes frequently had Ali more or less helpless on the ropes but refrained from attempting a knock-out. Ali retired after ten rounds.

Above right: A 'white hope' emerged to challenge Holmes in 1982 in the person of unbeaten Gerry Cooney, a New Yorker of Irish ancestry. Holmes proved much too skilful for the newcomer, whose manager was forced to enter the ring to save his man in the 13th round.

4in (1.93m) and 240lb (109kg) a huge man from Marion City, and Gerrie Coetzee, the South African heavyweight champion, who was not much smaller. The two met in Pretoria, South Africa, on 20 October 1979 and Tate took the decision and the title.

So Holmes and Tate were each calling themselves 'the heavyweight champion', and the public, used to many years of Ali and his antics and challengers, were suddenly apathetic in the extreme.

Holmes, the WBC title-holder, proved the more durable. In 1980 he knocked out Lorenzo Zanon, the European champion from Italy, at Las Vegas, and eight weeks later forced the referee to stop his contest with Leroy Jones, on the same night as John Tate's WBA reign ended with his first defence. He was knocked out in the last round at Knoxville by Mike Weaver, one of Holmes' conquests. In fact, Larry Holmes emerged as the true successor to Ali, since he began a long and successful WBC reign, while many of the boxers whom he beat contested the WBA crown, at this stage almost a secondary event.

Weaver, in fact, did manage two successful defences. In 1980 he went to Sun City, Bophuthatswana, and knocked out Gerrie Coetzee, making his second attempt on the title, in the 13th round. He then went almost a year without a contest before, in October 1981, taking on James 'Quick' Tillis, from Chicago, who had won all his 20 contests, 16 of them inside the distance. Weaver outpointed him, at the Horizon Arena, Rosemont, Illinois, then put his title into storage for over a year before stepping into the ring at Caesars Palace, Las Vegas, to defend against Michael Dokes. Dokes, from Akron, Ohio, put Weaver down in the first minute and the referee stopped the contest after 63 seconds. Weaver, and some of the spectators, thought the referee was a little premature.

While Weaver was sitting on his title, Holmes defended successfully no fewer than eight times. He continued 1980 by beating Leroy Jones in Las Vegas and Scott Ledoux in Bloomington, Minneapolis; then he accepted a challenge from former champion Muhammad Ali. Ali had not fought since regaining the title for the third time over two years before. In challenging Holmes he saw the prospect of a fourth world title win, plus the obvious box-office rewards for a fight between the two champions. It was billed at Caesars Palace, Las Vegas, as for the vacant title.

Ali had got his weight down to below what was his best when at his prime, but in all respects was not the man he was. In fact, at 38 years old, he had little to offer apart from one or two glimpses of his former glory. Holmes won as he pleased, and seemed reluctant to punish the former champion, frequently stepping back and glancing at the referee as a suggestion that it might be stopped. It was a relief to most onlookers when Ali's corner decided it should be stopped after 10 rounds and retired him.

In 1981 Holmes outpointed Trevor Berbick, a tough boxer born in Jamaica, but who had been fighting out of Canada, where he was the heavyweight champion. He had had 20 contests, with 19 wins and a draw, and gave Holmes a good battle before losing the decision. The former champion Leon Spinks was far less trouble, being comprehensively battered for three rounds before the referee stopped the contest.

Renaldo Snipes, a young unbeaten heavyweight from New York was next in against the champion, but was stopped in the 11th at the Civic Arena, Pittsburgh. Holmes then rested for seven months before accepting a challenge from Gerry Cooney, a huge unbeaten 26-year-old from New York. Cooney had two or three good names among his 25 victims, and had earned a title shot with a first round knockout of 38-year-old Ken Norton. Cooney, of Irish descent, was built up as a 'white hope', there not having been a white champion since Johansson. The fight was at Caesars Palace on 11 June 1982, and Holmes put on a masterly display, completely outboxing the strong but raw challenger and forcing Cooney's manager to climb into the ring in the 13th round, thus causing the referee to stop the one-sided bout.

Tex Cobb, from Houston, was Holmes' next challenger. A big puncher, he was not renowned for his science, and it was a surprise when the fight went the distance. The verdict was an easy win for Holmes, but his failure to stop Cobb made a few wonder if the champion, now just turned 33, was at last beginning to feel the pace.

Lucien Rodriguez, from France, the reigning European champion, came over to challenge at Scranton, Philadelphia, and he, too, went the distance but lost the verdict. Two months later Tim Witherspoon, a solid unbeaten 25-year-old from Philadelphia, was given a chance at the Dunes, Las Vegas. He was comparatively inexperienced with only 15 fights in less than four years on his record, but he gave Holmes his toughest defence to date. Holmes fought defensively, which swayed one judge to give the verdict to Witherspoon, but Larry took the split decision.

Scott Frank, another unbeaten young pretender, but with a less impressive record than Witherspoon, came next and was easily disposed of at Harrah's, Atlantic City, the referee stepping in in the fifth round. Marvis Frazier, the son of Joe Frazier the former champion, was then given a chance at Caesars Palace. Coached by his father, the 23-year-old Marvis had had ten contests and won them all, the most recent being a points win in Atlantic City over a lethargic Joe Bugner, but he had no chance with Holmes. As he rushed in to attack so the champion picked him off with jabs and finally sent over a right which led the referee to come to the assistance of the challenger in the first round.

Holmes now had a disagreement with the WBC, and a fortnight or so after beating Frazier, he gave up the title. As it happened, a new body, the International Boxing Federation, had been formed in 1983, with headquarters in Newark, New Jersey. This body was already proclaiming 'world champions', particularly in the lighter weights, and when Holmes agreed to fight under their banner in 1984 they had a ready-made world heavyweight champion who brought them plenty of credibility.

Meanwhile, on the WBA succession, Michael Dokes had given Mike Weaver a return contest after his controversial one-round stoppage. The fight was at the Dunes Hotel, Las Vegas, on 20 May 1983, and the two swapped punches throughout. It was desperately close, and a majority draw was the decision, two of the judges being unable to separate the boxers while the third narrowly gave it to Dokes. The champion therefore retained his title, which he soon put on the line against Gerrie Coetzee, the South African, at the Coliseum Arena, Richfield, Ohio. On his third try at the title Coetzee's right hand delivered the goods when it knocked out Dokes in the tenth. Coetzee became the first South African to hold a version of the heavyweight title and the first white boxer for 24 years to do so.

In 1983, while Holmes and Coetzee had been the WBC and WBA champions, there was a move by a South African syndicate to match them and unify the title, but unfortunately this was prevented by political considerations. The WBC wanted Holmes to defend against their leading contender, Greg Page, and it was Holmes' refusal to do so, and to take the match (or mismatch) with Marvis Frazier instead, which caused the ill-feeling between them.

The WBC now proposed to recognize as their champion the winner of a contest between Greg Page and Witherspoon, which took place at Las Vegas on 9 March 1984. Page was a 25-year-old from Louisville, Kentucky, a big man of around 240lb (109kg). He was the US champion, a points defeat by Trevor Berbick being the only blot on a 24-fight record. Witherspoon, nearly a year older, had the one narrow defeat by Holmes as his only reverse. In a hard fight Witherspoon took a narrow decision.

However, Witherspoon surprisingly lost his new crown five months later, when he fought Pinklon Thomas at the Riviera Casino, Las Vegas. Thomas, from Pontiac, Philadelphia, was unbeaten in 25 contests, with Gerrie Coetzee, the reigning WBA champion being the only opponent so far he had not beaten — the two had fought a draw at Atlantic City 18 months previously. This was another hard fight for Witherspoon, and this time it was his opponent who took the decision and became the new WBC title-holder.

Less than three months later Holmes resumed his career under IBF recognition by facing James 'Bonecrusher' Smith, a relatively inexperienced boxer from Magnolia, North Carolina. Despite the fact that he was 29, he had had only 15 contests, losing one (his first), and his only notable win was against the English contender Frank Bruno, on whom he had inflicted a first defeat by knocking him out in the last round after being out-fought in the previous nine. Holmes, as expected, outboxed Smith, whose eye was cut in the 11th round, causing a stoppage in the next.

The heavyweight year of 1984 ended in a strange manner in Sun City, where Gerrie Coetzee defended against Greg Page, the defeated WBC challenger, who had also since lost his American title to David Bey. The fight took a decisive turn when Coetzee went down at the end of the sixth round from blows delivered apparently after the bell. He was down again in the seventh and knocked out in the eighth, although it then transpired that the knock-out had come 50 seconds after the round should have ended.

So the end of 1984 saw the heavyweight championship considerably devalued, in what had begun to resemble a game of musical chairs, with three associations naming three men as champions, each of whom had won only one title fight under the respective association's auspices. It was far removed from the days of Dempsey, Louis and even Ali.

Larry misses the record

Holmes, the most authentic champion, was the first to defend in 1985, and he outpointed David Bey, from Philadelphia, the new US champion, previously unbeaten in 14 fights. Two months later he outpointed Carl Williams in Reno, to record his 48th win in an unbeaten career, 21 of them coming in world title fights. Holmes was now one short of Marciano's record of 49 straight wins, and decided to try to equal this record by facing Michael Spinks, the undisputed light-heavyweight champion and brother of former champion Leon, whom Holmes had already beaten. Spinks, unbeaten in 27 bouts himself, built himself up to heavyweight proportions, but few believed that he would beat the natural heavyweight, despite the fact that Holmes was now nearly 36 and clearly well past his best. In the event Spinks had retained his speed and was able to avoid most of the attacks of the more static Holmes, while scoring himself in short bursts. He won the decision, although it was a very narrow and controversial one, and Holmes himself was bitterly disappointed at it.

Spinks' victory established two records: he became the first light-heavyweight champion to win a version of the heavyweight championship, and he completed with his brother the first pair of boxers to hold a version of the heavyweight title. It is necessary, of course, to emphasize 'a version', because the three-way title could not rank with that which those up to Ali had won.

Complaining of robbery by the Las Vegas authorities, which earned him a fine, Holmes could do little but return there to attempt to regain his lost crown seven months later. The return fight followed a similar pattern to the first, with Spinks again getting the split decision amid much booing, and Holmes again expressing his disgust. It was not quite the end of the road for Holmes.

Meanwhile, each of the other championships had also changed hands. Greg Page's WBA reign lasted less than five months when he took on Tony Tubbs, a Cincinnati heavyweight who did not belie his name, at Buffalo. Tubbs was unbeaten in 21 fights, and made it 22 by outpointing Page in a dull contest to take the title. Tubbs himself had a short reign, because he, too, lost on his first defence, losing a narrow decision after a gruelling battle with Tim Witherspoon, the former WBC champion, at Atlanta. Pinklon Thomas did a little better than Page and Tubbs, because he took on ex-WBA champion Mike Weaver at Las Vegas and actually made a successful defence, knocking him out in the eighth round. However, he, too, lasted only until May 1986, when he suffered a surprise first defeat at the hands of Trevor Berbick. Berbick put on an impressive display to outpoint Thomas at Las Vegas.

In 1986 the flamboyant promoter, Don King, in association with the US Home Box Office cable television channel, decided to unify the heavyweight scene with a series of matches involving the three champions and the leading contenders. The plan was that a single heavyweight champion would emerge by the end of 1987.

Tim Witherspoon travelled to London to defend the WBA part of the championship against the English contender Frank Bruno, who relinquished the European title to take part. Bruno fought gamely but showed his lack of experience at this level, and Witherspoon inflicted upon him his second defeat when he suddenly cut loose in the 11th round and floored Bruno, forcing the referee to intervene.

Enter Mike Tyson

A teenager from New York, Mike Tyson, had been building up a big reputation since beginning his fighting career in March 1985. In the 18 months to September 1986 he faced no fewer than 27 opponents, and beat them all, only two of them hearing the final bell. His punching power was awesome. He had to be rapidly incorporated into the Don King/ HBO programme, and it was planned that

Above: Mike Tyson began his professional career in 1985 and rapidly rose to the top. He effected a 'no-nonsense' attitude, appearing in the ring with black trunks and shoes and no socks. His manner of fighting equally eschewed frills, if not thrills. His object was to land a big punch as early as possible. One was usually enough to put his opponent into trouble.

he would face the WBC champion, Trevor Berbick, the winner to take on the WBA champion, with the boxer who won that to take on the IBF champion and thus unify the division. However, Michael Spinks upset the plans. After easily beating Steffan Tangstad, from Norway, the European champion, he relinquished the IBF crown in order to make a lucrative match with Gerry Cooney, rather than proceed with the eliminators and a possible premature showdown with Tyson.

Tyson's arrival at championship class came on 22 November 1986 when he challenged Trevor Berbick for the WBC title. Berbick wore long black socks as a retaliation for Tyson deciding to wear black trunks, also favoured by the champion. Perhaps in continuation of the psychological war, Berbick began the fight as if he were the puncher, and not on the defensive as expected. A looping left from the challenger plainly hurt and might have changed his mind for him, but he was determined to carry the fight. His ploy failed. Early in the second round a right dumped him on the Las Vegas Hilton's canvas, and from then on his senses were somewhat scrambled. Suddenly, a left hook so paralysed his legs that he fell, got to his feet, tottered across the ring, fell again and again tried to rise, only to stagger back and pitch face down on the boards. He desperately tried to get up but his legs were not with him and Tyson had achieved a spectacular knock-out. At 20 years and nearly five months he had beaten Patterson's record to become the youngest boxer to hold a version of the heavyweight title.

There was a big upset three weeks later at Madison Square Garden, New York, where Tony Tubbs had been scheduled to meet Tim Witherspoon for the WBA title and the right to meet Tyson. Tubbs cried off days before with a shoulder injury, and Bonecrusher Smith was picked to take his place. He was thought to have little chance with the champion. But Smith, beaten by both Witherspoon and Tubbs the previous year, decided to risk all on an early attack and he caught Witherspoon cold, sending him reeling with a tremendous right. Not giving Witherspoon time to recover, Smith blasted him down three times in the opening round to cause the referee to stop it according to a 'three knock-down' rule.

Smith met Tyson on 7 March 1987 at the Hilton Hotel, Las Vegas. It was a disappointing fight in that the Bonecrusher's main object seemed to be to save his own bones from being crushed. Smith went in for spoiling from the opening bell, being warned for holding as early as the second round, and when he suffered an early cut eye it seemed that survival was his sole aim. He survived, in that he was still standing at the final bell, and indeed in the last few seconds he put together a token attack, but all the judges had given practically every round to Tyson. Tyson allowed some petulance to show through his usual single-minded display at Smith's purely negative tactics. He was now the WBC and WBA champion.

While waiting for an IBF champion to tackle, Tyson defended his titles against Pinklon Thomas, perhaps the most talented of the remaining boxers to beat. The fight was on a Las Vegas Hilton bill on 30 May 1987 which featured two bouts advertised as for the heavyweight championship of the world, for on the undercard Tony Tucker was boxing James Douglas for the IBF title vacated by Michael Spinks.

Few gave Thomas much chance against Tyson, but he began positively enough, resisting Tyson's early flashing hooks with some solid jabbing of his own. However, it soon became clear that Tyson's artillery carried the heavier shells, and Thomas's left jabs were soon being used more as a measure to keep his man at a distance than to hurt him. Thomas was also clever at claiming Tyson at close quarters, but in the sixth one of the champion's typical sweeping hooks caught Thomas powerfully on the chin, and as the challenger staggered back so Tyson piled in with a vicious battery of hooks that sat Thomas on the boards. He struggled to beat the count, but Angelo Dundee, his trainer, leapt into the ring to stop it.

Tony Tucker, a 28-year-old from Grand Rapids, had had 34 contests in nearly seven years, and won all except one, declared a 'no contest' in 1982. Tall and supple, he was the favourite in his clash for the vacant IBF title with James 'Buster' Douglas from Ohio, whose record included three defeats, a draw and a 'no contest' in 28 bouts. The shorter Douglas took the early rounds, however, with some solid punching, and it was not until half-way that Tucker's superior boxing began to tell. In the tenth round he rocked Douglas and moved in mercilessly, driving his helpless opponent around the ring until the referee was forced to stop the one-sided exchanges. Tucker's win took him one step from being the undisputed champion — but he would first have to meet 'Iron' Mike Tyson.

The final unification bout of the heavyweight division took place at the Las Vegas Hilton on 1 August 1987. The fight was over 12 rounds rather than the then IBF distance of 15 rounds. Tucker stood 6ft 5in (1.96m) and looked down on Tyson, but was an outsider in the betting, 12-1 generally being on offer. Tucker fought as well as any against Tyson, and even got in a good uppercut in the first round, but seeing it had no effect took the usual line of self-preservation first. Tucker stayed on his feet for the whole of the fight, but the decision was in no doubt, and Tyson became the first undisputed heavyweight champion since, surprisingly, not Ali but Leon Spinks.

On 16 October 1987 Tyson defended his titles for the first time against the hard-punching Tyrell Biggs, from Philadelphia, who had built up an unbeaten record since his debut in 1984. Biggs was courageous but was cut above one eye and below the other, as well as around his lips, and after he had been down twice in the seventh round the fight was stopped with him helpless in his corner.

The old champion, Larry Holmes, now

Below: Tyson became the first undisputed world heavyweight champion for nearly ten years when he outpointed Tony Tucker in 1987 to add the IBF title to the WBA and WBC titles which he already held. The taller Tucker was one of Tyson's better opponents, but never looked like threatening him too much.

__Left:__ Michael Spinks and his supporters continued to claim the unbeaten Spinks was the true and people's champion after Spinks had relinquished the IBF crown. The showdown came on 27 June 1988 and after 91 seconds Spinks had been counted out, being no match for the champion, who had quickly run out of worthy challengers.

claimed he could beat Tyson, but whether with any real conviction or with an eye to a last big pay day it was difficult to tell. He was accommodated at Atlantic City on 22 January 1988. Holmes boxed on the retreat, but the champion, who was over 16 years younger, got him tangled in the ropes in the fourth, dropped him to the canvas with a quick combination and so attacked him when he rose that the referee was forced to step in and save him.

Tyson's next challenger was Tony Tubbs, the former WBA champion. The huge Tubbs got his chance in the exotic location of Tokyo on 21 March 1988. Tyson began with circumspection, but unleashed a left hook in the second round which sank Tubbs to the canvas and the referee's services were needed only to call a merciful halt.

All this was building up to the confrontation with Michael Spinks, the only boxer with a semblance of a chance not yet eliminated by Tyson. Spinks, when IBF champion, had opted out of the unification series in order to make money by defeating Gerry Cooney, a feat which was accomplished without alarms. Spinks and his backers still insisted that Spinks was the true champion, as *Ring* magazine continued to rate him. There was even an argument about who would have the champion's privilege of entering the ring second, a dispute which actually delayed the start.

The big fight took place at the Convention Center, Atlantic City, on 27 June 1988. Spinks looked cool and confident during the introductions, as befitted a man unbeaten as a professional, with many top boxing experts tipping him to win. But it is difficult to believe that he had not resigned himself to defeat ever since he backed out of the unification contests. He was, after all, just a blown-up light-heavyweight.

The great battle was all over in 91 seconds. Backed against the ropes, Spinks took a left uppercut, then a blow to the body which made him drop to the floor in pain. He rose, and threw a clumsy right at Tyson, a pawing punch that merely lined up his own chin for Tyson to hit. Over came a powerful right and, although it landed a little high, Spinks was laid flat with no prospect whatever of beating the count. Tyson clearly had no serious challengers.

THE CRUISER-WEIGHTS

The cruiserweight division was the name originally given to the light-heavyweight division in Britain. However, Britain later came into line with American practice, which had recognized a light-heavyweight division in 1903. The term cruiserweight was not used for many years, but it was resurrected in 1979 by the WBC. A glance at the weights of heavyweight champions over the years shows the champions getting progressively heavier. Before Sonny Liston, who won the title in 1962, it was the exception for a heavyweight champion to scale over 200lb (91kg). Floyd Patterson, Rocky Marciano, and Ezzard Charles, who all won the title since the war, were well under this mark (if fighting today, they might be fighting as cruiserweights). Today the champions always weigh over 200lb (91kg) with the bigger boxers like John Tate, Greg Page and Tony Tubbs approaching 240lb (109kg).

It seemed necessary to have a weight limit between light-heavy and heavy, so that boxers of around 180lb (82kg) would not be asked to give away anything up to about 60lb (27kg) should they wish to contest a title. The WBC first set their weight limit at 190lb (86kg), but in 1981 increased this to the more sensible 195lb (88kg). The WBA, who founded a cruiserweight division (although they called it junior heavyweight) in 1982, and the IBF, who followed a year later, both set their limit at 190lb (86kg)

The first WBC cruiserweight champion was Marvin Camel, of the USA, but not until his second encounter with the former light-heavyweight champion, Mate Parlov of Yugoslavia. Camel, part Indian, was given a draw when he fought in Split, Yugoslavia, but in 1980 he won the rematch in Las Vegas comfortably enough. However, he lost the title to Carlos de Leon, a good-looking Puerto Rican from Rio Piedras, who was to prove a long-running champion (although he did drop the title a couple of times) and is one of the best boxers to perform at this weight.

De Leon, in fact, after outpointing Camel and then stopping him in the return, lost the title to his first new challenger, S.T. Gordon, a hard hitter from Los Angeles who caught the champion in the second round at Cleveland and forced the referee to stop the fight. De Leon won it back in July 1983 in Las Vegas, outpointing his opponent, who had made one successful defence against Jesse Burnett.

By now the other associations had recognized their champions. Ossie Ocasio, from Puerto Rico, won the inaugural WBA title by outpointing South African Robbie Williams at Rand Stadium, Johannesburg. It was a split decision but Ocasio, who three years earlier had challenged Larry Holmes for the heavyweight title, proved a worthy champion. He outpointed Young Joe Louis and Randy Stephens, and stopped John Odhiambo before dropping the title to Piet Crous in Sun City, South Africa. Crous, from Brixton, South Africa, was a building society clerk who was South African light-heavyweight champion.

Meanwhile, Marvin Camel, the first WBC champion, became the first IBF champion when he stopped Rick Sekorski at Billings, Montana, in May 1983. He followed up by stopping the Canadian Rod MacDonald in Halifax, Canada, but dropped the title in Billings when Lee Roy Murphy, of Chicago, was given the decision after the fight doctor had refused to allow Camel to come out for the final round because of cut eyes. Camel was well ahead on points at the time, so this proved to be a very lucky decision for Murphy.

The WBC champion, Carlos de Leon, stopped Yacqui Lopez two months after regaining the title from S.T. Gordon; then he outpointed Bashiru Ali before being stopped by Alfonso Ratliff, from Memphis, who had exceptionally big feet. His only two defeats had been by Tim Witherspoon and Pinklon Thomas, two big heavyweight champions, so it was fitting that he should take a cruiserweight title. Unfortunately, little more than three months later he lost it to Bernard Benton, an unsophisticated slugger known as 'The Bull'. Benton was outpointed on his first defence by Carlos de Leon, who thus was WBC champion again.

Evander Holyfield unifies the championship

Piet Crous, the WBA champion, fought as champion twice in Sun City, stopping Randy Stephens but being knocked out himself by Dwight Muhammad Qawi, the former light-heavyweight champion from Baltimore, who had begun his career under the name of Dwight Braxton. Qawi stopped Leon Spinks, the conqueror of Ali, before dropping the title when outpointed by Evander Holyfield at Atlanta, USA, on 12 July 1986. Holyfield was a beaten semi-finalist in the 1984 Olympic Games, but was the first of the Olympic boxers of that year to become a world champion.

Lee Roy Murphy successfully defended the IBF title against Young Joe Louis, then against the Commonwealth champion from Lusaka, Zambia, Chisanda Mutti in Monte Carlo, and finally against Dorcey Gaymon, from Jacksonville, before losing his unbeaten record and title when stopped by Rickey Parkey from Morristown, in Marsala, Italy. Parkey, who had had four previous defeats, defended the title against Holyfield at Las Vegas two months later, and was stopped in three rounds, so Holyfield had unified the IBF and WBA titles.

Meanwhile, Carlos de Leon continued his

Left: Evander Holyfield (on the right) unified the cruiserweight division in 1988 after an unbeaten professional career. He then began to take on heavyweights, and in the photograph is seen fighting James 'Quick' Tillis, whom he stopped in the fifth round. He was regarded as the most likely challenger to trouble Tyson for the heavyweight crown.

Below: Dwight Muhammad Qawi had a good career as champion at both light-heavyweight and cruiserweight during the 1980s. He is photographed with his WBA cruiserweight belt, which he lost to Holyfield in 1986.

winning ways by stopping Michael Greer, of Memphis, at Giardini Naxos, Italy, and entered 1987 with another defence in Italy, at Bergamo, where he opened a cut over the eye of Italian Angelo Rottoli which caused the referee to stop it at the end of the fourth round.

Holyfield put his IBF and WBA titles at stake against Ossie Ocasio, the old WBA champion, at St Tropez on 15 August 1987, and stopped the veteran in the 11th round. On 5 December 1987 he took on another old-stager, Dwight Muhammad Qawi, from whom he had taken the WBA title 17 months earlier. As the fight was scheduled for 15 rounds the WBA title was not at stake, the WBA insisting on a 12-round limit for contests. It made little difference as Holyfield quickly got the upper hand and knocked out the challenger in the fourth round at Atlantic City.

Carlos de Leon, the WBC champion, was first to defend his title in 1988, easily outpointing José Maria Flores of Brazil on 22 January 1988 on the undercard of the Tyson–Holmes heavyweight championship bout.

The public wanted to see a unification contest between Holyfield and de Leon, and this took place on 9 April 1988 at Caesars Palace, Las Vegas. The three-times champion de Leon was the 11-1 underdog in the betting, and the three-years-younger Holyfield kept him on the defence for the eight rounds that the fight lasted. There were no knockdowns, but in the eighth Holyfield suddenly cut loose against an opponent trapped in a corner and incapable of replying. The referee stopped the contest and Holyfield was the undisputed cruiserweight champion.

CAESARS CAESARS

The Light-Heavyweights and Super-Middleweights

Boxers weighing a little more than 160lb (73kg) have been unlucky in the matter of fistic popularity. Too heavy for the middleweight division with its great traditions, and not heavy enough to tackle the real big boys, they have practised in a limbo called the light-heavyweight division, and more recently in other 'in-between' classes called cruiserweight and super-middleweight. There have been some great practitioners of the 'noble art' in these categories, for example Tommy Loughran, Billy Conn, Bob Foster, Michael Spinks, and above all Archie Moore, but all were moved to try to assert themselves, sooner or later, in the heavyweight ranks. It was not until 1986 that one temporarily succeeded, and Michael Spinks' victory over the ageing Larry Holmes for the IBF title was an aberration in the natural order of things soon put into perspective by Mike Tyson.

***Left:** 'Golden Boy' Danny Lalonde (left), the WBC light-heavyweight champion, took on Sugar Ray Leonard (right), making a third comeback, at Caesars Palace, Las Vegas, in 1988, and the WBC decided that the super-middleweight title would also be at stake. Leonard won to take both titles, making him a world champion at five weights.*

THE TERRITORY OF ANCIENT ARCHIE MOORE

The light-heavyweight division was born in 1903, and was the idea of a Chicago newspaperman, Lou Houseman, who combined his writing with boxing management and promotion. He managed a boxer called Jack Root, who was once a middleweight but who had outgrown the division. At the time the middleweight limit was generally accepted at 154lb (70kg). A man whose best weight was a few pounds above this was forced to take on heavyweights, often at a tremendous weight disadvantage.

Houseman's idea that there should be a division between middleweight and heavyweight was a sound one, and when he matched his man Root against another overgrown middleweight called Kid McCoy, and announced this as for the light-heavyweight championship of the world, the boxing press accepted the idea and the new weight division caught on. Until modern days, when new divisions began to proliferate, it was the only division to have started life in America, rather than England.

The light-heavyweight division has not been a popular one on the whole, although some of the greatest names in boxing have graced it. It failed to attract the public enthusiasm that the middleweight and heavyweight categories have, with the result that many of the champions have found that after establishing themselves they could make more money by challenging the heavyweights, and so have built up their weight to campaign with the heavy brigade. There have been a number of light-heavyweight champions who have fought for the heavyweight championship, but until Michael Spinks beat an ageing Larry Holmes for the IBF heavyweight title in 1985, none had succeeded in taking the heavier title.

The real McCoy

McCoy was the more interesting of the two boxers who fought for the inaugural championship. He had claimed both the welterweight world title (he tricked Tommy Ryan into losing it) and the middleweight title, which he did not defend. He then campaigned amongst the heavyweights, and fought James J. Corbett, the former heavyweight champion, at Madison Square Garden in 1900. McCoy was knocked out in the fifth round in a fight which was so obviously a fake that it led to the repeal of the Horton Law, which until then allowed boxing in New York, and it put an end for a time to public contests there. In fact, McCoy, who was a brilliant boxer at his best, so often failed to produce the goods that the public began to talk about his good performances as being 'the real McCoy'. He was 30 and past his best when he fought Root at Detroit on 22 April 1903, and Root, nearly four years younger, outpointed him to become the first light-heavyweight champion. The amazing McCoy, who had eight wives, made a second career in films after his 25 years in the ring, and ended by murdering a woman and committing suicide in 1940.

Root, who was an Austrian whose real name was Janos Ruthaly, did not reign long as champion. He was challenged by an Irishman, George Gardner, from Co. Clare, and was knocked out in 12 rounds at Fort Erie, Canada. In 1905 Root fought for the vacant heavyweight title after Jeffries' retirement but lost to Marvin Hart. Ironically, Gardner, in November 1903, lost his title on his first defence to another former heavyweight champion, Bob Fitzsimmons. Fitzsimmons won a decision over 20 rounds at San Francisco, and as he was also a former middleweight champion, became the first of only two men (Henry Armstrong is the other) to hold undisputed world titles at three different weights.

There was a good deal of chicanery in boxing in the early years of the century, and doubts have been cast on Fitzsimmons' victory, and on his subsequent loss of the title to Philadelphia Jack O'Brien, when he retired after 13 rounds at San Francisco in 1905. O'Brien was to claim the fight was fixed.

Jack O'Brien (real name Joseph Hagan, of Irish parents) was another who preferred to fight among the heavyweights. He never defended the light-heavyweight title, although when he challenged Tommy Burns for the heavyweight title in 1906 both men were well inside the light-heavy limit, and presumably Burns could have claimed the title had he won. The result was a draw, thought to have favoured O'Brien, who lost the decision in a return match six months later.

Another Irish-American, Jack 'the Giant-killer' Dillon, claimed the title in 1908 when O'Brien declined to fight him, but although he was a very busy boxer he, too, did little about the light-heavyweight title, preferring to beat heavyweights (hence his nickname). When he knocked out Hugo Kelly in Indianapolis in 1912 he won general recognition and successfully defended twice (not including 'no-decision' bouts), the second time against Battling Levinsky, whom he outpointed in Kansas City. However, on their next meeting, in Boston, Levinsky reversed the decision.

Levinsky, with 274 contests officially on his record, including three in one day, was another extremely busy boxer, but not in the light-heavyweight division. His real name was Barney Labrowitz, and he came from Phila-

delphia. He did not defend his title for nearly four years, and then he lost it to one of boxing's all-time greats, Georges Carpentier of France. Carpentier had arrived in America to make himself known to the American public before challenging Dempsey for the heavyweight title, in what turned out to be the first million-dollar fight. The best way to achieve this was to knock out Levinsky in the fourth round at Jersey City and become light-heavyweight champion.

Gorgeous Georges Carpentier

Carpentier, having failed in his attempt on the heavyweight title, first defended his title against Ted 'Kid' Lewis at Olympia, London, in 1922, knocking him out in the first round when Lewis turned his head to listen to what the referee was saying to them, and then later in the year against Battling Siki in Paris. The handsome war hero and his supporters were given a huge shock. Siki, a Senegalese, held the Croix de Guerre himself, but was in awe of Carpentier. For three rounds Carpentier did much as he liked, but seemed to be avoiding finishing the fight too soon, withholding his famous knock-out punch. This has led to suggestions that the fight was fixed and that Siki somehow double-crossed Carpentier, but it is more likely that 'Gorgeous Georges', holding the film rights, did not want the fight to end too quickly. If that were the case he made the mistake of hitting Siki after the bell at the end of the third. Siki spent the next three rounds in a completely unexpected assault on the champion, battering him to a sixth-round knock-out. The referee then tried to save the title of the idol of France by disqualifying Siki for tripping, but there was such a riot that after an hour the decision had to be reversed, and Siki was the new champion.

Unfortunately, the unsophisticated Siki could not handle his fame, behaved outrageously, took to the bottle, and was to be murdered when only 28. He lost the title on his first defence, when he met Mick McTigue, from Co. Clare, Ireland, who had been boxing for 12 years in the US and Canada. McTigue took on Siki in Dublin on St Patrick's Day, 1923, with the Irish Civil War in full swing. Gunfire from outside punctuated the cheering from inside the arena as McTigue outpointed Siki over 20 rounds to become world champion.

McTigue had two fights with 19-year-old Young Stribling, a Georgian with a big local following. In the first he was given a draw at Columbus, Georgia, a diplomatic home-town decision as McTigue was clearly the better. Even so, the referee had to be rescued from the mob. Stribling had the better of the return in Newark, New Jersey, but this was a no-decision contest. Stribling, whose mother was always with him at his fights, was to challenge Schmeling for the heavyweight championship in 1931. He was killed on his motorcycle a year or two later.

McTigue lost his title to Paul Berlenbach, from New York City, a former wrestling champion. Berlenbach won on points in the Yankee Stadium, in 1925. McTigue beat Berlenbach two years later when both were ex-champions. The unlucky McTigue was soon to lose the rewards of a long career in the 1929 Wall Street crash, and for most of the rest of his life to 1966 was confined in a mental institution.

Berlenbach was a good champion who successfully defended three times in 1925 and 1926, beating Jimmy Slattery, Jack Delaney and Young Stribling. Unscientific, he had a big punch which eventually tamed his challengers. However, Delaney, a French-

Above: *Georges Carpentier (left) and Ted 'Kid' Lewis fighting for Carpentier's light-heavyweight title in London in 1922. Lewis, who had been welterweight champion only three years earlier, was knocked out in the first round by a punch Carpentier threw after an intervention by the referee.*

Above: The end of Carpentier's reign. Battling Siki was born Louis Phal in Senegal, and was brought to Paris as a youth by a lady admirer who eventually abandoned him to washing dishes. He took up boxing, and Carpentier was his idol, but he surprisingly knocked out his idol in Paris in 1922.

Canadian whose real name was Chapdelaine, took his title at Brooklyn in 1926. Delaney was another big puncher, and a clever boxer, and his four fights with Berlenbach, two for the title, were classics which brought the light-heavyweight division much kudos and popularity. Delaney won three of them. Nearly 50,000 paid $461,789 to see him win the title, but even so he decided not to defend it but to try his luck with the heavyweights. He retired after a controversial loss to the future world champion Jack Sharkey, being knocked out in the first round with a body punch.

On Delaney giving up the light-heavyweight title, the National Boxing Association decided to recognize as champion the winner of a bout between Jimmy Slattery and Maxie Rosenbloom. Slattery, from Buffalo, won on points at Hartford. Meanwhile, Mike McTigue, after his defeat of Berlenbach, claimed the vacant title and was backed by the New York authorities. However, Tommy Loughran, a brilliant boxer from Philadelphia, outpointed him for it in New York on 7 October 1927.

Loughran was one of the division's best champions. He defended six times in little more than 18 months and beat the best men around in Jimmy Slattery, Leo Lomski, Pete Latzo, Mickey Walker, an outstanding middleweight champion, and James J. Braddock, later to be the heavyweight champion. Loughran did not possess a heavy punch, but his skill reminded older fans of James J. Corbett. Against Lomski, he was down twice for nine in the first round, and was saved by the bell, but proceeded to outbox Lomski for the remaining 14 rounds.

Loughran was another light-heavyweight who gave up the title to challenge for the heavyweight crown. He was more successful than most, earning a title fight with Carnera, ironically one of the biggest of all heavyweights. Loughran gave away a record 84lb (38kg) and was outpointed.

When Loughran left the division, the New York Commission recognized Jimmy Slattery, who beat Lou Scozza at Buffalo in 1930, as champion, and four months later Maxie Rosenbloom, who outpointed Slattery at Buffalo. Maxie Rosenbloom was a champion whose career lasted for 16 years, during which time he had 289 contests. A friend of George Raft, the film star, he had learned from him how to move and dance, and was essentially a long-range boxer, recording only 18 knockouts in all his fights (but being knocked out only twice himself). Because of a tendency to hit without properly closing his glove he was known as 'Slapsie Maxie'. He enjoyed a career as a 'heavy' in films after his retirement.

In April 1932 the NBA recognized George Nichols as champion after he outpointed Dave Maier in Chicago, but the following month withdrew this recognition when Nichols lost a non-title bout to Lou Scozza. Slapsie Maxie, who had meanwhile defended successfully against Abe Bain and Jimmy Slattery, promptly outpointed Scozza, but still the NBA could not find it within themselves to agree with New York, and in 1933 recognized Bob Goodwin as champion after he outpointed Joe Knight. Slapsie Maxie in 1933 outpointed Abe Stillman and Adolf Henser and then stopped the NBA champion of only three weeks, Goodwin, in four rounds in New York to gain universal recognition.

Rosenbloom's next defence was one of his best battles, with the ex-middleweight champion Mickey Walker. He got the decision after 15 gruelling rounds in New York. In 1934 he could only draw with Joe Knight in Miami, and then back in Madison Square Garden he surprisingly dropped the title to Bob Olin, a mediocre champion who lost it on his first defence to John Henry Lewis, a 21-year-old from Los Angeles. Lewis had already fought 58 times with four defeats, and by coincidence was to have an identical record in the second half of his career.

Lewis was a good champion, whose first two defences were against Englishmen. Jock McAvoy, the Rochdale Thunderbolt, was British middleweight champion. He went to America in 1935–6 and beat the best middleweights, including a one-round annihilation of Babe Risko, recognized as world champion in America. But McAvoy was allowed a title fight only at light-heavyweight, and was outpointed by Lewis. Lewis then went to Wembley and narrowly outpointed the British champion, Len Harvey, who hurt his right hand in the third round and boxed virtually one-handed. Lewis himself was suffering from a bigger handicap. Cataracts had made him blind in one eye, and he had begun to lose the sight of the other. In 1937 and 1938 he beat Bob Olin, Emilio Martinez and Al Gainer, but was refused a licence for a return with Harvey in London because of his eye condition. He challenged his friend Joe Louis for the heavyweight crown, was knocked out in the first and retired.

The New York Commission recognized Tiger Jack Fox, who outpointed Al Gainer in 1938, but two months later, on 3 February 1939, Melio Bettina of Bridgeport, Connecticut, stopped him in the ninth to become champion. The British, however, preferred the claims of Harvey and McAvoy, who had given Lewis his best fights, and these two met for the British version of the title at the White City Stadium in London on 10 July 1939. A British record 90,000 turned up to see the two great rivals, and Harvey, the day before his thirty-second birthday, outpointed McAvoy to become champion. Unfortunately for him, war soon broke out in Europe and he joined the services, being unable to press his claims or cash in.

On the other side of the Atlantic, the NBA and New York bodies agreed to recognize the winner of a bout between Bettina and Billy Conn as champion, and Conn took a well-deserved points win at Madison Square Garden, three days after Harvey's win in London. Conn was an extremely handsome and clever Irish-American from Pittsburgh, who had not boxed as an amateur, but who had become a professional when 18 as a welterweight and had, in four years, made himself an outstanding champion. He made three defences in less than a year, outpointing Bettina again in Pittsburgh, and then Gus Lesnevich twice, in New York and Detroit. Conn then followed the path of other outstanding light-heavyweight champions and ambitiously challenged the heavyweight champion, who at this time was Joe Louis. As related earlier, Conn almost beat Louis.

The NBA, on Conn's moving up a division, decided that the winner of a bout between Anton Christoforidis and Melio Bettina was for the title. Christoforidis got the decision in Cleveland in January 1941. He was a Greek from Messina, who, after fighting in Athens and Paris, had left for New York to seek and find fame and fortune. He held the title for only four months, however, before losing it to Gus Lesnevich, who outpointed him in New York.

Lesnevich, from Cliffside, New Jersey, was of Russian extraction, and proved a skilful, hard-punching champion. He twice outpointed Tami Mauriello in New York and gained recognition from all US bodies. He immediately tried his luck as a heavyweight, but lost to two middling performers before the United States intervention in the war caused a lessening in boxing activity on that side of the Atlantic, too.

In 1942 an afternoon match was arranged at Tottenham Hotspur's football ground, White Hart Lane, London, between Len Harvey, the British claimant to the title, and Freddie Mills, two men serving in the Royal Air Force. Mills, a strong, young, tearaway fighter, bundled the ageing Harvey out of the ring in the second round to stake a claim for the title.

The Lesnevich-Mills fights

With the end of more serious hostilities, it was time to tidy up the world title picture in 1946. Lesnevich travelled to Harringay Arena, London, to face Mills in one of the bloodiest battles seen in a British ring. Mills fought back from the brink of defeat in the second round, but was stopped in the tenth, leaving Lesnevich undisputed champion.

In 1947 and 1948 Lesnevich defended against Blackjack Billy Fox. Fox was controlled by gangsters, who had engineered a title challenge, and got Fox a return by bribing Jake LaMotta to throw a fight against him. LaMotta himself earned a middleweight title fight by this connivance. It did Fox no good, apart from the share of the gates he and his handlers received, for Lesnevich stopped him in the tenth and knocked him out in the first in two one-sided bouts.

Lesnevich then returned to London to give Mills a return, and this time Mills won the decision in a battle which could not equal the fire of that of two years earlier. Like Lesnevich, Mills had been fighting heavyweights, and had had some of the famed resilience knocked out of him. Eighteen months after winning the title he was knocked out by Joey Maxim in the tenth round at Earls Court.

Maxim had been boxing as a professional since 1941. He was born in Cleveland as Guiseppe Berardinelli, a name his manager changed to Maxim because his left reminded him of the rapid firing of a Maxim machine gun. He took the US title from Lesnevich before regaining the world title for America with his defeat of Mills.

Like many others, Maxim's first glance on becoming champion was towards the heavyweight division, where Ezzard Charles, who had already defended against Gus Lesnevich, was running out of credible opponents. Maxim, too, had twice fought Charles as a light-heavyweight, without success, but now his manager, Doc Kearns, saw the possibilities of a battle of the champions, and Maxim was taken on in a challenge for the heavyweight crown. Charles comfortably outpointed his old enemy in Chicago.

Maxim outpointed Bob Murphy in New York, and then was himself challenged by a man stepping up a division. The great Sugar Ray Robinson, the middleweight champion, tried to take Maxim's crown at the Yankee Stadium on 25 June 1952. It was the hottest day of the year at 40°C (104°F), so hot that referee Ruby Goldstein was forced to give up after ten rounds. Maxim was lucky, because the heat got to Robinson too. Robinson was comfortably ahead on points until the

__Right:__ Archie Moore (left), perhaps the best-ever light-heavyweight, regarded his victory over the tough Canadian Yvon Durelle as the high point of his career. He came back from four knock-downs to knock out his opponent in the 11th round. He said he felt fresh at the finish, and admitted later to have been about 46 at the time.

13th round, when he suddenly collapsed exhausted, falling face down on the canvas. He lasted the round but could not come out for the 14th, and the new referee, Ray Miller, held Maxim's hand aloft.

The reign of Ancient Archie

For over five years one of boxing's all-time greats had been waiting in the wings. Archie Moore had been trying to get a title fight, having beaten all the contenders, but the champions from Lesnevich onwards had not been interested. Now, by the simple device of granting Doc Kearns a share of his contract, he was given a shot against Maxim. Moore was by now 36 years old, and already having difficulty making the light-heavyweight limit, but he comfortably outpointed Maxim on 13 December 1952 in St Louis to become the new champion. Even so, he had to beat Maxim three times before he could look elsewhere. In June 1953 and January 1954 Ancient Archie outpointed Maxim again, first at Ogden, Utah, a close decision, then at Miami, an easier win. Despite being the oldest to win the title, Moore was to reign for nine years.

On 11 August 1954 Moore stopped Harold Johnson in the 14th in New York, then in 1955 knocked out Carl Bobo Olsen, the reigning middleweight champion. He lasted until the third round. During this time Moore was running a publicity campaign to get the heavyweight champion Rocky Marciano into the ring. He succeeded, and was Marciano's last opponent. Knocking Marciano down in the third round, Moore claimed that the referee lost him the fight by allowing the champion time to recover. Moore was knocked out in the ninth round.

In 1956 Moore travelled to London to stop Yolande Pompey in the 10th round of an all-action battle, then had another chance at the heavyweight title when matched with Floyd Patterson for the vacant crown. Archie was favourite, but was 18 years older than Patterson, and could not contain Patterson's speed and youth. He was knocked out in the fifth round.

There wasn't a light-heavyweight who could beat Moore, however. The authorities of New York and the NBA declared the title vacant in 1957 because of Moore's inactivity, but then agreed Moore and Tony Anthony should meet for it. Moore forced the referee to save his opponent from a battering in the seventh, so the status quo was maintained. It was 15 months before Moore defended again, and then he put up one of his best displays in knocking out Canadian Yvon Durelle, of New Brunswick, in the 11th round after being down three times and almost out himself in the first round. This match was at the Forum, Montreal, where Moore returned eight months later to knock out the same opponent in the third.

After another 14 months during which he did not defend his title, Moore was stripped by the NBA for inactivity. The new NBA

champion was Harold Johnson of Philadelphia, who stopped Jesse Bowdry in the ninth at Miami. Johnson was a good boxer who was himself a veteran by normal standards, being 32. However, Moore held four victories over him in five meetings, and the rest of the world for the time being continued to recognize Moore as champion.

In 1961 Johnson stopped Von Clay in Philadelphia and Moore outpointed Guilio Rinaldi, of Italy, the European champion, in New York. In 1962 Moore was stripped by the New York and European bodies for failing to meet either Johnson or Doug Jones. When Johnson outpointed Jones at Philadelphia in May 1962 he was universally recognized. Next month he went to Berlin to outpoint Gustav Scholz of Germany.

Johnson's reign came to an unsatisfactory end in June 1963 when he lost in a split decision to Willie Pastrano, a light-hitting boxer from Louisiana. Pastrano had a roly-poly physique, but was deceptively quick on his feet and a clever boxer. Pastrano surprised everybody by winning his first defence by stopping Gregorio Peralta, who had beaten him the year before. He then crossed the Atlantic to fight Terry Downes, the former middleweight champion. Downes boxed beautifully in their contest at Belle Vue, Manchester, and was ahead until Pastrano pulled off another surprise by flooring Downes with a desperate punch in the 11th, causing the referee to stop the fight.

However, another ex-middleweight finally

ended Pastrano's reign. José Torres, from Playa Ponces, Puerto Rico, was the light-middleweight silver medalist at the 1956 Olympic Games, being outpointed in the final by one of the greatest of all amateur boxers, Laszlo Papp of Hungary, who was winning his third gold medal. Managed by Cus d'Amato, the manager of Floyd Patterson, Torres stopped Pastrano at Madison Square Garden on 30 March 1965. Down for the first time in his career, Pastrano found he could not answer the bell for the tenth round.

It seemed the fashion for champions in this division to get their opportunities late, for Torres was already 29 when taking the championship. He did not hold the title long, but made the most of it, defending four times in the last seven months of 1966. Wayne Thornton and Eddie Colton were outpointed, then Chic Calderwood, of Scotland, the British champion, was knocked out in the second round at San Juan, Puerto Rico. Calderwood was killed in a car accident less than a month later.

Torres lost his title on his fourth defence — to a much older man! Dick Tiger, twice the middleweight champion, was 37 when he challenged Torres on 6 December 1966 and surprisingly proved too sharp for him over a dull 15 rounds. Despite Torres having all the physical advantages, Tiger outpointed him again in the return in May 1967. The Nigerian made one more successful defence, stopping Roger Rouse in the 12th round at Las Vegas before he dropped the title on 24 May 1968 to Bob Foster at Madison Square Garden. He was knocked out in the fourth round, his first knock-out. He retired in 1971 and sadly died the same year of cancer.

His conqueror, Bob Foster, was another of the division's outstanding champions. A deputy sheriff in Albuquerque, New Mexico, he stood 6ft 3in (1.91m) and was a lanky boxer, naturally with a long reach. But he still possessed a strong punch, as his challengers in 1969 and 1970 discovered. Frankie de Paula, Andy Kendall and Roger Rouse were all stopped inside the first four rounds, and Mark Tessman was knocked out in the tenth. The World Boxing Association, the body formed from the National Boxing Association, were not impressed with this record, however, and stripped Foster for not defending against top-ranked contenders, in particular Jimmy Dupree. As it happened, their new champion turned out to be Vicente Rondon of Venezuela, who stopped Dupree in six rounds in Caracas, Venezuela. Foster, meanwhile, had taken on his toughest assignment — the almost obligatory shot at the heavyweight title. Joe Frazier was the reigning champion, and proved altogether too strong for Foster, knocking him out in the second round at Detroit.

Rondon won his title in February 1971, a year which saw eight more light-heavyweight title fights, each of the champions defending successfully four times. Foster knocked out Hal Carroll, outpointed Ray Anderson and stopped Tommy Hicks and Brian Kelly. Rondon knocked out Piero del Papa and outpointed Eddie Jones, both fights in Caracas, then stopped Gomeo Brennan in Miami and knocked out Doyle Baird in Cleveland.

In April 1972 the two champions met in Miami, and Foster proved his superiority by knocking out the Venezuelan in the second round. Foster next knocked out Mike Fourie in the fourth, then travelled to Wembley to face England's 1968 Olympic middleweight champion, Chris Finnegan, whom he knocked out in the 14th round of an exciting contest. After this he fought Muhammad Ali, on Ali's comeback trial, and was knocked out in the eighth round. In 1973 he twice outpointed the South African Pierre Foure, once each in their respective home towns of Albuquerque and Johannesburg. But when, on 17 June, Foster fought again at Albuquerque, against a tough Argentinian, Jorge Ahumada, he was given a blatant home-town draw, after appearing to have been well beaten. Foster was by now in his thirty-sixth year, and when the WBC indicated that he should give Ahumada a return or take on England's John Conteh, he decided it was time to retire.

The WBC settled on the fight between Conteh and Ahumada at Wembley on 1 October 1974 as the key to their new champion. Conteh, from Liverpool, was a

***Right:** John Conteh was British, Commonwealth, European and world light-heavyweight champion. After three successful defences of his world crown he was idle because of management disputes, and was stripped.*

better boxer and also as strong as Ahumada, and took a clear decision to become the champion. The WBA, meanwhile, picked another Argentinian, Victor Galindez, to fight Len Hutchins of the USA in Buenos Aires, and Galindez became their champion when he forced Hutchins to retire after 12 rounds.

Conteh stopped Lonnie Bennett in the fifth round in his first defence, but Galindez was much the more active. In 1975 he twice went to Johannesburg to outpoint Pierre Foure in exciting battles and also outpointed Ahumada in New York, his fourth victory over him in five contests. Galindez continued his winning ways in 1976, stopping Norwegian Harald Skog in Oslo, and then fighting twice more in Johannesburg, where he was a favourite with the fans, if not the contenders, for he knocked out Richie Kates (with one second of the fight left) and outpointed Kosie Smith.

Conteh, who was subject to managerial disputes and began to manage himself, had been forced to lay off with injured hands, but he outpointed Yaqui Lopez in Copenhagen in 1976, and in March 1977 stopped Len Hutchins in three rounds in Liverpool.

Conteh and Galindez were outstanding fighters, but did not meet, and Conteh's reign ended in 1977, not in the ring but through his mixed-up attitude. He was stripped when he withdrew from a defence against Miguel Cuello, another Argentinian, scheduled for Monte Carlo. Jesse Burnett came in as substitute, but was knocked out in the ninth, so both light-heavyweight champions were now from Argentina.

Galindez went on a Roman holiday, outpointing Richie Kates and Yacqui Lopez there, then Eddie Gregory in Turin, then Lopez again in Reggio. Cuello also went to Italy to defend, but he lost his half of the title in his first defence, to Mate Parlov, a Yugoslav who had won the Olympic Games light-heavyweight gold medal in 1972. Parlov became the first communist world champion. Parlov's first defence was in Belgrade against Conteh, and he was given the split points decision, although many thought Conteh had had the edge.

Galindez left Europe to defend in New Orleans in September 1978, and received a temporary setback, being surprisingly stopped by Mike Rossman of Philadelphia. Rossman made one successful defence, stopping Aldo Traversaro in six rounds in Philadelphia, before he gave Galindez a return and was forced to retire after the ninth in New Orleans.

There began some swapping of WBC and WBA titles around this time. Marvin Johnson took the WBC title from Mate Parlov by stopping him in the tenth round in Marsala (Italy was seeing a lot of action in the late 1970s), but then dropped it to Matt Franklin from Philadelphia in Indianapolis. Franklin promptly changed his name to Matthew Saad Muhammad. Undismayed, Marvin Johnson stopped Galindez in 11 rounds in New Orleans to take the WBA title.

Matthew Saad Muhammad's first defence was against Conteh, who lost a narrow decision after 15 exciting rounds at Atlantic City. Conteh was disappointed in that it seemed the champion's badly cut eyebrow was healed by an illegal substance. It was Conteh's last real challenge to regain his crown — he was stopped in the fourth in an Atlantic City return in March 1980, when he fought badly, his heart clearly not in it.

To bring more confusion to the scene, Marvin Johnson was stopped in Knoxville two days later by Ernie Gregory, who changed his name to Mustapha Muhammad, so both halves of the championship were now held by boxers who had changed their names to Muhammad. Both were active in 1980 and 1981. Matthew Saad Muhammad beat Louis Pergaud from the Cameroons, Yaqui Lopez, Lotte Mwale from Zambia, Vonzell Johnson, Murray Sutherland and Jerry Martin. He was eventually stopped in the tenth round in Atlantic City by Dwight Braxton of Baltimore. In 1982 Braxton stopped Jerry Martin and then beat Matthew Saad Muhammad in a return, at which point he (Braxton) inconsiderately changed his name in celebration to Dwight Muhammad Qawi.

The other Muhammad, Mustapha, had a less spectacular run, stopping Jerry Martin and Rudi Koopmans, the Dutch European champion. However, in July 1981 he was challenged by Michael Spinks, and outpointed at Las Vegas.

Spinks tidies up the division

Spinks, the 1976 Olympic middleweight champion, and brother of former world champion Leon Spinks, was to make a big impact on both the light-heavyweight and heavyweight scenes. He was to prove an outstanding light-heavyweight champion, who finally unified the division and incidentally swept away all the Muhammads.

A clever boxer with an awkward style, whose skill camouflaged an ability to hit hard and dispatch an opponent in trouble, Spinks stopped Vonzell Johnson, Mustapha Wasaijja, Murray Sutherland, Jerry Celestine and Johnny Davis between November 1981 and September 1982. On 18 March 1983 he fought Dwight Muhammad Qawi, who had stopped Eddie Davis in his tracks four months earlier. Spinks outpointed Qawi at Atlantic City to become the undisputed champion, the first since Foster retired in 1974.

Spinks continued to dominate the division, stopping Oscar Rivadeneyra of Peru at Vancouver, Canada, outpointing Eddie Davis at Atlantic City, stopping David Sears in only three rounds again in Atlantic City, and stopping Jim MacDonald in eight rounds in Las Vegas. He then challenged Larry Holmes for the IBF heavyweight championship, and won, to become the first light-heavyweight champion to win the top crown, albeit only a third of it.

When he decided he would not defend the light-heavyweight title again, the championship split three ways, there by now being three ruling bodies specifying 'world champions'. The first to name a champion was the WBC, who recognized J.B. Williamson of Indianapolis after he had outpointed Prince Muhammad at Los Angeles on 10 December 1985. Next in line was the IBF, who nominated Slobodan Kacar, from Ferucica, Yugoslavia, as champion, after his points victory over ex-WBA champion Mustapha Muhammad in Pesaro, Italy, on 21 December 1985, and finally the WBA proclaimed Marvin Johnson, who had already held the WBA and WBC championships, after he stopped Leslie Stewart of Trinidad, the Commonwealth champion, who was forced to retire with severe eye cuts after seven rounds in Indianapolis on 9 February 1986.

So the merry-go-round of the 'alphabet boys', as the WBC, WBA and IBF came to be known, began again. Only Johnson of the three champions managed a successful defence, when he stopped Jean-Marie Emebe, born in Cameroon but based in France, in Indianapolis.

Williamson lost his title to Dennis Andries, a Guyana-born boxer fighting out of Hackney, London. Andries was a strong journeyman fighter with six defeats in 34 contests, but was much too aggressive for a lacklustre Williamson in London and comfortably outpointed him. Kacar, a 1980 Olympic champion at light-heavyweight, went to Los Angeles and met Bobby Czyz from Wanaque, USA, a crowd-pleasing, all-action fighter, who surprisingly stopped the more stylish Kacar, who was helpless before the hammer blows of Czyz in the fifth when the referee stepped in. Johnson kept his title until 23 May 1987, when he gave a return to Leslie Stewart at Port of Spain, Trinidad. Having beaten Stewart in his own home town of Indianapolis, the veteran Johnson found the challenger a different proposition. Down twice in the first round, he was saved by the bell, and needed all his bravery to last eight rounds, when he was forced to retire.

__Below:__ Dennis Andries took the WBC light-heavyweight title from J.B. Williamson but lost it when defending against Thomas Hearns, who was seeking a title at a third weight.

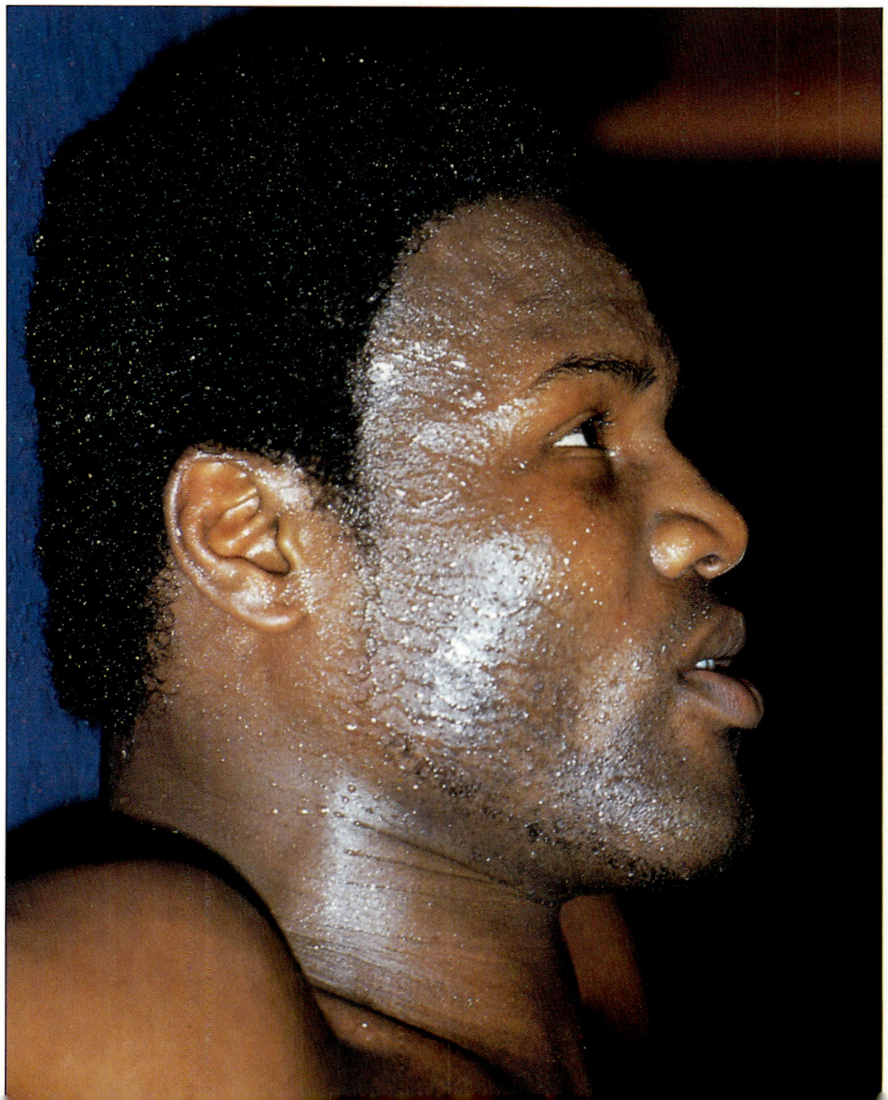

Above: *Andries made a successful 1986 defence of his title when knocking out British middleweight Tony Sibson, a victim of Marvin Hagler and Frank Tate when challenging for the world middleweight crown.*

Andries defended successfully in a local affair with Tony Sibson, the British middleweight champion, whom he stopped in nine rounds but then put his title on the line in Detroit, against the local hero, 'Hit Man' Thomas Hearns. Hearns was having his first fight at light-heavyweight, having held welterweight and light-middleweight titles and challenged unsuccessfully as a middleweight. It was an exciting contest in which the skill and speed of Hearns finally overcame Andries' superior strength. The turning point was a powerful right cross which sank Andries to the canvas in the sixth. Although he fought on bravely, the referee finally called a halt in the tenth. It was thus a third world title at different weights for Hearns, equalling the record of Fitzsimmons and Armstrong, although his titles were only partial ones.

Czyz continued his merry round of quick dismissals of IBF challengers, with early stoppages of David Sears, Willie Edwards and Jim MacDonald, but on 29 October, in Las Vegas, it suddenly went wrong. 'Prince' Charles Williams, of Cleveland, was dropped to the canvas early on, but fought back cleverly and closed the champion's right eye. Williams then got on top, and Czyz was forced to retire at the end of the ninth round. Williams made a successful defence on 10 June 1988, forcing Richard Caramanolis of France to retire in the 11th round at Annecy.

Leslie Stewart's reign as WBA champion did not last out 1987, for he lost on his first defence to Virgil Hill, an Olympic silver medalist in 1984, at Atlantic City. The referee stopped the contest in the fourth round in favour of the 23-year-old unbeaten American from Williston. Hill was a busy boxer in his first few months as champion. On 21 November 1987 he went to Paris to defend against Rufino Angulo, the French champion, and won a very easy decision. On 3 April 1988, before a home audience at Bismarck, North Dakota, he stopped Jean-Marie Emebe. On 6 June 1988 Hill kept his unbeaten record when outpointing Ramzi Hassan, from Chicago, at Las Vegas.

Meanwhile, Thomas Hearns left the WBC title vacant by deciding to move back to middleweight to attempt a fourth world title. The two boxers chosen to dispute the crown were Don Lalonde, from Winnipeg, and Eddie Davis, the veteran New Yorker, who was making his third challenge since 1982. The fight took place at Port of Spain, Trinidad, and Lalonde stopped Davis at the start of the second round, having almost knocked him out in the first. The blonde Lalonde, known as 'Golden Boy', defended on 29 May 1988 against Trinidad's only world champion, Leslie Stewart, who had held the WBA title eight months earlier. The match was at Port of Spain, but Stewart could not regain his laurels before his home crowd and was stopped in the fifth.

Lalonde then took part in a strange fight sanctioned by the WBC which broke its rules of not allowing a boxer to fight for a world title unless ranked in the top ten, nor allowing a boxer to hold a title at two weights. It was an indication that in the boxing business the only constant is the search for quick money.

Lalonde was matched with Sugar Ray Leonard, perhaps the outstanding boxer of the 1980s, who was a former world champion at welterweight, light-middleweight and middleweight, but who had three times retired and had not fought for 19 months. The WBC moreover agreed to recognize the super-middleweight class and to recognize the winner of the fight as light-heavyweight and super-middleweight champion.

So that the fight could be for the latter championship, Lalonde was required to weigh in at 168lb (75kg), thus putting his light-heavyweight title at risk while coming down to 7lb (3kg) below the limit for that class. The object of it all (as well as the pay-night) was to give Leonard the chance to become the first boxer to win world titles at five weights.

After all this cynicism, the fight itself, on 7 November 1988 at Caesars Palace, Las Vegas, was a good one. Lalonde fought well, and put Leonard down in the fourth, but Leonard was much too fast and skilful for the champion and eventually won with a stoppage in the ninth round. He thus won his five titles, and soon afterwards relinquished the two latest ones, although keeping his options open regarding a fourth retirement.

Left: *World light-heavyweight champion Dennis Andries gets sent to the canvas by Thomas Hearns in the eighth round. Hearns went on to win the WBC title in the tenth.*

THE SUPER-MIDDLE-WEIGHTS

The super-middleweight class was instituted by the IBF in 1984. The weight limit was set at 168lb (76kg), i.e. 8lb (3.6kg) above the middleweight limit and 7lb (3.2kg) below the light-heavyweight limit. The first men chosen to contest the championship were Murray Sutherland, a Scot who fought in the USA, and Ernie Singletary. Sutherland won on points on 28 March 1984.

Four months after winning this title, Sutherland accepted a challenge from Chong-Pal Park, from Chunranam-Do, South Korea, who for five years had held, except for a break of three months, the Orient and Pacific Boxing Federation middleweight title. Sutherland went to Seoul and was knocked out in the 11th round on 22 July 1984. Park, a clever boxer, was active as world champion, defending seven times in less than three years. He knocked out Roy Gumbs of Britain in the second round, outpointed Vinnie Curto in Seoul and knocked him out in the last round of the return in Los Angeles. He had a technical draw with Lindell Holmes of Detroit, the US champion, in Chungju, when the fight was stopped in the second round with both boxers suffering from an accidental clash of heads. He outpointed Marvin Mack of Philadelphia, stopped his Aborigine challenger Doug Sam, of Brisbane, in Seoul in another last-round victory after a tough fight, and outpointed Lindell Holmes in their return match in Inchon, a split decision.

After he had disposed of Emanuel Otti in four rounds, the WBA decided to recognize the class and nominated Jesus Gallardo to meet Park for their version. Park knocked out Gallardo in the second on 12 December 1987.

Park was forced to give up the IBF title to pursue his WBA ambitions. He kept the WBA crown by knocking out an Indonesian, Polly Pasireron, at Chungju, South Korea, in the fifth round with fierce body punching. On 23 May 1988 he took on Fulgencio Obelmejias, the only man to have beaten him, at Suanbao, and the Venezuelan took his title.

Meanwhile, the IBF, whose title fights were still over 15 rounds, nominated Graciano Rocchigiani from Rheinhesen, West Germany, and Vince Boulware, from Harrisburg, USA, to dispute their vacant championship. The fight was at Düsseldorf, and the unbeaten Rocchigiani became only the third German world champion when he stopped Boulware in the eighth round, a terrific left to the body being the final damaging punch. On 3 June 1988, Rocchigiani outpointed Nickey Walker in Berlin to keep the crown.

The WBC recognized the division on 7 November 1988 when agreeing that the winner of the light-heavyweight title fight between Don Lalonde and Sugar Ray Leonard would be recognized also as super-middleweight champion. As related above, Sugar Ray Leonard won but then relinquished the title.

Budweiser

The Middleweights and Light-Middleweights

Perhaps 160lb (73kg) is an ideal weight for a fighting man. This is the middleweight limit, and over the years there have been more outstanding warriors and outstanding battles in this division than in any other. Any gallery of great boxers would have to include Jack Dempsey (called 'the Nonpareil'), Tommy Ryan, the tragic Stanley Ketchel, Les Darcy, Harry Greb, Mickey Walker, Tony Zale, Marcel Cerdan, Sugar Ray Robinson, Randolph Turpin, Carlos Monzon and Marvin Hagler, not to mention the man who shared a ring with them for some of boxing's best remembered bouts: Bob Fitzsimmons, Billy Papke, Rocky Graziano, Jake LaMotta, Carmen Basilio, Tommy Hearns and others. Strength, speed, skill and stamina seem to mix most memorably in the middleweights.

Left: *Marvin Hagler (facing camera) and Thomas Hearns battle for the undisputed middleweight title at Caesars Palace, Las Vegas, in 1985. Hagler kept the title with a third-round stoppage. Although lasting only three rounds, the fight was one of the most exciting of the 1980s, with both men giving everything in all-out aggression throughout.*

WHERE POWER AND SPEED MAKE CHAMPIONS

In the old bare-knuckle days, the smaller men who were unable to fight the champions on equal terms would fight each other, and the concept of a 'lightweight' champion emerged, as opposed to the 'heavyweight' champion. Caleb Baldwin, weighing less than 140lb (64kg) was recognized as a lightweight champion in the 18th century. Men whom we would now think of as middleweights fought the big men, and indeed many of the bare-knuckle champions were middleweights by today's standards.

In the 19th century boxers began to be more conscious of their own weight and to claim to be champion at a particular weight. Nat Langham, from Hinckley, Leicestershire, who weighed about 150lb (68kg), was one of the great boxers of his day, and from 1843 to 1857 he was regarded as the 'middleweight' champion of England. Langham, himself beaten only once (by heavyweight Harry Orme), was the only man to beat the great Tom Sayers, who weighed no more than he did but became the champion of England at any weight. When 37 years old, Langham fought a 60-round draw in a grudge fight with Ben Caunt, the 210-lb (95.5-kg) ex-heavyweight champion, who himself was 43 and had been retired for 12 years.

On 13 April 1867, Tom Chandler beat Dooney Harris in 33 rounds at San Francisco for a $5,000 side-bet, for what he called the 'championship of his class'. Chandler weighed about 156lb (71kg). This championship passed through George Rooke to Professor Mike Donovan, who retired in 1882.

In 1884 George Fulljames of Canada claimed the title and challenged the world, for what he called 'the middleweight championship', setting it at 154lb (70kg).

Fulljames's challenge was accepted by an Irishman from Kildare, John Kelly, who had been taken to America as a boy and who fought under the name Jack Dempsey. Dempsey won in 22 rounds at Great Kills, Staten Island, New York (some reference books say Toronto, Fulljames's home town), and became the first to be recognized as world middleweight champion.

Dempsey, who in his career fought with bare knuckles, skin-tight gloves and the later gloves, was one of the ring's great figures. He was a perfect stylist, and became known as Jack Dempsey, 'the Nonpareil'. He was the second boxer to have been given this nickname (meaning 'having no equal'). Jack Randall, a Londoner of 5ft 6in (1.68m) and 136lb (62kg) had been unbeatable at his weight from 1815 to his retirement in 1821, winning many matches for large side-stakes, and he was boxing's original 'Nonpareil'.

Dempsey knocked out Jack Fogarty and George LaBlanche, a Canadian known as 'The Marine' in 1886, and Johnny Reagan in 1887. This title fight was unique in being held in two rings. Having already been postponed because of police interference and by fog, the battle began at Huntington, Long Island. When the tide came in after eight rounds the ring was flooded, and the two men and the 25 officials and spectators boarded a tug and re-erected the ring 25 miles upstream. Reagan lasted 45 rounds, but was outclassed.

Dempsey suffered a rare defeat in 1889 when he was knocked out in the 32nd round in a return with George LaBlanche. LaBlanche claimed the title but was not acknowledged as champion for two reasons. First, he weighed 161lb (73kg), 7lb (3.2kg) over the limit, and second he achieved the knock-out with a 'pivot blow'. Missing with a left hook, LaBlanche pivoted on his heel and caught Dempsey with his elbow on the way back, a sort of backhander. Dempsey was knocked unconscious, and although the referee gave LaBlanche the fight the public would not allow him the championship. The blow was made illegal. Dempsey then knocked out Billy McCarthy, an Australian, in the 28th round.

Bob Fitzsimmons, from Cornwall, who had emigrated to New Zealand as a blacksmith and fought in Australia, arrived in the United States on 10 May 1890 and, on 14 January 1891, took Dempsey's title. Fitzsimmons floored Dempsey 13 times and asked him to retire, but Dempsey replied: 'A champion never quits'. He was knocked out in the 13th round, and his backers, for whom he had won much money over the years, lost a fortune. Dempsey retired, and died four years later.

Fitzsimmons knocked out Dan Creedon, a New Zealander who later claimed the English title, in two rounds in 1894 and then moved up to challenge the heavyweights, a more lucrative proposition, and where he was to be equally successful. Fitzsimmons during his reign moved the limit up by 4lb (1.8kg) to 158lb (72kg) for his fight with Creedon.

Many claimed the crown on Fitzsimmons giving it up, including Kid McCoy, Philadelphia Jack O'Brien and Tommy Ryan, the welterweight champion. On 2 March 1896 McCoy took Ryan's welterweight title on a ruse (see Welterweight chapter) and claimed the middleweight crown as well, emphasizing his claim with a decision over Creedon in 1897. But McCoy then followed Fitzsimmons' example and decided to campaign as a heavyweight. Ryan knocked out George Green of San Francisco in 1898 and was acknowledged champion. Ryan, from New York, was a classy boxer who in a long career lost only three fights. He successfully defended the middleweight title six times, in New York, Fort Erie (Canada), London and Louisville, where his 17-round defeat of Tommy West was a bloody encounter.

The Michigan Assassin

Ryan retired in 1907, and the crown was claimed by another of the ring's greats, Stanley Ketchel. From Grand Rapids, Michigan, the son of a Polish immigrant, Ketchel drew over 20 rounds with Joe Thomas for the vacant title on 4 July 1907, then beat him on a knockout in the 32nd round in September. He confirmed this victory with a points win in December, then knocked out Mike (Twin) Sullivan in the first round in 1908. In his next fight, he knocked out Jack (Twin) Sullivan, who was also claiming the title, in the 20th and this established Ketchel's claim — he was now universally recognized.

One of the toughest of all fighters, Ketchel reigned for three years, until 1910, except for a spell of 11 weeks in 1908, when he was relieved of the championship by Billy Papke. Papke was another of the toughest of all fighters. He was known as the 'Illinois Thunderbolt', and when he met Ketchell, the 'Michigan Assassin', the sparks flew. Ketchel had beaten Papke on points in June 1908, but when they met in September Papke floored Ketchel with a tremendous right to the throat as Ketchel expected the handshake after the referee's instructions. Ketchel did not recover and was stopped in the 12th, having taken tremendous punishment. However, in November Ketchel regained his title and no doubt much satisfaction by pounding Papke to an 11th round knock-out in a savage battle.

Ketchel knocked out Philadelphia Jack O'Brien, the light-heavyweight champion, in 1909 but as O'Brien had been campaigning as a heavyweight for three years, Ketchel did not claim the light-heavy title. Ketchel also fought the heavyweight champion, the fearsome Jack Johnson in 1909, and suffered a painful defeat, losing some teeth in the process. The fight was probably a fix, but appeared to get out of hand due to Ketchel's exuberance.

Ketchel fought 16 title fights between 1907 and 1910 and was taking a short holiday on a ranch in Montana when he was murdered by a cowhand through jealousy.

Ketchel's murder threw the middleweight division into turmoil, and there was not another universally recognized champion until 1917. Papke was recognized in Great Britain (he had tried to claim the title when Ketchel fought Johnson, Ketchel having said he was giving it up) on the strength of beating Jim Sullivan, the British champion, in London in 1911. He also gained International Boxing Union recognition with three defences in Paris in 1912, but in 1913, also in Paris, he lost on a disqualification for persistent butting to Frank Klaus, a German-American from Pittsburgh. Klaus was already claiming the title on the strength of a decision over Jack Dillon in 1912, and now he had IBU recognition.

In the meantime, Frank Mantell, a German fighting in America, had claimed the title with a 1912 decision over Papke, but Papke claimed this was a non-title bout. Mantell was recognized in America, but when he was beaten by Pat O'Keefe in London, this thread of the championship was forgotten. Klaus returned to Pittsburgh and was surprisingly knocked out in 1913 by George Chip, from Scranton, Pennsylvania, which gave the American authorities an American

Below: Stanley Ketchel (left) poses with his toughest opponent Billy Papke, before one of their three title fights in 1908. Papke won the second by ignoring the pre-fight handshake and flooring Ketchel with a terrific punch. The referee is Jack Welch and behind Ketchel is his manager, Willus Britt. In this photograph Papke's shorts have at one time been tastefully painted in, as he actually wore a much more revealing pair.

to recognize as champion. Chip repeated his win over Klaus, but was then surprisingly knocked out in the first round at the Broadway Arena, Brooklyn, by Al McCoy. Chip was stand-in for his brother against the moderate McCoy in a non-title bout, and apparently had not realized McCoy was a southpaw, and was downed by a left to the stomach.

A number of American boxers were unimpressed with McCoy's claim to the title. Two of them, Eddie McGoorty and Jeff Smith, went to Australia where there was a boxing boom in 1914 and 1915, and when the two met at Sydney on the first day of 1914 the fight was advertised as for the vacant middleweight championship. McGoorty knocked out Smith in the first round, and for two or three years the Australian version of the title had the more credibility.

Other top middleweights went to Australia, and the title was held in turn by Smith (who already had a victory over Chip on his record), Mick King and the man who turned out to be the best of all, Les Darcy. Darcy took the title from Smith in May 1915, and beat all the other contenders in turn, successfully defending 14 times to September 1916. His last defence was a ninth-round knock-out of George Chip, who had also gone to Australia to try to get his title back.

Al McCoy, meanwhile, beat Hugh Ross in America in 1916, and Darcy, having no doubt McCoy would present him with no problems, accepted an invitation to America to settle the issue. Unfortunately, World War I was now in progress, and Australians between 18 and 40 were forbidden to leave the country. Darcy slipped away on a cargo boat. Unfortunately for him, when he arrived in America he found that the USA had now entered the war, too. Darcy was branded a 'slacker' and his fight with McCoy did not materialize. A very disappointed Darcy could not get a fight in America, and within weeks died, the fanciful say of shame and a broken heart, but the more practical admit he contracted pneumonia.

McCoy fought Mike O'Dowd in a no-decision bout, but O'Dowd knocked him out in the sixth in New York to take the title. It was November 1917, Darcy was dead, the world was at war, so nobody now disputed O'Dowd's claim to the crown. It was the last fight under the Frawley Law which forbade decisions in New York — from now on points verdicts were recognized in New York, although not in some other US centres.

O'Dowd, of Irish extraction from St Paul, Minnesota, and called the 'St Paul Phantom', successfully defended four times, but was outpointed in May 1920 by Johnny Wilson, in Boston. Wilson, from New York, was a character with well-known underworld connections, and his victory was disputed. However, he won a return, but then was the centre of controversy again after a challenge from Bryan Downey, of Columbus, Ohio, in Cleveland. Downey put Wilson down three times in the seventh round, but was disqualifed on the third for attempting to hit the champion while he was down.

The Ohio Federation refused to accept this strange decision and recognized Downey as champion, while later the New York authorities declared the title vacant. Downey twice defended his Ohio title, including beating Mike O'Dowd, but then lost it to Jock Malone. Dave Rosenberg won the New York version, but quickly lost it to Mike O'Dowd. These two new champions did not defend. Malone lost a non-title fight and was stripped, while O'Dowd retired after a long career.

Wilson then lost the dubious claim he had (by virtue of the referee's eccentric decision, re: Downey). He was beaten on his next defence by Harry Greb, who decisively outpointed him at the Polo Grounds, New York, in August 1923. When Greb followed this by outpointing Downey in Pittsburgh, there was no reason for anybody to dispute that he was the champion.

Greb brought a period of stability to the middleweights. He was himself one of the most remarkable of all fighters. He appeared to scorn training, and he fought with the all-action style of the street fighter. He was no more particular about his methods, and was known as the 'Human Windmill'. The most remarkable thing about him is that he became one of boxing's greats while fighting for much of his career with only one good eye.

The tragic Greb and Flowers

Greb, from Pittsburgh, ruled for two and a half years, defending successfully six times, his most notable victory being over Mickey Walker, with whom, according to legend, he fought again that night outside a night-club. He lost his title on 26 February 1926 when outpointed by Tiger Flowers in New York. Flowers repeated the decision six months later.

Tiger Flowers was born Theodore Flowers in Camilla, Georgia, a name about as appropriate for a boxer as Jersey Joe Walcott's (Arnold Cream). He was a church deacon, and became known as the 'Georgia Deacon'. A polished fighter, he was the first black middleweight champion. His misfortune was that his reign came between those of two of boxing's greats, for no sooner had he seen off Harry Greb than he lost his title on his second defence to Mickey Walker. By coincidence both Greb and Flowers died within a year of losing the title, Greb after a nose operation and Flowers after an eye operation. They were both 32.

Mickey Walker, from Elizabeth, New Jersey, had been welterweight champion. He was one of the toughest and most persistent fighters of all time, earning the nickname of the 'Toy Bulldog'. He defended against Tommy Milligan in London, winning a huge bet, and twice against Ace Hudkins. He then relinquished the title to move up to the heavyweights, where he took on the best.

Walker's decision to give up the title caused the biggest mix-up in the middleweight ranks, and there was not to be an undisputed champion for another ten years.

The National Boxing Association were first to name a champion. They recognized Gorilla Jones after his defeat in August 1931 of Tiger Thomas at Milwaukee. In 1932 he successfully defended against Oddone Piazza and Young Terry, and in June 1932 went to Paris to defend against Marcel Thil of France. He lost on a disqualification for hitting low in the 11th round, and the International Boxing Union (which was to become the European Boxing Union) joined the NBA in recognizing Thil as champion. Thil then went to London and outpointed the British champion, Len Harvey.

The New York Commission recognized Ben Jeby of New York as their champion when he outpointed Chuck Devlin in November 1932. He defended against Frank Battaglia, Vince Dundee, with whom he drew, and Young Terry in 1933. Meanwhile, the NBA withdrew recognition from Thil for failure to defend and recognized Gorilla Jones again after he knocked out Sammy Slaughter. There were now three middleweight champions with backing for their claims: Jeby, Jones and Thil.

Lou Brouillard, from St Eugene, Quebec, a former welterweight champion, knocked out the New York champion, Ben Jeby, in New York in 1933. Brouillard held a decision over Mickey Walker and was as good a candidate as any, but his reign lasted a mere 11 weeks. On 30 October 1933 he was outpointed by Vince Dundee at Boston.

Dundee's real name was Vincent Lazzaro, whose parents were Italian. His elder brother, Joe Dundee, who was world welterweight champion in the 1920s was born in Rome, but Vince was born in Baltimore, Maryland, after his parents had emigrated.

Dundee defended successfully against Andy Callahan and Al Diamond but was outpointed by Teddy Yarosz at Pittsburgh on 11 September 1934. In the meantime the NBA had withdrawn recognition from Gorilla Jones on the grounds of two defeats in 1934 and the NBA joined the New York authorities in recognizing Teddy Yarosz. There were thus only two champions now: Yarosz, recognized in America, and Thil, recognized in Europe.

Thil had meantime defended three times in Paris, outpointing Kid Tunero in 1933 and Ignacio Ara and Gustav Roth in 1934. He continued being the most active and stable of the two champions. He drew with Carmelo Candel in Paris in 1934 and in 1935 he overcame Vilda Jaks, Ignacio Ara again and then outpointed Carmelo Candel. In 1936 and 1937 he defended against Lou Brouillard, the French-Canadian former New York champion, who went to Paris and was disqualified twice for low blows.

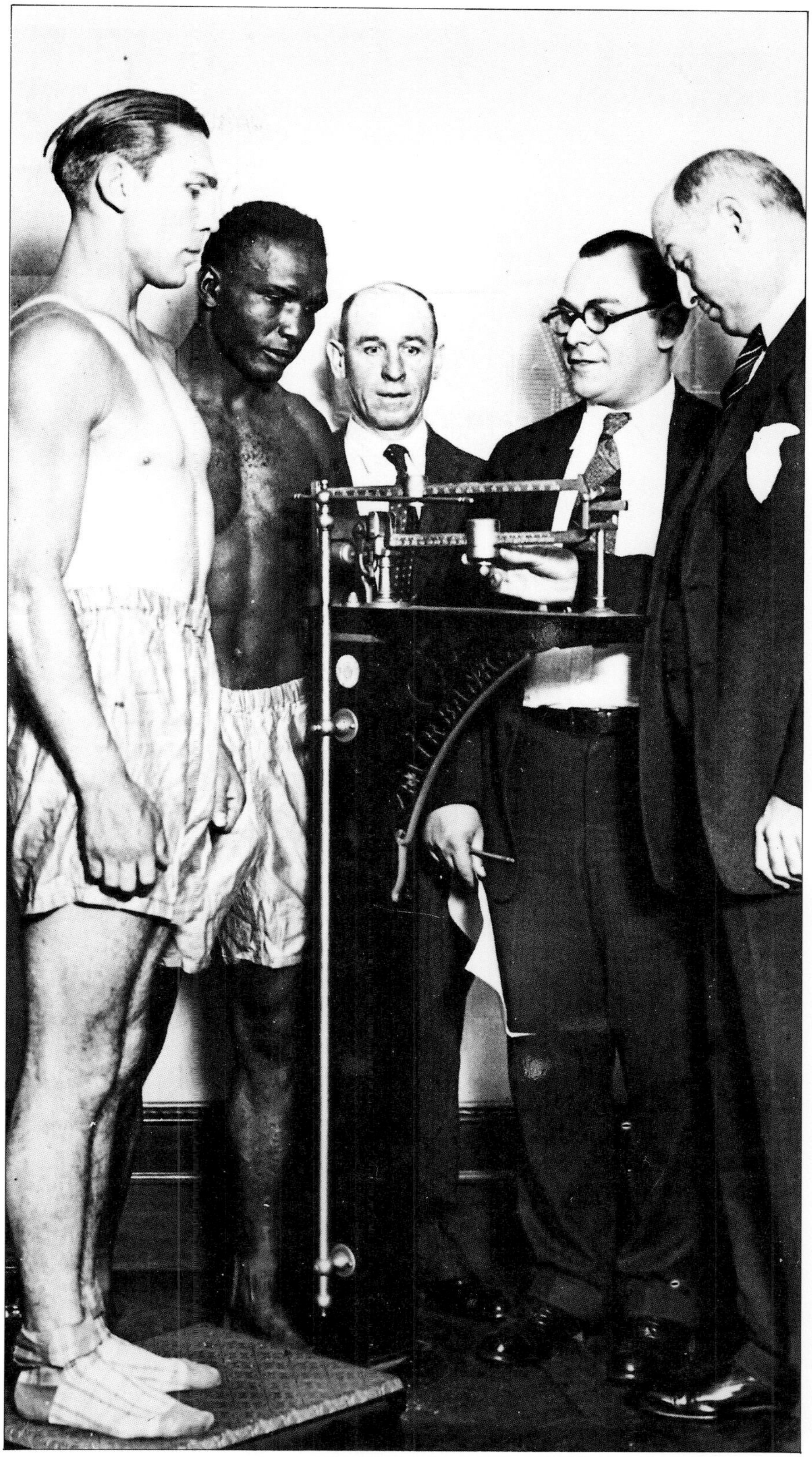

Yarosz lost his American version of the title on his first defence when Babe Risko, of Polish extraction, from Syracuse, New York, outpointed him in September 1935. However, the American strand of the championship did not look too good when the British champion, Jock McAvoy, during a tour of the United States, knocked Risko down six times before a first-round knockout in a non-title fight in 1936.

After one successful defence against Tony Fisher, Risko was outpointed in 1937 by Freddie Steele, a hard-hitting fighter from

Above: *Harry Greb weighs in for his title fight with Tiger Flowers in February 1926. Flowers won to end Greb's two and a half year reign. Greb died eight months later after an operation on his nose. Flowers, a church deacon, was the first black middleweight champion, and he, too, was dead within two years, dying after an eye operation.*

Tacoma, Washington. Steele beat Gorilla Jones, Risko again, Frank Battaglia and Ken Overlin.

Marcel Thil now went to New York and fought Fred Apostoli, from San Francisco, known as the 'Boxing Bell-hop' because he had been a hotel pageboy. Apostoli won when Thil's eyelid was cut, and the referee stopped the fight in the tenth round.

This result merely complicated the whole mess that the middleweight division was now in. Thil lost IBU recognition, but Apostoli did not accept it, because the New York Commission had refused to recognize the fight as a title fight, and in deference Apostoli forfeited IBU recognition. In return, the New York Commission ordered Steele, whom they recognized, to defend against Apostoli, who had already beaten him in a non-title fight. Steele refused, so the New York Commission stripped him and named Apostoli as champion. The NBA continued to support Steele. The IBU, without a champion, decided to recognize the winner of the European title bout between Edouard Tenet of France and Josef Besselmann of Germany on 7 April 1938. Tenet won on a 12th-round stoppage.

In 1938, therefore, Tenet, Steele and Apostoli all claimed the middleweight title. None retained a claim for long. Apostoli outpointed Glen Lee in April 1938, and decided to claim IBU recognition after all, and when Tenet lost his European title in July on his first defence, the IBU decided to back Apostoli in his claims. Steele stopped Carmen Barth, but was knocked out in the first round by Al Hostak in July 1938 in Seattle. Hostak, of Czech descent, from Minneapolis, was a big puncher who put away Steele in only one minute and 43 seconds. He was outpointed three months later by Solly Krieger, but won the title back in June 1939 by stopping Krieger in the fourth. He knocked out Eric Seelig, of Germany, in another first-round victory in Cleveland but lost his NBA title to Tony Zale in Seattle on 19 July 1940 in Seattle. Zale had already beaten him in a non-title bout, and forced Hostak to retire in the 13th round.

Meanwhile, Apostoli stopped Young Corbett III, but was then stopped himself by Ceferino Garcia in Madison Square Garden, New York, on 2 October 1939. Garcia, from Manila, in the Philippines, had twice challenged for the welterweight title, losing to Barney Ross and Henry Armstrong, and was 29 when he found himself middleweight champion. He knocked out Glen Lee and was then challenged by Henry Armstrong. Armstrong, one of boxing's all-time greats, had become the second boxer in history after Bob Fitzsimmons to hold world titles at three weights. He was now trying for a fourth. Armstrong conceded 11lb (5kg) to Garcia, and the two fought a ten-round draw in Los Angeles. Garcia lost his title in his next defence, when outpointed by Ken Overlin, of Decator, Illinois, another veteran of nearly 30. Overlin, a clever boxer, had been knocked out by Freddie Steele on a previous challenge. Overlin twice outpointed Steve Belloise, but in May 1941, having been champion for a year, he was outpointed by Billy Soose, from Farrell, Pennsylvania, who had attended Penn State College.

Soose's career began to go wrong after his title win, however. He began having weight problems, was outpointed in a non-title fight by Georgie Abrams and was knocked out by Ceferino Garcia. The New York and IBU authorities decided to withdraw recognition from him.

Luckily the NBA champion, Tony Zale, looked a steady champion. He knocked out Steve Mamakos in Chicago in 1941, and then gave another chance to Al Hostak, knocking him out in the second round. On 28 November 1941 Zale took on Georgie Abrams, who had three times beaten Soose and was regarded as the leading American contender. When Zale outpointed Abrams he was recognized universally as champion.

By now Europe had been at war for over two years, and with the United States entering the war and Zale joining the US Navy, there was no world middleweight action for five years.

The Zale–Graziano epics

Zale, from Gary, Indiana, worked in the steel mills. Of a Polish family, his fighting characteristics were a strong punch and extreme toughness. He became known as the 'Man of Steel'. He was one of the great middleweights and in his first defence after the war (after five warm-up knock-out wins) he met one who was not far behind him. Rocky Graziano, from New York, was brought up in the slums, and had had plenty of trouble in his 24 years before he challenged Zale for the title. Reformatories, remand homes, theft charges — his had been the sort of deprived and unsupervised life usually described as 'running wild'. He had even disgraced himself in the forces, striking an officer and deserting because he could not take the discipline. He had found his salvation in boxing, and by the time he met Zale had stopped 32 of his opponents.

Zale was by now 33, and he was the opposite of Graziano — a quiet religious man. They made the perfect match: old/young, Pole/Italian, introvert/extrovert, immovable object/irresistible force. They met at the Yankee Stadium, with the younger Graziano the favourite at about 3-1. The fight has become legendary. Zale floored Graziano with a perfect punch to begin the first round, but by the end of it Graziano was pummelling the champion. The fight see-sawed for all of its six rounds, with Zale looking on the point of being knocked out when he suddenly dragged up the energy to knock out his opponent. Even then Graziano, on gaining his feet and senses, had to be restrained from attempting to carry on.

The fight did much to restore boxing to its place as a great spectator sport after the war, and incidentally to give back to the middleweight division its pride.

There had to be a rematch, of course, but New York would not stage it. The New York Commission had discovered that Graziano had failed to report a bribe offered him to lose a warm-up fight with Reuben Shank. The actual fight had been cancelled, because Graziano injured a shoulder. But not reporting the bribe attempt cost Graziano his New York licence.

The rematch was at Chicago, ten months later. It was another sell-out and another great battle. This time Zale began on top, splitting the challenger's eye in the first, and after the third round, in which Graziano was dropped, it seemed it could not last another round. However, Graziano lasted two more, and then, when the referee examined his swollen eye, pleaded for a last round. Into this desperate round Graziano put all the savagery in his make-up and fought by instinct, his only object being to remove the man in front of him. He succeeded. The referee stepped in with Zale hanging over the ropes. It took some seconds for Graziano to be awoken from the trance in which he had been fighting and to realize he was the new champion.

New troubles faced Graziano as the dishonourable discharge from the army became known, and questions were asked about how such a man could be allowed to fight for a world championship. It took almost a year to get the rubber match staged. Newark, New Jersey, was the venue, and although Zale was now 35, he had negotiated the interim better than Graziano. The third fight was not as exciting as the others, and Zale won with a third round knock-out.

The golden age

The Zale–Graziano battles started a golden age for middleweights that has lasted more or less until today. Zale's final despatch of Graziano was his last championship victory. The next middleweight immortal was waiting in the wings.

Marcel Cerdan was born in Sidi-bel-Abbès, Algeria, the son of a butcher, and before World War I he just had time to become European welterweight champion. After the war, he fought as a middleweight, became European champion, and went to America in 1946, by which time he was 30. He beat contenders Georgie Abrams, Harold Green and Lavern Roach, despite Roach getting a 24-second count while the referee and timekeeper argued over the legitimacy of the knockdown. At last Cerdan was given a shot at Zale's title.

Although the fight attracted 20,000 to the Roosevelt Stadium, Jersey City, on 21 September 1948, Zale was fully expected to win. Americans had hardly seen a decent French boxer, but Cerdan outfought the champion all the way. The fight had a curious ending. Zale was helpless against the ropes as the bell ended the 11th round, and as Cerdan went back to his corner, so Zale's legs gave way, and he collapsed. The Man of Steel could not continue and Cerdan was the new champion.

Cerdan's first challenger was Jake LaMotta, another who, like him, had waited a long time for a title chance. LaMotta, from the Bronx, New York City, and known as 'The Bronx Bull', was another of the division's colourful characters. He admitted later in life that to get a title shot he had had to throw a fight. Much of the promotion of boxing in those years was connected to the underworld.

__Below:__ Tony Zale gets a solid left to the chin of Rocky Graziano in the third of their great fights, one a year from 1946. Graziano won the second to hold the title briefly, but Zale won the decider. The three contests comprise one of the most exciting series ever fought by two men.

Cerdan went to the United States to defend against LaMotta, taking him on in Briggs Stadium, Detroit, on 16 June 1949. Cerdan had had a marvellous career, losing only three fights in 122, two on a disqualification and one on a decision which he subsequently had reversed, but bad luck now took over and dealt him the cruellest misfortune. In the third round of his defence, he dislocated his right shoulder. He bravely fought on to the end of the ninth, but could not come out for the tenth.

A return fight was arranged, and he was confident, but LaMotta was injured and the fight was postponed. Cerdan decided to fly back home to Casablanca, a decision which cost him his life, for the plane bringing him back for the return fight crashed without survivors. Graziano, Cerdan and LaMotta were all larger than life characters of whose lives feature films were made.

LaMotta cashed in on the championship that had cost him so much to acquire (he claimed it cost him $20,000 as well as a thrown fight to earn the chance) by outpointing Tiberio Mitri of Italy, the European champion, and knocking out Laurent Dauthuille of France, both fights taking place in 1950. Dauthuille already held a decision over LaMotta, and was thoroughly outpointing LaMotta at Detroit, and got to within 30 seconds of the title. He was finishing with a last-round flourish when suddenly LaMotta threw a desperation punch which scattered Dauthuille's wits and the Bronx Bull followed up to knock out his man with 13 seconds remaining.

LaMotta's nemesis was yet another great middleweight champion. Sugar Ray Robinson had already fought LaMotta four times, and beaten him on three occasions. LaMotta's victory over Robinson was Robinson's only professional defeat so far.

Robinson had been regarded, quaintly, as world champion by the Pennsylvania Commission after outpointing Robert Villemain, of France, in Philadelphia in June 1950. Knock-out wins over Jose Basora and Carl 'Bobo' Olson followed and on 14 February 1961 he entered the ring with LaMotta for the fifth time at Chicago. Although it was St Valentine's Day, there was no love lost between the two men. Eventually, as in their previous three meetings, Robinson's classy boxing overcame the Bronx Bull's bravery and more basic methods. In the later stages LaMotta's aim was to stay on his feet, and this he defiantly did, leaning on the ropes as the referee stopped the contest in favour of Robinson, who became universal world champion, rather than Pennsylvania's only.

The Detroit-born Robinson, who had been welterweight champion for four years, was regarded at the time as the best pound-for-pound boxer in the world. He had been unbeaten for eight years since his defeat by LaMotta. He celebrated his new status by taking his colourful entourage on a holiday-cum-business tour of Europe. His pink Cadillac was seen in Paris, Zurich, Antwerp, Liège, Berlin and Turin, as Sugar Ray gave painful boxing lessons to some of Europe's leading middleweights.

Turpin beats Robinson

On 10 July 1951 Robinson stepped into the ring at the Exhibition Hall, Earls Court, London, to climax his tour with a world title defence against the British and European champion, Randolph Turpin. Turpin was a hard-hitting, tough fighter whose awkward style unsettled Robinson. A large crowd saw one of the biggest upsets in boxing as Robinson, unbeaten for 91 fights over eight years, was well outpointed by Turpin. The former naval cook from Leamington was the new middleweight champion.

There was a return fight clause in the contract, and the two met again at the Polo Grounds, New York, only 64 days later on 12 September 1951. This contest drew record receipts for a fight outside the heavyweight division of $767,626, from a crowd of 61,370. Everybody wanted to see the man who had beaten the by now legendary Sugar Ray Robinson.

This contest was fairly even until the tenth round, when Turpin appeared to get the ascendancy when he split Robinson's left eyebrow. With the referee Ruby Goldstein

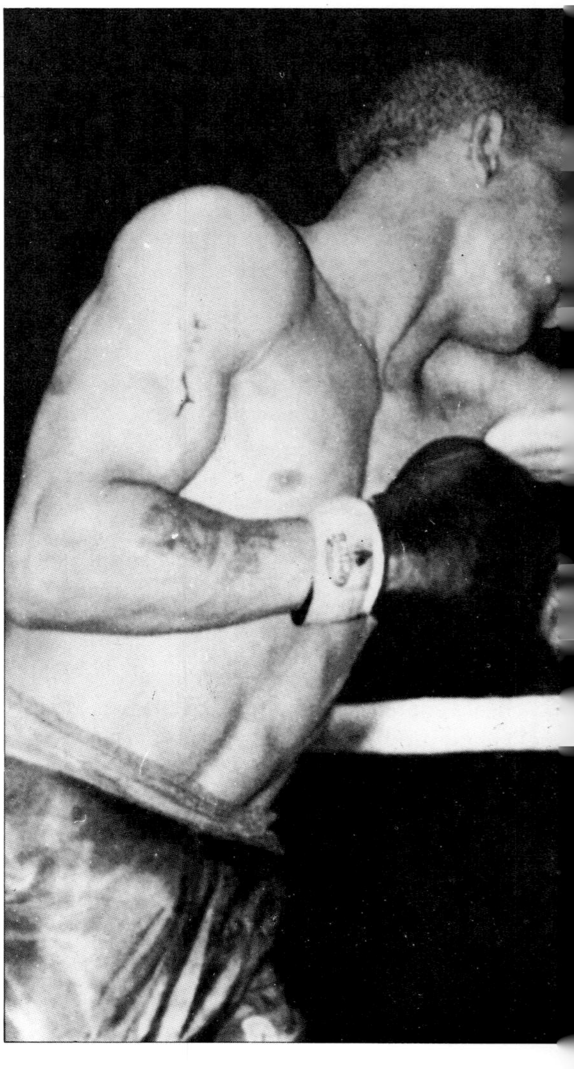

***Right:** Sugar Ray Robinson ducks below a left from Randolph Turpin in their title fight at Earls Court, London, in 1951. Turpin outpointed Robinson in a masterly display, but a tangled private life kept him from becoming a long-reigning champion.*

showing concern at the injury, Robinson launched a desperate attack, and caught the champion with a terrific right, following up with a flurry of blows which dropped Turpin for a count of seven. Turpin rose, but Robinson piled in the punches as Turpin swayed helplessly on the ropes. With eight seconds of the round remaining, the referee stopped the contest, and Robinson had reclaimed his crown. There was some controversy over the verdict, as had Turpin lasted to the end of the round, he might well have been in better condition than Robinson for the next.

Robinson rested for six months, and then outpointed Carl 'Bobo' Olson in San Francisco, and the following month he knocked out Rocky Graziano in the third round. Two months later Robinson attempted to win a world championship at a third weight by challenging light-heavyweight king Joey Maxim, and, as reported earlier, he was beaten as much by heat exhaustion as anything else. Just before the end of 1952 Robinson, aged 31, announced his retirement.

Turpin regained the crown in the eyes of the European Boxing Union by outpointing Charles Humez of France in London. Olson outpointed Paddy Young for the American title, and Turpin went to Madison Square Garden, New York, to fight Olson on 21 October 1953. Turpin's private life had by now become a muddle, compounded when he was met in New York by a girl who claimed he had promised to marry her on his visit two years earlier. Turpin was to be arrested and accused of rape before he left America, but meanwhile he fought against Olson as if he had no interest in the contest, and was comfortably outpointed.

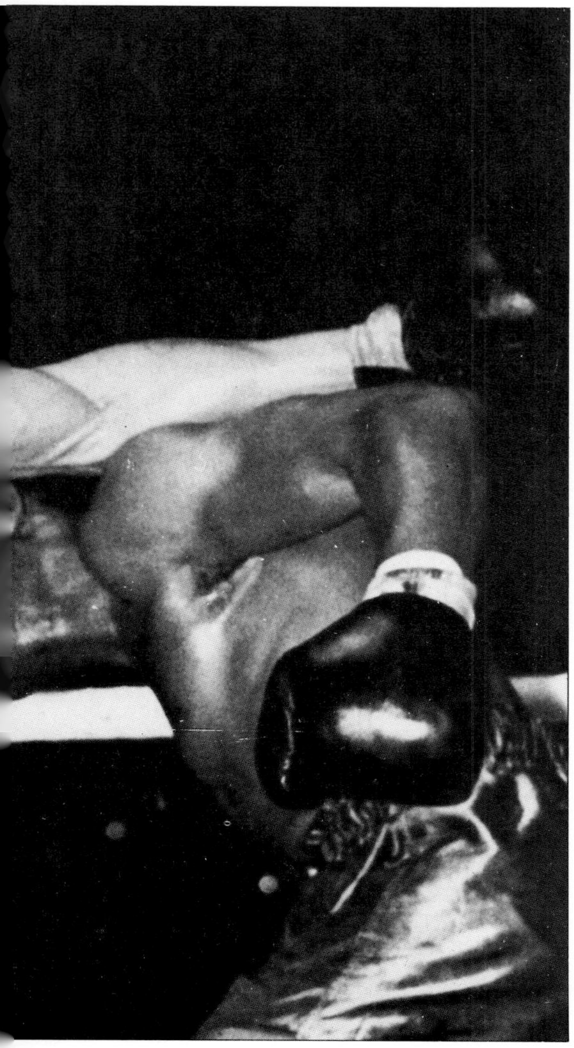

Olson, from Honolulu, Hawaii, defended successfully three times in 1954, outpointing Kid Gavilan in Chicago, and Rocky Castellani in San Francisco, and then stopping Pierre Langlois. In June 1955 he attempted to add the light-heavyweight crown to his middleweight one by challenging Archie Moore, but he lasted only three rounds before Ancient Archie knocked him out.

Meanwhile, Sugar Ray Robinson had been having tax problems, and his theatrical career was not flourishing, so he decided on a comeback. It began badly with a points defeat by Ralph 'Tiger' Jones, and his trainer and manager forsook him, but on 9 December 1955 he was given a chance to regain his old middleweight title. In the Chicago Stadium the 34-year-old knocked out Olson in the second round to become middleweight champion for the third time. On 18 May 1956 he repeated the treatment with a fourth-round knock-out in Los Angeles.

Robinson, however, was not the force he was, and dropped the title to Gene Fullmer, a tough 25-year-old Mormon from West Jordan, Utah, who knocked Robinson out of the ring in the seventh round at Madison Square Garden on the way to a clear-cut points win. However, four months later, in May 1957, the amazing Robinson knocked out Fullmer in a return at Chicago to win the title for the fourth time.

Two days after this feat Robinson celebrated his 36th birthday, and the ageing champion was now challenged by the welterweight champion, Carmen Basilio, who was a mere 30. Basilio, from Canastota, New York, was a much shorter man than Robinson. He was an all-action, two-fisted puncher and the Yankee Stadium fans saw a fierce, bloody battle on 23 September 1957. It was a desperately close contest between two men who did not much care for each other, and Basilio outlasted Robinson to cram non-stop punching into the last round and take a split decision.

Once again Robinson's career seemed to be over, but once again the great boxer provided a surprise. A return fight in March 1961 in Chicago was as bitterly fought as the first. Robinson gained the crucial advantage in the fifth round when he damaged Basilio's left eye to the extent that the champion fought the remainder of the contest with this eye tightly closed. Basilio fought savagely and bravely, but Robinson gained a split decision. In both fights two judges scored comfortably for one man but the third judge scored emphatically for the loser.

***Above:** Sugar Ray Robinson misses with an uppercut against the crouching Carmen Basilio. Both former welterweight champions, they fought two tremendous and bloody battles for the middleweight title in 1957 and 1958, winning one each, both verdicts being split decisions.*

Robinson's winning of the middleweight crown for the fifth time remains a record for any division. However, he did not defend it for a year, by which time he had passed his 38th birthday, and the NBA decided to withdraw recognition from him on the grounds of inactivity.

The NBA matched the two men who had won and lost the title to Robinson for their vacant crown: Gene Fullmer and Carmen Basilio. The two fought at San Francisco on 28 August 1959, and Fullmer won a hard contest when the referee stopped the bout in the 14th round. Three months later he successfully defended with a decision over Spider Webb at Logan.

Robinson, still recognized in New York, Europe and elsewhere, at last defended on 22 January 1960 against Paul Pender, a fireman from Brookline, Massachusetts. Pender was nine years younger than Robinson but even so it was a surprise when he outpointed the champion in Boston, where he was highly regarded. Again, it was a split decision, with one judge markedly disagreeing with the others. Pender was a scientific boxer who suffered from brittle hands, which once restricted him to only six fights in five years. Most expected Robinson to win the return in Boston five months later, but Pender outpointed him with yet another split decision in which the judges disagreed by a wide margin.

Fullmer kept his NBA title with a draw with Joey Giardello and then stopped Basilio in the 12th round. He then gave Robinson another chance to take the title for the sixth time. The two met at Las Vegas on 3 December 1960 and Robinson, now in his 40th year, boxed superbly to gain a draw. There was another remarkable variation in score-cards, one having it a draw, while another card had Robinson an 11 rounds to 4 winner, and the third gave 9 rounds to Fullmer and 5 to Robinson with one level. Most thought Robinson did enough to earn the verdict, and there had to be a return. At Las Vegas in March 1961 Fullmer won a unanimous decision, a fight which ended the marvellous championship days of Sugar Ray Robinson.

Fullmer, no doubt relieved at seeing off the aged warrior, did not have it all his own way when he next defended, against Florentino Fernandez, a Cuban who fought out of Miami. Once again Fullmer kept his title with a split decision.

In December 1961 Benny 'Kid' Paret, another Cuban, challenged Fullmer less than three months after regaining the world welterweight crown from Emile Griffith. Fullmer knocked out Paret in the tenth at Las Vegas.

It was ten months before Fullmer defended again, and then he took on Dick Tiger, from Orlu, Nigeria, who had campaigned in England, winning the Commonwealth title before trying his luck in the United States. The classy, boxing Tiger unanimously outpointed the rougher, less stylish Fullmer over 15 rounds at San Francisco. The return contest in Las Vegas on 23 February 1963 was a different affair and was marked a draw, Tiger keeping his crown.

Meanwhile Pender, whose title claims were recognized by all except the NBA after his two defeats of Robinson, stopped Terry Downes in Boston in the seventh round in January 1961 when the British champion suffered severe cuts to his nose. Pender outpointed Carmen Basilio three months later, but lost his title when he gave Downes a return on 11 July 1961. The bout was at Wembley, Pender's first title fight outside Boston. In another tough match, Pender was forced to retire at the end of the ninth round.

Downes, from Paddington, London, had gone to America when 15 and stayed there for six years during which time he joined the US Marines and won the US All-Services amateur title. A colourful, aggressive fighter, his weakness was a tendency to cut around the eyes and nose. Downes was not champion for long — in April 1962 he went to Boston for the rubber match and was outpointed.

This was Pender's last title fight. He wanted to unify the championship by boxing Fullmer, but the fight failed to come off, and because Pender's management failed to fix another fight in the time stipulated by the New York Commission he was stripped in November 1962 and lost recognition by all other authorities.

When Tiger kept his WBA (formed out of the NBA in 1962) title by drawing with Fullmer in February 1963, he was universally recognized as champion. Pender claims he was anxious to fight Tiger to clean up the sorry affair but Tiger's connections declined, at which point Pender announced his retirement in disgust, having not had the chance to lose his title in the ring. At least Tiger confirmed his own claims to the crown by giving Fullmer a third chance to beat him. The match was at Ibadan, Nigeria, a first world title fight for West Africa. Fullmer was forced to retire in the seventh round.

After disposing of Fullmer, however, Tiger dropped the title on his next defence. Joey Giardello, from Brooklyn, had been boxing for 15 years and had earned one title shot, drawing with Fullmer in 1960. He now fought Tiger (who at 34 was a year older) at Atlantic City, and his style of long-range jabbing and elusive defence presented Tiger with a problem he could not solve. Giardello (real name Carmen Titelli) outpointed Rubin 'Hurricane' Carter in Philadelphia and then gave Tiger a return in October 1965 in New York. Tiger this time unanimously outpointed Giardello to regain his crown.

Again Tiger did not hold the title long, because six months later he faced Emile Griffith, the welterweight champion, a man who had first won a world title five years earlier. Griffith, from the Virgin Islands, was over eight years younger than Tiger, and was a brilliant boxer as well as a tough, durable fighter. He had Tiger on the canvas on the way to a points decision in Madison Square Garden, New York. Griffith was following Robinson and Basilio up from welter champion to middleweight champion.

Griffith's first two defences were in the Madison Square Garden against Joey Archer, an Irish-American from New York. They were two very close decisions. In the first bout Archer was given a draw by one judge, and in the second all three judges gave Griffith eight of the 15 rounds, with Archer scoring seven, six and six.

Griffith, Benvenuti and the Garden

Griffith then had three bouts with an outstanding European champion, Nino Benvenuti, from Trieste, Italy. A classical boxer, Benvenuti had been the welterweight champion at the 1960 Olympics in Rome, and had held the world light-middleweight title. He was a firm favourite with the Italian crowds. Benvenuti took on Griffith at Madison Square Garden on 17 April 1967 and used his greater reach to advantage, outboxing Griffith on a unanimous decision.

Emile Griffith, however, had already come back twice to win the welterweight crown from opponents who had outpointed him, and he maintained the tradition in the heavier class by outpointing Benvenuti when the two were rematched in a return at Shea Stadium, New York.

There had to be a decider between two outstanding champions, and the fight inaugurated the current Madison Square Garden arena. This was the fourth Madison Square Garden, a name associated with sport and show business in New York since 1879, but in particular with boxing. The first Garden was converted from a derelict railway building by William A. Vanderbilt and was used for concerts, political meetings and the like, staging its first fight in 1882, when a British middleweight known as Tug Wilson (real name Joe Collins) won $500 by staying four rounds with the great John L. Sullivan, by means of clinching and going down whenever hit. This arena was rebuilt in 1890, and covered a block between Madison Avenue and Fourth Avenue, with a huge tower above. The designer, Stafford White, was murdered in the Theater Roof Garden by Harry Thaw, a wealthy jealous husband. The case became a classic, White having seduced Thaw's wife in his studio, where the architect had made numerous conquests with the aid of a red velvet swing. The case of the girl in the red velvet swing became the subject of books and a Hollywood film.

This arena housed fights until 5 May 1925, when it was pulled down and a new Garden built. This was called 'The House That Tex Built' because it was erected by the famous boxing promoter, Tex Rickard. It opened in November 1925 with a six-day bicycle race, its first major boxing match being the light-heavyweight championship bout between Paul Berlenbach and Jack Delaney on 11 December 1925. Rickard was succeeded as promoter at this Garden by William F. Carey, James J. Johnston, Mike Jacobs, James D. Norris and, from 1958, Truman Gibson among others.

The current Madison Square Garden was built above and beside Penn Station on Seventh Avenue, between 31st and 32nd Streets, and continues the tradition of presenting shows of all kinds, including boxing. The first boxing programme was on 4 March 1968, and featured the fights in which Joe Frazier stopped Buster Mathis to win the vacant WBC version of the heavyweight title, and the rubber match for the undisputed middleweight crown between Griffith and Benvenuti, which, as they say in cinematic circles, is where we came in.

It was again a brilliant fight between two thoroughly professional boxers, and at the end the judges made it very close. Benvenuti took the decision, with one judge marking it equal and the other two giving it to the Italian by two rounds.

The handsome Benvenuti now defended before his own fans, to whom the charismatic 'Nino' was a romantic and worshipped figure. He outpointed Don Fullmer at San Remo, won on a disqualification over Fraser Scott in Naples, and knocked out Luis Rodriguez, the former welterweight champion, in the first round in Rome. He then knocked out Tom Bethea in eight rounds in Umag, Yugoslavia, the first world title fight to be held in a communist country.

Benvenuti's next defence was in Rome, against a tall Argentinian from Santa Fe, Carlos Monzon. Monzon's strengths were a long reach, a heavy punch and an ice-cold temperament. In the metaphorical heat of a Rome arena, where Monzon must have felt like the Christian thrown to the lions, he kept cool and delivered a crushing right to the champion's chin in the 12th round, which spelt the end for Nino in one of boxing's bigger upsets.

Carlos Monzon

The result was to take on more of the look of the expected as Monzon's career progressed, and he proved to be another of the outstanding champions in this division of great boxers.

Unlike many world champions from the continents of North and South America, Monzon was prepared to put his title on the line in European rings. First of all, he had to give Benvenuti a return, and the Italian could not bring himself back to the top flight after the years of adulation. The contest took place in Monte Carlo in May 1971 and Monzon this time took less than three rounds to knock out the ex-champion.

Monzon embarked on a very busy career, taking on any challenger provided the purse was satisfactory. He began by defending in Buenos Aires, giving his countrymen the chance to see the new champion. The challenger was the evergreen Emile Griffith, who was stopped in the 14th round when the referee intervened.

In 1972 there were four defences. In May he went back to Rome to face the veteran Denny Moyer, of the USA, who had been the first of the light-middleweight world champions when the WBA instituted that class in 1962. The referee stopped the contest in the fifth round. In June Monzon went to Paris to take on Jean-Claude Bouttier, the European champion. Bouttier was forced to retire at the end of the 12th round. Two months later Monzon was in Copenhagen, where he fought the Dane, Tom Bogs, who was to succeed Bouttier as the European champion. Bogs took a beating before the referee stepped in to save him in the fifth round.

In November 1972 Monzon was taken the distance back in Buenos Aires by Benny Briscoe of Philadelphia, but the points verdict was unanimous for the champion. In February 1973 Emile Griffith was back again fighting for a world title (it was not to be his last attempt), and he gave Monzon a very difficult bout at Monte Carlo. Although

Griffith fought well, there was no doubt that Monzon had won the decision, which was unanimous.

Monzon's second defence in 1973 was a rematch with Jean-Claude Bouttier, again in Paris. Again the Argentinian was taken the distance, but there was no arguing with the verdict in his favour. In February 1974 he was challenged by another good champion, José Napoles of Cuba, who had been welterweight champion, apart from a short spell, since 1969. But the old boxing adage, 'a good big 'un will always beat a good little 'un' held good. Monzon even had two years on his side, and Napoles was forced to retire in the sixth.

Now, after 11 years of undisputed champions, the WBC denied recognition to Monzon for his failure to defend against their preferred contender, Rodrigo Valdez. The WBC had been formed in 1963 in response to the formation in 1962 of the WBA. The WBA had succeeded the NBA, which had originally been formed in 1921 to break the championship monopoly of the New York authorities. At its inauguration there were 51 boxing commissions, mostly in the USA, which supported it. The WBC was formed by the British Boxing Board of Control, the European Boxing Union, the boards of many other countries of the world and the boxing

***Above:** Carlos Monzon in training in 1972 before his title defence in Paris with the European champion, Jean-Claude Bouttier of France, which Monzon won on a 12th-round retirement. Monzon had the best record of any modern middleweight with 14 successful defences before retiring unbeaten.*

commissions of those states in America not affiliated to the WBA. The WBC was, therefore, much more of an international body.

The WBC decided to recognize as champion the winner of a Monte Carlo bout between Valdez and Bennie Briscoe. Valdez won by a knockout in the seventh round.

Valdez, from Bolívar, Colombia, was a tough all-action puncher, four years younger than Monzon. For the next two years the two champions defended their halves of the title impressively. In 1974 Monzon fought at home in Buenos Aires and knocked out Tony Mundine, from Sydney, Australia, while Valdez defended his title in Paris against Gratien Tonna of Marseille, and won with an 11th-round knockout.

Below: *Alan Minter, with his back to the camera, in his second victory over Vito Antuofermo, from whom he took the title in 1980. Minter and Antuofermo were both subject to cuts, in Minter's case around the eyes, which accounted for nearly all his defeats.*

Each defended twice in 1975. Valdez stopped Ramon Mendes, an Argentinian, in Cali, in Colombia, and outpointed Rudy Robles at Cartagena, Colombia. Monzon forced the referee to come to the rescue in the tenth round of a bout with Tony Licata of New Orleans, at Madison Square Garden, and then went to Marseille to knock out in the fifth Valdez's victim, Gratien Tonna. In March 1976 Valdez stopped Max Cohen in Paris, and three months later took on Carlos Monzon on neutral ground at Monte Carlo. Monzon, who was now 34, outpointed Valdez to win a unanimous decision and unify the championship again. A year later, on 30 July 1977, Monzon once again outpointed Valdez and retired. His 14 successful defences was a record for the division.

Luckily, for once, a great champion's retirement did not throw the division into confusion, as all bodies were prepared to recognize the winner of a contest between Valdez and Benny Briscoe as champion. It was Briscoe's third attempt at the middleweight crown, and once again he was to be disappointed, as Valdez outpointed him in Campione d'Italia, Switzerland. Now Valdez, with Monzon retired, at last had the satisfaction of being undisputed world champion. However, he did not enjoy this status long, as another trip to Italy in April 1978 saw him drop the title to Hugo Corro, like his old rival, Monzon, an Argentinian. Corro, from Mendoza, outpointed Valdez at San Remo to become the youngest middleweight titleholder for a little while, being only 25, and having been a professional for less than five years. Corro was a clever boxer with a good punch, and back in Buenos Aires he gave his countrymen a chance to see him as champion with a successful defence against Ronnie Harris, who had won the Olympic gold medal at lightweight for the USA in 1968. Corro won the decision. He gave Valdez a return in Buenos Aires and confirmed his form with another points win.

Corro next put the title at stake in Monte Carlo, which was seeing a lot of good middleweight action at this time. His opponent was an Italian, Vito Antuofermo, from Bari, who had been the European light-middleweight champion in 1976. He had, however, begun his professional career in New York, and after dropping his European title to Maurice Hope had returned to campaign in the United States. His main attributes were courage and durability, for he won many of his contests by wearing down his opponents, while usually taking plenty of punishment himself. It was the case in the title fight with Corro, for Antuofermo took everything that Corro could hand him and emerged the points winner after 15 gruelling rounds.

Antuofermo's first defence was against Marvin Hagler, from Newark, New Jersey. Hagler had an impressive record, and was expected to beat the comparatively raw Antuofermo, but Antuofermo showed his quality at its best in their encounter at Caesars Palace, Las Vegas. Although many thought Hagler's better boxing had earned him the decision over the tough Italian, the judges marked it a draw and the gallant Vito kept his title.

He did not win another title fight, however, for on his second defence, also at Caesars Palace, on 16 March 1980, he was comfortably outpointed by Alan Minter, from Crawley, Sussex in England. Minter, like Antuofermo, had a tendency to bleed, and cuts round his eyes were to prove his biggest handicap at the top level. He was, however, a good boxer with a knock-out punch and he handed the brave Antuofermo more damage than the Italian could return. A return three months later at Wembley proved too much for Antuofermo, who was so badly cut up by Minter that he was forced to retire after eight rounds.

'Marvelous' Marvin Hagler

Minter might have had a longer career as champion had his mandatory challenger not been Marvin Hagler, who took him on at Wembley on 27 September 1980. Minter was confidently expected to win by his countrymen on the strength of the form-line through Antuofermo, but Hagler this time fought a much more controlled and calculatingly destructive fight. Minter's face was cut so badly by the third round that the referee was forced to stop the fight. There were some ugly scenes as some of Minter's disappointed supporters threw beer cans into the ring and hurled racial abuse at the new champion. Hagler was escorted from the ring without being crowned as the champion.

Hagler proved to be one of the outstanding champions in the division, building up a list of successful defences which threatened as the years passed to equal that of Monzon.

Already 28 when he won the title, Hagler made three defences in 1981. Fulgencio Obelmejias, from San José, Venezuela, was his first challenger. The winner of all his 30 bouts, Obelmejias lasted only eight rounds in Boston before the referee intervened. Vito Antuofermo, after his draw little more than 18 months previously was given another chance, but after his experiences with Minter he was not now of the category to worry Hagler, and was forced to retire in the fourth. Mustafo Hamsho, born in Latakia, Syria, but boxing out of New York, promised sterner opposition, having lost only two early fights, but he, too, was stopped, in the 11th round at Rosemont, Illinois. The newly formed International Boxing Federation recognized Hagler as its champion after this contest, and indeed there were no logical alternatives.

In 1982 Hagler's title defences lasted no more than six rounds, for William 'Caveman' Lee was stopped in the first at Atlantic City, and Fully Obelmejias, in his second attempt, was stopped in five in San Remo, Italy.

'Marvelous' Marvin Hagler, with his shaven head, was now regarded as one of the best champions in the world, feared by his opponents for his destructive punching with either hand and his meanness when on top. Tony Sibson, from Leicester, went to a city with another English name, Worcester, to be the first of Hagler's three 1983 challengers, but Worcester, Massachusetts, proved inhospitable as Sibson was stopped in the sixth round and taken to hospital in a snowstorm to have 17 stitches applied to cuts around his eyes. Wilford Scypion did less well at Providence, being knocked out in the fourth round, but Roberto Duran, the old campaigner who had held titles at lightweight, welterweight and light-middleweight, gave Hagler his hardest fight yet at Caesars Palace, Las Vegas, on 10 November 1983. Duran, fighting at middleweight in what seemed the twilight of a great career, was not expected to trouble Hagler, always a fully fledged middle-

Above: *Marvin Hagler, who changed his name to 'Marvelous' Marvin Hagler, and was just as accurately described by one victim, Tony Sibson, as a 'master of disaster'. Hagler was middleweight champion for six and a half years in the 1980s and was involved in some of the decade's most memorable contests, notably those with Duran, Hearns and Leonard.*

Below: Hearns and Hagler posing before their middleweight title fight in 1985. Hagler is 'wearing' his WBC and WBA middleweight belts, while Hearns is wearing his WBC light-middleweight belt.

Below right: There was no posing in the ring. In the photograph Hagler is landing a left to Hearns' chin during the three rounds of mayhem which comprised the fight.

weight, but Hagler seemed tentative for once in the presence of another legend of the ring, and although he won clearly, he was taken the distance for the first time as champion.

Hagler was soon back to his more destructive ways. In March 1984 Juan Roldan of Argentina was stopped in the tenth at Las Vegas, and in October Mustafa Hamsho was given another chance but this time lasted only three rounds in New York.

On 16 April 1985 Hagler took on another of the big names of the 1980s, Thomas 'Hit Man' Hearns from Detroit. Hearns had been beaten only once, by Sugar Ray Leonard when unifying the welterweight title. He had already been welterweight and light-middleweight champion. Although, like Duran, Hearns was not a natural middleweight, he was four years younger than Hagler, who was now nearly 31, and the boxing world looked forward to an outstanding battle. It wasn't disappointed.

The fight took place at Caesars Palace, Las Vegas, and was three rounds of non-stop, controlled savagery. Both men began at a furious pace and rocked each other with tremendous punches. Hearns, a tall man for a middleweight, did not attempt to use his long reach to keep Hagler at bay, but preferred to mix it from the beginning, relying on his own devastating punching power and on Hagler's known habit of starting slowly. However, Hagler knew that this was a contest in which he needed to be at his sharpest from the beginning, and he, too, began with blazing attacks. Hagler proved the stronger, and rocked Hearns in the first round, and although Hearns had his own successes, causing the ringside doctor to study the cuts around Hagler's eye, he could not match the champion's capacity to take the punches. In the third round the referee stopped the bout after Hearns had been down and rose in a groggy condition.

Hagler's 1986 opponent was John 'The Beast' Mugabi, who was born in Kampala, Uganda, and had learned his boxing in England. He was unbeaten in 25 fights, none of which had gone the distance, and only three of which had got beyond the fourth round. He, too, at 26, was expected to test the champion, who was approaching veteran stage, and did have the better of the early rounds in Las Vegas, where the contest was fought in pouring rain. However, Hagler gradually got on top as Mugabi tired, and he knocked out the challenger in the 11th round.

The Leonard–Hagler bonanza

Hagler was then challenged by Sugar Ray Leonard, another former welter and light-middleweight champion. This fight was the most eagerly awaited encounter for many years, but it did not please the WBA and the IBF, who did not look kindly on Hagler's absence from the ring for over a year. These two bodies wanted him to fight Herol Graham of England, the leading contender, and withdrew recognition from him when he opted for the big pay-day of a meeting with Leonard.

Leonard had retired twice. As unbeaten welterweight champion he had retired in 1982 because of a detached retina in his eye. He had made a one-fight comeback in 1984 and although he won had retired again, so when he eventually fought Hagler on 6 April 1987 he had not fought in public for nearly three years.

Leonard was the 3-1 underdog, but surprised everybody by the dazzling display he put up. Hagler was the aggressor, but periodically Leonard would stop his running to deliver rapid combinations to Hagler, bewildering in their hand speed. The more pedestrian Hagler began to get telling blows home in the fifth round however, and from then on the fight resolved itself into Hagler's continuous forward drive, getting home as many heavy blows as he could, and Leonard's clever defensive work mixed with retaliatory bursts of dazzling punching. Occasionally Leonard looked in trouble, but always he managed to find energy to fight back, and ended the fight with his speed unimpaired. Seldom has a fight and its verdict caused so much discussion and disagreement. Many saw it as a triumph for Leonard's superb boxing, while others saw his display as flashy and superficial, with the real solid work coming from Hagler. The judges arrived at a split decision, two marking it close, one giving it to Leonard by two points, the other to Hagler by the same margin, but the third judge awarded the fight to Leonard by a comfortable eight points.

So Leonard triumphed in the battle of the two outstanding fighters of the first half of the 1980s. He retired again immediately, leaving the middleweight division without a champion.

The IBF were the first to find a new champion. They decided that the winner of the Frank Tate and Michael Olajide bout at Las Vegas on 10 October 1987 would be the champion. Tate, from Houston, Texas, was a surprise winner, scoring knockdowns and taking the unanimous decision.

The WBA chose the winner of the contest between Sumbu Kalambay and Iran Barkley to be their middleweight champion. Kalambay won on points in Livorno, Italy, on 23 October 1987. Kalambay was born in Zaire, but had become based in Italy, and was the European champion. He was already 31, and many thought the highest honours had passed him by. He was a surprise winner, but a very popular one in Italy.

***Above:** Sugar Ray Leonard was the man to topple Hagler in one of the richest fights in history. It was also one of the ring's outstanding fights, fought by two of the best practitioners of the 1980s. Although Leonard took the decision, there was much controversy over the verdict, and neither boxer lost any prestige.*

Above: *When Sugar Ray Leonard retired for the third (but not last) time after becoming middleweight champion, the division which had long enjoyed stability soon found itself with three champions. One was Frank Tate (facing camera), the 1984 Olympic champion, who won the IBF title and is seen successfully defending it against Tony Sibson, whom he knocked out at Stafford in 1988.*

Hearns' fourth title

The WBC favoured the winner of a bout between Thomas Hearns and Juan Roldan on 29 October 1987 at Las Vegas. Hearns, after his defeat by Hagler, had gone up yet another weight to take the WBC light-heavyweight title from Dennis Andries, and, consequently, his second assault on the middleweight crown was an attempt to win a world title at a fourth weight, a feat which had never before been accomplished. The two put up a tremendous show into the fourth round, when Hearns caught Roldan with a tremendous right to knock him out. Tate established himself with a knock-out victory over British champion Tony Sibson at Stafford on 7 February 1988, a defeat that decided Sibson to retire. However, he was then stopped on 28 July 1988 by Michael 'Second To' Nunn, from Iowa, who defended in November with a knock-out of Juan Roldan, and looked a brilliant unbeaten new champion.

Kalambay was very impressive in 1988. On 5 March he defended against Mike McCallum, the light-middleweight champion, at Pésaro in Italy. McCallum, an excellent champion whose victims included Don Curry, one of the leading welterweights of the 1980s, was fully expected to win, but Kalambay again surprised everybody by decisively outpointing the Jamaican and giving him his first defeat. Kalambay next took on Robbie Sims, the half-brother of Marvin Hagler. Hagler was at the ringside at Ravenna, Italy, on 12 June 1988 to see the clever Kalambay again produce a thoroughly professional performance to earn a comfortable points verdict.

Strangely enough, Thomas Hearns, the WBC champion, and the one thought most impregnable, was the one to lose his crown in 1988. On 6 June 1988 he fought Iran Barkley, who had already lost to Kalambay, at the Las Vegas Hilton. Hearns was comfortably in control in the first two rounds and seemed on the point of victory with Barkley cut over both eyes and in the mouth. But, with the fight progressing in the same way in the third, a desperate right swing by Barkley floored Hearns, who although he got to his feet at eight could not hold off Barkley's clubbing blows, the referee coming to his rescue as he slumped on the ropes. It was Hearns' third defeat in 47 fights and he spoke of retirement. Iran 'The Blade' Barkley, from New York, had previously suffered four defeats in a five-and-a-half-year career. For a while the middleweight division seemed to be awaiting its next great champion.

THE LIGHT-MIDDLE-WEIGHTS

One of the more reasonable 'intermediate' weights to be introduced recently into boxing is that between welterweight and middleweight. The 13lb (6kg) difference between the welter limit of 147lb (67kg) and the middleweight limit of 160lb (73kg) was one of the largest, and a handicap to a boxer whose best fighting weight was around 150lb (68kg). Even Sugar Ray Robinson had to overcome this difficulty, as his best weight for much of his career was well below the middleweight limit.

The new weight limit when the class was introduced in 1962 was 154lb (70kg). The newly-formed WBA was the first body to introduce the weight, calling it 'junior middleweight'. When the WBC followed in

1969 the weight limit was the same, but this body called the division the 'super-welterweight' division. In the 1980s, when the IBF recognized a champion at this weight, the division was called the 'junior middle-weight'. None of the bodies used the obvious name, with the traditional light-heavyweight division as a precedent, of calling it the 'light-middleweight' division.

The first champion was Denny Moyer, of Portland, Oregon, who outpointed Joey Ciambra, of Buffalo, New York, in his home town. He made only one successful defence, against Stan Harrington, in Honolulu, Hawaii, before being outpointed twice in 1963 by Ralph Dupas, of New Orleans, a veteran who had already fought for the lightweight and welterweight titles.

Dupas, having won the title in his home town, as had Moyer, then took it to Milan to face Sandro Mazzinghi — a reckless disregard of the omens — for the Italian knocked him out in the ninth round. Mazzinghi, whose birthplace was actually Pontedera, then stopped Dupas in a rematch in Sydney, Australia, to confirm his status. The Italian was a rough handful, immensely strong, and he kept the title through 1964 with successful defences against Tony Montano and Fortunato Manca, in Genoa and Rome respectively.

Mazzinghi met his match in his fellow Italian Nino Benvenuti, later a good middleweight champion. The polished ex-Olympic champion was too skilful for Mazzinghi, and knocked him out in the sixth round in Milan, later outpointing him in Rome to retain the crown.

The Italian monopoly was temporarily halted in June 1966, however, when Benvenuti made the mistake of his predecessors and took the crown to Seoul, South Korea, and promptly left it there, surprisingly outpointed by Ki-Soo Kim, the local man from Buk-Chong. Both fighters were unbeaten as professionals, but Benvenuti held an amateur decision over Kim. Kim was his country's first world champion. He defended successfully in Seoul against former challenger Stan Harrington and Freddie Little, and then, proving that boxers never learn, defended against Sandro Mazzinghi in Milan, who predictably outpointed the Korean to regain the title.

Mazzinghi's first defence of his second reign was in Rome against Freddie Little, from Picayune, Mississippi. This proved to be a most controversial contest. Mazzinghi was early hampered by a bad cut, and was having much the worst of the fight, when he decided he could not come out for the ninth round. Instead of awarding the fight to Little on a retirement, the German referee, Herbert Tomser, declared it a no-contest on the grounds that under European Boxing Union rules this was the verdict for a fight ended by injury before the half-way mark. Since Mazzinghi had continued to the end of the eighth this seemed a dubious decision by any judgement, and Little was justifiably disgusted. When Little returned to the USA he discovered that the WBA had declared the title vacant.

The WBC recognized the division when the vacant title was disputed by Little and Stan Hayward at Las Vegas, and Little, who was fighting out of Las Vegas, duly won the decision in his home town. Little had had a four-year break in the middle of his career, when he had become a schoolteacher, and he now found himself champion approaching 33 years old. He seemed not to have gained wisdom, for he made his three defences overseas, overcoming the division's hoodoo by knocking out Hisao Minami in Osaka, Japan, and outpointing Gerhard Piaskowy in Berlin before tempting fate once too often and being outpointed in Monza, Italy, by Carmelo Bossi.

Bossi, from Milan, was a silver medalist in the 1960 Rome Olympics. He put his new title at stake in Madrid in April 1971 against a Spaniard, José Hernandez, and like Little overcame tradition, but only just, by earning a draw. However, he was then tempted to tackle Koichi Wajima, from Hokkaido, Japan, in Tokyo. Wajima outpointed Bossi and proved to be one of the division's best champions, although he was helped, perhaps, by making all his defences in Japan. From May 1972 to February 1974 he defeated Domenico Tiberia, Matt Donovan, Ryu Sorimachi, Silvani Bertini and Miguel de Oliveira, having also previously drawn with de Oliveira.

Wajima then lost his title to Oscar 'Shotgun' Albarado, from Texas, who defied the odds by going to Tokyo in June 1974 and knocking out the champion 66 seconds from the end of the 15 rounds. Albarado then stopped Sorimachi in Tokyo, but when he gave Wajima a return he was outpointed.

There came a split in the championship because the WBC stripped Wajima for failing to defend against their contender, de Oliveira, who had fought two close battles with Wajima, drawing the first. The WBC recognized de Oliveira, from São Paulo, Brazil, when he outpointed José Duran at Monte Carlo in May 1975.

Wajima lost his WBA title a month later when Jae-Do Yuh, of Korea, stopped him in the seventh. Yuh defended against Masahiro Misako, but then lost the title back to Wajima, who did what Albarado had previously done to him, by winning with a last-round knock-out. It was Wajima's third spell as champion, but it lasted only three months, as he was knocked out in the 14th round by José Duran, from Madrid, who had been beaten for the WBC crown by de Oliveira.

De Oliveira meanwhile had lost this title on his first defence to Elisha Obed in Paris. Obed, a big puncher from Nassau in the Bahamas, successfully defended in his home town against Tony Gardner, and in the Ivory

Below: Maurice Hope (on the right) boxing Rocky Mattioli at Wembley in 1980. Hope won the light-middleweight title from Mattioli in 1979 and was making his second successful defence.

Coast against Sen Robinson, before dropping the WBC crown to Eckhard Dagge, of West Germany, in Berlin. Dagge, a big-punching Berliner, outpointed Emile Griffith, the 38-year-old ex-champion at welter and middleweight, got a lucky draw with Maurice Hope in Berlin and dropped his title in August 1977 to Rocky Mattioli, an Italian born in Ripa Testine who had been brought up in Australia, and had been Australian welterweight champion.

Mattioli's first defence of his WBC crown was in Melbourne, where before his old fans he knocked out Elisha Obed. He then returned to Pescara, Italy, to stop José Duran, but in his next defence, at San Remo, Italy, in March 1979, he was forced to retire in the eighth round against the southpaw Maurice Hope.

Hope, who was born in Antigua, West Indies, but brought up in England, was one of the division's better champions, and stopped Mike Baker at Wembley in 1979, Rocky Mattioli at Wembley in 1980 and outpointed Carlos Herrera before accepting a challenge from Wilfred Benitez, of New York, at Las Vegas. Benitez was a former light-welterweight and welterweight champion, whose only defeat at the time was in a terrific fight with the great Sugar Ray Leonard, and he knocked out Hope in the 12th round to take his third world title.

The WBA strand of the championship, meanwhile, had passed from José Duran, on his first defence, to Miguel Castellini, from Santa Rosa, Argentina. He won the title in Madrid in October 1976 but five months later made the mistake of the earlier champions of taking it to the country of the challenger, in this case Eddie Gazo, from San Lorenzo, Nicaragua, who outpointed him. Gazo resisted the last challenges of the old warrior, three-times winner Koichi Wajima, and Kenji Shibata, both in Tokyo, and of Chae-Keun Lim, in Inchon, South Korea, but in August 1978 he went to Akita, Japan, and left the championship with Masashi Kudo, from Gojonomi. Kudo, who won on a split decision, was a good champion who beat Ho-In Joo and Manuel Gonzalez twice before he was outpointed by Ayub Kalule at Akita in October 1979. It was Kudo's first and only defeat, for he then retired.

Ayub Kalule was born in Kampala, Uganda, and was another of the division's best champions, like his contemporary, Maurice Hope. He was a southpaw, based in Denmark, his four successful defences being in that country. He outpointed Steve Gregory and stopped Emiliano Villa, both in Copenhagen, and outpointed Marijan Benes in Randers and Bushy Bester in Aarhus. Then, like Hope, he was tempted to America to defend against one of the outstanding boxers of the 1980s, Sugar Ray Leonard.

Leonard was the reigning welterweight champion, and he took Kalule's title at Houston, the referee stopping the contest in the ninth round. So, by June 1981, the light-middleweight division boasted two of the world's better champions: Wilfred Benitez (WBC) and Sugar Ray Leonard (WBA).

Leonard did not defend his crown. He chose instead to concentrate on the welterweight division. This meant the WBA had to find a new champion, and they recognized Tadashi Mihara, of Japan, who outpointed Rocky Fratto of the USA at Rochester. Mihara's reign lasted only three months, because back in Tokyo he was challenged by Davey Moore and stopped in the sixth round.

Davey Moore, of New York, had the same name as the featherweight champion who had died after a knock-out in 1963. The second

Moore was a crowd-pleasing puncher who won the title on only his ninth professional fight. He kept busy, knocking out Charlie Weir, a South African, in Johannesburg, stopping Ayub Kalule, making another challenge, in Atlantic City, and knocking out Gary Guiden in the fourth round, before running up against Roberto Duran. It was the 32nd birthday of the former light and welterweight champion, and it was a surprise when his experience overcame the comparative youth of Moore and he registered an eighth-round stoppage. Duran immediately relinquished the title to challenge Hagler for the middleweight title. Benitez, meanwhile, had numbered Duran among his defeated challengers. He had also outpointed Carlos Santos, before he lost his title in December 1982 to Thomas Hearns. It was the second of Hearns' four world titles, as he outpointed Benitez at New Orleans.

In 1984 the IBF recognized the light-middleweight division, so a third champion entered the records when Mark Medal, from Jersey City, stopped Earl Hargrove in the fifth round at Atlantic City. The WBC champion was Hearns, who was extremely busy in 1984, defeating Luigi Minchello in Detroit and stopping Fred Hutchings in Saginaw. Between these two wins he fought Roberto Duran, who after his brave show against Hagler, returned to the lower division to try to take Hearns' crown. However, Hearns knocked the veteran out in the second round.

The third champion of 1984 was Mike McCallum, who took the vacant WBA title with a points win over Sean Mannion in Madison Square Garden. McCallum, born in Jamaica but fighting mainly in the USA, was an impressive performer. He and Hearns were solid champions who were ultimately to relinquish their titles to move up to middleweight, and the most unstable of the three championships was that of the new IBF.

Mark Medal lost this title on his first defence, when outpointed by Carlos Santos, from Santurce, Puerto Rico. He outpointed Louis Arcares in Paris, but was then stripped of the title for failing to defend against Davey Moore. However, six months after being stripped, Santos was fighting for the vacant title. His opponent was Buster Drayton, who outpointed him at East Rutherford. Drayton, from Philadelphia, had already suffered nine defeats before becoming champion. However, he stopped Davey Moore in Juan-les-Pins, France, and then went to nearby Cannes and stopped Said Skouma.

Drayton met his match, however, when the Canadian Matthew Hilton outpointed him in Montreal, Hilton's home town. The brilliant 22-year-old Canadian was unbeaten, and remained so after accepting a challenge from Jack Callahan at Atlantic City on 16 October 1987. The American took a bad beating in the first two rounds and could not come up for a third. However, Hilton lost the title to Robert Hines of Philadelphia.

Hearns continued to rule the WBC roost until stopping Mark Medal on 23 June 1986 at Caesars Palace, Las Vegas. He then relinquished the light-middleweight title to move up to the higher divisions, fighting as both a middleweight and a light-heavyweight. The new WBC champion was Duane Thomas, who surprisingly stopped John Mugabi at Las Vegas. The finish was controversial, as Mugabi was temporarily blinded in the third round and gave up fighting with his glove held to his eye. The referee was obliged to stop the contest and award Thomas the decision, with Mugabi's handlers claiming a thumb in the eye. Thomas, from Detroit, a clever boxer whose only defeat had been administered by Buster Drayton, lost his crown on the first time of asking, when he defended at Bordeaux, France, against Lupe Aquino, born in Tijuana, Mexico, but based at Chula Vista, USA. Aquino gave Thomas a beating to take the clear points decision.

Aquino made the mistake of choosing for his first defence Perugia, in Italy, with an Italian, Gianfranco Rosi, as his opponent. Rosi, from Assisi, fought an inspired contest to win a decisive points verdict. On 3 January 1988 Rosi gave another chance to Duane Thomas at Genoa, and stopped him in the seventh round, but on 8 July 1988 he was forced to retire at San Remo, Italy, against Don Curry, the former welterweight king, who became the new WBC champion.

McCallum beats Curry

Meanwhile, after taking the WBA title, Mike McCallum stopped Luigi Minchillo in the 14th round in Milan, Italy. In 1985 he stopped David Braxton, of Detroit, in the eighth round at Miami. Neither of McCallum's 1986 challengers lasted the distance. Julian Jackson was stopped in two rounds in Miami, and Said Skouma was knocked out in the ninth in Paris. In April 1987 McCallum completely outboxed the former welterweight champion Milton McCrory before stopping him in the tenth round at Phoenix, USA.

Despite McCallum's excellent record, he was not expected to be able to cope with another former welterweight king, Donald Curry, when they met at Las Vegas on 18 July 1987. Curry as a welterweight had crushed McCrory in less than two rounds, and was regarded as a strong threat to the light-middleweights. The fight was evenly fought until the fifth round, when a superb left hook from the champion flattened Curry, knocking him out with a single blow.

McCallum relinquished the WBA title after this to move up to the middleweight ranks. Julian Jackson, whom he had already easily beaten, was matched with In-Chul Baek, of South Korea, for the vacant crown. The match was at Las Vegas on 21 October 1987 and Jackson, from the Virgin Islands, became the new champion when the referee stopped the fight in the third. In July 1988 he beat Buster Drayton in his first defence.

The Welterweights and Light-Welterweights

The boxing writer A.J. Liebling thought Mysterious Billy Smith and Honey Mellody, both welterweight champions, had the best ring names. If Honey Mellody suggests a sweet boxer, then other welterweights, like Ted Lewis (the Crashing, Dashing Kid), Henry Armstrong (Homicide Hank) and Thomas Hearns (the Hit Man) had nicknames suggesting the more painful side of the game. All of these are men who have graced this division, alongside the evergreen Jack Britton, Jimmy 'Babyface' McLarnin, Barney Ross, Emile Griffith, the hat-maker, Jose Napoles, the 'exile' from Cuba, Don Curry, and, to revert to the sweet theme, Lloyd 'Honey' Honeyghan and the two Sugar Rays, Robinson and Leonard.

Left: *Lloyd Honeyghan rising in the ring like some apparition after his successful WBC welterweight defence against Maurice Blocker in April 1987. Blocker had the satisfaction of staying the distance against the destructive Honeyghan.*

SUGAR AND SPICE AND THINGS NOT NICE

The welterweight division is now recognized by all bodies to have an upper limit of 147lb (67kg). It came into being during the late 19th century along with the middleweight class, when the boxing fraternity began to recognize that something was needed between light and heavyweights.

Paddy Duffy of Boston, Massachusetts, is usually regarded as the first welterweight champion, setting the limit at 142lb (64kg). He knocked out William McMillan on 30 October 1888 at Fort Foote, Virginia. However, Duffy died in 1890, and the championship did not get under way in earnest until 1892. On 14 December of that year Mysterious Billy Smith knocked out Danny Needham at San Francisco and was recognized as champion. He was born Amos Smith at Eastport, Maine, and after boxing under that name changed it to Billy Smith. When a newspaper referred to this 'Mysterious Billy Smith' who was doing so well, the name stuck. He knocked out an Australian, Tom Williams, at Coney Island, but lost his title to Tommy Ryan, from Redwood, New York, who outpointed him over 20 rounds at Minneapolis. Ryan was one of the great champions of the 1890s, who was to lose only three fights in a long career. He beat Nonpareil Jack Dempsey, the former middleweight champion, in 1895 with a third-round knockout, ten months before Dempsey died. A return with Mysterious Billy Smith at Coney Island, New York, was stopped by the police after 18 rounds.

Ryan then lost the title to Kid McCoy. McCoy was an erstwhile sparring partner of Ryan, and he persuaded Ryan to give him a title fight on the grounds that he was sick and needed the purse. However, he surprised Ryan, who did not train too hard for what he thought was a formality, and turned up in peak condition. He floored Ryan 12 times on his way to a knock-out in the 15th round.

At this time the middleweight title was dormant, and McCoy claimed that as a result of his win, while Ryan continued to style himself as welterweight champion. He fought Mysterious Billy Smith again, winning on a disqualification (Smith was often disqualified), and after two more defences decided to move up to middleweight, McCoy in the meantime having himself moved up to the heavyweight class.

Mysterious Billy Smith then claimed back the title, as he had beaten Ryan in an overweight match. He drew with Joe Walcott, with whom he had a number of battles, and twice with Andy Walsh, all over 25 rounds, and also drew over 20 rounds with Charley McKeever, but he beat George Green, Matty Matthews, Jim Judge, Charley McKeever (twice), Billy Edwards, George Lavigne and his old enemy Joe Walcott. All this was in less than 18 months at the end of the century, but on his first defence in the new century, on 15 January 1900, he lost the title to Rube Ferns, again on a disqualification.

Ferns, from Pittsburgh, Kansas, was a knock-out specialist, who had a three-battle sequence with Matty Matthews, a good boxer from Brooklyn. Ferns won the rubber match to end with the title after Matthews had held it for five months. Ferns knocked out the lightweight champion, Frank Erne, at Fort Erie, Canada, but then lost his title to Joe Walcott, when stopped at the same venue.

From the West Indies, Walcott was known as the 'Barbados Demon'. He was a strong, durable champion, whose name came to the fore in the 1930s and 1940s when the future heavyweight champion, born Arnold Cream, adopted his name and became Jersey Joe Walcott. Walcott defended in London against Tommy West, whom he outpointed. He drew with Billy Woods, but lost his title on a disqualification in the 20th round with Dixie Kid, a good all-round boxer from Fulton, Missouri, whose real name was Aaron Brown. Walcott bitterly disputed the verdict, and the two met again 13 days later, when the decision was a draw. However, Dixie Kid outgrew the division and within months Walcott had reclaimed the title and fought a draw with Joe Gans, the great lightweight champion.

Billy 'Honey' Mellody took the title from Walcott with two victories at Chelsea, Massachusetts, but his six-month reign ended in April 1907 when Mike 'Twin' Sullivan outpointed him. Sullivan, one of twin boxers from Cambridge, Massachusetts, made three successful defences, in the middle of which he challenged the great Stanley Ketchel for the middleweight crown. Sullivan, unfortunately, had to relinquish the title because of an eye injury.

There followed a very confused period among the welterweights, with a number of boxers laying claim to the title. From 1908 to 1915 there were two strands to the championship, which were the US/Australian strand and the British/French strand.

The United States regarded Jimmy Gardner, an Irishman fighting out of Boston, as champion after a victory and a draw in contests with Jimmy Clabby. Gardner outgrew the division and US recognition fell on Clabby, who went to Australia to register wins in Sydney and Brisbane to gain Australian recognition. However, he, too, became too heavy, and the Australians recognized Waldemar Holberg, a Dane from Copenhagen, who outpointed an American, Ray Bronson, in Melbourne. Holberg was essentially a rough in-fighter who suffered from frequent disqualifications, one of which lost him his title to Tom McCormick, an Irish soldier fighting out of Plymouth. McCormick, who was to die two years later in World War I, lost the title, after one successful defence, to Matt Wells, from Walworth, a supremely clever boxer who outpointed McCormick in Sydney. At this time there was a boxing boom in Australia, following the Jack Johnson heavyweight title win there in 1908, and centred around the great Australian middleweight, Les Darcy. Wells won the Australian version of the welterweight title in 1914. He then went to the USA, where the Americans, searching for somebody to recognize as champion, were pleased to approve Mike Glover, an Irish-American from Lawrence, Mississippi, when he outpointed Wells. When Glover was himself outpointed by Jack Britton, a classical boxer from Clinton, New York, the USA had an outstanding welterweight champion.

Meanwhile, British and French recognition had been won by Harry Lewis. A New York Jew, real name Henry Besterman, he had beaten Honey Mellody by a fourth-round knock-out in a no-decision bout in 1908, and on the strength of this claimed the title when Sullivan relinquished it. Two fights in Paris with Willie Lewis were advertised as being for the title, and both were drawn. After a victory in Paris he beat Young Joseph, the British champion, in London and was granted British recognition as well as French.

While he was champion Lewis raised the welterweight limit to 147lb (67kg), the weight fixed by the National Sporting Club in 1909 for British championships. Lewis ceased to be recognized as champion in 1912 after two non-title defeats by Johnny Mathieson.

Jack Britton and Ted 'Kid' Lewis

The welterweight confusion was finally settled in 1915. Ted 'Kid' Lewis, from Aldgate, London, had, like others, followed the boxing boom to Australia, and then moved on to the United States. On 31 August 1915 he outpointed Jack Britton in Boston, and, as he also already had beaten Mike Glover, he was regarded universally as the welterweight champion, a status he emphasized with a repeat performance four weeks later.

Lewis, born Gershon Mendeloff, was an English Jew, and Britton, born William J. Breslin, was an Irish-American. They were two outstanding boxers who dominated the welterweight scene for over seven years, in which time one or the other was champion. They fought each other 20 times, mostly in no-decision bouts. Britton won 11 title fights and drew five, while Lewis won nine title fights and drew one. Of the decisions rendered in contests between them, Britton won four times and Lewis three, with one drawn. When Lewis was outpointed in 1921 to give Britton a 4-3 lead over him, he returned to England.

Britton's last successful defence was against Benny Leonard, one of the greatest of all lightweight champions, who was attempting to add the welter crown to his laurels. The match was one which filled the Metropolitan Velodrome in New York. Leonard was as clever a boxer as Britton, and 11 years his junior, and looked to be doing enough when he dropped Britton to one knee with a punch to the chin in the 13th, but then the classic boxer Leonard unaccountably cuffed Britton as he rested on his knee, and was disqualified by the referee.

Britton lost his title for the last time in his next fight. This time the 37-year-old was giving away nearly 16 years to the 21-year-old Mickey Walker, destined to be another of boxing's all-time great champions. Walker, from Elizabeth, New Jersey, outpointed Britton in a battle of superb craftsmanship and heavy punching at Madison Square Garden on 1 November 1922.

***Above:** Ted Kid Lewis from Aldgate was a busy all-action fighter who fought for titles at weights up to light-heavyweight, but the 'Crashing, Dashing Kid' was best at welterweight and dominated the division with Jack Britton in the years after World War I.*

Above: *Mickey Walker was one of the best welterweight champions, and later became an outstanding middleweight, and even fought one-time heavyweight champion, Max Schmeling.*

Walker was called 'the Toy Bulldog'. He was champion for three and a half years, in the middle of which he challenged for the middleweight title, where the champion was Harry Greb. It was a golden era for boxing and Harry Greb, whom Walker thought was the best fighter he had met, outpointed him. Walker's welterweight reign came to an end with a points defeat by Pete Latzo. Walker was already beginning to outgrow the division, and a few months later he was middleweight champion.

Latzo was a 23-year-old from Coloraine, Pennsylvania, who made two successful defences, but then lost a very close and disputed decision to Joe Dundee at the Polo Grounds, New York. Latzo was apparently still growing and had had great difficulty making the weight. Only a year later he was to have the first of two fights with Tommy Loughran for the light-heavyweight championship!

Joe Dundee was born in Rome, but his younger brother Vince was born in Baltimore. Both were to win world titles. Dundee took 13 months to defend, knocking out Hilario Martinez, and after another delay was stripped by the NBA, who matched Jackie Fields with Young Jack Thompson for the title. Jackie Fields took the points decision in his native Chicago and then beat Dundee on a second-round disqualification in Detroit. Dundee had been down twice in the first.

Fields had won the Olympic featherweight gold medal in 1924 in Paris when only 16, and cried because he beat his pal Joe Salas in the final. Even then he was using the ring-name of Fields, although his real name was Jacob Finkelstein. Fields lost the title on his first defence, which took the championship into the 1930s. He was outpointed by Young Jack Thompson, from Los Angeles, in Detroit. The early 1930s was a period when the welterweight title changed hands rapidly. It was a period when the division appeared to be at the mercy of shady operators, and it was difficult for some boxers to get a title shot. Thompson, who was only the second black boxer to win the championship, lost on points on his first defence to Tommy Freeman at Cleveland. Freeman, from Hot Springs, Arkansas, was a very busy fighter who had 185 fights in his career, six of them in just over three months as champion. After five wins he was forced to retire in the 12th when giving a rematch to Young Jack Thompson, again in Cleveland.

Thompson again lost on his first defence, this time to Lou Brouillard, a rugged French-Canadian southpaw from St Eugene, Quebec. Brouillard won on points in Boston, but he too held the title little more than three months before dropping it to former champion Jackie Fields at Chicago. Brouillard went on to win a version of the middleweight championship. Fields held on to the title for a year, but he, too, lost it on his first defence, being outpointed by Young Corbett III. This boxer had been born as Ralph Capabianca Giordino in Campania, Italy, but had begun his career in America, taking the name of the first heavyweight champion. Corbett lost the title after only three months to Jimmy McLarnin, who knocked him out in the first round at Los Angeles. Corbett went on to challenge for the middleweight title, while McLarnin began a new golden age for welterweights which lasted for the rest of the decade.

Jimmy 'Baby Face' McLarnin, born in Inchacore, Ireland, had fought out of Vancouver, where he was brought up, since the age of 17 in 1923 and had beaten the world's best boxers from flyweight upwards, although he had been outpointed in his one title shot, by lightweight champion Sammy

Mandell in 1928. He made no mistake with his welterweight chance, but unfortunately found himself contemporary with another great boxer, Barney Ross. Ross was an American Jew from New York who had three great battles with McLarnin, given spice by the Irish-Jewish rivalry in American rings of the day. Three years younger than McLarnin, he, too, had fought his way up the weight scale, and had been lightweight champion and light-welterweight champion in 1933, and was the NBA light-welterweight champion when he became McLarnin's first challenger for the welterweight title on 28 May 1934.

The Ross-McLarnin battles

Ross won the first encounter on a split decision. McLarnin was warned four times for low punches which might have swayed the verdict, with which many disagreed, although one judge and the referee gave it to Ross by huge margins. The fight was at the Madison Square Garden Corporation's new Long Island Bowl arena, and the large crowd of over 30,000 were anxious to see a rematch. It came four months later at the same venue, and in another tremendous contest which swayed one way and another the referee was again called upon to separate the boxers as the two judges disagreed. This time he chose McLarnin, and the general opinion of the verdict was that it was wrong. However, two split decisions, one for each fighter, meant a lucrative third match, and this took place exactly a year after the first, at New York's Polo Grounds before over 30,000 fans.

The rubber match lived up to the others, and both men were pummelling each other at the bell which ended 45 rounds of exciting scrapping between them. This time the verdict was unanimous — Ross had won — but it was, nevertheless, greeted with booing and many good judges disagreed. Ross, however, was the man to emerge as an outstanding welterweight champion.

Ross made successful defences in 1936 and 1937, in his second defence outpointing Ceferino Garcia, of the Philippines, who later was middleweight champion, in a terrific bout on a Carnival of Champions bill at the Polo Grounds, New York.

Ross lost his title on 31 May 1938 to a fistic phenomenon, Henry Armstrong. Armstrong, with his slow heartbeat, was perpetual motion in the ring, and one of boxing's busiest champions, fighting no fewer than 27 times in 1937. Like McLarnin and Ross, he had risen up the weight scale. In October 1937 he won the featherweight championship, and was seeking to add a second world title when tackling Ross at the Long Island Bowl.

Ross did not possess a real knock-out punch, and he found it impossible to prevent the all-action Armstrong from swarming all over him. Despite easing up in the later stages to allow Ross to finish on his feet Armstrong won comfortably, inflicting enough punishment on the champion to make him retire.

The great Henry Armstrong

Armstrong, born in Columbus, Mississippi, but brought up in St Louis, was known as 'Homicide Hank', and he certainly killed off the hopes of many welterweights during the next three years. He successfully defended the title no fewer than 19 times, a record for the division.

Also during this period, Armstrong won the lightweight title when he outpointed Lou Ambers, and challenged for a version of the middleweight title, getting a draw with Ceferino Garcia, coming within an ace of winning a world title at a fourth weight. Ceferino Garcia was one of the welterweight challengers he beat in his reign to October 1940. Other notable boxers he beat were Baby Arizmendi, the former featherweight champion, and Ernie Roderick, the British champion. These two, plus Garcia and Ross, were the only challengers to take him the distance.

Perhaps Armstrong went to the wall once too often, for he lost his title on 4 October 1940 only 11 days after he had successfully defended against Phil Furr. His conqueror was Fritzie Zivic, the youngest of five boxing brothers from Pittsburgh, Pennsylvania. The family ranged from bantam to middleweight and were a rough, tough bunch, of whom Fritzie was the toughest, engaging in a schedule not much less arduous than Armstrong's. Zivic won on points, giving Armstrong a bad beating and flooring him for the first time. A rematch on 17 January 1941 was watched by a record 23,000 at Madison Square Garden, and again Zivic battered Armstrong so that the referee was forced to intervene in the 12th round.

__Below:__ Henry Armstrong held the welterweight title at a time when he was also featherweight and lightweight champion, a unique record. He defended the welterweight crown 19 times.

Zivic's first challenger, six months later, was Freddie 'Red' Cochrane, from Elizabeth, New Jersey, who was a surprise winner at Newark. However, Cochrane had no chance to cash in, because America entered World War II and he enlisted in the navy. When he returned to the ring he was knocked out twice by middleweight Rocky Graziano after leading on points, and then lost the title to Marty Servo, from Schenectady, New York, who knocked him out in four rounds. Servo gained precedence over Sugar Ray Robinson, who had already twice outpointed him, by guaranteeing Cochrane $50,000, so in a sense he 'bought' the title, his purse not covering that amount.

Servo was matched with Sugar Ray Robinson for the title but in the meantime he, like Cochrane had done, took on Graziano in a non-title contest. Graziano gave him a fierce beating from the first bell, and although the fight was stopped as early as the second round, Servo's nose was so badly injured that he was forced to give up the Robinson fight and the title. He fought only twice more.

The New York Commission wanted an elimination contest for the title, but were forced to name Robinson as champion when other leading welters declined to meet him. In December 1946 Tommy Bell challenged Robinson and was outpointed at Madison Square Garden, whereupon Robinson was universally accepted as the new champion.

Robinson, from Detroit, was to prove himself one of the greatest boxers in the history of the sport, but his main renown was to come later in the middleweight division. He remained welterweight champion for over four years, beating off five challengers, of whom the best was Kid Gavilan, a future champion. Robinson's second challenger, Jimmy Doyle, died after being stopped in the eighth, hitting his head on the canvas when being knocked down, the bell saving the count-out. During this time Robinson gained recognition in Pennsylvania as middleweight champion, and when in 1951 he beat LaMotta to become undisputed middleweight champion, he relinquished the welterweight crown.

Robinson's final victim, Charlie Fasari, was matched with Johnny Bratton at Chicago for the NBA title, and Bratton won a split decision in the town he fought from, although he was born in Little Rock. Bratton, who owed his title shot to his Chicago connections, lost on his first defence two months later to Kid Gavilan, who was granted New York recognition as well as NBA. Gavilan beat Billy Graham and Bobby Dykes on split decisions, both of which were bitterly disputed, and then stopped Gil Turner before a crowd of 39,000 at the Municipal Stadium, Philadelphia. This victory gained him universal recognition as world champion.

Gavilan, born Gerardo Gonzalez at Camagüey, Cuba, began his career in Havana, and developed a punch peculiar to himself, an uppercut with a twisting motion which was called a 'bolo' punch. He was champion for over two years, beating Graham again, decisively this time, and Carmen Basilio, a tough future champion who, at the time, was claiming New York recognition, and was only beaten on a split decision.

Gavilan, the master of split decision victories, lost his title to Johnny Saxton in Philadelphia on 20 October 1954, losing to a unanimous decision that most observers thought a poor verdict. Saxton had been a brilliant amateur, who as a professional had high-profile underworld management in the notorious Blinky Palermo.

Saxton's reign lasted less than six months, and he lost on his first defence to Tony de Marco, born Leonard Liotta in Boston, Massachusetts. A knock-out specialist, he stopped Saxton in the 14th round in his home town. However, de Marco lasted only ten weeks as champion, as he was stopped in turn in the 12th at Syracuse by Carmen Basilio. There was a return six months later in Boston, but the popular de Marco's home supporters had to witness exactly the same result, in a tremendous battle in which the immensely durable Basilio was himself almost knocked out in the seventh round.

Basilio now had three fights with Saxton, the first of which he lost at the Chicago Stadium. It was a unanimous decision of the judges, but everybody else who saw the fight appeared unanimous that Basilio had won it. Basilio had to wait six months, until September 1956, for his revenge, when he stopped Saxton in the ninth at Syracuse. In February 1957 he knocked him out in the second round at Cleveland to end Saxton's title pretensions for good.

Basilio now took on Sugar Ray Robinson for the middleweight crown, and in one of those gruelling battles in which he specialized, he won. He thus relinquished the welterweight title to move up a division.

Luckily there was no disagreement regarding his successor. The NBA and New York authorities agreed on an elimination competition involving George Barnes of Australia, de Marco, Isaac Logart of Cuba, Vince Martinez of Paterson, New Jersey, Gaspar Ortega of Mexico and Gil Turner of Philadelphia. Barnes declined the trip to America and de Marco lost to Virgil Akins, who took his place. Akins was matched with Martinez in the final at St Louis, and stopped him in the fourth round to become the new welterweight champion.

Akins had won the title almost by stealth, but he held it for only six months exactly, and his decline became as rapid as his rise, an eye injury finally ending his career in 1962. His conqueror was Don Jordan, born in the Dominican Republic but based in Los Angeles. Jordan outpointed Akins in Los Angeles. Jordan in later life gave an interview to Peter Heller for his book *In this Corner!* in which he claimed to have been born with webbed fingers, and to have been called

'Duck' by his parents and 18 brothers and sisters. He claimed to have been a hired assassin in the jungle from the age of ten, using poison darts in the necks of his victims, of whom there were 30 in one month. He spent much of his early days as a youth in California in reform schools, and after staking a man to the ground and setting fire to him was sent to prison. He became an amateur boxer and went to the 1952 Olympics, where he claimed he was disqualified for carrying his hands below his waist. He turned professional, and fought mainly as a lightweight, but seized his opportunity to become welterweight champion.

Jordan repeated his win over Akins, then outpointed Denny Moyer who was to become the first light-middleweight champion. However, in March 1960 he lost the title when outpointed by Benny 'Kid' Paret. Paret was born in Santa Clara, Cuba, beginning his career in that country but switching to America when professional boxing was banned there. He was a strong, durable boxer but not a big hitter, who therefore won most of his fights the hard way. He made one successful defence but then lost on a 13th-round knock-out at Miami Beach to the man who was to be his Nemesis, Emile Griffith.

Benny Paret dies on TV

Griffith was born at St Thomas, in the Virgin Islands, and moved to New York to become one of boxing's greatest champions. His fight with Paret was close until the unexpected knock-out, and after one successful defence Paret was given a return at Madison Square Garden. Again it was close, with both judges giving it to Paret, although the referee gave it to Griffith. The crowd seemed to agree with the referee, and on 24 March 1962 a third meeting between them was held, again at Madison Square Garden.

This was a tragic fight. The two men had an altercation at the weigh-in. Griffith, again in an interview with Peter Heller from the book mentioned before, tells how Paret taunted him with homosexuality (Griffith had been an apprentice in a hat-making factory, an odd occupation for a boxer, leading press stories to link him with millinery). In the fight Griffith was floored and says Paret mocked him with hand on hip. Griffith was angry, and his trainer, to concentrate his attention, told him to keep punching if he got his opponent in difficulties. This happened in the 12th, when Paret was trapped on the ropes and took numerous punches before the fight was stopped. He never recovered consciousness. It was a fight which had a big effect on the American public, who had watched the fatal blows on ABC-TV.

Griffith remained welterweight champion for over three more years, except for a period of 11 weeks or so when he lost a decision to Luis Rodriguez, from Camagüey, Cuba. It was a unanimous decision at the Dodgers Stadium, Los Angeles, but a close one, and many would have given it the other way. Griffith regained the crown three months later, this time on a split decision at Madison Square Garden, where the biggest margin on the cards was the 10-5 verdict one judge gave to Rodriguez. A year later there was a third match at Las Vegas, and Griffith again took the split decision. The unlucky Rodriguez later challenged Benvenuti unsuccessfully for the middleweight title.

One of Griffith's successful defences featured a stoppage of Jorge Fernandez, an unlucky Argentinian. Griffith struck him low in the ninth round, and Fernandez was given five minutes to recover. When he failed to do so the verdict was granted to Griffith.

Griffith moved up to the middleweight division in 1966 and won the title, relin-

Left: The tragic ending to the world title fight in which Emile Griffith knocked out Benny 'Kid' Paret at Madison Square Garden in 1962. Paret was knocked unconscious and rushed to hospital but he remained in a coma and died some days later.

***Right:** Jose Napoles avoids a long left from challenger John H Stacey in their 1975 title fight. Napoles was the division's best for over six years, but was finally stopped by the younger Stacey.*

quishing the welterweight crown. The NBA recognized Curtis Cokes, who outpointed Manuel Gonzalez at New Orleans in the final of an eliminating tournament. Ernie Lopez, Ted Whitfield and Luis Rodriguez also took part. Cokes, from Dallas, Texas, was a surprise winner, especially over Rodriguez, whom he stopped in the last round of the semi-final. He proved a good champion, outpointing Jean Josselin, of France, the European champion, in his first defence in Dallas.

Charlie Shipes was recognized by the Californian commission in December 1966 after stopping Percy Manning, but Cokes stopped him in eight rounds at Oakland in October 1967 to gain universal recognition. Cokes defended successfully five times in all in a reign of over two and a half years before he lost the crown to José Napoles in Los Angeles on 18 April 1969.

Napoles was an excellent champion who ruled, with a minor hiccup, for six years. Born in Oriente, Cuba, Napoles was a craftsman, an all-round boxer who also had a knock-out punch. With professional boxing banned in Cuba, he made his home in Mexico. He battered Cokes to a stoppage at the end of the 13th round, when both of Cokes' eyes were almost shut, and the referee decided he had no chance of winning. It was Napoles 41st win by the quick route in 61 bouts. He gave Cokes a return in Mexico City, and stopped him when Cokes, again with both eyes badly damaged, could not come out for the 11th round.

Napoles' next challenger was the great former champion, Emil Griffith, who was back well inside the welterweight limit after winning and losing the middleweight title. The fight was at the Inglewood Forum, Los Angeles, and Napoles scored an easy points win.

After a defence against Ernie Lopez, Napoles, now recognized as a great champion, was surprisingly stopped on a cut eye in the fourth round by Billy Backus, a 9-1 outsider, at Syracuse, in December 1970. Backus, of Canastota, New York, was a southpaw nephew of Carmen Basilio. He kept the title for six months, but when he faced Napoles in a return in Los Angeles, the referee was forced to come to his rescue in the eighth on the advice of the ringside doctor.

Napoles outpointed Hedgemon Lewis in a close fight at the Inglewood Forum, Los Angeles, and travelled to Europe for two of his next three defences, knocking out Ralph Charles of West Ham, London, the British champion, at Wembley, and outpointing Roger Menetrey, of France, the European champion, at Grenoble. He also defended in Canada, outpointing Clyde Gray at Toronto and inflicting upon him his first defeat in 43 bouts.

Meanwhile, Hedgemon Lewis had been recognized in New York as champion with two wins in 1972 over Billy Backus. Napoles went to Paris in 1974 and fought Carlos Monzon for the middleweight title but was beaten. On his return across the Atlantic he stopped Hedgemon Lewis in nine rounds at Mexico City.

Napoles was not at his best after his tangle with Monzon, however. He disposed of Horacio Saldano of Argentina, but in 1975 he nearly lost his title at Acapulco when the ringside doctor stopped his fight with Armando Muniz, a Mexican based in Los Angeles, because Napoles had severe eye injuries. The referee gave Napoles the verdict, called a 'technical decision', on the grounds that the injuries were caused by butts.

Napoles now gave up the WBA title to concentrate on the WBC title, but it was academic as his championship career had nearly reached the end. At Mexico City he gave Muniz a return and won a unanimous decision, but then he was stopped in the sixth round at Mexico City by John H. Stracey, the British and European champion. Stracey, a skilful boxer from Bethnal Green, London, had almost pulled out of the bout. Nervous about fighting at altitude to start with, he was dismayed to find all the officials for the bout Mexican. He survived a first round knock-down to pound Napoles to defeat.

Stracey stopped Hedgemon Lewis to end his title pretensions for good, but lost his championship on 22 June 1976 when he was stopped by Carlos Palomino at Wembley. Palomino, born in San Luis, Mexico, boxed out of Los Angeles. He was a deceptively skilful boxer, particularly strong with body punches, and it was these which suddenly destroyed Stracey in the 12th round.

Meanwhile, the WBA had recognized Angel Espada as champion after he had outpointed Canada's Clyde Gray at San Juan, Puerto Rico, on 28 June 1975. Espada was a big-punching Puerto Rican from Salinas, who also stopped Alfonso Hayman at San Juan before taking his title to Mexicali, Mexico, and dropping it to Pipino Cuevas.

Cuevas was only 18 years, 203 days old on winning the title, one of the youngest world champions in boxing history. From Mexico City, he was a knock-out specialist. He was occasionally outpointed himself, but practically all his own victories came before the scheduled distance had elapsed.

Cuevas and Palomino won the WBA and WBC titles respectively in 1976 and it was two and a half years and 14 world title fights before either was deposed.

Palomino made four defences in 1977, knocking out Dave 'Boy' Green of England, at Wembley, and beating Armando Muniz, Everaldo Azevedo and Jose Palacios at Los Angeles. In 1978 he stopped Ryu Sorimachi and Mimoun Mohatar at Las Vegas and then returned to Los Angeles to outpoint Armando Muniz. In his first fight in 1979 he was outpointed by another great champion, Wilfred Benitez, at San Juan, Puerto Rico. Benitez, from the Bronx, New York, was a former light-welterweight champion, and was still only 20 years old. He was part of another golden age for welterweights. He defended successfully against Harold Weston, who had lost previously to Cuevas, but then ran up against one of the outstanding boxers of the 1980s, Sugar Ray Leonard. Leonard, an Olympic champion in 1976, had become the new golden boy of boxing, and challenged Benitez at Caesars Palace, Las Vegas, on 30 November 1979. Even the challenger earned a million dollars for this battle. Benitez fought back from a third-round knockdown but was stopped in the last few seconds of the fight, when he finally ran out of steam.

Meanwhile, Cuevas had defended his WBA title even more often than Palomino, and his run lasted into the 1980s. In 1976 he defended in Japan, and was one of the few champions to return with his title when he knocked out Shoji Tsujimoto in the sixth round. In 1977 he made three defences: two second-round knockouts of Miguel Campanino and Clyde Gray and an 11th round stoppage of Angel Espada, from whom he had won the title. He also made three defences in 1978, stopping Harold Weston in the ninth, Billy Backus in the first and Pete Ranzany in the second. In 1979 there were three more defences, against Scott Clark, Randy Shields, who took him the distance, and Angel Espada again. In 1980 he stopped Harold Volbrecht, the South African champion, but then he, too, ran up against one of the legendary figures of the 1980s, Thomas Hearns. Hearns was as explosive a puncher as Cuevas, and when the two met at Hearns' 'home' venue of Detroit, it was the 'Hit Man' whose punching told first, and Cuevas was stopped for the first time in his career in the second round.

Strangely, by the time Hearns won the world title, Leonard had temporarily lost his. On 20 June 1980 he was challenged by Roberto Duran of Panama, a veteran who had held the lightweight title since 1972. Leonard was a warm favourite even against such a man as Duran, but on a rainy night at Montreal before 46,000 fans the old champion fought with all his macho swagger and aggression, roughing up Leonard whenever possible and maintaining his snarling belligerence to the end. He managed to take Leonard out of his smooth stride enough to record the only defeat Leonard suffered until his successful third comeback in 1988. It was a unanimous decision, but only by a single point on two score-cards and two on the other.

The two had to meet again, and five months later faced each other at the Superdome, New Orleans. This time Leonard boxed brilliantly, and having got on top began taunting Duran, inviting him to come forward. The fight was a brilliant contrast to their first, with the rapier baffling the bludgeon. Duran become so bewildered at having nobody to fight, in the sense that Leonard refused to stand up and mix it, that in the eighth round he turned his back on his tormentor and with the words which became famous in boxing circles, 'no mas' (no more) he retired. For Duran, the macho man, it was a humiliation that he would find difficult to live down, but for Leonard it was a tremendous triumph for boxing skill.

Above: *The climax of the great unification contest between WBC champion Sugar Ray Leonard and WBA champion Thomas Hearns in 1981. Hearns built up a lead but Leonard suddenly took charge in the 13th round and in the photograph has Hearns groggy with a right. Leonard won by a 14th round stoppage.*

Sugar beats the Hit Man

The paths of Leonard (WBC) and Hearns (WBA) now took parallel paths towards an inevitable meeting, if that is not a geometrical impossibility. Leonard stopped Larry Bonds and then took the WBA light-middleweight title from Ayub Kalule, a title he straightaway relinquished to return to the welterweight ranks and a meeting with Hearns. Hearns stopped Luis Primera, Randy Shields and Pablo Baez before he and Leonard met at Caesars Palace, Las Vegas. The fight was a multi-million dollar affair that everybody wanted to see, and proved to be an outstanding battle. The unbeaten Hearns made a quick start, as was his habit, but could not destroy Leonard, although he built up a points lead. In the 13th round Leonard suddenly began a tremendous rally, and put Hearns down twice, one a genuine knock-down and one ruled a slip, as Hearns visibly wilted. Halfway through the 14th the referee had to come to the assistance of the exhausted and beaten Hearns.

Leonard's eye had been damaged in this fight, possibly starting the trouble that caused him to retire after a detached retina was diagnosed and after he had made one defence of the unified title, stopping Bruce Finch.

It was not surprising that the WBA and WBC now split again and chose different champions, but it was surprising that after such a run of outstanding title-holders the two new ones were also of excellent standard. Don Curry, in particular, who won WBA recognition by outpointing Jun-Sok Hwang, of South Korea, at Fort Worth, was to be regarded at one time as the best pound-for-pound boxer in the world. Curry, from Fort Worth, was called the Cobra, but the title win was a difficult one for him, as he was not only down during the contest but hurt his hand in hitting his opponent, a recurring weakness.

The WBC version of the title was won by Milton McCrory, a tall skilful boxer who fought out of Detroit. McCrory was called the Ice Man for his cool demeanour in tight corners. He fought two battles with the British champion Colin Jones, a hard-hitting Welshman, before earning recognition. The first, in Reno, was adjudged a draw when most thought McCrory won, and the second was given to him on a split decision when there were plenty who thought Jones won.

The two champions, like Leonard and Hearns, fought their way to a showdown. Curry was slightly the busier, travelling all the way to Marsala in Italy to knock out Roger Stafford in the first round, outpointing Marlon Starling in Atlantic City, which won him IBF recognition, stopping Elio Diaz at Fort Worth and Nino la Rocca at Monte Carlo, and then in Birmingham stopping Colin Jones, who had fought McCrory, in the fourth, the challenger suffering a badly split nose.

McCrory defended twice in Detroit, stopping Milton Guest and Gilles Ebilia, both in the sixth round, and then, like Curry, defended in Europe, outpointing Pedro Vilella in Paris and stopping Carlos Trujillo in Monte Carlo.

Lloyd Honeyghan shocks Curry

The two unbeaten champions met at Las Vegas on 6 December 1985, and Curry proved much too strong for McCrory, flooring him twice before the knock-out was administered half-way through the second round. Curry disposed of Edouardo Rodriguez, also in two rounds, at Fort Worth, in the first defence of his unified title, but then was surprisingly beaten by his British challenger, Lloyd Honeyghan, at Atlantic City. Again, both men were unbeaten, but Curry was a hot favourite, only to find Honeyghan far too strong and aggressive. Curry was outboxed, outpunched and demoralized, retiring at the end of the sixth round.

The flamboyant Honeyghan, who began wearing glamour gear in the ring, was born in Jamaica, but fought out of Bermondsey, London. He was one of only two boxers (Hagler was the other) to hold undisputed world titles, but he relinquished the WBA title before he could make a defence. This was because the WBA had named Harold Volbrecht, a South African, as a contender. Honeyghan's withdrawal was a protest against apartheid, but it was also a business decision, because the WBC suspend for two years a boxer who meets a South African.

Honeyghan went on to stop Johnny Bumphus at Wembley in two rounds for the IBF title, and outpoint Maurice Blocker in a close match to retain his WBC title (the IBF insisted on title fights being over 15 rounds, while WBC defences were over 12 rounds, therefore the titles had to be defended separately). On 30 August 1987 Honeyghan went to Marbella, Spain, and stopped Gene 'Mad Dog' Hatcher, the former light-welterweight champion, in the first round of a contest postponed because of storms.

On 28 October 1987 Honeyghan was surprisingly beaten for the WBC title by Jorge Vaca, from Guadalajara, the Mexican champion, and not a man regarded as likely to trouble him. The match took a peculiar turn in the eighth round. An accidental butt cut Vaca's eye and the fight was stopped. Under WBC rules, the points total at the end of the previous round applies, after each judge deducts one point from the total of the boxer causing the cut, i.e. Honeyghan. This rule cost the champion his title and gave him his first defeat. Vaca won by a split decision. Without the deduction the fight would have been a draw, and Honeyghan would have kept the title. As it was, mix-ups in his private life had caused him to fight without sparkle, and he had no complaints. Another oddity followed in that the IBF, whose championship was not at stake, nevertheless stripped Honeyghan after this defeat. The illogicality of such decisions means that while the champion can lose his title, the challenger cannot win it. It is another aspect of the control of championships by the 'alphabet boys' (WBC, WBA, and IBF) which considerably devalues world titles.

On 29 March 1988 Honeyghan knocked out Vaca in the third round of a return at Wembley and regained the WBC title, but of course not the IBF. In July he stopped Yung-Kil Chung of Korea.

The WBA title, which Honeyghan shed of his own free will in 1986, was duly won by Mark Breland, who knocked out the South African Harold Volbrecht for the vacant title at Atlantic City on 6 February 1987. Breland, from Brooklyn, was the 1984 Olympic welterweight champion, an elegant boxer whose predicted rise to the top of the professional ranks proceeded smoothly to the acquisition of the title unbeaten.

Breland *v.* Honeyghan was being hyped as an outstanding showdown when Breland surprisingly lost his title to Marlon Starling. Starling, from Hartford, had previously challenged Curry and lost, but at Columbia, South Carolina, the clever Starling knew far too much for Breland and knocked him out in the 11th round. Starling defended his title against Fujio Ozaki of Japan at Atlantic City in February 1988 with an uninspiring points win, and on 16 April 1988 gave Breland a return at the Las Vegas Hilton. In a very disappointing fight with little action, the judges marked it a draw, so Starling kept the title, most observers agreeing it did not deserve to change hands.

In July 1988 Starling lost the title in very unsatisfactory circumstances when knocked out at the end of the sixth round at Atlantic City by Tomas Molinares, the knock-out blow landing well after the bell had sounded. Till then, Starling had been well in front.

On 23 April 1988 Simon Brown of Jamaica, fighting out of Washington, stopped Tyrone Trice at the Palais des Sports, Berck-sur-Mer, France, in the 14th round to take the title the IBF had removed from Honeyghan. Brown fought a rough fight, delivering a blow or two to an opponent sitting on the canvas. His only defeat to date was inflicted by WBA champion Starling. He successfully defended against Jorge Vaca and Mauro Martelli.

***Below:** Lloyd Honeyghan being congratulated after his shock 1985 victory over champion Don Curry, previously regarded as invincible. Honeyghan stopped Curry in the sixth to become undisputed welterweight champion.*

THE LIGHT-WELTER-WEIGHTS

The light-welterweight class came into being in 1926, twice fell into disuse, and over the years has produced a few brilliant champions.

The category came into being in a unique manner. Mike Collins, the publisher of *The Boxing Blade*, managed a few boxers, one being Myron 'Pinkie' Mitchell, whose brother, Ritchie, fought Benny Leonard for the lightweight championship. Pinkie was at an awkward weight that made him too heavy for the lightweight class, and too light for the welterweight class, where he fought champion Jack Britton in a no-contest bout. So Collins announced in his paper the inauguration of a light-welterweight division, with a weight limit of 140lb (64kg), and invited his readers to vote for the first champion. Not surprisingly, Pinkie Mitchell was elected, and proclaimed champion by the publisher/ manager in November 1922.

This harmless circulation caper would have been a one-issue talking point, but an in-between class was needed, and 140lb (64kg) was a very convenient weight level. Mitchell was not seriously regarded as a champion, but on 21 September 1926 a contest between him and Mushy Callahan was recognized by the New York and NBA authorities as for the light-welterweight championship, and the division was under way. Callahan, from New York City, was only 20, and not an outstanding boxer, but he duly outpointed Mitchell, who is probably the only man ever regarded as a world champion who lost more bouts than he won.

Callahan made three successful defences, but when he decided to go to London to fight Jack 'Kid' Berg, who had already beaten him in Brooklyn, the New York authorities decided that the new weight was not one they really wanted to sponsor, and abolished the class. However, Jack 'Kid' Berg, who *was* an outstanding boxer, was recognized by the NBA when he forced Callahan to retire with an eye injury at the end of the tenth round. Lord Lonsdale, the famous boxing patron after whom the Lonsdale belts are named, stood up when the 'light-welterweight' fight was announced to protest that there was 'no such thing', a view which many boxing fans hold about all the intermediate weights.

Berg, whose real name was Judah Bergman, was born in London's East End, and became known as the 'Whitechapel Whirlwind'. He fought regularly on both sides of the Atlantic, and in the early 1930s he defended his title successfully in Newark, New York, Chicago and Detroit, before surprisingly being knocked out in the third round by Tony Canzoneri in Chicago, a man whom he had recently beaten. The match was for Canzoneri's lightweight title, but since both men were naturally inside the junior welterweight limit, Canzoneri also claimed that title, although some of Berg's subsequent fights were also advertised as being for it. Oddly enough Canzoneri officially defended successfully only twice: when he subsequently defended his lightweight title against Berg and Kid Chocolate, he specified that these contests were for the lightweight crown only, and not the light-welterweight.

Canzoneri, born in Slidell, Louisiana, was an outstanding boxer who had also been featherweight champion. He dropped the title on points to Johnny Jadick, of Philadelphia, who won it before his own supporters and who repeated the feat six months later. However, Jadick ran out of luck at New Orleans and lost a decision to Battling Shaw, from Nuevo Laredo, Mexico, who had recently based himself in New Orleans and whose real name was José Perez Flores. However, Canzoneri went to New Orleans and regained the title, beating him on points.

Canzoneri, who, while losing temporarily the light-welterweight crown, had retained his lightweight title, lost both at once on 23 June 1933 to Barney Ross. Ross, another of the division's great champions, outpointed Canzoneri over 10 rounds at Chicago. Ross defended the light-welterweight title eight times, and also beat Canzoneri again with only the lightweight title at stake. On 28 May 1935 Ross won the welterweight title in the first of his three battles with Jimmy McLarnin, and relinquished the light-welterweight title to fight as a full welterweight. The division then fell into disuse until after World War II.

An attempt to revive the championship in 1946 did not last long. Tippy Larkin (real name Antonio Pilleteri) from Garfield, New Jersey, had failed in a challenge for the lightweight title of Beau Jack, but was recognized by the Massachusetts and then the New York commissions with wins over Willie Joyce in Boston and New York; then he moved up to welterweight, lost a fight with Ike Williams and ceased to be recognized, at which the division again slumbered, this time for 13 years.

It was revived in 1959 for Carlos Ortiz and Kenny Lane, who were frustrated lightweight contenders. Ortiz won in the second round when Lane was cut at Madison Square Garden. Ortiz, a Puerto Rican, was a good champion who knocked out Battling Torres in Los Angeles and then had a series of three contests with Duilio Loi of Trieste, Italy, a good all-round boxer who had a long career as Italian and European champion at light and welterweight. Ortiz got a decision in San Francisco, and Loi two in Milan to keep the title. Ortiz returned to the lightweights for a long reign. Loi ended three contests with Eddie Perkins (drew, lost, won) still with the title, and retired.

***Above:** Tony Canzoneri (left) and Jimmy McLarnin before a light-welterweight contest on 8 May 1936. The two men fought in many divisions: Canzoneri was successively feather, light and light-welterweight champion; McLarnin was a welterweight champion.*

Roberto Cruz of the Philippines knocked out Battling Torres for the vacant title on 21 March 1963, but three months later Perkins outpointed him to regain it. Perkins, born in Clarksdale, Mississippi, won in the Philippines, Japan and Jamaica, but dropped the title to Carlos Hernandez, from Caracas, Venezuela, a strong puncher who outpointed Perkins in his home town. After two successful defences Hernandez lost in Rome to Sandro Lopopolo on a split decision, one judge making it a draw. Lopopolo, born in Milan, had been a silver medalist at the Rome Olympics. He lost the title when he left Italy to defend in Tokyo. Paul Fujii, born in Honolulu, Hawaii, but basing his career in Japan, stopped him in the second round. Fujii surprisingly retired two weeks before a match with Pedro Adigue, only to change his mind and defend against Nicolino Loche, from Mendoza, Argentina, a fast, skilful boxer, who stopped him and took his title at Tokyo. Meanwhile, the WBC had stripped Fujii on his 'retirement' and recognized Adigue, from Palanan, in the Philippines, when he outpointed Adolf Pruitt in Manila. Fujii's change of mind thus provoked a split championship, and the strands have remained separate.

Loche reigned for over three years and made five successful defences before being outpointed by Alfonso Frazer, a knock-out specialist from Panama City. He made only one successful defence, however, before handing on to the long-reigning Antonio Cervantes, of Bolívar, Colombia. Cervantes was another hard-punching boxer, who had previously unsuccessfully challenged Loche. Loche was to be one of his victims as he defended successfully no fewer than ten times in his first spell as champion. He had been champion nearly three and a half years before being outpointed by the brilliant Wilfred Benitez at San Juan, Puerto Rico.

Benitez earns a record

Benitez, in this contest, became the youngest-ever world champion at 17 years, 173 days. He made two successful defences before being stripped by the WBA for failing to give Cervantes a return. Benitez continued to be recognized by the New York authorities in 1977 when he stopped Guerrero Chavez, but he relinquished the title to move up to more success among the welterweights.

This allowed Antonio Cervantes to resume his WBA career, and he took the vacant title by stopping Carlos Giminez at Maracaibo in Venezuela. Cervantes made six more defences, taking his title to Thailand, Botswana, South Korea and Colombia before finally losing it to Aaron Pryor on a fourth-round knock-out at Cincinnati on 2 August 1980. He had won 18 title fights in the division in a period of over seven years.

Pedro Adigue, the new WBC champion in 1968, lost on his first defence to Bruno Arcari in Rome, and Arcari, from Latina, Italy, had almost as good a run as Cervantes. A southpaw, he built up an excellent record, making eight successful defences in four years before relinquishing the title with weight problems. All his defences were in Italy.

The vacant WBC title was won in 1974 by Perico Fernandez, of Zaragoza, Spain, a tough boxer with a good punch, who after one defence left his title in Bangkok, Thailand, when forced to retire against Saensak Muangsurin. Muangsurin was a Thai kick-boxer having only his third recorded bout under Queensberry Rules. He briefly dropped the title to another Spaniard, Miguel Velasquez, on a foul in Madrid, hitting him after the bell after twice having him down legitimately, but quickly won it back in Segovia. He made eight successful defences in his two periods as champion before losing finally to a South Korean, Sang-Hyun Kim, who stopped him in Seoul. Kim made two successful defences and was succeeded by Saoul Mamby, a Jamaican boxing out of New York, who had already challenged Saensak Muangsurin unsuccessfully in Thailand.

Mamby assumed the WBC title in 1980, as did Pryor the WBA, and the two ruled for the early years of the 1980s.

The 1980s have still failed to see an undisputed champion. Pryor was an outstanding champion before running into difficulties with drugs. He defended the WBA crown successfully eight times, including a stoppage of former WBC champion Sang-Hyun Kim. Perhaps his best victories were two against Alexis Arguello, a brilliant boxer who had given up world championships undefeated at three lower weights, but who could not handle Pryor. Pryor gave up the WBA title because of his well-publicized drug problem, but within months returned to fight for the new IBF title, which he won with a points victory over Nicky Furlano in Toronto. After one defence in 1985 he forfeited the title through inactivity, and retired with a 100 per cent record after 36 bouts. He was a strong, crashing, all-action fighter who might have become one of the all-time greats.

On Pryor giving up the WBA title, Johnny Bumphus, from Tacoma, won it but immediately dropped it to Gene Hatcher. He made one successful defence, against Ubaldo Sacco, but then lost the title to him, only for Sacco to pass it on to Patrizio Oliva of Naples, Italy.

Oliva won the light-welterweight gold medal at the 1980 Moscow Olympics, and was a polished professional, who successfully defended twice in Italy before being knocked out in the third round at Ribera by Juan Coggi, from Rosario, Argentina. It was Oliva's first defeat in his 49 contests, and he retired. Coggi defended successfully in May 1988 against Sang-Ho Lee of South Korea.

Saoul Mamby, meanwhile, made five successful WBC defences, before being outpointed in June 1982 by Leroy Haley, from Las Vegas, who repeated the feat before he was outpointed in turn by Bruce Curry, the older brother of the welterweight champion.

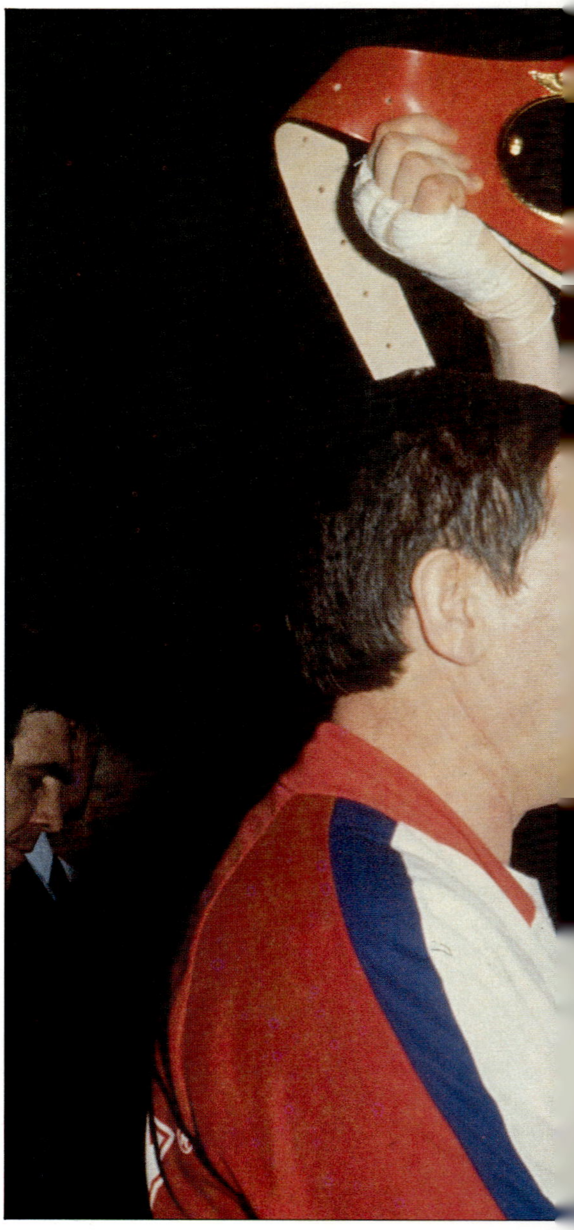

Curry, after defending in Japan, beat Haley again but was then stopped by Bill Costello, from New York, whose three successful defences included points wins over former champions Mamby and Haley. Costello was stopped by the unbeaten Lonnie Smith of Denver. But in May 1986 Smith was stopped in his first defence by Rene Arredondo, from Apatzingán, Mexico, the brother of the former WBC junior lightweight champion Ricardo Arredondo. He lost on his first defence when knocked out in the first round in Tokyo by Tsuyoshi Hamada, from Nagagusuku. After a successful defence in Tokyo, Hamada dropped the title when Arredondo won it back by going to Tokyo and stopping the champion, who suffered cuts in the sixth.

Four months later Arredondo lost the championship to Roger Mayweather, from Grand Rapids, a former junior lightweight champion. Mayweather carried the title into 1988 with a knock-out of Mauricio Aceves of Mexico in Los Angeles in March, and a points win over American Harold Brazier of South Bend, at Las Vegas in June. Rodolfo Gonzales and Vinny Pazienza were further 1988 victims.

After Pryor had inaugurated the IBF championship and retired, his last victim, Gary Hinton, of Philadelphia, won the vacant title by outpointing Antonio Reyes Cruz, from the Dominican Republic, at Lucca, Italy. In October 1986 Hinton was knocked out by Joe Manley, of Lima, but he held the title only four months before being stopped by Terry Marsh, of Basildon, Essex, the British champion. Marsh was a colourful character who won the title in a huge circus tent in his home town. Although unbeaten as a boxer, he preferred to retain his job as a fireman than to box full time. He made a successful defence in July 1987, stopping Akio Kameda, of Japan, at the Albert Hall, London, but then revealed that he had epilepsy, and retired.

Marsh's next challenger was to have been Frankie Warren, who was paired with James McGirt of New York for the vacant title. It was a surprise when McGirt, who had been outpointed by Warren in 1986, stopped him in the 12th round in February 1988. McGirt beat Howard Davis, but was then stopped by Meldrick Taylor of Philadelphia.

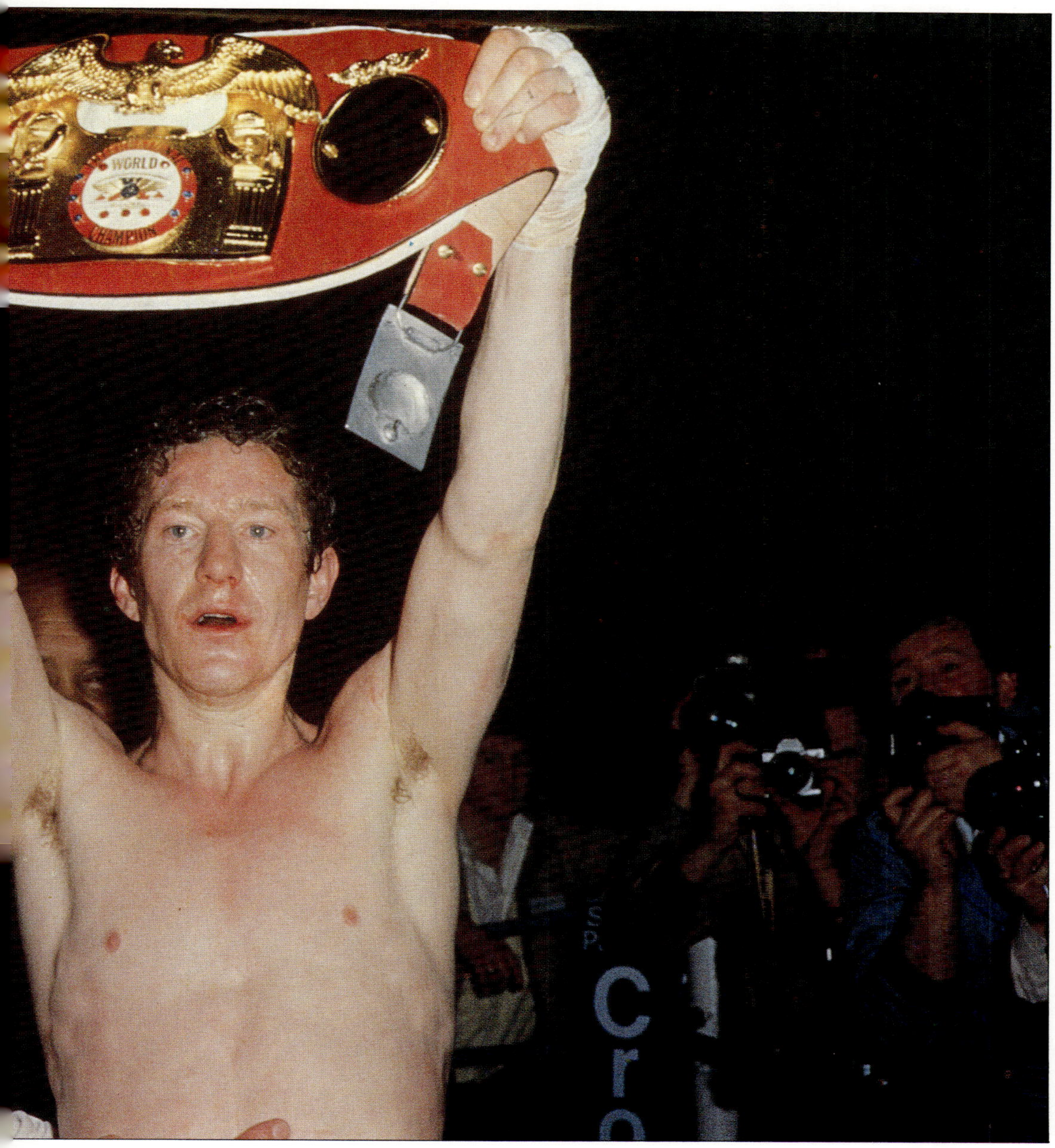

Left: *Terry Marsh, the Essex fireman, celebrates his world title win over Joe Manley in 1987 by holding up his new IBF belt. Marsh was forced to retire with epilepsy as the unbeaten world light-welterweight champion.*

USA SPORTS
USA SPORTS

The Lightweights and Junior Lightweights

The lightweight division is one where outstanding skill and finesse live side-by-side with legalized brutality, making this class one of the most diverse. Sometimes the ultra-skilful boxer has been contemporary with the most macho fighter, and some memorable conflicts have ensued. The elegant Joe Gans and the well-named Battling Nelson made one such match. The brilliant Ken Buchanan and the fire-eating Roberto Duran made another. Ad Wolgast, Tony Canzoneri and Hector 'Macho' Camacho were among those who breathed aggression, Willie Ritchie, Joe Brown and Jim Watt were of the skilful breed, while some of the best — Freddy Welsh, Benny Leonard and Alexis Arguello — could box and scrap with equal facility.

***Left:** Roberto Duran towards the end of a career which went on and on. Duran won world titles at three weights but was at his best as a lightweight, where he was a champion from 1972 until he relinquished the title because of weight difficulties in 1978.*

THE CLASS WHERE ANYTHING GOES

In bare-knuckle days, 'lightweight' was probably the first of the class divisions, as we know them now, to be named. The heavyweight champion would have been known as just the champion. When smaller men began to proclaim they could beat the best of their weight, they would be called 'lightweight' champions. In the 1790s Caleb Baldwin was regarded as the lightweight champion, and in turn Dutch Sam (Samuel Elias), his only conqueror, might have claimed the title as he never weighed more than 135lb (61kg). Jack Randall, the 'Nonpareil', was regarded as the lightweight champion around 1815, and others who followed were Dick Curtis, Barney Aaron, Sam Collyer, Owney Geoghan and Abe Hicken.

In more modern days the first lightweight champion is sometimes given as Arthur Chambers, after he had beaten another Englishman, Billy Edwards, on a disqualification at Squirrel Island, Canada. Chambers won an elimination contest after Abe Hicken, who claimed the American title, retired. When Chambers retired, Nonpareil Jack Dempsey claimed he was lightweight champion, but established a better claim to be middleweight champion, backing his friend Jack McAuliffe as the lightweight king. McAuliffe was regarded as the best in America, so when Jem Carney, the best in Britain, went to Revere, Massachusetts, to fight him, the fight was designated as for the world championship, and this is regarded, by some experts, as the first genuine world middleweight title bout, but the men did not wear gloves as the Queensberry Rules required.

McAuliffe, from Cork, Ireland, weighed 126lb (57kg), and Carney, from Birmingham, 129lb (59kg). After elaborate precautions to get the crowd assembled within a barn without the police noticing, a savage bout took place, lasting 74 rounds, when Carney, having had McAuliffe down in the 70th, was about to finish him off. Unfortunately for him, a St Louis gambler had backed McAuliffe and stood to lose a fortune and he and his friends proceeded to disrupt the fight and force the referee to call it a draw, so Carney was never acknowledged as a world champion.

McAuliffe was luckier, of course, being based in America, and he was held to have made further 'defences' after this 'draw' and took part in the three-day 'Carnival of Champions' which ended with James J. Corbett becoming the world heavyweight champion. On the first day McAuliffe 'retained' his title. McAuliffe was an excellent boxer, one of the few to go through a career unbeaten, so the gambler's intervention was particularly significant for him.

After the goings on in Revere in 1887 it was not until 1896 that a second world lightweight title fight was generally recognized. On this occasion it was the American champion, George 'Kid' Lavigne, who journeyed to London to meet the British champion, Dick Burge. This was the first lightweight world title fight with gloves. Lavigne, a French Canadian from Bay City, Michigan, was known as the 'Saginaw Kid', after his base, while Burge, from Cheltenham, was the conqueror of Carney. The fight was at the National Sporting Club, and Lavigne won a 17th-round knock-out. Burge gained extra fame as a promoter at the famous Blackfriars Ring in London. Lavigne made five successful defences, the best win being over the ex-welterweight champion Joe Walcott, who retired by agreement on being unable to knock out Lavigne in 12 rounds. Lavigne also drew with Frank Erne from Zurich, Switzerland, who boxed in New York, over 20 rounds, but in 1899 Erne took his title with a 20-round points win.

Erne, a clever upstanding boxer, made two defences, one a 12th-round stoppage of Joe Gans, from Baltimore, Maryland. Gans, known as the 'Old Master', received a cut eye and immediately asked the referee if he could quit, a mysterious request, as he appeared in little distress. Less than two months later Gans knocked out Erne in the first minute to take the title, causing considerable talk. It is generally held that Gans, like all black boxers of the period, was forced to throw an occasional fight to keep in business.

In the next two and a half years Gans had a winning run of 16 defences, dominating the division. He was so superior that in 1902 Jimmy Britt claimed a 'white lightweight championship' on beating Frank Erne but Gans so thoroughly beat Britt in San Francisco that Britt preferred to strike low and accept disqualification in the 20th round rather than be knocked out.

Tex Rickard begins business

Britt was knocked out by a Dane, 'Battling' Nelson, in September 1905, which led the greatest of all fight promoters, Tex Rickard, to enter the business. A gambling saloon proprietor in Goldfield, Nevada, he was asked how to put Goldfield, a prosperous mining town, on the map. Rickard went ahead and did it by promoting the lightweight championship of the world between the black holder and the white pretender.

Rickard put the unheard of lightweight purse of 30,000 dollars of gold in his window, for the press to photograph, built a huge wooden stadium and publicized the fight shrewdly as a racist battle. The whole plan worked. Goldfield became famous, and

Rickard made a profit and went on to his huge promotions of the 1920s.

Nelson, from Copenhagen, who used to claim that 'Battling' was one of his real names, was a tremendously tough (and rough) fighter, who was also called the 'Durable Dane'. He gave Gans a tremendous scrap, but Gans' superior skill finally got on top. Nelson became so frustrated that in the 42nd round — the longest world title bout under Queensberry Rules — Nelson hit Gans so low his disqualification was immediate and unchallenged.

Gans made four more defences before facing Nelson again in San Francisco in 1908. Gans was now 33, and having difficulty making the weight. He was probably also suffering from the consumption which killed him two years later. Nelson's style of constantly boring forward gave the Old Master no rest, and he was knocked out in the 17th round. He suffered a 21st-round knock-out in the return.

Nelson, undisputed champion at last, made two defences and then ran into a man as aggressive and tough as himself — and also one with as little regard for the rules. He was Ad Wolgast, from Cadillac, Michigan. Their fight was as foul-filled as any seen in the history of boxing. While each gave as good as he got in the line of dubious fighting, Wolgast just had the edge overall, and the referee finally stopped the bout in his favour in the 40th round.

Wolgast made six successful defences, his toughest being against the unlucky Birmingham boxer Owen Moran, who twice had fought draws for the world featherweight title, when many thought he might have been given the verdict. He was knocked out in the 13th round when trying at the heavier weight, but only by a typical Wolgast blow that had him clutching his stomach well below the belt region as he writhed on the canvas in agony.

The 'double knock-out'

Wolgast's next and last successful defence had one of the most bizarre endings to a world title fight ever seen. Wolgast's opponent was Mexican Joe Rivers, based at Los Angeles, and in the 13th round of a furious contest each landed simultaneously with crushing blows — Rivers with a left hook to the chin and Wolgast with an uppercut that came from the floor and to many seemed to get no higher than the groin before thudding into Rivers. Both men went down for what could have been the count for either. But referee Jack Welch, who had officiated in the Moran fight, favoured Wolgast again to the extent of helping him to his feet and almost propping him up while he completed the count on Rivers. The fight has gone into the records as the 'double knock-out'. A riot ensued after the referee's behaviour.

Wolgast's reign came to an end in perhaps the inevitable manner in his next defence against Willie Ritchie. Ritchie was a clever boxer from San Francisco, who in his home town held his own to the 16th round with Wolgast, who was then disqualified for two

Tex Rickard (above left) was probably the most successful of all boxing promoters. He began his career in boxing by promoting the 1906 world lightweight title clash between the black Joe Gans and the 'Durable Dane' Battling Nelson (above). Nelson lost but was later to become champion, while Rickard promoted the great Dempsey fights at the Madison Square Garden in the 1920s.

low blows. His biggest mistake was probably not to have Welch as referee for once.

Ritchie defended twice successfully, firstly against the hard-done-by Mexican Joe Rivers, whom he knocked out.

Meanwhile, the National Sporting Club in London had set limits for the eight standard championship weights, the lightweight being set at 135lb (61kg). When Freddie Welsh drew with Packy McFarland of the USA in London on 30 May 1910, the fight had been announced as for the world title, and when he outpointed Hughie Mehegan of Australia at this weight at Olympia, London, on 16 December 1912, the NSC recognized Welsh as world champion. In America, the weight class had been limited to 133lb (60kg). Welsh's claims were enhanced by the fact that he had beaten Ritchie in America in 1911, and, in fact, had been avoided by previous champions Gans, Nelson and Wolgast.

Welsh enticed Ritchie to come to Olympia, London, to settle matters on 7 July 1916, by fighting for nothing. The theatrical impresario Charles B. Cochran achieved the match by promising Ritchie £5,000. Both men were extremely good all-rounders (the term 'box-fighters' was coined to describe a man good at everything) and their 20-round scrap paraded all the skills, Welsh getting the narrowest of points verdicts to be undisputed champion.

Welsh, from Pontypridd, whose real name was Frederick Hall Thomas, immediately returned to the USA to campaign, and held the title for nearly three years, during which time he beat, on a disqualification, Ad Wolgast. Many of Welsh's defences were no-decision affairs, however, and it was in one of these that he lost his title. He was knocked out by Benny Leonard, another of the legendary lightweights, at the Manhattan Casino, New York, on 28 May 1917. Welsh had had the edge in two previous no-decision contests, so the result was a surprise, but Leonard was to become one of the greatest champions in any division, and perhaps the greatest of all Jewish champions.

Born Benjamin Leiner, in New York, he was a clever boxer who also possessed a good punch, more than once coming back from the brink of defeat to win title fights with his punching power. Three of the most remarkable of these were against Charley White, who knocked him out of the ring, Richie Mitchell, who had him dazed, and Lew Tendler. After seven successful defences spread over six years Leonard retired in 1923, while still champion.

The New York authorities recognized Jimmy Goodrich as champion in July 1925 when he won an elimination competition, his final opponent, Stanislaus Loayza, breaking an ankle in the first round and retiring in the second. Goodrich (real name James Noran) from Scranton, Pennsylvania, was succeeded by Rocky Kansas, from Buffalo, New York, after five months, but he reigned only for seven, being outpointed by Sammy Mandell, who hailed from Rockford, Illinois.

Mandell was an apparently indestructible puncher, who reigned for four years, and beat outstanding men in Tony Canzoneri, a future champion, and Jimmy McLarnin, who went on to take the welterweight title.

Canzoneri gained the crown by way of Al Singer, a hard-hitting New Yorker, who knocked out Mandell in 106 seconds at Madison Square Garden, but who, after losing in a non-title fight to McLarnin, lost the title four months later by being knocked out by Canzoneri in 66 seconds, a unique double.

This was Canzoneri's second world title. He had been featherweight champion and was to succeed also at light-welterweight. He was 22 when he won the crown, and he defended against Jack 'Kid' Berg (from whom he incidentally took the light-welterweight crown), Kid Chocolate and Billy Petrolle, three top-class fighters, before dropping the title to a fourth, Barney Ross. Ross was also to win at three weights, but he began at lightweight, and took Canzoneri's title with two points wins before moving upwards. Canzoneri regained the title by outpointing Lou Ambers for the vacant championship, but after one more defence he lost two points verdicts to Ambers, who took over.

Ambers (real name Louis d'Ambrosio), from Herkimer, New York, was a popular, tough two-fisted boxer who held the title for 15 months before losing it to the great Henry Armstrong, who thus won his third world title. Armstrong remains the only boxer to hold three world titles simultaneously, and one of only two (Fitzsimmons being the other) to hold world titles at three of the 'classic' eight divisions as set out by the National Sporting Club in 1909. Despite Ambers being down twice, the verdict was a split decision, Armstrong getting it by the closest of margins. A year later, at the Yankee Stadium, Ambers regained the title with a unanimous decision, Armstrong losing points for repeated foul blows.

The championship became split for nearly two years when Ambers was stripped by the NBA for refusing to meet Davey Day, whom he had outpointed three years earlier. Day was outpointed by Sammy Angott for their vacant title. Angott unified the title in 1941 by outpointing Lew Jenkins, who had stopped Ambers for the New York version in 1940. Angott (real name Engotti, from Washington) had an unpopular style, being fond of holding after landing a blow to prevent a counter. He surprised the boxing world by retiring in 1942, when only 28 years old. 'The Clutch' made a comeback after a year or two, but meanwhile the championship had again been split, and remained so until after the war.

New York was first to name a champion, when Beau Jack, born Sidney Walker in Augusta, Georgia, beat Tippy Larkin, a future light-welterweight champion. Jack, a shoe-shine boy who had joined a boys' club and learned to box, dropped his title to Bob Montgomery, from Sumter, South Carolina, won it back but then lost it to him again.

The Maryland commission named Slugger White, who beat Willie Joyce in Baltimore, as champion, and when Sammy Angott returned to outpoint White in Los Angeles, Angott was recognized by the NBA once more. Angott lost the NBA title to Juan Zarita, a veteran from Guadalajara, who became only the second Mexican boxer to win a world title. Zarita was knocked out by Ike Williams, from Brunswick, Georgia, in 1945, and after he and the New York champion Bob Montgomery had each defended a few times, they met at Philadelphia in August 1947 to reunify the title, Williams winning by a sixth-round knock-out.

Ike Williams kept the undisputed title for over three years before being stopped in the 14th round by Jimmy Carter on 25 May 1951. Williams had been knocked out of the ring in the 10th round.

Carter, from Aiken, South Carolina, but based in New York, was a busy boxer who, having outpointed Lauro Salas of Monterrey, Mexico, another busy fighter, in 1952, dropped the title to him a month later only to regain it by the end of the year in a rubber match. In 1954 Paddy de Marco, from Brooklyn, outpointed Carter but again Carter won it back eight months later in San Francisco. Carter dropped the title a third time in 1955 to Wallace 'Bud' Smith, and this time the rematch later in the year produced the same result — a points victory for Smith.

Smith, from Cincinnati, lost his first defence in 1956, however, to a man who was to become one of the division's best champions, Joe Brown. Brown, from New Orleans, Louisiana, was 30 when he at last got the chance of the title, and was already styled 'Old Bones'. He was tall for a lightweight, and had a long reach, but unlike many lanky boxers could also punch. In fact, his first four challengers, including Smith, were all stopped. His most meritorious wins were against Ralph Dupas, a future light-middleweight champion, Kenny Lane and European champion Dave Charnley, whom he beat twice, on the second occasion in London on a decision that many disagreed with. Brown eventually lost his title in his 12th defence (he was then nearly 36) to another of the division's best titleholders, Carlos Ortiz.

Ortiz, a Puerto Rican boxing from New York, had previously been holder of the light-welterweight title, beating Kenny Lane, one of Brown's unsuccessful challengers. Having lost that title in two fights with Duilio Loi in 1960 and 1961, Ortiz stepped down a weight and easily outpointed the ageing Brown in Las Vegas on 21 April 1962. Ortiz made four successful defences, including one in Tokyo, before underestimating Ismael Laguna, a smart boxer from Panama, dropping the title to him on a split decision in April 1965. However, Ortiz won it back in the return seven months later, while Ismael Laguna's

Left: *Bob Montgomery (on the left) taking the title from Beau Jack in 1944. It was the third contest between them, Montgomery having taken Jack's title in 1943 and Jack having won it back again later that year.*

turn was to come again in five years' time.

A curious Ortiz defence was against Sugar Ramos, of Matanzas, in Cuba, the hard-punching former featherweight champion, who three years earlier had been concerned in the featherweight contest following which Davey Moore had died. Referee Billy Conn (the man who nearly beat Louis) stopped the fight in Ortiz's favour in the fifth round, with Ramos badly cut. However, the Mexico City crowd rioted, and the WBC official, Ramon Velasquez, ordered the fight to continue. When Ortiz refused, Velasquez named Ramos the champion. This decision was cancelled on 48 hours' reflection, the WBC commanding the two boxers to meet in a return for the vacant title. After having disposed of Flash Elorde in the meantime, Ortiz stopped Ramos again and regained undisputed recognition.

Ortiz's fine run came to an end on 29 June 1968, when after 11 title fight victories he was outpointed at Santo Domingo by Carlo Teo Cruz, of the Dominican Republic. Cruz was a fast boxer, but not outstanding, and after outpointing Mando Ramos, he was stopped by him in a return in Los Angeles. Cruz was killed in an air crash in 1970 when looking forward to a rubber match with Ramos.

Ramos, from Long Beach, California, was a popular puncher based in Los Angeles, and was only 20 when he won the title. He beat Yoshiaki Numata, the junior lightweight champion, but lost his crown when forced to retire after the ninth round against Ismael Laguna, both his eyes being cut.

Laguna, from Colón, Panama, was thus winning the title for a second time, but he managed only one successful defence, against Ishimatsu Suzuki (who was to change his name to Guts Ishimatsu) before being outpointed by the brilliant Scottish boxer, Ken Buchanan. Buchanan, from Edinburgh, was put in a strange position by this victory. Because the WBC wanted Laguna to give Ramos a return, they did not recognize this title fight. The WBA did, but as the British Board of Control was not affiliated at the time to the WBA, they could not recognize Buchanan either. So Britain's first lightweight champion since Freddie Welsh was for a time not recognized in his own country. A contest between Buchanan and Ramos was arranged to clear up the discrepancy, but Ramos was forced to withdraw at the last minute. Ruben Navarro was named as substitute, and when Buchanan outpointed him, he was recognized universally as champion.

It was not, however, the end of his troubles. Buchanan naturally awarded a rematch to Laguna, but by now the WBC's leading challenger was Pedro Carrasco, of Huelva, Spain, the former European champion, so Buchanan was stripped of the WBC version. The odd situation now was that the BBBC, who were affiliated with the WBC, should have followed suit and withdrawn recognition from Buchanan also. But, having come in for enough press and public criticism for their earlier decision, they now threw logic out of the window and continued to recognize Buchanan, thus perhaps expressing the right opinion of the 'alphabet boys'.

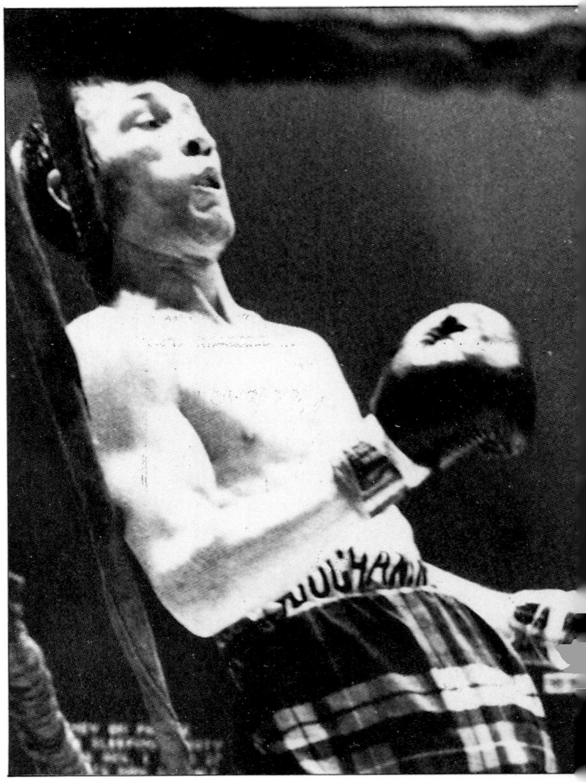

Roberto Duran the Macho Man

Sadly, what happened next was that Buchanan, who put up a superb performance to repeat his win over Laguna despite a badly cut eye, lost the WBA title on his next defence to the rough, tough Roberto Duran, of Panama. The direction his future career would take was signposted by a swaggering, no-fouls barred display that won him a stoppage at the end of the 13th round, with Buchanan unable to continue after a blow which he claimed was: (a) so low it was in the groin and (b) was delivered after the bell.

The Madison Square Garden receipts were a record for lightweights — Buchanan had impressed them earlier with his superb skill, and Duran had impressed them with his machismo. What was particularly galling for Buchanan was that Duran refused him a return, for which he was merely admonished.

Carrasco duly won the vacant WBC title when Mando Ramos was disqualified in the 11th round for persistent high and low blows — below the belt and on the top of the head — but Ramos won two subsequent points decisions in Los Angeles and Madrid. All three contests had their controversies. The referee's decision in the first was considered by the WBC to be perverse, so they ordered the rematch. They then ordered the third bout on the grounds that the split decision in the second had been influenced by Ramos' home supporters. Then the Spaniards objected to the third decision: (a) because they thought it a bad decision and (b) because they claimed a drug test on Ramos was positive. Be that as

it may, the WBC and WBA now had separate champions, a state of affairs which got even worse in the 1980s when the IBF recognized a third champion.

While Duran ruled the WBA championship for five and a half years, the WBC champions were much less stable. Ramos avoided a possible fourth meeting with Carrasco (who retired in disgust) by being stopped by Chango Carmona, a hard-punching fighter from Mexico City. Indeed Ramos needed hospital care afterwards. Carmona himself was champion for less than two months, as Rudolfo Gonzalez stopped him in the 12th in Los Angeles.

Gonzalez, from Jalisco in Mexico, was a knockout specialist who won most of his contests by the short route. He remained champion for 18 months, successfully defending twice before being knocked out in the eighth by Guts Ishimatsu, who had previously challenged Laguna and Duran. Ishimatsu held the title for just over two years, making five successful defences, the most notable being against ex-champion Ken Buchanan, whom he outpointed in Tokyo. He was himself outpointed in May 1976 by Esteban de Jesus, from Carolina, Puerto Rico. De Jesus was an aggressive boxer who carried a good punch in each hand, and who had previously unsuccessfully challenged Duran (and also Antonio Cervantes for the light-welterweight title). He made three defences before his admiring fans in Puerto Rico before taking on Roberto Duran in a contest to unify the title.

All this time Duran, the WBA champion, who had been only ten days older than 21 when winning the title from Buchanan, had made 11 defences, only the last of which, against Edwin Viruet, had gone the distance. He had stopped both Guts Ishimatsu and Esteban de Jesus, two men who had then gone on to win the WBC title. So Duran, who appeared supreme at this weight, was a firm favourite to beat de Jesus again when the two champions met at Las Vegas. De Jesus' best hope arose from the fact that in 1972 he had beaten Duran, the only boxer to have beaten him at the time. Duran, however, was now a different proposition, and he knocked out de Jesus in the 12th round.

Unfortunately, Duran had been finding it increasingly difficult to make the weight, and having unified the title at last, he relinquished it at the end of 1978 to move up to the welterweight class.

Each ruling body named a different champion, of course. For the WBC it was Jim Watt, a clever Scottish southpaw, who after years in the shadow of Buchanan, had almost retired, but now found a chance arriving at the age of nearly 31, and took it, stopping Alfredo Pitalua in the 12th round before his own supporters in the Kelvin Hall, Glasgow. This was to be the venue of four stirring title defences which thrilled the Glasgow audiences. Watt's last successful defence was against Sean O'Grady, who ironically had become WBA champion before Watt lost his crown on his next defence.

The WBA's new champion on the retirement from the division of Duran had been Ernesto Espana, from La Flor, Venezuela, who knocked out Claude Noel, the Trinidadian Commonwealth champion, at San Juan, Puerto Rico. One successful defence had led to a stoppage by Hilmer Kenty, who was born in Austin, Texas, but fought out of Detroit. Kenty made three successful defences before Sean O'Grady outpointed him at Atlantic City.

Above: *The end of the 13th round in the classic boxer v fighter lightweight title clash of 1972. Champion Ken Buchanan sways against the ropes (left) as challenger Roberto Duran bores in. The round ended with the referee (right) trying to pull Duran off as he piled into Buchanan, some punches landing low. Buchanan was unable to come out for the 14th round.*

O'Grady was a good puncher from Oklahoma City who was managed by his father. Unfortunately, having won the crown with only two defeats, he forfeited it as his father, who nursed him carefully, was unwilling to take WBA instruction on the logical contenders.

The WBC strand of the championship was much the stronger at this time because Watt's conqueror had been Alexis Arguello, from Managua, Nicaragua, one of the outstanding boxers of the 1970s and early 1980s. He had been featherweight and junior lightweight champion, relinquishing both titles to take on the lightweight, and he outfought Watt to take the title on a unanimous decision at Wembley on 20 June 1981.

Arguello made four successful defences, all inside-the-distance wins, before relinquishing the title in 1983 to move up to light-welterweight, where at last his run had to end. He was clearly the best lightweight in the world, as at the time of his retirement from the division, the WBA champion was Ray Mancini, whom he had stopped at Atlantic City on his first defence.

Mancini had acquired the WBA title by knocking out Arturo Frias in the first round. Frias, from Montebello, California, had himself won it from Claude Noel, who had become WBA champion when O'Grady had been deposed. Mancini, from Youngstown, Ohio, was an exciting all-or-nothing fighter, whose fights were always likely to be short ones. He became one of the television fans' favourites and earned himself the nickname of 'Boom Boom'. Although his title victory was won in the first round, he himself had been floored and groggy. His first winning defence was against Ernesto Espana, a former champion, and his second against Deuk-Koo Kim, who sadly did not regain consciousness after a 14th-round stoppage. He also stopped Orlando Romero and Bobby Chacon, the former junior lightweight champion. He was finally beaten by Livingstone Bramble, who was born in St Croix, in the Virgin Islands, but fought out of Atlantic City. Bramble, who at the time sported the dreadlock hairstyle, was a fast puncher who stopped Mancini in the 14th at Buffalo in June 1984 and then outpointed him in a return eight months later in Reno. Bramble stopped Tyrone Crawley before being knocked out by Edwin Rosario, of Santurce, Puerto Rico, in the second round at Miami. The fight was on the same bill as the WBC title fight, and Bramble and the WBC champion, Hector Camacho, were both expected to win and set up a profitable unification bout, so Rosario's win was a big upset.

Rosario had already been WBC champion, having won the crown when Arguello relinquished it in 1983. He had outpointed José Luis Ramirez, from Huatabampo, Mexico. He had stopped Roberto Elizondo and outpointed Howard Davis, two men who had previously challenged unsuccessfully, but had then been stopped by Ramirez in the fourth round at San Juan, Puerto Rico. Ramirez at the time had the excellent record of having been beaten only four times in 93 fights, all four defeats by world champions: Ruben Olivares, Alexis Arguello, Ray Mancini and Edwin Rosario.

Ramirez lost the title to Hector Camacho, whose nickname did not need much inventing — 'Macho' Camacho. Born at Bayanion, Puerto Rico, but based in New York, he was an excellent boxer who could also punch, and had relinquished the junior lightweight title to challenge for the lightweight crown. Camacho outpointed Ramirez in an exciting 12-rounder at Las Vegas.

Camacho's first defence was another points win over Rosario, a split decision which was much resented by the loser, and his second was another points win over Cornelius Bosa-Edwards, a former junior lightweight champion (this was the night in September 1986 already mentioned, when Rosario became WBA champion). Camacho then relinquished the title because of weight difficulties to move up to light-welterweight.

Meanwhile, the IBF had recognized a champion. On 30 January 1984, Charlie 'Choo Choo' Brown beat Melvin Paul at Atlantic City for the IBF laurels, but he lost on his first defence to Harry Arroyo. Arroyo stopped Charlie 'White Lightning' Brown (a second lightweight Charlie Brown) and Terence Alli, but was outpointed by Jimmy Paul (a second lightweight Paul). Paul looked impressive in three defences before being outpointed on 5 December 1986 by the unbeaten Greg Haugen from Washington.

The lightweight division was in a transitional stage as 1987 began, therefore, with new champions representing the WBA and IBF, and the WBC not having a champion.

The IBF champion did not last long, for Haugen was beaten on his first defence by Vinny Pazienza, from Cranston, Rhode Island, who outpointed him in a very close match before his own supporters at Providence, Rhode Island. But Haugen regained the title in a dazzling display against a brave opponent at Atlantic City on 6 February 1988.

Haugen retained his title on 11 April 1988 after a remarkable reversed decision at Tacoma, Washington. His challenger was Miguel Santana from Puerto Rico. In the 11th round of a close, hard-fought contest, there was a bad clash of heads, and Haugen, with bad cuts over each eye, could not continue. Referee Jack Cassidy awarded the fight to Santana. However, 20 minutes later, the Washington State Boxing commissioner, Jimmy Rondeau, also the IBF vice-president, ruled that as the cut was the result of an unintentional butt, the result must be based on the score cards. Two judges had 106-103 for Haugen, while the third had 106-103 for Santana. So Haugen was named as the champion, but there was naturally much dissatisfaction with the verdict.

Chavez enters the Lightweights

The new WBA champion did not last through 1987 either, as Edwin Rosario, after knocking out Juan Nazario in August, met one of the rising stars of the late 1980s in Julio Cesar Chavez, from Culiacán, Mexico. The good-looking boxer with the big punch had moved up from the junior middleweight division where he had reigned as WBC champion for over three years and in one of the most anticipated lightweight fights for many a year he battered the brave Rosario so that the referee was forced to step in, in the 11th round. That Chavez was a star at his new weight was emphasized when he stopped Rodolfo Aguilar from Panama in the eighth round at the Hilton Center, Las Vegas. The 6ft (1.83m) Aguilar could not handle the 5ft 7in (1.70m) Chavez's punching power.

The only champion to reign through 1987 was the new WBC king, who turned out to be José Luis Ramirez, who outpointed Terrence Alli after a good hard contest at St Tropez, France, on 19 June 1987 for the title vacated by Camacho. Ramirez's first defence, on 12 March 1988, was extremely controversial. He had made France his base, and was defending in Paris against Pernell Whitaker, the 1984 Olympic champion, a fast boxer with an unbeaten run of 12 wins. Whitaker, from Norfolk, claimed after the fight to have a broken a bone in his left hand in the fourth round, but he boxed brilliantly for all that, catching Ramirez, the aggressor, with numerous punches throughout the fight. At the end one judge (former British referee Harry Gibbs) awarded the fight to Whitaker, but the other two gave it to Ramirez. The decision caused booing at the time, and *Ring* magazine called it outrageous. It caused much discussion later, but the veteran Ramirez still had his title.

However, on 29 October 1988 the WBC and WBA champions met, and Julio Cesar Chavez took both titles with a technical decision over Ramirez. A clash of heads in the 11th round left Ramirez unable to continue, and Chavez was declared the winner after the scorecards had been added up.

Above: Two stalwarts of the lightweight division in the 1980s battling for the title in 1986. Hector 'Macho' Camacho, left, took a 12-round decision over former champion Edwin Rosario, but Rosario won the title again when Camacho moved up to light-welterweight.

Left: Jim Watt (on the right) followed Ken Buchanan as a good Scottish lightweight world champion, but after exciting defences in Glasgow he was outpointed at Wembley by the outstanding Alexis Arguello, who won a world title at a third weight.

JUNIOR LIGHT-WEIGHTS

The junior lightweight class, now with a limit of 130lb (59kg), was started in 1921 by the New York boxing commission, but had some false starts — New York abolished it in 1929, and the whole weight class fell into disuse in 1933 and was not fully operative until 1959. The WBC call it the super-featherweight class.

When New York set the ball rolling, the first champion was Johnny Dundee (no relation to two later world champions, Vince and Joe — in fact Dundee was not the real name of any). Johnny Dundee was born Guiseppe Corrara in Sciacca, Italy, and was, because of the choice of boxing name by his Scottish manager, called 'The Scotch Wop', a nickname which stuck. He won the title through a fifth-round foul by George 'KO' Chaney, and defended successfully three times before losing it temporarily to Jack Bernstein, a routine boxer from New York, whose real name was John Dodick. With Bernstein's win the NBA also recognized the division, so the title could be called 'undisputed', although Britain and Europe were not to recognize the division for many years. Dundee won the title back but was finally beaten by Steve 'Kid' Sullivan from Brooklyn, another fighter with a comparatively poor record. His successor, Mike Ballerino, from Ashbury Park, New Jersey, was another nondescript champion but Tod Morgan, who beat him, was a little better, if only because he managed 11 successful defences. His real name was Bert Pilkington, and he came from Seattle, having over 200 fights in a 21-year career, but he lost a lot.

Benny Bass, who beat him, was born in Kiev, Russia, and boxed out of Philadelphia. Naturally, he was known as 'The Fish'. As betting money had made Bass a 5-1 on favourite, and he won with a second-round knockout, there were deep suspicions about this fight, which was investigated by the New York commission while both boxers' purses were withheld. Both boxers were cleared, but New York decided not to recognize the division any more. Two years later Morgan went to Australia to continue his career.

Bass made two successful defences but was then stopped by Kid Chocolate. Chocolate, whose real name was Eligio Sardinias, was from Cerro, in Cuba, and was a brilliant boxer with a good punch. He had title fights for all the championships from feather to light-welter, and held the featherweight and junior lightweight titles simultaneously. Surprisingly, he lost the junior lightweight crown to Frankie Klick, from San Francisco, on a seventh-round stoppage. Klick relinquished the title to fight as a light-welterweight and the division failed through apathy.

The Ohio boxing commission attempted to revive it in 1949, giving Sandy Saddler the title after a defeat of Orlando Zulueta, but it was not a happy revival because Saddler's only defence sparked a riot when the crowd thought his win over Lauro Salar had been achieved with a foul blow. Saddler then regained his featherweight title and the junior lightweight category again disappeared.

The NBA revived the title once more in 1959, the first champion being Harold Gomes, from Providence, Rhode Island, who outpointed a Texan, Paul Jorgensen, in his home town. However, he was stopped on 16 March 1960 by Gabriel 'Flash' Elorde from Bogo, in the Philippines. The brilliant new champion held the title for over seven years and really established the division for good. In 1964 he stopped Teruo Kosaka in Tokyo, and when he knocked out the same boxer in the return in Quezon City, the WBC also recognized the division. In the next few years Britain and Europe followed suit.

Flash Elorde lost the title at last on another visit to Tokyo, when he was outpointed by Yoshiaki Numata, from Hokkaidō, on a split decision.

Numata was knocked out in his first defence by his countryman, Hiroshi Kobayashi. Kobayashi drew on his first defence, with Rene Barrientos, of Balite, in the Philippines, in a decision in which two of the Tokyo judges marked it a draw and the other gave it to Barrientos. After Kobayashi had beaten James Valladeres, also in Tokyo, he lost WBC recognition for failing to give Rene Barrientos a return.

Barrientos was matched against Ruben Navarro, the Los Angeles-based Mexican, for the WBC crown and won a unanimous decision, but Barrientos then travelled to Tokyo again and was beaten by the former champion Yoshiaki Numata on a split decision, two judges giving it to Numata by a point, the other to Barrientos by three points. When Numata beat Barrientos again by another split decision, Barrientos retired.

So both strands of the championship were held by Japanese boxers, and they continued to defend, exclusively in Japan, until both were beaten in 1971. Kobayashi was forced to retire in the tenth round by Alfredo Marcano, from Sucre, Venezuela, a big puncher who usually stopped his victims before the final bell. Numata was knocked out by Ricardo Arredondo, also in the tenth. Arredondo, from Apatzingán, Mexico, was another destructive puncher, who had previously been outpointed by Kobayashi.

Suddenly, the activity in the junior lightweight ranks switched from Japan to Venezuela, Costa Rica and Mexico, to which was added Hawaii when Ben Villaflor outpointed Marcano on his second defence of the WBA crown. Ben Villaflor, from Negros, in the Philippines, drew his first defence, against Victor Echegaray, and lost the title on his next, to Kuniaki Shibata. However, after Shibata had also beaten Echegaray, Villaflor won it back with a first-round knock-out and then made five successful defences, two of which were draws. So Villaflor, while an excellent champion whose divided reign lasted four and a half years, was lucky with three draws (and one split decision).

During this time Ricardo Arredondo made five defences before losing the WBC crown to Kuniaki Shibata, who had just lost the WBA title to Villaflor. It is this sort of switching which makes the dual or triple control of title fights so annoying to the fans.

However, Shibata's second spell as champion was ended when he was knocked out in the second round by Alberto Escalera in Kasamatsu, Japan, on 5 July 1975. Escalera and his successor Alexis Arguello were to be long-running champions who took the WBC version of the title into the 1980s, and as the WBA champion Sam Serrano also enjoyed a long spell at the top the division now assumed a degree of continuity.

It did not look that way when Escalera began a record ten defences. The hard-working boxer from Carolina, Puerto Rico, began with a draw with Lionel Hernandez of Venezuela, when Hernandez scored the majority of the points on the score-cards. There was controversy, too, in Escalera's win over the Japanese Buzzsaw Yamabe. The referee stopped the contest in the sixth with Yamabe on the ropes, but the fans rioted on what they saw as a premature decision, and the Japanese commission altered the verdict to 'no decision' on the grounds that the referee had not consulted the ringside doctor. It was patently a decision to appease the fans, and has not gone into the records.

Another of Escalera's wins, over Tyrone Everett, of Philadelphia, was not greeted with universal approval, most thinking that the split decision favoured Escalera somewhat.

Arguello passes through

After ten defences, Escalera was stopped in the 13th round by Alexis Arguello, of Nicaragua, one of boxing's immortals. Arguello had relinquished the featherweight title, and on 28 January 1978 began a second reign as world champion when he won the WBC junior middleweight title.

Arguello proved as successful in his new division as in the old, making eight defences, including a 116-second knock-out of Diego Alcala, and stopping three men, Rafael Limon, Bobby Chacon and Rolando Navarrete, who were all to become champions after he moved up another weight in 1980.

Meanwhile the new WBA champion in 1976, Sam Serrano, who took the crown from Villaflor, also carried his title into the 1980s. Serrano was born in Toa Alta, Puerto Rico, and was a very clever southpaw, the majority of whose wins came from unanimous points decisions. He was stopped in August 1980 by Yasutsune Uehara, from Okinawa, Japan, who had previously unsuccessfully challenged Villaflor. Uehara beat Lionel Hernandez but in 1981 was outpointed in Wakayama by Serrano, who began a second spell as champion. He made two more successful defences, making 12 in all, and then was involved in a strange ending against Benedicto Villablanca of Chile; the fight being declared a 'no contest' by officials after Serrano had been stopped by a cut in the 11th round. The referee had given the Chilean the victory, and he was considerably put out by the controversial over-ruling.

Serrano lost his title on his next defence, being counted out in the eighth against Roger Mayweather, a tall boxer from Grand Rapids boxing out of Las Vegas. Mayweather knocked out the unfortunate Villablanca in the first round, but was himself given the same treatment by Rocky Lockridge. After two defences, Lockridge was beaten by Wilfredo Gomez, of Puerto Rico, who had held the light-featherweight title from 1977 to 1982 but had failed to win the featherweight title from Azumah Nelson. Gomez lost the title on his first defence to Alfredo Layne, who did likewise to Brian Mitchell, a South African who won in Sun City, where it was thought perhaps Layne had been affected by the climate. However, Mitchell proved a worthy and busy champion through 1988.

Meanwhile, on Arguello abdicating from the WBC kingdom in 1980, the new champion was his earlier victim, Rafael Limon, who stopped Idelfonso Betelmy in the last round at Los Angeles, but Limon was beaten in his first defence by Cornelius Boza-Edwards in Stockton. Boza was born in Uganda, and added the Edwards to his name in tribute to the Englishman who looked after him there and in London, from where he boxed. After beating Bobby Chacon, Boza-Edwards lost the title to Rolando Navarrete, of the Philippines, who in turn lost it to Rafael Limon, who thus regained it.

Limon, from Mexico City, was a knock-out specialist. He made one successful defence in his second spell as champion, but was then outpointed by Bobby Chacon, from Los Angeles. Chacon was stripped of the title because of contractual disputes. Promoter Don King claimed to have him under contract to fight Hector Camacho. Promoter Mickey Duff claimed the same for Boza-Edwards. The WBC allowed a contest with Boza-Edwards to take place but without title recognition (Chacon won), but then Chacon refused to fight Camacho for King (Duff allegedly offered him double).

Camacho duly stopped Limon for the vacant WBC title, but after one defence against Rafael Solis moved up to lightweight, leaving Chacon no doubt disillusioned with the promotion politics of the 1980s.

An outstanding champion won the title, vacant for a second time in a year, when Julio Cesar Chavez, unbeaten in 43 contests, added another one to the list by stopping Mario Martinez in Los Angeles. Chavez made eight successful defences, beating among others former champions Mayweather and Lockridge, before, in 1987, relinquishing the title to move up to lightweight.

The new WBC champion was Azumah Nelson, the former undefeated featherweight title-holder, who beat Mario Martinez on a bitterly disputed split decision. Fans booed and showered the Inglewood Forum ring as Nelson, down after a left hook in the 10th round, was given the decision. In June 1988 he beat Lupe Suarez to retain the title.

The IBF had recognized a junior lightweight champion in September 1984, when the Korean Hwan-Kil Yuh outpointed Rod Sequenan at Seoul. He retained the title at Pohang but lost it when travelling to Melbourne and being outpointed by Lester Ellis in 1985. Ellis, from Melbourne, lost it to Barry Michael from the same city, as the title became an all-Australian affair for a while. Michael defended it successfully in Darwin, Melbourne and Manchester, England, before back in England he lost a tough battle with former champion Rocky Lockridge. Michael was forced to retire after eight rounds. Lockridge beat Johnny de la Rosa and Harold Knight but was outpointed on 23 July 1988 at Sacramento by local boy Tony Lopez, who defended his new title by outpointing Juan Molina of Puerto Rico.

Stevie

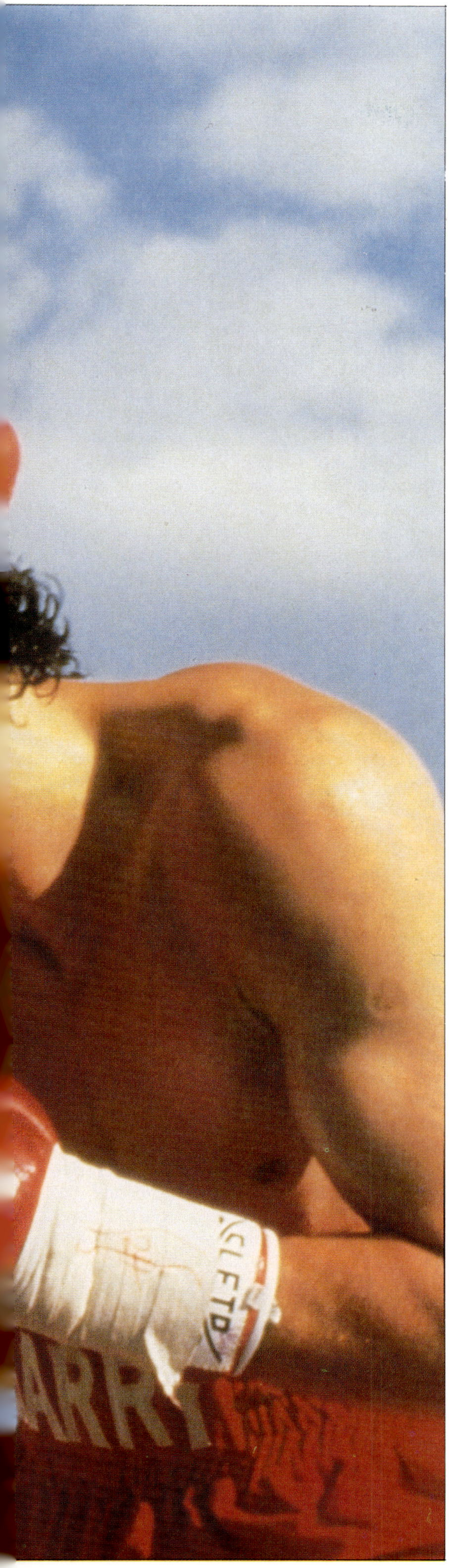

The Featherweights and Light-Featherweights

The featherweight class has seen a number of long-running and busy champions from many parts of the world. George Dixon, from Canada, known as 'Little Chocolate' was champion for practically all the 1890s, Abe Attell, from the USA, thanks to the 'no-decision' rule, for nearly as long, another American, Johnny Kilbane, for over 11 years, and, in recent times, Eusebio Pedroza, from Panama, for over seven years. One of the best of all feathers, 'Peerless' Jim Driscoll, was from Wales, Vicente Saldivar, an outstanding champion of the 1960s, and the tragic Salvador Sanchez, who was killed while still champion in 1982, were from Mexico, and a 1980s champion, Azumah Nelson, was from Ghana. Two featherweights whose names are often linked, Willie Pep and Sandy Saddler, ruled the division for over ten years, and fought four bitter battles as their careers overlapped in the late 1940s and early 1950s.

Left: *The popular Irish featherweight champion Barry McGuigan (right) was expected to enjoy a long reign but on his first defence in America he came up against an energy-sapping Las Vegas desert heat and succumbed to an opponent who came in as a substitute, Steve Cruz (left).*

THE DIVISION WHERE THE CHAMPIONS LAST

It is almost possible to take one's pick as to the first world featherweight champion, with claims being made for at least four: Dal Hawkins, Ike Weir, Billy Murphy and George Dixon. Hawkins, of San Francisco, beat Fred Bogan with a 91st-round knock-out at San Francisco on 3 and 4 June 1889. The fight was stopped at 5 am after 75 rounds and resumed next day. Hawkins outgrew the division, but this was really just the American title.

Ike Weir, from Lurgan, Co. Armagh, drew with Frank Murphy of England at Kouts, Indiana, on 31 March 1889, when police stopped the bout after 80 rounds in a fight advertised as being for the world title. Weir's claim lies in the fact that he was considered to be ahead. However, 'Torpedo' Billy Murphy, from Auckland, New Zealand, usually called Australian Billy Murphy, seemed to have the best claim yet when he drew at San Francisco with Frank Murphy, then knocked out Ike Weir in the 14th round, also in San Francisco. His trouble was that he returned to Australia so his claim was not taken seriously in America. He was beaten in Sydney by Young Griffo, a brilliant boxer whose real name was Albert Griffiths. This claim, however, gradually petered out.

The Americans asserted that the Young Griffo claim was merely for a British Empire title, and supported George Dixon, who stopped Cal McCarthy at Troy, New York, on 31 March 1891. Dixon gradually became accepted as the best, especially after beating Fred Johnson, the British best, in New York City in 1892.

George Dixon was a brilliant boxer from Halifax, Nova Scotia, Canada, who because of his size and colour was known as 'Little Chocolate'. Only 5ft 3½in (1.61m), he was really only a bantamweight, but he fought in the featherweight category. The weight varied in the early days from 120lb (54kg) to 130lb (59kg), overlapping the bantamweight class which rose to 122lb (55kg). The current limit of 126lb (57kg) was fixed in 1909.

Dixon held the title until July 1897, having defended 14 times successfully since beating McCarthy. He was held to three draws, one by Frank Erne, the future lightweight champion. He was once beaten by Erne but claimed the match was overweight, and subsequently beat Erne by the same token.

Dixon's manager raised the weight limit to 126lb (57kg) when tackling Solly Smith at San Francisco on 4 October 1907, and had to give up the crown when Smith won on points. However, he still claimed he was the true featherweight champion at 122lb (55kg), and this led the British authorities to recognize Ben Jordan, when Jordan outpointed Dixon over 25 rounds at New York on 1 July 1898. Jordan, from Bermondsey, London, successfully defended once, but then on another trip to the States he was knocked out by Eddie Santry in the 15th round in New York on 10 October 1899. The British thus declined to recognize Jordan, and Santry began to claim the title.

However, much of the confusion was due to the weights at which the bouts were made. Dixon had in the meantime continued to claim the title, now with justification, for he had beaten Dave Sullivan on a disqualification (Sullivan, from Cork, Ireland, having won it from Solly Smith, Dixon's conqueror). Dixon and Sullivan each weighed 118lb (53.5kg) only in this contest. Dixon destroyed Santry's claim (he doesn't usually appear in the records) by beating him in six rounds (without his, Dixon's, title at stake), then drawing with him (when it was).

Dixon eventually lost his title for good on 9 January 1900, when he was stopped in the ninth round by Terry McGovern. 'Terrible' Terry McGovern, from Johnstown, Pennsylvania, was a popular performer with a big punch and ferocious instincts. He had moved up from being bantamweight champion, and had a string of knock-outs behind him. Dixon was down several times before he retired.

Some of Terry's wins were a little dubious, however (the Gans lightweight fight has already been mentioned) and there was a scandal over his second defence against Oscar Gardner. McGovern was floored by a tremendous right in the second round, and the referee (McGovern's favourite) took so long over taking up the count that McGovern was down for at least 20 seconds, and was then allowed to hold for the rest of the round. He won in the next.

McGovern made six successful defences, all knock-outs by the seventh round. Then he was stopped himself by Young Corbett II, whose win was reminiscent of Gardner's near-miss. However, Corbett planned it beautifully, by so insulting McGovern's mother that the Irish-tempered Terry flew into a rage, boxed without care, and was knocked out. Corbett, from Denver, Colorado, whose real name was William H. Rothwell, had planned his tactics on James J. Corbett's mastery of the swashbuckling O'Sullivan in their heavyweight contest nine years earlier. Corbett made four defences, beating McGovern again in 1903 to prove it was no fluke, but then had to move up to lightweight, where he had no similar successes.

Having drawn and beaten George Dixon in 1901, when Dixon was campaigning for another title shot, a Jewish boxer from San Francisco, Abe Attell, claimed the crown on Corbett's abdication. After he had beaten Johnny Reagan and Harry Forbes, most

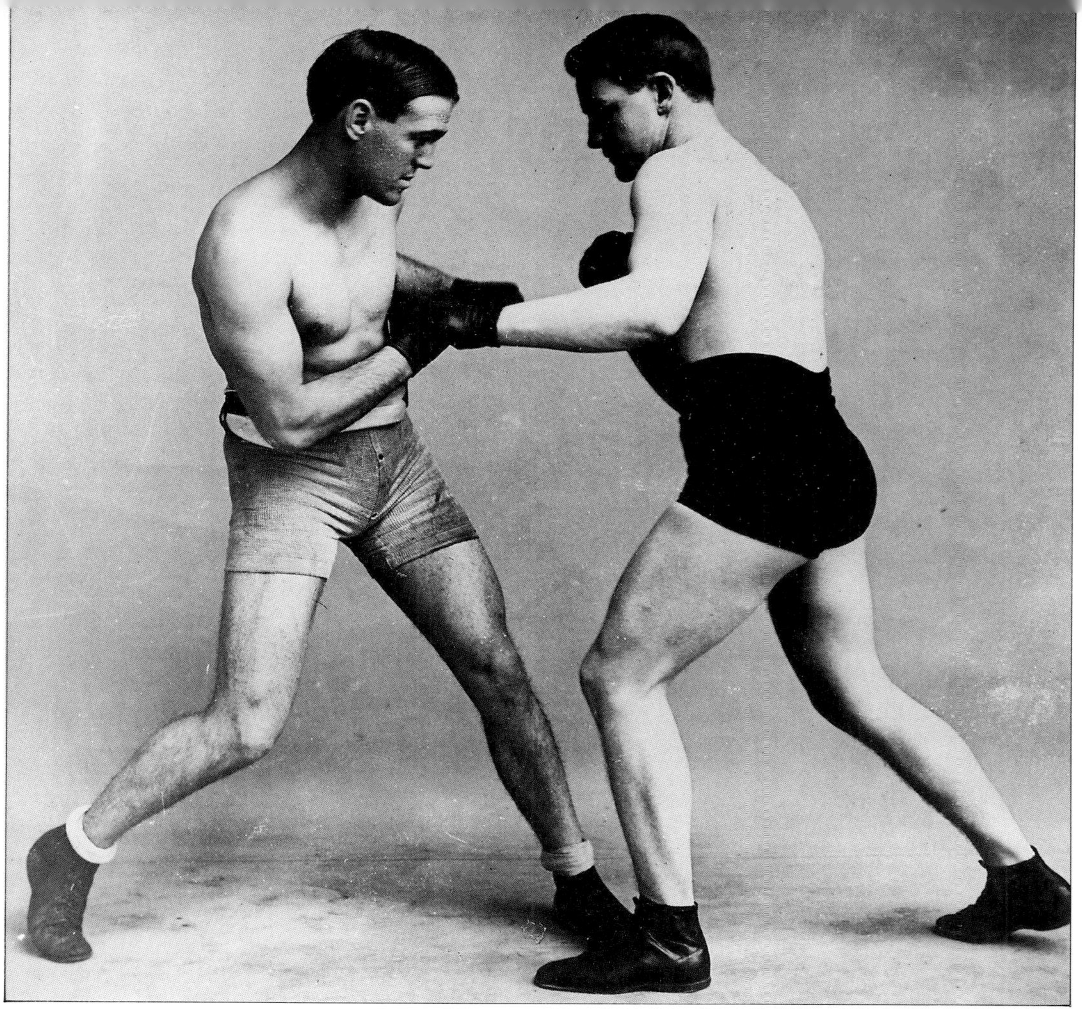

Left: 'Terrible' Terry McGovern (on the left) posing with Young Corbett II before their world title fight in 1901. Corbett took McGovern's title with a second-round knockout and destroyed the myth of McGovern, who did not recover his earlier pre-eminence.

commentators thought that his claim was best, but on 13 April 1904 he was knocked out by Tommy Sullivan at St Louis. Attell claimed that Sullivan was overweight and that therefore the title was not at stake. Both men claimed the title but Sullivan was less active and the consensus was that Attell was champion. After several more defences Attell knocked out Sullivan in 1908 and was undisputed champion.

However, in 1908 he also boxed two draws with Owen Moran, of Birmingham, who had arrived in the States to seek the title. The first was over 25 rounds at San Francisco, and Moran and his supporters were disgusted with the verdict. A return was arranged, with Attell wanting the distance reduced to 20 rounds — they compromised on 23, a unique distance for a world title fight. Again Moran was upset at the drawn verdict.

Jim Driscoll, the British champion, then went to the States to try to do better, but Attell would meet him only in a no-decision bout in New York. On 19 February 1919 the majority of the reporters agreed that Driscoll had won every single round. Attell would not meet him in a title bout, and the British and European authorities stripped him and regarded Driscoll as champion.

'Peerless' Jim Driscoll was one of the all-time great boxers. The Cardiff-born boxer of Irish family defended against Jean Poesy of France, and boxed a draw with the luckless Owen Moran, but Driscoll's retirement and World War I put an end to this line of the championship.

Meanwhile in America, Attell continued to defend, including a points win over Johnny Kilbane, who was the man eventually to topple him. Kilbane outpointed Attell over 20 rounds at Los Angeles on 22 February 1922. It was Attell's 28th title fight (although some reckon it more or fewer, because of the uncertainty of the conflicting claims of the boxers of the day). It was a great record for the 'Little Hebrew', but for most of the eight years or so he reigned Driscoll was the world's best featherweight.

Johnny Kilbane, from Cleveland, Ohio, was a boxer almost as clever as Attell, and with a good punch, but it was a great surprise when he clearly outpointed the champion. Nobody could take the title from him for over 11 years, but most of his bouts were of the no-decision kind, and there were few formal defences. Kilbane drew with Johnny Dundee over 20 rounds in 1913, after which Dundee won the junior lightweight title and wanted to challenge Kilbane again. When Kilbane refused to fight Dundee, the New York commission stripped him in 1922 and recognized Dundee after he had knocked out Danny Frush, a Londoner who had also lost to Kilbane.

Kilbane eventually lost his title to Eugene Criqui from Belleville, France, a pre-war flyweight contender, who had fought all around the world to end up as European featherweight champion. While serving in the war his jaw had been shattered by a bullet, and was held together by a silver plate which, he claimed, made it impossible to knock him out with a blow there. Travelling to New York, Criqui knocked out Kilbane on 2 June 1923 to win the crown and end Kilbane's 11-year spell as champion.

In the age of the veterans, the almost 30-year-old Criqui (who beat 34-year-old Kilbane) was then outpointed at the Polo Grounds, New York, by Johnny Dundee, who was three months younger than Criqui. So Dundee, the 'Scotch Wop', was now undisputed champion, but he immediately moved back to regain his junior lightweight title, which he had lost while featherweight champion.

Louis 'Kid' Kaplan became the new champion with a stoppage of Danny Kramer in New York in 1925. Kaplan was born in Russia, and was Russia's first world champion. However, his career was entirely American, mostly spent around New Jersey. A clever boxer, he was forced to relinquish the crown after three defences, being unable to make the weight.

Massachusetts proclaimed Honeyboy Finnegan champion in 1926 after a Boston win over Chick Suggs, but this progressed no further, Finnegan outgrowing the class.

Benny Bass, remarkably, like Kaplan, born in Russia, became the NBA champion with a win over Red Chapman at Philadelphia. Tony Canzoneri won the New York version with a win over Johnny Dundee, now once more an ex-champion at the next higher weight.

Canzoneri and Bass, who were both to win world titles at higher weights, then met for the undisputed championship and Canzoneri won with a unanimous points decision at Madison Square Garden. He held the title for only seven months, however, losing to Andre Routis, a Frenchman from Bordeaux. Routis, a strong boxer, won a decision with which Canzoneri's handlers disagreed. However, Routis was the unluckier boxer, because after one defence he was afflicted with eye trouble, and dropped the title on points to Bat Battalino in his home town of Hartford in 1929.

Christopher 'Battling' Battalino was a good scrapper who beat some excellent boxers in his six successful defences, including future champions in Kid Chocolate and Freddie Miller, and ex-Olympic and world flyweight champion Fidel LaBarba. Battalino lost his title in peculiar circumstances. He came in 3lb (1.4kg) overweight for a fight with his stablemate Freddie Miller, and was knocked down by a third-round punch which caused the referee to stop the fight, giving it to Miller. The contest was ruled 'no contest' by both the NBA and New York authorities, the implication being that it was fixed for Battalino to pass on the title to Miller. The championship was declared vacant. In an interview with Peter Heller years later for *In This Corner!* Battalino admitted the fight was a fake, and said he was forced into it by crooked managers and racketeers. He was suspended for 30 days.

One incidental disadvantage of Battalino's disgrace was that the championship was split, and remained so until after World War II.

Tommy Paul, of Buffalo, New York, outpointed Johnny Pena at Detroit to become the first new champion, on 26 May 1932, but he lost on his first defence to Freddie Miller, so the notorious plan of Battalino's management worked out all right in the end. Freddie Miller, from Cincinnati, reigned for over three years, and proved a good champion. A southpaw, he made nine successful defences, but during his reign actually engaged in 90 contests. He twice fought in Liverpool against one of Britain's cleverest boxers, Nel Tarleton, winning narrow points victories each time. He eventually lost his crown on his second challenge of 1936 from Petey Sarron, who after losing on points in Miami, outpointed the champion ten weeks later in Washington.

The New York authorities could not boast such a long-running champion, but had some good ones, none better than the first, Kid Chocolate, the NBA junior lightweight champion. Chocolate had had an unsuccessful try at the lightweight championship so now moved downwards to fight men of his own weight. He knocked out Lew Feldman to win the title and then defended against LaBarba and Seaman Tommy Watson, the British champion, before forfeiting recognition for failing to defend against Frankie Klick (Klick took his junior lightweight title).

Chocolate was succeeded by Baby Arizmendi, who had been outpointed by Freddie Miller 18 months earlier. Arizmendi (first name Alberto), from Torréon, Coahuila, Mexico, was known as 'Baby' for his smiling features, but in the ring he was far from gentle, being a crowd-pleasing, two-fisted attacker. He won the title by outpointing Mike Belloise, but immediately lost New York recognition by fighting for a Californian version of the title. This brought him a points victory over the great Henry Armstrong, just about to launch his attack on the world titles from feather to middle. However, in 1936 Armstrong outpointed Arizmendi for this version of the title.

Mike Belloise was recognized by the New York commission as champion in 1936, and defended against Britain's Dave Crowley, knocking him out in the ninth round at Madison Square Garden, but the New York authorities then withdrew recognition from Belloise because he too fought for the Californian title, where he was outpointed by Armstrong.

This was five months after Petey Sarron had taken Freddie Miller's NBA title, and the two were to meet to unify the championship. Before this Sarron, a tough boxer from Birmingham, Alabama, defended twice, including a second win against Freddie Miller in Johannesburg (it made their score 4-2 to Miller). When he defended against Armstrong at Madison Square Garden on 29 October 1937, with the NBA and Californian titles at stake, the New York authorities also agreed to recognize the winner. This proved to be Armstrong, who thus won the first of his three undisputed world titles.

Undisputed is a relative term here, because in fact the IBU had 24 days earlier recognized Maurice Holtzer of France as champion, when he outpointed the Belgian Phil Dolhem in Algiers. Holtzer made one defence but lost IBU recognition through ill health.

Armstrong, having won two more world titles, relinquished the featherweight crown, where he had long had weight difficulties, without defending it. Joey Archibald, from Providence, won the New York version with a points win over Mike Belloise, and Leo Rodak, from Chicago, the NBA version with a points win over Italy's Leone Efrati. Archibald then outpointed Rodak to unify the title, but was immediately shorn of NBA recognition for failing to defend against Petey Scalzo. Louisiana named Jimmy Perrin champion after he beat Bobby Ruffin at New Orleans, but disowned him after Petey Scalzo defeated him in a non-title bout. Scalzo was recognized by the NBA after knocking out Frankie Covelli at Washington in 1940, and successfully defended twice, against opponents whose names have proved more memorable than their records, Bobby 'Poison' Ivy and Phil Zwick. Scalzo, from New York, lost to Richie Lemos, of Los Angeles, who in turn lost in two contests with Jackie Wilson, a veteran from Kansas.

Wilson immediately handed over the NBA title in two 1943 bouts to Jackie Callura, of Hamilton, Ontario, who lost it in two more 1943 bouts to Phil Terranova of New York City. The roundabout continued. Two 1944 bouts in Boston saw Sal Bartolo, fighting in his home town, assume the uneasy crown. Bartolo actually made two successful defences before losing in June 1946 to Willie Pep, the New York champion, who thus unified the championship at last.

The Savage Saddler–Pep Battles

The New York progression after Archibald had replaced Armstrong had been less of an exercise in musical chairs. Archibald lost the title to Harry Jeffra, a Baltimore Italian (Ignacius Guiffi), a crowding fighter who had been bantamweight champion, but after Jeffra had made one defence Archibald regained the title, only to lose it in 1941 on an 11th-round knock-out to Albert 'Chalky' Wright, from Durango, Mexico, who was in the middle of a long career. Harry Jeffra complicated the issue a little when California recognized him as champion after a win over Lou Transparenti, but Wright stopped him and beat Lulu Constantino before losing the title to Willie Pep, who outpointed him in New York City, in 1942.

Willie Pep from Middletown, Connecticut, was a very fast and clever boxer who had begun his professional career in July 1940. He outpointed Sal Bartolo in his first defence, and then Chalky Wright in a return. Pep outpointed Phil Terranova, the former NBA champion, and followed this by again outpointing Sal Bartolo, who by now was the reigning NBA champion. Pep thus unified the championship, which was appropriate, as he was one of the greatest featherweights of all time, his only defeat at that stage having come in his 63rd fight when he took on ex-lightweight champion Sammy Angott.

After two defences of the unified crown, Pep, now with a record of 134 wins and a draw in 136 contests, took on Sandy Saddler in the first of four epic championship battles between the two men. Saddler surprisingly

Below: The third battle between Willie Pep (left) and Sandy Saddler in September 1950. Saddler had taken the title from the brilliant boxer Pep in 1948 but Pep had regained it with an outstanding exhibition in 1949. The strength and punching power of Saddler proved decisive in the rubber bout.

won the first contest with a fourth-round knock-out, but there were suspicions over a large swing in the betting odds which the New York commission noticed. The return, like the first contest, was at Madison Square Garden and it drew over 19,000 spectators. This time Pep put up a terrific performance, perhaps his best ever, and he clearly won on points. He made three more defences, including one against Ray Famechon of France, before having to face Saddler once more. This time it was Saddler's turn again. No indoor arena would be big enough for the rubber match, and over 38,000 packed the Yankee Stadium to see Pep retire after the seventh round with a dislocated shoulder. The fourth meeting, at the Polo Grounds, was a disgrace. Both men fouled persistently. Their great rivalry was so bitter that none would give best. Pep was forced to retire once again, this time after the eighth round, with bad cuts. Saddler was suspended for 30 days after this display, and Pep banned for ever from boxing in New York.

Saddler, a tall (5ft 8½in/1.74m) featherweight who had been born in Boston but brought up in Harlem, now joined the US Army. There was an interim title while he was away, won by Percy Bassett, then Teddy 'Red Top' Davis, but Saddler returned in 1956 to outpoint Davis and resume his reign. Alas, after only one more defence, a stoppage of Flash Elorde, who was to be an outstanding junior middleweight, Saddler badly injured an eye in a car accident, and was forced to retire. He was one of the great featherweights.

Luckily, the championship did not split. Hogan Kid Bassey, from Calabar, Nigeria, a good boxer with a hard punch, took the vacant title. He stopped Cherif Hamia, of Algeria, in Paris and then likewise Ricardo Moreno of Mexico City, but dropped the title when forced to retire after 13 rounds with eye injuries against Davey Moore. Moore, born in Lexington, Kentucky, was a tough, vigorous fighter who also forced Bassey to retire in the return. He then made four more defences, winning twice in Tokyo and once in Finland, and remained champion for four years.

Tragedy marked his last defence, however, for he was forced to retire at the end of the tenth round against Ultiminio 'Sugar' Ramos, and on arriving at his dressing room he collapsed, spending two days in a coma from which he did not recover.

Sugar Ramos, from Matanzas, Cuba, was another all-action fighter, like Moore, and carried a knock-out punch. Ramos made three defences, in Mexico City, Tokyo and Accra, the last a very controversial affair. His opponent was Floyd Robertson, a Ghanaian who held the British Empire title. Ramos was awarded a split decision that so incensed the Ghanaian authorities that they regarded Robertson as champion. The British referee voted for Robertson but the US and Mexican judges gave it to Ramos. Robertson was not recognized elsewhere, and lost another challenge 21 months later when knocked out by Ramos' successor, Vicente Saldivar.

Saldivar, from Mexico City, was one of the great South American boxers who began to dominate the lighter divisions around this time. A strong-punching southpaw, Saldivar won the title when forcing Ramos to retire at the end of the 11th at Mexico City on 25 September 1964.

Saldivar defended successfully seven times, three of his defences being against Howard Winstone, the clever Welshman from Merthyr Tydfil. Winstone was missing the tops of three fingers of his right hand, but was a brilliant craftsman, which made his fights with Saldivar, the puncher, so entertaining. The first was at Earls Court, the power of Saldivar taking the points decision. The second, at Cardiff, also went to Saldivar, but by the narrowest margin. In each fight Saldivar had to come strongly after Winstone had built up a lead on points. The third fight was at Mexico City, where Winstone was forced to retire at the end of the 13th round with cut eyes. Saldivar, who was only 23, then announced his retirement from the ring.

This must have been welcome news to Winstone, four years his senior, who took the WBC version of the title with a cut-eye stoppage of Japan's Mitsunori Seki at the Albert Hall, London, but his reign lasted only

***Right:** Welsh wizard Howard Winstone three times tried to take the featherweight title from Vicente Saldivar (on the left) and each time his points lead was wiped out by a strong Saldivar finish. In this third, 1967, encounter in Mexico City, Winstone was forced to retire after this 12th-round knockdown. Saldivar then announced his retirement from the ring, and Winstone later took the vacant crown.*

six months. José Legra, from Baracoa, Cuba, who boxed out of Spain and was European champion, stopped him in the fifth round at Porthcawl. Legra's reign did not last long, Johnny Famechon outpointing him at the Albert Hall, London, on 21 January 1969. Famechon came from a well-known family of French boxers (his uncle Ray had fought Pep for the title) but Johnny, although born in Paris, had gone to Australia to box and was Australian champion. Famechon, a skilful boxer, twice beat Masahiko 'Fighting' Harada, from Tokyo, but on 9 May 1970 was outpointed by Vicente Saldivar in Rome, the former champion proving that sometimes they do come back, at least once (a second comeback later still was unsuccessful).

Meanwhile, the WBA title on Saldivar's first retirement had been won by Paul Rojas, from San Pedro, California, like Winstone and Seki one of Saldivar's earlier victims. He outpointed Antonio Herrera and defended against Enrique Higgins before being outpointed in Los Angeles by Shozo Saijyo of Saitama, Japan. Saijyo defended successfully five times, and in 1971 there were actually two Japanese champions, as Saldivar, on his second spell, lost his WBC title on his first defence to Kuniaki Shibata from Hitachi, who was also later to become junior lightweight champion.

However, both Japanese champions had gone by 1972. First Saijyo was harried into a defence against Antonio Gomez, from Cumaná, Venezuela (the WBC stripped him of his title, then just before the fight was signed they reinstated him). Gomez, a game scrapper, stopped the champion in the fifth round in Tokyo. Shibata made all his three defences in Tokyo, stopping Raul Cruz in the first (for the first time in a world title fight the count continued after the round should have ended), but could only draw with Ernesto Marcel, a future champion. The Japanese lost his title on 19 May 1972 when he was knocked out in the third round by Clemente Sanchez, of Monterrey, Mexico.

Sanchez, in his home town, was stopped on his first defence by former champion José Legra (Sanchez was also 3lb (1.4kg) overweight), who was outpointed by Eder Jofre, a two-fisted puncher from São Paulo, Brazil. Jofre's first task as champion was to turn back the second comeback of Vicente Saldivar. Jofre knocked him out in the fourth round at Salvador, Brazil. Jofre then forfeited the WBC title for failing to defend against Alfredo Marcano, the former junior lightweight champion.

Meanwhile, Gomez made only one successful defence after taking the WBA title in 1971. He was then outpointed by Enresto Marcel, from Colón, Panama, a hard puncher who stopped many opponents. Marcel then made four successful defences, the last a points win over the great Alexis Arguello, who was soon to win titles at three weights. Perhaps Marcel, who was only 25, did not realize the strength of this achievement, for he retired while still champion. As Jofre had been stripped by the WBC, the middle of 1974 found neither main governing body with a featherweight champion.

The WBA was the first to find a champion, when Ruben Olivares, a former outstanding bantamweight champion from Mexico, knocked out Zensuke Utagawa of Japan at the Inglewood Forum, Los Angeles, but he lasted only four and a half months as WBA champion, being knocked out in the 13th round on 23 November 1974 by Alexis Arguello, making his second attempt at the title. Arguello made four defences, setting the style of his subsequent career by showing himself willing to travel — the defences were in Venezuela, Nicaragua, Tokyo and the United States, and none of them went the distance. After two years of being the best featherweight in the world, Arguello found 126lb (57kg) was too difficult a weight limit for him, and gave up the title to exert his mastery among the junior lightweights.

The vacant WBA title was taken by Rafael Ortega, from Panama City, who had begun his career as a flyweight, and who scored a narrow points victory over Francisco Coronado of Nicaragua. He managed one successful defence, against Flipper Uehara, in Tokyo, and then was beaten by Cecilio

Lastra from Santander, Spain, who outpointed him in his own country, at Torrelavega. Unfortunately for Lastra, his first defence four months later was in Panama City, the birthplace of the challenger, Eusebio Pedroza, and Pedroza was to prove to be another great featherweight. He ruled the WBA strand of the championship from 1978 to 1985.

Meanwhile, the WBC strand had been won after Jofre had been stripped by Bobby Chacon, a popular all-action performer from Los Angeles, who stopped Alfredo Marcano before his own supporters. Chacon knocked out Jesus Estrada but was then stopped by Ruben Olivares, the former WBA champion. Olivares' reign as WBC king was even shorter than his WBA tenure, lasting only three months, when he was outpointed at Los Angeles by David Kotey, from Accra, Ghana. Kotey had built up a reputation as a knockout specialist, but his win over Olivares was the narrowest possible split decision — all three judges had one point difference, two favouring Kotey.

Kotey's win was great news for Ghana, and 60,000 turned out to see his first defence in Accra, where he stopped Flipper Uehara in the 12th round. Kotey franked his form by then defending successfully in Tokyo against Shig Fukuyama, a third-round stoppage, and 100,000 turned up in Accra in November 1976 to see him defend against Danny 'Little Red' Lopez, born in Fort Duchesne, Utah, but based in California. Lopez was part-Indian, and brother of Ernie, who had challenged Napoles for the welterweight title. He had begun his career with 21 inside-the-distance wins, but was then stopped himself by Chacon and Fukuyama, so his battles were usually interesting. Unhappily for the home supporters, he outpointed Kotey.

Lopez made eight successful defences in his reign of over three years, including a stoppage of Kotey in a return. His most remarkable contests were against Juan Malvarez of Argentina, who floored him in the first round but was knocked out in the second, and Mike Ayala, of San Antonio. The referee counted Ayala out in the 11th round in his home city, but the Ayala corner protested and the timekeeper confirmed that Ayala had risen at 'nine', so the bout continued. Lopez knocked out Ayala four rounds later, in the last round.

The tragic Salvador Sanchez

Lopez's eventual conqueror was a man who looked like becoming as long-reigning a king as Pedroza was proving to be in the WBA half of the championship. Salvador Sanchez, from Santiago, Mexico, fought his way up from bantamweight, where he suffered his only defeat in his national championship challenge, and took the world featherweight title at Phoenix, Arizona. Sanchez had all the boxing talents and carried punching power in each fist. His nine successful defences included some against the best men at the weight, three of whom were to become champion. His toughest opponent, however, was the British champion, Pat Cowdell, whom he beat on a split decision at Houston, USA. His last defence was a stoppage of Azumah Nelson in July 1982, and three weeks later he was killed in a car crash.

By September the WBC had a new champion, Juan Laporte, a Puerto Rican, who stopped Mario Miranda, from Colombia, at New York. After two defences he was outpointed by another Puerto Rican, Wilfredo Gomez, who had been an outstanding light-featherweight champion for over five years. Gomez's reign as a featherweight, though,

Below: *Danny 'Red' Lopez throws a long right to the chin of Salvador Sanchez in their featherweight title fight in February 1980 at Phoenix, Arizona. Sanchez won by a stoppage and remained champion until killed in a road accident.*

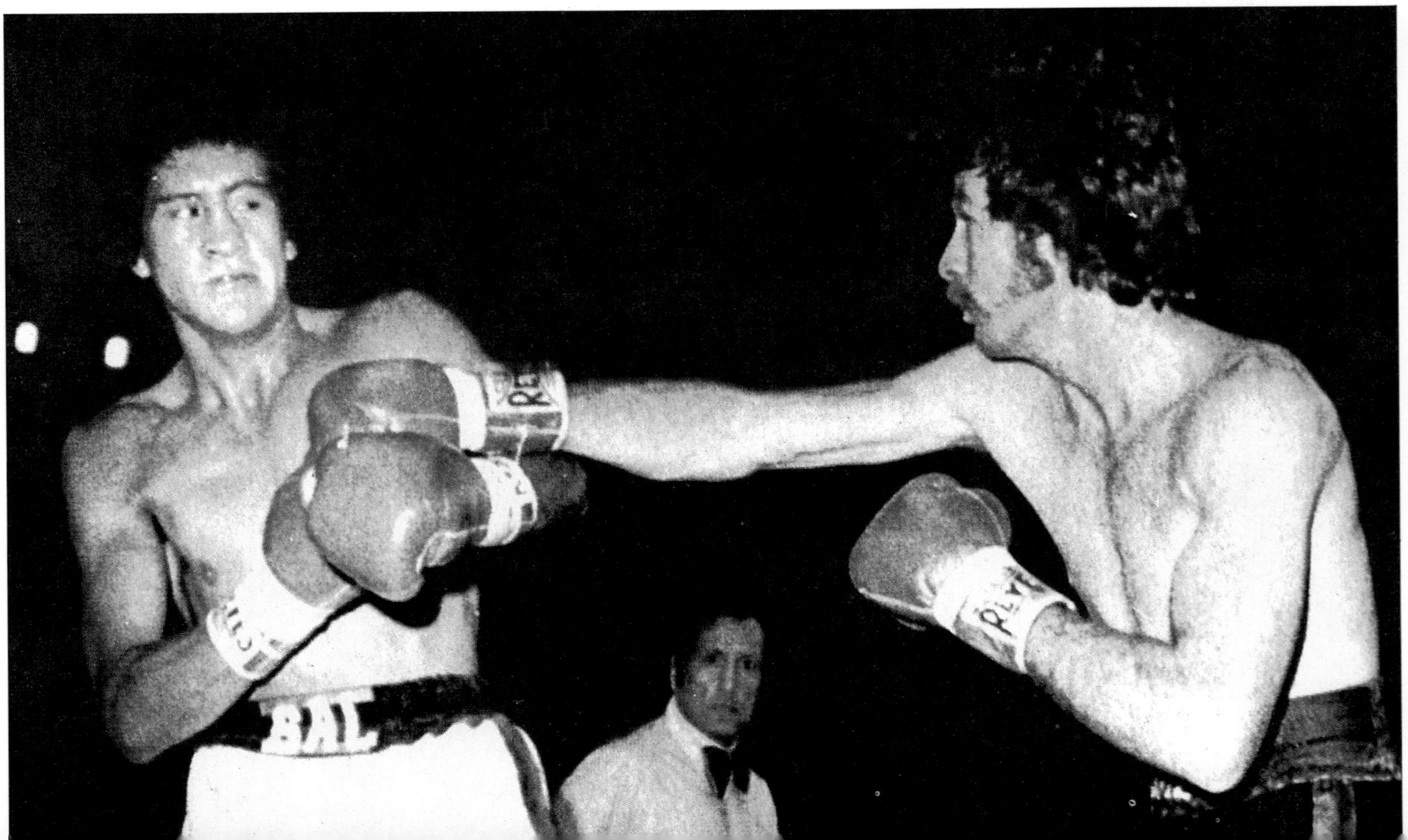

was short-lived, for on his first defence, on 8 December 1984, he was stopped in the 11th round in San Juan by Azumah Nelson, like Kotey from Accra, Ghana. Thus, the three successors of Sanchez were all men whom he had beaten.

Eusebio Pedroza, meanwhile, who had won the WBA half of the title in April 1978, was still beating all his challengers. The skilful Pedroza made no fewer than 19 successful defences, and future champions Laporte and junior middleweight Rocky Lockridge were among his victims. Pedroza took his title to many lands — Panama, Puerto Rico, Japan, USA, Papua New Guinea, South Korea, Venezuela, Italy and the West Indies — and returned with it, but he lost it on his first trip to England. At Loftus Road, the home of Queen's Park Rangers football club, Barry McGuigan of Clones, Ireland, outpointed him. McGuigan was immensely popular in both halves of Ireland and made defences in Belfast, Northern Ireland, and Dublin, Republic of Ireland. However, just when it seemed that a lucrative unification battle was possible with Azumah Nelson, the new WBC title-holder, McGuigan lost his title to a substitute, Steve Cruz of Texas, in the fierce heat of Las Vegas.

Cruz lost the title in his home town on his first defence, being stopped in the 12th round of a hard fight by Antonio Esparragoza of Venezuela. Esparragoza held the title into 1986 with a win over Pascual Aranda of Mexico and a draw with Marcos Villasana, also of Mexico. Villasana, twice an unsuccessful challenger to Azumah Nelson for the WBC title, almost upset Esparragoza, who faded in the later rounds but just held on. At the Sports Arena, Las Vegas, Villasana lost a point for a low blow in the fifth round. It cost him the title, as whereas one judge scored it comfortably for him, and another for Esparragoza, the third judge (Patricia Jarman) had it all square.

Azumah Nelson, meanwhile, continued impressively. He made six successful defences, including the two points wins over Villasana and a one-round destruction of Pat Cowdell, who had done so well against Sanchez. Nelson's second win over Villasana, on 29 August 1987, was not greeted happily by the Los Angeles fans, although it was unanimous, and Nelson decided to move up to the junior lightweight class, where he quickly won a title. The WBC featherweight title which he vacated was won by a man stepping up a class himself. Jeff Fenech, of Sydney, Australia, the light-featherweight champion, stopped Victor Callejas of Puerto Rico, another former light-featherweight champion, in the 10th round at Sydney on 7 March 1988. This was a world title at a third weight for Fenech, who won with two damaged hands and who, after 20 fights, had a reputation as one of the 1980s' best fighters.

The IBF did not recognize a featherweight champion until 4 March 1984, when Min-Keun Oh, of Kyunggi City, South Korea, beat Joko Arter for the title at Seoul. Oh won with a second-round knock-out, and defended successfully against Kelvin Lampkin and Irving Mitchell, but his countryman, Ki-Yung Chung, stopped him in the last round at Chŏnju in November 1985. He, too, made two successful defences in South Korea, but Antonio Rivera of Puerto Rico took the title away from the East by forcing Chung to retire at Osan in August 1986.

Rivera's first defence produced a terrific round of fighting. Calvin Grove of Coatesville, Pennsylvania, but fighting out of Houston, was the challenger, unbeaten in 31 fights, a record that looked like disappearing in the fourth round at Gamaches, France. He just beat the count from a tremendous left hook which had him groggy and cut under the eye. However, as Rivera tried to finish him he scored himself with an uppercut and a hook that floored Rivera. As the two then battled it out Rivera was dropped again and then stopped as Grove poured in punches. Grove kept his crown with a points victory over Myron Taylor. Taylor, from Philadelphia, was a late substitute at the Sands Hotel Casino, Atlantic City, for Bernard Taylor, earlier an unsuccessful challenger to Barry McGuigan. Grove extended his unbeaten sequence with a points win on 17 May 1988, but lost that and his title when narrowly outpointed by local boxer Jorge Paez at Mexicali, Mexico, on 4 August 1988.

Above: Eusebio Pedroza is down in his defence of his title in London in 1985. Pedroza's seven-year championship reign was about to come to an end before the fists of Barry McGuigan.

THE LIGHT-FEATHER-WEIGHTS

The light-featherweight division had one false start and very nearly another. In 1922 a contest between Jack 'Kid' Wolfe, of Cleveland, Ohio, and Joe Lynch, of New York, the reigning bantamweight champion, was advertised, at the Madison Square Garden, New York, as being for the light-featherweight title. The weight was set at 122lb (55kg), 4lb (2kg) below the featherweight limit. Wolfe won, but lost recognition on being overweight for a defence against Carl Duane, of New York (which Duane won) and the title fell into disuse. The WBC re-instated the division in 1976, calling it the super-bantamweight division. The WBA and IBF both used junior featherweight when instituting their class in 1977 and 1984 respectively. The weight limit is 122lb (55kg) for each.

Rigoberto Riasco of Panama City was the first champion, stopping Waruinge Nakayama in the eighth round at Panama City. Nakayama's real name was Philip Waruinge, and he was a Kenyan who boxed out of Japan. Riasco had fought mainly in Panama, and had been stopped by Alexis Arguello in a featherweight challenge the year before.

Riasco's second defence, against the South Korean Dong-Kyun Yum in Seoul, caused a scandal. The US referee and the Panamanian judge each gave it to Riasco, by margins of two and four points respectively. The South Korean judge gave it to Yum by seven points. The referee, Larry Rozadilla, raised Riasco's arm amid angry crowd scenes, for most observers thought Yum had done enough to win. After 25 minutes of pressure from many of the 15,000 fans, referee Rozadilla returned to the ring to announce that the heavy rain which had fallen throughout the fight had blurred his scorecard, and that re-examination revealed that Yum was the winner. His arm was duly raised and the WBC accepted the verdict.

However, back in America, Rozadilla informed the authorities that he had been forced to change his verdict not through a discovered error but through physical force, a gang of men having ordered him at gun-point to change his card. The WBC then reinstated Riasco.

Riasco, a fast fighter who had seized his chance late in his career, dropped the title on his next defence to Royal Kobayashi, of Japan. He was another who had failed to dislodge Arguello, but he stopped Riasco in Tokyo and promptly lost the title to Dong-Kyun Yum. So everything worked out well for the little Korean from Chung-Buk-Do in the end. He was knocked out, however, on his second defence by Wilfredo Gomez, of Puerto Rico, perhaps the division's best champion.

Gomez was a big punching, clever boxer who held the title for five and a half years, when he relinquished it after 17 successful defences. He suffered a defeat in that time when he challenged Salvador Sanchez for the featherweight title, but some of his beaten challengers were top-class, for example Carlos Zarate, the bantamweight champion, on whom Gomez inflicted his first defeat in 51 contests, and none lasted the distance.

Lupe Pintor, the bantamweight champion who succeeded Zarate, did best, staying into the 14th round on Gomez's last defence, on 3 December 1982. Weight difficulties forced Gomez up into the featherweight class, where he again became champion.

Meanwhile, the WBA strand had begun in 1977 with a Korean champion, Soo-Hwan Hong, from Seoul. He beat Hector Carrasquilla of Panama in Panama City, and got up off the floor four times to knock out his opponent in the third round. Hong was a former bantamweight champion, and made one defence being stopped by Ricardo Cardona, of Bolívar, Columbia. Cardona defended successfully five times, although his second defence, against Soon-Hyun Chang in Seoul, caused a bottle-throwing riot when the loser's local fans did not like the split decision. The scoring was not unlike that in the Riasco–Yum contest two years earlier, with the Korean judge giving Chung victory by a margin twice as large as the other two judges' verdicts for Cardona.

The Colombian lost his title in May 1980 when Leo Randolph, from Tacoma, Washington, a 1976 Olympic gold medalist at flyweight, stopped him in the last round at Seattle, but three months later Randolph was knocked out in the sixth in his native Washington by Sergio Palma, from Chaco, Argentina, an earlier victim of Cardona.

Palma, a tough, durable boxer, made five successful defences in 14 months, stopping Cardona, but he was eventually outpointed in Miami in June 1982 by Leonardo Cruz, of the Dominican Republic, whom he had already beaten in Buenos Aires.

An unbeaten Italian, Louis Stecca from San Arcángelo, took the title from Cruz after Cruz had made three defences, but he suffered his first defeat when stopped in his first defence in Guaynabo, Puerto Rico, by Victor Callejas. Callejas made two defences, including winning a return with Stecca, before losing WBA recognition for failing to defend against Louis Espinosa.

Espinosa, from Phoenix, USA, took the vacant title by stopping Tommy Valoy, of the Dominican Republic, on 16 January 1987. The hard-punching Espinosa downed Valoy in the fourth, and soon afterwards the referee was forced to intervene. After two defences, however, in August and September 1987,

***Left:** Lupe Pintor is down in the 14th round as the referee tries to intercept one last punch thrown by Wilfredo Gomez in the light-featherweight title fight in 1982. After this contest Gomez relinquished the WBC title to fight as a featherweight.*

Espinosa was outpointed in November by another boxer from the Dominican Republic, Juan Gervacio. It was a surprise victory for the challenger, but his reign lasted only to 27 February 1988, when Bernardo Pinango, the former bantamweight champion, born in Caracas, Venezuela, but fighting out of Panama, outpointed him in San Juan, Puerto Rico. A last-round knockdown helped Pinango get the decision, but this rapidly changing version of the championship saw yet another new champion on 28 May 1988 when Juan José Estrada, of Mexico, outpointed him at Tijuana.

After Gomez had given up the WBC title, Jaime Garza, of Santa Cruz, won the vacant title by stopping Bobby Berna in the second round in Los Angeles. He followed this up by knocking out Felipe Orozio in the third, but then suffered his first defeat in 40 contests when knocked out in the first round in Kingston, New York, by Juan 'Kid' Meza, from Mexicali, Mexico, who had been stopped by Gomez in 1982. Lupe Pintor, the former bantamweight champion, another of Gomez's title-fight victims, outpointed Meza on his second defence, but Pintor was less effective at the higher weight and was knocked out by Samart Payakarum, of Thailand, at Bangkok. This was only Payakarum's 12th fight, but he followed up with a defeat of Meza in December 1986. Meza was well outfought and knocked out in the last round.

Payakarum suffered his first defeat in May 1987, when his championship was taken in a tremendous punching battle at Sydney, Australia, by Jeff Fenech, the former bantamweight champion. The local boxer was put down for the first time in his career in the first round, but came back so well that he knocked out the champion in the fourth, and it was some minutes before Payakarum was fit enough to leave the ring.

Fenech stopped Greg Richardson, from Youngstown, in his first defence, and earned a technical decision in his second, against former bantamweight champion Carlos Zarate, when there was a clash of heads in the fourth round and Fenech's cheek was badly cut. The champion was awarded the contest, being ahead on all cards at the time. Fenech then relinquished the title to campaign among the featherweights.

On 2 February 1988 the veteran Mexican Zarate, nearly 37, fought for the vacant title but was stopped in the tenth round by Daniel Zaragoza, another former bantamweight king from Mexico City. Zaragoza proved much too strong and inflicted a fourth defeat on Zarate at the Inglewood Forum, Los Angeles. Zaragoza defended only a month later, boxing a draw with Seung Hoon-Lee.

The IBF strand of the championship had begun on 4 December 1983, when Bobby Berna of the Philippines, who had been stopped by Jaime Garza only six months earlier in a bid for the vacant WBC title, took the title when Seung-In Suh had been forced to retire in the 11th round in Seoul. But the Korean won a return in Seoul in April 1984, whereupon another Korean, Ji-Won Kim took it and defended it four times before retiring in 1986 — three of these occasions were very rapid knock-outs.

Another Korean, Seung-Hoon Lee won the vacant crown, and he too defended four times before giving it up to try to wrest the WBC crown from Daniel Zaragoza, and having to be content with a draw. His last defence was a split decision at Pohang, South Korea, against José Sanabria, a tall Venezuelan, and Sanabria had the satisfaction of winning the crown Seung-Hoon Lee abdicated with a fifth-round knock-out of Moises Fuentes of Colombia at Bucaramanga. In 1988 he successfully defended in Sicily and France against Vincenzo Belcastro and Fabrice Benichou.

HOTELS
SOUTHERN CROS

The Bantamweights and Light-Bantamweights

The bantamweight class in the west has in recent years been dominated by young fighters who quickly outgrow the division without becoming world champions. After British and American boxers provided the most champions up to World War I, the emphasis switched to South and Central America and the eastern countries. One of the best bantams, Panama Al Brown, was a lanky boxer who did not look like a bantam at all. Manuel Ortiz of the USA, Jimmy Carruthers of Australia, Eder Jofre of Brazil, Fighting Harada of Japan, Ruben Olivares of Mexico and Miguel Lora of Colombia have been among the best bantams since World War II.

***Left:** Jeff Fenech has opponent Tony Miller standing on one leg as he takes the Australian featherweight title at Melbourne in 1987. Fenech was already IBF world bantamweight champion, and later took world titles at light-featherweight and featherweight.*

THE GAMECOCKS OF THE ROPED SQUARE

The late 19th-century activity in the bantamweight class is complicated not only by several claimants to the world championship, that is shared by the other divisions, but also by the various weight limits that boxers arbitrarily gave to the class, and above that by the fact that in the 1890s George Dixon, the brilliant 'Little Chocolate' from Novia Scotia, fought everybody from bantamweight up to featherweight and, while he was the best in the world, it is not easy to know which championship he was claiming.

When on 27 June 1890 Dixon forced Nunc Wallace, regarded as British champion, to retire after 18 rounds at the Pelican Club, he was generally regarded as the world's best bantamweight. Later in the year he stopped Johnny Murphy in the 40th round in Providence, Rhode Island, but from then on his title bouts were regarded as featherweight contests. In those days many bantamweight claimants were boxing at 110lb (50kg) while Dixon set his limit at 112lb (51kg).

Other boxers whose names might be found in bantamweight roles of honour in the 1890s include Tommy Kelly, the 'Harlem Spider', and Jimmy Barry, unbeaten in 68 contests. Barry, of Chicago, was recognized in the USA with a win over New York's Caspar Leon in 1894, and consolidated his claim with a win over Walter Croot, of Britain, which ended tragically for Croot, whose skull struck the floor with great force, and he died with a brain injury. Barry retired in 1899.

Croot, however, had never been British champion, and a Briton with a better claim than anybody to the world crown was Billy Plimmer, who was British champion in 1892 when he outpointed Tommy Kelly at New York. Plimmer, an upstanding classical boxer from Birmingham, defended three times successfully in the United States, and then came back to England, where after one more successful defence his titles as British and world champion were taken by Thomas 'Pedlar' Palmer, who won on a disqualification when Plimmer's brother climbed into the ring to save him further punishment. Palmer, from Canning Town, London, made three defences, then was sent by a subscription among members of the National Sporting Club to America to sort out the championship with Terry McGovern, a 19-year-old from Johnstown, Pennsylvania, who was claiming the title on the retirement of Barry. A match took place at Tuckahoe, New York, which ended the British claim to the title for five years or so in a very unsatisfactory manner. Shortly after the fight began, the timekeeper accidentally struck the bell again. The referee sent the boxers to their corners, but then asked them to resume. Palmer, as if the fight were beginning afresh, extended his glove for the customary handshake, and McGovern seized the opportunity to sling a right which ended the contest in 75 seconds. McGovern raised the bantam limit to 116lb (53kg), but only managed one defence, a quick knock-out of Harry Forbes, before being forced to move up to featherweight.

Harry Harris, the 'Human Hairpin' from Chicago, was recognized in America as champion when he crossed to London in 1901 to outpoint Pedlar Palmer, but even the long, thin Harris had weight problems, and had to concede the title. Harry Forbes, from Rockford, Illinois, took over with a second round knockout of Dan Dougherty at St Louis, but after four quick defences he was knocked out in 1903 by Frankie Neil, a hard-punching Irish-American from San Francisco. On his fourth defence Neil travelled to London and was outpointed over 20 rounds by Joe Bowker, of Salford, Manchester, whose real name was Tommy Mahon. The clever Bowker made one defence, then moved up to featherweight.

Jimmy Walsh, of Newton, Massachusetts, and Britain's Digger Stanley claimed the title, so Stanley went to Chelsea, Massachusetts, to determine ownership, but was outpointed by Walsh who, however, also moved up to feather. In 1908 Walsh fought again as a bantam, reclaiming the crown, but his claim was not widely accepted. By then Britain had recognized Owen Moran, after a defeat of Al Demont, but he too could not maintain the weight.

Johnny Coulon, a Canadian from Toronto, established the best claim thereafter. Beginning with points wins over Kid Murphy, he maintained his position until June 1914, when he was knocked out by Kid Williams, who thus unified the title, for he was recognized by Great Britain and Europe.

Britain had named George 'Digger' Stanley, born, some say, in a caravan at Kingston-upon-Thames, who knocked out Joe Bowker, the former holder, in London in 1910 for the British bantamweight title, and since Bowker had not been beaten for the world title, that was regarded as at stake also. When Digger Stanley, on his third defence, outpointed Charles Ledoux, of France, on 22 April 1912, he was recognized by the IBU as well as Britain, and when Ledoux won the return in Dieppe, France, two months later, he was regarded as world champion. Ledoux took his half of the title to Los Angeles and was outpointed by Eddie Campi, of San Francisco, whose real name was Eddie de Campus. He, in turn, was knocked out by Kid Williams on 31 January 1914, and when

Above: Jimmy Wilde, the world flyweight champion, trying a right which Joe Lynch ducks beneath in their bout at the National Sporting Club in 1919. Wilde won although Lynch was to become world bantamweight champion the following year.

Williams beat Johnny Coulon in June he was recognized throughout the boxing world as champion. By now the weight limit had settled at 118lb (53.5kg).

Kid Williams was born in Copenhagen, his real name being Johnny Gutenko. He fought out of Baltimore, Maryland, and was short even for a bantamweight at 5ft 1in (1.55m), but was a good two-handed puncher.

Williams might have lost his title to Johnny 'Kowpie' Ertle of St Paul, Minnesota, being disqualified for low blows in a no-decision contest but it was generally ruled that a no-decision contest could be won only by a knock-out, so Williams remained the recognized champion. He drew twice over 20 rounds with Frankie Burns and Pete Herman, but was then outpointed by Herman, who also outpointed Burns, all these contests being in New Orleans. Herman then lost the title by being outpointed by Joe Lynch in New York.

Herman then came to England for a famous fight with the flyweight champion Jimmy Wilde, who had half-retired. The match had been made for the bantamweight title, and there was a suspicion in Britain that Herman 'loaned' the title to Lynch to prevent it being at risk. Wilde had already beaten Lynch. There was an argument over the weigh-in for the fight. Wilde claimed that there was an agreement for Herman to weigh in on the evening of the contest, to satisfy Wilde that he was not giving too much weight away. However, at the time, Herman refused, saying he had weighed in at lunchtime. Wilde declined to fight unless he weighed in, and eventually it took the Prince of Wales to persuade Wilde to fight. Herman stopped Wilde in the 17th round. He then returned to Brooklyn and regained the world title from Lynch.

However, Herman, from New Orleans, was already suffering from the eye trouble which ultimately caused his blindness, and he was outpointed in a surprise result on his next defence by Johnny Buff, of Perth Amboy, New Jersey. After one successful defence Buff was forced to retire in a match with Joe Lynch, who took the title for the second time. He beat Midget Smith but withdrew from a championship bout with Joe Burman two days beforehand (the cause being an accident). Abe Goldstein, of New York, who had boxed only two days before, was named as substitute, and the New York authorities announced that Burman was champion and the fight was a title fight. Goldstein then caused a surprise by winning, but he confirmed the form five months or so later by outpointing Joe Lynch at Madison Square Garden, in an exciting evening for both the Irish fans from the West Side and the Jewish supporters of Goldstein from Harlem.

Goldstein made two more defences before being outpointed by Eddie Martin, from Brooklyn, who was outpointed in turn by Charlie 'Phil' Rosenberg, another New York Jew. Rosenberg, on what would have been his third defence, against Bushy Graham (born Angelo Gerali in Italy), was overweight and the title was declared vacant, Rosenberg winning the overweight affair. Afterwards, it transpired that the two boxers had made a secret arrangement regarding the division of the purse, and both were suspended for a year by the New York authorities.

There was now a division in the championship. In 1927 Charles 'Bud' Taylor, of Terre Haute, Indiana, and 19-year-old Tony Canzoneri, later to be a world champion at three higher weights, were nominated to fight for the NBA title, and drew at Chicago, but Taylor won a return, only to relinquish the title because of weight-making difficulties. Pete Sanstol outpointed Archie Bell at Montreal for the, again, vacant title, but was then beaten by Panama Al Brown, who was already recognized by New York and Europe, and Brown thus unified the title.

The British version of the title, after Rosenberg's stripping, was won by Terry Baldock, of Poplar, London, who beat Archie Bell of America at the Albert Hall. Baldock's reign lasted only five months before he was outpointed by Willie Smith of Johannesburg, South Africa, the 1924 Olympic champion. Smith went to America to try to get a unifying bout with Bud Taylor, but returned disillusioned with the racketeering in American boxing. He moved up to featherweight without making a defence.

Bushy Graham, who had been suspended after his bout with champion Charlie Rosenberg, gained recognition in New York in May 1928 by outpointing Izzy Schwarz, but he, too, had weight problems and did not defend.

Al Brown won this title, with a points decision over Vidal Gregorio, and added European recognition to New York's by outpointing Knud Larson, at Copenhagen, although this was an overweight match so Brown's title was not at stake. When he outpointed Sanstol on a split decision in Montreal, Brown collected the NBA title and was undisputed champion.

The lanky Panama Al

Al Brown was born in Panama, and was frequently known as Panama Al Brown. He was 5ft 11in (1.80m), an extremely tall man for a bantamweight, and was a clever boxer who used his inches well. He was also a clever man who spoke many languages, and he was happy to risk his title in Europe, Canada and Britain, making 11 successful defences before he lost NBA recognition for failing to defend against a Mexican, Baby Casanova.

However, it was not Casanova who won the vacant title, it was Sixto Escobar, of Barcelona, Puerto Rico, who knocked out Casanova at Montreal. Escobar was a tough, hard-punching fighter. He lost the title on his second defence to Lou Salica of New York, who had been a brilliant amateur, but won it back in the return, and in August 1936 unified the championship again.

Meanwhile Al Brown, after one more defence, was surprisingly outpointed by Baltazar Sangchilli, in Valencia, Spain, the challenger's home town. A tough, busy fighter, Sangchilli (real name Hervoas) was Spain's first world champion. He went to New York where he fought many non-title fights before losing his crown in unfortunate circumstances on his first defence. He was well ahead of Tony Marino, of Pittsburgh, who was not in championship class, when he was paralysed with cramp in the 14th round and knocked out. Marino was stopped by Escobar on his first defence, Escobar thus becoming undisputed champion. Marino, sadly, died five months later after being outpointed in another contest.

Escobar was to drop and regain the title again (to Harry Jeffra of Baltimore, who later was featherweight champion). Escobar himself moved up to the featherweights in 1939.

George Pace was then named as champion by the NBA, and fought Lou Salica, favoured by New York, to a draw, thus retaining the title. Salica won the return at the Bronx Coliseum, New York, for universal recognition, leaving Pace as a man who was recognized by the NBA as champion but who never won a title fight.

In January 1942 Manuel Ortiz, of El Centro, California, earned recognition from his state as champion after a victory over Tony Olivera, and in August Ortiz outpointed Lou Salica, making his fourth defence, to become undisputed champion, and one of the division's most successful. From August 1942 to May 1950 Ortiz was undisputed champion for all but nine weeks, when Harold Dade of Chicago held the title after upsetting Ortiz on points at San Francisco — one of boxing's biggest surprises. Ortiz regained the crown at Los Angeles. In those seven and three-quarter years Ortiz fought in 22 world title fights, and won 20. One of his stranger victories was over David Young of Hawaii, at Honolulu, when Ortiz was unable to continue after the 13th round because of a low blow. After a 15-minute break Ortiz won on points.

Barefoot in Bangkok

Ortiz's final conqueror was Vic Toweel, from a famous boxing family of Benoni, South Africa. Toweel had been a brilliant amateur boxer, who took the title at Johannesburg on only his 14th professional contest. He was South Africa's first world champion, and made three defences, all in Johannesburg, before being knocked out in the first round by Jimmy Carruthers of Australia. Carruthers, from Paddington, New South Wales, had been an amateur in the 1948 Olympic Games with Toweel, where both had lost in an early round. Carruthers turned professional after

Left: *Panama Al Brown in training for a contest with former bantamweight champion Terry Baldock. Brown, an exceptionally tall bantam, made 12 successful defences of his world title, mostly in Europe.*

Toweel's success, convinced that if Toweel could win a world title, he could. He proved himself right, made three defences, and retired. The third defence was a remarkable affair. It took place in Bangkok, with Chamrern Songkitrat as the challenger, and was held in the open air in a storm. As large puddles formed in the ring, causing them to slip, the boxers agreed to fight in bare feet. Lights shattered occasionally in this 'Battle of the Typhoon', but with 60,000 present the fight went on, Carruthers winning on points.

When Carruthers retired, Robert Cohen, of Bône, Algeria, went to Bangkok to face Songkitrat for the vacant title and gained a split decision, but was then stripped by the NBA for failing to defend against Mexico's Raton Macias. He defended in Johannesburg against Vic Toweel's brother, Willie, and the fight was adjudged a draw. He lost the title when forced to retire against Mario D'Agata, of Arezzo, Italy, in Rome in June 1956.

D'Agata was a deaf mute who overcame this tremendous handicap to win a world title. He was outpointed on his first defence, however, by Alphonse Halimi, in Paris.

Meanwhile, the NBA title had been won by Raton Macias, of Mexico City, who knocked out Chamrern Songkitrat, making his third attempt, this time in San Francisco. Macias made two successful defences before meeting Halimi on 6 November 1957 for the undisputed title. Halimi, another Algerian, from Constantine, gave Macias a bad beating in the later rounds to take a clear points win.

However, having unified the championship, Halimi lost his next defence, against Joe Becerra, a tough Mexican from Guadalajara, who was a heavy-punching knock-out specialist. Halimi was beaten by this route in the eighth round in Los Angeles. He lasted one more round in the return and then Becerra outpointed Kenji Yonekura on a split decision in Tokyo. Becerra then took an eighth round knock-out in a non-title fight from Elroy Sanchez in Mexico and decided to retire. The championship split once more.

The British and European authorities recognized former champion Alphonse Halimi, after he outpointed Belfast's Freddie Gilroy in a disputed decision at Wembley. But Halimi lost the first defence of his second spell as champion when another Belfast boxer, Johnnie Caldwell, outpointed him, also at Wembley. Caldwell won a return, and then faced the NBA champion Eder Jofre at São Paulo, Brazil.

Jofre had won the vacant title by knocking out Elroy Sanchez, the cause of Becerra's retirement. Jofre, from São Paulo, was 24 when he won the title, and his third defence, against Caldwell, resulted in him becoming undisputed champion, as Caldwell was forced to retire in the tenth. Jofre was a brilliant two-fisted fighter who took his defences to eight before being forced to go the distance for the first time in a title fight — it spelt defeat as Fighting Harada outpointed him at Nagoya, Japan. It was a very close split decision, Jofre's first defeat in 51 fights. He retired, but three years later made a comeback to win the featherweight title.

Harada, from Setagaya, Tokyo, was meanwhile stepping up from the flyweight division, where he had briefly won the world title. Harada was a good champion who defended four times before being outpointed by Lionel Rose. He then moved up to featherweight and almost won a third title when challenging Johnny Famechon.

Lionel Rose was an Aborigine from Drouin, Australia, and a surprise winner over Harada, having been a substitute for Jesus Pimental, but the decision in Tokyo was unanimous, and he proved himself a good champion. He defended well in Tokyo, Los Angeles and Melbourne before running up against another of the outstanding South Americans who do so well in this division. Ruben Olivares, from Mexico City, was a ferocious hitter with a tremendous left hook, and he knocked out Rose in the fifth round at Los Angeles.

Olivares reigned for two and a half years, but did lose the title for six months of that time to Jesus 'Chuchu' Castillo, another Mexican who had the misfortune to be contemporary to Olivares, and to have lost a very close split decision to Rose. Olivares was finally stopped in March 1972 by Rafael Herrera of Julisco, Mexico. Herrera was outpointed in his first defence by Enrique Pinder, of Panama City, fighting in his home town. Pinder's win unfortunately heralded a split in the championship which has remained since 1972, for the WBC stripped him for failing to defend against Rodolfo Martinez.

As frequently happens in these situations, Martinez did not immediately win the vacant title. Matched with Rafael Herrera, Pinder's last victim, he was stopped in the 12th round at Monterrey, Mexico. After two defences, including one against Romeo Anaya, who had briefly held the WBA version, and a very close split decision over Venice Borkorsor of Bangkok, Herrera was stopped by Martinez, who became champion. Martinez, from Tepito, Mexico, was a swarming all-action boxer who won most of his contests by the short route. He made three defences, one of which was against the unlucky Borkorsor, who again was on the wrong end of a split decision.

Martinez was knocked out in May 1976 by Carlos Zarate, another boxer from Tepito, Mexico, whose stoppage record was remarkable, only one boxer taking him the distance in his first 50 contests. Nine of these wins were successful defences of his title. His first defeat came when he challenged another outstanding champion, Wilfredo Gomez, for his light-featherweight title. Zarate's second defeat came when he lost his title after three years to Lupe Pintor, another Mexican, from Cuajimalpa. Like the rest, Pintor carried a heavy punch, but his victory over Zarate was a split decision of extraordinary scoring. Two judges gave it to Pinter by a single point, while the third had Zarate eight points to the good.

Despite the controversial nature of his victory Pintor was nevertheless a good champion. He did not face Zarate again, as Zarate retired, only to return as a light featherweight, but he defended eight times successfully. One defence ended tragically for the lanky Welsh fighter Johnny Owen, the British, Commonwealth and European

Left: ***EBU champion Johnny Caldwell down in the tenth round of his title fight with NBA champion Eder Jofre in 1962. Caldwell retired later in the round in São Paulo. Jofre was champion for over four years.***

champion, who was so thin he was called 'Matchstick'; Owen died after 46 days in a coma following a 12th-round knock-out. In December 1982 Pintor, like Zarate, challenged Wilfredo Gomez for the light-featherweight crown, and was stopped in the 14th round. Pintor was then badly injured in a motorcycle accident which prevented him boxing, and in July 1983, by which time he had not defended his bantamweight title in over a year, he forfeited WBC recognition.

Meanwhile, back ten years in the 1973 WBA version of the championship, Enrique Pinder had no sooner been stripped of WBC recognition than he lost his WBA crown when knocked out in the third round by Romeo Anaya, of Cahuare, Mexico. Anaya defended twice, and then took the title to Johannesburg, where the local boy, Arnold Taylor, took it from him in an exciting battle. Taylor was down four times, but a left hook and right cross knocked out Anaya in the 14th round of a spectacular, all-action match. Taylor's only defence, at Durban, was another gruelling affair. He and Soo-Hwan Hong, of Seoul, South Korea, suffered damage as both went all out for victory, Taylor in particular ending with a huge swelling which closed his eye, before Hong was awarded the decision. Taylor, who retired in 1976, was sadly killed in a car accident five years later.

Hong, who later won the light-featherweight title, was knocked out in his second defence by Alfonso Zamora, one of the outstanding Mexicans in the division. He and Zarate ruled the two halves of the championship for over three and a half years, but did not meet to unify it, although Zarate won a non-title fight in 1977. Zamora was another tremendous puncher, whose six winning title fights lasted only 27 rounds. A second-round victim was Eusebio Pedroza, who two years later was to begin a long reign as featherweight champion. Zamora was knocked out himself in 1977 by Jorge Lujan, of Colón, Panama, who scored a big surprise, but proved himself to be an excellent boxer. Lujan made five defences, including a trip to Tokyo, before being outpointed by Julian Solis, an unbeaten 23-year-old from Rio Piedras, Puerto Rico. Solis had the misfortune to find Jeff Chandler, another outstanding champion, waiting in the wings, and Chandler stopped him in the 14th in his first defence in Miami.

Chandler, from Philadelphia, Pennsylvania, made nine successful defences, and reigned for three and a half years. Although he twice made trips to Tokyo, on one of which he drew with Eijiro Murata, an unlucky boxer who also drew with Pintor, most of his defences were in Atlantic City, which is where he lost his title to Richard (or Ricardo) Sandoval, of California. Sandoval won an exciting scrap with a last-round knock-out. Sandoval retired after his third defence in 1986 when he was stopped by Gaby Canizales of Laredo, Texas, and did not recover consciousness for several minutes. Canizales lost the title in his next contest, three months later, when outpointed by Bernardo Pinango, Venezuelan-born, but fighting from Panama. After three defences, he relinquished the title to fight as a light-featherweight.

The title changed hands rapidly after this: Takuya Muguruma, of Osaka, knocked out Azael Moran of Panama City to win, but lost

Right: *Miguel Lora of Colombia scores with a right to the head of Wilfredo Vasquez of Puerto Rico. 'Happy' Lora was successfully defending his WBC bantamweight title.*

on his first defence to Chan-Yung Park of South Korea, who did likewise to Wilfredo Vasquez of Bayamón, Puerto Rico, a previous unsuccessful challenger to Miguel Lora, the WBC champion. Vasquez went to Osaka and drew with former champion Muguruma, but he lost his title in May 1988 to Kaokor Galaxy, of Petchaboon, Thailand. The unbeaten Galaxy survived a fifth-round knockdown to come back strongly and take a split decision, winning the title in his 18th fight. This contest made history, for Kaokor's twin brother, Kaosai, was the reigning WBA light-bantamweight champion. While many sets of brothers have held world titles, this was the first example of twins being world champions. Kaosai won a non-title fight on the same bill, and after a quick shower was in his brother's corner for the historic win.

Galaxy lost his title on his first defence on a technical decision at Seoul on 14 August 1988 to Sung-Kil Moon of Korea after a clash of heads.

In the WBC strand of the championship, Pintor's motorcycle accident in 1983 allowed Albert Davila, of Pomona, who had previously failed in challenges to Zarate, Lujan and Pintor, to assume the title with a knockout of Kiko Bejines of Mexico in Los Angeles. Bejines was knocked out in the 12th round and never recovered consciousness, a tragic coincidence because it was in the same ring and in the same round that Johnny Owen had suffered the same fate three years before. Davila, after one successful defence, was forced to give up the crown with a back injury.

The new champion was Daniel Zaragoza, who won by the disqualification of Fred Jackson for butting. Zaragoza was outpointed by Miguel Lora three months later, and moved up to the light-featherweight class, where he won another world title.

Miguel 'Happy' Lora, of Montería, Colombia, brought some order to what was becoming a very messy division with defences into 1988, which saw him beat Wilfredo Vasquez, a future champion Enrique Sanchez, former champion Albert Davila on a come-back, Antonio Avelar, Ray Minus, Lucio Lopez and Davila again before being outpointed at Las Vegas on 29 October 1988 by surprise winner Raul Perez of Mexico.

The IBF recognized the bantamweight division in 1984, Satoshi Shingaki becoming the first champion by stopping Elmer Magallano, at Kawashiwara, Japan. Shingaki made one defence in Japan before being stopped in Sydney, by the Australian Jeff Fenech. Fenech made three defences in Sydney before weight problems forced him into the light-featherweight class, where he again became champion before moving up again and becoming featherweight champion.

Kelvin Seabrooks, of Charlotte, a man whose 34-bout record showed 13 defeats, took the vacant title with a fifth-round knockout of local boy Miguel Maturana, at Cartagena, Colombia, and kept the title when he met the Frenchman, Thierry Jacob, at Calais. A clash of heads ended the fight in the ninth round, both boxers's corners claiming victory, but the official verdict after the confusion was 'no contest'. Seabrooks stopped Ernie Cataluna and Fernando Beltran to keep the title but in July 1988 he was stopped in the 15th round by Orlando Canizales, of Laredo, Texas, who took the crown.

THE LIGHT-BANTAMWEIGHTS

A class between the flyweights and the bantamweights hardly seemed necessary, since there were only six pounds between the two limits, but the proliferation of weight classes has exceeded even that of governing bodies. Of the latter the WBC have been to the fore in creating new divisions, and they kicked off the super-flyweight class, as they now call it, in 1980. Boxing had got along without it for a few hundred years, but of course the WBA and IBF had to have an equivalent class of their own, so by 1984 there were three champions at the weight. The WBA and IBF call the division the junior bantamweight, the WBC's original title for it. This book will stay with its system and call it light-bantamweight. The weight limit is 115lb (52kg), 3lb (1.4kg) more than flyweight and 3lb (1.4kg) less than bantamweight.

The first champion, on 2 February 1980, was Rafael Orono, of Sucre, Venezuela, who outpointed Seung-Hoon Lee, at Caracas, in

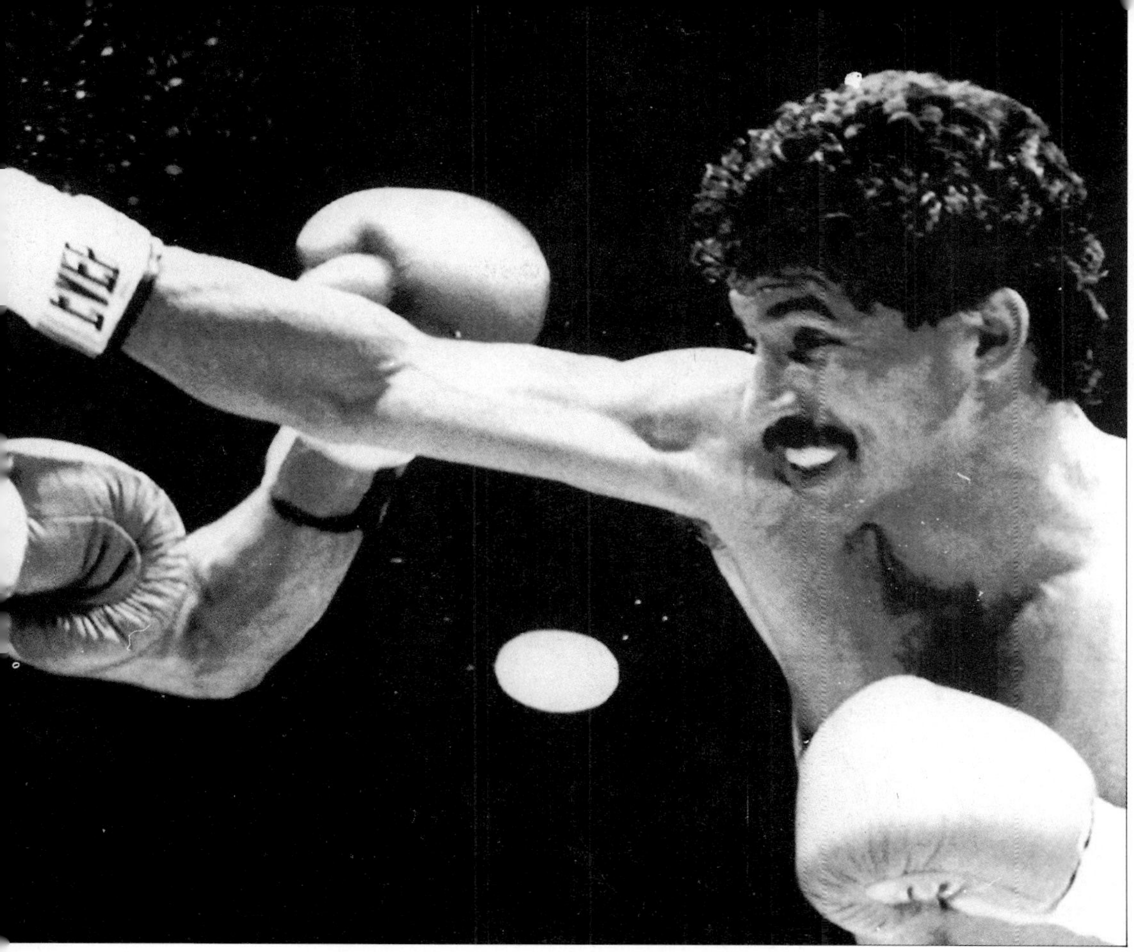

only his 11th contest. He was 21. He defended three times that year, but was knocked out by Chul-Ho Kim, of Ohsan, South Korea, who was only 19. He had made five defences by 1982, but was then knocked out by former champion Rafael Orono, by now a veteran of 24. He made four defences in his second spell, before being outpointed by Payao Poonterat.

Meanwhile, the WBA had instituted the class, and they recognized Gustavo Ballas, of Villa María, Argentina, who beat Sok-Chul Baek, but he was champion for less than three months, losing to Rafael Pedroza of Panama, a cousin of Eusebio, the reigning featherweight champion. However, he was outpointed by Jiro Watanabe, one of the best at this weight. Watanabe was champion of one body or the other for nearly four years, making 11 'defences'. In fact, Watanabe made six defences of the WBA title by March 1984, but was then stripped for not meeting Kaosai Galaxy, the main contender. Instead, he outpointed Payao Poonterat, the WBC champion, who had made one defence since beating Orono. The opportunity to unify the two strands was therefore missed, but Watanabe continued happily beating his WBC opponents until March 1986 when he was outpointed by Gilberto Roman, an extremely busy boxer from Mexicali, Mexico, having his 44th contest since turning professional less than five years earlier. He continued fighting frequently as champion, making seven defences by May 1987 when he lost the title to Santos Laciar, from Huinca Renancó, Argentina, with whom he had previously fought a draw. Laciar lost at the first defence to Jesus Rojas, of Colombia, who stopped one former champion in Gustavo Ballas, but on 8 April 1988 was outpointed by another, Gilberto Roman, who successfully defended twice in 1988.

Meanwhile, when Watanabe was stripped by the WBA in 1984, Kaosai Galaxy of Petchaboon, Thailand, won the title in Bangkok by knocking out Eusebio Espinal. He proved to be as good a champion as Watanabe. By January 1988 he had made seven successful defences, including defeats of former WBC champion Orono and former IBF champion Elly Pical. He then had the pleasure of seeing his twin brother Kaokor, who had begun professional boxing nearly five years after Kaosai, win a version of the bantamweight title.

The IBF strand of the division had its first champion on 10 December 1984 when Joo Do-Chun, of South Korea, beat Ken Kasugai in Osaka, Japan. He made five defences, all in South Korea, before he ventured abroad and Elly Pical, from Saparua-Maluku, Indonesia, stopped him in Jakarta. Pical confined himself to Jakarta, making one defence before losing to Cesar Polanco, of the Dominican Republic, but winning the title back and defending successfully once before forfeiting the IBF title to challenge Galaxy for the WBA crown. The contest was in Jakarta, but Galaxy won by a 14th-round knock-out.

South Koreans Tae-Il Chang and Soon-Chun Kwon fought for the vacant IBF title in the former's home town of Puson, and Chang got the split decision, after a close battle. However, the former holder, Elly Pical, won his old title back by beating him in Jakarta, and kept it on 20 February 1988 with a tremendous battle with Raul Diaz, of Bucaramanga, Colombia, who floored him three times before Pical came back to win a narrow points decision.

CHARLIE MAGRI
SPORTS
C.M.

The Flyweights and the Smaller Men

The very small boxers have always held fascination for the fans. Because of their speed they usually pack twice as much action into a round as the heavyweights, and a few of them have packed a terrific punch, too. The division got off to a good start with Jimmy Wilde, one of the best pound-for-pound boxers of all time. Pancho Villa, Fidel LaBarba, Frankie Genaro and Benny Lynch carried on the high tradition until World War II. From 1950 the champions came mostly from Japan, Thailand, South and Central America and South Korea, with Pascual Perez, Pone Kingpetch, Chartchai Chionoi, Santos Laciar and Sot Chitalada being among the better champions.

Left: *European champion Charlie Magri (left) boxing British champion Duke McKenzie at Wembley in May 1986 for both titles, taken by McKenzie with a fifth-round stoppage. Magri was world flyweight champion in 1983 and McKenzie won the world title in 1988.*

IN THE FOOTSTEPS OF JIMMY WILDE

The flyweight division came into being when the National Sporting Club in London drew up the weights for British championship bouts in 1909. The NSC was an unofficial ruling body in Britain, and largely formed the British Boxing Board of Control in the 1920s. The weight limit set for flyweights was 112lb (51kg), and the first British champion was Sid Smith of Bermondsey, London, who outpointed Joe Wilson over a memorable 20 rounds.

On 11 April 1913 Smith went to Paris and outpointed the French champion, Eugene Criqui, and was acknowledged by British and European authorities as world champion. Soon afterwards Smith was stopped by another Londoner, Bill Ladbury of New Cross, at the famous Blackfriars Ring. This match was at catchweights, and although advertised as for the championship, some do not regard it as such. Smith, however, relinquished his claim.

Percy Jones, of Porth, Wales, outpointed Ladbury at the NSC and was recognized as champion, and beat Eugene Criqui in a defence, but he forfeited the title when overweight for a match with Joe Symonds of Plymouth. Jones and Ladbury were both killed as a result of World War I — Ladbury in France in 1916, while Jones died as a result of his injuries in 1922.

Although Symonds beat Jones he was not recognized because of the overweight of Jones. However, he claimed the title, with more justification than many world champions of the period, and some class Symonds' defeat of Tancy Lee, the British champion, on 18 October 1915 as a world title fight.

Britain and Europe recognized Jimmy Wilde, one of boxing's immortals, as champion when he stopped Symonds on 14 February 1916. Wilde had previously beaten Symonds and lost to Lee. Wilde's defeat of Johnny Rosner, of New York, at Liverpool in 1916 emphasized his claim, and defeats of Tancy Lee and Johnny Hughes were advertised as world title bouts.

Meanwhile, America had recognized the class, and the man who had emerged to claim the US championship was Young Zulu Kid, an Italian-born boxer whose real name was Giuseppe di Melfi, but who boxed out of New York with his fanciful ring name. He came to London in 1916, and despite the war the serving soldier Wilde was allowed to meet him on the grounds that the stadium (the Central Hall, Holborn, a derelict ex-storage shed for the delivery company Carter Paterson) would be turned afterwards into a YMCA hostel to help the war effort. Wilde had little trouble in knocking out the Zulu Kid (although it lasted 11 rounds) and he was now recognized universally as champion. This fight is sometimes listed as the first for the world title, which seems unreasonable as in other weight classes it was not thought necessary to wait for an international bout before there could be a champion.

The Ghost with a Hammer in his Hand

Jimmy Wilde, from Tylorstown, Wales, was 5ft 2½in (1.59m) and never more than 108lb (49kg), and with skinny legs and arms he looked most unlike a boxer. He had built up strength with work down the mines, and skill with hundreds of boxing booth fights, and during his career he not only beat the world's best flyweights but also many bantams and feathers. He earned several nicknames, the most expressive being 'The Ghost with a Hammer in his Hand'. Wartime curtailed his opportunities for cashing in on his title, and as a soldier he could not be paid. One promoter got around this, and when Wilde beat American bantamweight Joe Conn, Mrs Wilde was handed a bag of diamonds.

Unfortunately for Wilde, some of his best years would have been the four years of the war. In 1919 he beat the American bantamweights Joe Lynch (the following year world champion) and Pal Moore, and in 1920 toured America, beating all-comers. Unfortunately, in 1921, he was badly beaten by bantamweight champion Pete Herman (whom he thought tricked him over the weigh-in, Wilde having to concede nearly 14lb [6kg]), and more or less retired. However, when asked to defend the flyweight championship in New York in 1923 against Pancho Villa, he felt obliged to go, and took another bad beating, whereupon he retired for good, with over 100 knock-outs to his name.

Pancho Villa, of Iloilo, Philippines, was a tough boxer with knock-out power in his fists. Only 22 when he took the title, he outpointed four challengers and then took on the 18-year-old Jimmy McLarnin, later to be world welterweight champion. Villa had had a wisdom tooth extracted before the fight, and the punches he took to the jaw necessitated further treatment, an abscess and blood poisoning followed, and he died on the operating table ten days after the contest, on 4 July 1925.

Two Olympic flyweight champions contested the vacant title: Frankie Genaro (1920) and Fidel LaBarba (1924). LaBarba got the decision and American recognition, which after one defence he made universal when he outpointed Glaswegian Elky Clark, the British champion, in Madison Square Garden. However LaBarba, still only 21, then retired for a spell to enter Stanford University.

There was disagreement over the new champion. The NBA backed Albert 'Frenchy' Belanger, a popular Canadian from Toronto, who outpointed Genaro in his home town.

New York favoured Izzy Schwartz, an agile New Yorker, who outpointed Newsboy Brown, a boxer who fought mainly in California but who was born David Montrose in Russia. California actually recognized Newsboy Brown as champion after he outpointed Johnny McCoy.

When Johnny Hill, from Strathmiglo, Fife, Scotland, outpointed Newsboy Brown in London in 1928, Great Britain was able to follow California and name Hill champion, but this strand of the championship ended when Hill, surprisingly, lost a non-title fight to France's Emile Pladner, whom he had already beaten for the European title. It transpired that Hill was probably already seriously ill at the time, for he died seven months later.

Meanwhile, Genaro had taken the NBA title in a return with Belanger, but surprisingly, he was knocked out in 56 seconds by Emile Pladner, who was recognized by both Europe and the NBA. Pladner, from Clermont-Ferrand, then lost the title on the return by hitting low in the fifth round, both bouts being in Paris.

Izzy Schwartz, the New York champion, proved the soundest of the claimants, defending four times before losing in 1929 to Willie La Morte, who for some reason did not gain New York recognition, although by beating Schwartz again he put him out of contention, and by 'defending' against Frisco Grande he had a strong claim. New York preferred instead an elimination tournament, in the final of which Midget Wolgast of Philadelphia, Pennsylvania, outpointed Black Bill of Cuba. Of course, that was not his real name (Wolgast, that is). He was born Joseph Loscalzo and took his fighting name from Adolphus Wolgast, the former bantamweight champion.

Wolgast was an extremely fast boxer, who then beat La Morte, who collapsed with a heart spasm as he returned to his corner at the end of the fifth round, and was forced to retire.

Meanwhile Genaro, the NBA and European choice, another fast boxer, was doing well in his second spell. He won in Paris, then defeated La Morte and Belanger, and was matched with Wolgast in New York to unify the championship. Unfortunately, the decision was a draw, so each boxer kept half a title. Genaro returned to Europe where he boxed another draw, with a Spaniard, Victor Ferrand, in Madrid. Ferrand was extremely unlucky, as IBU rules required a five-point margin in the scores before a title could change hands, and the referee's score card showed Ferrand only four points ahead.

After two more defences Genaro lost the title when knocked out in the second round by Victor 'Young' Perez of Tunis, who was stopped in his first defence a year later by Jackie Brown, in the challenger's home town of Manchester. Brown defended four times successfully, three against Valentin Angelmann, of Colmar, France, twice outpointing him and then boxing a draw. Jackie Brown then lost recognition by the IBU for not meeting Angelmann a fourth time after the draw, and soon afterwards in September 1935 lost the NBA title when knocked out in the second round (after 11 knockdowns) by Scotland's Benny Lynch, one of the greatest of all flyweights.

While all this activity was going on, Midget Wolgast did not defend the New York title for four years. When he did, a week after Lynch had won the NBA version, he was outpointed by Small Montana (real name Benjamin Gan) of the Philippines, who had based himself in California. He won in Oakland, and California recognized him as well as New York. When the IBU recognized Angelmann as champion after a stoppage of Kid Davis in Paris, there were three claimants to the championship, but this was now to be cleared up. After one defence, Angelmann's recognition by the IBU lapsed, ostensibly because of weight problems but also because Angelmann was beaten in non-title fights, twice by future champion Peter Kane.

Above: *Probably the greatest of all world flyweight champions, Jimmy Wilde, who often had to fight men much heavier than himself. Wilde was champion for over seven years.*

The brilliant Benny Lynch

When Small Montana came to Wembley to meet Lynch on 19 January 1937 it was the first unifying contest in this division since 1930, and the two put on a display worthy of the occasion, Lynch winning with a brilliant exhibition of boxing and fighting.

Lynch, from Clydesdale, had a problem — alcohol — which was to destroy him, but at his peak he was outstanding, and his tremendous defence against Peter Kane, which he won by a 13th-round knock-out, was watched by 40,000 at Shawfield Park, Glasgow. Alas, it was his last defence. He scaled more than 6lb (3kg) over the limit for a challenge from Jackie Jurich, of San Jose, California, and although he won the overweight match, he was stripped of his title. Eight years later he was found dead of malnutrition.

Jackie Jurich fought Peter Kane for the vacant title, and Kane won on points at Anfield, Liverpool. Kane, from Golborne, Lancashire, was only 20 but already a seasoned professional with a tremendous punch. After losing to Lynch he had drawn with him in an overweight contest. His most striking physical characteristic was large staring eyes, like those of Eddie Cantor, the film comedian.

Unfortunately, within a year of Kane winning the title, England was at war and he was unable to cash in. During the war in Europe the NBA proclaimed Little Dado, of the Philippines, champion, but this was never followed up and he did not fight for the title.

During the war, Kane fought Jackie Paterson, of Springfield, Ayrshire, and the Scot knocked him out in 61 seconds. Paterson was a hard-hitting southpaw who also enjoyed success as a bantam while flyweight champion. The Scottish fans hoped for another Lynch and after the war 50,000, a new Scottish record, packed Hampden Park, Glasgow, to see his first defence, against Joe Curran, of Liverpool. Paterson won on points.

Alas, Paterson's reign followed Lynch's in a manner not desired. He was unable to make the weight for a defence against Dado Marino of Honolulu and was stripped of the crown. Three months later Marino faced Rinty Monaghan, of Belfast, for the vacant crown, and Monaghan won on points at Harringay, London. Monaghan was recognized by the NBA, but the British Boxing Board of Control were unable to recognize him because Paterson had taken out an injunction against them, preventing them sanctioning any contest not including him as for the title. However, the matter was soon cleared up for five months later Paterson met Monaghan in the King's Hall, Belfast, and Monaghan knocked out Paterson, who had weakened himself to make the weight, in the seventh round. Paterson, like Lynch, had a sad end. He did not keep the money he made from boxing, losing much of it on gambling, and, having emigrated to South Africa, he was killed in 1966 in a street fight.

John Joseph Monaghan was a very popular figure who acquired the nickname 'Rinty' from the famous dog, Rin Tin Tin, of the movies. His habit was to sing to the crowds after victory — 'When Irish Eyes are Smiling' was the theme. Monaghan fought Maurice Sandeyron of France, the European champion, for both titles and outpointed him, and then drew with Terry Allen. All these fights were popular Irish occasions at the King's Hall, Belfast. Six months after the draw with Allen, Monaghan announced his retirement. Terry Allen won the vacant title with a points win over Honore Pratesi, of Marseilles. Allen, whose real name was Edward Govier, was a barrow-boy from Islington, and a sharp puncher, but his reign lasted only 98 days. He took the title to Honolulu and was outpointed by Dado Marino.

Dado Marino, from Honolulu, was just short of 34 years when he won the title. He became the first grandfather ever to become a world champion. He had previously tried to wrest the bantamweight title from Manuel Ortiz. He beat Allen in a return 15 months later but lost the title in Tokyo to Yoshio Shirai. Shirai, from Tokyo, defended successfully four times, all points wins in Tokyo, including one over Allen, before he himself was outpointed in Tokyo by Pascual Perez, of Argentina, in November 1954.

The diminutive Perez

Perez, from Mendoza, was only 4ft 11in (1.50m) and only 105lb (48kg), but he was one of the hardest hitting of all flyweights. He knocked out Shirai in the return and continued to beat all-comers for five and a half years and was champion into the 1960s. He made nine successful defences, five of which finished inside the distance, including a one-round demolition of British champion Dai Dower in Buenos Aires. When his reign came to an end at last it was in Bangkok, where Pone Kingpetch, of Hui Hui, Thailand, outpointed him on a split verdict. Kingpetch, however, stopped Perez in a return in Los Angeles, the first time he had fought outside Bangkok. He proved he could win abroad with two defences in Tokyo before Fighting Harada knocked him out there, but he regained the title in Tokyo with a split decision (one judge marking a draw). He was then knocked out in the first round by Hiroyuki Ebihara, of Tokyo, but back in Bangkok regained the title for a second time with another split decision. Kingpetch's reign ended at last with a points defeat by Salvadore Burruni in Rome in April 1965. Kingpetch died of pneumonia in 1982.

Burruni was stripped of the WBA title for failing to meet Horacio Accavallo, and lost his WBC title when outpointed at Wembley by Walter McGowan, a Scot from Burnbank, Lanarkshire. McGowan was a brilliant boxer

Above: A memorable world flyweight bout at Wembley in 1937 was that in which the champion Benny Lynch (back to camera) outpointed Small Montana after a brilliant exhibition of boxing.

who had the misfortune to suffer badly from cuts. He overcame one on his eye to take the title. Burruni was unlucky for he had defended his European title successfully against McGowan and would have expected a rubber match, but McGowan lost the title on his first defence and Burruni did not get another chance. McGowan had a badly split nose which caused his stoppage against Chartchai Chionoi, the local man, in Bangkok. Chionoi took over where Kingpetch left off, winning and losing versions of the flyweight title for almost eight years. A brilliant boxer and fighter, he made four successful defences in his first spell as champion including another win over McGowan, whose eye was cut when he was well ahead, and a 13th-round stoppage of Efren Torres, who also was well ahead, and with three rounds to go about to win the title. However, Torres won it in Mexico City in 1969 when Chionoi himself was cut over the left eye.

Efren Torres, from Mexico, made one successful defence in Guadalajara, but was then unanimously outpointed by Chionoi in Bangkok. Chionoi's second reign lasted nine months, until he was stopped in the second round by Erbito Salavarria, from Manila, in the Philippines. Chionoi's future activities were to be under the WBA banner. Salavarria made two defences, the second a draw with Betulio Gonzalez, but he was stripped after this contest because, it was alleged, he used an illegal stimulant. Salavarria, too, had a second reign with the WBA.

Gonzalez, from Maracaibo, Venezuela, was another long-running champion in both divisions. His first spell lasted until his second defence, when he retired against Venice Borkorsov of Thailand, who outpointed Salavarria before relinquishing the title to move up to bantamweight, where he twice challenged unsuccessfully for a world title.

Meanwhile, after Burruni had been stripped by the WBA in 1965, Horacio Accavallo, of Parque Patricias, Argentina, won the title by outpointing Katsuyoshi Takayama in Tokyo, in one of those split decisions common in Tokyo at the time, where two judges give the fight comfortably to the winner, and the third narrowly to the loser. Accavallo, a brilliant boxer, made three defences, the last a split decision in Buenos Aires against Hiroyuki Ebihara, and retired.

Ebihara, a previous champion, won the vacant title but, for a second time, was outpointed on his first defence by Bernabe Villacampo, of Toledo, Philippines, who also lost first time to Berkrerk Chartvanchai of Bangkok, who maintained the tradition by being outpointed by Masao Ohba of Japan. Ohba, from Sumidaku, brought some order to the WBA strand and was a good champion, making five defences, beating those persistent champions and challengers Betulio Gonzalez and Chartchai Chionoi, but sadly Ohba was killed in a car crash in Tokyo in January 1973.

As Borkorsov relinquished the WBC crown in July 1973, the WBA and WBC were both for a spell without champions. Chionoi and Gonzalez helped them out.

First to find a champion was the WBA, and Chionoi won when Fritz Chervet, of Switzerland, was stopped with a cut eye. Chionoi made two defences, including a split decision over Chervet of wildly fluctuating scores, but then conceded the title when weighing in 3.5lb (1.6kg) overweight for a defence against Susumu Hanagata. He was stripped and Hanagata awarded the title after stopping him in the overweight bout.

The title was then won from Hanagata by Erbito Salavarria, a former champion, who took it on a split decision at Toyama, Japan. He was stopped in the last round of his first defence by Alfonso Lopez of Panama, who beat Shojo Oguma on a typical Tokyo split decision, but was stopped at Los Angeles by Gustavo 'Guty' Espadas of Mérida, Mexico.

Espadas, a boxer who crowded his opponents, defended successfully five times before losing to Betulio Gonzalez, by now having his third spell as champion, who outpointed Espadas at Maracay, Venezuela, in one of the split decisions which seemed to plague the flyweight division.

Gonzalez, as related, had enjoyed his second spell as champion when he had taken the vacant WBC title in 1973 with a points win over Miguel Canto, and had defended twice before being outpointed by Shoji Oguma in Tokyo. It was, of course, a split decision, with one judge favouring Gonzalez, by four points. Oguma lost at Sendai, Japan, on his first defence to Miguel Canto, on a split decision. To prove split decisions were not Japanese copyright, Canto then beat Gonzalez on one at Monterrey, Mexico.

Miguel Canto, from Mérida, the same town as Guty Espadas, who shared the WBA/WBC flyweight championship with him for over two years, was an outstanding champion who successfully defended 14 times, beating Gonzalez twice and Oguma twice. Six of these were split verdicts. He lost on 18 March 1979 to Chan-He Park, of Pusan, South Korea, who outpointed him in his home town.

Park made five successful defences, beating Canto again, and also his fellow-townsman Espadas, before being outpointed on 18 May 1980 by Shoji Oguma, who became title-holder for the second time. Oguma, after two defences, lost to Antonio Avelar, of Guadalajara, Mexico, a knock-out specialist who on his second defence was knocked out in the first round by Prudencio Cardona, of Colombio. The WBC title then changed hands with nobody making a successful defence through Freddie Castillo of Mexico, Eloncio Mercedes of the Dominican Republic, Charlie Magri of England, Frank Cedeno of the Philippines and Koji Kobayashi of Japan. He was knocked out in the second round by Gabriel Bernal of Huetamo, Mexico, who did manage a successful defence before being outpointed by Sot Chitalada in Bangkok. The Thailander had previously fought for the light-flyweight title, and he won the flyweight title in only his eighth contest. He was another to graduate from the foot-boxing school. Chitalada proved a good champion, and made six successful defences before losing on points to Yong-Kang Kim of South Korea at Pohang on 24 July 1988.

To revert to the WBA, Betulio Gonzalez, on winning the title in 1978, defended three times, twice against Shoji Oguma, as persistent as he in chasing the title, before being outpointed by Luis Ibarra, of Panama, who soon passed the crown on to Tae-Shik Kim,

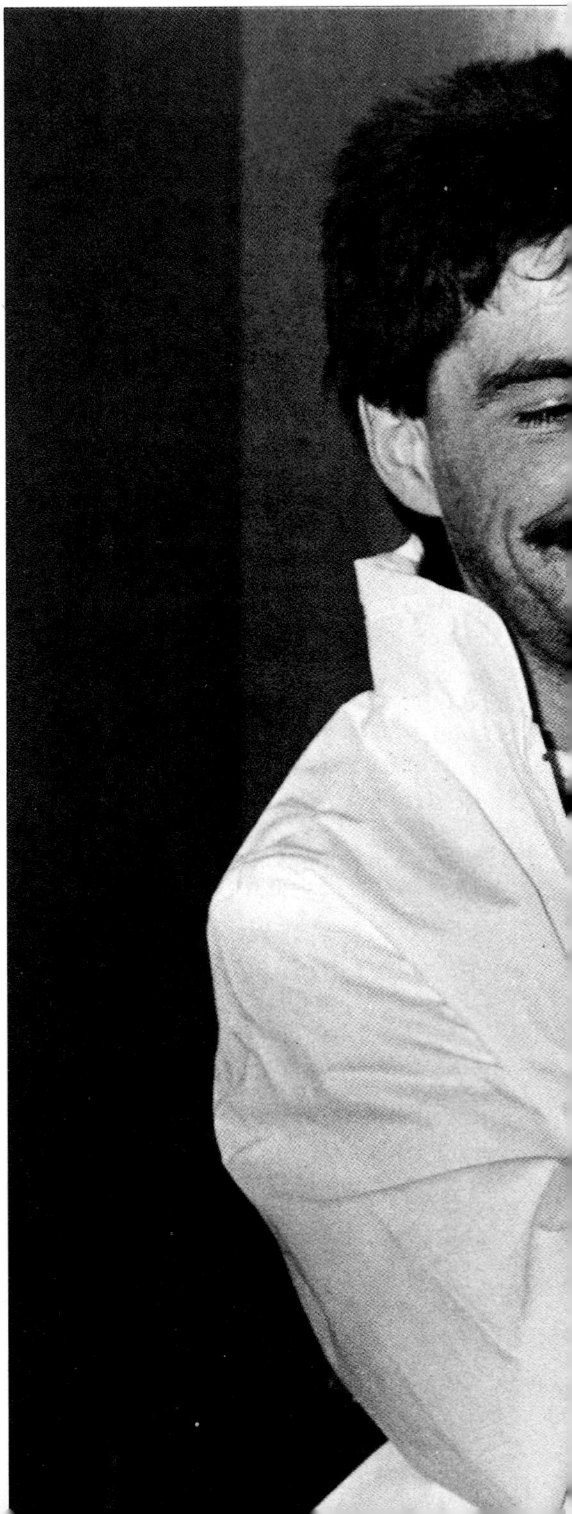

who knocked him out in the second round in Seoul. Kim, from Kanwon-Do, South Korea, was a big puncher, who on his second defence was outpointed by Peter Mathebula, from Mohlakeng in the Transvaal, the first black South African to win a world title. He defended in Soweto, but was stopped in the seventh by Santos Laciar, a very busy boxer from Huinca Renancó, Argentina. Laciar was beaten by Luis Ibarra on his first defence but for the second time Ibarra dropped the title, to Juan Herrera, on *his* first defence. Herrera, another flyweight from Mérida, Mexico, made a successful defence — against Betulio Gonzalez — but then gave the crown back to Laciar, who stopped him in Mérida. Laciar's first defence this time was against Gonzalez, making his last effort to win the title for the fourth time, and Laciar outpointed the veteran 33-year-old, who then retired. Laciar proved a good champion in his second spell, making nine successful defences in nearly three years before relinquishing the title to campaign as a light-bantamweight.

The new WBA champion in October 1985 was Hilario Zapata, from Panama City, an outstanding light-flyweight champion, who successfully moved up a class and outpointed Alonzo Gonzales for the title. He had previously failed in an attempt to beat Laciar. On his sixth defence he was outpointed by the unbeaten Fidel Bassa, of Colombia.

Bassa was a good puncher who occasionally showed himself vulnerable to a punch, so his fights were usually exciting. One such was his first defence against Dave 'Boy' McAuley in the King's Hall, Belfast in May 1987. McAuley was down in the first, but fought back to put the champion down in the third, and from then on it was a tremendous scrap.

Left: Dave 'Boy' McAuley, the local challenger, demonstrating what he intended to do to flyweight champion Fidel Bassa during their title fight in Belfast in 1987. He succeeded in knocking down Bassa, but in an exciting match of fluctuating fortunes Bassa scored the knockout in the 13th round.

***Above:** Dave McAuley (facing camera) and Fidel Bassa, who retained his title, during their 1987 contest at the King's Hall, Belfast.*

The Irish challenger almost won in the ninth, putting Bassa down twice (a third time would have ended it) but the game champion had the last word with a terrific right in the 13th which knocked out McAuley. Bassa then drew with Zapata in Panama City, and by October 1988 had successfully defended five times, including another points win over McAuley in Belfast, in a good battle in which the champion fought more cagily than before.

The International Boxing Federation began its flyweight division in 1983 and it has been dominated by boxers from Korea and the Philippines. On Christmas Eve 1983 Soon-Chun Kwon knocked out Rene Busayong in Seoul, and made six successful defences, all in South Korea. Two of these were draws with Chon-Kwan Chung, who on their third meeting on 20 December 1985 stopped the champion in the fourth. His reign was short-lived, for he passed the title to Bi-Won Chung, who soon lost it to Hi-Sup Shin, who on 22 February 1987 was knocked out in the fifth round by Dodie Penalosa, a previous unsuccessful challenger to Zapata.

In September 1987, for the first time, an IBF flyweight world title fight took place outside South Korea, when Penalosa, of the Philippines, defended in Manila, but a Korean won the title back, for Penalosa was knocked out in the 11th round by Chang-Ho Choi. In January 1988 Choi lost his title on points to Rolando Bohol of the Philippines, who retained it in May 1988 with a decision over Cho-Woon Park, of South Korea. Bohol, however, lost the title on his first defence, when Duke McKenzie of Croydon, the British and European champion, knocked him out in the 11th round at Wembley.

LIGHT FLYWEIGHTS

The WBC instituted the light-flyweight class in 1975. The weight limit was 108lb (49kg), i.e. 4lb (2kg) below the flyweight limit. Franco

Udella of Cágliari, Italy, a 1974 challenger to Betulio Gonzalez for the flyweight title, was the first champion. He won on a disqualification when a kidney punch by Valentin Martinez led to him leaving the ring in agony. He relinquished the title when illness prevented him keeping a date with Rafael Lovera, of Paraguay. Lovera faced Louis Estaba, from Puerto La Cruz, Venezuela, a 34-year-old who won so easily that Lovera was investigated and found to be an impostor with no boxing experience at all.

It was a deeply embarrassing scandal for the WBC and all those who claim boxing is rigidly controlled from the point of view of the safety of competitors. Probably Estaba was embarrassed, too, that the fake challenger lasted four rounds. Estaba, however, redeemed this inauspicious start by making 11 successful defences, before losing to Freddie Castillo, who stopped him in Caracas. Castillo lost to Sor Vorasingh of Bangkok on his first defence, and he lost on his second to Sung-Jun Kim, from Kyungnam in South Korea, who lost three months later to Shigeo Nakajima of Ibaraki, Japan. He was beaten on his first defence by a man who made the division a career for three years, Hilario Zapata, of Panama City. He made eight defences then lost to a second-round knockout by Amado Ursua of Mexico, but he regained the title from Tadashi Tomori, of Japan, who beat Ursua on his first defence. Zapata made two more defences before losing the title finally to Jung-Koo Chang in 1983 and moving up to flyweight. Chang, from Pusan, South Korea, known as 'The Hawk', began a long series of defences, which by 27 June 1988 had reached 14, and he had been champion for over five years. His only defeat had been against Zapata in a previous challenge, and his victims included Sot Chitalada, the flyweight champion, on whom he inflicted his first defeat.

The WBA strand of the championship (called junior flyweight) produced fewer long-running champions. The first contest was on 23 August 1975 and Jaime Rios, of Panama City, won it by outpointing Rigoberto Marcano. Juan Guzman of the Dominican Republic beat Rios; then Yoko Gushiken of Okinawa beat him and held the title for nearly four and a half years. He made 13 successful defences, but Pedro Flores, of Mexico, beat him at the second attempt in March 1981.

Flores lost the title on his first defence to Hwan-Jin Kim, of Korea, who managed one successful defence before losing to Katsuo Tokashiki of Japan. He made five successful defences before losing to Lupe Madera of Mexico, who had been outpointed and then held to a draw in two previous challenges to him. Madera's victory was fortuitous in a sense, for a clash of heads in the fourth round left him badly cut and unable to continue, and the title went to him on the strength of the first three rounds, this being the minimum distance the WBA required for such a decision to be rendered. Madera, however, won a return on points before losing to Francisco Quiroz of the Dominican Republic. Quiroz's second defence was a loss to Joey Olivo, of Los Angeles, who also made one successful defence before the unbeaten Myung-Woo Yuh, of Korea, outpointed him in Seoul on December 1985. Yuh, a strong skilful boxer, carried the title into 1988, when on 6 November he made his eighth successful defence.

The IBF entered the scene in 1983, also calling the division junior flyweight. The first champion was Dodie Penalosa of the Philippines, who stopped Satoshi Shingaki at Seoul on 10 December. Penalosa made three defences but forfeited the title in July 1986 when he challenged Hilario Zapata for the WBA flyweight title. The title then passed to Korea, when Jum-Hwan Choi gradually took control to win a unanimous decision over Cho-Woon Park. Choi proved a difficult man to beat and by November 1988 had made five successful defences.

MINI-FLYWEIGHTS OR STRAW-WEIGHTS

In 1987, the WBC started a new class which they called strawweight, setting a weight limit of 105lb (48kg), 3lb (1.4kg) less than light-flyweights.

The first champion, on 18 October 1987, was 18-year-old Hiroki Ioka of Japan, who outpointed Mai Thomburifarm of Thailand at Osaka. The tall 5ft 6½in (1.69m) boxer won impressively before 8,000 fans at the Kinki University Auditorium. He stopped Korean Kyung-Yung Lee at Osaka and kept his title in June 1988 with a draw with Napa Kiatwanchi of Thailand in Osaka.

The IBF called their corresponding class the mini-flyweight division, and their first champion was the Korean, Kyung Yung Lee, but he forfeited the crown by choosing to challenge the WBC champion Hiroki Ioka and losing. The vacant title was won in March 1988 by the Thailander, Samuth Sithnaroepul, who was awarded a controversial technical decision when his contest with Pretty Boy Lucas was stopped in the 11th round, Lucas being badly cut over the right eye.

The WBA, also calling the class mini-flyweight, named Leo Gamez, of Venezuela, their first champion when he beat Bong-Jun Kim, of Korea, in a close battle at Pusan in January 1988, all three judges giving it to him by a single point after a gruelling struggle. In April 1988 he defended successfully with a victory over Japan's Kenji Yokozawa.

EVERLAST
MOM

The Great Boxers

Boxers are so diverse, with a champion like Primo Carnera weighing the equivalent of two and a half flyweights, that it is impossible to rank them in a specific order. Styles have changed, not only between the wrestling style of the prize ring and the punching style of today. An old film of a Dempsey fight, say, bears little correspondence with a modern encounter between champions like Hagler and Leonard. Even within one era and one weight there is room for a wide diversity — Ali and Frazier were quite different boxers, but both good champions. This section highlights some of the best, from Ali in one corner to Zale in the other.

Left: *Larry Holmes had one of the best records of any heavyweight champion, winning 21 title fights. Having lost the title and his unbeaten record to Michael Spinks, he enjoyed a final pay day when tackling the latest champion from the gallery of all-time greats, Mike Tyson. Tyson was too strong for the fading Holmes and won easily by a fourth-round stoppage.*

Below: Muhammad Ali was one of the most brilliant of champions, combining the size, strength and weight of a top heavyweight with the speed and agility of many a lightweight. He was as good for boxing with his tongue as with his fists, for nobody in recent times could stir up as much interest or controversy with his opinions on the fight game.

Muhammad ALI

b 1942

Muhammad Ali styled himself 'The Greatest', and few would argue. He is probably the best-known boxer of all time, and at his peak was the most famous sportsman in the world.

He was born Cassius Marcellus Clay in Louisville, Kentucky, took an interest in boxing when 12, became an outstanding amateur, and won the light-heavyweight Olympic title in Rome. Sponsored by a group of local millionaires, he turned professional and soon attracted notice with his habit of predicting the round in which he would win. He became extremely unpopular with his bragging, and fans turned up to see if anybody could button 'The Louisville Lip'.

After defeating Archie Moore, he earned a heavyweight title shot against the formidable Sonny Liston when 22, and put up an incredible display of hyper-activity at the weigh-in which his own doctor described as 'self-induced hysteria'. However, he won the fight and proved unbeatable until stripped of the title because of his refusal to submit to being drafted during the Vietnam War. During this time he had joined the Black Muslim movement and changed his name from Cassius Clay, under which he fought until he won the title, to Muhammad Ali. He was out of boxing for three years, but eventually returned, and even won his argument with the US Army over Vietnam, a sentence of five years being cancelled.

During his comeback he challenged Joe Frazier, who had assumed his title, and suffered his first defeat, but amazingly he regained the championship with a tremendous display against George Foreman. Having then lost it to Leon Spinks, he regained it again to become the first to win the title three times. He retired and tried to win it a fourth time from Larry Holmes, but was well past his best and soundly beaten.

It could be argued that nobody beat Ali in his prime, three of his defeats coming after his long lay-off (and each emphatically avenged) and the other two coming when he mistakenly came back from retirement.

Many claim that Ali is the greatest of all boxers. He was a perfect physical specimen at 6ft 3in (1.91m) and around 215lb (98kg), one of the biggest of heavyweights. However, he moved so nimbly that he looked like a middleweight in action. 'He floats like a butterfly and stings like a bee' was one of the more famous remarks made of him. He had an acute boxing intelligence and adapted his style to suit his opponent. Some opponents were dominated by his sheer personality.

Although he split public opinion over his Vietnam War stand, by the end of his remarkable career he was universally admired. He proved a charismatic and outgoing star of the media. For around 20 years he was the biggest name in boxing, keeping the fans thoroughly entertained both in and out of the ring. As soon as he retired he began to suffer from ill health. His speech became slurred and he lost his customary snap — it is to be hoped he regains it.

Alexis ARGUELLO

b 1952

Tall and slim, Arguello was a skilful boxer who won titles at three weights and was not frightened to risk them in many parts of the world. That he had a punch to back up the clinical efficiency of his boxing is demonstrated by the fact that he won three-quarters of his 86 contests inside the distance.

He was born in Managua, the capital of Nicaragua, on 19 April 1952. He turned professional when sixteen and a half. After 35 bouts he challenged Ernesto Marcel for the WBA featherweight title but was outpointed. However, in November 1974, he knocked out Ruben Olivares for the title. He defended this four times and then gave it up to become a junior lightweight, and in January 1978 he stopped Alberto Escalera, who was making his eleventh defence, for the WBC title. Arguello proved himself the best at this weight by making eight defences, then he decided to tackle the lightweights.

In June 1981 he beat Jim Watt at Wembley to become the WBC champion. Having defended this title four times Arguello, for the third time, relinquished a title unbeaten in order to challenge the light-welterweights and try to become the first boxer to win a world title at four weights. This time he was taking on too much and two terrific bouts with Aaron Pryor resulted in defeats. He was now in his thirties and decided enough was enough.

Arguello had 22 world title bouts, winning 19, in eight countries: Panama, USA, Venezuela, Nicaragua, Japan, Puerto Rico, Italy and England.

Henry ARMSTRONG

b 1912–d 1988

Henry Armstrong's record of being the only boxer to hold three undisputed world titles simultaneously will probably never be equalled. Nowadays there are few undisputed champions, and boxers must relinquish a title at one weight to challenge at another. Armstrong's feat is remarkable, too, in that each of his titles was at one of the original eight weights — there were no in-between 'junior' weights amongst them. For a short time he ruled the world from 118lb (54kg) to 147lb (67kg).

He was born Henry Jackson on a plantation in Columbus, Mississippi, on 12 December 1912. His mother was half-Cherokee Indian, and his father the son of a white man and a black slave. He began boxing in St Louis as an amateur, and when he went to San Francisco, he took the name of his trainer, Harry Armstrong, to continue as an amateur and disguise the fact that he had boxed a few bouts as a professional. He began to get somewhere in boxing after Al Jolson, the film star, bought his contract. George Raft was also a behind-the-scenes backer.

Eddie Mead managed him, and to make him marketable (Joe Louis was all the rage at the time) the scheme to win the triple championship was hatched. First he beat Petey Sarron for the featherweight title on 29 October 1937. On 31 May 1938 he fought Barney Ross for the welterweight title. The fight was postponed ten days after the weigh-in, in which time Armstrong desperately shed weight to regain fighting fitness, while Ross, who had had difficulty making the weight, put on so much that Armstrong reckoned there was about 25lb (11kg) between them on the night. Ross knew he was well beaten and retired.

The middle title, the lightweight, came on 17 August 1938, when Lou Ambers was outpointed. Henry then relinquished the featherweight crown, lost the lightweight and concentrated on the welterweights. He challenged Ceferino Garcia for a version of the middleweight title, but Garcia, whom he had beaten as a welter, held him to a draw.

Armstrong's secret was an exceptionally slow heart beat. He needed to warm up before a fight, and during it he was perpetual motion. He was called 'Hurricane Hank' and 'Homicide Hank', never giving his opponent a rest. He retired in 1945, and eventually decided to become a minister in St Louis. He died there in 1988.

Max BAER

b 1909–d 1959

Max Baer's right arm delivered one of the biggest punches in boxing history. It took him to the heavyweight championship, but he enjoyed life too much to dedicate himself to boxing and lost the title on a huge upset.

He was born in Omaha, Nebraska, on 11 February 1909, the son of a cattle butcher. He was known as the 'Livermore Larruper', and demolished many opponents before on 14 June 1934 he gave away about 50lb (23kg) to Primo Carnera and took from him the championship. Baer found fame on the radio, where his easy personality came across, and developed a clowning, playboy image. He underestimated his first challenger, James J. Braddock, and was outpointed. He was then defeated by the up-and-coming Joe Louis and did not get another shot at the title, although his younger brother Buddy twice unsuccessfully challenged Louis.

He died on 21 November 1959 in Hollywood, California.

Jem BELCHER

b 1781 – d 1811

Jem Belcher was born in Bristol on 15 April 1781, and was bare-knuckle champion of England from about 1800 when he beat the Irishman, Andrew Gamble. Belcher was the best champion since John Jackson, but lost an eye in 1803 which caused his retirement. He made a comeback and did remarkably well, putting up two great shows against Tom Cribb. At last he was persuaded to give up and take an inn in Soho, where he died aged only 30, respected by the whole of the boxing world, who erected a stone to his memory when he was buried in St Anne's Churchyard.

William Thompson BENDIGO

b 1811 – d 1880

William Thompson was one of triplets born to a family of 21 in Nottingham on 11 October 1811. The triplets were called Shadrach, Meshach and Abednego, the last becoming Bendigo to the Fancy. Although he weighed only around 165lb (75kg) he fought in 1835 his local rival Ben Caunt, some 45lb (20kg) heavier, and won on a foul. Bendigo was a rough, provoking fighter, who had a band of ruffians called 'Nottingham Lambs' to support him. They caused a riot when Caunt beat Bendigo on a disqualification in 1838.

Bendigo won the championship of England in 1839 from James Burke, the 'Deaf 'Un', and retired, but on a comeback again beat Caunt, who was disqualified. Bendigo was continually in trouble for drunkenness and assault, and had 28 spells in prison, but was also credited with saving three people from drowning. He was converted in prison, and joined a religious sect, the Good Templars, and preached all over the country. He died after a fall downstairs in 1880, and a huge stone memorial of a life-sized lion is erected to his memory in Nottingham cemetery.

Wilfred BENITEZ

b 1958

Wilfred, who began his career as Wilfredo, Benitez was born in the Bronx, New York, on 12 September 1958, one of a family of eight. A fast, skilful boxer and two-fisted puncher, he had early successes as a professional and went on to win titles at three weights.

Benitez turned professional in 1973, when 15, and on 6 March 1976 he outpointed Antonio Cervantes to become WBA light-welterweight champion. At 17 years 173 days he was the youngest of all world champions. This title he forfeited seven months later for failing to give Cervantes a return, but he moved up to welterweight and in January 1979 outpointed Carlos Palomino for the WBC title. After two defences he lost this title in November when he suffered his first defeat. Sugar Ray Leonard stopped him in the last round of a tremendous battle. Undeterred, Benitez next moved to light-middleweight, and in May 1981 knocked out Maurice Hope for the WBC crown. He defended this twice before suffering his second defeat, with Thomas Hearns getting a decision in December 1982.

Nino BENVENUTI

b 1938

Benvenuti became an Italian hero in the 1960 Rome Olympics, winning the welterweight gold medal, and he proved to be one of the best Italian professionals from 1961. Born in Trieste on 26 July 1938, his first world title as a pro was the WBA light-middleweight, which he took from his countryman Sandro Mazzinghi in 1965. A year later he lost it to Ki-Soo Kim, and moved up to middleweight where he prospered. He won the undisputed title in April 1967 from Emile Griffith, lost the return, but won the rubber match. A handsome and stylish boxer, he made four successful defences before surprisingly losing in November 1970 to Carlos Monzon. He retired, having won a very respectable 82 of his 90 bouts.

Jack 'Kid' BERG

b 1909

Jack Berg was named Judah Bergman when he was born at Whitechapel, London, on 28 June 1909, but it was as 'Kid' Berg, or the 'Whitechapel Whirlwind', that he became famous. He went to America in 1928 and two years later won the world light-welterweight title, which he took from Mushy Callahan, but it was not a division recognized in England. Two of his last fights resulted in points wins over the great Kid Chocolate, then at the height of his powers, on whom he inflicted his first defeat.

Berg was best as a lightweight but could not get a title chance until beaten twice by Tony Canzoneri, whom he had previously beaten. He finally retired in 1945 after 21 years and 192 fights.

Left: Jack 'Kid' Berg had a 21-year career in which he fought most of the best lightweights and light-welterweights on both sides of the Atlantic. He had nearly 200 contests, and was world light-welterweight champion in the 1930s.

James J. BRADDOCK

b 1906

Braddock's rags-to-riches story is so romantic he was called the 'Cinderella Man'. An Irish-American born in New York City on 7 June 1906, he fought as welter up to heavyweight, his best performance being a challenge to Tommy Loughran for the light-heavyweight title, before he more or less retired during the 1930s depression to join the breadline to support his family.

In 1934 he was picked to fight Corn Griffin, an up-and-coming heavyweight, and surprisingly beat him. Three fights later he was boxing Max Baer for the championship, and pulled off a 10-1 upset with a win. He was an inactive champion for two years and was then knocked out by Joe Louis, but had made such a deal with Louis' manager that he never more needed poor relief to survive.

Jack BRITTON

b 1885–d 1962

Jack Britton was a brilliant counter-punching classical welterweight, whose long career has not perhaps earned its full recognition.

He was born William Breslin in Clinton, New York, on 14 October 1885, and began a professional career in 1905. In 1915 he claimed the world's welterweight title with a win over Mike Glover. He promptly lost it to Ted 'Kid' Lewis, with whom he was to share the title for the next seven years. He fought Lewis 20 times, mostly no-decision bouts, but he won four to Lewis' three. Britton was challenged by Benny Leonard, the outstanding lightweight champion, and was outpointing him when Leonard was disqualified. He lost his title in 1922 to Mickey Walker, 16 years his junior. When he retired in 1927 he had been boxing for 22 years, having had 299 contests.

Jack BROUGHTON

b 1704–d 1789

Jack Broughton was known as the 'Father of Boxing'. Born in Cirencester in 1704, he was seen by James Figg in Bristol and brought to London where he became champion with a win over George Taylor. He opened an Academy and took Figg's place as instructor to his influential patrons.

Broughton drew up his rules after the death of one of his challengers, George Stevenson. Broughton's Rules, published in 1743, obtained widespread recognition before being superseded by the London Prize Ring Rules, based upon them, in 1838. Broughton lost his title in 1750 to Jack Slack, on a famous occasion which cost his patron, the Duke of Cumberland, a fortune.

One of Broughton's civilizing innovations in boxing was the introduction of mufflers, or thin gloves to protect the features of the aristocracy at his establishment. Although falling out with the Duke of Cumberland, he died a rich man at 85, was a Yeoman of the Guard, and has a paving stone to his memory in Westminster Abbey.

'Panama' Al BROWN

b 1902–d 1951

Al Brown was a black boxer called 'Panama' after his birthplace (on 5 July 1902), and was extraordinary for a bantamweight in standing 5ft 11in (1.80m). He won New York recognition as bantamweight champion after outpointing Vidal Gregorio in New York in 1929. He gained universal recognition in August 1931 with a defeat of Pete Sanstol, recognized by the NBA.

Brown was champion for six years. He defended only once in the US, preferring Europe and Canada for his bouts. He was an intellectual, speaking seven languages. As a boxer his reach gave him great advantages, and he could punch well for a thin man. He lost the title eventually to a Spaniard, Baltazar Sangchilli, but fought on for seven years before retiring in 1942. He died in 1951.

Tommy BURNS

b 1881–d 1955

Of all heavyweight champions, Tommy Burns is perhaps the most under-rated. His real name was Noah Brusso and he was born in Chesley, Ontario, on 17 June 1881, a French Canadian.

He took the world title on 23 February 1906 from Marvin Hart, who won it when Jeffries retired. Burns managed himself, and very astutely. He made 11 successful defences, and until Ali was the only heavyweight champion willing to risk his title regularly outside the country of his birth — he defended in the USA, England, Ireland, France and Australia.

Although the shortest of all heavyweight champions at 5ft 7in (1.70m), he had a good reach and was able to beat some important challengers.

His reputation suffered perhaps by the story of the flight from Jack Johnson, who eventually caught up with him in Australia and easily took his crown in 1908, but even that was possibly stage-managed by Burns, who earned a huge purse to climax his career. He died in 1955.

Tony CANZONERI

b 1908–d 1959

Tony Canzoneri was an Italian-American shoeshine boy from Slidell, Louisiana, who won world titles at three weights and fought for another.

He was born on 6 November 1908, began boxing professionally as a bantamweight in 1925 and twice challenged for the bantamweight title in 1927, aged 18, first drawing and then being outpointed by Bud Taylor. However, he won the New York featherweight crown later in the year by outpointing Johnny Dundee, and gained universal recognition next year by beating Benny Bass. Losing this, he moved up to lightweight, and won the title in 1930 with a first-round knock-out of Al Singer.

He beat challenger Jack 'Kid' Berg in 1931, and since Berg was light-welterweight champion was regarded as having won that, too, both men obviously being under the limit. Having dropped the heavier title to Johnny Sadick, he regained it, but lost both his titles in 1933 to Barney Ross. He then won back the lightweight title, losing it eventually to Lou Ambers in 1937.

An aggressive, busy fighter, Canzoneri was popular wherever he fought. He retired at the end of 1939, and died on 9 December 1959.

Primo CARNERA

b 1906–d 1967

Primo Carnera was regarded as a physical freak in his day: he stood 6ft 5¾in (2m) and weighed around 266lb (120kg), by far the heaviest man to win a world title. Born in Sequals, Venice, Italy, on 26 October 1906, he did various jobs before Leon See, a French manager, saw his boxing potential. After bouts in London and Paris, he was taken to America, where he was exploited by American managers connected with gangsterism. Piloted to a world title fight with Jack Sharkey, he became world champion in June 1933 and defended twice before losing a year later to Max Baer.

When he retired in 1936, the amiable 'Ambling Alp' was penniless, and took to wrestling to earn enough for a liquor store in California. He eventually returned to Sequals, where he died in 1967.

Georges CARPENTIER

b 1894–d 1975

Georges Carpentier was one of the greatest of European boxers, and certainly the most famous boxer ever produced by France. Born in Lens, France, on 12 January 1894 he took up 'English' boxing after specializing in the French *savate*, in which the feet can be used. Before he was 16 he was the French lightweight champion, and by 18 French and European welterweight champion. Four months later he was European middleweight champion with a win over British champion Jim Sullivan, and when he was 19 was European heavyweight champion with a knockout victory over Britain's Bombardier Billy Wells.

As if all this were not enough, Carpentier was so handsome he drew ladies to the ring as spectators, and was known as the 'Orchid Man'. Although never a heavyweight he won the 'white heavyweight championship of the world' (in the days when Johnson was the real champion) by beating 'Gunboat' Smith on a foul. Nineteen days later war broke out, and naturally 'Gorgeous Georges', a lover of fast cars, became a hero in the air force, winning the *Croix de Guerre* for bravery.

After the war he won the world light-heavyweight title by knocking out Battling Levinsky, and then fought Jack Dempsey for the world title in the first fight to take a million dollars in gate money: $1,789,238. Dempsey was regarded as a wartime 'slacker' and even many Americans were supporting the great Georges.

Alas, he was not a man who could beat a top-class heavyweight and, breaking his thumb on Dempsey's head in the second round, he was knocked out in the fourth. Carpentier was conceding about 24lb (11kg).

He lost his light-heavyweight title in a surprise defeat by Battling Siki, his greatest admirer, and was never quite the same afterwards. He lost to Gene Tunney in 1924 in America, refusing to come out for the last round after what he claimed was a low blow.

Carpentier was a brilliant boxer with a devastating right hand, an idol wherever he went, and he was well-managed by his friend François Descamps. After his retirement in 1927, he opened a bar in Paris, appeared in variety halls and remained a much-loved figure until his death in Paris in 1975.

Marcel CERDAN

b 1916–d 1949

After Carpentier, Cerdan is the greatest of all French boxers. He was born (first name Marcellin) in Sidi-bel-Abbès, Algeria, on 22 July 1916, a butcher's son. He was a professional at 17, but World War II spoiled his progress. European welterweight champion before the war, he was a middleweight afterwards. A Belgian, Cyrille Delannoit, was the first to beat him in 1948 (apart from two disqualifications), but he avenged this defeat, and on 21 September, aged 32, got his chance at the world title by challenging Tony Zale in Jersey City. Despite a third-round hand injury Cerdan beat the great Zale one-handed, Zale being in a sorry state at the end of the 12th round.

Cerdan then defended against Jake LaMotta, the 'Bronx Bull', in Detroit, and had the misfortune to pull a muscle in his shoulder in the third round. He could not overcome this handicap and retired after the ninth. Cerdan was on his way back to America for the return when his plane crashed in the Azores, killing all aboard, on 27 October 1949.

Cerdan had a not-too-discreet love affair with French singer Edith Piaf. The two were idols in France, and his death was mourned by the whole nation.

Ezzard CHARLES

b 1921–d 1970

Ezzard Charles was a clever boxer who won the world heavyweight title despite being one of the lightest men to win it — only Burns this century was probably lighter.

He was born in Lawrenceville, Georgia, on 7 July 1921, and began boxing professionally in 1940 as a light-heavyweight. In June 1949, when Joe Louis retired, he was matched with Jersey Joe Walcott for the vacant heavyweight title (NBA version) and won. He was universally recognized in 1950, when he beat Louis, making a comeback. He remained champion until July 1951 when he lost to his old rival Walcott, whom he'd already beaten twice for the title. Later Walcott beat him again, and he twice unsuccessfully challenged Marciano, putting up tremendous opposition to the unbeaten champion.

Charles, who was called the 'Cincinnati Flash' and the 'Cincinnati Cobra', unhappily spent his last years in a wheelchair and he died in 1970 aged only 48.

Below: *The profile which caused a noticeable increase in the number of female spectators at matches just after World War I. Georges Carpentier was a champion from the age of 15, reaching his peak as the world light-heavyweight champion in the early 1920s.*

Below: *James J. Corbett as heavyweight champion of the world in 1896. The pose is that of a bare-knuckle boxer, but Gentleman Jim was the first modern champion, in temperament and science as well as in the donning of gloves.*

Julio Cesar CHAVEZ

b 1962

Julio Cesar Chavez, who began a professional career in February 1980, was still unbeaten in 1988 and was becoming one of the top attractions in boxing. Born in Ciudad Obregón, Mexico, on 12 July 1962, the good-looking Chavez, who carries a knock-out punch in each hand, had by September 1984 won his first 33 fights, and in the next he took the vacant WBC junior lightweight title with a stoppage of Mario Martinez. Chavez then began an impressive series of defences in which he beat many champions, among them Roger Mayweather, Rocky Lockridge and Juan Laporte. In 1987, after nine defences, Chavez moved up to lightweight, and scored his most impressive victory to date with a stoppage of Edwin Rosario, the WBA champion. Having assumed the title, Chavez defended in 1988 against Rodolfo Aguilar and then added the WBC title by beating Jose Luis Ramirez, by which time he was unbeaten after 62 contests.

Kid CHOCOLATE

b 1910–d 1988

Kid Chocolate's real name was Eligio Sardinias, and he was born in Cerro, Cuba, on 6 January 1910. A superb amateur boxer, he carried his brilliance into the professional ranks and after four years was challenging for the world featherweight title, being outscored by the more experienced Bat Battalino. However, he won the junior lightweight title from Benny Bass in July 1931, and took the vacant New York version of the featherweight title with a knock-out over Lew Feldman in 1932. He failed in a bid for the lightweight title, being outpointed by Tony Canzoneri.

Chocolate was a slim-waisted, good-moving, skilful boxer, with a punch. Known as the 'Havana Bon Bon', he was among the best in the world. However, he lost both his titles in 1933 when, it was said, he had not only squandered a fortune (six cars, 70 suits) but was, at 23, severely ill with syphilis. Nevertheless, he had many more bouts before retiring in 1938, when he had lost only 10 of 148 contests. After being 'discovered' in Havana in 1988 after rumours that he was dead, he then died on 8 August 1988.

Billy CONN

b 1917

How close Billy Conn came to everlasting fistic fame! A superb light-heavyweight champion he fought Joe Louis for the heavyweight title in 1941. Well ahead in the 13th round, Conn was set for a sensational win, but his Irish fighting blood prompted him to try to knock out Louis, and the Brown Bomber stopped him with his best punch.

Conn was born in Pittsburgh, Pennsylvania, on 8 October 1917 and began his professional career in 1935 as a welterweight, never having boxed as an amateur. In 1937 he beat four former world champions: Babe Risko, Vince Dundee, Teddy Yarosz and Young Corbett III. He fought Melio Bettina for the light-heavyweight title in 1939 and won on points. After three defences he relinquished the title to challenge Louis.

Conn was a clever boxer who studied his opponents' styles. A handsome man and good dresser, he was talented as an artist. He had lost his sparkle when he resumed boxing after the war and soon retired.

John CONTEH

b 1951

Born in Liverpool on 27 May 1951, John Conteh was ABA champion at middleweight and light-heavyweight, and he continued to delight the fans when he turned professional, beating his first opponent on 18 October 1971. A brilliant combination puncher, he was European light-heavyweight champion after 19 contests, beating Rudige Schmidtke in 1973. The following year he won the WBC world title when outpointing Jorge Ahumada at Wembley. He made three successful defences, beating Lonnie Bennett, Yaqui Lopez and Len Hutchins, but began having problems, twice breaking his hand. When he withdrew from a defence against Miguel Cuello he was stripped. He later challenged Mate Parlov for the title but lost a bitterly disputed split decision in Belgrade. In 1979 and 1980 he twice went to Atlantic City to try to wrest the title from Matthew Saad Muhammed but failed, and retired, having suffered only four defeats in an excellent career.

James J. CORBETT

b 1866–d 1933

The world's first heavyweight champion, James J. Corbett ended and began an era of boxing history. He not only began the reign of Queensberry heavyweight champions as opposed to the prize ring days, he brought science to boxing, replacing the bravery and strength of Sullivan with skill, finesse and tactics.

Born on 1 September 1866 in San Francisco, he was a bank clerk, who took up amateur boxing and turned professional in 1884. After a draw with the West Indian Peter Jackson, he knocked out Sullivan to end the Boston Strong Boy's career. Corbett defended successfully only once, against an Englishman, Charlie Mitchell, and then lost the title to another, Bob Fitzsimmons, when paralysed by a blow to the solar plexus. He nearly won back the championship from James J. Jeffries, outpointing him until being knocked out, and then lost to Jeffries again.

Tom CRIBB

b 1781–d 1848

Tom Cribb, born in Hansham in Gloucestershire on 8 July 1781, came to London, joined the navy, had some scraps and became a bare-knuckle fighter. He had early success, beating the veteran George Maddox after 76 gruelling rounds, but in 1805 he suffered his only defeat, by George Nichols. He beat Bill Richmond, a black American, then in 1805 beat Jem Belcher for the championship of England.

Cribb then just beat Bob Gregson, after looking beaten, and the brave, one-eyed Belcher again. Cribb was given a handsome cup and retired. However, there appeared another black American, Tom Molyneaux, who threatened to claim the championship, so Cribb had to come back. He beat Molyneaux in 1810, although it needed some trickery. He had to beat him again a year later and did so, Molyneaux having suffered hardships in the meantime. Crowds of over 20,000 watched Cribb uphold England's honour, and he was a hero for life.

Above: Tom Cribb earned the esteem of his fellow-Englishmen when he kept the title of champion at home by beating off the challenge of the black American Tom Molyneaux, postponing the appearance of the first black heavyweight champion for 100 years.

Les DARCY

b 1895–d 1916

When the world middleweight championship was in turmoil around 1915, Australian Les

Darcy had claims to being the best in the world. He was born in Maitland, New South Wales, in 1895. He built up a physique as a blacksmith's apprentice, did well as an amateur boxer and became a professional at 16. A skilful puncher, he soon was the best middleweight in Australia and in 1915 he beat the New Yorker Jeff Smith who was claiming the middleweight crown. Darcy made 12 defences of his title in a year, and was then invited to America to meet Al McCoy.

Unfortunately, Australia was at war with Germany, and men between 18 and 40 were forbidden to leave the country. Darcy slipped away, but then America entered the war, and having reached there, he was shunned. He suffered an abscess on a tooth, developed fever, got worse and died, aged 21.

Jack DEMPSEY

b 1895–d 1983

Jack Dempsey was one of the toughest heavyweights the world has seen. He was born in Manassa, Colorado, on 24 June 1895, as William Harrison Dempsey, and took the fighting name Jack in deference to the old middleweight. His professional career, which started in 1914, took off after a disappointing beginning when he met Jack 'Doc' Kearns, a young manager with an eye for publicity who got him a bout with Jess Willard, the giant heavyweight champion. Dempsey won with a savage exhibition on 4 July 1919, and he and Kearns, together with promoter Tex Rickard, were ready to make their fortunes.

Clever publicity which branded Dempsey a war slacker, drew the first million-dollar gate when he fought hero Georges Carpentier, and there was another million-dollar pay day as he beat Louis Firpo. There was a hiccup, however, when Dempsey went off to make films in Hollywood, and fell in love with and married his co-star, Estelle Taylor. She and Kearns did not agree, and he went amid much expensive litigation.

The champion did not fight for three years, and then in 1926 faced ex-marine Gene Tunney before 120,757 spectators in Chicago. They were soaked by a deluge and shocked when Tunney outpointed Dempsey. However, Tunney also won the return, despite the famous long count, when he was down for at least 14 seconds. Dempsey retired, making an unconvincing comeback four years later.

He remarried, became a referee, and then the owner of a famous New York restaurant. He died in 1983, aged 88.

Below: The Broadway restaurant of former heavyweight champion Jack Dempsey from a postcard of the 1930s. On one wall was a huge painting of his 1919 defeat of Jess Willard. The restaurant was pulled down a few years before he died in 1983.

Jack 'Nonpareil' DEMPSEY

b 1862–d 1895

The original Jack Dempsey was born in Co. Kildare, Ireland, on 15 December 1862. His real name was John Kelly. He emigrated to America as a boy and, after being a wrestler, became a boxer and claimed the world's lightweight title. On 13 June 1884 he beat George Fulljames in 22 rounds and, generally, was regarded as the middleweight champion. He established a reputation that earned him the nickname 'The Nonpareil'. After reigning for five years he was knocked out by George LaBlanche, but the Canadian marine had used a pivot punch, and the boxing world would not recognize LaBlanche as champion.

Dempsey was dethroned eventually by Bob Fitzsimmons of England, a surprise winner, in 1891, but proved his courage in refusing to throw in the towel as he took a tremendous beating. He retired, and died in 1895. His lonely, unkept grave was discovered in the woods in Oregon and after a famous poem had been written about him, a proper gravestone was raised by public subscription.

George DIXON

b 1870–d 1909

George Dixon was born in Halifax, Novia Scotia, on 29 July 1870 and early earned the nickname 'Little Chocolate' for his size (5ft 3½in/1.61m), and colour. He was a brilliant boxer, whose defeat of Nunc Wallace in 18 rounds in 1890 made him world bantamweight champion. When he stopped Cal McCarthy in Troy, New York, in 22 rounds in 1891 he claimed the featherweight championship, and a victory over Fred Johnson the following year gained him universal recognition. Dixon was beaten by Solly Smith in 1897, after being a world champion for seven years, but claimed the title was not at stake and continued to bill himself as champion. However, nine months later he lost to Ben Johnson, an Englishman, in New York.

Dixon had caused some confusion in the featherweight ranks but regained American recognition in 1898 when Dave Sullivan was disqualified against him, and was accepted universally again in 1899, when he beat Will Curley. Altogether he won 26 contests billed as world championships. He finally lost his title when well beaten by Terry McGovern in January 1900. He fought on for seven years, but suffered a number of defeats. He died on 6 January 1909, aged only 38.

Jim DRISCOLL

b 1881–d 1925

Driscoll was one of the masters of boxing. Having learned his business in the booths, he was such a classical exponent of the noble art that he was called 'Peerless' Jim Driscoll.

He was born in Cardiff on 15 December 1881 of Irish parents, and learned to box as a printer's apprentice with old newspapers used as 'gloves'. Handsome and modest, his supreme skill made him a favourite at the National Sporting Club in London, where he won the British Commonwealth and European titles. In 1909 he went to New York to challenge Abe Attell for the world title. He could obtain only a 'no-decision' contest and, although outclassing Attell, could not knock him out. He was recognized as champion in Britain and Europe, however, in 1911 when Attell would not defend against him. It was a bit late for Driscoll, who retired in 1913; the only defeat on his record was a disqualification against Freddie Welsh, who became world lightweight champion. Sadly, he was persuaded to return after the war, but retired for good when suffering his second defeat, being stopped by Charles Ledoux, of France, in the 16th round, having outboxed him. He was 38, and already suffering from the first stages of the consumption which killed him six years later.

Roberto DURAN

b 1951

Roberto Duran, born in Guarare, Panama, on 16 June 1951, was made to fight. He began in the streets, and did not modify his style when he became a professional in 1967. Throughout his boxing career he breathed belligerence and aggression, and there were no niceties in the ring where he was concerned.

Having lost two contests comparatively early, he was unbeaten for 13 years, during which time he fought some of the world's best boxers. He took the WBA lightweight championship from Ken Buchanan in 1972 in a rough display in which low blows and hitting after the bell played their part, and for nearly six years proved he was the world's best, defending 12 times and only once being taken the distance. He then moved up to welterweight, and in 1980 inflicted a first defeat on Sugar Ray Leonard to take the WBC crown.

Five months later he lost the return in a manner which surprised the world — the great macho man turned his back on Leonard and retired, completely frustrated by Leonard's skill. He needed to restore his tarnished reputation, and stopped Davey Moore in 1983 to win a world title at a third weight — light-middleweight. He did not defend this title but later in the year took on 'Marvelous' Marvin Hagler, the awesome middleweight champion. He proved again his fighting heart by taking Hagler the distance — the only challenger to do so in Hagler's 13 title wins.

By now Duran was 32, but would not give up the fight game, and continued boxing into 1988, suffering an occasional defeat, but already established as a ring legend.

Above: *Roberto Duran built up a long unbeaten record and a reputation as a fighter with whom nobody could take a chance. He is the only man to beat Sugar Ray Leonard, and was the unbeaten lightweight champion for over five years.*

Below: *Australian Jeff Fenech wearing his WBC championship belt. A world champion at three weights in his first 20 unbeaten professional contests, he had not been fully tested as 1989 began.*

Flash
ELORDE
b 1935–d 1985

Gabriel 'Flash' Elorde was born in Bogo, in the Philippines, on 22 March 1935. He turned professional when 16 and became an excellent boxer, being an oriental champion at all weights from bantam to light. In an active career he had 44 title fights (15 for world titles) and was involved in at least one each year from 1952 to 1967.

Elorde failed in a world title challenge to Sandy Saddler at featherweight in 1956 before winning the junior lightweight title in March 1960 with a knock-out of Harold Gomes. He became one of the division's best champions, reigning for over seven years and making ten successful defences before being outpointed by Yoshiaki Numata in June 1967. During this time he also made two attempts on Carlos Ortiz's lightweight title, each time losing in the 14th round. He retired in 1967, but made a comeback two years later and fought to 1971.

Jeff
FENECH
b 1964

Born in Sydney on 28 May 1964, Jeff Fenech became a professional at 20 and within five years had proved himself one of the best boxers to emerge from Australia for a long while. In only his seventh contest, in April 1985, he stopped Satoshi Shingaki in Sydney to win the IBF bantamweight title. After three Sydney defences he gave this up to take the WBC light-featherweight title in May 1987 with a stoppage of Samart Payakarun. Two defences of this, and Fenech moved up a division again, and in March 1988 stopped Victor Callejas to win the WBC featherweight crown.

Fenech fights in a non-stop style, always coming forward and throwing punches. He inflicted on Callejas only his second defeat, and improved his own record to 20 wins out of 20, 16 inside the distance. He had already held world titles at three weights, and although his title bouts had been in Sydney, there seemed no reason why he should not be a star into the 1990s.

James
FIGG
b 1695–d 1734

Figg (or Fig) was the first prize ring champion, or at least the first to gain prominence. He was born in Thame, Oxfordshire, around 1695, and he became a master of all types of swords, cudgels and staves. He taught the art of defence at an amphitheatre in London's Oxford Road, with a card designed by Hogarth, who along with literary giants like Swift and Pope was among his clients.

He challenged all-comers, and when he defeated Ned Sutton, the Gravesend Pipemaker in his Great Tiled Booth on the Green at Southwark, he was accounted the champion. He fought Sutton successfully with bare fists and cudgels, only just winning the fist fight by an arm-lock, after Sutton had been backed at 4-1 on. Figg died around 1734.

Bob
FITZSIMMONS
b 1863–d 1917

Bob Fitzsimmons has his place in history as being the first man to win undisputed world titles at three weights — in fact only Armstrong emulated him.

He was born in Helston, Cornwall, on

26 May 1863, and when a boy went to New Zealand, helping in the family blacksmith business, developing strength in the shoulders. He began boxing there and was discovered by Jem Mace, the bare-knuckle champion, on a tour. He turned professional in 1883, moved to Australia, and in 1890 went to America. A year later he won the middleweight title, knocking out Jack Dempsey the 'Nonpareil'. Having reigned for over four years he turned his attention to the heavyweights (there being no light-heavyweight division), and by taking out American citizenship and knocking off the championship contenders one by one he earned a title shot against Gentleman Jim Corbett in 1897.

Fitzsimmons never weighed more than 168lb (76kg) and was an unlikely shape for a heavyweight, having thin legs (which he sometimes disguised by padding his tights). He also had freckles and receding fair hair, and only his shoulders were those of a boxer. 'Ruby Robert' caused an upset by stopping Corbett, but by the time of his defence against the powerful James J. Jeffries two years and three months later, his prowess was so much acknowledged that he was firm favourite.

Jeffries was too strong, however, stopping him in the 11th round. He lost a second match with Jeffries, and then took advantage of the newly formed light-heavyweight division to become its second champion. This was in November 1903 and he was already past 40. He lost this title to Philadelphia Jack O'Brien two years later, but continued to box occasionally until he retired, aged 52, in 1914. He was probably the lightest man to win the world heavyweight title. He died of pneumonia in Chicago in 1917.

George FOREMAN

b 1948

George Foreman won the Olympic heavyweight gold medal in 1968, and when less then five years later he destroyed Joe Frazier in two rounds to become world champion, he looked set for a long reign.

He was born in Marshall, Texas, on 22 January 1948, and grew to a strong 6ft 3in (1.91m) and 220lb (100kg). He made two easy defences but then was surprisingly outboxed and knocked out by the 32-year-old Ali on his comeback. Foreman fought on in a desultory way for a while but retired in 1977, his punching power having earned him 42 inside-the-distance wins in 47 contests. He became a pastor, and blew up to over 300lb (136kg). However, in 1987 he began a comeback at 243lb (110kg) and (with a shaven head) soon rattled up a string of quick victories which, even though he was past 40, caused some to talk of another title challenge.

Above: Bob Foster, the Albuquerque sheriff, was light-heavyweight champion for over six years before retiring while still champion. He defended 14 times and his later defeats were by heavyweights.

Bob FOSTER

b 1938

Bob Foster, born in Albuquerque, New Mexico, on 15 December 1938, grew into a 6ft 3in (1.91m) light-heavyweight, who was one of the best champions at his weight but found tackling heavyweights too demanding.

Foster had already lost to heavyweights Doug Jones and Ernie Terrell by the time he took the light-heavyweight title in 1968 with a knock-out of Dick Tiger. He lost WBA recognition in 1970 by failing to meet their contender, but unified the title again in 1972 when knocking out Vicente Rondon. He successfully defended 14 times in all before retiring in 1974. During this time he challenged Joe Frazier for the heavyweight championship, but was knocked out in the second round.

Above: Joe Frazier had his best battles with Muhammad Ali, being the first to beat him. Ali and Foreman were his masters, but he was in the top flight of heavyweights for eight years, and world champion for nearly five.

Joe FRAZIER

b 1944

Frazier owed a 1964 Olympic gold medal to an injury to Buster Mathis, who beat him in the trials, but 'Smokin' Joe' proved the better as a professional. When Ali was stripped of the heavyweight title in 1967 Frazier stopped Mathis for the WBC title, gained 'universal' recognition in 1970 with a defeat of the WBA champion, Doug Ellis, and popular recognition in 1971 when he inflicted a first defeat on Ali, returning after a long lay-off.

Frazier was born in Beaufort, South Carolina, on 12 January 1944. Short, with heavy legs, Frazier's style of fighting was to keep coming forward, boring in under the guard of his usually taller opponents. He could not cope with the big George Foreman, who took his title in 1973 on his tenth defence. This style complemented Ali's, however, and they had three great fights, Ali winning the last two — the last when Frazier challenged him for the crown which Ali regained from Foreman. Foreman and Ali, twice each, were the only boxers to have beaten him when he retired to train his son Marvis for a title shot.

Joe GANS

b 1874–d 1910

Gans was a superb boxer who suffered at the turn of the century the frustration of having to lose important fights to white boxers, one of the drawbacks of being black at that time.

Born in Baltimore, Maryland, on 25 November 1874, he was a professional by 1891, and after a string of good performances he earned a lightweight title fight in March 1900 against Frank Erne, whom he outboxed for 12 rounds and then retired with a cut eye. Many thought his retirement premature and suspicious. Later in the year he was knocked out in two rounds by Terry McGovern, in a fight universally regarded as being a fake.

After this, however, Gans was unbeaten for eight years, except for a loss to the much heavier Sam Langford. He knocked out Erne in the first round to win the lightweight title in 1902; then he challenged Joe Walcott for the welter crown in 1904, but was held to a draw over 20 rounds. He twice beat future welterweight king Mike Twin Sullivan, however. His lightweight reign lasted for over six years, the highlight being his great 1906 confrontation with Battling Nelson, whom he beat after 42 bruising rounds in Tex Rickard's first promotion in Goldfield, Nevada.

Nelson was the man to take Gans' title at last, with two defeats in 1908. He was then 34 years old and no doubt suffering from the consumption that killed him two years later. A great counter-puncher, he was known as the 'Old Master' and, undoubtedly, was one of the ring geniuses of his era.

Wilfredo GOMEZ

b 1956

Wilfredo Gomez was a big-punching light-featherweight who at one time won 32 successive fights inside the distance, a lot for a boxer in the lighter divisions.

He was born in Puerto Rico on 29 October 1956 and began boxing professionally in 1974. In only his 17th bout he won the WBC light-featherweight title with a knock-out of Dong-Kyun Yum. He proved outstanding at this weight, defending 17 times before relinquishing the title to move up to featherweight in 1983. None of these defences went the distance. He won the WBC featherweight title in March 1984 by outpointing Juan Laporte, but he was stopped later in the year by Azumah Nelson. In 1985 he outpointed Rocky Lockridge for the junior lightweight title, but lost it on his first defence to Alfredo Layne. He was a champion at three weights, and won 20 title fights — an excellent record.

Rocky GRAZIANO

b 1922

It was his style rather than the statistics of his career that made Rocky Graziano such a favourite of the 1940s. He was born on 1 January 1922 Rocco Barbella of Italian parents in an East Side New York flat, and was always in trouble with the law, serving time in reform school and prison, where he assaulted a guard. A street fighter, he reacted to discipline no better in the army, hitting an officer and deserting.

His ring career flourished, however, and he fought Tony Zale three times for the world middleweight title from 1946 to 1948, winning the second fight and being champion for nearly a year. He even had trouble with the boxing authorities, being suspended for failure to report a bribery attempt. He tried to win the title again in 1952 but was beaten by Sugar Ray Robinson.

An uncomplicated tearaway fighter, whose sole ambition was to remove the man before him, he was equally successful on retirement as a natural television celebrity and actor, and a film was made of his rugged life entitled, appropriately, *Somebody Up There Likes Me*.

Harry GREB

b 1894–d 1926

Harry Greb was one of the greatest all-action fighters, a man called 'The Human Windmill'. Born in Pittsburgh, Pennsylvania, on 6 June 1894, Greb became a pro in 1913 and had a hectic career of nearly 300 fights, 44 in 1919 alone. His style was to wear down his opponents by whatever method, and there is no doubt he did not care for the niceties of rules.

He won the middleweight title in 1923 and lost it to Tiger Flowers in 1926, but he also beat many light-heavyweights and even heavyweight Bill Brennan, just before he fought Dempsey for the title. He was the only man to beat Gene Tunney (for the American light-heavyweight title), putting him in hospital, but the heavier Tunney beat him four times.

Greb was said to scorn training and to enjoy the high life, but, in fact, he was a serious fighter. Eye trouble meant that for the latter part of his career he fought while blind in one eye.

After a return fight with Flowers in 1926 he had a glass eye fitted, but within a few weeks needed an operation on his nose following an accident and, tragically, he died under the anaesthetic.

Emile GRIFFITH

b 1938

Griffith was born at St Thomas in the Virgin Islands on 3 February 1938. Going to New York to work in a hat factory, he was spotted as a potential boxer and enjoyed a long career in championship class.

He won the world welterweight title in 1961 from Benny 'Kid' Paret, lost it back to him and then regained it in a fight after which Paret died, a tragedy which had a deep effect on the fight game. He then lost and regained the title to Luis Rodriguez, and after three further defences turned to the middleweight class. In 1966 he outpointed Dick Tiger for the title, finally losing it in 1968 after three fights with Nino Benvenuti, the Italian winning the rubber match.

Griffith was a brilliant boxer, who could mix rough fighting with his skill. He tried to regain the welterweight title from José Napoles and the middleweight title twice from Carlos Monzon; late in his career, he challenged for the light-middleweight title, losing to Eckhard Dagge. He finally retired in 1977, when he was 39.

Below: *Harry Greb, world middleweight champion from 1923 until 1926, fought while blind in one eye for the latter part of his career.*

Below: 'Marvelous' Marvin Hagler before the battle with Sugar Ray Leonard which ended his 6½ years as undisputed middleweight champion. It was his first defeat for 11 years, and for three or four years in the 1980s he was boxing's outstanding champion.

Marvin HAGLER
b 1952

For a period in the mid-1980s Hagler, who enlarged his name by special registration to Marvelous Marvin Hagler, was not only the only undisputed champion in the world but generally regarded as the best.

Born in Newark, New Jersey, on 23 May 1952, he turned professional in 1973, and possessed a killer punch in both hands as well as a keen fighting brain. He challenged for the middleweight title in 1979 but was held to a draw by Vito Autuofermo. However, he stopped Alan Minter in September 1980 at Wembley and began a long run as champion. He defended successfully 12 times, and built an awesome reputation for destruction, especially after his three-round conquest of Thomas Hearns. He finally lost the title in April 1987 in one of the biggest fights of recent years, to Sugar Ray Leonard. However, there were many who thought Hagler's solid style deserved the split decision as much as Leonard's dazzling manner. By the end of 1988 Hagler had not fought again, but there was no official retirement.

Masahiko HARADA
b 1943

Fighting Harada was born on 5 April 1943 at Setagaya, Tokyo, and became one of Japan's best fighters, winning titles at two weights and almost a third. He won the world flyweight title, by knocking out Pone Kingpetch in October 1962, when he was only 19. He lost this in the return match, but two years later outpointed Eder Jofre (he was the only man to beat Jofre) for the bantamweight crown. He held this for nearly three years before losing it to Lionel Rose of Australia, having defended brilliantly four times.

Harada then turned his attention to the featherweights, where he twice challenged Johnny Famechon. On the first occasion he lost by a single point after referee Willie Pep had announced a draw at first. Harada's title fights were at three of the original eight weights, and his two championships were undisputed, so it really was an impressive record.

Len HARVEY
b 1907–d 1976

Len Harvey, born at Stoke Climsland, Cornwall, on 11 July 1907, began his professional career when twelve and a half years old. He was one of Britain's greatest boxers, fighting at all the weights from fly to heavy, although at his heaviest he was no more than 170lb (77kg). He drew for the British welterweight title, and won the middle, light-heavy and heavyweight crowns.

Harvey did not possess a punch, but was one of the most skilful boxers ever. He was outpointed by Marcel Thil in a bid for the world middleweight title in 1932, and by John Henry Lewis in a bid for the light-heavyweight title in 1936. Lewis' eye trouble prevented a rematch, and Harvey was recognized by the BBBC as world light-heavyweight champion when he outpointed Jock McAvoy in July 1939. Two months later England was at war and Harvey had no chance to cash in on his fame. After a gap in his career of three years he was knocked out by Freddie Mills, who shortly became undisputed world champion. It was only the second time in 22 years Harvey had been stopped — the other was on a cut eye.

Thomas HEARNS
b 1958

Thomas Hearns was one of the big boxing names of the 1980s. Born in Memphis, Tennessee, on 18 October 1958, he began his professional career in 1977 and became the star of the Kronk gymnasium in Detroit.

Hearns made his first impression among the welterweights, where he was tall and fast, and possessed such a lethal punch that he was called the 'Hit Man'. He won the WBA title in 1980 by stopping Pipino Cuevas in the second round, but lost it a year later when Sugar Ray

Leonard, one of boxing's immortals, came from behind to stop him in the 14th. In 1982 he outpointed Wilfred Benitez, another of the best of the period, to win the WBC light-middleweight title, which he relinquished after four defences, including a quick knock-out of Roberto Duran, to challenge Mavin Hagler for the middleweight crown. In a sensational fight he was stopped in the third round, his second defeat.

Spotting a chance to win a version of the light-heavyweight title, Hearns challenged Dennis Andries, the WBC champion, and stopped him in Detroit. With Leonard's defeat of Hagler, there were suddenly three chances to win a middleweight title and thus a world title at a record four weights. Hearns seized it in October 1986 with a knock-out of Juan Domingo Roldan for the WBC version. It was one of 1988's great shocks when Iran Barkley stopped him in the third round on his first defence to inflict his third defeat.

Hearns challenged Fully Obelmejias for the WBA super-middleweight title in 1988, and when Obelmejias withdrew he beat substitute James Kinchen on a split decision. A splinter organization from the WBA, the World Boxing Organization, 'sanctioned' the fight as being for the super-middleweight title, enabling Hearns to claim five world titles, but the boxing world in general paid no heed to the claims.

Larry HOLMES

b 1949

Like Corbett, who succeeded the great Sullivan as heavyweight champion, and Charles, who succeeded Louis, Holmes, who succeeded Ali, did not get his due plaudits. He was an excellent champion, for about six years clearly the best heavyweight in the world and even Marciano could not claim that.

Holmes was born in Cuthbert, Georgia, on 3 November 1949, and turned professional in 1973. He was sound if unspectacular, a good boxer with a punch, who fought unbeaten to 1978 before getting a crack at the WBC title, awarded to Ken Norton. Holmes outpointed him and began a succession of 19 defences which ran to September 1985, during which he beat Weaver, Berbick, Leon Spinks, Cooney, Snipes, Cobb, Witherspoon and 'Bonecrusher' Smith, all leading contenders, among other easier opponents including Ali on an ill-advised comeback. He was never in serious danger of defeat.

He then found he had an unbeaten record of 48 wins, one fewer than the legendary Marciano's, and determined to equal or beat Rocky's 49. He faced the light-heavyweight champion Michael Spinks on his next defence. It was one too many and he was outpointed in a controversial decision. He then lost a return, even more controversially, and, with all records disappeared, he challenged the new young king Mike Tyson, to suffer a third defeat.

Holmes was bitter about his lack of public recognition and rightly so, for his was an outstanding record.

***Left:** Thomas Hearns was one of a triumvirate of boxers in the 1980s who all fought each other: Hagler, Leonard and himself. Although he lost to both the others, they were his only defeats until near the end of his career, and they were two of the 1980s' most memorable fights. He was the first to win world titles at four weights.*

***Below:** Larry Holmes won his first 48 contests, and could have retired then as world champion. Unfortunately he was tempted to try to equal or beat the similar record of Rocky Marciano, who retired unbeaten with 49 victories, and this led to his downfall.*

Below: *Lloyd Honeyghan makes a forceful point into the microphone. After taking the undisputed welterweight title from Don Curry in 1986, he displayed a very forceful attitude in the ring, usually blasting his opponents to rapid defeats.*

Evander HOLYFIELD

b 1962

Evander Holyfield was conspicuous among the US Olympic boxers in 1984 in not winning a gold medal — he was disqualified in the semi-finals. But he has proved a great professional and was *The Ring*'s fighter of 1987.

Holyfield, born on 19 October 1962, made his professional debut in November 1984 and in his 12th contest, in July 1986, took the WBA cruiserweight crown from Dwight Muhammad Qawi. In 1987 he demolished Henry Tillman, the Olympic heavyweight champion, and made three other defences, adding the IBF title to his collection. In April 1988 he stopped Carlos de Leon, the WBC champion, to unify the cruiserweight division. Still unbeaten, the strong and skilful Holyfield announced his intention to go after the heavyweights, and was seen as a possible challenger to Mike Tyson.

Lloyd HONEYGHAN

b 1960

Lloyd Honeyghan was born in Jamaica on 22 April 1960 but was brought early to England, where he began his professional career at the end of 1980. A flashy fighter who likes flashy trunks, he is a fast and devastating puncher, who after 28 unbeaten fights earned a welterweight title fight in September 1988 with Don Curry, at the time regarded as the greatest pound-for-pound boxer in the world. It was a shock when Honeyghan completely outfought Curry, who retired at the end of the sixth.

Honeyghan and Hagler were at the time the only two undisputed world champions, but Honeyghan gave up the WBA crown when a South African, Harold Volbrecht, was named as the contender. He rapidly disposed of Johnny Bumphus, Maurice Blocker and Gene Hatcher, but lost the WBC title in a listless display to Jorge Vaca on a technical decision after a clash of heads, and was illogically stripped of the IBF title, which was not at stake. Honeyghan was having trouble with his private life and professional associations, but he overcame these to regain the WBC title, knocking out Vaca in 1988, and looked to be easily the best welterweight in the world, when applying himself to the task.

John JACKSON

b 1769–d 1845

Gentleman John Jackson was a bare-knuckle fighter who was born on 25 September 1769 and became champion of England in 1795, when he beat Daniel Mendoza. It was only his third fight and second win, whereupon he retired. He opened a training academy in Bond Street, London, and taught the aristocracy. He formed the Pugilistic Club in 1814, but this did not become the ruling body, pugilism remaining an illegal sport. Jackson was, nevertheless, an influential figure in boxing. He died in Grosvenor Street in 1845, and there is a magnificent memorial to him in Brompton Cemetery.

James J. *JEFFRIES*

b 1875–d 1953

Born in Carroll, Ohio, on 15 April, Jeffries became a boilermaker and grew to be a strong 6ft 2½in (1.89m), 220lb (100kg) giant who in his early days was a sparring partner to heavyweights like James J. Corbett. But his strength and power were such that when he began professional boxing in 1896, it took him only 13 fights to beat Bob Fitzsimmons and become heavyweight champion of the world.

'The Boilermaker' fought from a crouch which made him difficult to hit and, although no great boxer, his superb strength did the rest. He reigned for over four years, the only challenger to take him the distance (25 rounds) being Tom Sharkey, who suffered broken ribs from the body blows.

Jeffries retired unbeaten in 1905, having no more contenders to beat, but, sadly, was persuaded out of retirement in 1910 to challenge Jack Johnson, who humiliated him and spoiled a great record. Jeffries died in 1953.

Eder *JOFRE*

b 1936

Jofre was an outstanding bantamweight who became the first boxer from Brazil to win a world title. He was born in São Paulo on 26 March 1936, and turned professional on his 21st birthday. In November 1960 he stopped Eloy Sanchez to become NBA bantamweight champion, and in 1962 he unified the title. In 1965 and 1966 he was twice outpointed by Fighting Harada in Japan, the first a close split decision, to lose his crown. He retired but, three years later, returned as a featherweight, still a hard-punching, two-fisted fighter.

Jofre won the WBC featherweight title in 1973 outpointing José Legra and he defended it against Vicente Saldivar later in the year. He was then 37, and was stripped in 1974 for failing to sign for a defence. He retired in 1976.

Ingemar *JOHANSSON*

b 1932

From humiliation to supreme triumph was the boxing story of Ingemar Johansson. Born in Gothenburg, Sweden, on 16 October 1932, he was disgraced in the Olympic Games final of 1952 by disqualification for not giving of his best. He appeared scared of Ed Saunders, his big-hitting opponent.

However, on turning professional soon afterwards, he made sure it was his opponents who tasted the big punch, particularly from his right, which he called the 'Hammer of Thor'. He became European champion, and a shock first-round knock-out of the top contender for the world title, Eddie Machen, earned him a title shot against Floyd Patterson in 1959. In America, he seemed to defy the age-old rites of training, enjoying the company of his fiancée more than his sparring partners, but caused another shock by flooring Patterson seven times and taking the world title in a third-round knockout. His reign lasted only until the return a year later, and he was knocked out again in the rubber match, although once more he floored Patterson. He retired in 1964.

Above: *Power was the forte of James J. Jeffries, and his strength can be guessed at from this photograph. Nobody could withstand his terrific punches during his career, but he was persuaded into a comeback five years after retiring to fight the formidable Johnson and lost his unbeaten record.*

Above: *Jack Johnson in 1911 when he was heavyweight champion and invincible. A desperate search for a 'white hope' to beat him was put into operation, and there was a 'white heavyweight championship'. Only age eventually subdued Johnson.*

Jack JOHNSON

b 1878–d 1946

The first black heavyweight champion, Johnson was so disliked by white Americans that a search was made for a 'white hope' to beat him. None was found, and he remained champion until he was 37.

Johnson was born in Galveston, Texas, on 31 March 1878. He began boxing professionally, beating all who would fight him, including ex-champion Bob Fitzsimmons. When Burns won the heavyweight title in 1906, Johnson pursued him, even to Australia, where in 1908 he earned the chance at the title in Rushcutters Bay, Sydney. The 30-year-old Johnson won easily but his victory stirred white America to hatred. Johnson's arrogant manner did not help matters, nor his liking for white women as mistresses. Nobody could beat him in the ring and few tried. Middleweight champion Stanley Ketchel did, and lost some teeth. When the legendary hero James J. Jeffries was brought out of retirement to try, Johnson toyed with him, and there followed race riots and lynchings in many parts of America.

It was the Mann Act that spoiled Johnson's career. It forbade transporting women over state lines for immoral purposes, and a white prostitute was willing to certify that Johnson had done just that. He was convicted and sentenced to imprisonment for a year and a day, but skipped to Europe while on bail and defended his title in Paris.

War broke out in 1914 and Johnson fled Europe for Argentina. A promoter persuaded him that he would not serve his sentence if he returned to the USA without the championship. On 5 April 1915 Johnson was knocked out in the 26th round in Havana, Cuba, by the 'Giant Cowboy', Jess Willard. Johnson claimed later that the fight was arranged, and that his wife was 'paid out' just before he 'laid down', and historians have never been able to agree on the truth of this assertion, although the majority believe the 37-year-old was beaten squarely by age and tiredness.

Johnson returned to America to see his mother, but was forced to serve his sentence. In later life, and harmless to white supremacy, he was given the recognition he was due as one of the greatest of all boxers. He was still fighting exhibitions aged 66. He died in 1946 when driving one of his fast cars.

Stanley KETCHEL

b 1886–d 1910

Stanley Ketchel was regarded for a long time as the greatest of all middleweights, although there have been so many great ones over the years it is impossible to compare them. He was born in Grand Rapids, Michigan, of a Polish immigrant family on 14 September 1886, his real name being Stanislaus Kiecal. He was only 16 when he had his first professional fight, and with his rugged style, which scorned defence, he was soon a great favourite.

He claimed the middleweight championship in 1907 after beating Joe Thomas, and remained king of the division for three years, during which time he dropped the title for a few weeks to Billy Papke, who stopped him in 1908 after having tricked him at the start by not shaking hands — he punched him instead. Ketchel took ample revenge on Papke in the return. He beat Philadelphia Jack O'Brien, the light-heavyweight champion, and conceded around 35lb (16kg) when he took on Jack Johnson, the heavyweight champion, in 1909. He was knocked out.

Ketchel was known as the 'Michigan Assassin', but he himself was assassinated on 15 October 1910, when a jealous farmhand shot him one day while he breakfasted on holiday.

Jake LAMOTTA

b 1921

For his relentless punching and non-stop aggression, Jake LaMotta was nicknamed the 'Bronx Bull'. He was born on the lower East Side of New York on 10 July 1921, of an Italian father and Jewish mother. His first name was Giacobe.

LaMotta was a juvenile delinquent who, for a time, was at the same reform school as Rocky Graziano. He was a good amateur and turned professional before he was 20. He was the first to beat Sugar Ray Robinson, but to get a title shot LaMotta admitted he had to lose deliberately to Billy Fox for a betting coup, so corrupt was boxing at the time.

He won the middleweight title on 16 June 1949 when Marcel Cerdan, who suffered an injured shoulder, retired after ten rounds. Cerdan was killed on his way to the return.

LaMotta's most exciting defence was against Laurent Dauthuille, whom he knocked out with 13 seconds left, being well behind on points. LaMotta lost the title in 1951 to the great Sugar Ray Robinson, who beat him four times in five meetings. He retired in 1954 and his book, *Raging Bull*, was made into a full-length feature film.

Benny LEONARD

b 1896–d 1947

Benny Leonard, born Benjamin Leiner on 7 April 1896, is regarded both as one of the greatest of all lightweights and one of the greatest of all Jewish boxers. He began a professional career aged 15 and was known as a brilliant boxer with a damaging punch in both hands.

To win the world lightweight title in 1917 Leonard had to stop champion Freddie Welsh, which he did in the ninth round, because they were fighting under the Frawley Law, which did not allow decisions. It was the third time Leonard had faced Welsh, another great champion.

Leonard remained champion until his retirement more than seven years later, his only defeat coming when he was disqualified in a challenge for Jack Britton's welterweight title.

Six years after retiring Leonard decided to make a comeback, but when the 36-year-old lost on his 20th comeback fight to Jimmy McLarnin, he retired for good and became a referee.

He died while refereeing, from a heart attack, aged 51.

Sugar Ray LEONARD

b 1956

A 1976 Olympic gold medalist, good-looking, articulate Sugar Ray Leonard was regarded as the charismatic figure to take over from Ali as boxing's main attraction. It looked as if his career had ended prematurely when he retired with a detached retina, but he returned for an amazing triumph.

Born on 17 May 1956 at Wilmington, North Carolina, Leonard turned professional in 1977 and won the WBC welterweight title in 1979 after a tremendous scrap with Wilfred Benitez. On his second defence he suffered his only defeat, being outpointed by a determined Roberto Duran. But Leonard confirmed his class by so dazzling Duran in the return that Duran gave up in one of boxing's most famous capitulations. Leonard then won the WBA light-middleweight title by stopping Ayub Kalule, but gave this up to unify the welter division with a tremendous win over WBA champion Thomas Hearns.

This contest possibly began Leonard's eye trouble, and he retired in 1982 after an operation. In May 1984 he knocked out Kevin Howard, but retired again. After nearly three years he challenged Marvin Hagler for the WBC middleweight title. It was the richest fight on record, and he won on points with a skilful display of boxing. He retired again, only to make a third comeback on 7 November 1988, when he challenged and stopped Don Lalonde, the WBC light-heavyweight champion. As the WBC recognized the fight as being also for the new super-middleweight title, Leonard won two titles at once and became the first boxer in history to win world championships at five different weights.

__Below:__ Sugar Ray Leonard talks to the world. The most talented all-round boxer of the 1980s, his career was interrupted by eye trouble, so that he fought only 36 times in nearly 12 years, but most of his fights were big ones.

Above: *Sonny Liston was a boxer of such physique and reputation that when he fixed his opponents with a stare at once troubled and malevolent, many of them were beaten before they even climbed into the ring.*

Ted 'Kid' LEWIS

b 1894–d 1970

Born in Aldgate, London, on 24 October 1894, Gershon Mendeloff became, under his fighting name of Ted 'Kid' Lewis, one of Britain's greatest boxers. He was not quite 15 when he began his professional career and, four years later, he was British and Empire featherweight champion — a meteoric rise.

In 1915 Lewis went to America and became undisputed world welterweight champion by outpointing Jack Britton. The two men were to share the title for over seven years, and they fought each other 20 times, Britton having the edge 4-3, with one draw and 12 no-decisions. Lewis' last spell as world champion ended in 1919. In a 20-year career of 283 contests, in which he was called the 'Crashing, Dashing Kid', Lewis won nine titles from featherweight to middleweight: three British, two Empire, three European and the world title.

Charles 'Sonny' LISTON

b 1932–d 1970

Sonny Liston was the most menacing of modern heavyweights. When he took the title from Floyd Patterson with two one-round knock-outs in 1962 and 1963 he looked invincible.

Liston was born in St Francis, Arkansas, on 8 May 1932, one of 25 children of his father. He moved with his mother to St Louis as a boy, and throughout his teens was in trouble with the law, armed robbery being the worst of his crimes. In the penitentiary he learned boxing, and turned professional in 1953, but gangsterdom controlled him as a boxer. Despite losing only once, to Marty Marshall, who broke Liston's jaw and outpointed him (a defeat Liston avenged) he waited until 1962 for a title shot. The boxing authorities were not keen that a man of his record should become champion. Given his chance, he demolished Patterson, who twice failed to last a round.

Liston had a brooding manner and a baleful stare full of malice. He had a long reach and large fists, and gave the impression of being the immovable object. However, the incredible Cassius Clay (Muhammad Ali) was his challenger after Patterson, and suddenly in his first fight with Ali, Liston looked his age (it was at least nearly 32 — but his 'official' birth date has been questioned). Ali won when Liston retired, claiming a shoulder injury.

The return was a farce as Liston was knocked out in the first round with a punch few thought capable of knocking out such a big man, and with the referee getting into a muddle over the count. This fight is one of boxing's big mysteries, and many think Liston threw it, but if so the motive is not obvious.

Liston made a comeback, retiring finally in 1969. He had lost only four of 54 contests in more than 16 years. His death, too, was a mystery. He died at home on 30 December 1970, a year after his retirement, but his body was undiscovered for six days.

Tommy LOUGHRAN

b 1902–d 1982

One of the best light-heavyweight champions, Tommy Loughran found the lack of weight and punch too big a handicap when he chased after the heavyweight crown.

He was born in Philadelphia, Pennsylvania, on 29 November 1902, and began his professional career in 1919. He was a brilliant boxer with the classical straight left, but early in his career had trouble with Harry Greb, the opposite — a fighter — Greb winning 2-1 in their series of six (one draw, two no-decision). It took Loughran eight years and 100 contests to get a title chance, whereupon he beat Mike McTigue for the New York title, and then unified the light-heavyweight division by beating Jimmy Slattery.

Loughran defended his crown six times in less than two years (beating the middleweight champion Mickey Walker and the future heavyweight champion James J. Braddock), then challenged the heavyweights. He had sufficient success (beating Sharkey) to earn a title shot in 1934 against Primo Carnera, but Carnera was one of the biggest of all, and outpointed the 31-year-old Loughran, who conceded 86lb (39kg). Loughran fought on, suffering a few late-career defeats, before retiring in 1937. He died in 1982.

Joe LOUIS

b 1914–d 1981

Joe Louis' real name was Joseph Louis Barrow, and he was born in Lafayette, Alabama, on 13 May 1914, of Cherokee Indian stock. His family moved to Detroit, where he dodged violin lessons to learn to box. He was a good amateur, who turned professional in 1934. After 12 wins he knocked out Primo Carnera in New York before 62,000 fans, and quickly became the hottest property in boxing. He was called the 'Brown Bomber'. He made a point of beating former world heavyweight title-holders, but Max Schmeling caused one of the sport's biggest upsets when he knocked out Louis in 1936.

Louis, however, went on to win the world title by stopping Braddock in 1937, and in 1938 he avenged the only blot on his record by annihilating Schmeling in one round.

Joe Louis, whom some still claim was the best of all heavyweights, reigned from 1937 to 1949, making a record 25 successful defences. The war years curtailed his activity, but in the late 1930s and early 1940s he fought so often he was said to be on a 'bum-of-the-month' campaign. Only three of his challengers went the distance and only one of those, Tommy Farr, was not stopped subsequently.

Louis retired while still champion in 1949 but, unfortunately, financial (tax) problems forced him to return in 1950, when he was beaten by Ezzard Charles, who had assumed the title. While he was still seeking another chance, he was stopped by future champion Rocky Marciano and retired permanently.

Louis fought behind a left jab, always shuffling forward to score with both fists. He was ruthless when an opponent was facing a knock-out. The first black heavyweight champion after Johnson, whose victories caused riots, his demeanour was of great importance and was so exemplary that he became immensely popular with black and white supporters. Sadly, his financial problems were not eased, and he was forced to use his name first by wrestling and then as a host in a Las Vegas casino. He died in Las Vegas in 1981.

__Below:__ Joe Louis had the longest uninterrupted spell as heavyweight champion and defended the title more often than anybody else. Sadly, problems of unpaid tax prevented him retiring for good while still supreme.

Benny LYNCH

b 1913 – d 1946

Benny Lynch was born in Clydesdale, Scotland, on 12 April 1913 and became one of the greatest of flyweights. He was a boxing artist, but could also punch with extreme savagery. He learned his skills in a travelling boxing booth and turned professional when 18. In 1935 he drew a non-title bout with world flyweight champion Jackie Brown, and given a title chance six months later he knocked him down ten times in two rounds to win the NBA crown. He unified the division with a win over Small Montana in 1937.

All Lynch's four title fights were exciting affairs where his brilliance was exhibited to the full. However, drink was destroying him, and he lost the title when 6½lb (3kg) overweight for a defence against Jackie Jurich in 1937. His last fight was to be in October 1938, when he was knocked out for the only time. He was only 25 and, eight years later he was dead — dying poor, heartbroken and a physical wreck.

Right: Benny Lynch was a brilliant flyweight whose world title fights delighted Scottish fans of the 1930s, but in the manner of true tragedy he destroyed himself with drink.

Jem MACE

b 1831 – d 1910

Jem Mace straddled the bare-knuckle and gloved eras. He was champion of England (and, therefore, the world) from about 1861, eventually ceasing to be champion through age, rather than being beaten.

Mace was born in Beeston, Norfolk, on 18 April 1831. He toured the countryside playing the violin as well as boxing. He had a Romany appearance and was called the 'Swaffham Gypsy'. He became champion by beating Sam Hurst, the Stalybridge Infant. He lost the title in 1862 to Tom King but regained it in 1866. In 1870 he went to America and beat the American champion Tom Allen.

His influence on the sport was immense. He is regarded as the father of modern scientific boxing. He helped spread the noble art in South Africa, Australia and New Zealand, where he discovered Bob Fitzsimmons, a future champion. In America, he was an influence on Jim Corbett, the first heavyweight champion. Later on he toured England with his boxing show, giving exhibitions until he was 70. He died in Newcastle in 1910 and is buried in Liverpool.

Rocky MARCIANO

b 1923 – d 1969

Rocco Francis Marchegiano was born in Brockton, Massachusetts, on 1 September 1923 and became a destructive fighter known as the 'Brockton Blockbuster'. He is the only world heavyweight champion to retire for good with a perfect record: 49 contests, 49 wins.

At 5ft 10½in (1.79m) and 194lb (88kg) he was not big for a heavyweight, nor was he

Far right: The young Rocky Marciano on the brink of becoming the first heavyweight champion of the world to retire for good unbeaten. Marciano's style was non-stop aggression, and none was strong enough to resist.

scientific. His only assets were a punch, durability and stamina. He was not too concerned with the rules — he just kept clubbing opponents until they went down. Matchmaker Al Weill was not impressed when Marciano sought a trial, but he was given a chance, and just kept winning, through strength alone. Eventually he gave the great Joe Louis, who was on a comeback trail, his last beating and earned a chance at Jersey Joe Walcott's title. Marciano won with a knock-out after being outpointed for 12 rounds. This was his 43rd contest, and he defended the title six times before retiring in 1956 with his unique record. Of his 49 victims, 43 failed to last the distance.

Marciano was brutal inside the ring, but a gentle family man outside it. He lost his life on 31 August 1969 when the private plane in which he was being taken to a meeting crashed. It was the day before his 46th birthday.

Terry McGOVERN

b 1880–d 1918

'Terrible' Terry McGovern had a short but explosive career. He was born in Johnstown, Pennsylvania, on 9 March 1880, became a newspaper seller and started boxing for money at 17. He was not 20 when he won the bantamweight title with a one-round victory over Pedlar Palmer. Next year he won the featherweight title by stopping George Dixon. He beat the lightweights Joe Gans and Frank Erne and, less than 18 months after winning the featherweight title, had knocked out his first six challengers. However, Young Corbett II then knocked him out twice and the rapid progress of the apparently invincible McGovern was over. He fought on for four years before retiring, and died in 1918, just before his 38th birthday.

Jimmy McLARNIN

b 1906

Jimmy McLarnin was born in Inchacore, Belfast, N. Ireland, on 19 December 1906, but was taken to Vancouver as a boy, where under his influential trainer, Pop Foster, he became an outstanding champion.

McLarnin, known as 'Babyface', began professional boxing aged 17, and by the time he was 22 he was challenging Sammy Mandell for the lightweight title, but was outpointed. He won the welterweight championship in 1933 with a first-round knock-out of Young Corbett III. This followed wins over Mandell, Al Singer, Billy Petrolle, Lou Brouillard and Benny Leonard. He lost his title after three great battles with Barney Ross, who won the decisive one, and retired.

Freddie MILLS

b 1919–d 1965

Freddie Mills was an aggressive, two-fisted puncher who learned his boxing in West Country boxing booths. He was born in Parkstone, Dorset, on 26 June 1919 and was a professional before he was 17. During World War II, in which he served in the RAF, he beat Jock McAvoy and, in 1942, Len Harvey, to be recognized in Britain as world light-heavyweight champion. However, in 1946 he met Gus Lesnevich, the American claimant, who beat him after a great battle, but Mills, who was having his first contest for 15 months, outpointed Lesnevich in a return two years later to become undisputed champion.

Mills, a durable, gutsy fighter, frequently fought heavyweights and took bad beatings from British champion Bruce Woodcock and the giant American Joe Baksi, defeats which told on him, and he lost his world title in 1950 to Joey Maxim. He retired immediately, became a television personality, and owned a night club in London. In 1965 he was found shot dead in his car outside his club, and the circumstances of his death were never satisfactorily explained.

Carlos MONZON

b 1942

Carlos Monzon fought in the middleweight division, traditionally one with the greatest champions, and Monzon's record in this company is unsurpassed.

He was born in Santa Fe, Argentina, on 7 August 1942, a poor boy from a family of ten children. He began boxing as an amateur, studied the principles carefully, and turned professional in 1963. He suffered three early defeats but avenged them all, and in 1970 took his first long trip away from Argentina to challenge Nino Benvenuti for the middleweight title. Unknown to most supporters outside his own country, he caused a great upset with a 12th-round knock-out. He then defended his title in many parts of the world, and when he retired nearly seven years later he was still undisputed champion, having defended 14 times. The three early defeats were all he suffered in 102 contests.

Tragedy entered Monzon's private life in 1988. His third wife died after a fall from a balcony, and Monzon was charged with murder.

Archie MOORE

b 1916

Archie Moore's record is one of the most impressive of all boxers. He was world light-heavyweight champion for nearly ten years — and would have been for longer had his chance come sooner.

He was born Archibald Lee Wright in Benoit, Mississippi, on 13 December 1916 — although his mother claimed that this 'official' date was wrong, and that he was born in 1913. He took the name Moore from his uncle Cleveland Moore, who looked after him when his parents separated. After a delinquent childhood, he turned professional in 1935, but was poorly managed in a difficult time for black fighters. A serious accident and pneumonia also held him back, and he waited until the end of 1952 before he was given a title chance. He then outpointed Joey Maxim three times to become light-heavyweight champion. By this time he was already at least 36.

He was more or less unbeatable at this weight where he was a knock-out specialist. In 1955 he fought Rocky Marciano for the heavyweight championship and had Marciano down before losing. A year later he was beaten by Floyd Patterson for the vacant title.

In 1960, after eight defences, the NBA stripped the 44-year-old Moore of their version of the light-heavyweight title for inactivity, but he continued to defend the New York and European version until 1961, when he lost recognition from these bodies also.

He finally retired to his ranch in 1963 and appeared in an occasional film. In 215 fights over 28 years he won 183, 129 inside the distance.

Jose NAPOLES

b 1940

Jose Napoles was one of the best post-war welterweight champions. He was born in Oriente, Santiago, Cuba, on 13 April 1940, and began a professional career in 1958. He was forced to box in Mexico because of Cuba's attitude to professional boxing. In 1969 he won the world title with a victory over Curtis Cokes.

In December 1970 he surprisingly lost it for six months to Billy Backus, who damaged his eye, but he retrieved it and held on to it until December 1975, when John H. Stracey beat him. He was by then 35, and the year before had unsuccessfully challenged Carlos Monzon for the middleweight title.

Ruben OLIVARES

b 1947

Olivares was one of the hardest hitting of all the smaller men, 77 of his 87 victories coming inside the distance. Born in Mexico City on 14 January 1947 he turned professional soon after his 17th birthday.

Olivares fought for world titles as a bantam and featherweight. He first won the undisputed bantam title in August 1969 with a knock-out of Lionel Rose, and was champion for two and a half years, during which time Chuchu Castillo took the title for six months by winning the second of three bouts with him. He lost the belt in 1972 to Rafael Herrera, but in July 1974 he won the WBA featherweight title by stopping Zensuke Utegawa. He soon lost this to Alexis Arguello, but six months later knocked out Bobby Chacon for the WBC crown. He held this for three months until David Kotey won a decision to end his days as a champion, although he challenged Eusebio Pedroza as late as 1979. In all he had 13 world title fights, winning eight. He retired in 1981, with 87 wins and three draws in 102 bouts.

Carlos ORTIZ

b 1935

Born in Ponce, Puerto Rico, on 9 September 1936, Carlos Ortiz was an excellent boxer, who after a good amateur career in New York turned professional in 1955. Four years later he won the NBA light-welterweight title with a two-round stoppage of Kenny Lane.

Ortiz became a well-travelled champion, losing this title after 15 months to Duilio Loi in Milan. Ortiz then moved down to lightweight and in April 1962 surprisingly outpointed Joe Brown for the undisputed championship. In 1965 he lost and regained the title in two contests with Ismael Laguna, not relinquishing his crown for good until outpointed by Carlos Teo Cruz in 1968. He retired in 1972 when stopped for the first time in his career (by Ken Buchanan). Of his 70 contests he won 61, including 14 world title victories over more than eight years.

Manuel ORTIZ

b 1916–d 1970

Manuel Ortiz was one of the best of the world's bantamweight champions. He was born in Corona, California, of Mexican parents, on 2 July 1916. He became a hard-hitting professional in 1938, and in January 1942 was recognized by California as world bantamweight champion with a win over Tony Olivera.

He outpointed Lou Salica in August for universal recognition and did not lose the title for good until he was outpointed in Johannesburg by Vic Toweel, who was 13 years his junior.

He was champion for over eight years, despite a period of two months in 1947 when the title was held by Harold Dade, who scored an upset points win over him in January — Ortiz won the title back in March when the pair met again. He fought on until he was 39, retiring in 1955.

He died in 1970.

Floyd PATTERSON

b 1935

Floyd Patterson was one of the most interesting of heavyweight champions. He was born in Waco, North Carolina, on 4 January 1935. A delinquent child, he was taught boxing at a reform school, and won an Olympic gold medal in 1952. Of the three records he set, the first was to be the first Olympic champion to become the heavyweight champion of the world.

Patterson, at 6ft (1.83m) and 190lb (86kg) was not big for a modern heavyweight, and under his manager, Cus d'Amato, he adopted a strange style, holding his gloves high in front of his face and leaping in with hooks when he launched attacks. In 1956 he won the vacant title caused by Marciano's retirement with a knock-out of light-heavyweight champion Archie Moore. At 21 years 10 months and 26 days he established another record in being the youngest world heavyweight champion.

Cus d'Amato would have nothing to do with the International Boxing Club which then held the contracts of many leading heavyweights, so many of Patterson's defences were easy — but one expected to be so was not. Ingemar Johansson surprised him with seven knockdowns and a third-round stoppage. However, Patterson regained the title a year later to create his third record — he became the first man to regain the crown.

In 1962, nearly six years after first winning the title, Patterson lost it for good when stopped in the first round by Sonny Liston. Patterson's retiring nature was emphasized when he slipped out of the arena in disguise. He lost again to Liston in one round, and later challenged Ali and Jimmy Ellis for the title, unsuccessfully.

He retired in 1972 after 20 years as a professional.

Above: Floyd Patterson was a courageous boxer who was frequently knocked down but usually got up to win. His two spells as heavyweight champion added up to nearly five years.

Eusebio PEDROZA

b 1953

Pedroza proved to be a wily and long-lasting featherweight champion and a hard-punching professional. Born in Panama City on 2 March 1953, he turned professional when 20, and in his 16th fight challenged Alfonso Zamora for the bantamweight title, but was knocked out. On 15 April 1978 he won the WBA featherweight crown by knocking out Cecilio Lastra. Pedroza made no fewer than 19 successful defences, and remained champion for over seven years before he was finally outpointed by Barry McGuigan in June 1985. It was a great run, made more impressive by the fact that five of his victims were past or future world champions.

Willie
PEP
b 1922

Willie Pep was an outstanding featherweight, so fast and difficult to hit that he was called 'Will o' the Wisp'.

Born in Middletown, Connecticut, on 19 September 1922 (his surname was actually Papaleo), he was an excellent amateur who turned professional in 1940.

Pep was a very busy boxer. In November 1942 he won New York recognition as world champion when he outpointed Chalky Wright. He was only 20 years old at this time. When he beat the NBA champion Sal Bartolo in 1946 he was undisputed champion. He had held a version of the championship for nearly six years when he fought Sandy Saddler in 1948, and had lost only one of his previous 136 fights — that to lightweight champion Sammy Angott. Saddler, surprisingly, knocked him out in the fourth round. Pep later regained the title with his best performance, a brilliant points win, but in 1950 and 1951 Saddler beat him in two savage and dirty fights to end his championship days. Pep was suspended in New York after the second fight.

He retired in 1958 but made a surprising comeback seven years later at the ripe old age of 43, having ten more contests before deciding to become a referee. He had an excellent personal record, having won 230 of his 242 bouts.

Pascual
PEREZ
b 1926–d 1977

Pascual Perez was an amazing champion — and had the distinction of becoming the first Argentinian to win a world title. He was born in Mendoza on 4 March 1926 and won the flyweight gold medal at the 1948 Olympics in London.

Perez turned professional against the wishes of his family when he was past 26. He quickly won his first 50 fights, and in November 1954 he outpointed Yoshio Shirai in Tokyo for the world title.

Perez was only 4ft 11in (1.50m) and 106lb (48kg), but was a terrific hitter. He was an excellent champion, who ran up a sequence of 52 unbeaten contests.

He made nine successful defences of his title before losing it to Pone Kingpetch in Bangkok, having been champion for five and a half years. He was then 34, but he boxed on for another four years. He won 83 of 91 fights, 56 inside the distance.

A tough, though diminutive fighter, Pascual Perez died in 1977 aged only 50.

Aaron
PRYOR
b 1955

Pryor was born in Cincinnati, Ohio, on 20 October 1955, and turned professional soon after his 21st birthday. In August 1980 he won the WBA light-welterweight title with a fourth round knock-out of the brilliant Antonio Cervantes.

To September 1983 Pryor made eight defences, none of which went the distance. Two were against triple champion Alexis Arguello, attempting a world title at a fourth weight. After his second victory over Arguello, Pryor retired, still only 28. A hard-hitting, very aggressive fighter, he was finding fighting drugs tough. Pryor, however, quickly received the blessing of the IBF, and was their inaugural champion in June 1984, outpointing Nicky Furlano. In 1985 he outpointed challenger Gary Hinton, later forfeiting his title through inactivity. He won all his 36 contests, 33 inside the distance.

Sugar Ray
ROBINSON
b 1921

Some claim Sugar Ray Robinson was the most complete boxer of all. He was born Walker Smith in Detroit, Michigan, on 3 May 1921, and began professional boxing in 1940. He obtained the name Ray Robinson when he deputized for an absent boxer and he kept the name. He acquired the 'Sugar' when somebody told his trainer George Gainsford that his boxer was 'as sweet as sugar'.

Robinson began as a lightweight and moved up to welterweight, where after 40 wins he was outpointed by Jake LaMotta, a defeat he avenged four times. In the next eight years Robinson was unbeaten in 91 contests. In 1946 he won the vacant welterweight title by outpointing Tommy Bell. He made five defences of the welterweight title over four years, then won Pennsylvanian recognition as middleweight champion when outpointing Robert Villemain in 1950 and universal recognition in 1951 when stopping Jake LaMotta. Robinson thereupon gave up the welterweight title at which he was invincible and defended his middleweight crown. He was to win it five times in all.

The second defeat of his career was in 1951 by Randolph Turpin, but he regained the title 64 days later. In 1952 he gave up the title and fought Joey Maxim for the light-heavyweight crown. He was ahead on points when he retired, exhausted, after 13 rounds in a New York heatwave. He retired and began a cabaret act, but made a comeback in 1955, aged 34. Amazingly, he regained the middle-

Left: *Sugar Ray Robinson in 1962, near the end of a long career during which he won the world welterweight championship and the middleweight championship five times. For some years he was unbeatable at his weight.*

weight crown from Carl 'Bobo' Olson. He then lost it and regained it from Gene Fullmer and Carmen Basilio. Ultimately, he forfeited the title in 1959 for inactivity, but challenged unsuccessfully four times thereafter, once getting a draw with Fullmer. He did not retire finally until 1965, when in his 45th year.

Robinson won 175 of 202 contests in 25 years, and had 22 world championship bouts.

Barney ROSS

b 1909–d 1967

Ross was born Barnet Rosofsky in New York City on 23 December 1909. An excellent amateur, he turned professional in 1929 to help support the family after his father, a grocer, had been murdered by gunmen.

Ross was one of the last of a line of great pre-war Jewish champions. He became one of the fastest of welterweights, an all-action fighter. In June 1933 he won the lightweight and junior welterweight titles from Tony Canzoneri. In May 1934 he added the welterweight title when he outpointed Jimmy McLarnin. Ross was then forced to relinquish the lightweight title because of weight difficulties, but he kept the light-welterweight title, defending eight times until April 1935. He was then forced to relinquish this to concentrate on the welters, and the 'junior' title fell into disuse.

Ross' victory over the Irishman McLarnin was the first of three contests between them which excited their ethnic supporters in New York. All three ended in controversial decisions, but it was Ross who won the deciding bout, and continued as champion until May 1938. He was then beaten by another all-action performer, Henry Armstrong, and retired. He won 73 and lost only four of his 81 bouts. He was awarded the Congressional Medal of Honour while serving as a marine at Guadalcanal in World War II, and afterwards fought drug addiction arising from the treatment of his wounds before dying of cancer in 1967.

Tommy RYAN

b 1870–d 1948

Tommy Ryan's real name was Joseph Youngs, and he was born of a French father and English mother in Redwood, New York, on 31 March 1870. He became a clever middleweight who also carried a knock-out punch.

Ryan won first the welterweight title in July 1894 with a 20-round decision over Mysterious Billy Smith. In 1896 he lost to Kid McCoy, who tricked him into thinking he was ill, so Ryan did not train, but McCoy subsequently showed more interest in claiming the middleweight title, so Ryan continued as welter king. In 1898 Ryan himself moved up to middleweight, and won the title by knocking out George Green. He kept this title until he retired in 1904.

Because of the confusion among the weight classes in the 1890s it is not clear which of Ryan's fights were title fights, but he probably took part in 14, losing only one. He lost only the odd four of 104 contests in his career. He died in 1948.

Sandy SADDLER

b 1926

Saddler was a tall featherweight at 5ft 8½in (1.74m), who, unlike many tall boxers, possessed a devastating punch, particularly his left hook. He was born in Boston, Massachusetts, on 23 June 1926 and turned professional in 1944.

The son of a West Indian, he was brought up in Harlem, New York, and after four years of impressive victories he earned a world title fight with the legendary Willie Pep. It was a major upset when Saddler scored a fourth-round knock-out. Pep won a return on points, but the stronger and rougher Saddler won two further bitter battles to establish himself as champion. During this time Ohio revived the junior lightweight division, and acknowledged Saddler as world champion when he outpointed Orlando Zulueta in 1949, but this division fell into disuse again when Saddler regained the featherweight title.

Saddler then spent three years in the US Army, during which time Teddy 'Redtop' Davis was installed as an 'interim' champion. Saddler beat him in 1955 and stopped Flash Elorde in 1956, but a road accident injured his eye so badly he was forced to retire. He won 144 of his 162 contests.

Vicente SALDIVAR

b 1943–d 1985

Vicente Saldivar had a rapid rise to the top, retired, and then fought his way to the top again. He was born of a poor family in Mexico City on 13 May 1943. After an excellent amateur career he turned professional as a hard-hitting featherweight in 1961, and in September 1964 he stopped Sugar Ramos to become world champion. After eight defences, the last two against Howard Winstone of Wales, he retired, his only defeat in 34 contests being an early disqualification. He was only 26, and after two and a half years began a comeback. He beat both of Winstone's successors as WBC champion, José Legra and Johnny Famechon, to become champion again in 1970. However, after seven months he lost the title to Kuniaki Shibata. He retired again, but in 1973 made another comeback, and had another shot at the title, losing to Eder Jofre. These three were the only defeats he suffered in his 41-fight career, 27 of his 38 wins coming inside the distance. Sadly, he died of a heart attack in July 1985, aged only 42.

Salvador SANCHEZ

b 1958–d 1982

The tragic Sanchez was killed in his prime, when he was one of the outstanding world champions. He was born on 3 February 1958 in Santiago, Mexico, and turned professional three months after his 17th birthday. A points defeat when challenging for the Mexican bantamweight title was to prove his only reverse and he developed into a skilful two-fisted boxer with a terrific punch. On 2 February 1980 he won the WBC featherweight title with a stoppage of Danny Lopez. In the next two and a half years he made nine successful defences, four of his challengers being past or future champions. He died in a road accident on 12 August 1982, with one defeat in 45 contests.

Tom SAYERS

b 1826–d 1865

Although he weighed no more than 155lb (70kg) or so, Sayers was one of the best bare-knuckle champions, often beating men much bigger than himself. He was born in Brighton on 25 May 1826, and went to London to become a prize fighter. His only defeat on his way to the championship was inflicted, ironically, by a lighter man, Nat Langham, the middleweight champion, who closed both Sayers' eyes, causing him to retire in 61 rounds.

Sayers won the championship in beating William Perry, the 'Tipton Slasher' in 1857. Perry was four inches (10cm) taller and at least 40lb (18kg) heavier, but Sayers won in 95 minutes. Tom beat off three challengers, then faced the American champion, John C. Heenan, in the great fight at Farnborough, Hampshire. The fight was declared a draw after two hours 20 minutes, and both men were given a silver belt. It was Sayers' last fight. He died in 1865, and there is a huge memorial to him in Highgate Cemetery, where he is buried.

Max SCHMELING

b 1905

Max Schmeling is best remembered for the savage beating Joe Louis gave him in a world title fight in 1938, which is unfair to him, as he was an excellent boxer, with a booming right hand, who did not receive due fairness from Americans.

He was born in Brandenburg, Germany, on 28 September 1905. He became European heavyweight champion and in June 1930 he won the vacant world title when Jack Sharkey was disqualified against him — he is the only heavyweight champion to win the title on a disqualification. He lost the title to Sharkey in a return two years later, in a close fight which many thought he had won.

In 1936 he became the only man to beat Joe Louis before Louis' first retirement. He worked out a weakness in the Brown Bomber's armoury and knocked him out in a big upset. It made Schmeling the leading contender for Braddock's title, but a secret deal between the managers of Braddock and Louis prevented Schmeling getting his chance. He was nearly 33 when Louis knocked him out on his last challenge. Schmeling bore Louis no grudge, and helped him in later years when Louis was down on his luck.

Jack SHARKEY

b 1902

Sharkey was born in Binghamton, New York, on 26 October 1902. His real name was Joseph Paul Zukauskas, his parents being Lithuanian. He fought out of Boston, and because he was an ex-sailor he was known as the 'Boston Gob'. He was also known as the

'Sobbing Sailor', because he was very temperamental and emotional.

He was a good heavyweight who concentrated on body punching, so when he got a shot at the vacant title in 1930 it was not altogether a shock when he was disqualified against Schmeling for a low blow. He won the title two years later by outpointing Schmeling, but surprisingly lost it on his first defence to the giant Italian, Primo Carnera. Three years later, when 34, he lost to the rising star Joe Louis and retired.

Mysterious Billy SMITH

b 1891–d 1937

Amos Smith, born in Eastport, Maine, on 15 May 1891, called himself Billy as a more appropriate fighting name, and acquired the 'Mysterious' when he switched his operations from the East Coast to the West, and a fan wrote to a boxing paper asking who this 'mysterious Billy Smith' was.

He was the world welterweight champion in 1892, when he knocked out Danny Needham. He lost the title in 1894 to Tommy Ryan, but when Ryan moved up to middleweight in 1898, Smith regained it. He was a tough fighter who remained champion until disqualified against Rube Ferns in 1900. He retired in 1902, and died in Portland, Oregon.

Leon SPINKS

b 1953

Leon Spinks was born in St Louis, Missouri, on 11 July 1953, and he and his younger brother Michael both won gold medals in the 1976 Olympic Games. Leon immediately turned professional and in only his eighth professional bout (in February 1978) was given a shot at the heavyweight title held by Muhammad Ali. He boxed in brilliant fashion, and shook the fistic world by gaining a split decision over the lethargic Ali. His reign lasted only until the return seven months later. He was well beaten by Larry Holmes in a later challenge and retired, although he came back in 1988.

Michael SPINKS

b 1956

Leon Spinks' younger brother was also born in St Louis, on 13 July 1956. He, too, turned professional in 1977 after winning a 1976 Olympic gold medal, but his career was different from his brother's. He carefully fought his way up the light-heavyweight rankings until given a chance, after 16 wins, against Mustapha Muhammad for the WBA title in 1981.

Spinks won and proved an outstanding champion. After five defences he unified the championship by outpointing Dwight Muhammad Qawi, the WBC champion, in 1983. After four defences of the undisputed title, he moved up to heavyweight and became IBF champion in September 1985 with a bitterly disputed points victory over the veteran Larry Holmes.

Thus, the Spinks brothers became the first pair to win a version of the heavyweight title, and Michael became the first to succeed of a long line of light-heavyweight champions who had tried to win the heavier title.

When a plan was afoot to unify the heavyweight division in the late 1980s, Spinks opted out rather than face Mike Tyson, and beat Gerry Cooney instead. However, the showdown between the two unbeaten champions eventually took place on 27 June 1988 and Spinks was crushed in 91 seconds.

Above: *Leon Spinks in training for a heavyweight title fight with Muhammad Ali. Spinks' feat in winning boxing's top prize in only his eighth professional bout is unlikely to be bettered, but his career went rapidly downhill afterwards.*

John L. SULLIVAN

b 1858–d 1918

John L. (for Lawrence) Sullivan was born in Roxbury, Boston, Massachusetts, on 15 October 1858. He was an immensely strong prize-fighter, whose boast was that he could lick 'any sonofabitch in the house'. He was called the 'Boston Strong Boy'. He won the American championship in 1882 when he beat Paddy Ryan, and although he did not beat the best in England, there is little doubt that around this time Sullivan was the best in the world.

Sullivan was a larger than life character, an Irish 'broth of a boyo', whose great talent seemed not impaired by his liking for strong drink. He became the most popular boxer there has ever been in America. In 1889 he had a tremendous battle with Jake Kilrain, whom he beat after 75 rounds. His fans presented him with a magnificent belt containing 397 diamonds.

Some claim Sullivan to be the first world heavyweight champion, but the first match in which he fought with gloves that could be classed as a world title fight was the one in which he suffered his only defeat. James J. Corbett, who studied boxing science, knocked out the old braggart in 1892, and to him is accorded the honour of being the first champion. John L. reformed. He married his childhood sweetheart and together they toured America lecturing on the evils of drink. Sullivan died in 1918.

Dick TIGER

b 1929–d 1971

Dick Tiger was born in Amaigo, Orlu, Nigeria, on 14 August 1929 as Dick Ihetu. He did a little boxing as an amateur, turned professional at 23, then pursued his career in Liverpool. He beat future middleweight champion Terry Downes and then went to America.

Eventually, in 1962, the hard-hitting Tiger won the WBA middleweight title from Gene Fullmer, and after a draw and another victory over Fullmer was recognized as undisputed champion. Tiger lost and regained the title in contests with Joey Giardello, but then lost it finally in April 1966 to Emile Griffith. Tiger then went after the light-heavyweight title and in December 1966 outpointed José Torres to win it. This title he held for nearly 18 months (during which time he fought in the Nigerian civil war) before losing to Bob Foster. Tiger was now in his 39th year.

He retired, but sadly died of cancer in 1971, aged only 42.

Gene TUNNEY

b 1897–d 1978

Tunney's real Christian names were James Joseph, and he was born in Greenwich Village, New York, on 25 May 1897 of well-off parents. Boxing gloves as an 11th birthday present, rather than the usual poverty, set him on the road to fistic fame. He turned professional against his parents' wishes at 18, but his career was soon interrupted by World War I, in which he served as a marine. He became a services champion, and back home became US light-heavyweight champion (he lost the title in his only career defeat, to Harry Greb, but avenged this defeat four times).

Tunney then began beating the heavyweight contenders until he earned a title shot with Jack Dempsey. Tunney was a student of boxing, and he easily outpointed the primitive Dempsey to become champion. He won the return in the 'Battle of the Long Count', in which he was down for 14 seconds, defended once more and then retired. He married an heiress, became a successful businessman and was a friend of George Bernard Shaw. His son became a US congressman. He died rich and respected.

Randolph TURPIN

b 1928–d 1966

Randolph Turpin, born in Leamington, Warwickshire, on 7 June 1928, was from a boxing family — his brother Dick was the first black boxer to win a British title. He had a good amateur career, and turned professional aged 18.

Turpin was a skilful boxer with an individual style, holding his hands low and often launching attacks from a crouch. He had a big punch with either hand. Turpin won the British middleweight title from Albert Finch six months after Finch had taken it from his brother, and in 1951 thrilled British fans with a brilliant victory over Sugar Ray Robinson for the world title. He was champion for only 64 days, Robinson beating him in New York in a desperate attack when his eye had been cut.

Unfortunately, that marked the end of Turpin as a world-class fighter, although he regained European recognition when Robinson retired. A unification contest in America with Carl 'Bobo' Olson was fought against the background of rape charges and other major domestic problems, and he lost tamely. He fought on until 1962, sometimes showing flashes of his old brilliance, but then had to indulge in wrestling to try to solve his financial problems. In 1966 he shot himself at his home.

Mike TYSON

b 1966

Mike Tyson burst upon the boxing scene in 1986, when a string of impressive knock-out victories demanded that he be incorporated into a series of contests that were planned to unify the world heavyweight championship.

Tyson was born on 30 June 1966 and brought up in Brownsville, a tough area of New York. As a boy he kept pigeons, and it was the killing of one of them by an older boy that first released the aggression that was to become famous. The 10-year-old beat up the bigger boy and realized his strength. He became a mugger and terror of the streets, and at 13 was in a detention centre. His salvation was Cus d'Amato and his gym in Catskill. The trainer of world champions Floyd Patterson and José Torres became his legal guardian and coached Tyson towards the heavyweight championship of the world.

Tyson turned professional in 1985, and in exactly 18 months had won his first 27 contests, all but two inside the distance, 21 inside the first three rounds, 15 in the first. This earned him a WBC title shot with Trevor Berbick, whom he destroyed in two rounds.

Tyson was 20 years, 4 months and 22 days old, becoming in succession to Patterson the youngest heavyweight champion. Sadly, d'Amato had died the previous year, but the young tearaway was well managed by Jim Jacobs and Bill Cayton, two men with boxing at heart.

Tyson at 5ft 11in (1.80m) is not tall for a heavyweight and frequently needs to punch upwards. However, unlike Patterson, he does so from a firm stance. He stalks his opponents, and his hand speed is extremely fast. Tyson's image is of the bad guy — he enters the ring without a robe, without socks and with plain black trunks, allowing no softening of the picture. His most noticeable physical attribute in repose is his 19¾-in (50cm) neck.

After disposing of Berbick, he added the WBA title to the WBC with a defeat of James 'Bonecrusher' Smith, then, interspersed with defences of these titles, he annexed the IBF crown by beating Tony Tucker, quickly beat ex-champion Larry Holmes and then removed the only pretender to the crown, the unbeaten Michael Spinks, in 91 seconds.

This brought his career to June 1988, little more than three years after his debut. With no opposition in the ring, his private life became the centre of attention. Manager Jim Jacobs had died and Tyson fell out with Cayton, and there followed legal squabbles over his contract concerning Cayton and promoter Don King, who wanted to guide the champion. Marriage to TV actress Robin Givens ('Beauty and the Beast' said the papers) led to reports that a strong-willed mother-in-law was also influencing the young man's life. Then, a late-night Harlem brawl with a former opponent left him with a hair-line fracture of the hand, and a car crash with a tree knocked him out for 20 minutes. One newspaper suggested he was suicidal and was seeing a psychiatrist.

At 22, Tyson, who earned over $20 million for the Spinks fight alone, was feeling the pressure of his fame. As a boxer, he was already among the legends.

__Below:__ Mike Tyson looking to be in gentle mood. The trail of destruction he left on his way to the heavyweight title aged 20 was rapid and comprehensive, only two men going the distance in 28 contests.

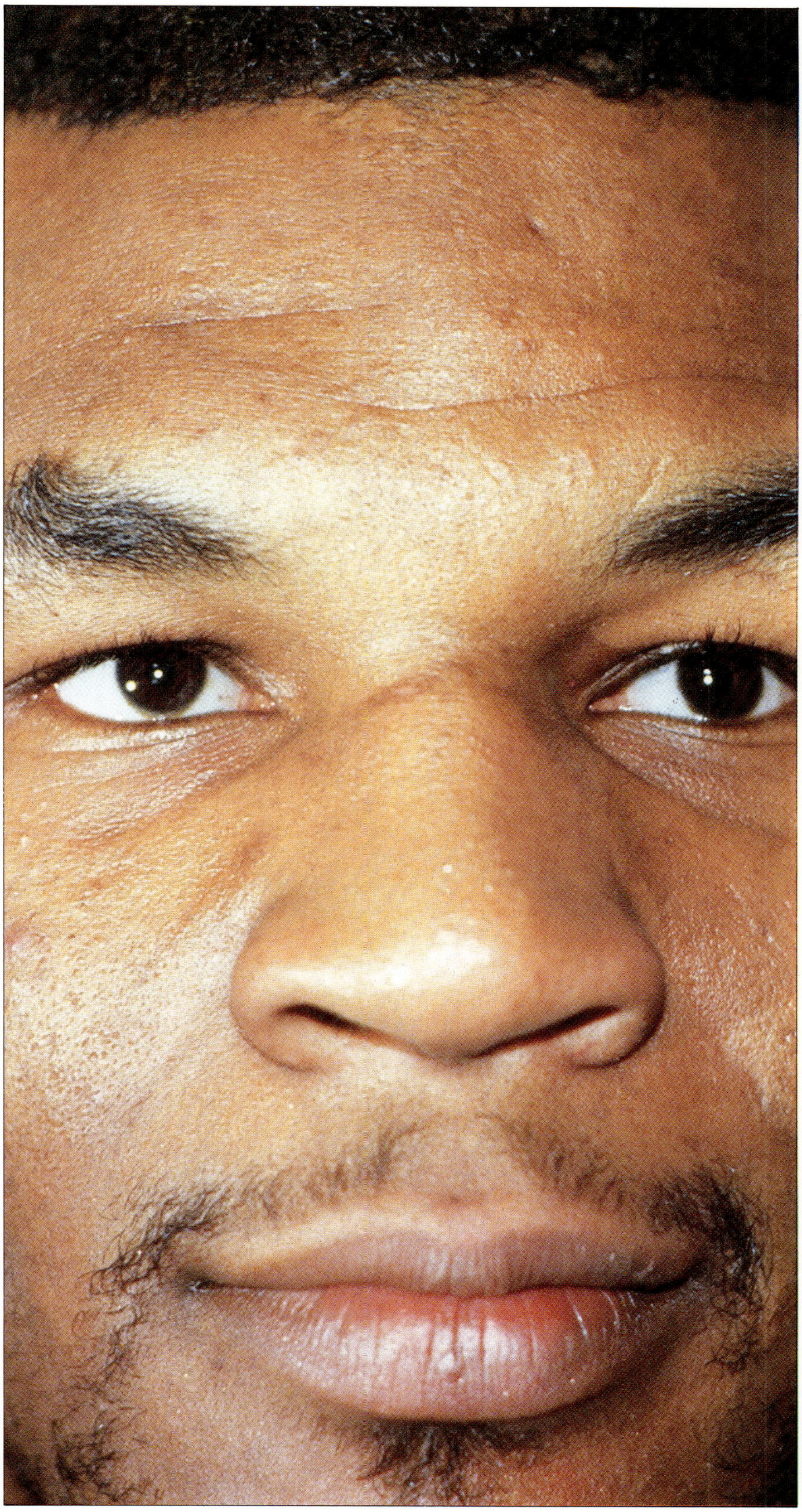

Right: Persistence paid off for Jersey Joe Walcott, who won the world heavyweight title on his fifth attempt. In fact, he fought eight times for the title, winning twice, all after the age of 33.

Pancho VILLA

b 1901–d 1925

Pancho Villa was not Mexican, but a Filipino, born in Iloilo on 1 August 1901. When he began professional boxing in 1919 he took the name of the Mexican revolutionary. Within six years both boxer and rebel had met untimely deaths. After winning the oriental flyweight and bantamweight titles Villa went to New York, where he was instantly popular. Tex Rickard, the great promoter, put up a large purse for Jimmy Wilde to come out of semi-retirement and defend his flyweight title against Villa in New York. Villa smashed Wilde to defeat, and with his all-action style made a fortune in the next two years with a number of exciting wins. Then, in July 1925, he took on Jimmy McLarnin soon after having a wisdom tooth removed. He took a lot of punishment around the mouth, and needed an operation. He died under anaesthetic on 14 July 1925.

Jersey Joe WALCOTT

b 1914

Walcott's real name was not that of a boxer: Arnold Raymond Cream. He was born at Merchantville, New Jersey, on 31 January 1914. He turned professional as a featherweight at 16 and took the name of the former welterweight champion Joe Walcott, whom he resembled facially, and added the 'Jersey' for his state.

Walcott's career divides into two parts. He retired in 1944, aged 30, after a routine career with no great success. He had a wife and six children and took a job in a soup factory in Camden to support them. He then agreed to six fights for a local promoter opening a hall and did so well that he was invited to box an exhibition with Joe Louis, the heavyweight champion. This became a title fight, and though Louis was given the decision, everybody, including the champion, thought Walcott was badly treated. He was given a return, and then, when Louis retired, fought Ezzard Charles for the vacant title. Charles won, but later defended twice against Walcott, and on the second occasion, in July 1951, Walcott won with a knock-out. It was his fifth challenge, he had been fighting for 21 years, and he was 37½, the oldest man to win the heavyweight championship. Just over a year later he was knocked out by Rocky Marciano in the 13th round after being ahead. He retired, became a referee and a mayor of Camden and, being a religious man, he helped the New Jersey Police fight juvenile delinquency.

Mickey WALKER

b 1901–d 1981

Mickey Walker was one of the toughest, bravest and hardest hitting of middleweights, and he even fought heavyweights. He was called the 'Toy Bulldog'.

Walker was born in Elizabeth, New Jersey on 13 July 1901. He turned professional in 1919 as a welterweight, and in his 46th contest he won the world title from the veteran Jack Britton in November 1922. In 1925 he challenged Harry Greb for the middleweight title, but lost. In May 1926, after three successful defences of his welterweight title, he was outpointed by Pete Latzo and moved up to middleweight. Six months later he won the title by outpointing Tiger Flowers. In 1929, while champion, he was outpointed by Tommy Loughran for the light-heavyweight title. After four defences, the 5ft 7in (1.70m) Walker relinquished the middleweight title in 1931 to tackle the heavyweights. His best performance was a draw with Jack Sharkey, who soon was to become heavyweight champion, but he was badly beaten by the recent ex-champion Max Schmeling.

After his retirement in 1935 Walker had several jobs (and six wives) and was acclaimed as a primitive painter. He died in 1981.

Freddie WELSH

b 1886–d 1927

Freddie Welsh was a great lightweight,

extremely quick on his feet and a powerful in-fighter. He was born in Pontypridd, Wales, on 5 March 1886, and turned professional in 1905, when he was in America. His real name was Frederick Hall Thomas.

He became British and Empire champion, but none of Joe Gans, Battling Nelson or Ad Wolgast would give him a shot at the world title. Eventually, Willie Ritchie did, and in 1914 Welsh narrowly outpointed him over 20 rounds at Olympia. Welsh returned to the USA for the rest of his career. He remained champion until May 1917 when Benny Leonard stopped him in a no-decision contest. Welsh was 31 and decided to retire. In his career of 168 contests, nearly half no-decision, he was beaten only four times.

After leaving boxing he lost his money in a health farm, and was poor when he died in 1927, aged only 41.

Jimmy WILDE

b 1892–d 1969

Wilde was an outstanding flyweight, who frequently beat bigger men, and pound-for-pound was one of the greatest of all boxers. He was born in Tylorstown, Wales, on 15 May 1892. He was only 5ft 2½in (1.59m) and never weighed more than 108lb (49kg), often much less. He had a boyish face and skinny arms and legs, but developed great hitting power through work in the mines, where his size meant he worked in the narrower seams, hewing coal in cramped surroundings. He boxed in the booths, and during his career probably fought over 800 contests of all kinds.

Wilde turned professional in 1911, and won the world flyweight title when stopping Joe Symonds in February 1916. When he beat the American champion, Young Zulu Kid, ten months later, he was recognized throughout the world. Two of his best wins came in 1919, over the American bantamweights Joe Lynch (later world champion) and Pal Moore. In 1920 he made a tour of America, and was unbeaten in 12 fights.

Wilde's hitting power earned him numerous nicknames, like the 'Mighty Atom', and 'Tylorstown Terror', but perhaps the best was the 'Ghost with a Hammer in his Hand'. His style was to attack with his hands held low, around his waist.

In 1921 the 29-year-old Wilde suffered a bad defeat by Pete Herman, a good world bantamweight champion, to whom he conceded 14lb (6kg), and who stopped him in the 17th round. He retired, but against advice went to America in 1923 to defend the flyweight title against Pancho Villa. He put up a tremendous performance but was knocked out. He became a boxing journalist, and died in 1969.

Tony ZALE

b 1913

Tony Zale had two tries at a boxing career, and the second was very successful. He was born Anthony Florian Zaleski of Polish parents at Gary, Indiana, on 29 May 1913 and worked in the steel mills of the town while enjoying a successful amateur career. He turned professional at 21, but after 28 contests in a year lost interest and went back to the mills. Two years later he began again and, in July 1940, earned NBA recognition as middleweight champion with a stoppage of Al Hostak. When he beat Georgie Abrams in 1941 he was universally recognized.

Zale was extremely tough, and earned himself the nickname of the 'Man of Steel'. He needed his toughness for the battles he will be remembered for — the three contests with challenger Rocky Graziano. In 1946, after war service, he came from almost certain defeat to win; in 1947 Graziano did the same; but the Man of Steel won the decider in 1948. The fights took their toll, and the 35-year-old lost his title in his next defence to Marcel Cerdan, and retired.

Below: *Tony Zale showing how he would try to crush Rocky when he met challenger Graziano in 1946. If anything, the human Rocky proved even harder to crack. Zale eventually won two of the three matches in their two-year saga.*

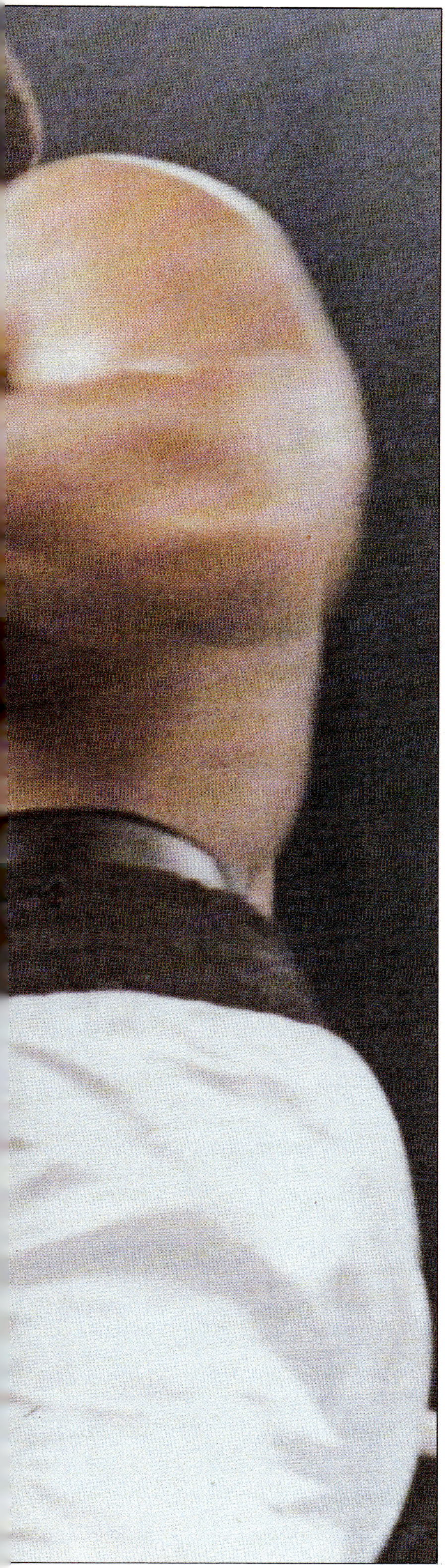

The Big Fights

Throughout the history of boxing, there have been contests which for one reason or another have risen to such heights that all who witnessed them never forget how privileged they were. This section describes a few that have reached that peak, from the illicit international battle between the English and American champions in 1860 to the dollar bonanza of the much-hyped middle-weight shoot-out between Hagler and Leonard in 1987. On the way are featured such greats as Fitzsimmons, Gans, Johnson, the Wolgast-Rivers 'double knock-out', Dempsey and the 'long count', the Zale-Graziano series, LaMotta's extraordinary comeback, Rocky Marciano, Moore's most memorable win and the 'thrilla in Manila'.

Left: *Muhammad Ali (right) in tentative mood as Joe Frazier covers up during their classic battle in Manila in 1975. It was the third match between the two and this confirmed his mastery with a desperately close win.*

Above: *The scene as Bob Fitzsimmons (back to camera) fights James J. Corbett for the world heavyweight championship in 1897. There seem to be plenty of seats available in the arena near Carson City.*

Tom Sayers v. *John C. Heenan*

Championship of the World, 17 April 1860, Farnborough Common, Hampshire

Tom Sayers, at about 152lb (69kg) was champion of England; John C. Heenan, the 'Benecia Boy', at about 195lb (88kg), was champion of America and challenged Sayers to a championship of the world. The challenge was accepted, and the press of England and America, not to mention France, journeyed to England to report on the great prize fight — the first international contest between two white men.

The only snag was that prize fighting was illegal. On the morning of the fight the boxers travelled to London in secret, Sayers in a horse-box from his training headquarters at Newmarket and Heenan from a barn in Wiltshire where he had prepared himself.

Long special trains left London Bridge at about 3.30am carrying fans to the fight (tickets £3, destination unknown). For 16 miles the Metropolitan Police watched the trains, but after that they were beyond their jurisdiction. The venue turned out to be Farnborough Common, Hampshire. Present when the fighters entered the ring was the cream of society: politicians, writers, artists, and so on.

All the physical advantages, including age (27 to 34) were with the American challenger, but Sayers was a vastly experienced fighter. He scored first with a left which drew blood. Heenan picked him up, threw him to the ground and fell upon him. Thus, the rounds proceeded until a blow from Heenan broke a bone in Sayers' right forearm, but Sayers got punches to Heenan's right eye, and closed it.

Sayers now concentrated on shutting Heenan's other eye, while Heenan, in delivering a punch to Sayers' head, broke a bone in his own left hand. Both men were now virtually one-armed, but Heenan's face was becoming a bloody mess, while Sayers was becoming exhausted by Heenan constantly throwing him and falling on him.

The 37th round proved a turning point. Law officers arrived but were kept at bay. More important, Heenan, realizing he had little time before he was blinded, desperately grabbed Sayers' throat, and, with Sayers' head on the top rope, began throttling him, ignoring Sayers' blows. Sayers' face began to go black. Then chaos ensued. Somebody cut the rope. The crowd spilled into the ring, and the referee disappeared as the police tried to show some authority.

Order was restored, however, and the battle continued without a referee for five more rounds. The police then intervened again, and the verdict was given as a draw. Needless to say, partisans disagreed as to who would have won. The greatest prize-fight ever fought had lasted 2 hours 20 minutes.

Bob Fitzsimmons v. *James J. Corbett*

Heavyweight Championship of the World, 17 March 1897, Carson City, Nevada

Gentleman Jim Corbett had brought science to boxing and earned public disapproval by beating John L. Sullivan, the biggest popular idol boxing had produced. The immaculate Corbett seemed invincible, particularly as his main rival was a balding, spindly-legged, freckled Englishman who had arrived in America via New Zealand and won the middleweight title. At first Corbett would not deign to notice the challenge of Bob Fitzsimmons, devoting himself to the stage. When he did, it was to insult him. Fitzsimmons stored up the slights, awaiting the day he could avenge them, although it seemed he would wait a long time, as two proposed meetings fell foul of the law, Fitzsimmons on one occasion being arrested for conspiring to arrange a prize-fight.

However, the day arrived when the two men met in the ring: St Patrick's Day. Fitzsimmons, with his wasp waist and blacksmith's shoulders, was something of a boxing innovator himself, using short hooks with a swivel of the body which gave his punches power out of proportion to his weight, which was some 16lb (7kg) less than Corbett's. He began on the attack, but the cool Corbett was soon in control, countering neatly to the head and avoiding Fitzsimmons' punches. Fitzsimmons, at 33, was more than three years older than Corbett, and when in the fifth round Corbett drew first blood by opening Fitzsimmons' lip, 'Ruby Robert' suddenly looked tired. In the sixth, he was down, but recovered well, and suddenly the fight took a swing.

Mrs Fitzsimmons, who was in a private box, has been given the credit for reminding her husband of one of his strengths. Going to his corner she told him to 'hit him in the slats' (the body). Fitz did, and it had the effect of slowing Corbett. Fitzsimmons told his wife he would now win.

Fitzsimmons had perfected a punch which he delivered off the wrong foot — in effect he shifted his stance to southpaw as he delivered a left. In the 14th round the perfect opportunity arose for him to deliver it and he sank a hard left just below Corbett's heart. Corbett fell to the floor, the wind knocked out of him, grey-faced and paralysed. He was counted out on his face. When he recovered he wanted to fight on, but it was too late — the world had a new heavyweight champion.

A doctor was reported as describing the target as the 'solar plexus', and a part of the body previously unknown to the layman became familiar to all boxing followers.

Joe Gans v. *Battling Nelson*

Lightweight Championship of the World, 3 September 1906, Goldfield, Nevada

With Jim Jeffries, the heavyweight champion, retired, boxing activity was quiet in 1906, so when the sports scribes heard that an unknown promoter called Tex Rickard was proposing to put up $30,000 for a lightweight fight, a sum unheard of among the little men, they descended on Goldfield, Nevada, to find the strength of the story.

The story was true. Gold had been discovered near Goldfield in 1904, and the booming tent city had decided to promote itself. A constantly replenished lake — of beer — in the main street was one suggestion, but Rickard, who had moved in with a gambling saloon, proposed the fight. He knew that the black Gans, one of the greatest boxers the world has seen, was the champion, but that Nelson had won a 'white championship' and thought he could beat Gans. Rickard realized the value of the 'black *v.* white' publicity angle, and was confident the prize money itself would inspire interest. He was right.

Gans had lost five of his 144 bouts, but some of these defeats were not genuine. As a black boxer he had to obey orders and throw an occasional fight to keep in business. He was still poor, despite his brilliance. He jumped at the proposition. Nelson was shrewdly managed. With Gans willing to fight for almost anything, he eventually signed for $23,000 to the champion's $10,000. His forte was durability. He was willing to take punches all evening, knowing that sooner or later he would sink his opponent.

Rickard built an arena and 6,000 fans filled Goldfield for the fight. It was a hot, exhausting day, all in favour of Nelson, who had insisted on the weight limit being reduced to 133lb (60kg), causing Gans to shed weight, and on an 18ft (5.5m) ring, suitable to his own close quarter work. The contract was for a match to a finish, which meant 45 rounds.

The match began at 3.22 pm and for ten rounds or more the superb Gans outboxed his stockier opponent — but that was to be expected. Gradually, Nelson, with his butting, elbowing and general rough-house tactics, began to get into the fight. At one point he had Gans groggy, but Gans fought back. At last even Nelson found his capacity for taking blows exhausted. He was being continually warned, and his face was a mass of blood. In the 42nd round he was warned again for rough work in a clinch, and as they parted, he deliberately punched Gans in the groin. Referee George Siler immediately disqualified him and went to help the stricken champion.

Gans had been in the habit of letting his mother know that they could afford to eat bacon when he earned a good purse, and that day's telegram confirmed that he was 'bringing home the bacon'.

Jack Johnson v. *James J. Jeffries*

Heavyweight Championship of the World, 4 July 1910, Reno, Nevada

The most hated boxer of all time was Jack Johnson. The main reason was that he was black. The second was that he was undoubtedly the best heavyweight in the world. The third was that he knew this and flaunted it, which led to the fourth, that he 'didn't know his place'. He even consorted with white women — and married three. Of course, only the whites hated Johnson, but they were in the majority and were the rulers.

When Johnson beat Burns to take the title in 1908, the novelist Jack London was at the ringside. He urged that the golden smile be removed from Johnson's face. Unfortunately, there was nobody to do it — except, possibly, one man.

Jim Jeffries had retired unbeaten as heavyweight champion in 1905. To many he seemed invincible, but he had been living at ease on his alfalfa farm. He refused to put the black man in his place. However, as the arrogant Johnson swaggered his way through America's heavyweight boxers and white women, the pressure increased on Jeffries to do the decent thing, and eventually he agreed to try. The match could hardly fail to be a sell-out, and at Meyer's Hotel in Hoboken, New Jersey, promoters submitted sealed envelopes for the rights. Tex Rickard's offer of £101,000 was accepted, partly because the showman had submitted some of it in $1,000 bills, which is paper fighters can understand better than a contract, and partly because he had taken the precaution of offering the two boxers $10,000 each under the table.

Although Rickard would have preferred San Francisco, the 'Battle of the Century' took place in Reno, and everybody seemed to be there. Most expected Jeffries to win, and he was a warm betting favourite. He appeared in a suit, worn over his fighting gear, and was rapturously cheered. Johnson, in black and white bathrobe, was cheered by his supporters but probably noticed too the jeers and the band playing a tune with the line 'all coons look alike to me'. Jeffries was introduced as champion. All this must have seemed a minor irritation to the brave Johnson, who had received threats that he would be shot.

The fight began in hot conditions at 2.30 pm. Jeffries attacked but Johnson parried all his efforts and began to toy with him. He spoke to him as he jabbed: 'How do you like that, Mister Jeff?', and carried on a conversation with Corbett, who was in Jeffries' corner: 'Did you see that, Jimmy?'

After displaying his contempt for the proceedings, Johnson suddenly sprang at Jeffries in the 15th round and with a succession of blows knocked him down for the first time in his life. Jeffries rose but was clearly ripe for the knock-out. The crowd screamed at Rickard, who was refereeing the fight himself, to stop it to save the white man the indignity of being knocked out by the black. However, Jeffries went down a third and final time, and although it was reported that Rickard completed the count, the official result was 'referee stopped contest'.

Savage race riots followed the humiliation of the white man. Rickard, for whom Jeffries was an idol, swore he would not promote any black *v.* white contest again. This was ironic in view of his first-ever venture, the deliberately racial Gans *v.* Nelson contest of 1906.

Ad Wolgast v. *Joe Rivers*

Lightweight Championship of the World,
4 July 1912, Vernon, California

Ad Wolgast was a lightweight who made full use of lax refereeing standards before World War I. Everything in the book was fine for Ad, who just to make sure he would not be unduly penalized had his own favourite referee, Jack Welch, to see fair or fairish play. Wolgast's defence of his title against Mexican Joe Rivers in 1912 has entered the history books as the nearest to a double-knock-out there has been.

Rivers (real name Joe Ybarra) was only 19, a popular and successful featherweight moving up a division. Wolgast had just won the title in a 40-round 'war' with Battling Nelson. Welch, who turned out to be the most significant man in the ring, was a top referee who officiated in many important fights, and was known to be a man who tolerated rough-house tactics.

Rivers began the better and faster, and cut Wolgast's ear and eye, but Wolgast fought back with some inside work, and the match developed into a tough, rough scrap, with both men taking punishment and neither giving way. During one skirmish in the 11th round they nearly wrestled each other out of the ring.

Rivers was slightly ahead and Wolgast showed reluctance to come out for the 13th, but he did, and a maul developed in the centre of the ring. Suddenly, Rivers measured Wolgast with a left and sent over a perfect right. At the same time Wolgast launched a full-blooded left to the area of Rivers' groin. The blows landed together, and both boxers crumpled to the floor, Wolgast falling on Rivers. Ignoring cries that Wolgast had fouled Rivers, referee Welch took up the count . . . at the same time helping Wolgast to his feet and supporting him to his corner. At 'ten' he lifted Wolgast's arm in victory, and fled the ring before a riot started.

Eye-witness accounts vary on the exact happenings of this extraordinary round. Many, including the timekeeper, claimed the bell went before Welch reached 'ten', so neither man was perhaps knocked out in the 'double knock-out'. Welch's explanation, given much later, was that Rivers was down first, so he counted over him, and there was no reason why he should not help Wolgast.

The strange end to the story is that Wolgast was confined in an institution from 1920, having lost his memory, and his most regular visitor was Rivers.

Gene Tunney v. *Jack Dempsey*

Heavyweight Championship of the World,
22 September 1927, Soldier's Field, Chicago

The second fight between Gene Tunney and Jack Dempsey is probably the most famous fight in boxing history. Interest in the sport was at its peak (the gate receipts for this fight were not beaten for 49 years, and only then because of inflation). Dempsey had become a legend, and the outcome hinged on the most controversial incident in boxing — the famous 'long count'.

Tunney, a clever boxer, had taken the title from Dempsey, a pure and simple slugger, a year and a day before. Dempsey was now better prepared, and was fancied to win the title back. Until the seventh round, the calm Tunney outpointed Dempsey and was well ahead. However, in the seventh a hard left hook from Dempsey knocked Tunney to the ropes, where he stood bewildered as Dempsey piled in punch after punch until Tunney slid to the canvas.

Referee Dave Barry moved to take up the count, but then saw Dempsey standing at hand ready to pounce on Tunney again. Before the fight it had been emphasized that in the event of a knockdown, the upright boxer must go immediately to the farthest neutral corner before the count could start. This Dempsey had blatantly failed to do in his defeat of Firpo, and again his instincts had got the better of him. Dempsey at first ignored Barry's attempt to move him away, then went to the wrong corner. By the time Dempsey was properly positioned, Barry had taken up the count, and Tunney had risen at 'nine', it was estimated the champion had been down for *at least* 14 seconds.

Even so, Dempsey was rushing across the ring as Tunney rose, but Tunney was able to avoid another knockdown punch to the end of the round. Tunney recovered in the eighth, and even clipped a tired Dempsey to the canvas. He continued to outpoint Dempsey for an easy win, but the hysteria of the seventh round was talked about for years.

Tunney claimed later that he was in control, and could have got up at 'nine' no matter when the count had begun. Dempsey, who kept silent for years, agreed near the end of his life that this was probably so. Even now, more than 60 years later, there are men who still talk of the look in Tunney's eyes when he slid down, and are prepared to swear that Dempsey's impetuosity cost him the richest prize in sport.

Rocky Graziano v. *Tony Zale*

Middleweight Championship of the World, 16 July 1947, Chicago Stadium

The three battles between Tony Zale and Rocky Graziano have gone into boxing history as the most savage series fought by two men. Each fought with courage and at times desperation, and neither yielded an inch.

It started on 27 September 1946 at the Yankee Stadium, New York, when Zale, the champion, beat Graziano after being all but out himself on two occasions. The great battle demanded a return, and ten months later it was set for Chicago.

The two men were opposites in some ways. Zale was quiet, religious, upright, while Graziano was the ex-delinquent, the 'Dead End Kid', the street fighter whose instinct was to win at all costs. However, there were similarities — both were tough and determined, and neither knew when they were beaten.

Zale began the second fight, watched by the then indoor record attendance of 18,547, with a strong attack. By the end of the first round Graziano was sore around the ribs and his left eye was closing. Graziano fought back and halfway through the second round, a right to the jaw had Zale groggy. In the third Zale split Graziano's eye and knocked him down, and appeared to be on top. Zale continued pressing in the fourth, and with Graziano's left eye pouring blood and his right beginning to puff up, he began to take plenty of punishment and the referee showed concern. At the end of the round he advised Graziano to retire, but Rocky insisted on one more round, and was granted it.

Rocky put all he had into the fifth, abandoning all pretence of the 'noble art' and pouring into Zale, swinging at random. Zale was bewildered, and a long right from Graziano smashed into the side of his head. The tide began to turn, and more rights found their way home as Graziano piled in flurry upon flurry of blows. At the bell Zale was the rockier, and Graziano had a last chance of glory.

In the sixth Zale tried to regain the initiative, but a right cross landed on his jaw and as others followed he was suddenly floundering. Zale went down, and when he rose Graziano went berserk. He just tore into Zale until after two minutes 10 seconds of the round the champion was draped helpless over the middle rope with his back to Graziano who continued pouring in blows. The referee stopped it and tried to pull Graziano off, but suddenly Graziano was fighting everything that moved, and his seconds had to grab him and drag him to his corner, slapping his face to break his trance.

Graziano, the poor boy, was world champion. Zale won the rubber match, but neither fighter was as good after their encounters. They will always be paired in boxing history.

***Below:** The end of the saga of Zale and Graziano. In the third of their epic fights, this one at Newark, New Jersey, Zale knocks out Graziano in the third round to leave the situation as it was when they first fought two years earlier, with Zale as world middleweight champion.*

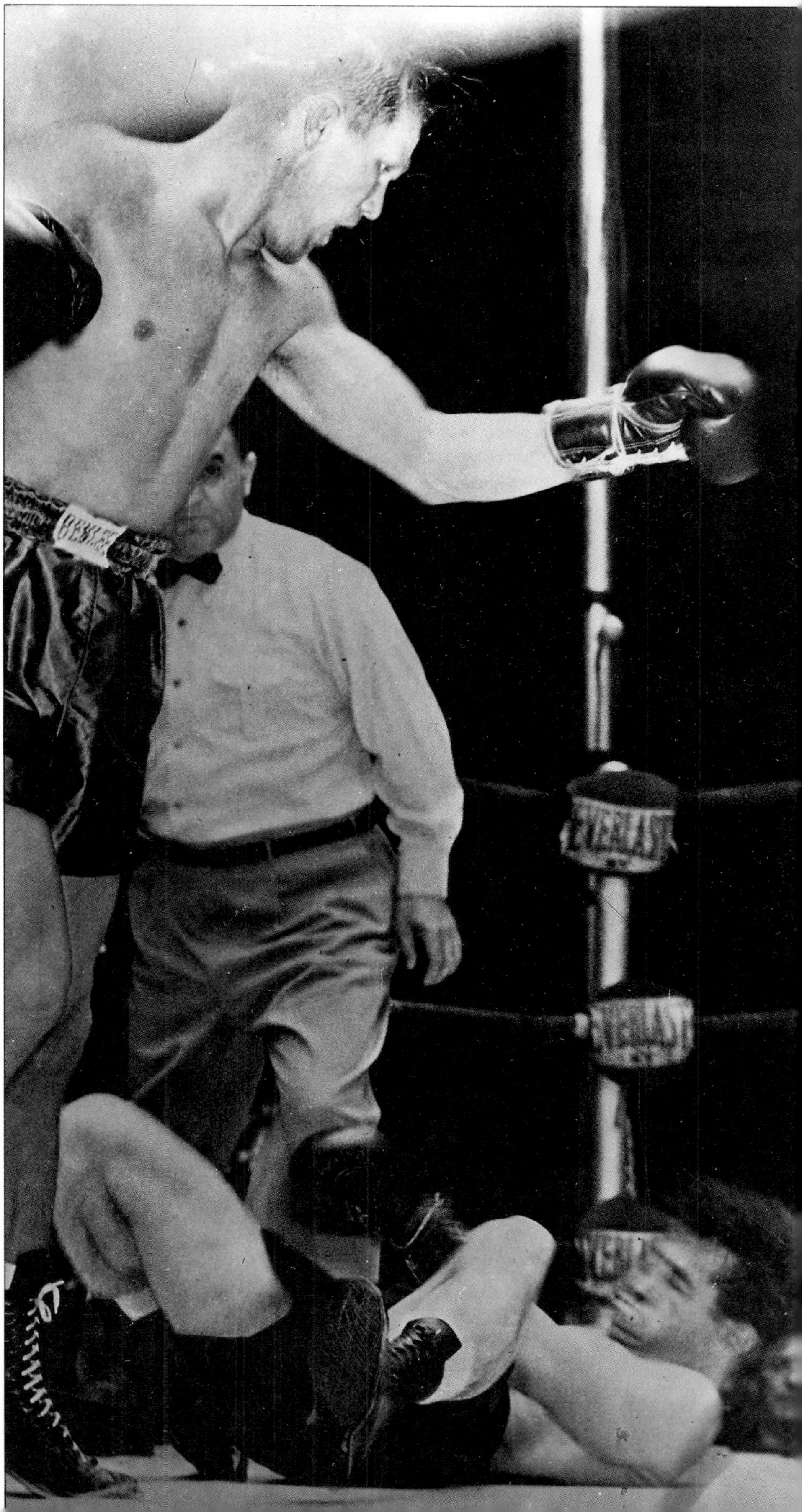

Right: *One of the best executed punches in heavyweight championship boxing. Rocky Marciano catches champion Jersey Joe Walcott with a perfect right hand to the chin.*

Jake LaMotta v. *Laurent Dauthuille*

Middleweight Championship of the World, 13 September 1950, Detroit

In a golden age of middleweights, Jake LaMotta did well to hold the world title for 20 months. He was lucky to wrest it from an injured Marcel Cerdan, but with Zale, Graziano, Cerdan and Sugar Ray Robinson among his contemporaries any boxer needs a little luck. He might also be called lucky in his defence against Laurent Dauthuille, but this could also be called a brilliant fight-back.

LaMotta waited a long time for a chance to win the title. One setback while waiting was a narrow defeat in a savage Montreal encounter by Dauthuille, who rallied from a bad start to have LaMotta groggy at the bell. So it was brave of LaMotta to take on the Frenchman on his second defence, but LaMotta was brave. He did not fight with science, he fought with heart. He was called the 'Bronx Bull' and his method was that of a raging animal, courageous and uncomplicated.

The fight began, unlike their first, with Dauthuille taking command from the start and building up a big lead as he moved around LaMotta, putting in scoring punches at will. In the middle rounds a desperate LaMotta was warned for low blows. The more he tried to bullock his way through Dauthuille's guard, so the more the challenger picked him off with crisp counters.

In the 12th LaMotta tried the only subtle tactic in his armoury — pretending to be hurt. It had worked in the past, and it worked temporarily now as Dauthuille followed up a stricken opponent only to walk into a fierce rally. However, it looked like a last fling as LaMotta again looked bewildered in the 13th and 14th.

LaMotta knew that he had to knock out Dauthuille in the last round to keep his title. Strangely, instead of boxing on the retreat, Dauthuille began as if he, too, needed a big finish. Perhaps he really thought LaMotta, his left eye almost shut, was ready for the kill. La Motta took more blows to the head, but then, with less than a minute left, caught Dauthuille with a long left that sent the Frenchman staggering backwards. LaMotta followed up, throwing his last strength into a succession of punches with both hands. What is more he remained cool enough for many of them to connect. Dauthuille slumped to the canvas, pinning down the bottom rope. He could not get up as the referee counted ten. There were 13 seconds of the fight left.

Rocky Marciano v. *Jersey Joe Walcott*

Heavyweight Championship of the World, 23 September 1952, Municipal Stadium, Philadelphia

Jersey Joe Walcott's elevation to boxing immortality at 37½ after being a journeyman most of his career is one of boxing's most romantic and surprising stories. The story of Rocky Marciano, his second challenger, has its romantic aspect, too, for Marciano, when 19 months old, almost died from pneumonia. When the two met in the ring in 1952 both were rock-hard fighters, one with all the guile of 22 years' experience, the other with the strength of 37 quick wins in 42 fights, and the knowledge he had never been off his feet.

This last fact was history halfway through the first round, when Walcott's educated left hook dumped Rocky on the floor for a count of four. He caught him again before the end of the round, and those who had bet 9-5 on the young lion being too strong for old Jersey Joe were worried about their investment.

Marciano fought back and cut Walcott's eye, but he himself had a deep cut on the top of his head. The fight swung in round seven. Some of the solution used to stem the blood got into Marciano's eye. The Marciano corner blamed Walcott's, but Marciano's biography quoted evidence that it was his own corner that nearly blinded him. Walcott punished the champion for six rounds and was well in front with three to go.

Perhaps Walcott now decided to coast cagily through the last nine minutes. If so, it was a mistaken policy. After 30 seconds of the 13th he found himself on the ropes, and moved to throw a right. However, Marciano beat him to it and delivered one of the cleanest knock-out blows in boxing history. It was a solid right that connected flush on Walcott's jaw, distorting his face and scrambling his senses. He slithered down the ropes, his arm catching the middle one and temporarily halting his progress before he pitched forward with no hope of rising. Old Jersey Joe's career was over, but Marciano was to prove an exciting champion with a unique boxing record.

Carmen Basilio v. *Sugar Ray Robinson*

Middleweight Championship of the World, 23 September 1957, Yankee Stadium, New York

In his prime Sugar Ray Robinson was virtually unbeatable — indeed he fought for eight years in 91 bouts without defeat in the welterweight and middleweight divisions. His record shows 19 defeats in 202 contests but most of those came near the end of his career. It is often forgotten that Robinson won the middleweight title three times *after* his first retirement, aged 31.

Robinson was 36 when he defended his middleweight championship (part four) against Carmen Basilio in 1957. Basilio was a tough fighter for anybody to take on. He was the welterweight champion, having won the title three times. His forte was courage and durability. He stood only 5ft 6½in (1.69m) and conceded reach to most of his opponents, so his method was to get inside and work. He had built a reputation for tough battles, two with Tony De Marco being particularly remembered.

Robinson was tall and elegant and seemed to have all the advantages when the two shook hands before 38,072 fans at the Yankee Stadium. The champion was even 6lb (3kg) heavier. However, the vital statistic, not apparent when looking at them, was that Basilio was six years the younger.

Sugar Ray began by outscoring Basilio with his long left jab, as the challenger, fighting from a crouch, tried unsuccessfully to rush Robinson off his feet. It was to be a bloody fight, and Basilio's nose was soon pouring blood, followed by his left eye. However, Basilio was used to this, and he began to get into the fight from the fourth round. By the seventh he was beginning to get to the champion, whose legs were feeling the strain. The hooks and swings started to connect. Robinson began to do his work at the end of rounds to impress the judges.

The 11th was a big round, with Robinson making a determined rally but being unable to maintain it, and Basilio was handing out the punishment at the end. Robinson steadied himself again in the 12th, and accurate punching suddenly found Basilio running out of steam at last — he just survived.

The excitement was now intense, as both men had given everything, and it seemed a good shot from either could be decisive. Robinson did his best to land it in the 13th and 14th but Basilio, his face a mass of blood, kept coming back, and in the 15th the gallant little man staged a big non-stop punching effort of his own. At the end both men were exhausted. The referee gave it 9-6 to Robinson, but the two judges gave it 9-5-1 and 8-6-1 for Basilio. There was a worthy new title-holder, but the amazing Robinson was to win it back in an equally gory battle, which Basilio fought one-eyed from the fifth, and ironically, won in the view of the referee, while the two judges this time gave it to Robinson.

Above: *The effect of the punch. Jersey Joe is temporarily held up by the middle rope but soon will pitch forwards on to his face and in ten seconds will be an ex-heavyweight champion.*

Archie Moore v. *Yvon Durelle*

Light-heavyweight Championship of the World, 10 December 1958, Montreal Forum

There is no doubt that Archie Moore was a fistic genius. Having struggled in his early career with bad managers, and then encountered a series of accidents, injuries and illnesses, he did not get a world title shot until 1952. Archie's age was then officially 36 years and four days, but his mother always insisted that he was three years older, and after his retirement, Moore was inclined to agree with her. So he might have begun a champion's career at nearly 40, when most boxers have long since retired. Amazingly, he was never beaten for this title, although he did not retire until over ten years later.

Of his 215 fights, the one most fans remember is the encounter with the Commonwealth light-heavyweight champion, the Canadian Yvon Durelle. Durelle was a big-swinging but unscientific former lumberjack, whose punches carried such power that over half his wins were by the short route. But he was a 3-1 underdog against Ancient Archie, despite Archie being possibly as old as 44.

He looked it in the first round, as Durelle clubbed a muscled right to Moore's head and Moore subsided to the canvas. The referee (former heavyweight champion Jack Sharkey) counted to 'nine' before a wobbly Moore rose, only to be dropped again. Moore rose, and fought by instinct, but took another right and another nine count before the safety of the bell gave him a rest — it looked all over at last for the Ancient One.

In the second round Moore rallied, but by the third Durelle was catching him and in the fifth Moore was down again.

Incredibly, in the sixth Moore began to have some success by poking out a straight left, and in the seventh he actually put Durelle down for a short count. Suddenly, Durelle's frantic efforts to knock out Moore seemed to have tired him more than his opponent.

With both men practically exhausted, it was Moore who had the boxing skill to make his punches tell. A succession of blows from all angles finally caused Durelle to collapse to the boards in the 10th round, where he was when the bell rang, the referee having reached 'eight'. Durelle could hardly bring himself to the centre of the ring for the 11th round, and a crisp right to the chin put him down for the count. Moore had done it again and, incidentally, recorded his 127th win inside the distance, beating Young Stribling's record.

Muhammad Ali v. *Joe Frazier*

Heavyweight Championship of the World, 1 October 1975, Coliseum, Manila

Ali's was as great a career as that of any boxer, and the man who was fashioned to be his opponent, and whose name will always be linked with him, is Joe Frazier. The two had first fought for the title when both were unbeaten champions in 1971 and Frazier inflicted upon Ali his first defeat. They had met again in 1974, when both were ex-champions, and Ali had won. Now that Ali was world champion again, he was fighting Frazier once more for sport's richest prize. It was the rubber match, and it was billed, rightly as it happened, as 'The Thrilla in Manila'.

The crowd of 25,000 was reinforced by television millions all round the world. The styles of the two men were complementary: Frazier bullocking forward constantly, Ali, taller, heavier, faster, more agile, being the matador to Frazier's bull.

It is a boxing mystery why the multi-talented Ali, who could destroy such powerful big men as George Foreman, should have had such difficulty with Frazier. No doubt, like many things with Ali, it was partly in the mind. He promised that this fight would end quickly, and began as if to keep his word, buckling Frazier's legs in the first and looking on the point of victory in the third as he hit him at will.

Inevitably, the persistent Frazier got through occasionally and, in the fifth and sixth, he started reaching Ali, particularly with two shattering hooks which caused the champion distress. Ali now concentrated on survival for a spell. By the tenth it was level, with both on the limits of their endurance, but Frazier appearing to be the man going forward.

***Right:** The athletic Muhammad Ali, on his toes, has just caught Joe Frazier with a left to the side of the head as Frazier prepares to throw a left hook. The 1975 'Thrilla in Manila' was won by champion Ali but was a hard fight for both.*

It needed a supreme effort from Ali and, in the 11th, he began to make it, scoring with long punches. The 12th was decisive. Using all his reserves of strength, Ali beat a tattoo on Frazier's face so that it suddenly seemed to get misshapen as lumps appeared all over it. At the end of the 14th the stumbling Frazier, mouth dripping blood, could hardly see, and the referee helped him back to his corner. Frazier's manager, Eddie Futch, would not let Frazier out for another round, and the great battle was over.

Ali himself sank to the canvas, exhausted. After the fight, he was serious for once, confessing that he had almost retired after the tenth, and describing the experience as the closest thing to death he knew.

There were no more wisecracks and jibes at Frazier. The two men did not need to sell any more fight tickets, and at last they could admit their respect for each other.

Sugar Ray Leonard v. *Marvin Hagler*

Middleweight Championship of the World, 6 April 1987, Caesars Palace, Las Vegas

There were those who said that Sugar Ray Leonard should not be allowed to fight Marvin Hagler for the middleweight title. They were right. A man who had retired with a detached retina, returned for one fight and retired again, and for whom that fight was the only one in over five years, should not be fighting the outstanding champion of the 1980s. The WBA and IBF agreed. They stripped Hagler for not meeting England's Herol Graham. However, Leonard himself happened to be just about the most charismatic fighter of the early 1980s — and money talked, as it always has done in boxing.

And how it talked! The *average* price per seat was over $500. The 15,336 seats were sold months in advance. About 30,000 disappointed applicants watched on closed circuit television. Over 300 million viewers saw the bout later in about 50 countries. The fight revenue in all exceeded £100 million, and the tourist bonanza in Las Vegas was estimated to be worth three times this amount.

Leonard was a double world champion who had lost once in 34 fights, a defeat by Roberto Duran spectacularly avenged. Hagler had not been beaten for over 11 years and had been undisputed world champion for nearly seven.

Hagler was a natural middleweight, at 33 perhaps nearing the end of his career. Leonard had been a great welterweight, but had built up his weight to only ½lb (1kg) less than Hagler. He was two years younger, but because of his lay-off an unknown quantity. Hagler was 3-1 favourite.

It was the richest fight of all time. It had been discussed and analysed for months, and the world's press descended on Las Vegas to file their descriptions and render their verdicts. The fight lived up to all expectations, even to a controversial decision.

Leonard fought in snatches, while Hagler all the while tried to bring his supposedly greater strength and superior condition to bear. Sugar Ray won the first four rounds with his speed. He tormented Hagler, who could not reach him with his comparatively plodding efforts. However, Leonard could not dance for 12 rounds and in the fifth, battle really commenced when Marvelous Marvin caught him with an uppercut which turned his legs to jelly, and he was pummelling Sugar Ray at the bell. Hagler edged the next three rounds, catching Leonard more frequently while Leonard was forced to keep out of trouble and try to impress the judges with flurries of punches delivered with a hand speed that bewildered Hagler.

The ninth was a big round with Leonard beginning with a burst but being forced to give ground as the champion came back to hammer in some wicked blows. The last three rounds were hard to assess. Every time Hagler looked about to assume control Leonard produced some crisp counterpunching bursts. Leonard also indulged in clowning, inviting Hagler to hit his face and exaggerating his dancing. Hagler was content to go about his business, but Leonard captured the attention.

It was a split decision. One judged voted 115-113 for Leonard, another by the same score for Hagler. The third decided by a whopping 118-110 for Leonard. Arguments about who is the better man will remain.

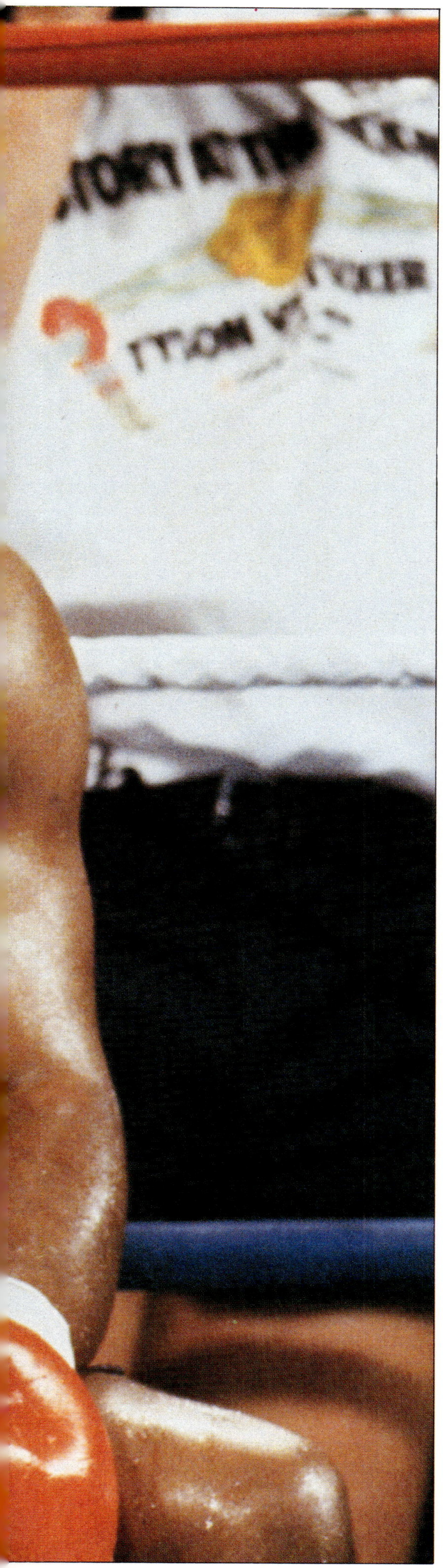

Records

This section lists the world championship contests weight by weight, beginning with the advent of gloves. In the beginning it was complex, as the weights were not standardized, the glove and bare-knuckle eras overlapped, and there were many claimants to many crowns. Then all became light, as eight weight classes became more or less universally accepted and (believe it or not, fans of today) from 1917 to 1921 there were eight undisputed world champions, one at each weight. From 1921, 'in-between' weights like junior lightweight and light-featherweight began to be introduced, and at all weights different authorities began naming different champions. Nowadays, there are no fewer than 18 weight divisions, and with three widely accepted authorities (WBC, WBA and IBF) naming champions (there are others with less recognition), there could be 54 men claiming to be world champions. Boxing is much the poorer for all this multiplicity of championships. The following lists are based on several different sources, and there is unlikely to be universal agreement on the validity of all the claims to world titles.

Left: *Mike Tyson, the youngest man to win the world heavyweight championship, was also for a period in 1988 the only undisputed world champion, as the ruling bodies competed with each other to name new champions.*

The following lists of world championship contests at each weight are as complete as possible.

The abbreviations of the appropriate governing bodies are as follows:

Abbreviations

W =won
KO =knock out
PTS =points
RTD=retired
RSC=referee stopped contest
DIS =disqualified

N.B. Dates in *italics* (ie *7 Sep 92*) refer to the 1800s.

WBA	World Boxing Association
WBC	World Boxing Council
IBF	International Boxing Federation
NBA	National Boxing Association (superseded by the WBA)
NY	New York Boxing Commission (now members of the WBC)
EBU	European Boxing Union
IBU	International Boxing Union (fore-runner of the EBU)
GB	Great Britain (denoting usually the National Sporting Club until 1929 and the British Boxing Board of Control thereafter)
USA	United States of America
FR	France
AUSTR	Australia
CALIF	California
LOUIS	Louisiana
MARY	Maryland
MASS	Massachusetts
PEN	Pennsylvania

Boxers who during their championship career changed their names are referred to by their ultimate name. Previous names of champions are:

Muhammad Ali: *Cassius Clay*
Wildred Benitez: *Wilfredo Benitez*
Guts Ishimatsu: *Ishimatsu Susuki*
Eddie Mustapha Muhammad: *Eddie Gregory*
Matthew Saad Muhammad: *Matt Franklin*
Dwight Muhammad Qawi: *Dwight Braxton*

HEAVYWEIGHT

(*Current weight limit:* unlimited)

DATE	
7 Sep 92	James J. Corbett W KO 21 John L. Sullivan, *New Orleans, USA*
25 Jan 94	James J. Corbett W KO 3 Charlie Mitchell, *Jacksonville, USA*
17 Mar 97	Bob Fitzsimmons W KO 14 James J. Corbett, *Carson C, USA*
9 Jun 99	James J. Jeffries W KO 11 Bob Fitzsimmons, *New York C, USA*
3 Nov 99	James J. Jeffries W PTS 25 Tom Sharkey, *New York C, USA*
6 Apr 00	James J. Jeffries W KO 1 Jack Finnegan, *Detroit, USA*
11 May 00	James J. Jeffries W KO 23 James J. Corbett, *New York C, USA*
15 Nov 01	James J. Jeffries W RTD 5 Gus Ruhlin, *San Francisco, USA*
25 Jul 02	James J. Jeffries W KO 8 Bob Fitzsimmons, *San Francisco, USA*
14 Aug 03	James J. Jeffries W KO 10 James J. Corbett, *San Francisco, USA*
26 Aug 04	James J. Jeffries W KO 2 Jack Munroe, *San Francisco, USA*
	James J. Jeffries relinquished title (retired)
3 Jul 05	Marvin Hart W RSC 12 Jack Root, *Reno, USA*
23 Feb 06	Tommy Burns W PTS 20 Marvin Hart, *Los Angeles, USA*
2 Oct 06	Tommy Burns W KO 15 Jim Flynn, *Los Angeles, USA*
28 Nov 06	Tommy Burns DREW 20 Jack O'Brien, *Los Angeles, USA*
8 May 07	Tommy Burns W PTS 20 Jack O'Brien, *Los Angeles, USA*
4 July 07	Tommy Burns W KO 1 Bill Squires, *Los Angeles, USA*
2 Dec 07	Tommy Burns W KO 10 Gunner Moir, *London, England*
10 Feb 08	Tommy Burns W KO 4 Jack Palmer, *London, England*
17 Mar 08	Tommy Burns W KO 1 Jem Roche, *Dublin, Ireland*
18 Apr 08	Tommy Burns W KO 5 Jewey Smith, *Paris, France*
13 Jun 08	Tommy Burns W KO 8 Bill Squires, *Paris, France*
24 Aug 08	Tommy Burns W KO 13 Bill Squires, *Sydney, Australia*
2 Sep 08	Tommy Burns KO 6 Bill Lang, *Melbourne, Australia*
26 Dec 08	Jack Johnson W RSC 14 Tommy Burns, *Sydney, Australia*
16 Oct 09	Jack Johnson W KO 12 Stanley Ketchel, *Los Angeles, USA*
4 Jul 10	Jack Johnson W RSC 15 James J. Jeffries, *Reno, USA*
4 Jul 12	Jack Johnson W RSC 9 Jim Flynn, *Las Vegas, USA*
19 Dec 13	Jack Johnson DREW 10 Jim Johnson, *Paris, France*
27 Jun 14	Jack Johnson W PTS 20 Frank Moran, *Paris, France*
5 Apr 15	Jess Willard W KO 26 Jack Johnson, *Havana, Cuba*
4 Jul 19	Jack Dempsey W RTD 3 Jess Willard, *Toledo, USA*
6 Sep 20	Jack Dempsey W KO 3 Billy Miske, *Benton Harbor, USA*
14 Dec 20	Jack Dempsey W KO 12 Bill Brennan, *New York C, USA*
2 Jul 21	Jack Dempsey W KO 4 Georges Carpentier, *Jersey C, USA*
4 Jul 23	Jack Dempsey W PTS 15 Tommy Gibbons, *Shelby, USA*
14 Sep 23	Jack Dempsey W KO 2 Luis Firpo, *New York C, USA*
23 Sep 26	Gene Tunney W PTS 10 Jack Dempsey, *Philadelphia, USA*
22 Sep 27	Gene Tunney W PTS 10 Jack Dempsey, *Chicago, USA*
26 Jul 28	Gene Tunney W RSC 11 Tom Heeney, *New York C, USA*
	Gene Tunney relinquished title (retired)
12 Jun 30	Max Schmeling W DIS 4 Jack Sharkey, *New York C, USA*
3 Jul 31	Max Schmeling W RSC 15 Young Stribling, *Cleveland, USA*
21 Jun 32	Jack Sharkey W PTS 15 Max Schmeling, *New York C, USA*
29 Jun 33	Primo Carnera W KO 6 Jack Sharkey, *New York C, USA*
22 Oct 33	Primo Carnera W PTS 15 Paolino Uzcudun, *Rome, Italy*

DATE	
1 Mar 34	Primo Carnera W PTS 15 Tommy Loughran, *Miami, USA*
14 Jun 34	Max Baer W RSC 11 Primo Carnera, *New York C, USA*
13 Jun 35	James J. Braddock W PTS 15 Max Baer, *New York C, USA*
22 Jun 37	Joe Louis W KO 8 James J. Braddock, *Chicago, USA*
30 Aug 37	Joe Louis W PTS 15 Tommy Farr, *New York C, USA*
23 Feb 38	Joe Louis W KO 3 Nathan Mann, *New York C, USA*
1 Apr 38	Joe Louis W KO 5 Harry Thomas, *Chicago, USA*
22 Jun 38	Joe Louis W KO 1 Max Schmeling, *New York C, USA*
25 Jan 39	Joe Louis W RSC 1 John Henry Lewis, *New York C, USA*
17 Apr 39	Joe Louis W KO 1 Jack Roper, *Los Angeles, USA*
28 Jun 39	Joe Louis W RSC 4 Tony Galento, *New York C, USA*
20 Sep 39	Joe Louis W KO 11 Bob Pastor, *Detroit, USA*
9 Feb 40	Joe Louis W PTS 15 Arturo Godoy, *New York C, USA*
29 Mar 40	Joe Louis W KO 2 Johnny Paychek, *New York C, USA*
20 Jun 40	Joe Louis W RSC 8 Arturo Godoy, *New York C, USA*
16 Dec 40	Joe Louis W RTD 6 Al McCoy, *Boston, USA*
31 Jan 41	Joe Louis W KO 5 Red Burman, *New York C, USA*
17 Feb 41	Joe Louis W KO 2 Gus Dorazio, *Philadelphia, USA*
21 Mar 41	Joe Louis W RSC 13 Abe Simon, *Detroit, USA*
8 Apr 41	Joe Louis W RSC 9 Tony Musto, *St Louis, USA*
23 May 41	Joe Louis W DIS 7 Buddy Baer, *Washington, USA*
18 Jun 41	Joe Louis W KO 13 Billy Conn, *New York C, USA*
29 Sep 41	Joe Louis W RSC 6 Lou Nova, *New York C, USA*
9 Jan 42	Joe Louis W KO 1 Buddy Baer, *New York C, USA*
27 Mar 42	Joe Louis W KO 6 Abe Simon, *New York C, USA*
19 Jun 46	Joe Louis W KO 8 Billy Conn, *New York C, USA*
18 Sep 46	Joe Louis W KO 1 Tami Mauriello, *New York C, USA*
5 Dec 47	Joe Louis W PTS 15 Jersey Joe Walcott, *New York C, USA*
25 Jun 48	Joe Louis W KO 11 Jersey Joe Walcott, *New York C, USA*
	Joe Louis relinquished title (retired)
22 Jun 49	Ezzard Charles W PTS 15 Jersey Joe Walcott, *Chicago, USA* (NBA)
10 Aug 49	Ezzard Charles W RSC 7 Gus Lesnevich, *New York C, USA* (NBA)
14 Oct 49	Ezzard Charles W KO 8 Pat Valentino, *San Francisco, USA* (NBA)
6 Jun 50	Lee Savold W RTD 4 Bruce Woodcock, *London, England* (GB/EBU)
	Lee Savold ceased to be recognized by GB/EBU on the announcement that Joe Louis was making a comeback
15 Aug 50	Ezzard Charles W RSC 14 Freddie Beshore, *Buffalo, USA* (NBA)
27 Sep 50	Ezzard Charles W PTS 15 Joe Louis, *New York C, USA*
5 Dec 50	Ezzard Charles W KO 11 Nick Barone, *Cincinnati, USA*
12 Jan 51	Ezzard Charles W RSC 10 Lee Oma, *New York C, USA*
7 Mar 51	Ezzard Charles W PTS 15 Jersey Joe Walcott, *Detroit, USA*
30 May 51	Ezzard Charles W PTS 15 Joey Maxim, *Chicago, USA*
18 Jul 51	Jersey Joe Walcott W KO 7 Ezzard Charles, *Pittsburgh, USA*
5 Jan 52	Jersey Joe Walcott W PTS 15 Ezzard Charles, *Philadelphia, USA*
23 Sep 52	Rocky Marciano W KO 13 Jersey Joe Walcott, *Philadelphia, USA*
15 May 53	Rocky Marciano W KO 1 Jersey Joe Walcott, *Chicago, USA*
24 Sep 53	Rocky Marciano W RSC 11 Roland LaStarza, *New York C, USA*

DATE	
17 Jun 54	Rocky Marciano W PTS 15 Ezzard Charles, *New York C, USA*
17 Sep 54	Rocky Marciano W KO 8 Ezzard Charles, *New York C, USA*
16 May 55	Rocky Marciano W RSC 9 Don Cockell, *San Francisco, USA*
21 Sep 55	Rocky Marciano W KO 9 Archie Moore, *New York C, USA*
	Rocky Marciano relinquished title (retired)
30 Nov 56	Floyd Patterson W KO 5 Archie Moore, *Chicago, USA*
29 Jul 57	Floyd Patterson W RSC 10 Tommy Jackson, *New York C, USA*
22 Aug 57	Floyd Patterson W KO 6 Pete Rademacher, *Seattle, USA*
18 Aug 58	Floyd Patterson W RTD 12 Roy Harris, *Los Angeles, USA*
1 May 59	Floyd Patterson W KO 11 Brian London, *Indianapolis, USA*
26 Jun 59	Ingemar Johansson W RSC 3 Floyd Patterson, *New York C, USA*
20 Jun 60	Floyd Patterson W KO 5 Ingemar Johansson, *New York C, USA*
13 Mar 61	Floyd Patterson W KO 6 Ingemar Johansson, *Miami, USA*
4 Dec 61	Floyd Patterson W KO 4 Tom McNeeley, *Toronto, Canada*
25 Sep 62	Sonny Liston W KO 1 Floyd Patterson, *Chicago, USA*
22 Jul 63	Sonny Liston W KO 1 Floyd Patterson, *Las Vegas, USA*
25 Feb 64	Muhammad Ali W RTD 6 Sonny Liston, *Miami, USA*
	Muhammad Ali forfeited WBA recognition for signing a 'return-fight clause' in his contract with Liston
5 Mar 65	Ernie Terrell W PTS 15 Eddie Machen, *Chicago, USA* (WBA)
25 May 65	Muhammad Ali W KO 1 Sonny Liston, *Lewiston, USA* (WBC)
1 Nov 65	Ernie Terrell W PTS 15 George Chuvalo, *Toronto, Canada* (WBA)
22 Nov 65	Muhammad Ali W RSC 12 Floyd Patterson, *Las Vegas, USA* (WBC)
29 Mar 66	Muhammad Ali W PTS 15 George Chuvalo, *Toronto, Canada* (WBC)
21 May 66	Muhammad Ali W RSC 6 Henry Cooper, *London England* (WBC)
28 Jun 66	Ernie Terrell W PTS 15 Doug Jones, *Houston, USA* (WBA)
6 Aug 66	Muhammad Ali W KO 3 Brian London, *London, England* (WBC)
10 Sep 66	Muhammad Ali W RSC 12 Karl Mildenberger, *Frankfurt, W Germany* (WBC)
14 Nov 66	Muhammad Ali W RSC 3 Cleveland Williams, *Houston, USA* (WBC)
6 Feb 67	Muhammad Ali W PTS 15 Ernie Terrell, *Houston, USA*
22 Mar 67	Muhammad Ali W KO 7 Zora Folley, *New York C, USA*
	Muhammad Ali forfeited title owing to inactivity following his refusal to be drafted for the Vietnam War
4 Mar 68	Joe Frazier W RSC 11 Buster Mathis, *New York C, USA* (WBC)
27 Apr 68	Jimmy Ellis W PTS 15 Jerry Quarry, *Oakland, USA* (WBA)
24 Jun 68	Joe Frazier W RTD 2 Manuel Ramos, *New York C, USA* (WBC)
14 Sep 68	Jimmy Ellis W PTS 15 Floyd Patterson, *Stockholm, Sweden* (WBA)
10 Dec 68	Joe Frazier W PTS 15 Oscar Bonavena, *Philadelphia, USA* (WBC)
22 Apr 69	Joe Frazier W KO 1 Dave Zyglewicz, *Houston, USA* (WBC)
23 Jun 69	Joe Frazier W RSC 7 Jerry Quarry, *New York C, USA* (WBC)
16 Feb 70	Joe Frazier W RTD 4 Jimmy Ellis, *New York C, USA*

DATE	
18 Nov 70	Joe Frazier W KO 2 Bob Foster, *Detroit, USA*
8 Mar 71	Joe Frazier W PTS 15 Muhammad Ali, *New York C, USA*
15 Jan 72	Joe Frazier W RSC 4 Terry Daniels, *New Orleans, USA*
26 May 72	Joe Frazier W RSC 4 Ron Stander, *Omaha, USA*
22 Jan 73	George Foreman W RSC 2 Joe Frazier, *Kingston, Jamaica*
1 Sep 73	George Foreman W KO 1 Jose Roman, *Tokyo, Japan*
26 Mar 74	George Foreman W RSC 2 Ken Norton, *Caracas, Venezuela*
30 Oct 74	Muhammad Ali W KO 8 George Foreman, *Kinshasha, Zaire*
24 Mar 75	Muhammad Ali W RSC 15 Chuck Wepner, *Cleveland, USA*
16 May 75	Muhammad Ali W RSC 11 Ron Lyle, *Las Vegas, USA*
1 Jul 75	Muhammad Ali W PTS 15 Joe Bugner, *Kuala Lumpar, Malaysia*
1 Oct 75	Muhammad Ali W RTD 14 Joe Frazier, *Manila, Philippines*
20 Feb 76	Muhammad Ali W KO 5 Jean-Pierre Coopman, *San Juan, Puerto Rico*
30 Apr 76	Muhammad Ali W PTS 15 Jimmy Young, *Landover, USA*
25 May 76	Muhammad Ali W RSC 5 Richard Dunn, *Munich, W Germany*
28 Sep 76	Muhammad Ali W PTS 15 Ken Norton, *New York C, USA*
16 May 77	Muhammad Ali W PTS 15 Alfredo Evangelista, *Landover, USA*
29 Sep 77	Muhammad Ali W PTS 15 Earnie Shavers, *New York C, USA*
15 Feb 78	Leon Spinks W PTS 15 Muhammad Ali, *Las Vegas, USA*
	Leon Spinks forfeited WBC recognition (failure to defend against Ken Norton). Norton was named as WBC champion
9 Jun 78	Larry Holmes W PTS 15 Ken Norton, *Las Vegas, USA* (WBC)
15 Sep 78	Muhammad Ali W PTS 15 Leon Spinks, *New Orleans, USA* (WBA)
	Muhammad Ali relinquished WBA version of title (retired)
10 Nov 78	Larry Holmes W KO 7 Alfredo Evangelista, *Las Vegas, USA* (WBC)
23 Mar 79	Larry Holmes W RSC 7 Ossie Ocasio, *Las Vegas, USA* (WBC)
22 Jun 79	Larry Holmes W RSC 12 Mike Weaver, *New York C, USA* (WBC)
28 Sep 79	Larry Holmes W RSC 11 Earnie Shavers, *Las Vegas, USA* (WBC)
20 Oct 79	John Tate W PTS 15 Gerrie Coetzee, *Pretoria, S Africa* (WBA)
3 Feb 80	Larry Holmes W KO 6 Lorenzo Zanon, *Las Vegas, USA* (WBC)
31 Mar 80	Mike Weaver W KO 15 John Tate, *Knoxville, USA* (WBA)
31 Mar 80	Larry Holmes W RSC 8 Leroy Jones, *Las Vegas, USA* (WBC)
7 Jul 80	Larry Holmes W RSC 7 Scott Ledoux, *Minneapolis, USA* (WBC)
2 Oct 80	Larry Holmes W RTD 10 Muhammad Ali, *Las Vegas, USA* (WBC)
23 Oct 80	Mike Weaver W KO 13 Gerrie Coetzee, *Sun C, S Africa* (WBA)
11 Apr 81	Larry Holmes W PTS 15 Trevor Berbick, *Las Vegas, USA* (WBC)
12 Jun 81	Larry Holmes W RSC 3 Leon Spinks, *Detroit, USA* (WBC)
3 Oct 81	Mike Weaver W PTS 15 James Tillis, *Rosemont, USA* (WBA)
6 Nov 81	Larry Holmes W RSC 11 Renaldo Snipes, *Pittsburgh, USA* (WBC)
11 Jun 82	Larry Holmes W RSC 13 Gerry Cooney, *Las Vegas, USA* (WBC)
26 Nov 82	Larry Holmes W PTS 15 Tex Cobb, Houston, USA (WBC)

***Left:** Muhammad Ali attempting a right to the smaller Leon Spinks, who covers up, during their second fight in 1978, in which Ali recovered the title he had lost to Spinks seven months earlier.*

DATE

10 Dec 82 Michael Dokes W RSC 1 Mike Weaver, *Las Vegas, USA* (WBA)
27 Mar 83 Larry Holmes W PTS 12 Lucien Rodriguez, *Scranton, USA* (WBC)
20 May 83 Michael Dokes DREW 15 Mike Weaver, *Las Vegas, USA* (WBA)
20 May 83 Larry Holmes W PTS 12 Tim Witherspoon, *Las Vegas, USA* (WBC)
10 Sep 83 Larry Holmes W RSC 5 Scott Frank, *Atlantic C USA,* (WBC)
23 Sep 83 Gerrie Coetzee W KO 10 Michael Dokes, *Richfield, USA* (WBA)
25 Nov 83 Larry Holmes W RSC 1 Marvis Frazier, *Las Vegas, USA* (WBC)
Larry Holmes relinquished the WBC version of the title to box exclusively for the IBF
9 Mar 84 Tim Witherspoon W PTS 12 Greg Page, *Las Vegas, USA* (WBC)
31 Aug 84 Pinklon Thomas W PTS 12 Tim Witherspoon, *Las Vegas, USA* (WBC)
9 Nov 84 Larry Holmes W RSC 12 James Smith, *Las Vegas, USA* (IBF)
1 Dec 84 Greg Page W KO 8 Gerrie Coetzee, *Sun C, S Africa* (WBA)
15 Mar 85 Larry Holmes W RSC 10 David Bey, *Las Vegas, USA* (IBF)
29 Apr 85 Tony Tubbs W PTS 15 Greg Page, *Buffalo, USA* (WBA)
20 May 85 Larry Holmes W PTS 15 Carl Williams, *Reno, USA* (IBF)
15 Jun 85 Pinklon Thomas W KO 8 Mike Weaver, *Las Vegas, USA* (WBC)
21 Sep 85 Michael Spinks W PTS 15 Larry Holmes, *Las Vegas, USA* (IBF)
17 Jan 86 Tim Witherspoon W PTS 15 Tony Tubbs, *Atlanta, USA* (WBA)
22 Mar 86 Trevor Berbick W PTS 12 Pinklon Thomas, *Las Vegas, USA* (WBC)
19 Apr 86 Michael Spinks W PTS 15 Larry Holmes, *Las Vegas, USA* (IBF)
19 Jul 86 Tim Witherspoon W RSC 11 Frank Bruno, *Wembley, England* (WBA)
6 Sep 86 Michael Spinks W RSC 4 Steffen Tangstad, *Las Vegas, USA* (IBF)
Michael Spinks forfeited title (refusal to defend against Tony Tucker)
22 Nov 86 Mike Tyson W RSC 2 Trevor Berbick, *Las Vegas, USA* (WBC)
12 Dec 86 James Smith W RSC 1 Tim Witherspoon, *New York C, USA* (WBA)
7 Mar 87 Mike Tyson W PTS 12 James Smith, *Las Vegas, USA* (WBA/WBC)
30 May 87 Mike Tyson W RSC 6 Pinklon Thomas, *Las Vegas, USA* (WBA/WBC)
30 May 87 Tony Tucker W RSC 10 James Douglas, *Las Vegas, USA* (IBF)
1 Aug 87 Mike Tyson W PTS 12 Tony Tucker, *Las Vegas, USA*
16 Oct 87 Mike Tyson W RSC 7 Tyrell Biggs, *Atlantic City, USA*
22 Jan 88 Mike Tyson W RSC 4 Larry Holmes, *Atlantic City, USA*
21 Mar 88 Mike Tyson W RSC 2 Tony Tubbs, *Tokyo, Japan*
27 Jun 88 Mike Tyson W KO 1 Michael Spinks, *Atlantic City, USA*
25 Feb 89 Mike Tyson W RSC 5 Frank Bruno, *Las Vegas, USA*

***Above:** Tim Witherspoon (on the left) visited London in 1986 to successfully defend his WBA title against Frank Bruno.*

CRUISERWEIGHT

(*Current weight limit:* 195lb/88.5kg (WBC); 190lb/86.2kg (WBA and IBF). The WBA calls the class 'Junior Heavyweight')

DATE

8 Dec 79 Marvin Camel DREW 15 Mate Parlov, *Split, Yugoslavia* (WBC)
31 Mar 80 Marvin Camel W PTS 15 Mate Parlov, *Las Vegas, USA* (WBC)
25 Nov 80 Carlos de Leon W PTS 15 Marvin Camel, *New Orleans, USA* (WBC)
13 Feb 82 Ossie Ocasio W PTS 15 Robbie Williams, *Johannesburg, S Africa* (WBA)
24 Feb 82 Carlos de Leon W RSC 8 Marvin Camel, *Atlantic C, USA* (WBC)
27 Jun 82 S.T. Gordon W RSC 2 Carlos de Leon, *Cleveland, USA* (WBC)
15 Dec 82 Ossie Ocasio W PTS 15 Young Joe Louis, *Chicago, USA* (WBA)
16 Feb 83 S.T. Gordon W RSC 8 Jesse Burnett, *E Rutherford, USA* (WBC)
20 May 83 Ossie Ocasio W PTS 15 Randy Stephens, *Las Vegas, USA* (WBA)
21 May 83 Marvin Camel W RSC 9 Rick Sekorski, *Billings, USA* (IBF)
17 Jul 83 Carlos de Leon W PTS 12 S.T. Gordon, *Las Vegas, USA* (WBC)
21 Sep 83 Carlos de Leon W RSC 4 Yaqui Lopez, *San Jose, USA* (WBC)
13 Dec 83 Marvin Camel W RSC 5 Rod MacDonald, *Halifax, Canada* (IBF)
9 Mar 84 Carlos de Leon W PTS 12 Anthony Davis, *Las Vegas, USA* (WBC)
5 May 84 Ossie Ocasio W RSC 15 John Odhiambo, *San Juan, Puerto Rico* (WBA)
2 Jun 84 Carlos de Leon W PTS 12 Bashiru Ali, *Oakland, USA* (WBC)
6 Oct 84 Lee Roy Murphy W RSC 14 Marvin Camel, *Billings, USA* (IBF)
1 Dec 84 Piet Crous W PTS 15 Ossie Ocasio, *Sun C, S Africa* (WBA)
20 Dec 84 Lee Roy Murphy W RSC 12 Young Joe Louis, *Chicago, USA* (IBF)
30 Mar 85 Piet Crous W RSC 3 Randy Stephens, *Sun C, S Africa* (WBA)
6 Jun 85 Alfonso Ratliff W PTS 12 Carlos de Leon, *Las Vegas, USA* (WBC)

DATE

27 Jul 85 Dwight Muhammad Qawi W KO 11 Piet Crous, *Sun C, S Africa* (WBA)
21 Sep 85 Bernard Benton W PTS 12 Alfonso Ratliff, *Las Vegas, USA* (WBC)
19 Oct 85 Lee Roy Murphy W KO 12 Chisanda Mutti, *Monte Carlo* (IBF)
22 Mar 86 Carlos de Leon W PTS 12 Bernard Benton, *Las Vegas, USA* (WBC)
23 Mar 86 Dwight Muhammad Qawi W RSC 6 Leon Spinks, *Reno, USA* (WBA)
19 Apr 86 Lee Roy Murphy W KO 9 Dorcey Gaymon, *San Remo, Italy* (IBF)
12 Jul 86 Evander Holyfield W PTS 15 Dwight Muhammad Qawi, *Atlanta, USA* (WBA)
10 Aug 86 Carlos de Leon W RSC 8 Michael Greer, *Giardini Naxos, Italy* (WBC)
25 Oct 86 Rickey Parkey W RSC 10 Lee Roy Murphy, *Marsala, Italy* (IBF)
14 Feb 87 Evander Holyfield W RSC 7 Henry Tillman, *Reno, USA* (WBA)
21 Feb 87 Carlos de Leon W RTD 4 Angelo Rottoli, *Bergamo, Italy* (WBC)
28 Mar 87 Rickey Parkey W RSC 12 Chisanda Mutti, *Camaiore, Italy* (IBF)
15 May 87 Evander Holyfield W RSC 3 Rickey Parkey, *Las Vegas, USA* (IBF)
15 Aug 87 Evander Holyfield W RSC 11 Ossie Ocasio, *St Tropez, France* (WBA/IBF)
5 Dec 87 Evander Holyfield W CO 4 Dwight Muhammad Qawi, *Atlantic City, USA* (WBA/IBF)
22 Jan 88 Carlos de Leon W PTS 12 José Maria Flores, *Atlantic City, USA* (WBC)
9 Apr 88 Evander Holyfield W RSC 8 Carlos de Leon, *Las Vegas, USA*

LIGHT-HEAVYWEIGHT

(*Current weight limit:* 175lb/79.5kg)

DATE

22 Apr 03 Jack Root W PTS 10 Kid McCoy, *Detroit, USA* (USA)
4 Jul 03 George Gardner W KO 12 Jack Root, *Fort Erie, Canada* (USA)
25 Nov 03 Bob Fitzsimmons W PTS 20 George Gardner, *San Francisco, USA*
20 Dec 05 Jack O'Brien W RTD 13 Bob Fitzsimmons, *San Francisco, USA*
28 Nov 06 Jack O'Brien DREW 20 Tommy Burns, *Los Angeles, USA*
Jack O'Brien relinquished title to campaign as heavyweight
28 May 12 Jack Dillon W KO 3 Hugo Kelly, *Indianapolis, USA*
28 Apr 14 Jack Dillon W PTS 10 Al Norton, *Kansas C, USA*
25 Apr 16 Jack Dillon W PTS 15 Battling Levinsky, *Kansas C, USA*
24 Oct 16 Battling Levinsky W PTS 12 Jack Dillon, *Boston, USA*
3 May 20 Battling Levinsky W PTS 12 Clay Turner, *Portland, USA*
12 Oct 20 Georges Carpentier W KO 4 Battling Levinsky, *Jersey C, USA*

DATE

11 May 22 Georges Carpentier W KO 1 Ted Kid Lewis, *London, England*
24 Sep 22 Battling Siki W KO 6 Georges Carpentier, *Paris, France*
17 Mar 23 Mike McTigue W PTS 20 Battling Siki, *Dublin, Ireland*
4 Oct 23 Mike McTigue DREW 10 Young Stribling, *Columbus, USA*
30 May 25 Paul Berlenbach W PTS 15 Mike McTigue, *New York C, USA*
11 Sep 25 Paul Berlenbach W RSC 11 Jimmy Slattery *New York C, USA*
11 Dec 25 Paul Berlenbach W PTS 15 Jack Delaney, *New York C, USA*
10 Jun 26 Paul Berlenbach W PTS 15 Young Stribling *New York C, USA*
16 Jul 26 Jack Delaney W PTS 15 Paul Berlenbach, *New York , USA*
Jack Delaney relinquished title to campaign as heavyweight
30 Aug 27 Jimmy Slattery W PTS 10 Maxie Rosenbloom, *Hartford, USA* (NBA)
7 Oct 27 Tommy Loughran W PTS 15 Mike McTigue, *New York C, USA* (NY)
12 Dec 27 Tommy Loughran W PTS 15 Jimmy Slattery, *New York C, USA*
6 Jan 28 Tommy Loughran W PTS 15 Leo Lomski, *New York C, USA*
1 Jun 28 Tommy Loughran W PTS 15 Pete Latzo, *New York C, USA*
16 Jul 28 Tommy Loughran W PTS 10 Pete Latzo, *Wiles Barre, USA*
8 Mar 29 Tommy Loughran W PTS 10 Mickey Walker, *Chicago, USA*
18 Jul 29 Tommy Loughran W PTS 15 James J. Braddock, *New York C, USA*
Tommy Loughran relinquished title (moved up to heavyweight)
10 Feb 30 Jimmy Slattery W PTS 15 Lou Scozza, *Buffalo, USA* (NY)
25 Jun 30 Maxie Rosenbloom W PTS 15 Jimmy Slattery, *Buffalo, USA* (NY)
22 Oct 30 Maxie Rosenbloom W RSC 11 Abe Bain, *New York C, USA* (NY)
5 Aug 31 Maxie Rosenbloom W PTS 15 Jimmy Slattery, *New York C, USA* (NY)
13 Mar 32 George Nichols W PTS 10 Dave Maier, *Chicago, USA* (NBA)
George Nichols ceased to be recognized by the NBA following a defeat by Lou Scozza in a non-title bout, May, 1932
4 Jul 32 Maxie Rosenbloom W PTS 15 Lou Scozza, *Buffalo, USA* (NY)
22 Feb 33 Maxie Rosenbloom W PTS 10 Al Stillman, *St Louis, USA* (NY)
1 Mar 33 Bob Godwin W PTS 10 Joe Knight, *Palm Beach, USA* (NBA)
10 Mar 33 Maxie Rosenbloom W PTS 15 Adolf Heuser, *New York C, USA* (NY)
24 Mar 33 Maxie Rosenbloom W RSC 4 Bob Godwin, *New York C, USA*
3 Nov 33 Maxie Rosenbloom W PTS 15 Mickey Walker, *New York C, USA*
5 Feb 34 Maxie Rosenbloom DREW 15 Joe Knight, *Miami, USA*
16 Nov 34 Bob Olin W PTS 15 Maxie Rosenbloom, *New York C, USA*
31 Oct 35 John Henry Lewis W PTS 15 Bob Olin, *St Louis, USA*
13 Mar 36 John Henry Lewis W PTS 15 Jock McAvoy, *New York C, USA*
9 Nov 36 John Henry Lewis W PTS 15 Len Harvey, *Wembley, England*
3 Jun 37 John Henry Lewis W RSC 8 Bob Olin, *St Louis, USA*
23 Apr 38 John Henry Lewis W KO 4 Emilio Martinez, *Minneapolis, USA*
28 Oct 38 John Henry Lewis W PTS 15 Al Gainer, *New Haven, USA*
John Henry Lewis relinquished title (retired)
29 Nov 38 Tiger Jack Fox W PTS 15 Al Gainer, *New York C, USA* (NY)
3 Feb 39 Melio Bettina W RSC 9 Tiger Jack Fox, *New York C, USA* (NY)
10 Jul 39 Len Harvey W PTS 15 Jock McAvoy, *London, England* (GB)
13 Jul 39 Billy Conn W PTS 15 Melio Bettina, *New York C, USA*
25 Sep 39 Billy Conn W PTS 15 Melio Bettina, *Pittsburgh, USA*
17 Nov 39 Billy Conn W PTS 15 Gus Lesnevich, *New York C, USA*
5 Jun 40 Billy Conn W PTS 15 Gus Lesnevich, *Detroit, USA*
Billy Conn relinquished title to campaign as heavyweight
13 Jan 41 Anton Christoforidis W PTS 15 Melio Bettina, *Cleveland, USA* (NBA)
22 May 41 Gus Lesnevich W PTS 15 Anton Christoforidis, *New York C, USA*
26 Aug 41 Gus Lesnevich W PTS 15 Tami Mauriello, *New York C, USA*
14 Nov 41 Gus Lesnevich W PTS Tami Mauriello, *New York C, USA*
20 Jun 42 Freddie Mills W KO 2 Len Harvey, *London, England* (GB)
14 May 46 Gus Lesnevich W RSC 10 Freddie Mills, *London, England*
28 Feb 47 Gus Lesnevich W RSC 10 Billy Fox, *New York C, USA*
5 Mar 48 Gus Lesnevich W KO 1 Billy Fox, *New York C, USA*
26 Jul 48 Freddie Mills W PTS 15 Gus Lesnevich, *London, England*
24 Jan 50 Joey Maxim W KO 10 Freddie Mills, *London, England*
22 Aug 51 Joey Maxim W PTS 15 Bob Murphy, *New York C, USA*
25 Jun 52 Joey Maxim W RTD 13 Sugar Ray Robinson, *New York C, USA*
17 Dec 52 Archie Moore W PTS 15 Joey Maxim, *St Louis, USA*
24 Jun 53 Archie Moore W PTS 15 Joey Maxim, *Ogden, USA*
27 Jan 54 Archie Moore W PTS 15 Joey Maxim, *Miami, USA*
11 Aug 54 Archie Moore W RSC 14 Harold Johnson, *New York C, USA*
22 Jun 55 Archie Moore W KO 3 Carl Bobo Olson, *New York C, USA*
5 Jun 56 Archie Moore W RSC 10 Yolande Pompey, *London, England*
20 Sep 57 Archie Moore W RSC 7 Tony Anthony, *Los Angeles, USA*
10 Dec 58 Archie Moore W KO 11 Yvon Durelle, *Montreal, Canada*
12 Aug 59 Archie Moore W KO 3 Yvon Durelle, *Montreal, Canada*
Archie Moore forfeited NBA recognition (inactivity)

DATE

7 Feb 61 Harold Johnson W RSC 9 Jesse Bowdry, *Miami, USA* (NBA)
24 Apr 61 Harold Johnson W RSC 2 Von Clay *Philadelphia, USA* (NBA)
10 Jun 61 Archie Moore W PTS 15 Giulio Rinaldi, *New York C, USA* (NY/EBU)
Archie Moore forfeited NY/EBU recognition (failure to defend against either Harold Johnson or Doug Jones)
29 Aug 61 Harold Johnson W PTS 15 Eddie Cotton, *Seattle, USA* (NBA)
12 May 62 Harold Johnson W PTS 15 Doug Jones, *Philadelphia, USA*
23 Jun 62 Harold Johnson W PTS 15 Gustav Scholz, *Berlin, W Germany*
1 Jun 63 Willie Pastrano W PTS 15 Harold Johnson, *Las Vegas, USA*
10 Apr 64 Willie Pastrano W RSC 5 Greg Peralta, *New Orleans, USA*
30 Nov 64 Willie Pastrano W RSC 11 Terry Downes, *Manchester, England*
30 Mar 65 José Torres W RSC 9 Willie Pastrano, *New York C, USA*
21 May 66 José Torres W PTS 15 Wayne Thornton, *New York C, USA*
15 Aug 66 José Torres W PTS 15 Eddie Cotton, *Las Vegas, USA*
15 Oct 66 José Torres W KO 2 Chick Calderwood, *San Juan, Puerto Rico*
16 Dec 66 Dick Tiger W PTS 15 José Torres, *New York C, USA*
16 May 67 Dick Tiger W PTS 15 José Torres, *New York C, USA*
17 Nov 67 Dick Tiger W RSC 12 Roger Rouse, *Las Vegas, USA*
24 May 68 Bob Foster W KO 4 Dick Tiger, *New York C, USA*
23 Jan 69 Bob Foster W RSC 1 Frankie de Paula, *New York C, USA*
24 May 69 Bob Foster W RSC 4 Andy Kendall, *Springfield, USA*
4 Apr 70 Bob Foster W RSC 3 Roger Rouse, *Missoula, USA*
27 Jun 70 Bob Foster W KO 10 Mark Tessman, *Baltimore, USA*
Bob Foster forfeited WBA recognition (failure to defend against Jimmy Dupree)
27 Feb 71 Vicente Rondon W RSC 6 Jimmy Dupree, *Caracas, Venezuela* (WBA)
2 Mar 71 Bob Foster W KO 4 Hal Carroll, *Scranton, USA* (WBC)
24 Apr 71 Bob Foster W PTS 15 Ray Anderson, *Tampa, USA* (WBC)
5 Jun 71 Vicente Rondon W KO 1 Piero del Papa, *Caracas, Venezula* (WBA)
21 Aug 71 Vicente Rondon W PTS 15 Eddie Jones, *Caracas, Venezuela* (WBA)
26 Oct 71 Vicente Rondon W RSC 12 Gomeo Brenna, *Miami, USA* (WBA)
29 Oct 71 Bob Foster W RSC 8 Tommy Hicks, *Scranton, USA* (WBC)
15 Dec 71 Vicente Rondon W KO 8 Doyle Baird, *Cleveland, USA* (WBA)
16 Dec 71 Bob Foster W RSC 3 Brian Kelly, *Oklahoma C, USA* (WBC)
7 Apr 72 Bob Foster W KO 2 Vicente Rondon, *Miami, USA*
27 Jun 72 Bob Foster W KO 4 Mike Quarry, *Las Vegas, USA*
26 Sep 72 Bob Foster W KO 14 Chris Finnegan, *Wembley, England*
21 Aug 73 Bob Foster W PTS 15 Pierre Fourie, *Albuquerque, USA*
1 Dec 73 Bob Foster W PTS 15 Pierre Fourie, *Johannesburg, S Africa*
17 Jun 74 Bob Foster DREW 15 Jorge Ahumada, *Albuquerque, USA*
Bob Foster relinquished title (retired)
1 Oct 74 John Conteh W PTS 15 Jorge Ahumada, *Wembley, England* (WBC)
7 Dec 74 Victor Galindez W RTD 12 Len Hutchins, *Buenos Aires, Argentine* (WBA)
11 Mar 75 John Conteh W RSC 5 Lonnie Bennett, *Wembley, England* (WBC)
7 Apr 75 Victor Galindez W PTS 15 Pierre Fourie, *Johannesburg, S Africa* (WBA)
30 Jun 75 Victor Galindez W PTS 15 Jorge Ahumada, *New York C, USA* (WBA)
13 Sep 75 Victor Galindez W PTS 15 Pierre Fourie, *Johannesburg, S Africa* (WBA)
28 Mar 76 Victor Galindez W RTD 3 Harald Skog, *Oslo, Norway* (WBA)
22 May 76 Victor Galindez W KO 15 Richie Kates, *Johannesburg, S Africa* (WBA)
5 Oct 76 Victor Galindez W PTS 15 Kosie Smith, *Johannesburg, S Africa* (WBA)
9 Oct 76 John Conteh W PTS 15 Yaqui Lopez, *Copenhagen, Denmark* (WBC)
5 Mar 77 John Conteh W RSC 3 Len Hutchins, *Liverpool, England* (WBC)
John Conteh forfeited WBC version of title (withdrew from a scheduled defence against Miguel Cuello)
21 May 77 Miguel Cuello W KO 9 Jesse Burnett, *Monte Carlo* (WBC)
18 Jun 77 Victor Galindez W PTS 15 Richie Kates, *Rome, Italy* (WBA)
17 Sep 77 Victor Galindez W PTS 15 Yaqui Lopez, *Rome, Italy* (WBA)
20 Nov 77 Victor Galindez W PTS 15 Mustapha Muhammad, *Turin, Italy* (WBA)
7 Jan 78 Mate Parlov W KO 9 Miguel Cuello, *Milan, Italy* (WBC)
6 May 78 Victor Galindez W PTS 15 Yaqui Lopez, *Reggio, Italy* (WBA)
17 Jun 78 Mate Parlov W PTS 15 John Conteh, *Belgrade, Yugoslavia* (WBC)
15 Sep 78 Mike Rossman W RSC 13 Victor Galindez, *New Orleans, USA* (WBA)
2 Dec 78 Marvin Johnson W RSC 10 Mate Parlov, *Marsala, Italy* (WBC)
5 Dec 78 Mike Rossman W RSC 6 Aldo Traversaro, *Philadelphia, USA* (WBA)

DATE

14 Apr 79 Victor Galindez W RTD 9 Mike Rossman, *New Orleans, USA* (WBA)
22 Apr 79 Matt Saad Muhammad W RSC 8 Marvin Johnson, *Indianapolis, USA* (WBC)
18 Aug 79 Matt Saad Muhammad W PTS 15 John Conteh, *Atlantic C, USA* (WBC)
30 Nov 79 Marvin Johnson W RSC 11 Victor Galindez, *New Orleans, USA* (WBA)
29 Mar 80 Matt Saad Muhammad W RSC 4 John Conteh, *Atlantic C, USA* (WBC)
31 Mar 80 Mustapha Muhammad W RSC 11 Marvin Johnson, *Knoxville, USA* (WBA)
11 May 80 Matt Saad Muhammad W RSC 5 Louis Pergaud, *Halifax, Canada* (WBC)
13 July 80 Matt Saad Muhammad W RSC 14 Yaqui Lopez, *McAfee, USA* (WBC)
20 Jul 80 Mustapha Muhammad W RSC 10 Jerry Martin, *McAfee, USA* (WBA)
28 Nov 80 Matt Saad Muhammad W KO 4 Lotte Mwale, *San Diego, USA* (WBC)
29 Nov 80 Mustapha Muhammad W RSC 3 Rudi Koopmans, *Los Angeles, USA* (WBA)
28 Feb 81 Matt Saad Muhammad W RSC 11 Vonzell Johnson, *Atlantic C, USA* (WBC)
25 Apr 81 Matt Saad Muhammad W KO 9 Murray Sutherland, *Atlantic C, USA* (WBC)
18 Jul 81 Michael Spinks W PTS 15 Mustapha Muhammad, *Las Vegas, USA* (WBA)
26 Sep 81 Matt Saad Muhammad W RSC 11 Jerry Martin, *Atlantic C, USA* (WBC)
7 Nov 81 Michael Spinks W RSC 7 Vonzell Johnson, *Atlantic C, USA* (WBA)
19 Dec 81 Dwight Muhammad Qawi W RSC 10 Matt Saad Muhammad, *Atlantic C, USA* (WBC)
13 Feb 82 Michael Spinks W RSC 6 Mustapha Wasajja, *Atlantic C, USA* (WBA)
21 Mar 82 Dwight Muhammad Qawi W RSC 6 Jerry Martin, *Las Vegas, USA* (WBC)
11 Apr 82 Michael Spinks W RSC 8 Murray Sutherland, *Atlantic C, USA* (WBA)
12 Jun 82 Michael Spinks W RSC 8 Jerry Celestine, *Atlantic C, USA* (WBA)
7 Aug 82 Dwight Muhammad Qawi W RSC 6 Matt Saad Muhammad, *Philadelphia, USA* (WBC)
18 Sep 82 Michael Spinks W RSC 9 Johnny Davis, *Atlantic C, USA* (WBA)
20 Nov 82 Dwight Muhammad Qawi W RSC 11 Eddie Davis, *Atlantic C, USA* (WBC)
18 Mar 83 Michael Spinks W PTS 15 Dwight Muhammad Qawi, *Atlantic C, USA*
25 Nov 83 Michael Spinks W RSC 10 Oscar Rivadeneyra, *Vancouver, Canada*
25 Feb 84 Michael Spinks W PTS 12 Eddie Davis, *Atlantic C, USA*
23 Feb 85 Michael Spinks W RSC 3 David Sears, *Atlantic C, USA*
6 Jun 85 Michael Spinks W RSC 8 Jim MacDonald, *Las Vegas, USA*
Michael Spinks relinquished title to campaign as a heavyweight
10 Dec 85 J.B. Williamson W PTS 12 Prince Muhammed, *Los Angeles, USA* (WBC)
21 Dec 85 Slobodan Kacar W PTS 15 Mustafa Muhammad, *Pesaro, Italy* (IBF)
9 Feb 86 Marvin Johnson W RSC 7 Leslie Stewart, *Indianapolis, USA* (WBA)
30 Apr 86 Dennis Andries W PTS 12 J.B. Williamson, *London, England* (WBC)
6 Sep 86 Bobby Czyz W RSC 5 Slobodan Kacar, *Las Vegas, USA* (IBF)
10 Sep 86 Dennis Andries W RSC 9 Tony Sibson, *London, England* (WBC)
20 Sep 86 Marvin Johnson W RSC 13 Jean-Marie Emebe, *Indianapolis, USA* (WBA)
26 Dec 86 Bobby Czyz W RSC 1 David Sears, *West Orange, USA* (IBF)
21 Feb 87 Bobby Czyz W KO 2 Willie Edwards, *Atlantic C, USA* (IBF)
7 Mar 87 Thomas Hearns W RSC 10 Dennis Andries, *Detroit, USA* (WBC)
Thomas Hearns relinquished title to campaign as a middleweight
3 May 87 Bobby Czyz W RSC 6 Jim MacDonald, *Atlantic C, USA* (IBF)
23 May 87 Leslie Stewart W RTD 8 Marvin Johnson, *Port of Spain, Trinidad* (WBA)
5 Sep 87 Virgil Hill W RSC 4 Leslie Stewart, *Atlantic City, USA* (WBA)
29 Oct 87 Charles Williams W RTD 9 Bobby Czyz, *Las Vegas, USA* (IBF)
21 Nov 87 Virgil Hill W PTS 12 Rufino Angulo, *Paris, France* (WBA)
27 Nov 87 Don Lalonde W RSC 2 Eddie Davis, *Port-of-Spain, Trinidad* (WBC)

DATE	
3 Apr 88	Virgil Hill W RSC 11 Jean-Marie Emebe, *Bismarck, USA* (WBA)
29 May 88	Don Lalonde W RSC 5 Leslie Stewart, *Port-of-Spain, Trinidad* (WBC)
6 Jun 88	Virgil Hill W PTS 12 Ramzi Hassan, *Las Vegas, USA* (WBA)
10 Jun 88	Charles Williams W RTD 11 Richard Caramanolis, *Annecy, France* (IBF)
21 Oct 88	Charles Williams W RSC 3 Rufino Angulo, *Ville D'Ornon, France* (IBF)
7 Nov 88	Sugar Ray Leonard W RSC 9 Don Lalonde, *Las Vegas, USA* (WBC)
11 Nov 88	Virgil Hill W RSC 10 Willy Featherstone, *Bismarck, USA* (WBA)

SUPER-MIDDLEWEIGHT

(*Current weight limit:* 168lb/76kg)

DATE	
28 Mar 84	Murray Sutherland W PTS 15 Ernie Singletary, *Atlantic C, USA* (IBF)
22 Jul 84	Chong-Pal Park W KO 11 Murray Sutherland, *Seoul, S Korea* (IBF)
2 Jan 85	Chong-Pal Park W KO 2 Roy Gumbs, *Seoul, S Korea* (IBF)
30 Jun 85	Chong-Pal Park W PTS 15 Vinnie Curto, *Seoul, S Korea* (IBF)
11 Apr 86	Chong-Pal Park W KO 15 Vinnie Curto, *Los Angeles, USA* (IBF)
6 Jul 86	Chong-Pal Park T DRAW 2 Lindell Holmes, *Chungju, S Korea* (IBF)
14 Sep 86	Chong-Pal Park W PTS 15 Marvin Mack, *Pusan, S Korea* (IBF)
25 Jan 87	Chong-Pal Park W RSC 15 Doug Sam, *Seoul, S Korea* (IBF)
3 May 87	Chong-Pal Park W PTS 15 Lindell Holmes, *Inchon, S Korea* (IBF)
26 Jul 87	Chong-Pal Park W RSC 4 Emmanuel Otti, *Kwangju, S Korea* (IBF)
6 Dec 87	Chong-Pal Park W RSC 2 Jesus Gallardo, *Seoul, S Korea* (WBA)
	Chong-Pal Park relinquished title (IBF) to concentrate on WBA title
1 Mar 88	Chong-Pal Park W KO 5 Polly Pasieron, *Chungju, S Korea* (WBA)
12 Mar 88	Graciano Rocchigiani W RSC 8 Vince Boulware, *Dusseldorf, W Germany* (IBF)
23 May 88	Fully Obelmejias W PTS 12 Chong-Pal Park, *Suanbo, S Korea* (WBA)
3 Jun 88	Graciano Rocchigiani W PTS 15 Nicky Walker, *Berlin, W Germany* (IBF)
7 Oct 88	Graciano Rocchigiani W RTD 11 Chris Reid, *Berlin, W Germany* (IBF)
7 Nov 88	Sugar Ray Leonard W RSC 9 Don Lalonde, *Las Vegas, USA* (WBC)

MIDDLEWEIGHT

(*Current weight limit:* 160lb/72.5kg)

DATE	
30 Jun 84	Jack Dempsey W KO 22 George Fulljames, *New York, USA*
3 Feb 86	Jack Dempsey W KO 27 Jack Fogarty, *New York, USA*
4 Mar 86	Jack Dempsey W KO 13 George LaBlanche, *New York, USA*
27 Feb 89	George LaBlanche W KO 32 Jack Dempsey, *San Francisco, USA*
	LaBlanche's win was not recognized as he used a pivot punch, which was made illegal
18 Feb 90	Jack Dempsey W KO 28 Bill McCarthy, *San Francisco, USA*
14 Jan 91	Bob Fitzsimmons W KO 13 Jack Dempsey, *New Orleans, USA*
26 Sep 94	Bob Fitzsimmons W KO 2 Dan Creedon, *New Orleans, USA*
	Bob Fitzsimmons relinquished title to campaign as a heavyweight
2 Mar 96	Kid McCoy W KO 15 Tommy Ryan, *New York, USA*
17 Dec 97	Kid McCoy W PTS 15 Dan Creedon, *New York C, USA*
	Kid McCoy relinquished title to campaign as a heavyweight
25 Feb 98	Tommy Ryan W KO 18 George Green, *San Francisco, USA*
13 Jun 98	Tommy Ryan W RSC 14 Tommy West, *New York C, USA*
24 Oct 98	Tommy Ryan W PTS 20 Jack Bonner, *New York C, USA*
18 Sep 99	Tommy Ryan W 10 Frank Craig, *New York C, USA*
4 Mar 01	Tommy Ryan W RTD 17 Tommy West, *Louisville, USA*
24 Jun 02	Tommy Ryan W KO 3 Johnny Gorman, *London, England*
15 Sep 02	Tommy Ryan W KO 6 Kid Carter, *Fort Erie, Canada*
	Tommy Ryan relinquished title (retired)
4 Jul 07	Stanley Ketchel DREW 20 Joe Thomas, *Marysville, USA*
2 Sep 07	Stanley Ketchel W KO 32 Joe Thomas, *San Francisco, USA*
12 Dec 07	Stanley Ketchel W PTS 20 Joe Thomas, *San Francisco, USA*
22 Feb 08	Stanley Ketchel W KO 1 Mike Twin Sullivan, *San Francisco, USA*
9 May 08	Stanley Ketchel W KO 20 Jack Twin Sullivan, *San Francisco, USA*
4 Jun 08	Stanley Ketchel W PTS 10 Billy Papke, *Milwaukee, USA*
31 Jul 08	Stanley Ketchel W KO 3 Hugo Kelly, *San Francisco, USA*
18 Aug 08	Stanley Ketchel W KO 2 Joe Thomas, *San Francisco, USA*
7 Sep 08	Billy Papke W RSC 12 Stanley Ketchel, *Los Angeles, USA*
26 Nov 08	Stanley Ketchel W KO 11 Billy Papke, *San Francisco, USA*
2 Jun 09	Stanley Ketchel W KO 4 Tony Caponi, *Schnectady, USA*
9 Jun 09	Stanley Ketchel W RSC 3 Jack O'Brien, *Philadelphia, USA*
5 Jul 09	Stanley Ketchel W PTS 20 Billy Papke, *San Francisco, USA*
27 May 10	Stanley Ketchel W KO 2 Willie Lewis, *New York C, USA*
10 Jun 10	Stanley Ketchel W KO 5 Jim Smith, *New York C, USA*
	Stanley Ketchel was murdered while still champion
8 Jun 11	Billy Papke W RTD 9 Jim Sullivan, *London, England* (GB)
22 Feb 12	Frank Mantell W PTS 20 Billy Papke, *Sacramento, USA* (USA)
30 Mar 12	Frank Mantell W PTS 20 Jack Henrick, *Los Angeles, USA* (USA)
	Frank Mantell lost US recognition after several non-title defeats
29 Jun 12	Billy Papke W RSC 16 Marcel Moreau, *Paris, France* (IBU)
23 Oct 12	Billy Papke W DIS 17 Georges Carpentier, *Paris, France* (IBU)
4 Dec 12	Billy Papke W KO 7 George Bernard, *Paris, France* (IBU)
5 Mar 13	Frank Klaus W DIS 15 Billy Papke, *Paris, France* (IBU)
11 Oct 13	George Chip W KO 6 Frank Klaus, *Pittsburgh, USA* (USA)
23 Dec 13	George Chip W KO 5 Frank Klaus, *Pittsburgh, USA* (USA)
1 Jan 14	Eddie McGoorty W KO 1 Dave Smith, *Sydney, Australia* (AUSTR)
7 Feb 14	Eddie McGoorty W PTS 20 Pat Bradley, *Sydney, Australia* (AUSTR)
14 Mar 14	Jeff Smith W PTS 20 Eddie McGoorty, *Sydney, Australia* (AUSTR)
6 Apr 14	Al McCoy W KO 1 George Chip, *New York C, USA* (USA)
13 Apr 14	Jeff Smith W KO 16 Pat Bradley, *Sydney, Australia* (AUSTR)
6 Jun 14	Jeff Smith W PTS 20 Jimmy Clabby, *Sydney, Australia* (AUSTR)
28 Nov 14	Mick King W PTS 20 Jeff Smith, *Sydney, Australia* (AUSTR)
26 Dec 14	Jeff Smith W PTS 20 Mick King, *Sydney, Australia* (AUSTR)
23 Jan 15	Jeff Smith W DIS 5 Les Darcy, *Sydney, Australia* (AUSTR)
20 Feb 15	Jeff Smith W PTS 20 Mick King, *Melbourne, Australia* (AUSTR)
23 May 15	Les Darcy W DIS 2 Jeff Smith, *Sydney, Australia* (AUSTR)
12 Jun 15	Les Darcy W RTD 10 Mick King, *Sydney, Australia* (AUSTR)
31 Jul 15	Les Darcy W RSC 15 Eddie McGoorty, *Sydney, Australia* (AUSTR)
4 Sep 15	Les Darcy W PTS 20 Billy Murray, *Sydney, Australia* (AUSTR)
9 Oct 15	Les Darcy W RTD 6 Fred Dyer, *Sydney, Australia* (AUSTR)
23 Oct 15	Les Darcy W PTS 20 Jimmy Clabby, *Sydney, Australia* (AUSTR)
27 Dec 15	Les Darcy W RTD 8 Eddie McGoorty, *Sydney, Australia* (AUSTR)
15 Jan 16	Les Darcy W PTS 20 George Brown, *Sydney, Australia* (AUSTR)
25 Mar 16	Les Darcy W KO 7 Les O'Donnell, *Sydney, Australia* (AUSTR)
8 Apr 16	Les Darcy W PTS 20 George Brown, *Sydney, Australia* (AUSTR)
13 May 16	Les Darcy W RTD 4 Alex Costica, *Sydney, Australia* (AUSTR)
3 Jun 16	Les Darcy W KO 2 Buck Crouse, *Sydney, Australia* (AUSTR)
24 Jun 16	Les Darcy W KO 12 Dave Smith, *Sydney, Australia* (AUSTR)

***Right:** A painful blow to the stomach of Jake LaMotta by Sugar Ray Robinson. Robinson won a version of the middleweight title five times, a record for any division. He first won the undisputed title with a 13th-round stoppage of LaMotta at Chicago in 1951.*

DATE	
26 Jun 16	Al McCoy W PTS 15 Hugh Ross, *Bridgeport, USA* (USA)
9 Sep 16	Les Darcy W PTS 20 Jimmy Clabby, *Sydney, Australia* (AUSTR)
30 Sep 16	Les Darcy W KO 9 George Chip, *Sydney, Australia* (AUSTR)
	Les Darcy died and the Australian version ceased
14 Nov 17	Mike O'Dowd W KO 6 Al McCoy, *New York C, USA*
17 Jul 19	Mike O'Dowd W KO 3 Al McCoy, *St Paul, USA*
6 Nov 19	Mike O'Dowd W KO 2 Billy Kramer, *Paterson, USA*
1 Mar 20	Mike O'Dowd W KO 2 Jack McCarron, *Philadelphia, USA*
30 Mar 20	Mike O'Dowd W KO 5 Joe Eagen, *Boston, USA*
6 May 20	Johnny Wilson W PTS 12 Mike O'Dowd, *Boston, USA*
17 Mar 21	Johnny Wilson W PTS 15 Mike O'Dowd, *New York C, USA*
27 Jul 21	Johnny Wilson W DIS 7 Bryan Downey, *Cleveland, USA*
22 Feb 22	Bryan Downey W PTS 12 Frank Carbone, *Canton, USA* (OHIO)
15 May 22	Bryan Downey W PTS 12 Mike O'Dowd, *Columbus, USA* (OHIO)
14 Aug 22	Dave Rosenberg W PTS 15 Phil Krug, *New York C, USA* (NY)
18 Sep 22	Jock Malone W PTS 12 Bryan Downey, *Columbus, USA* (OHIO)
30 Nov 22	Mike O'Dowd W DIS 8 Dave Rosenberg, *New York C, USA* (NY)
	Mike O'Dowd relinquished NY version of title (retired)
24 Jul 23	Jock Malone W PTS 12 Bryan Downey, *Columbus, USA* (OHIO)
	Jock Malone ceased to be recognized by Ohio following a defeat by Lou Bogash in a non-title bout, October, 1923)
31 Aug 23	Harry Greb W PTS 15 Johnny Wilson, *New York C, USA*
3 Dec 23	Harry Greb W PTS 10 Bryan Downey, *Pittsburgh, USA*
18 Jan 24	Harry Greb W PTS 15 Johnny Wilson, *New York C, USA*
24 Mar 24	Harry Greb W RSC 12 Fay Keiser, *Baltimore, USA*
26 Jun 24	Harry Greb W PTS 15 Ted Moore, *New York C, USA*
2 Jul 25	Harry Greb W PTS 15 Mickey Walker, *New York C, USA*
13 Nov 25	Harry Greb W PTS 15 Tony Marullo, *New Orleans, USA*
26 Feb 26	Tiger Flowers W PTS 15 Harry Greb, *New York C, USA*
19 Aug 26	Tiger Flowers W PTS 15 Harry Greb, *New York C, USA*
3 Dec 26	Mickey Walker W PTS 10 Tiger Flowers, *Chicago, USA*
30 Jun 27	Mickey Walker W KO 10 Tommy Milligan, *London, England*
21 Jun 28	Mickey Walker W PTS 10 Ace Hudkins, *Chicago, USA*
29 Oct 29	Mickey Walker W PTS 10 Ace Hudkins, *Los Angeles, USA*

DATE	
30 Jul 30	Mickey Walker W KO 3 Willie Oster, *Newark, USA*
	Mickey Walker relinquished title (to campaign as heavyweight)
25 Aug 31	Gorilla Jones W PTS 10 Tiger Thomas, *Milwaukee, USA* (NBA)
25 Jan 32	Gorilla Jones W RSC 6 Oddone Piazza, *Milwaukee, USA* (NBA)
26 Apr 32	Gorilla Jones W PTS 12 Young Terry, *Trenton, USA* (NBA)
11 Jun 32	Marcel Thil W DIS 11 Gorilla Jones, *Paris, France* (NBA/IBU)
4 Jul 32	Marcel Thil W PTS 15 Len Harvey, *London, England* (NBA/IBU)
	Marcel Thil ceased to be recognised by the NBA (the authority once again supported the claims of Gorilla Jones)
11 Nov 32	Ben Jeby W PTS 15 Chuck Devlin, *New York C, USA* (NY)
13 Jan 33	Ben Jeby W RSC 12 Frank Battaglia, *New York C, USA* (NY)
30 Jan 33	Gorilla Jones W KO 7 Sammy Slaughter, *Cleveland, USA* (NBA)
	Gorilla Jones ceased to be recognized by the NBA after non-title defeats in 1934
17 Mar 33	Ben Jeby DREW 15 Vince Dundee, *New York C, USA* (NY)
10 Jul 33	Ben Jeby W PTS 15 Young Terry, *Newark, USA* (NY)
9 Aug 33	Lou Brouillard W KO 7 Ben Jeby, *New York C, USA* (NY)
2 Oct 33	Marcel Thil W PTS 15 Kid Tunero, *Paris, France* (IBU)
30 Oct 33	Vince Dundee W PTS 15 Lou Brouillard, *Boston, USA* (NY)
8 Dec 33	Vince Dundee W PTS 15 Andy Callahan, *Boston, USA* (NY)
26 Feb 34	Marcel Thil W PTS 15 Ignacio Ara, *Paris, France* (IBU)
1 May 34	Vince Dundee W PTS 15 Al Diamond, *Paterson, USA* (NY)
3 May 34	Marcel Thil W PTS 15 Gustav Roth, *Paris, USA* (IBU)
11 Sep 34	Teddy Yarosz W PTS 15 Vince Dundee, *Pittsburgh, USA* (NY/NBA)
15 Oct 34	Marcel Thil DREW 15 Carmelo Candel, *Paris, France* (IBU)
4 May 35	Marcel Thil W RTD 14 Vilda Jaks, *Paris, France* (IBU)
3 Jun 35	Marcel Thil W PTS 15 Ignacio Ara, *Madrid, Spain* (IBU)
28 Jun 35	Marcel Thil W PTS 10 Carmelo Candel, *Paris, France* (IBU)
19 Sep 35	Babe Risko W PTS 15 Teddy Yarosz, *Pittsburgh, USA* (NY/NBA)
20 Jan 36	Marcel Thil W DIS 4 Lou Brouillard, *Paris, France* (IBU)
10 Feb 36	Babe Risko W PTS 15 Tony Fisher, *Newark, USA* (NY/NBA)
11 Jul 36	Freddie Steele W PTS 15 Babe Risko, *Seattle, USA* (NY/NBA)
1 Jan 37	Freddie Steele W PTS 10 Gorilla Jones, *Milwaukee, USA* (NY/NBA)
15 Feb 37	Marcel Thil W DIS 6 Lou Brouillard, *Paris, France* (IBU)

DATE	
19 Feb 37	Freddie Steele W PTS 15 Babe Risko, *New York C, USA* (NY/NBA)
11 May 37	Freddie Steele W KO 3 Frank Battaglia, *Seattle, USA* (NY/NBA)
11 Sep 37	Freddie Steele W KO 4 Ken Overlin, *Seattle, USA* (NY/NBA)
	Freddie Steele ceased to be recognized by NY (failure to defend against Fred Apostoli)
23 Sep 37	Fred Apostoli W RSC 10 Marcel Thil, *New York C, USA* (IBU)
	Apostoli did not claim IBU recognition due to an agreement with the New York authorities, but Thil lost IBU recognition
19 Feb 38	Freddie Steele W RTD 7 Carmen Barth, *Cleveland, USA* (NBA)
1 Apr 38	Fred Apostoli W PTS 15 Glen Lee, *New York C, USA* (NY)
7 Apr 38	Edouard Tenet W RTD 12 Josef Besselmann, *Berlin, Germany* (IBU)
	Edouard Tenet ceased to be recognized by the IBU following a defeat by Bep van Klaveren in a European title defence, July, 1938
26 Jul 38	Al Hostak W KO 1 Freddie Steele, *Seattle, USA* (NBA)
1 Nov 38	Solly Krieger W PTS 15 Al Hostak, *Seattle, USA* (NBA)
18 Nov 38	Fred Apostoli W RSC 8 Young Corbett III, *New York C, USA* (NY/IBA)
27 Jun 39	Al Hostak W RSC 4 Solly Krieger, *Seattle, USA* (NBA)
2 Oct 39	Ceferino Garcia W RSC 7 Fred Apostoli, *New York C, USA* (NY/IBA)
11 Dec 39	Al Hostak W KO 1 Eric Seelig, *Cleveland, USA* (NBA)
23 Dec 39	Ceferino Garcia W KO 13 Glen Lee, *Manila, Philippines* (NY/IBA)
1 Mar 40	Ceferino Garcia DREW 10 Henry Armstrong, *Los Angeles, USA* (NY/IBA)
23 May 40	Ken Overlin W PTS 15 Ceferino Garcia, *New York C, USA* (NY/IBA)
19 Jul 40	Tony Zale W RTD 13 Al Hostak, *Seattle, USA* (NBA)
1 Nov 40	Ken Overlin W PTS 15 Steve Belloise, *New York C, USA* (NY/IBA)
13 Dec 40	Ken Overlin W PTS 15 Steve Belloise, *New York C, USA* (NY/IBA)
21 Feb 41	Tony Zale W KO 14 Steve Mamakos, *Chicago, USA* (NBA)
9 May 41	Billy Soose W PTS 15 Ken Overlin, *New York C, USA* (NY/IBA)
	Billy Soose ceased to be recognized by NY following a defeat by Georgie Abrams in a non-title bout, July, 1941
28 May 41	Tony Zale W KO 2 Al Hostak, *Chicago, USA* (NBA)
28 Nov 41	Tony Zale W PTS 15 Georgie Abrams, *New York C, USA*
27 Sep 46	Tony Zale W KO 6 Rocky Graziano, *New York C, USA*
16 Jul 47	Rocky Graziano W RSC 6 Tony Zale, *Chicago, USA*
10 Jun 48	Tony Zale W KO 3 Rocky Graziano, *Newark, USA*
21 Sep 48	Marcel Cerdan W RSC 12 Tony Zale, *Jersey C, USA*
16 Jun 49	Jake LaMotta W RTD 10 Marcel Cerdan, *Detroit, USA*
5 Jun 50	Sugar Ray Robinson W PTS 15 Robert Villemain, *Philadelphia, USA* (PEN)
12 Jul 50	Jake LaMotta W PTS 15 Tiberio Mitri, *New York C, USA* (NY/NBA)
25 Aug 50	Sugar Ray Robinson W KO 1 Jose Basora, *Scranton, USA* (PEN)
13 Sep 50	Jake LaMotta W KO 15 Laurent Dauthuille, *Detroit, USA* (NY/NBA)
26 Oct 50	Sugar Ray Robinson W KO 12 Carl Bobo Olson, *Philadelphia, USA* (PEN)
14 Feb 51	Sugar Ray Robinson W RSC 13 Jake LaMotta, *Chicago, USA*
10 Jul 51	Randolph Turpin W PTS 15 Sugar Ray Robinson, *London, England*
12 Sep 51	Sugar Ray Robinson W RSC 10 Randolph Turpin, *New York C, USA*
13 Mar 52	Sugar Ray Robinson W PTS 15 Carl Bobo Olson, *San Francisco, USA*
16 Apr 52	Sugar Ray Robinson W KO 3 Rocky Graziano, *Chicago, USA*
	Sugar Ray Robinson relinquished title (retired)
9 Jun 53	Randolph Turpin W PTS 15 Charles Humez, *London, England* (EBU)
21 Oct 53	Carl Bobo Olson W PTS 15 Randolph Turpin, *New York C, USA*
2 Apr 54	Carl Bobo Olson W PTS 15 Kid Gavilan, *Chicago, USA*
20 Aug 54	Carl Bobo Olson W PTS 15 Rocky Castellani, *San Francisco, USA*
15 Dec 54	Carl Bobo Olson W RSC 11 Pierre Langlois, *San Francisco, USA*
9 Dec 55	Sugar Ray Robinson W KO 2 Carl Bobo Olson, *Chicago, USA*
18 May 56	Sugar Ray Robinson W KO 4 Carl Bobo Olson, *Los Angeles, USA*
2 Jan 57	Gene Fullmer W PTS 15 Sugar Ray Robinson, *New York C, USA*
1 May 57	Sugar Ray Robinson W KO 5 Gene Fullmer, *Chicago, USA*
23 Sep 57	Carmen Basilio W PTS 15 Sugar Ray Robinson, *New York C, USA*
25 Mar 52	Sugar Ray Robinson W PTS 15 Carmen Basilio, *Chicago, USA*
	Sugar Ray Robinson forfeited NBA recognition (inactivity)
28 Aug 59	Gene Fullmer W RSC 14 Carmen Basilio, *San Francisco, USA* (NBA)
4 Dec 59	Gene Fullmer W PTS 15 Spider Webb, *Logan, USA* (NBA)
22 Jan 60	Paul Pender W PTS 15 Sugar Ray Robinson, *Boston, USA* (NY/EBU)
20 Apr 60	Gene Fullmer DREW 15 Joey Giardello, *Bozeman, USA* (NBA)
10 Jun 60	Paul Pender W PTS 15 Sugar Ray Robinson, *Boston, USA* (NY/EBU)
29 Jun 60	Gene Fullmer W RSC 12 Carmen Basilio, *Salt Lake C, USA* (NBA)
3 Dec 60	Gene Fullmer DREW 15 Sugar Ray Robinson, *Los Angeles, USA* (NBA)
14 Jan 61	Paul Pender W RSC 7 Terry Downes, *Boston, USA* (NY/EBU)
4 Mar 61	Gene Fullmer W PTS 15 Sugar Ray Robinson, *Las Vegas, USA* (NBA)
22 Apr 61	Paul Pender W PTS 15 Carmen Basilio, *Boston, USA* (NY/EBU)

DATE	
11 Jul 61	Terry Downes W RTD 9 Paul Pender, *Wembley, England* (NY/EBU)
5 Aug 61	Gene Fullmer W PTS 15 Florentino Fernandez, *Ogden, USA* (NBA)
9 Dec 61	Gene Fullmer W KO 10 Benny Kid Paret, *Las Vegas, USA* (NBA)
7 Apr 62	Paul Pender W PTS 15 Terry Downes, *Boston, USA* (NY/EBU)
	Paul Pender forfeited NY/EBU recognition (failure to defend within stipulated period)
23 Oct 62	Dick Tiger W PTS 15 Gene Fullmer, *San Francisco, USA* (WBA)
23 Feb 63	Dick Tiger DREW 15 Gene Fullmer, *Las Vegas, USA*
10 Aug 63	Dick Tiger W RTD 7 Gene Fullmer, *Ibadan, Nigeria*
7 Dec 63	Joey Giardello W PTS 15 Dick Tiger, *Atlantic C, USA*
14 Dec 64	Joey Giardello W PTS 15 Rubin Carter, *Philadelphia, USA*
21 Oct 65	Dick Tiger W PTS 15 Joey Giardello, *New York C, USA*
25 Apr 66	Emile Griffith W PTS 15 Dick Tiger, *New York C, USA*
13 Jul 66	Emile Griffith W PTS 15 Joey Archer, *New York C, USA*
23 Jan 67	Emile Griffith W PTS 15 Joey Archer, *New York C, USA*
17 Apr 67	Nino Benvenuti W PTS 15 Emile Griffith, *New York C, USA*
29 Sep 67	Emile Griffith W PTS 15 Nino Benvenuti, *New York C, USA*
4 Mar 68	Nino Benvenuti W PTS 15 Emile Griffith, *New York C, USA*
14 Dec 68	Nino Benvenuti W PTS 15 Don Fullmer, *San Remo, Italy*
4 Oct 69	Nino Benvenuti W DIS 7 Fraser Scott, *Naples, Italy*
22 Nov 69	Nino Benvenuti W KO 1 Luis Rodriguez, *Rome, Italy*
23 May 70	Nino Benvenuti W KO 8 Tom Bethea, *Umag, Yugoslavia*
7 Nov 70	Carlos Monzon W KO 12 Nino Benvenuti, *Rome, Italy*
8 May 71	Carlos Monzon W RSC 3 Nino Benvenuti, *Monte Carlo*
25 Sep 71	Carlos Monzon W RSC 14 Emile Griffith, *Buenos Aires, Argentine*
4 Mar 72	Carlos Monzon W RSC 5 Denny Moyer, *Rome, Italy*
17 Jun 72	Carlos Monzon W RTD 12 Jean-Claude Bouttier, *Colombes, France*
19 Aug 72	Carlos Monzon W RSC 5 Tom Bogs, *Copenhagen, Denmark*
11 Nov 72	Carlos Monzon W PTS 15 Bennie Briscoe, *Buenos Aires, Argentine*
2 Jun 72	Carlos Monzon W PTS 15 Emile Griffith, *Monte Carlo*
29 Sep 73	Carlos Monzon W PTS 15 Jean-Claude Bouttier, *Paris, France*
9 Feb 74	Carlos Monzon W RTD 6 Jose Napoles, *Paris, France*
	Carlos Monzon forfeited WBC recognition (failure to defend against Rodrigo Valdez)
25 May 74	Rodrigo Valdez W KO 7 Bennie Briscoe, *Monte Carlo* (WBC)
5 Oct 74	Carlos Monzon W KO 7 Tony Mundine, *Buenos Aires, Argentine* (WBA)
30 Nov 74	Rodrigo Valdez W KO 11 Gratien Tonna, *Paris, France* (WBC)
31 May 75	Rodrigo Valdez W RSC 8 Ramon Mendez, *Cali, Colombia* (WBC)
30 Jun 75	Carlos Monzon W RSC 10 Tony Licata, *New York C, USA* (WBA)
16 Aug 75	Rodrigo Valdez W PTS 15 Rudy Robles, *Cartagena, Colombia* (WBC)
13 Dec 75	Carlos Monzon W KO 5 Gratien Tonna, *Paris, France* (WBA)
28 Mar 76	Rodrigo Valdez W RTD 4 Max Cohen, *Paris, France* (WBC)
26 Jun 76	Carlos Monzon W PTS 15 Rodrigo Valdez, *Monte Carlo*
30 Jul 77	Carlos Monzon W PTS 15 Rodrigo Valdez, *Monte Carlo*
	Carlos Monzon relinquished title (retired)
5 Nov 77	Rodrigo Valdez W PTS 15 Bennie Briscoe, *Campione d'Italia, Switzerland*
22 Apr 78	Hugo Corro W PTS 15 Rodrigo Valdez, *San Remo, Italy*
5 Aug 78	Hugo Corro W PTS 15 Ronnie Harris, *Buenos Aires, Argentine*
11 Nov 78	Hugo Corro W PTS 15 Rodrigo Valdez, *Buenos Aires, Argentine*
30 Jun 79	Vito Antuofermo W PTS 15 Hugo Corro, *Monte Carlo*
30 Nov 79	Vito Antuofermo DREW 15 Marvin Hagler, *Las Vegas, USA*
16 Mar 80	Alan Minter W PTS 15 Vito Antuofermo, *Las Vegas, USA*
28 Jun 80	Alan Minter W RTD 8 Vito Antuofermo, *Wembley, England*
27 Sep 80	Marvin Hagler W RSC 3 Alan Minter, *Wembley, England*
17 Jan 81	Marvin Hagler W RSC 8 Fully Obelmejias, *Boston, USA*
13 Jun 81	Marvin Hagler W RTD 4 Vito Antuofermo, *Boston, USA*
3 Oct 81	Marvin Hagler W RSC 11 Mustafa Hamsho, *Rosemont, USA*
7 Mar 82	Marvin Hagler W RSC 1 Caveman Lee, *Atlantic C, USA*
30 Oct 82	Marvin Hagler W RSC 5 Fully Obelmejias, *San Remo, Italy*
11 Feb 83	Marvin Hagler W RSC 6 Tony Sibson, *Worcester, USA*
27 May 83	Marvin Hagler W KO 4 Wilford Scypion, *Providence, USA*
10 Nov 83	Marvin Hagler W PTS 15 Roberto Duran, *Las Vegas, USA*
30 Mar 84	Marvin Hagler W RSC 10 Juan Domingo Roldan, *Las Vegas, USA*
19 Oct 84	Marvin Hagler W RSC 3 Mustafa Hamsho, *New York C, USA*
15 Apr 85	Marvin Hagler W RSC 3 Thomas Hearns, *Las Vegas, USA*
10 Mar 86	Marvin Hagler W KO 11 John Mugabi, *Las Vegas, USA*
	Marvin Hagler forfeited WBA/IBF recognition (failure to meet Herol Graham inside the stipulated period and subsequently boxing Leonard)
6 Apr 87	Sugar Ray Leonard W PTS 12 Marvin Hagler, *Las Vegas, USA* (WBC)
	Sugar Ray Leonard relinquished title (retired)
10 Oct 87	Frank Tate W PTS 15 Michael Olajide, *Las Vegas, USA* (IBF)

DATE

23 Oct 87 Sumbu Kalambay W PTS 15 Iran Barkley, *Livorno, Italy* (WBA)
29 Oct 87 Thomas Hearns W KO 4 Juan Domingo Roldan, *Las Vegas, USA* (WBC)
7 Feb 88 Frank Tate W KO 10 Tony Sibson, *Stafford, England* (IBF)
5 Mar 88 Sumbu Kalambay W PTS 12 Mike McCallum, *Pesaro, Italy* (WBA)
6 Jun 88 Iran Barkley W RSC 3 Thomas Hearns, *Las Vegas, USA* (WBC)
12 Jun 88 Sumbu Kalambay W PTS 12 Robbie Sims, *Ravenna, Italy* (WBA)
28 Jul 88 Michael Nunn W RSC 9 Frank Tate, *Las Vegas, USA* (IBF)
4 Nov 88 Michael Nunn W KO 8 Juan Domingo Roldan, *Las Vegas, USA* (IBF)
8 Nov 88 Sumbu Kalambay W KO 7 Doug De-Witt, *Monte Carlo* (WBA)

LIGHT-MIDDLEWEIGHT

(*Current weight limit:* 154lb/70kg. The WBA and IBF call the class 'Junior Middleweight' and the WBC call the class 'Super-welterweight')

DATE

20 Oct 62 Denny Moyer W PTS 15 Joey Giambra, *Portland, USA* (WBA)
19 Feb 63 Denny Moyer W PTS 15 Stan Harrington, *Honolulu, Hawaii* (WBA)
29 Apr 63 Ralph Dupas W PTS 15 Denny Moyer, *New Orleans, USA* (WBA)
17 Jun 63 Ralph Dupas W PTS 15 Denny Moyer, *Baltimore, USA* (WBA)
7 Sep 63 Sandro Mazzinghi W KO 9 Ralph Dupas, *Milan, Italy* (WBA)
2 Dec 63 Sandro Mazzinghi W RSC 13 Ralph Dupas, *Sydney, Australia* (WBA)
3 Oct 64 Sandro Mazzinghi W RSC 12 Tony Montano, *Genoa, Italy* (WBA)
11 Dec 64 Sandro Mazzinghi W PTS 15 Fortunato Manca, *Rome, Italy* (WBA)
18 Jun 65 Nino Benvenuti W KO 6 Sandro Mazzinghi, *Milan, Italy* (WBA)
17 Dec 65 Nino Benvenuti W PTS 15 Sandro Mazzinghi, *Rome, Italy* (WBA)
25 Jun 66 Ki-Soo Kim W PTS 15 Nino Benvenuti, *Seoul, S Korea* (WBA)
17 Dec 66 Ki-Soo Kim W PTS 15 Stan Harrington, *Seoul, S Korea* (WBA)
3 Oct 67 Ki-Soo Kim W PTS 15 Freddie Little, *Seoul, S Korea* (WBA)
25 May 68 Sandro Mazzinghi W PTS 15 Ki-Soo Kim, *Milan, Italy* (WBA)
25 Oct 68 Sandro Mazzinghi NC 9 Freddie Little, *Rome, Italy* (WBA)
Mazzinghi was forced to retire because of a cut at the end of the eighth round, and because the referee's decision was controversial, the WBA declared the title vacant
17 Mar 69 Freddie Little W PTS 15 Stan Hayward, *Las Vegas, USA*
9 Sep 69 Freddie Little W KO 2 Hisai Minami, *Osaka, Japan*
20 Mar 70 Freddie Little W PTS 15 Gerhard Piaskowy, *Berlin, W Germany*
9 Jul 70 Carmelo Bossi W PTS 15 Freddie Little, *Monza, Italy*
29 Apr 71 Carmelo Bossi DREW 15 Jose Hernandez, *Madrid, Spain*
31 Oct 71 Koichi Wajima W PTS 15 Carmelo Bossi, *Tokyo, Japan*
7 May 72 Koichi Wajima W KO 1 Domenico Tiberia, *Tokyo, Japan*
3 Oct 72 Koichi Wajima W KO 3 Matt Donovan, *Tokyo, Japan*
9 Jan 73 Koichi Wajima DREW 15 Miguel de Oliviera, *Tokyo, Japan*
19 Apr 73 Koichi Wajima W PTS 15 Ryu Sorimachi, *Osaka, Japan*
14 Aug 73 Koichi Wajima W RTD 12 Silvani Bertini, *Sappora, Japan*
5 Feb 74 Koichi Wajima W PTS 15 Miguel de Oliviera, *Tokyo, Japan*
3 Jun 74 Oscar Albarado W KO 15 Koichi Wajima, *Tokyo, Japan*
8 Oct 74 Oscar Albarado W RSC 7 Ryu Sorimachi, *Tokyo, Japan*
21 Jan 75 Koichi Wajima W PTS 15 Oscar Albarado, *Tokyo, Japan*
Koichi Wajima forfeited WBC recognition (failure to defend against Miguel de Oliveira)
7 May 75 Miguel de Oliveira W PTS 15 Jose Duran, *Monte Carlo* (WBC)
7 Jun 75 Jae-Do Yuh W RSC 7 Koichi Wajima, *Kitakyushi, Japan* (WBA)
11 Nov 75 Jae-Do Yuh W RSC 6 Masahiro Misako, *Shizuoka, Japan* (WBA)
13 Nov 75 Elisha Obed W RTD 10 Miguel de Oliviera, *Paris, France* (WBC)

DATE

17 Feb 76 Koichi Wajima W KO 15 Jae-Do Yuh, *Tokyo, Japan* (WBA)
28 Feb 76 Elisha Obed W KO 2 Tony Gardner, *Nassau, Bahamas* (WBC)
23 Apr 76 Elisha Obed W PTS 15 Sea Robinson, *Abidjan, Ivory Coast* (WBC)
18 May 76 Jose Duran W KO 14 Koichi Wajima, *Tokyo, Japan* (WBA)
18 Jun 76 Eckhard Dagge W RTD 10 Elisha Obed, *Berlin, W Germany* (WBC)
18 Sep 76 Eckhard Dagge W PTS 15 Emile Griffith, *Berlin, W Germany* (WBC)
8 Oct 76 Miguel Castellini W PTS 15 Jose Duran, *Madrid, Spain* (WBA)
5 Mar 77 Eddie Gazo W PTS 15 Miguel Castellini, *Managua, Nicaragua* (WBA)
15 Mar 77 Eckhard Dagge DREW 15 Maurice Hope, *Berlin, W Germany* (WBC)
7 Jun 77 Eddie Gazo W RSC 11 Koichi Wajima, *Tokyo, Japan* (WBA)
6 Aug 77 Rocky Mattioli W KO 5 Eckhard Dagge, *Berlin, W Germany* (WBC)
13 Sep 77 Eddie Gazo W PTS 15 Kenji Shibata, *Tokyo, Japan* (WBA)
18 Dec 77 Eddie Gazo W PTS 15 Chae-Keun Lim, *Inchon, S Korea* (WBA)
11 Mar 78 Rocky Mattioli W KO 7 Elisha Obed, *Melbourne, Australia* (WBC)
14 May 78 Rocky Mattioli W RSC 5 Jose Duran, *Pescara, Italy* (WBC)
9 Aug 78 Masashi Kudo W PTS 15 Eddie Gazo, *Akita, Japan* (WBA)
13 Dec 78 Masashi Kudo W PTS 15 Ho-In Joo, *Osaka, Japan* (WBA)
4 Mar 79 Maurice Hope W RTD 8 Rocky Mattioli, *San Remo, Italy* (WBC)
13 Mar 79 Masashi Kudo W PTS 15 Manuel Gonzalez, *Tokyo, Japan* (WBA)
20 Jun 79 Masashi Kudo W RSC 12 Manuel Gonzalez, *Yokkaichi, Japan* (WBA)
25 Sep 79 Maurice Hope W RSC 7 Mike Baker, *Wembley, England* (WBC)
24 Oct 79 Ayub Kalule W PTS 15 Masashi Kudo, *Akita, Japan* (WBA)
6 Dec 79 Ayub Kalule W PTS 15 Steve Gregory, *Copenhagen, Denmark* (WBA)
17 Apr 80 Ayub Kalule W RTD 11 Emiliano Villa, *Copenhagen, Denmark* (WBA)
12 Jun 80 Ayub Kalule W PTS 15 Marijan Benes, *Randers, Denmark* (WBA)
12 Jul 80 Maurice Hope W RSC 11 Rocky Mattioli, *Wembley, England* (WBC)
6 Sep 80 Ayub Kalule W PTS 15 Bushy Bester, *Aarhus, Denmark* (WBA)
26 Nov 80 Maurice Hope W PTS 15 Carlos Herrera, *Wembley, England* (WBC)
24 May 81 Wilfred Benitez W KO 12 Maurice Hope, *Las Vegas, USA* (WBC)

Below: Maurice Hope (left) is congratulated by unsuccessful challenger, Rocky Mattioli, after their 1980 title fight.

***Above:** Don Curry (right) and champion Mike McCallum during their WBA light-middleweight title fight at Las Vegas in 1987. McCallum won with a knock-out.*

DATE	
25 Jun 81	Sugar Ray Leonard W RSC 9 Ayub Kalule, *Houston, USA* (WBA)
	Sugar Ray Leonard relinquished title to concentrate on the welterweight division
7 Nov 81	Tadashi Mihara W PTS 15 Rocky Fratto, *Rochester, USA* (WBA)
14 Nov 81	Wilfred Benitez W PTS 15 Carlos Santos, *Las Vegas, USA* (WBC)
30 Jan 82	Wilfred Benitez W PTS 15 Roberto Duran, *Las Vegas, USA* (WBC)
2 Feb 82	Davey Moore W RSC 6 Tadashi Mihara, *Tokyo, Japan* (WBA)
26 Apr 82	Davey Moore W KO 5 Charlie Weir, *Johannesburg, S Africa* (WBA)
17 Jul 82	Davey Moore W RSC 10 Ayub Kalule, *Atlantic C, USA* (WBA)
3 Dec 82	Thomas Hearns W PTS 15 Wilfred Benitez, *New Orleans, USA* (WBC)
29 Jan 83	Davey Moore W KO 4 Gary Guiden, *Atlantic C, USA* (WBA)
16 Jun 83	Roberto Duran W RSC 8 Davey Moore, *New York C, USA* (WBA)
	Roberto Duran relinquished title to campaign as a middleweight
11 Feb 84	Thomas Hearns W PTS 12 Luigi Minchillo, *Detroit, USA* (WBC)
11 Mar 84	Mark Medal W RSC 5 Earl Hargrove, *Atlantic C, USA* (IBF)
15 Jun 84	Thomas Hearns W KO 2 Roberto Duran, *Las Vegas, USA* (WBC)
15 Sep 84	Thomas Hearns W RSC 3 Fred Hutchings, *Saginaw, USA* (WBC)
19 Oct 84	Mike McCallum W PTS 15 Sean Mannion, *New York C, USA* (WBA)
2 Nov 84	Carlos Santos W PTS 15 Mark Medal, *New York C, USA* (IBF)
1 Dec 84	Mike McCallum W RSC 14 Luigi Minchillo, *Milan, Italy* (WBA)
1 Jun 85	Carlos Santos W PTS 15 Louis Acaries, *Paris, France* (IBF)
	Carlos Santos forfeited title (failure to defend against Davey Moore)
28 Jul 85	Mike McCallum W RSC 8 David Braxton, *Miami, USA* (WBA)
4 Jun 86	Buster Drayton W PTS 15 Carlos Santos, *E Rutherford, USA* (IBF)
23 Jun 86	Thomas Hearns W RSC 8 Mark Medal, *Las Vegas, USA* (WBC)
	Thomas Hearns relinquished title to campaign as a middleweight
23 Aug 86	Mike McCallum W RSC 2 Julian Jackson, *Miami, USA* (WBA)

DATE	
24 Aug 86	Buster Drayton W RSC 10 Davey Moore, *Juan les Pins, France* (IBF)
25 Oct 86	Mike McCallum W KO 9 Said Skouma, *Paris, France* (WBA)
5 Dec 86	Duane Thomas W RSC 3 John Mugabi, *Las Vegas, USA* (WBC)
27 Mar 87	Buster Drayton W RTD 10 Said Skouma, *Cannes, France* (IBF)
19 Apr 87	Mike McCallum W RSC 10 Milton McCrory, *Phoenix, USA* (WBA)
27 Jun 87	Matthew Hilton W PTS 15 Buster Drayton, *Montreal, Canada* (IBF)
12 Jul 87	Lupe Aquino W PTS 12 Duane Thomas, *Bordeaux, France* (WBC)
18 Jul 87	Mike McCallum W KO 5 Don Curry, *Las Vegas, USA* (WBA)
	Mike McCallum relinquished title to campaign as a middleweight
2 Oct 87	Gianfranco Rosi W PTS 12 Lupe Aquino, *Perugia, Italy* (WBC)
16 Oct 87	Matthew Hilton W RTD 2 Jack Callahan, *Atlantic City, USA* (IBF)
21 Nov 87	Julian Jackson W RSC 3 In-Chul Baek, *Las Vegas, USA* (WBA)
3 Jan 88	Gianfranco Rosi W RSC 7 Duane Thomas, *Genoa, Italy* (WBC)
8 Jul 88	Don Curry W RTD 9 Gianfranco Rosi, *San Remo, Italy* (WBC)
30 Jul 88	Julian Jackson W RSC 3 Buster Drayton, *Atlantic City, USA* (WBA)
4 Nov 88	Robert Hines W PTS 12 Matthew Hilton, *Las Vegas, USA* (IBF)

WELTERWEIGHT

(*Current weight limit:* 147lb/66.7kg)

DATE	
30 Oct 88	Paddy Duffy W KO 17 William McMillan, *Fort Foote, USA*
	Paddy Duffy died in 1890 while still champion
14 Dec 92	Mysterious Billy Smith W KO 14 Danny Needham, *San Francisco, USA*
17 Apr 93	Mysterious Billy Smith W KO 2 Tom Williams, *New York C, USA*
26 Jul 94	Tommy Ryan W PTS 20 Mysterious Billy Smith, *Minneapolis, USA*
18 Jan 95	Tommy Ryan W KO 3 Nonpareil Jack Dempsey, *New York C, USA*
27 May 95	Tommy Ryan NC 18 Mysterious Billy Smith, *New York C, USA*
2 Mar 96	Kid McCoy W KO 15 Tommy Ryan, *New York C, USA*
	Kid McCoy relinquished title to campaign as a middleweight
25 Nov 96	Tommy Ryan W DIS 9 Mysterious Billy Smith, *New York C, USA*
23 Dec 96	Tommy Ryan W KO 4 Bill Payne, *Syracuse, USA*
24 Feb 97	Tommy Ryan W KO 9 Tom Tracy, *Syracuse, USA*
	Tommy Ryan relinquished title to campaign as a middleweight
4 Apr 98	Mysterious Billy Smith DREW 25 Joe Walcott, *Bridgeport, USA*
29 Jul 98	Mysterious Billy Smith W PTS 25 George Green, *New York C, USA*
25 Aug 98	Mysterious Billy Smith W PTS 25 Matty Matthews, *New York C, USA*
5 Sep 98	Mysterious Billy Smith DREW 25 Andy Walsh, *New York C, USA*
3 Oct 98	Mysterious Billy Smith W KO 20 Jim Judge, *Scranton, USA*
7 Oct 98	Mysterious Billy Smith W PTS 25 Charley McKeever, *New York C, USA*
6 Dec 98	Mysterious Billy Smith W PTS 20 Joe Walcott, *New York C, USA*
24 Jan 99	Mysterious Billy Smith W KO 14 Billy Edwards, *New York C, USA*
10 Mar 99	Mysterious Billy Smith W RSC 14 George Lavigne, *San Francisco, USA*
29 Jun 99	Mysterious Billy Smith DREW 20 Charley McKeever, *New York C, USA*
4 Aug 99	Mysterious Billy Smith DREW 25 Andy Walsh, *New York C, USA*
8 Nov 99	Mysterious Billy Smith W PTS 20 Charley McKeever, *New York C, USA*
15 Jan 00	Rube Ferns W DIS 21 Mysterious Billy Smith, *Buffalo, USA*
13 Aug 00	Rube Ferns W RTD 15 Eddie Connolly, *Buffalo, USA*
1 Sep 00	Rube Ferns W PTS 15 Matty Matthews, *Detroit, USA*
16 Oct 00	Matty Matthews W PTS 15 Rube Ferns, *Detroit, USA*
29 Apr 01	Matty Matthews W PTS 20 Tom Couhig, *Louisville, USA*
24 May 01	Rube Ferns W KO 10 Matty Matthews, *Toronto, Canada*
23 Sep 01	Rube Ferns W KO 9 Frank Erne, *Fort Erie, Canada*
18 Dec 01	Joe Walcott W RSC 5 Rube Ferns, *Fort Erie, Canada*
23 Jun 02	Joe Walcott W PTS 15 Tommy West, *London, England*
2 Apr 03	Joe Walcott DREW 20 Billy Woods, *Los Angeles, USA*
29 Apr 04	Dixie Kid W DIS 20 Joe Walcott, *San Francisco, USA*
12 May 04	Dixie Kid DREW 20 Joe Walcott, *San Francisco, USA*
	Dixie Kid relinquished title (unable to make weight)
30 Sep 04	Joe Walcott DREW 20 Joe Gans, *San Francisco, USA*
16 Oct 06	Honey Mellody W PTS 15 Joe Walcott, *Chelsea, Mass, USA*
29 Nov 06	Honey Mellody W RSC 12 Joe Walcott, *Chelsea, Mass, USA*
23 Apr 07	Mike Twin Sullivan W PTS 20 Honey Mellody, *Los Angeles, USA*
1 Nov 07	Mike Twin Sullivan W PTS 20 Frank Field, *Goldfield, USA*
27 Nov 07	Mike Twin Sullivan W KO 13 Kid Farmer, *Los Angeles, USA*
23 Apr 08	Mike Twin Sullivan W PTS 25 Jimmy Gardner, *Los Angeles, USA*
	Mike Twin Sullivan relinquished title (eye injury)
7 Nov 08	Jimmy Gardner W PTS 15 Jimmy Clabby, *New Orleans, USA* (USA)
26 Nov 08	Jimmy Gardner DREW 20 Jimmy Clabby, *New Orleans, USA* (USA)
	Jimmy Gardner ceased to be recognized in the USA (unable to make the weight)
19 Feb 10	Harry Lewis DREW 25 Willie Lewis, *Paris, France* (FR)
23 Apr 10	Harry Lewis DREW 25 Willie Lewis, *Paris, France* (FR)
4 May 10	Harry Lewis W KO 3 Peter Brown, *Paris, France* (FR)
27 Jun 10	Harry Lewis W RTD 7 Young Joseph, *London, England* (GB/FR)
5 Sep 10	Jimmy Clabby W KO 13 Guy Buckles, *Sheridan, USA* (USA)
2 Nov 10	Jimmy Clabby W RSC 7 Bob Bryant, *Sydney, Australia* (USA/AUSTR)
26 Dec 10	Jimmy Clabby W KO 1 Gus Devitt, *Brisbane, Australia* (USA/AUSTR)
	Jimmy Clabby relinquished title to campaign as a middleweight
25 Jan 11	Harry Lewis W KO 4 Johnny Summers, *London, England* (GB/FR)
	Harry Lewis ceased to be recognized in GB and France (this followed two losing contests against Johnny Mathieson in 1912)
1 Jan 14	Waldemar Holberg W PTS 20 Ray Bronson, *Melbourne, Australia* (AUSTR)

DATE	
24 Jan 14	Tom McCormick W DIS 6 Waldemar Holberg, *Melbourne, Australia* (AUSTR)
14 Feb 14	Tom McCormick W KO 1 Johnny Summers, *Sydney, Australia* (AUSTR)
21 Mar 14	Matt Wells W PTS 20 Tom McCormick, *Sydney, Australia* (AUSTR)
1 Jun 15	Mike Glover W PTS 12 Matt Wells, *Boston, USA* (USA)
22 Jun 15	Jack Britton W PTS 12 Mike Glover, *Boston, USA* (USA)
31 Aug 15	Ted Kid Lewis W PTS 12 Jack Britton, *Boston, USA*
27 Sep 15	Ted Kid Lewis W PTS 12 Jack Britton, *Boston, USA*
26 Oct 15	Ted Kid Lewis W PTS 12 Joe Mandot, *Boston, USA*
2 Nov 15	Ted Kid Lewis W PTS 12 Milburn Saylor, *Boston, USA*
23 Nov 15	Ted Kid Lewis W KO 1 Jimmy Duffy, *Boston, USA*
1 Mar 16	Ted Kid Lewis W PTS 20 Harry Stone, *New Orleans, USA*
24 Apr 16	Jack Britton W PTS 20 Ted Kid Lewis, *New Orleans, USA*
6 Jun 16	Jack Britton W PTS 12 Mike O'Dowd, *Boston, USA*
17 Oct 16	Jack Britton W PTS 12 Ted Kid Lewis, *Boston, USA*
14 Nov 16	Jack Britton DREW 12 Ted Kid Lewis, *Boston, USA*
21 Nov 16	Jack Britton W PTS 12 Charley White, *Boston, USA*
25 Jun 17	Ted Kid Lewis W PTS 20 Jack Britton, *Dayton, USA*
13 Nov 17	Ted Kid Lewis W RSC 4 Johnny McCarthy, *San Francisco, USA*
17 May 18	Ted Kid Lewis W PTS 20 Johnny Tillman, *Denver, USA*
17 Mar 19	Jack Britton W KO 9 Ted Kid Lewis, *Canton, USA*
1 Dec 19	Jack Britton W KO 11 Billy Ryan, *Canton, USA*
31 May 20	Jack Britton W PTS 15 Johnny Griffiths, *Akron, USA*
23 Aug 20	Jack Britton DREW 12 Lou Bogash, *Bridgeport, USA*
6 Sep 20	Jack Britton W PTS 10 Ray Bronson, *Cedar Point, USA*
7 Feb 21	Jack Britton W PTS 15 Ted Kid Lewis, *New York C, USA*
3 Jun 21	Jack Britton DREW 10 Dave Shade, *Portland, USA*
10 Jun 21	Jack Britton DREW 10 Frank Barrieau, *Portland, USA*
17 Feb 22	Jack Britton DREW 15 Dave Shade, *New York C, USA*
26 Jun 22	Jack Britton W DIS 13 Benny Leonard, *New York C, USA*
1 Nov 22	Mickey Walker W PTS 15 Jack Britton, *New York C, USA*
2 Jun 24	Mickey Walker W PTS 10 Lew Tendler, *Philadelphia, USA*
1 Oct 24	Mickey Walker W KO 6 Bobby Barrett, *Philadelphia, USA*
21 Sep 25	Mickey Walker W PTS 15 Dave Shade, *New York C, USA*
20 May 26	Pete Latzo W PTS 10 Mickey Walker, *Scranton, USA*
29 Jun 26	Pete Latzo W KO 5 Willie Harmon, *Newark, USA*
9 Jul 26	Pete Latzo W DIS 4 George Levine, *New York C, USA*
3 Jun 37	Joe Dundee W PTS 15 Pete Latzo, *New York C, USA*
7 Jul 28	Joe Dundee W KO 8 Hilario Martinez, *Philadelphia, USA*
25 Mar 29	Jackie Fields W PTS 10 Young Jack Thompson, *Chicago, USA* (NBA)
25 Jul 29	Jackie Fields W DIS 2 Joe Dundee, *Detroit, USA*
9 May 30	Young Jack Thompson W PTS 15 Jackie Fields, *Detroit, USA*
5 May 30	Tommy Freeman W PTS 15 Young Jack Thompson, *Cleveland, USA*
9 Jan 31	Tommy Freeman W PTS 10 Pete August, *Hot Springs, USA*
26 Jan 31	Tommy Freeman W PTS 10 Eddie Murdoch, *Oklahoma C, USA*
5 Feb 31	Tommy Freeman W KO 5 Duke Trammel, *Memphis, USA*
9 Feb 31	Tommy Freeman W KO 5 Al Kid Kober, *New Orleans, USA*
1 Mar 31	Tommy Freeman W PTS 10 Alfredo Gaona, *Mexico C, Mexico*
14 Apr 31	Young Jack Thompson W RTD 12 Tommy Freeman, *Cleveland, USA*
23 Oct 31	Lou Brouillard W PTS 15 Young Jack Thompson, *Boston, USA*
28 Feb 32	Jackie Fields W PTS 10 Lou Brouillard, *Chicago, USA*
22 Feb 33	Young Corbett III W PTS 10 Jackie Fields, *San Francisco, USA*
29 May 33	Jimmy McLarnin W KO 1 Young Corbett III, *Los Angeles, USA*
28 May 34	Barney Ross W PTS 15 Jimmy McLarnin, *New York C, USA*
17 Sep 34	Jimmy McLarnin W PTS 15 Barney Ross, *New York C, USA*
28 May 35	Barney Ross W PTS 15 Jimmy McLarnin, *New York C, USA*
27 Nov 36	Barney Ross W PTS 15 Izzy Jannazzo, *New York C, USA*
23 Sep 37	Barney Ross W PTS 15 Ceferino Garcia, *New York C, USA*
31 May 38	Henry Armstrong W PTS 15 Barney Ross, *New York C, USA*
25 Nov 38	Henry Armstrong W PTS 15 Ceferino Garcia, *New York C, USA*
5 Dec 38	Henry Armstrong W RSC 3 Al Manfredo, *Cleveland, USA*
10 Jan 39	Henry Armstrong W PTS 10 Baby Arizmendi, *Los Angeles, USA*
4 Mar 39	Henry Armstrong W RSC 4 Bobby Pacho, *Havana, Cuba*
16 Mar 39	Henry Armstrong W KO 1 Lew Feldman, *St Louis, USA*
31 Mar 39	Henry Armstrong W KO 12 Davey Day, *New York C, USA*
25 May 39	Henry Armstrong W PTS 15 Ernie Roderick, *London, England*
9 Oct 39	Henry Armstrong W RSC 4 Al Manfredo, *Des Moines, USA*
13 Oct 39	Henry Armstrong W KO 2 Howard Scott, *Minneapolis, USA*
20 Oct 39	Henry Armstrong W KO 3 Richie Fontaine, *Seattle, USA*
24 Oct 39	Henry Armstrong W PTS 10 Jimmy Garrison, *Los Angeles, USA*
30 Oct 39	Henry Armstrong W RSC 4 Bobby Pacho, *Denver, USA*

DATE	
11 Dec 39	Henry Armstrong W KO 7 Jimmy Garrison, *Cleveland, USA*
4 Jan 40	Henry Armstrong W KO 5 Joe Ghnouly, *St Louis, USA*
24 Jan 40	Henry Armstrong W RSC 9 Pedro Montanez, *New York C, USA*
26 Apr 40	Henry Armstrong W RSC 7 Paul Junior, *Boston, USA*
24 May 40	Henry Armstrong W RSC 5 Ralph Zanelli, *Boston, USA*
21 Jun 40	Henry Armstrong W RSC 3 Paul Junior, *Portland, USA*
23 Sep 40	Henry Armstrong W KO 4 Phill Furr, *Washington, USA*
4 Oct 40	Fritzie Zivic W PTS 15 Henry Armstrong, *New York C, USA*
17 Jan 41	Fritzie Zivic W RSC 12 Henry Armstrong, *New York C, USA*
29 Jul 41	Red Cochrane W PTS 15 Fritzie Zivic, *Newark, USA*
1 Feb 46	Marty Servo W KO 4 Red Cochrane, *New York C, USA*
	Marty Servo relinquished title (retired)
20 Dec 46	Sugar Ray Robinson W PTS 15 Tommy Bell, *New York C, USA*
24 Jun 47	Sugar Ray Robinson W RSC 8 Jimmy Doyle, *Cleveland, USA*
19 Dec 47	Sugar Ray Robinson W RSC 6 Chuck Taylor, *Detroit, USA*
28 Jan 48	Sugar Ray Robinson W PTS 15 Bernard Docusen, *Chicago, USA*
11 Jul 49	Sugar Ray Robinson W PTS 15 Kid Gavilan, *Philadelphia, USA*
9 Aug 50	Sugar Ray Robinson W PTS 15 Charlie Fusari, *Jersey C, USA*
	Sugar Ray Robinson relinquished title to campaign as a middleweight
14 Mar 51	Johnny Bratton W PTS 15 Charlie Fusari, *Chicago, USA* (NBA)
18 May 51	Kid Gavilan W PTS 15 Johnny Bratton, *New York C, USA* (NBA/NY)
29 Aug 51	Kid Gavilan W PTS 15 Billy Graham, *New York C, USA* (NBA/NY)
4 Feb 52	Kid Gavilan W PTS 15 Bobby Dykes, *Miami, USA* (NBA/NY)
7 Jul 52	Kid Gavilan W RSC 11 Gil Turner, *Philadelphia, USA*
3 Oct 52	Kid Gavilan W PTS 15 Billy Graham, *Havana, Cuba*
11 Feb 53	Kid Gavilan W RTD 9 Chuck Davey, *Chicago, USA*
6 Jun 53	Carmen Basilio W PTS 12 Billy Graham, *Syracuse, USA* (NY)
25 Jul 53	Carmen Basilio DREW 12 Billy Graham, *Syracuse, USA* (NY)
18 Sep 53	Kid Gavilan W PTS 15 Carmen Basilio, *Syracuse, USA*
13 Nov 53	Kid Gavilan W PTS 15 Johnny Bratton, *Chicago, USA*
20 Oct 54	Johnny Saxton W PTS 15 Kid Gavilan, *Philadelphia, USA*
1 Apr 55	Tony de Marco W RSC 14 Johnny Saxton, *Boston, USA*
10 Jun 55	Carmen Basilio W RSC 12 Tony de Marco, *Syracuse, USA*
30 Nov 55	Carmen Basilio W RSC 12 Tony De Marco, *Boston, USA*
14 Mar 56	Johnny Saxton W PTS 15 Carmen Basilio, *Chicago, USA*
12 Sep 56	Carmen Basilio W RSC 9 Johnny Saxton, *Syracuse, USA*
22 Feb 57	Carmen Basilio W KO 2 Johnny Saxton, *Cleveland, USA*
	Carmen Basilio relinquished title to campaign as a middleweight
5 Jun 58	Virgil Akins W RSC 4 Vince Martinez, *St Louis, USA*
5 Dec 58	Don Jordan W PTS 15 Virgil Akins, *Los Angeles, USA*

DATE	
24 Apr 59	Don Jordan W PTS 15 Virgil Akins, *St Louis, USA*
10 Jul 59	Don Jordan W PTS 15 Denny Moyer, *Portland, USA*
27 May 60	Benny Kid Paret W PTS 15 Don Jordan, *Las Vegas, USA*
10 Dec 60	Benny Kid Paret W PTS 15 Federico Thompson, *New York C, USA*
1 Apr 61	Emile Griffith W KO 13 Benny Kid Paret, *Miami, USA*
3 Jun 61	Emile Griffith W RSC 12 Gaspar Ortega, *Los Angeles, USA*
30 Sep 61	Benny Kid Paret W PTS 15 Emile Griffith, *New York C, USA*
24 Mar 62	Emile Griffith W RSC 12 Benny Kid Paret, *New York C, USA*
13 Jul 62	Emile Griffith W PTS 15 Ralph Dupas, *Las Vegas, USA*
8 Dec 62	Emile Griffith W RTD 9 Jorge Fernandez, *Las Vegas, USA*
21 Mar 63	Luis Rodriguez W PTS 15 Emile Griffith, *Los Angeles, USA*
8 Jun 63	Emile Griffith W PTS 15 Luis Rodriguez, *New York C, USA*
12 Jun 64	Emile Griffith W PTS 15 Luis Rodriguez, *Las Vegas, USA*
22 Sep 64	Emile Griffith W PTS 15 Brian Curvis, *Wembley, England*
30 Mar 65	Emile Griffith W PTS 15 Jose Stable, *New York C, USA*
10 Dec 65	Emile Griffith W PTS 15 Manuel Gonzalez, *New York C, USA*
	Emile Griffith relinquished title to campaign as a middleweight
24 Aug 66	Curtis Cokes W PTS 15 Manuel Gonzalez, *New Orleans, USA* (WBA)
28 Nov 66	Curtis Cokes W PTS 15 Jean Josselin, *Dallas, USA* (WBA)
7 Dec 66	Charlie Shipes W RSC 10 Percy Manning, *Hayward, USA* (CALIF)
19 May 67	Curtis Cokes W RSC 10 Francois Pavilla, *Dallas, USA* (WBA)
2 Oct 67	Curtis Cokes W RSC 8 Charlie Shipes, *Oakland, USA*
16 Apr 68	Curtis Cokes W RSC 5 Willie Ludick, *Dallas, USA*
21 Oct 68	Curtis Cokes W PTS 15 Ramon la Cruz, *New Orleans, USA*
18 Apr 69	Jose Napoles W RSC 13 Curtis Cokes, *Los Angeles, USA*
29 Jun 69	Jose Napoles W RTD 10 Curtis Cokes, *Mexico C, Mexico*
17 Oct 69	Jose Napoles W PTS 15 Emile Griffith, *Los Angeles, USA*
15 Feb 70	Jose Napoles W RSC 15 Ernie Lopez, *Los Angeles, USA*
3 Dec 70	Billy Backus W RSC 4 Jose Napoles, *Syracuse, USA*
4 Jun 71	Jose Napoles W RSC 8 Billy Backus, *Los Angeles, USA*
14 Dec 71	Jose Napoles W PTS 15 Hedgemon Lewis, *Los Angeles, USA*
28 Mar 72	Jose Napoles W KO 7 Ralph Charles, *Wembley, England*
10 Jun 72	Jose Napoles W RSC 2 Adolph Pruitt, *Monterrey, Mexico*
16 Jun 72	Hedgemon Lewis W PTS 15 Billy Backus, *Syracuse, USA* (NY)
8 Dec 72	Hedgemon Lewis W PTS 15 Billy Backus, *Syracuse, USA* (NY)
28 Feb 73	Jose Napoles W KO 7 Ernie Lopez, *Los Angeles, USA*
23 Jun 73	Jose Napoles W PTS 15 Roger Menetrey, *Grenoble, France*
22 Sep 73	Jose Napoles W PTS 15 Clyde Gray, *Toronto, Canada*
3 Aug 74	Jose Napoles W RSC 9 Hedgemon Lewis, *Mexico C, Mexico*
14 Dec 74	Jose Napoles W KO 3 Horacio Saldano, *Mexico C, Mexico*

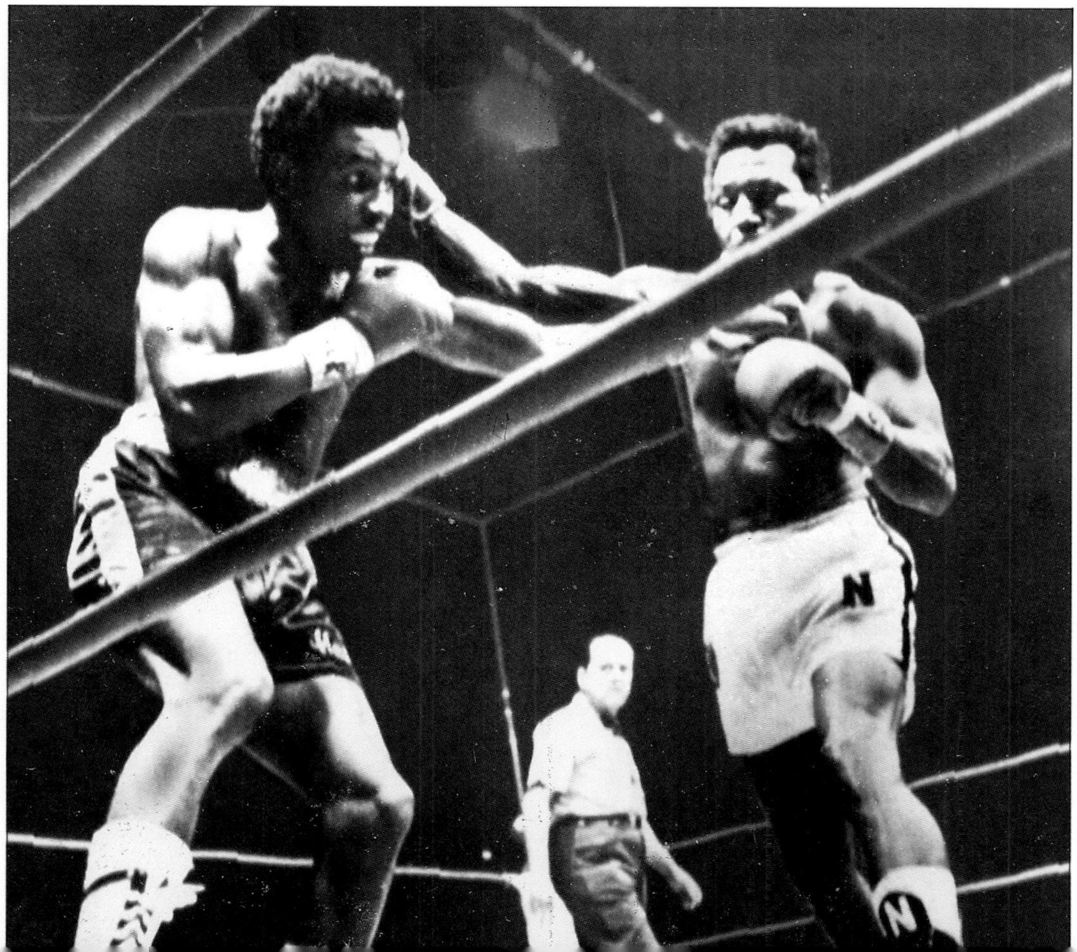

***Left:** Jose Napoles, known as 'Mantequilla' because he was as smooth as butter, gets a right to the head of welterweight challenger Hedgemon Lewis before the fight was stopped in his favour in 1974.*

Above: *Lloyd Honeyghan (on the right) boxing Maurice Blocker in London in 1987 for the world welterweight title. Honeyghan won on points.*

DATE	
30 Mar 75	Jose Napoles W TD 12 Armando Muniz, *Acapulco, Mexico* *Jose Napoles relinquished WBA title to concentrate on the WBC title (the requirements of the two bodies clashed)*
28 Jun 75	Angel Espada W PTS 15 Clyde Gray, *San Juan, Puerto Rico* (WBA)
12 Jul 75	Jose Napoles W PTS 15 Armando Muniz, *Mexico C, Mexico* (WBC)
11 Oct 75	Angel Espada W PTS 15 Johnny Gant, *San Juan, Puerto Rico* (WBA)
6 Dec 75	John H. Stracey W RSC 6 Jose Napoles, *Mexico C, Mexico* (WBC)
20 Mar 76	John H. Stracey W RSC 10 Hedgemon Lewis, *Wembley, England* (WBC)
27 Apr 76	Angel Espada W RS 8 Alfonso Hayman, *San Juan, Puerto Rico* (WBA)
22 Jun 76	Carlos Palomino W RSC 12 John H. Stracey, *Wembley, England* (WBC)
17 Jul 76	Pipino Cuevas W RSC 2 Angel Espada, *Mexicali, Mexico* (WBA)
27 Oct 76	Pipino Cuevas W KO 6 Shoji Tsujimoto, *Kanazawa, Japan* (WBA)
22 Jan 77	Carlos Palomino W RSC 15 Armando Muniz, *Los Angeles, USA* (WBC)
12 Mar 77	Pipino Cuevas W KO 2 Miguel Campanino, *Mexico C, Mexico* (WBA)
14 Jun 77	Carlos Palomino W KO 11 Dave Boy Green, *Wembley, England* (WBC)
6 Aug 77	Pipino Cuevas W KO 2 Clyde Gray, *Los Angeles, USA* (WBA)
13 Sep 77	Carlos Palomino W PTS 15 Everaldo Azevedo, *Los Angeles, USA* (WBC)
19 Nov 77	Pipino Cuevas W RSC 11 Angel Espada, *San Juan, Puerto Rico* (WBA)
10 Dec 77	Carlos Palomino W KO 13 Jose Palacios, *Los Angeles, USA* (WBC)
11 Feb 78	Carlos Palomino W KO 7 Ryu Sorimachi, *Las Vegas, USA* (WBC)
4 Mar 78	Pipino Cuevas W RSC 9 Harold Weston, *Los Angeles, USA* (WBA)
18 Mar 78	Carlos Palomino W RSC 9 Mimoun Mohatar, *Las Vegas, USA* (WBC)
20 May 78	Pipino Cuevas W RSC 1 Billy Backus, *Los Angeles, USA* (WBA)
27 May 78	Carlos Palomino W PTS 15 Armando Muniz, *Los Angeles, USA* (WBC)
9 Sep 78	Pipino Cuevas W RSC 2 Pete Ranzany, *Sacramento, USA* (WBA)
14 Jan 79	Wilfred Benitez W PTS 15 Carlos Palomino, *San Juan, Puerto Rico* (WBC)
29 Jan 79	Pipino Cuevas W RSC 2 Scott Clark, *Los Angeles, USA* (WBA)
25 Mar 79	Wilfred Benitez W PTS 15 Harold Weston, *San Juan, Puerto Rico* (WBA)
30 Jul 79	Pipino Cuevas W PTS 15 Randy Shields, *Chicago, USA* (WBA)
30 Nov 79	Sugar Ray Leonard W RSC 15 Wilfred Benitez, *Las Vegas, USA* (WBC)
8 Dec 79	Pipino Cuevas W RSC 10 Angel Espada, *Los Angeles, USA* (WBA)

DATE	
31 Mar 80	Sugar Ray Leonard W KO 4 Dave Boy Green, *Landover, USA* (WBC)
6 Apr 80	Pipino Cuevas W KO 5 Harold Volbrecht, *Houston, USA* (WBA)
20 Jun 80	Roberto Duran W PTS 15 Sugar Ray Leonard, *Montreal, Canada* (WBC)
2 Aug 80	Thomas Hearns W RSC 2 Pipino Cuevas, *Detroit, USA* (WBA)
25 Nov 80	Sugar Ray Leonard W RTD 8 Roberto Duran, *New Orleans, USA* (WBC)
6 Dec 80	Thomas Hearns W KO 6 Luis Primera, *Detroit, USA* (WBA)
28 Mar 81	Sugar Ray Leonard W RSC 10 Larry Bonds, *Syracuse, USA* (WBC)
25 Apr 81	Thomas Hearns W RSC 12 Randy Shields, *Phoenix, USA* (WBA)
25 Jun 81	Thomas Hearns W RSC 4 Pablo Baez, *Houston, USA* (WBA)
16 Sep 81	Sugar Ray Leonard W RSC 14 Thomas Hearns, *Las Vegas, USA*
15 Feb 82	Sugar Ray Leonard W RSC 3 Bruce Finch, *Reno, USA* *Sugar Ray Leonard relinquished title (retired)*
13 Feb 83	Don Curry W PTS 15 Jun-Sok Hwang, *Fort Worth, USA* (WBA)
19 Mar 83	Milton McCrory DREW 12 Colin Jones, *Reno, USA* (WBC)
13 Aug 83	Milton McCrory W PTS 12 Colin Jones, *Las Vegas, USA* (WBC)
3 Sep 83	Don Curry W RSC 1 Roger Stafford, *Marsala, Italy* (WBA)
14 Jan 84	Milton McCrory W RSC 6 Milton Guest, *Detroit, USA* (WBC)
4 Feb 84	Don Curry W PTS 15 Marlon Starling, *Atlantic C, USA* (WBA/IBF)
15 Apr 84	Milton McCrory W RSC 6 Gilles Ebilia, *Detroit, USA* (WBC)
21 Apr 84	Don Curry W RTD 7 Elio Diaz, *Fort Worth, USA* (WBA/IBF)
22 Sep 84	Don Curry W RSC 6 Nino la Rocca, *Monte Carlo* (WBA/IBF)
19 Jan 85	Don Curry W RSC 4 Colin Jones, *Birmingham, England* (WBA/IBF)
9 Mar 85	Milton McCrory W PTS 12 Pedro Vilella, *Paris, France* (WBC)
14 Jul 85	Milton McCrory W RSC 3 Carlos Trujillo, *Monte Carlo* (WBC)
6 Dec 85	Don Curry W KO 2 Milton McCrory, *Las Vegas, USA* (WBA/WBC)
9 Mar 86	Don Curry W KO 2 Eduardo Rodriguez, *Fort Worth, USA* (WBA)
27 Sep 86	Lloyd Honeyghan W RTD 6 Don Curry, *Atlantic C, USA* *Lloyd Honeyghan relinquished WBA title when South African Harold Volbrecht was named as contender on the grounds of apartheid*
6 Feb 87	Mark Breland W KO 7 Harold Volbrecht, *Atlantic C, USA* (WBA)
22 Feb 87	Lloyd Honeyghan W RSC 2 Johnny Bumphus, *Wembley, England* (IBF)
18 Apr 87	Lloyd Honeyghan W PTS 12 Maurice Blocker, *London, England* (WBC)
22 Aug 87	Marlon Starling W KO 11 Mark Breland, *Columbia USA* (WBA)
30 Aug 87	Lloyd Honeyghan W RSC 1 Gene Hatcher, *Marbella, Spain* (WBC)
28 Oct 87	Jorge Vaca W TD 8 Lloyd Honeyghan, *Wembley, England* (WBC) *Lloyd Honeyghan was stripped of his IBF title after this defeat*
5 Feb 88	Marlon Starling W PTS 12 Fujio Ozaki, *Atlantic City, USA* (WBA)
29 Mar 88	Lloyd Honeyghan W KO 3 Jorge Vaca, *Wembley, England* (WBC)

DATE	
16 Apr 88	Marlon Starling DREW 12 Mark Breland, *Las Vegas, USA* (WBA)
23 Apr 88	Simon Brown W RSC 14 Tyrone Trice, *Berck-sur-Mer, France* (IBF)
16 Jul 88	Simon Brown W RSC 3 Jorge Vaca, *Kingston, Jamaica* (IBF)
29 Jul 88	Tomas Molinares W KO 6 Marlon Starling, *Atlantic City, USA* (WBA)
29 Jul 88	Lloyd Honeyghan W RSC 5 Jung-Kil Chung, *Atlantic City, USA* (WBC)
14 Oct 88	Simon Brown W PTS 12 Mauro Martelli, *Lausanne, Switzerland* (IBF)

LIGHT-WELTERWEIGHT

(*Current weight limit:* 140lb/63.5kg. The WBA and IBF call the class 'Junior Welterweight' and the WBC calls the class 'Super-lightweight')

DATE	
21 Sep 26	Mushy Callahan W PTS 10 Pinkey Mitchell, *Los Angeles, USA* (NY/NBA)
14 Mar 27	Mushy Callahan W KO 2 Andy Divodi, *New York C, USA* (NY/NBA)
31 May 27	Mushy Callahan W PTS 10 Spug Myers, *Chicago, USA* (NY/NBA)
28 May 29	Mushy Callahan W KO 3 Fred Mahan, *Los Angeles, USA* (NY/NBA)
	New York abolished the division
18 Feb 30	Jack Kid Berg W RTD 10 Mushy Callahan, *London, England* (NBA)
29 May 30	Jack Kid Berg W RSC 4 Al Delmont, *Newark, USA* (NBA)
12 Jun 30	Jack Kid Berg W RSC 10 Herman Perlick, *New York C, USA* (NBA)
3 Sep 30	Jack Kid Berg W PTS 10 Buster Brown, *Newark, USA* (NBA)
23 Jan 31	Jack Kid Berg W PTS 10 Goldie Hess, *Chicago, USA* (NBA)
10 Apr 31	Jack Kid Berg W PTS 10 Billy Wallace, *Detroit, USA* (NBA)
24 Apr 31	Tony Canzoneri W KO 3 Jack Kid Berg, *Chicago, USA* (NBA)
13 Jul 31	Tony Canzoneri W PTS 10 Cecil Payne, *Los Angeles, USA* (NBA)
29 Oct 31	Tony Canzoneri W PTS 10 Phillie Griffin, *Newark, USA* (NBA)
18 Jan 32	Johnny Jadick W PTS 10 Tony Canzoneri, *Philadelphia, USA* (NBA)
18 Jul 32	Johnny Jadick W PTS 10 Tony Canzoneri, *Philadelphia, USA* (NBA)
20 Feb 33	Battling Shaw W PTS 10 Johnny Jadick, *New Orleans, USA* (NBA)
21 May 33	Tony Canzoneri W PTS 10 Battling Shaw, *New Orleans*, USA (NBA)
23 Jun 33	Barney Ross W PTS 10 Tony Canzoneri, *Chicago, USA* (NBA)
26 Jul 33	Barney Ross W RSC 6 Johnny Farr, *Kansas C, USA* (NBA)
17 Nov 33	Barney Ross W PTS 10 Sammy Fuller, *Chicago, USA* (NBA)
7 Feb 34	Barney Ross W PTS 12 Pete Nebo, *New Orleans, USA* (NBA)
5 Mar 34	Barney Ross DREW 10 Frankie Klick, *San Francisco, USA* (NBA)
27 Mar 34	Barney Ross W PTS 10 Bobby Pacho, *Los Angeles, USA* (NBA)
10 Dec 34	Barney Ross W PTS 12 Bobby Pacho, *Cleveland, USA* (NBA)
28 Jan 35	Barney Ross W PTS 10 Frankie Klick, *Miami, USA* (NBA)
9 Apr 35	Barney Ross W PTS 12 Harry Woods, *Seattle, USA* (NBA)
	Barney Ross relinquished title to concentrate on defending his welterweight title. The division fell into disuse
29 Apr 46	Tippy Larkin W PTS 12 Willie Joyce, *Boston, USA* (MASS)
13 Sep 46	Tippy Larkin W PTS 12 Willie Joyce, *New York C, USA* (MASS/NY)
	Tippy Larkin ceased to be recognized by NY and Massachusetts because of a defeat by Ike Williams in a non-title bout, June, 1947. The division again fell into disuse
12 Jun 59	Carlos Ortiz W RTD 2 Kenny Lane, *New York C, USA* (NBA)
4 Feb 60	Carlos Ortiz W KO 10 Battling Torres, *Los Angeles, USA* (NBA)
15 Jun 60	Carlos Ortiz W PTS 15 Duilio Loi, *San Francisco, USA* (NBA)
1 Sep 60	Duilio Loi W PTS 15 Carlos Ortiz, *Milan, Italy* (NBA)
10 May 61	Duilio Loi W PTS 15 Carlos Ortiz, *Milan, Italy* (NBA)
21 Oct 61	Duilio Loi DREW 15 Eddie Perkins, *Milan, Italy* (NBA)
14 Sep 62	Eddie Perkins W PTS 15 Duilio Loi, *Milan, Italy* (NBA)
15 Dec 62	Duilio Loi W PTS 15 Eddie Perkins, *Milan, Italy* (NBA)
	Duilio Loi relinquished NBA version of title (retired)
21 Mar 63	Roberto Cruz W KO 1 Battling Torres, *Los Angeles, USA* (WBA)
15 Jun 63	Eddie Perkins W PTS 15 Roberto Cruz, *Manila, Philippines* (WBA)
4 Jan 64	Eddie Perkins W RSC 13 Yoshinori Takahashi, *Tokyo, Japan* (WBA)

DATE	
18 Apr 64	Eddie Perkins W PTS 15 Bunny Grant, *Kingston, Jamaica* (WBA)
18 Jan 65	Carlos Hernandez W PTS 15 Eddie Perkins, *Caracas, Venezuela*
15 May 65	Carlos Hernandez W RSC 4 Mario Rossito, *Maracaibo, Venezuela*
10 Jul 65	Carlos Hernandez W KO 3 Percy Hayles, *Kingston, Jamaica*
30 Apr 66	Sandro Lopopolo W PTS 15 Carlos Hernandez, *Rome, Italy*
21 Oct 66	Sandro Lopopolo W RSC 7 Vicente Rivas, *Rome, Italy*
30 Apr 67	Paul Fujii W RTD 2 Sandro Lopopolo, *Tokyo, Japan*
16 Nov 67	Paul Fujii W KO 4 Willi Quatuor, *Tokyo, Japan*
	Paul Fujii forfeited WBC recognition (failure to defend against Pedro Adigue)
12 Dec 68	Nicolino Loche W RTD 9 Paul Fujii, *Tokyo, Japan* (WBA)
14 Dec 68	Pedro Adigue W PTS 15 Adolph Pruitt, *Quezon C, Philippines* (WBC)
3 May 69	Nicolino Loche W PTS 15 Carlos Hernandez, *Buenos Aires, Argentine* (WBA)
11 Oct 69	Nicolino Loche W PTS 15 Joao Henrique, *Buenos Aires, Argentine* (WBA)
1 Feb 70	Bruno Arcari W PTS 15 Pedro Adigue, *Rome, Italy* (WBC)
16 May 70	Nicolino Loche W PTS 15 Adolph Pruitt, *Buenos Aires, Argentine* (WBA)
10 Jul 70	Bruno Arcari W DIS 6 Rene Roque, *Lignano, Italy* (WBC)
30 Oct 70	Bruno Arcari W KO 3 Raymundo Dias, *Genoa, Italy* (WBC)
6 May 71	Bruno Arcari W PTS 15 Joao Henrique, *Rome, Italy* (WBC)
3 Apr 71	Nicolino Loche W PTS 15 Domingo Barrera, *Buenos Aires, Argentine* (WBA)
26 Jun 71	Bruno Arcari W RSC 9 Enrique Jana, *Palermo, Italy* (WBC)
10 Oct 71	Bruno Arcari W KO 10 Domingo Corpas, *Genoa, Italy* (WBC)
11 Dec 71	Nicolino Loche W PTS 15 Antonio Cervantes, *Buenos Aires, Argentine* (WBA)
10 Mar 72	Alfonso Frazer W PTS 15 Nicolino Loche, *Panama C, Panama* (WBA)
10 Jun 72	Bruno Arcari W KO 12 Joao Henrique, *Genoa, Italy* (WBC)
17 Jun 72	Alfonso Frazer W RTD 4 Al Ford, *Panama C, Panama* (WBA)
28 Oct 72	Antonio Cervantes W KO 10 Alfonso Frazer, *Panama C, Panama* (WBA)
2 Dec 72	Bruno Arcari W PTS 15 Costa Azevedo, *Turin, Italy* (WBC)
16 Feb 73	Antonio Cervantes W PTS 15 Josua Marquez, *San Juan, Puerto Rico* (WBA)
17 Mar 73	Antonio Cervantes W RTD 9 Nicolino Loche, *Maracay, Venezuela* (WBA)
19 May 73	Antonio Cervantes W RSC 5 Alfonso Frazer, *Panama C, Panama* (WBA)
8 Sep 73	Antonio Cervantes W RSC 5 Carlos Giminez, *Bogota, Colombia* (WBA)
4 Dec 73	Antonio Cervantes W PTS 15 Lion Furuyama, *Panama C, Panama* (WBA)
16 Feb 74	Bruno Arcari W DIS 8 Tony Ortiz, *Turin, Italy* (WBC)
	Bruno Arcari relinquished title (unable to make weight)
2 Mar 74	Antonio Cervantes W KO 6 Chang-Kil Lee, *Cartagena, Colombia* (WBA)
27 Jul 74	Antonio Cervantes W KO 2 Victor Ortiz, *Cartagena, Colombia* (WBA)
21 Sep 74	Perico Fernandez W PTS 15 Lion Furuyama, *Rome, Italy* (WBC)
26 Oct 74	Antonio Cervantes W KO 8 Shinchi Kadoto, *Tokyo, Japan* (WBA)
19 Apr 75	Perico Fernandez W KO 9 Joao Henrique, *Barcelona, Spain* (WBC)
17 May 75	Antonio Cervantes W PTS 15 Esteban de Jesus, *Panama C, Panama* (WBA)
15 Jul 75	Saensak Muangsurin W RTD 8 Perico Fernandez, *Bangkok, Thailand* (WBC)
15 Nov 75	Antonio Cervantes W RTD 7 Hector Thompson, *Panama C, Panama* (WBA)
25 Jan 76	Saensak Muangsurin W PTS 15 Lion Furuyama, *Tokyo, Japan* (WBC)
6 Mar 76	Wilfred Benitez W PTS 15 Antonio Cervantes, *San Juan, Puerto Rico* (WBA)
31 May 76	Wilfred Benitez W PTS 15 Emiliano Villa, *San Juan, Puerto Rico* (WBA)
30 Jun 76	Miguel Velasquez W DIS 4 Saensak Muangsurin, *Madrid, Spain* (WBC)
16 Oct 76	Wilfred Benitez W RSC 3 Tony Petronelli, *San Juan, Puerto Rico* (WBA)
	Wilfred Benitez forfeited WBA recognition (failure to defend against Antonio Cervantes)
29 Oct 76	Saensak Muangsurin W RSC 2 Miguel Velasquez, *Segovia, Spain* (WBC)
15 Jan 77	Saensak Muangsurin W RSC 15 Monroe Brooks, *Chiang, Thailand* (WBC)

DATE	
2 Apr 77	Saensak Muangsurin W KO 6 Guts Ishimatsu, *Tokyo, Japan* (WBC)
17 Jun 77	Saensak Muangsurin W PTS 15 Perico Fernandez, *Madrid, Spain* (WBC)
25 Jan 77	Antonio Cervantes W RSC 5 Carlos Giminez, *Maracaibo, Venezuela* (WBA)
3 Aug 77	Wilfred Benitez W RSC 15 Guerrero Chavez, *New York C, USA* (NY) *Wilfred Benitez ceased to be recognized by NY (moved up to welterweight)*
20 Aug 77	Saensak Muangsurin W RSC 6 Mike Everett, *Roi-Et, Thailand* (WBC)
22 Oct 77	Saensak Muangsurin W PTS 15 Saoul Mamby, *Korat, Thailand* (WBC)
5 Nov 77	Antonio Cervantes W PTS 15 Adriano Marrero, *Maracay, Venezuela* (WBA)
29 Dec 77	Saensak Muangsurin W RTD 13 Jo Kimpuani, *Chanthabun, Thailand* (WBC)
8 Apr 78	Saensak Muangsurin W KO 13 Francisco Moreno, *Hat Yai, Thailand* (WBC)
28 Apr 78	Antonio Cervantes W KO 6 Tonga Kiatvayupakdi, *Udon, Thailand* (WBA)
26 Aug 78	Antonio Cervantes W RSC 9 Norman Sekgapane, *Botswana* (WBA)
30 Dec 78	Sang-Hyun Kim W KO 13 Saensak Muangsurin, *Seoul, S Korea* (WBC)
18 Jan 79	Antonio Cervantes W PTS 15 Miguel Montilla, *New York C, USA* (WBA)
3 Jun 79	Sang-Hyun Kim W PTS 15 Fitzroy Guisseppi, *Seoul, S Korea* (WBC)
25 Aug 79	Antonio Cervantes W PTS 15 Kwang-Min Kim, *Seoul, S Korea* (WBA)
4 Oct 79	Sang-Hyun Kim W KO 11 Masahiro Yokai, *Tokyo, Japan* (WBC)
23 Feb 80	Saoul Mamby W KO 14 Sang-Hyun Kim, *Seoul, S Korea* (WBC)
29 Mar 80	Antonio Cervantes W RSC 7 Miguel Montilla, *Cartagena, Colombia* (WBA)
7 July 80	Saoul Mamby W RSC 13 Esteban de Jesus, *Bloomington, USA* (WBC)
2 Aug 80	Aaron Pryor W KO 4 Antonio Cervantes, *Cincinnati, USA* (WBA)
2 Oct 80	Saoul Mamby W PTS 15 Maurice Watkins, *Las Vegas, USA* (WBC)
22 Nov 80	Aaron Pryor W RSC 6 Gaetan Hart, *Cincinnati, USA* (WBA)
12 Jun 81	Saoul Mamby W PTS 15 Jo Kimpuani, *Detroit, USA* (WBC)
27 Jun 81	Aaron Pryor W RSC 2 Lennox Blackmore, *Las Vegas, USA* (WBA)
29 Aug 81	Saoul Mamby W PTS 15 Thomas Americo, *Jakarta, Indonesia* (WBC)
14 Nov 81	Aaron Pryor W RSC 7 Dujuan Johnson, *Cleveland, USA* (WBA)
20 Dec 81	Saoul Mamby W PTS 15 Obisia Nwankpa, *Lagos, Nigeria* (WBC)
21 Mar 82	Aaron Pryor 2 RSC 12 Miguel Montilla, *Atlantic C, USA* (WBA)
26 Jun 82	Leroy Haley W PTS 15 Saoul Mamby, *Cleveland, USA* (WBC)
4 Jul 82	Aaron Pryor W RSC 6 Akio Kameda, *Cincinnati, USA* (WBA)
20 Oct 82	Leroy Haley W PTS 15 Juan Giminez, *Cleveland, USA* (WBC)
12 Nov 82	Aaron Pryor W RSC 14 Alexis Arguello, *Miami, USA* (WBA)
13 Feb 83	Leroy Haley W PTS 12 Saoul Mamby, *Cleveland, USA* (WBC)
2 Apr 83	Aaron Pryor W RSC 3 Sang-Hyun Kim, *Atlantic C, USA* (WBA)
18 May 83	Bruce Curry W PTS 12 Leroy Haley, *Las Vegas, USA* (WBC)
7 Jul 83	Bruce Curry W RSC 7 Hidekazu Akai, *Osaka, Japan* (WBC)
9 Sep 83	Aaron Pryor W KO 10 Alexis Arguello, *Las Vegas, USA* (WBA) *Aaron Pryor relinquished title (retired)*
19 Oct 83	Bruce Curry W PTS 12 Leroy Haley, *Las Vegas, USA* (WBC)
22 Jan 84	Johnny Bumphus W PTS 15 Lorenzo Garcia, *Atlantic C, USA* (WBA)
29 Jan 84	Bill Costello W RSC 10 Bruce Curry, *Beaumont, USA* (WBC)
1 Jun 84	Gene Hatcher W RSC 11 Johnny Bumphus, *Buffalo, USA* (WBA)
22 Jun 84	Aaron Pryor W PTS 15 Nicky Furlano, *Toronto, Canada* (IBF)
15 Jul 84	Bill Costello W PTS 12 Ronnie Shields, *Kingston NY, USA* (WBC)
3 Nov 84	Bill Costello W PTS 12 Saoul Mamby, *Kingston NY, USA* (WBC)
15 Dec 84	Gene Hatcher W PTS 15 Ubaldo Sacco, *Fort Worth, USA* (WBA)
16 Feb 84	Bill Costello W PTS 12 Leroy Haley, *Kingston NY, USA* (WBC)
2 Mar 85	Aaron Pryor W PTS 15 Gary Hinton, *Atlantic C, USA* (IBF) *Aaron Pryor forfeited title (inactive)*
21 Jul 85	Ubaldo Sacco W RSC 9 Gene Hatcher, *Campione, Italy* (WBA)
21 Aug 85	Lonnie Smith W RSC 8 Bill Costello, *New York C, USA* (WBC)
15 Mar 86	Patrizio Oliva W PTS 15 Ubaldo Sacco, *Monte Carlo* (WBA)
26 Apr 86	Gary Hinton W PTS 15 Antonio Reyes Cruz, *Lucca, Italy* (IBF)
5 May 86	Rene Arredondo W RSC 5 Lonnie Smith, *Los Angeles, USA* (WBC)
24 Jul 86	Tsuyoshi Hamada W KO 1 Rene Arredondo, *Tokyo, Japan* (WBC)
6 Sep 86	Patrizio Oliva W RSC 3 Brian Brunette, *Naples, Italy* (WBA)
30 Oct 86	Joe Manley W KO 10 Gary Hinton, *Hartford, USA* (IBF)
2 Dec 86	Tsuyoshi Hamada W PTS 12 Ronnie Shields, *Tokyo, Japan* (WBC)
10 Jan 87	Patrizio Oliva W PTS 15 Rodolfo Gonzalez, *Agrigento, Italy* (WBA)
4 Mar 87	Terry Marsh W RSC 10 Joe Manley, *Basildon, England* (IBF)
1 Jul 87	Terry Marsh W RTD 6 Akio Kameda, *London, England* (IBF) *Marsh relinquished title (retired)*
4 Jul 87	Juan M. Coggi W KO 3 Patrizio Oliva, *Riberia, Italy* (WBA)
22 Jul 87	Rene Arredondo W RSC 6 Tsuyoshi Hamada, *Tokyo, Japan* (WBC)
12 Nov 87	Roger Mayweather W RSC 6 Rene Arredondo, *Los Angeles, USA* (WBC)
14 Feb 88	James McGirt W RSC 12 Frankie Warren, *Corpus Christi, USA* (IBF)
24 Mar 88	Roger Mayweather W KO 3 Mauricio Aceves, *Los Angeles, USA* (WBC)
7 May 88	Juan M. Coggi W KO 2 Sang-Ho Lee, *Abruzzi, Italy* (WBA)
6 Jun 88	Roger Mayweather W PTS 12 Harold Brazier, *Las Vegas, USA* (WBC)
31 Jul 88	James McGirt W KO 1 Howard Davis, *New York C, USA* (IBF)
3 Sep 88	Meldrick Taylor W RSC 12 James McGirt, *Atlantic C, USA* (IBF)
22 Sep 88	Roger Mayweather W RSC 12 Rodolfo Gonzales, *Los Angeles, USA* (WBC)
7 Nov 88	Roger Mayweather W PTS 12 Vinny Pazienza, *Las Vegas, USA* (WBC)

LIGHTWEIGHT

(*Current weight limit:* 135lb/61.2kg)

DATE	
1 Jun 96	George Lavigne W KO 17 Dick Burge, *London, England*
27 Oct 96	George Lavigne W KO 24 Jack Everhardt, *New York C, USA*
8 Feb 97	George Lavigne W PTS 25 Kid McPartland, *New York C, USA*
28 Apr 97	George Lavigne W 11 Eddie Connolly, *New York C, USA*
29 Oct 97	George Lavigne W RTD 12 Joe Walcott, *San Francisco, USA*
17 Mar 98	George Lavigne DREW 20 Jack Daly, *Cleveland, USA*
28 Sep 98	George Lavigne DREW 20 Frank Erne, *New York C, USA*
25 Nov 98	George Lavigne W PTS 20 Tom Tracy, *San Francisco, USA*
3 Jul 99	Frank Erne W PTS 20 George Lavigne, *Buffalo, USA*
4 Dec 99	Frank Erne DREW 25 Jack O'Brien, *New York C, USA*
23 Mar 00	Frank Erne W RTD 12 Joe Gans, *New York C, USA*
12 May 02	Joe Gans W KO 1 Frank Erne, *Fort Erie, Canada*
27 Jun 02	Joe Gans W KO 3 George McFadden, *San Francisco, USA*
24 Jul 02	Joe Gans W KO 15 Rufe Turner, *Oakland, USA*
17 Sep 02	Joe Gans W KO 5 Gus Gardner, *Baltimore, USA*
13 Oct 02	Joe Gans W KO 5 Kid McPartland, *Fort Erie, Canada*
1 Jan 03	Joe Gans W DIS 11 Gus Gardner, *New Britain, USA*
11 Mar 03	Joe Gans W RTD 11 Steve Crosby, *Hot Springs, USA*
29 May 03	Joe Gans W KO 10 Willie Fitzgerald, *San Francisco, USA*
4 Jul 03	Joe Gans W KO 5 Buddy King, *Butte, USA*
12 Jan 04	Joe Gans W PTS 10 Willie Fitzgerald, *Detroit, USA*
31 Oct 04	Joe Gans W DIS 5 Jimmy Britt, *San Francisco, USA*
3 Sep 06	Joe Gans W DIS 42 Battling Nelson, *Goldfield, USA*
1 Jan 07	Joe Gans W KO 8 Kid Herman, *Tonopah, USA*
9 Sep 07	Joe Gans W RTD 6 Jimmy Britt, *San Francisco, USA*
27 Sep 07	Joe Gans W PTS 20 George Memsic, *Los Angeles, USA*
1 Apr 08	Joe Gans W KO 3 Spike Robson, *Philadelphia, USA*
14 May 08	Joe Gans W RSC 11 Rudy Unholz, *San Francisco, USA*
4 Jul 08	Battling Nelson W KO 17 Joe Gans, *San Francisco, USA*
9 Sep 08	Battling Nelson W KO 21 Joe Gans, *San Francisco, USA*
29 May 09	Battling Nelson W KO 23 Dick Hyland, *San Francisco, USA*
22 Jun 09	Battling Nelson W KO 5 Jack Clifford, *Oklahoma C, USA*

***Below:* Benny Leonard (right) shakes hands with Lew Tendler before defending his lightweight title in 1923.**

DATE	
22 Feb 10	Ad Wolgast W RSC 40 Battling Nelson, *Richmond, USA*
30 May 10	Freddie Welsh DREW 20 Packy McFarland, *London, England* (GB)
17 Mar 11	Ad Wolgast W RSC 9 George Memsic, *Los Angeles, USA*
31 Mar 11	Ad Wolgast W RTD 5 Antonio la Grave, *San Francisco, USA*
26 April 11	Ad Wolgast W RSC 2 One-Round Hogan, *New York C, USA*
27 May 11	Ad Wolgast W RTD 17 Frankie Burns, *San Francisco, USA*
4 Jul 11	Ad Wolgast W KO 13 Owen Moran, *San Francisco, USA*
4 Jul 12	Ad Wolgast W KO 13 Joe Rivers, *Los Angeles, USA*
28 Nov 12	Willie Ritchie W DIS 16 Ad Wolgast, *San Francisco, USA*
16 Dec 12	Freddie Welsh W PTS 20 Hughie Mehegan, *London, England* (GB)
4 Jul 13	Willie Ritchie W KO 11 Joe Rivers, *San Francisco, USA*
17 Apr 14	Willie Ritchie W PTS 20 Tommy Murphy, *San Francisco, USA*
7 Jul 14	Freddie Welsh W PTS 20 Willie Ritchie, *London, England*
4 Jul 16	Freddie Welsh W DIS 11 Ad Wolgast, *Denver, USA*
4 Sep 16	Freddie Welsh W PTS 20 Charley White, *Colorado Springs USA*
28 May 17	Benny Leonard W RSC 9 Freddie Welsh, *New York C, USA*
25 Jul 17	Benny Leonard W KO 3 Johnny Kilbane, *Philadelphia, USA*
5 Jul 20	Benny Leonard W KO 9 Charley White, *Benton Harbor, USA*
26 Nov 20	Benny Leonard W RSC 14 Joe Welling, *New York C, USA*
14 Jan 21	Benny Leonard W RSC 6 Richie Mitchell, *New York C, USA*
10 Feb 22	Benny Leonard W PTS 15 Rocky Kansas, *New York C, USA*
4 Jul 22	Benny Leonard W RSC 8 Rocky Kansas, *Michigan C, USA*
23 Jul 23	Benny Leonard W PTS 15 Lew Tendler, *New York C, USA*
	Benny Leonard relinquished title (retired)
13 Jul 25	Jimmy Goodrich W RSC 2 Stanislaus Loayza, *New York C, USA* (NY)
7 Dec 25	Rocky Kansas W PTS 15 Jimmy Goodrich, *Buffalo, USA*
3 Jul 26	Sammy Mandell W PTS 10 Rocky Kansas, *Chicago, USA*
21 May 28	Sammy Mandell W PTS 15 Jimmy McLarnin, *New York C, USA*
2 Aug 29	Sammy Mandell W PTS 10 Tony Canzoneri, *Chicago, USA*
17 Jul 30	Al Singer W KO 1 Sammy Mandell, *New York C, USA*
14 Nov 30	Tony Canzoneri W KO 1 Al Singer, *New York C, USA*
24 Apr 31	Tony Canzoneri W KO 3 Jack Kid Berg, *Chicago, USA*
10 Sep 31	Tony Canzoneri W PTS 15 Jack Kid Berg, *New York C, USA*
20 Nov 31	Tony Canzoneri W PTS 15 Kid Chocolate, *New York C, USA*
4 Nov 32	Tony Canzoneri W PTS 15 Billy Petrolle, *New York C, USA*
23 Jun 33	Barney Ross W PTS 10 Tony Canzoneri, *Chicago, USA*
12 Sep 33	Barney Ross W PTS 15 Tony Canzoneri, *New York C, USA*
	Barney Ross relinquished title to campaign as a welterweight
10 May 35	Tony Canzoneri W PTS 15 Lou Ambers, *New York C, USA*
4 Oct 35	Tony Canzoneri W PTS 15 Al Roth, *New York C, USA*
3 Sep 36	Lou Ambers W PTS 15 Tony Canzoneri, *New York C, USA*
7 May 37	Lou Ambers W PTS 15 Tony Canzoneri, *New York C, USA*
23 Sep 37	Lou Ambers W PTS 15 Pedro Montanez, *New York C, USA*
17 Aug 38	Henry Armstrong W PTS 15 Lou Ambers, *New York C, USA*
22 Aug 39	Lou Ambers W PTS 15 Henry Armstrong, *New York C, USA*
	Lou Ambers forfeited NBA recognition (failure to defend against Davey Day)
3 May 40	Sammy Angott W PTS 15 Davey Day, *Louisville, USA* (NBA)
10 May 40	Lew Jenkins W RSC 3 Lou Ambers, *New York C, USA* (NY)
22 Nov 40	Lew Jenkins W RSC 2 Pete Lello, *New York C*, USA (NY)
2 May 41	Sammy Angott W PTS 12 Dave Castilloux, *Louisville, USA* (NBA)
19 Dec 41	Sammy Angott W PTS 15 Lew Jenkins, *New York C, USA*
15 May 42	Sammy Angott W PTS 15 Allie Stolz, *New York C, USA*
	Sammy Angott relinquished title (retired)
18 Dec 42	Beau Jack W KO 3 Tippy Larkin, *New York C, USA* (NY)
4 Jan 43	Slugger White W PTS 15 Willie Joyce, *Baltimore, USA* (MARY)
21 May 43	Bob Montgomery W PTS 15 Beau Jack, *New York C, USA* (NY)
27 Oct 43	Sammy Angott W PTS 15 Slugger White, *Los Angeles, USA* (NBA)
19 Nov 43	Beau Jack W PTS 15 Bob Montgomery, *New York C, USA* (NY)
3 Mar 44	Bob Montgomery W PTS 15 Beau Jack, *New York C, USA* (NY)
8 Mar 44	Juan Zurita W PTS 15 Sammy Angott, *Los Angeles, USA* (NBA)
18 Apr 45	Ike Williams W KO 2 Juan Zurita, *Mexico C, Mexico* (NBA)
30 Apr 46	Ike Williams W RSC 8 Enrique Bolanos, *Los Angeles, USA* (NBA)
28 Jun 46	Bob Montgomery W KO 13 Allie Stolz, *New York C, USA* (NY)
4 Sep 46	Ike Williams W KO 9 Ronnie James, *Cardiff, Wales* (NBA)
26 Nov 46	Bob Montgomery W KO 8 Wesley Mouzon, *Philadelphia, USA* (NY)
4 Aug 47	Ike Williams W KO 6 Bob Montgomery, *Philadelphia, USA*
25 May 48	Ike Williams W PTS 15 Enrique Bolanos, *Los Angeles, USA*
12 Jul 48	Ike Williams W RSC 6 Beau Jack, *Philadelphia, USA*
23 Sep 48	Ike Williams W KO 10 Jesse Flores, *New York C, USA*
21 Jul 49	Ike Williams W RSC 4 Enrique Bolanos, *Los Angeles, USA*
5 Dec 49	Ike Williams W PTS 15 Freddie Dawson, *Philadelphia, USA*
25 May 51	Jimmy Carter W RSC 14 Ike Williams, *New York C, USA*
14 Nov 51	Jimmy Carter W PTS 15 Art Aragon, *Los Angeles, USA*

DATE	
1 Apr 52	Jimmy Carter W PTS 15 Lauro Salas, *Los Angeles, USA*
14 May 52	Lauro Salas W PTS 15 Jimmy Carter, *Los Angeles, USA*
15 Oct 52	Jimmy Carter W PTS 15 Lauro Salas, *Chicago, USA*
24 Apr 53	Jimmy Carter W RSC 4 Tommy Collins, *Boston, USA*
12 Jun 53	Jimmy Carter W RSC 13 George Araujo, *New York C, USA*
11 Nov 53	Jimmy Carter W KO 5 Armand Savoie, *Montreal, Canada*
5 Mar 54	Paddy de Marco W PTS 15 Jimmy Carter, *New York C, USA*
17 Nov 54	Jimmy Carter W RSC 15 Paddy de Marco, *San Francisco, USA*
29 Jun 55	Wallace Bud Smith W PTS 15 Jimmy Carter, *Boston, USA*
19 Oct 55	Wallace Bud Smith W PTS 15 Jimmy Carter, *Cincinnati, USA*
24 Aug 56	Joe Brown W PTS 15 Wallace Bud Smith, *New Orleans, USA*
13 Feb 57	Joe Brown RSC 10 Wallace Bud Smith, *Miami, USA*
19 Jun 57	Joe Brown W RSC 15 Orlando Zulueta, *Denver, USA*
4 Dec 57	Joe Brown W RSC 11 Joey Lopes, *Chicago, USA*
7 May 58	Joe Brown W RSC 8 Ralph Dupas, *Houston, USA*
23 Jul 58	Joe Brown W PTS 15 Kenny Lane, *Houson, USA*
11 Feb 59	Joe Brown W PTS 15 Johnny Busso, *Houston, USA*
3 Jun 59	Joe Brown W RTD 8 Paolo Rossi, *Washington, USA*
2 Dec 59	Joe Brown W RTD 5 Dave Charnley, *Houston, USA*
28 Oct 60	Joe Brown W PTS 15 Cisco Andrade, *Los Angeles, USA*
18 Apr 61	Joe Brown W PTS 15 Dave Charnley, *London, England*
28 Oct 61	Joe Brown W PTS 15 Bert Somodio, *Quezon C, Philippines*
21 Apr 62	Carlos Ortiz W PTS 15 Joe Brown, *Las Vegas, USA*
3 Dec 62	Carlos Ortiz W KO 5 Teruo Kosaka, *Tokyo, Japan*
7 Apr 63	Carlos Ortiz W RSC 13 Doug Vaillant, *San Juan, Puerto Rico*
15 Feb 64	Carlos Ortiz W RSC 14 Flash Elorde, *Manila, Philippines*
11 Apr 64	Carlos Ortiz W PTS 15 Kenny Lane, *San Juan, Puerto Rico*
10 Apr 65	Ismael Laguna W PTS 15 Carlos Ortiz, *Panama C, Panama*
13 Nov 65	Carlos Ortiz W PTS 15 Ismael Laguna, *San Juan, Puerto Rico*
20 Jun 66	Carlos Ortiz W RSC 12 Johnny Bizzarro, *Pittsburgh, USA*
22 Oct 66	Carlos Ortiz W RSC 5 Sugar Ramos, *Mexico C, Mexico*
28 Nov 66	Carlos Ortiz W KO 14 Flash Elorde, *New York C, USA*
1 Jul 67	Carlos Ortiz W RSC 4 Sugar Ramos, *San Juan, Puerto Rico*
16 Aug 67	Carlos Ortiz W PTS 15 Ismael Laguna, *New York C, USA*
29 Jun 68	Carlos Teo Cruz W PTS 15 Carlos Ortiz, *St Domingo, Puerto Rico*
28 Sep 68	Carlos Teo Cruz W PTS 15 Mando Ramos, *Los Angeles, USA*
18 Feb 69	Mando Ramos W RSC 11 Carlos Teo Cruz, *Los Angeles, USA*
4 Oct 69	Mando Ramos W RSC 6 Yoshiaki Numata, *Los Angeles, USA*
3 Mar 70	Ismael Laguna W RTD 9 Mando Ramos, *Los Angeles, USA*
7 Jun 70	Ismael Laguna W RSC 13 Guts Ishimatsu, *Panama C, Panama*
26 Sep 70	Ken Buchanan W PTS 15 Ismael Laguna, *San Juan, Puerto Rico* (WBA)
12 Feb 71	Ken Buchanan W PTS 15 Ruben Navarro, *Los Angeles, USA*
	Ken Buchanan forfeited WBC recognition (failure to defend against Pedro Carrasco)

***Above:** Champion Ken Buchanan (left) successfully defending his title against Ismael Laguna in 1971.*

DATE	
13 Sep 71	Ken Buchanan W PTS 15 Ismael Laguna, *New York C, USA* (WBA)
5 Nov 71	Pedro Carrasco W DIS 11 Mando Ramos, *Madrid, Spain* (WBC)
18 Feb 72	Mando Ramos W PTS 15 Pedro Carrasco, *Los Angeles, USA* (WBC)
26 Jun 72	Roberto Duran W RSC 13 Ken Buchanan, *New York C, USA* (WBA)
28 Jun 72	Mando Ramos W PTS 15 Pedro Carrasco, *Madrid, Spain* (WBA)
15 Sep 72	Chango Carmona W RSC 8 Mando Ramos, *Los Angeles, USA* (WBC)
10 Nov 72	Rodolfo Gonzalez W RTD 12 Chango Carmona, *Los Angeles, USA* (WBC)
20 Jan 73	Roberto Duran W KO 5 Jimmy Robertson, *Panama C, Panama* (WBA)
17 Mar 73	Rodolfo Gonzalez W RSC 9 Ruben Navarro, *Los Angeles, USA* (WBC)
2 Jun 73	Roberto Duran W RSC 8 Hector Thompson, *Panama C, Panama, USA* (WBA)
8 Sep 73	Roberto Duran W RSC 10 Guts Ishimatsu, *Panama C, Panama* (WBA)
27 Oct 73	Rodolfo Gonzalez W RTD 10 Antonio Puddu, *Los Angeles, USA* (WBC)
16 Mar 74	Roberto Duran W RSC 11 Esteban de Jesus, *Panama C, Panama* (WBA)
11 Apr 74	Guts Ishimatsu W KO 8 Rodolfo Gonzalez, *Tokyo, Japan* (WBC)
13 Sep 74	Guts Ishimatsu DREW 15 Tury Pineda, *Nagoya, Japan* (WBC)
28 Nov 74	Guts Ishimatsu W KO 12 Rodolfo Gonzalez, *Osaka, Japan* (WBC)
21 Dec 74	Roberto Duran W RSC 1 Masataka Takayama, *San Jose, Costa Rica* (WBA)
27 Feb 75	Guts Ishimatsu W PTS 15 Ken Buchanan, *Tokyo, Japan* (WBC)
2 Mar 75	Roberto Duran W KO 14 Ray Lampkin, *Panama C, Panama* (WBA)
5 Jun 75	Guts Ishimatsu W PTS 15 Tury Pineda, *Osaka, Japan* (WBC)
4 Dec 75	Guts Ishimatsu W KO 14 Alvaro Rojas, *Tokyo, Japan* (WBC)
14 Dec 75	Roberto Duran W KO 15 Leoncio Ortiz, *San Juan, Puerto Rico* (WBA)
8 May 76	Esteban de Jesus W PTS 15 Guts Ishimatsu, *Bayamon, Puerto Rico* (WBC)
22 May 76	Roberto Duran W KO 14 Lou Bizzarro, *Erie, USA* (WBA)
10 Sep 76	Esteban de Jesus W KO 7 Hector Medina, *Bayamon, Puerto Rico* (WBC)
15 Oct 76	Roberto Duran W KO 1 Alvaro Rojas, *Los Angeles, USA* (WBA)
29 Jan 77	Roberto Duran W KO 13 Vilomar Fernandez, *Miami, USA* (WBA)
12 Feb 77	Esteban de Jesus W RSC 6 Buzzsaw Yamabe, *Bayamon, Puerto Rico* (WBC)
25 Jun 77	Esteban de Jesus W KO 11 Vicente Mijares, *Bayamon, Puerto Rico* (WBC)
17 Sep 77	Roberto Duran W PTS 15 Edwin Viruet, *Philadelphia, USA* (WBA)
21 Jan 78	Roberto Duran W KO 12 Esteban de Jesus, *Las Vegas, USA*
	Roberto Duran relinquished title to campaign as a welterweight
17 Apr 79	Jim Watt W RSC 12 Alfredo Pitalua, *Glasgow, Scotland* (WBC)
16 Jun 79	Ernesto Espana W KO 13 Claude Noel, *San Juan, Puerto Rico* (WBA)
4 Aug 79	Ernesto Espana W RSC 9 Johnny Lira, *Chicago, USA* (WBA)
3 Nov 79	Jim Watt W RSC 9 Roberto Vasquez, *Glasgow, Scotland* (WBC)
2 Mar 80	Hilmer Kenty W RSC 9 Ernesto Espana, *Detroit, USA* (WBA)
14 Mar 80	Jim Watt W RSC 4 Charlie Nash, *Glasgow, Scotland* (WBC)
7 Jun 80	Jim Watt W PTS 15 Howard Davis, *Glasgow, Scotland* (WBC)
2 Aug 80	Hilmer Kenty W RSC 9 Yong-Ho Oh, *Detroit, USA* (WBA)
20 Sep 80	Hilmer Kenty W RSC 4 Ernesto Espana, *San Juan, Puerto Rico* (WBA)
1 Nov 80	Jim Watt W RSC 12 Sean O'Grady, *Glasgow, Scotland* (WBC)
8 Nov 80	Hilmer Kenty W PTS 15 Vilomar Fernandez, *Detroit, USA* (WBA)
12 Apr 81	Sean O'Grady W PTS 15 Hilmer Kenty, *Atlantic C, USA* (WBA)
	Sean O'Grady forfeited WBA recognition (contractual dispute)
20 Jun 81	Alexis Arguello W PTS 15 Jim Watt, *Wembley, England* (WBC)
12 Sep 81	Claude Noel W PTS 15 Gato Gonzalez, *Atlantic C, USA* (WBA)
3 Oct 81	Alexis Arguello W RSC 14 Ray Mancini, *Atlantic C, USA* (WBC)
21 Nov 81	Alexis Arguello W KO 7 Robert Elizondo, *Las Vegas, USA* (WBC)
5 Dec 81	Arturo Frias W KO 8 Claude Noel, *Las Vegas, USA* (WBA)
30 Jan 82	Arturo Frias W TD 9 Ernesto Espana, *Atlantic C, USA* (WBA)
13 Feb 82	Alexis Arguello W RSC 6 Bubba Busceme, *Beaumont, USA* (WBC)
8 May 82	Ray Mancini W RSC 1 Arturo Frias, *Las Vegas, USA* (WBA)
22 May 82	Alexis Arguello W KO 5 Andy Ganigan, *Las Vegas, USA* (WBC)
	Alexis Arguello relinquished title to campaign as a light-welterweight
24 Jul 82	Ray Mancini W RSC 6 Ernesto Espana, *Warren, USA* (WBA)
13 Nov 82	Ray Mancini W RSC 14 Deuk-Koo Kim, *Las Vegas, USA* (WBA)

DATE	
1 May 83	Edwin Rosario W PTS 12 Jose Luis Ramirez, *San Juan, Puerto Rico* (WBC)
15 Sep 83	Ray Mancini W KO 9 Orlando Romero, *New York C, USA* (WBA)
14 Jan 84	Ray Mancini W RSC 3 Bobby Chacon, *Reno, USA* (WBA)
30 Jan 84	Charlie Choo Choo Brown W PTS 15 Melvin Paul, *Atlantic C, USA* (IBF)
17 Mar 84	Edwin Rosario W RSC 1 Robert Elizondo, *San Juan, Puerto Rico* (WBC)
15 Apr 84	Harry Arroyo W RSC 14 Charlie Choo Choo Brown, *Atlantic C, USA* (IBF)
1 Jun 84	Livingstone Bramble W RSC 14 Ray Mancini, *Buffalo, USA* (WBA)
23 Jun 84	Edwin Rosario W PTS 12 Howard Davis, *San Juan, Puerto Rico* (WBC)
1 Sep 84	Harry Arroyo W RSC 8 Charlie W.L. Brown, *Youngstown, USA* (IBF)
3 Nov 84	Jose Luis Ramirez W RSC 4 Edwin Rosario, *San Juan, Puerto Rico* (WBC)
12 Jan 85	Harry Arroyo W RSC 11 Terrence Alli, *Atlantic C, USA* (IBF)
16 Feb 85	Livingstone Bramble W PTS 15 Ray Mancini, *Reno, USA* (WBA)
6 Apr 85	Jimmy Paul W PTS 15 Harry Arroyo, *Atlantic C, USA* (IBF)
30 Jun 85	Jimmy Paul W RSC 14 Robin Blake *Las Vegas, USA* (IBF)
10 Aug 85	Hector Camacho W PTS 12 Jose Luis Ramirez, *Las Vegas, USA* (WBC)
16 Feb 86	Livingstone Bramble W RSC 13 Tyrone Crawley, *Reno, USA* (WBA)
4 Jun 86	Jimmy Paul W PTS 15 Irleis Perez, *E Rutherford, USA* (IBF)
13 Jun 86	Hector Camacho W PTS 12 Edwin Rosario, *New York C, USA* (WBC)
15 Aug 86	Jimmy Paul W PTS 15 Darryl Tyson, *Detroit, USA* (IBF)
26 Sep 86	Hector Camacho W PTS 12 Cornelius Boza-Edwards, *Miami, USA* (WBC) *Hector Camacho relinquished title to campaign as a light-welterweight*

DATE	
26 Sep 86	Edwin Rosario W KO 2 Livingstone Bramble, *Miami, USA* (WBA)
5 Dec 86	Greg Haugen W PTS 15 Jimmy Paul, *Las Vegas, USA* (IBF)
7 Jun 87	Vinny Pazienza W PTS 15 Greg Haugen, *Providence, USA* (IBF)
19 Jun 87	Jose Luis Ramirez W PTS 12 Terrence Alli, *St Tropez, France* (WBC)
1[illegible] Aug 87	Edwin Rosario W KO 8 Juan Nazario, *Chicago, USA* (WBA)
10 Oct 87	Jose Luis Ramirez W KO 5 Cornelius Boza-Edwards, *Paris, France* (WBC)
2[illegible] Nov 87	Julio Cesar Chavez W RSC 11 Edwin Rosario, *Las Vegas, USA* (WBA)
16 Feb 88	Greg Haugen W PTS 15 Vinny Pazienza, *Atlantic City, USA* (IBF)
12 Mar 88	Jose Luis Ramirez W PTS 12 Pernell Whitaker, *Paris, France* (WBC)
11 Apr 88	Greg Haugen W TD 11 Miguel Santana, *Tacoma, USA* (IBF)
16 Apr 88	Julio Cesar Chavez W RSC 6 Rodolfo Aguilar, *Las Vegas, USA* (WBA)
23 Oct 88	Greg Haugen W RSC 10 Gert Bo Jacobsen, *Copenhagen, Denmark* (IBF)
29 Oct 88	Julio Cesar Chavez W TD 11 Jose Luis Ramirez, *Las Vegas, USA* (WBA/WBC)

Below: *Hector 'Macho' Camacho, a lightweight champion of the 1980s, looking good outside the ring.*

JUNIOR LIGHTWEIGHT

(*Current weight limit:* 130lb/59kg. The WBA and IBF call this class 'Junior Lightweight', the WBC calls the class 'Super-featherweight')

DATE	
18 Nov 21	Johnny Dundee W DIS 5 KO Chaney *New York C, USA* (NY)
6 Jul 22	Johnny Dundee W PTS 15 Jackie Sharkey, *New York C, USA* (NY)
28 Aug 22	Johnny Dundee W PTS 15 Pepper Martin, *New York C, USA* (NY)
2 Feb 23	Johnny Dundee W PTS 15 Elino Flores, *New York C, USA* (NY)
30 May 23	Jack Bernstein W PTS 15 Johnny Dundee, *New York C, USA* (NY/NBA)
25 Jun 23	Jack Bernstein W KO 5 Freddie Jacks, *Philadelphia, USA* (NY/NBA)
17 Dec 23	Johnny Dundee W PTS 15 Jack Bernstein, *New York C, USA* (NY/NBA)
20 Jun 24	Kid Sullivan W PTS 10 Johnny Dundee, *New York C, USA* (NY/NBA)
18 Aug 24	Kid Sullivan W PTS 15 Pepper Martin, *New York C, USA* (NY/NBA)
15 Oct 24	Kid Sullivan W KO 5 Mike Ballerino, *New York C, USA* (NY/NBA)
1 Apr 25	Mike Ballerino W PTS 10 Kid Sullivan, *Philadelphia, USA* (NY/NBA)
6 Jul 25	Mike Ballerino W PTS 15 Pepper Martin, *New York C, USA* (NY/NBA)
2 Dec 25	Tod Morgan W RTD 10 Mike Ballerino, *Los Angeles, USA* (NY/NBA)
3 Jun 26	Tod Morgan W RTD 6 Kid Sullivan, *New York C, USA* (NY/NBA)
30 Sep 26	Tod Morgan W PTS 15 Joe Glick, *New York C, USA* (NY/NBA)
19 Oct 26	Tod Morgan W PTS 10 Johnny Dundee, *San Francisco, USA* (NY/NBA)
19 Nov 26	Tod Morgan W PTS 15 Carl Duane, *New York C, USA* (NY/NBA)
28 May 27	Tod Morgan W PTS Vic Foley, *Vancouver, Canada* (NY/WBA)
16 Dec 27	Tod Morgan W DIS 14 Joe Glick, *New York C, USA* (NY/NBA)
24 May 28	Tod Morgan W PTS 15 Eddie Martin, *New York C, USA* (NY/NBA)
18 Jul 28	Tod Morgan W PTS 15 Eddie Martin, *New York C, USA* (NY/NBA)
3 Dec 28	Tod Morgan DREW 10 Santiago Zorilla, *San Francisco, USA* (NY/NBA)
5 Apr 29	Tod Morgan W PTS 10 Santiago Zorilla, *Los Angeles, USA* (NY/NBA)
20 May 29	Tod Morgan W PTS 10 Baby Sal Sorio, *Los Angeles, USA* (NY/NBA)
20 Dec 29	Benny Bass W KO 2 Tod Morgan, *New York C, USA* (NY/NBA) *Benny Bass ceased to be recognized by NY (NY abolished weight division)*
3 Feb 30	Benny Bass W RSC 4 Davey Abad, *St Louis, USA* (NBA)
5 Jan 31	Benny Bass W PTS 10 Lew Massey, *Philadelphia, USA* (NBA)
15 Jul 31	Kid Chocolate W RSC 7 Benny Bass, *Philadelphia, USA* (NBA)
10 Apr 32	Kid Chocolate W PTS 15 Davey Abad, *Havana, Cuba* (NBA)
4 Aug 32	Kid Chocolate W PTS 10 Eddie Shea, *Chicago, USA* (NBA)
1 May 33	Kid Chocolate W PTS 10 Johnny Farr, *Philadelphia, USA* (NBA)

DATE

4 Dec 33 Kid Chocolate W PTS 10 Frankie Wallace, *Cleveland, USA* (NBA)
26 Dec 33 Frankie Klick W RSC 7 Kid Chocolate, *Philadelphia, USA* (NBA)
Frankie Klick relinquished title to campaign as a light-welterweight. The division fell into disuse
6 Dec 49 Sandy Saddler W PTS 10 Orlando Zulueta, *Cleveland, USA* (OHIO)
18 Apr 50 Saddler Saddler W RSC 9 Lauro Salas, *Cleveland, USA* (OHIO)
Sandy Saddler ceased to be recognized by Ohio (failure to defend after regaining the featherweight title)
20 Jul 59 Harold Gomes W PTS 15 Paul Jorgensen, *Providence, USA* (NBA)
16 Mar 60 Flash Elorde W KO 7 Harold Gomes, *Quezon C, Philippines* (NBA)
17 Aug 60 Flash Elorde W KO 1 Harold Gomes, *San Francisco, USA* (NBA)
19 Mar 61 Flash Elorde W PTS 15 Joey Lopes, *Manila, Philippines* (NBA)
16 Dec 61 Flash Elorde W RSC 1 Sergio Caprari, *Manila, Philippines* (NBA)
23 Jun 62 Flash Elorde W PTS 15 Auburn Copeland, *Manila, Philippines* (NBA)
16 Feb 63 Flash Elorde W PTS 15 Johnny Bizzarro, *Manila, Philippines* (WBA)
16 Nov 63 Flash Elorde W DIS 11 Love Allotey, *Quezon C, Philippines* (WBA)
27 Jul 64 Flash Elorde W RSC 12 Teruo Kosaka, *Tokyo, Japan* (WBA)
5 Jun 65 Flash Elorde W KO 15 Teruo Kosaka, *Quezon C, Philippines*
4 Dec 65 Flash Elorde W PTS 15 Kang-Il Suh, *Quezon C, Philippines*
22 Oct 66 Flash Elorde W PTS 15 Vicente Derado, *Quezon C, Philippines*
15 Jun 67 Yoshiaki Numata W PTS 15 Flash Elorde, *Tokyo, Japan*
14 Dec 67 Hiroshi Kobayashi W KO 12 Yoshiaki Numata, *Tokyo, Japan*
30 Mar 68 Hiroshi Kobayashi DREW 15 Rene Barrientos, *Tokyo, Japan*
6 Oct 68 Hiroshi Kobayashi W PTS 15 Jaime Valladeres, *Tokyo, Japan*
Hiroshi Kobayashi forfeited WBC recognition (failure to defend against Rene Barrientos)
15 Feb 69 Rene Barrientos W PTS 15 Ruben Navarro, *Quezon C, Philippines* (WBC)
6 Apr 69 Hiroshi Kobayashi W PTS 15 Antonio Amaya, *Tokyo, Japan* (WBA)
9 Nov 69 Hiroshi Kobayashi W PTS 15 Carlos Canete, *Tokyo, Japan* (WBA)
5 Apr 70 Yoshiaki Numata W PTS 15 Rene Barrientos, *Tokyo, Japan* (WBC)
23 Aug 70 Hiroshi Kobayashi W PTS 15 Antonio Amaya, *Tokyo, Japan* (WBA)
27 Sep 70 Yoshiaki Numata W KO 5 Paul Rojas, *Tokyo, Japan* (WBC)
3 Jan 71 Yoshiaki Numata W PTS 15 Rene Barrientos, *Shizuaka, Japan* (WBC)
3 Mar 71 Hiroshi Kobayashi W PTS 15 Ricardo Arredondo, *Tokyo, Japan* (WBA)
30 May 71 Yoshiaki Numata W PTS 15 Lionel Rose, *Hiroshima, Japan* (WBC)
29 Jul 71 Alfredo Marcano W RTD 10 Hiroshi Kobayashi, *Aomori, Japan* (WBA)
10 Oct 71 Ricardo Arredondo W KO 10 Yoshiaki Numata, *Sendai, Japan* (WBC)
7 Nov 71 Alfredo Marcano W RSC 4 Kenji Iwata, *Caracas, Venezuela* (WBA)
29 Jan 72 Ricardo Arredondo W PTS 15 Jose Marin, *San Jose, Costa Rica* (WBC)
22 Apr 72 Ricardo Arredondo W KO 5 William Martinez, *Mexico C, Mexico* (WBC)
25 Apr 72 Ben Villaflor W PTS 15 Alfredo Marcano, *Honolulu, Hawaii* (WBA)
5 Sep 72 Ben Villaflor DREW 15 Victor Echegaray, *Honolulu, Hawaii* (WBA)
15 Sep 72 Ricardo Arredondo W KO 12 Susumu Okabe, *Tokyo, Japan* (WBC)
6 Mar 73 Ricardo Arredondo W PTS 15 Apollo Yoshio, *Fukuoka C, Japan* (WBC)
12 Mar 73 Kuniaki Shibata W PTS 15 Ben Villaflor, *Honolulu, Hawaii* (WBA)
19 Jun 73 Kuniaki Shibata W PTS 15 Victor Echegaray, *Tokyo, Japan* (WBA)
1 Sep 73 Ricardo Arredondo W RSC 6 Morito Kashiwaba, *Tokyo, Japan* (WBC)
18 Oct 73 Ben Villaflor W KO 1 Kuniaki Shibata, *Honolulu, Hawaii* (WBA)
28 Feb 74 Kuniaki Shibata W PTS 15 Ricardo Arredondo, *Tokyo, Japan* (WBC)
14 Mar 74 Ben Villaflor DREW 15 Apollo Yoshio, *Toyama, Japan* (WBA)
27 Jun 74 Kuniaki Shibata W PTS 15 Antonio Amaya, *Tokyo, Japan* (WBC)
3 Aug 74 Kuniaki Shibata W RSC 15 Ramiro Bolanos, *Tokyo, Japan* (WBC)
24 Aug 74 Ben Villaflor W RSC 2 Yasutsune Uehara, *Honolulu, Hawaii* (WBA)
13 Mar 75 Ben Villaflor W PTS 15 Hyun-Chi Kim, *Quezon C, Philippines* (WBA)
27 Mar 75 Kuniaki Shibata W PTS 15 Ould Makloufi, *Fukuoka C, Japan* (WBC)
5 Jul 75 Alfredo Escalera W KO 2 Kuniaki Shibata, *Kasamatsu, Japan* (WBC)
20 Sep 75 Alfredo Escalera DREW 15 Leonel Hernandez, *Caracas, Venezuela* (WBC)
12 Dec 75 Alfredo Escalera W RSC 9 Sven-Erik Paulsen, *Oslo, Norway* (WBC)
12 Jan 76 Ben Villaflor W RSC 13 Morito Kashiwaba, *Tokyo, Japan* (WBA)
20 Feb 76 Alfredo Escalera W RSC 13 Jose Fernandez, *San Juan, Puerto Rico* (WBC)
1 Apr 76 Alfredo Escalera W RSC 6 Buzzsaw Yamabe, *Nara, Japan* (WBC)
13 Apr 76 Ben Villaflor DREW 15 Sam Serrano, *Honolulu, Hawaii* (WBA)
1 Jul 76 Alfredo Escalera W PTS 15 Buzzsaw Yamabe, *Nara, Japan* (WBC)
18 Sep 76 Alfredo Escalera W RTD 12 Ray Lunny, *San Juan, Puerto Rico* (WBC)

DATE

16 Oct 76 Sam Serrano W PTS 15 Ben Villaflor, *San Juan, Puerto Rico* (WBA)
30 Nov 76 Alfredo Escalera W PTS 15 Tyrone Everett, *Philadelphia, USA* (WBC)
15 Jan 77 Sam Serrano W RSC 11 Alberto Herrera, *Guayaquil, Ecuador* (WBA)
17 Mar 77 Alfredo Escalera W RSC 6 Ronnie McGarvey, *San Juan, Puerto Rico* (WBC)
16 May 77 Alfredo Escalera W KO 8 Carlos Becerril, *Landover, USA* (WBC)
26 Jun 77 Sam Serrano W PTS 15 Leonel Hernandez, *Cruz, Venezuela* (WBA)
27 Aug 77 Sam Serrano W PTS 15 Apollo Yoshio, *San Juan, Puerto Rico* (WBA)
10 Sep 77 Alfredo Escalera W PTS 15 Sigfredo Rodriguez, *San Juan, Puerto Rico* (WBC)
19 Nov 77 Sam Serrano W RSC 10 Tae-Ho Kim, *San Juan, Puerto Rico* (WBA)
28 Jan 78 Alexis Arguello W RSC 13 Alfredo Escalera, *Bayamon, Puerto Rico* (WBC)
18 Feb 78 Sam Serrano W PTS 15 Mario Martinez, *San Juan, Puerto Rico* (WBA)
29 Apr 78 Alexis Arguello W RSC 5 Rey Tam, *Los Angeles, USA* (WBC)
3 Jun 78 Alexis Arguello W KO 1 Diego Alcala, *San Juan, Puerto Rico* (WBC)
8 Jul 78 Sam Serrano W RSC 9 Oh-Young Ho, *San Juan, Puerto Rico* (WBA)
10 Nov 78 Alexis Arguello W PTS 15 Arturo Leon, *Las Vegas, USA* (WBC)
29 Nov 78 Sam Serrano W PTS 15 Takas Maruki, *Nagoya, Japan* (WBA)
4 Feb 79 Alexis Arguello W KO 13 Alfredo Escalera, *Rimini, Italy* (WBC)
18 Feb 79 Sam Serrano W PTS 15 Julio Valdez, *San Juan, Puerto Rico* (WBA)
14 Apr 79 Sam Serrano W RSC 8 Nkosana Mgxaji, *Capetown, S Africa* (WBA)
8 Jul 79 Alexis Arguello W RSC 11 Rafael Limon, *New York C, USA* (WBC)
16 Nov 79 Alexis Arguello W RTD 7 Bobby Chacon, *Los Angeles, USA* (WBC)
20 Jan 80 Alexis Arguello W RSC 11 Ruben Castillo, *Tuscon, USA* (WBC)
3 Apr 80 Sam Serrano W RSC 13 Battle Hawk Kazama, *Nara, Japan* (WBA)
27 Apr 80 Alexis Arguello W RSC 4 Rolando Navarette, *San Juan, Puerto Rico* (WBC)
Alexis Arguello relinquished title to campaign as a lightweight
2 Aug 80 Yasutsune Uehara W KO 6 Sam Serrano, *Detroit, USA* (WBA)
20 Nov 80 Yasutsune Uehara W PTS 15 Leonel Hernandez, *Tokyo, Japan* (WBA)
11 Dec 80 Rafael Limon W RSC 15 Ildefonso Bethelmy, *Los Angeles, USA* (WBC)
8 Mar 81 Cornelius Boza-Edwards W PTS 15 Rafael Limon, *Stockton, USA* (WBC)
9 Apr 81 Sam Serrano W PTS 15 Yasutsune Uehara, *Wakayama, Japan* (WBA)
30 May 81 Cornelius Boza-Edwards W RTD 13 Bobby Chacon, *Las Vegas, USA* (WBC)
29 Jun 81 Sam Serrano W PTS 15 Leonel Hernandez, *Caracas, Venezuela* (WBA)
29 Aug 81 Rolando Navarrete W KO 5 Cornelius Boza-Edwards, *Reggio, Italy* (WBC)
10 Dec 81 Sam Serrano W RSC 12 Hikaru Tomonari, *San Juan, Puerto Rico* (WBA)
16 Jan 82 Rolando Navarrete W KO 11 Chung-Il Choi, *Manila, Philippines* (WBC)
29 May 82 Rafael Limon W KO 12 Rolando Navarette, *Las Vegas, USA* (WBC)
5 Jun 82 Sam Serrano NC 11 Benedicto Villablanca, *Santiago, Chile* (WBA)
18 Sep 82 Rafael Limon W RSC 7 Chung-Il Choi, *Los Angeles, USA* (WBC)
11 Dec 82 Bobby Chacon W PTS 15 Rafael Limon, *Sacramento, USA* (WBC)
Bobby Chacon forfeited WBC recognition (contractual dispute)
19 Jan 83 Roger Mayweather W KO 8 Sam Serrano, *San Juan, Puerto Rico* (WBC)
20 Apr 83 Roger Mayweather W RSC 8 Jorge Alvarado, *San Jose, USA* (WBA)
7 Aug 83 Hector Camacho W RSC 5 Rafael Limon, *San Juan, Puerto Rico* (WBC)
17 Aug 83 Roger Mayweather W KO 1 Benedicto Villablanca, *Las Vegas, USA* (WBA)
18 Nov 83 Hector Camacho W KO 5 Rafael Solis, *San Juan, Puerto Rico* (WBC)
Hector Camacho relinquished title to campaign as a lightweight
26 Feb 84 Rocky Lockridge W KO 1 Roger Mayweather, *Beaumont, USA* (WBA)
22 Apr 84 Hwan-Kil Yuh W PTS 15 Rod Sequenan, *Seoul, S Korea* (IBF)
12 Jun 84 Rocky Lockridge W RSC 11 Taej-In Moon, *Anchorage, Alaska* (WBA)
13 Sep 84 Julio Cesar Chavez W RSC 8 Mario Martinez, *Los Angeles, USA* (WBC)
16 Sep 84 Hwan-Kil Yuh W KO 6 Sak Galexi, *Pohang, S Korea* (IBF)

DATE

27 Jan 85 Rocky Lockridge W RSC 6 Kamel Bou Ali, *Riva del Garda, Italy* (WBA)
15 Feb 85 Lester Ellis W PTS 15 Hwan-Kil Yuh, *Melbourne, Australia* (IBF)
19 Apr 85 Julio Cesar Chavez W RSC 6 Ruben Castillo, *Los Angeles, USA* (WBC)
26 Apr 85 Lester Ellis W KO 13 Rod Sequenan, *Melbourne, Australia* (IBF)
19 May 85 Wilfredo Gomez W PTS 15 Rocky Lockridge, *San Juan, Puerto Rico* (WBA)
7 Jul 85 Julio Cesar Chavez W RSC 2 Roger Mayweather, *Las Vegas, USA* (WBC)
12 Jul 85 Barry Michael W PTS 15 Lester Ellis, *Melbourne, Australia* (IBF)
22 Sep 85 Julio Cesar Chavez W PTS 12 Dwight Pratchett, *Las Vegas, USA* (WBC)
18 Oct 85 Barry Michael W RSC 4 Jin-Shik Choi, *Darwin, Australia* (IBF)
15 May 86 Julio Cesar Chavez W RSC 5 Faustino Barrios, *Paris, France* (WBC)
23 May 86 Barry Michael W RSC 4 Mark Fernandez, *Melbourne, Australia* (IBF)
24 May 86 Alfredo Layne W RSC 9 Wilfredo Gomez, *San Juan, Puerto Rico* (WBA)
13 Jun 86 Julio Cesar Chavez W RSC 7 Refugio Rojas, *New York C, USA* (WBC)
3 Aug 86 Julio Cesar Chavez W PTS 12 Rocky Lockridge, *Monte Carlo* (WBC)
23 Aug 86 Barry Michael W PTS 12 Najib Daho, *Manchester, England* (IBF)
27 Sep 86 Brian Mitchell W RSC 10 Alfredo Layne, *Sun C, S Africa* (WBA)
12 Dec 86 Julio Cesar Chavez W PTS 12 Juan Laporte, *New York C, USA* (WBC)
27 Mar 87 Brian Mitchell DREW 15 Jose Rivera, *San Juan, Puerto Rico* (WBA)
18 Apr 87 Julio Cesar Chavez W RSC 3 Francisco Tomas da Cruz, *Nimes, France* (WBC)
31 Jul 87 Brian Mitchell W RSC 14 Francisco Fernandez, *Panama C, Panama* (WBA)
9 Aug 87 Rocky Lockridge W RTD 8 Barry Michael, *Windsor, England* (IBF)
21 Aug 87 Julio Cesar Chavez W PTS 12 Danilo Cabrera, *Tijuana, Mexico* (WBC)
Chavez relinquished title to campaign as a lightweight
3 Oct 87 Brian Mitchell W PTS 15 Daniel Londas, *Gravelines, France* (WBA)
25 Oct 87 Rocky Lockridge W RSC 10 Johnny de la Rosa, *Tucson, USA* (IBF)
19 Dec 87 Brian Mitchell W RTD 8 Salvadore Curcetti, *Capo d'Orlando, Italy* (WBA)
29 Feb 88 Azumah Nelson W PTS 12 Mario Martinez, *Los Angeles USA* (WBC)
2 Apr 88 Rocky Lockridge W PTS 15 Harold Knight, *Atlantic City, USA* (IBF)
26 Apr 88 Brian Mitchell W PTS 12 Jose Rivera, *Madrid, Spain* (WBA)
4 Jun 88 Brian Mitchell W PTS 12 Danilo Cabrera, *Johannesburg, S Africa* (WBA)
25 Jun 88 Azumah Nelson W RSC 9 Lupe Suarez, *Atlantic City, USA* (WBC)
23 Jul 88 Tony Lopez W PTS 12 Rocky Lockridge, *Sacramento, USA* (IBF)
27 Oct 88 Tony Lopez W PTS 12 Juan Molina, *Sacramento, USA* (IBF)
2 Nov 88 Brian Mitchell W PTS 12 Jim MacDonnell, *London, England* (WBA)

FEATHERWEIGHT

(*Current weight limit:* 126lb/57.2kg)

DATE

13 Jan 90 Billy Murphy W KO 14 Ike Weir, *San Francisco, USA* (AUSTR)
3 Sep 90 Young Griffo W PTS 15 Billy Murphy, *Sydney, Australia* (AUSTR)
Young Griffo's title claim lapsed when he failed to press it
31 Mar 91 George Dixon W RSC 22 Cal McCarthy, *Troy, USA*
28 Jul 91 George Dixon W KO 5 Abe Willis, *San Francisco, USA*
27 Jun 92 George Dixon W KO 14 Fred Johnson, *New York C, USA*
6 Sep 92 George Dixon W KO 8 Jack Skelly, *New Orleans, USA*
7 Aug 93 George Dixon W KO 3 Eddie Pierce, *New York C, USA*
25 Sep 93 George Dixon W KO 7 Solly Smith, *New York C, USA*
27 Aug 95 George Dixon W PTS 25 Johnny Griffin, *Boston, USA*
5 Dec 95 George Dixon DREW 10 Frank Erne, *New York C, USA*
17 Mar 96 George Dixon W KO 8 Jerry Marshall, *Boston, USA*
16 Jun 96 George Dixon DREW 20 Martin Flaherty, *Boston, USA*
25 Sep 96 George Dixon DREW 20 Tommy White, *New York C, USA*
22 Jan 97 George Dixon W KO 6 Billy Murphy, *New York C, USA*
15 Feb 97 George Dixon DREW 20 Jack Downey, *New York C, USA*
26 Apr 97 George Dixon W PTS 20 Johnny Griffin, *New York C, USA*
23 Jul 97 George Dixon DREW 20 Dal Hawkins, *San Francisco, USA*
4 Oct 97 Solly Smith W PTS 20 George Dixon, *San Francisco, USA* (USA)
1 Jul 98 Ben Jordan W PTS 25 George Dixon, *New York C, USA* (GB)
7 Jul 98 Solly Smith W DIS 7 Billy O'Donnell, *Buffalo, USA* (USA)
1 Aug 98 Solly Smith DREW 25 Tommy White, *New York C, USA* (USA)
26 Sep 98 Dave Sullivan W RTD 5 Solly Smith, *New York C, USA* (USA)
11 Nov 98 George Dixon W DIS 10 Dave Sullivan, *New York C, USA* (USA)
29 Nov 98 George Dixon W PTS 25 Oscar Gardner, *New York C, USA* (USA)
17 Jan 99 George Dixon W KO 10 Young Pluto, *New York C, USA* (USA)
15 May 99 George Dixon W PTS 20 Kid Broad, *Buffalo, USA* (USA)
29 May 99 Ben Jordan W KO 9 Harry Greenfield, *London, England* (GB)
Ben Jordan ceased to be recognized by GB following a defeat by Eddie Santry in October, 1899
2 Jun 99 George Dixon W PTS 25 Joe Bernstein, *New York C, USA* (USA)
11 Jul 99 George Dixon W PTS 20 Tommy White, *Denver, USA* (USA)
11 Aug 99 George Dixon DREW 20 Eddie Santry, *New York C, USA* (USA)
2 Nov 99 George Dixon W PTS 25 Will Curley, *New York C, USA*
21 Nov 99 George Dixon W PTS 25 Eddie Lenny, *New York C, USA*
9 Jan 00 Terry McGovern W RSC 9 George Dixon, *New York C, USA*
1 Feb 00 Terry McGovern W KO 5 Eddie Santry, *Chicago, USA*
9 Mar 00 Terry McGovern W KO 3 Oscar Gardner, *New York C, USA*
12 Jun 00 Terry McGovern W KO 3 Tommy White, *New York C, USA*
2 Nov 00 Terry McGovern W KO 7 Joe Bernstein, *Louisville, USA*
30 Apr 01 Terry McGovern W KO 4 Oscar Gardner, *San Francisco, USA*
29 May 01 Terry McGovern W KO 5 Aurelio Herrera, *San Francisco, USA*
28 Nov 01 Young Corbett II W KO 2 Terry McGovern, *Hartford, USA*
16 Oct 02 Young Corbett II W RTD 8 Joe Bernstein, *Baltimore, USA*
14 Jan 03 Young Corbett II 18 Austin Rice, *Hot Springs, USA*
26 Feb 03 Young Corbett II DREW 20 Eddie Hanlon, *San Francisco, USA*
31 Mar 03 Young Corbett II W KO 11 Terry McGovern, *San Francisco, USA*
Young Corbett II lost general recognition (weight making difficulties)
3 Sep 03 Abe Attell W PTS 20 Johnny Reagan, *St Louis, USA*
1 Feb 04 Abe Attell W RSC 5 Harry Forbes, *St Louis, USA*
23 Jun 04 Abe Attell W PTS 20 Johnny Reagan, *St Louis, USA*
13 Oct 04 Tommy Sullivan W KO 5 Abe Attell, *St Louis, USA*
Tommy Sullivan forfeited title (inactivity)
22 Feb 06 Abe Attell W PTS 15 Jimmy Walsh, *Chelsea, Mass, USA*
15 Mar 06 Abe Attell W DIS 3 Tony Moran, *Baltimore, USA*
11 May 06 Abe Attell DREW 20 Kid Herman, *Los Angeles, USA*
4 Jul 06 Abe Attell W PTS 20 Frankie Neil, *Los Angeles, USA*
30 Oct 06 Abe Attell W PTS 20 Harry Baker, *Los Angeles, USA*
16 Nov 06 Abe Attell W PTS 15 Billy de Coursey, *San Diego, USA*
7 Dec 06 Abe Attell W KO 8 Jimmy Walsh, *Los Angeles, USA*
18 Jan 07 Abe Attell W KO 8 Harry Baker, *Los Angeles, USA*
24 May 07 Abe Attell W PTS 20 Kid Solomon, *Los Angeles, USA*
29 Oct 07 Abe Attell W KO 4 Freddie Weeks, *Los Angeles, USA*
1 Jan 08 Abe Attell DREW 25 Owen Moran, *San Francisco, USA*
31 Jan 08 Abe Attell W RTD 13 Frankie Neil, *San Francisco, USA*
28 Feb 08 Abe Attell W KO 7 Eddie Kelly, *San Francisco, USA*
30 Apr 08 Abe Attell W KO 4 Tommy Sullivan, *San Francisco, USA*
7 Sep 08 Abe Attell DREW 23 Owen Moran, *San Francisco, USA*
14 Jan 09 Abe Attell W KO 10 Freddie Weeks, *Goldfield, USA*
4 Feb 09 Abe Attell W KO 7 Eddie Kelly, *New Orleans, USA*

DATE	
26 Mar 09	Abe Attell W KO 8 Frankie White, *Dayton, USA*
28 Feb 10	Abe Attell W KO 6 Harry Forbes, *New York C, USA*
22 Aug 10	Abe Attell W KO 3 Eddie Marino, *Calgary, Canada*
5 Sep 10	Abe Attell W KO 17 Billy Lauder, *Calgary, Canada*
24 Oct 10	Abe Attell W PTS 10 Johnny Kilbane, *Kansas City, USA*
13 Nov 10	Abe Attell DREW 15 Frank Conley, *New Orleans, USA*
	Abe Attell forfeited GB/IBU recognition (failure to defend against Driscoll)
22 Feb 12	Johnny Kilbane W PTS 20 Abe Attell, *Los Angeles, USA* (USA)
21 May 12	Johnny Kilbane DREW 12 Jimmy Walsh, *Boston, USA* (USA)
3 Jun 12	Jim Driscoll W KO 12 Jean Poesy, *London, England* (GB/IBU)
14 Oct 12	Johnny Kilbane W PTS 12 Eddie O'Keefe, *Cleveland, USA* (USA)
3 Dec 12	Johnny Kilbane W RSC 8 Monte Attell, *Cleveland, USA* (USA)
27 Jan 13	Jim Driscoll DREW 20 Owen Moran, *London, England* (GB/IBU)
	Jim Driscoll ceased to be recognized by the IBU/GB after relinquishing the European featherweight title in July 1913
29 Apr 13	Johnny Kilbane DREW 20 Johnny Dundee, *Los Angeles, USA* (USA)
16 Sep 13	Johnny Kilbane W PTS 12 Jimmy Walsh, *Boston, USA*
4 Sep 16	Johnny Kilbane W KO 3 KO Chaney, *Cedar Point, USA*
26 Mar 17	Johnny Kilbane DREW 12 Eddie Wallace, *Bridgeport, USA*
21 Apr 20	Johnny Kilbane W KO 7 Alvie Miller, *Lorain, USA*
17 Aug 21	Johnny Kilbane W KO 7 Danny Frush, *Cleveland, USA*
	Johnny Kilbane lost New York recognition (failure to meet Johnny Dundee)
15 Aug 22	Johnny Dundee W KO 9 Danny Frush, *New York C, USA* (NY)
2 Jun 23	Eugene Criqui W KO 6 Johnny Kilbane, *New York C, USA* (NBA)
26 Jul 23	Johnny Dundee W PTS 15 Eugene Criqui, *New York C, USA*
	Johnny Dundee relinquished title to campaign as junior lightweight
2 Jan 25	Kid Kaplan W RTD 9 Danny Kramer, *New York C, USA*
27 Aug 25	Kid Kaplan DREW 15 Babe Herman, *Waterbury, USA*
18 Dec 25	Kid Kaplan W PTS 15 Babe Herman, *New York C, USA*
28 Jun 26	Kid Kaplan W KO 10 Bobby Garcia, *Hartford, USA*
	Kid Kaplan relinquished title (unable to make weight)
15 Nov 26	Honeyboy Finnegan W PTS 10 Chick Suggs, *Boston, USA* (MASS)
	Honeyboy Finnegan ceased to be recognized by Massachusetts (unable to make weight)
12 Sep 27	Benny Bass W PTS 10 Red Chapman, *Philadelphia, USA* (NBA)
24 Oct 27	Tony Canzoneri W PTS 15 Johnny Dundee, *New York C, USA* (NY)
10 Feb 28	Tony Canzoneri W PTS 15 Benny Bass, *New York C, USA*
28 Sep 28	Andre Routis W PTS 15 Tony Canzoneri, *New York C, USA*
27 May 29	Andre Routis W RSC 3 Buster Brown, *Baltimore, USA*
23 Sep 29	Bat Battalino W PTS 15 Andre Routis, *Hartford, USA*
15 Jul 30	Bat Battalino W KO 5 Ignacio Fernandez, *Hartford, USA*
12 Dec 30	Bat Battalino W PTS 15 Kid Chocolate, *New York C, USA*
22 May 31	Bat Battalino W PTS 15 Fidel la Barba, *New York C, USA*
1 Jul 31	Bat Battalino W PTS 10 Bobby Brady, *Jersey C, USA*
23 Jul 31	Bat Battalino W PTS 10 Freddie Miller, *Cincinnati, USA*
4 Nov 31	Bat Battalino W PTS 10 Earl Maestro, *Chicago, USA*
27 Jan 32	Bat Battalino NC Freddie Miller, *Cincinnati, USA*
	Bat Battalino forfeited title (overweight for the above defence)
26 May 32	Tommy Paul W PTS 10 Johnny Pena, *Detroit, USA* (NBA)
13 Oct 32	Kid Chocolate W KO 12 Lew Feldman, *New York C, USA* (NY)
9 Dec 32	Kid Chocolate W PTS 15 Fidel la Barba, *New York C, USA* (NY)
13 Jan 33	Freddie Miller W PTS 10 Tommy Paul, *Chicago, USA* (NBA)
28 Feb 33	Freddie Miller W PTS 10 Baby Arizmendi, *Los Angeles, USA* (NBA)
21 Mar 33	Freddie Miller W PTS 10 Speedy Dado, *Los Angeles, USA* (NBA)
19 May 33	Kid Chocolate W PTS 15 Seaman Tommy Watson, *New York C, USA* (NY)
	Kid Chocolate forfeited NY recognition (failure to defend against Frankie Klick)
1 Jan 34	Freddie Miller W PTS 10 Jackie Sharkey, *Cincinnati, USA* (NBA)
30 Aug 34	Baby Arizmendi W PTS 15 Mike Belloise, *New York C, USA* (NY)
	Baby Arizmendi forfeited NY recognition for contesting California title
21 Sep 34	Freddie Miller W PTS 15 Nel Tarleton, *Liverpool, England* (NBA)
1 Jan 35	Baby Arizmendi W PTS 12 Henry Armstrong, *Mexico C, Mexico* (CALIF)
17 Feb 35	Freddie Miller W KO 1 Jose Girones, *Barcelona, Spain* (NBA)
12 Jun 35	Freddie Miller W PTS 15 Nel Tarleton, *Liverpool, England* (NBA)
22 Oct 35	Freddie Miller W PTS 15 Vernon Cormier, *Boston, USA* (NBA)
18 Feb 36	Freddie Miller W PTS 12 Johnny Pena, *Seattle, USA* (NBA)
2 Mar 36	Freddie Miller W PTS 15 Petey Sarron, *Miami, USA* (NBA)
11 May 36	Petey Sarron W PTS 15 Freddie Miller, *Washington, USA* (NBA)
22 Jul 36	Petey Sarron W PTS 15 Baby Manuel, *Dallas, USA* (NBA)

***Above:** Battling Battalino, the world featherweight champion for over two years, in training. He lost his title after a match with Freddie Miller, the fighters having come to an illegal arrangement.*

DATE	
4 Aug 36	Henry Armstrong W PTS 10 Baby Arizmendi, *Los Angeles, USA* (CALIF)
3 Sep 36	Mike Belloise W KO 9 Dave Crowley, *New York C, USA* (NY)
	Mike Belloise forfeited NY recognition for contesting California title
27 Oct 36	Henry Armstrong W PTS 10 Mike Belloise, *Los Angeles, USA* (CALIF)
4 Sep 37	Petey Sarron W PTS 12 Freddie Miller, *Johannesburg, S Africa* (NBA)
5 Oct 37	Maurice Holtzer W PTS 15 Phil Dolhem, *Algiers, Algeria* (IBU)
29 Oct 37	Henry Armstrong W KO 6 Petey Sarron, *New York C, USA* (NY/NBA)
	Henry Armstrong relinquished title to campaign as a welterweight
19 Feb 38	Maurice Holtzer DREW 15 Maurice Dubois, *Geneva, Switzerland* (IBU)
	Maurice Holtzer ceased to be recognized by the IBU after relinquishing the EBU featherweight title in July, 1938
17 Oct 38	Joey Archibald W PTS 15 Mike Belloise, *New York C, USA* (NY)

DATE	
29 Dec 38	Leo Rodak W PTS Leone Efrati, *Chicago, USA* (NBA)
18 Apr 39	Joey Archibald W PTS 15 Leo Rodak, *Providence, USA*
	Joey Archibald forfeited NBA recognition (refused to defend against Petey Scalzo)
28 Sep 39	Joey Archibald W PTS 15 Harry Jeffra, *Washington, USA* (NY)
8 May 40	Jimmy Perrin W PTS 15 Bobby Ruffing, *New Orleans, USA* (LOUIS)
	Jimmy Perrin ceased to be recognized by Louisiana following a defeat by Petey Scalzo in a non-title bout, August, 1940
15 May 40	Petey Scalzo W KO 6 Frankie Covelli, *Washington, USA* (NBA)
20 May 40	Harry Jeffra W PTS 15 Joey Archibald, *Baltimore, USA* (NY)
10 Jul 40	Petey Scalzo W RSC 15 Bobby Poison Ivy, *Hartford, USA* (NBA)
29 Jul 40	Harry Jeffra W PTS 15 Spider Armstrong, *Baltimore, USA* (NY)
12 May 41	Joey Archibald W PTS 15 Harry Jeffra, *Washington, USA* (NY)
19 May 41	Petey Scalzo W PTS 15 Phil Zwick, *Milwaukee, USA* (NBA)
1 Jul 41	Richie Lemons W KO 5 Petey Scalzo, *Los Angeles, USA* (NBA)
11 Sep 41	Chalky Wright W KO 11 Joey Archibald, *Washington, USA* (NY)
15 Sep 41	Harry Jeffra W PTS 12 Lou Transparenti, *Baltimore, USA* (MARY)
18 Nov 41	Jackie Wilson W PTS 12 Richie Lemons, *Los Angeles, USA* (NBA)
16 Dec 41	Jackie Wilson W PTS 12 Richie Lemons, *Los Angeles, USA* (NBA)
19 Jun 42	Chalky Wright W RSC 10 Harry Jeffra, *Baltimore, USA* (NY)
25 Sep 42	Chalky Wright W PTS 15 Lulu Constantino, *New York C, USA* (NY)
20 Nov 42	Willie Pep W PTS 15 Chalky Wright, *New York C, USA* (NY)
18 Jan 43	Jackie Callura W PTS 15 Jackie Wilson, *Providence, USA* (NBA)
18 Mar 43	Jackie Callura W PTS 15 Jackie Wilson, *Boston, USA* (NBA)
8 Jun 43	Willie Pep W PTS 15 Sal Bartolo, *Boston, USA* (NY)
16 Aug 43	Phil Terranova W KO 8 Jackie Callura, *New Orleans, USA* (NBA)
27 Dec 43	Phil Terranova W RSC 6 Jackie Callura, *New Orleans, USA* (NBA)
10 Mar 44	Sal Bartolo W PTS 15 Phil Terranova, *Boston, USA* (NBA)
5 May 44	Sal Bartolo W PTS 15 Phil Terranova, *Boston, USA* (NBA)
29 Sep 44	Willie Pep W PTS 15 Chalky Wright, *New York C, USA* (NY)
15 Dec 44	Sal Bartolo W PTS 15 Willie Roache, *Boston, USA* (NBA)
19 Feb 45	Willie Pep W PTS 15 Phil Terranova, *New York C, USA* (NY)
3 May 46	Sal Bartolo W KO 6 Spider Armstrong, *Boston, USA* (NBA)
7 Jun 46	Willie Pep W KO 12 Sal Bartolo, *New York C, USA*
22 Aug 47	Willie Pep W KO 12 Jock Leslie, *Flint, USA*
24 Feb 48	Willie Pep W RSC 10 Humberto Sierra, *Miami, USA*
29 Oct 48	Sandy Saddler W KO 4 Willie Pep, *New York C, USA*
11 Feb 49	Willie Pep W PTS 15 Sandy Saddler, *New York C, USA*
20 Sep 49	Willie Pep RSC 7 Eddie Compo, *Waterbury, USA*
16 Jan 50	Willie Pep W KO 5 Charley Riley, *St Louis, USA*
17 Mar 50	Willie Pep W PTS 15 Ray Famechon, *New York C, USA*
8 Sep 50	Sandy Saddler W RTD 8 Willie Pep, *New York C, USA*
26 Sep 51	Sandy Saddler W RTD 9 Willie Pep, *New York C, USA*
25 Feb 55	Sandy Saddler W PTS 15 Teddy Davis, *New York C, USA*
18 Jan 56	Sandy Saddler W RSC 13 Flash Elorde, *San Francisco, USA*
	Sandy Saddler relinquished title (retired)
24 Jun 57	Hogan Kid Bassey W RSC 10 Cherif Hamia, *Paris, France*
1 Apr 58	Hogan Kid Bassey W KO 3 Ricardo Moreno, *Los Angeles, USA*
18 Mar 59	Davey Moore W RTD 13 Hogan Kid Bassey, *Los Angeles, USA*
19 Aug 59	Davey Moore W RTD 10 Hogan Kid Bassey, *Los Angeles, USA*
29 Aug 60	Davey Moore W PTS 15 Kazuo Takayama, *Tokyo, Japan*
8 Apr 61	Davey Moore W KO 1 Danny Valdez, *Los Angeles, USA*
13 Nov 61	Davey Moore W PTS 15 Kazuo Takayama, *Tokyo, Japan*
17 Aug 62	Davey Moore W RSC 2 Olli Maki, *Helsinki, Finland*
21 Mar 63	Sugar Ramos W RTD 10 Davey Moore, *Los Angeles, USA*
13 Jul 63	Sugar Ramos W PTS 15 Rafiu King, *Mexico C, Mexico*
28 Feb 64	Sugar Ramos W RTD 6 Mitsunori Seki, *Tokyo, Japan*
9 May 64	Sugar Ramos W PTS 15 Floyd Robertson, *Accra, Ghana*
26 Sep 64	Vicente Saldivar W RTD 11 Sugar Ramos, *Mexico C, Mexico*
6 Dec 64	Vicente Saldivar W RSC 11 Delfino Rosales, *Guanajuato, Mexico*
7 May 65	Vicente Saldivar W RSC 15 Raul Rojas, *Los Angeles, USA*
7 Sep 65	Vicente Saldivar W PTS 15 Howard Winstone, *London, England*
12 Feb 66	Vicente Saldivar W KO 2 Floyd Robertson, *Mexico C, Mexico*
7 Aug 66	Vicente Saldivar W PTS 15 Mitsunori Seki, *Mexico C, Mexico*
29 Jan 67	Vicente Saldivar W RSC 7 Mitsunori Seki, *Mexico C, Mexico*
15 Jun 67	Vicente Saldivar W PTS 15 Howard Winstone, *Cardiff, Wales*
14 Oct 67	Vicente Saldivar W RTD 12 Howard Winstone, *Mexico C, Mexico*
	Vicente Saldivar relinquished title (retired)
14 Dec 67	Raul Rojas W PTS 15 Antonio Herrera, *Los Angeles, USA* (WBA)
23 Jan 68	Howard Winstone W RSC 9 Mitsunori Seki, *London, England* (WBC)
28 Mar 68	Raul Rojas W PTS 15 Enrique Higgins, *Los Angeles, USA* (WBA)
24 Jul 68	Jose Legra W RSC 5 Howard Winstone, *Porthcawl, Wales* (WBC)
28 Sep 68	Shozo Saijyo W PTS 15 Raul Rojas, *Los Angeles, USA* (WBA)
21 Jan 69	Johnny Famechon W PTS 15 Jose Legra, *London, England* (WBC)
9 Feb 69	Shozo Saijyo W PTS 15 Pedro Gomez, *Tokyo, Japan* (WBA)

DATE	
28 Jul 69	Johnny Famechon W PTS 15 Fighting Harada, *Sydney, Australia* (WBC)
7 Sep 69	Shozo Saijyo W KO 2 Jose Pimental, *Sapporo, Japan* (WBA)
6 Jan 70	Johnny Famechon W KO 14 Fighting Harada, *Tokyo, Japan* (WBC)
8 Feb 70	Shozo Saijyo W PTS 15 Godfrey Stevens, *Tokyo, Japan* (WBA)
9 May 70	Vicente Saldivar W PTS 15 Johnny Famechon, *Rome, Italy* (WBC)
5 Jul 70	Shozo Saijyo W PTS 15 Frankie Crawford, *Sendai, Japan* (WBA)
11 Dec 70	Kuniaki Shibata W RSC 12 Vicente Saldivar, *Tijuana, Mexico* (WBC)
28 Feb 71	Shozo Saijyo W PTS 15 Frankie Crawford, *Utsonomuja, Japan* (WBA)
3 Jun 71	Kuniaki Shibata W KO 1 Raul Cruz, *Tokyo, Japan* (WBC)
2 Sep 71	Antonio Gomez W RSC 5 Shozo Saijyo, *Tokyo, Japan* (WBA)
11 Nov 71	Kuniaki Shibata DREW 15 Ernesto Marcel, *Matsuyama, Japan* (WBC)
6 Feb 72	Antonio Gomez W KO 7 Raul Martinez, *Maracay, Venezuela* (WBA)
19 May 72	Clemente Sanchez W KO 3 Kuniaki Shibata, *Tokyo, Japan* (WBC)
19 Aug 72	Ernesto Marcel W PTS 15 Antonio Gomez, *Maracay, Venezuela* (WBA)
3 Dec 72	Ernesto Marcel W RSC 6 Enrique Garcia, *Panama C, Panama* (WBA)
16 Dec 72	Jose Legra W RSC 10 Clemente Sanchez, *Monterrey, Mexico* (WBC)
5 May 73	Eder Jofre W PTS 15 Jose Legra, *Brasilia, Brazil* (WBC)
14 Jul 73	Ernesto Marcel W RTD 11 Antonio Gomez, *Panama C, Panama* (WBA)
8 Sep 73	Ernesto Marcel W KO 9 Spider Nemoto, *Panama C, Panama* (WBA)
21 Oct 73	Eder Jofre W KO 4 Vicente Saldivar, *Salvador, Brazil* (WBC)
	Eder Jofre forfeited WBC recognition (failure to defend against Alfredo Marcano)
13 Feb 74	Ernesto Marcel W PTS 15 Alexis Arguello, *Panama C, Panama* (WBA)
	Ernesto Marcel relinquished title (retired)
9 Jul 74	Ruben Olivares W RSC 7 Zensuke Utagawa, *Los Angeles, USA* (WBA)
7 Sep 74	Bobby Chacon W RSC 9 Alfredo Marcano, *Los Angeles, USA* (WBC)
23 Nov 74	Alexis Arguello W KO 13 Ruben Olivares, *Los Angeles, USA* (WBA)
1 Mar 75	Bobby Chacon W KO 2 Jesus Estrada, *Los Angeles, USA* (WBC)
15 Mar 75	Alexis Arguello W RSC 8 Leonel Hernandez, *Caracas, Venezuela* (WBA)
31 May 75	Alexis Arguello W RSC 2 Rigoberto Riasco, *Managua, Nicaragua* (WBA)
20 Jan 75	Ruben Olivares W RSC 2 Bobby Chacon, *Los Angeles, USA* (WBC)
20 Sep 75	David Kotey W PTS 15 Ruben Olivares, *Los Angeles, USA* (WBC)
12 Oct 75	Alexis Arguello W KO 5 Royal Kobayashi, *Tokyo, Japan* (WBA)
6 Mar 76	David Kotey W RSC 12 Flipper Uehara, *Accra, Ghana* (WBC)
19 Jun 76	Alexis Arguello W KO 3 Salvatore Torres, *Los Angeles, USA* (WBA)
	Alexis Arguello relinquished title to campaign as a junior lightweight
16 Jul 76	David Kotey W RSC 3 Shig Fukuyama, *Tokyo, Japan* (WBC)
5 Nov 76	Danny Lopez W PTS 15 David Kotey, *Accra, Ghana* (WBC)
15 Jan 77	Rafael Ortega W PTS 15 Francisco Coronada, *Panama C, Panama* (WBA)
29 May 77	Rafael Ortega W PTS 15 Flipper Uehara, *Okinawa, Japan* (WBA)
13 Sep 77	Danny Lopez W RSC 7 Jose Torres, *Los Angeles, USA* (WBC)
17 Dec 77	Cecilio Lastra W PTS 15 Rafael Ortega, *Torrelavega, Spain* (WBA)
15 Feb 78	Danny Lopez W RSC 6 David Kotey, *Las Vegas, USA* (WBC)
15 Apr 78	Eusebio Pedroza W KO 13 Cecilio Lastra, *Panama C, Panama* (WBA)
23 Apr 78	Danny Lopez W RSC 6 Jose de Paula, *Los Angeles, USA* (WBC)
2 Jul 78	Eusebio Pedroza W RSC 12 Ernesto Herrera, *Panama C, Panama* (WBA)
15 Sep 78	Danny Lopez W KO 2 Juan Malvarez, *New Orleans, USA* (WBC)
21 Oct 78	Danny Lopez W DIS 4 Fel Clemente, *Pesaro, Italy* (WBC)
27 Nov 78	Eusebio Pedroza W PTS 15 Enrique Solis, *San Juan, Puerto Rico* (WBA)
9 Jan 79	Eusebio Pedroza W RTD 13 Royal Kobayashi, *Tokyo, Japan* (WBA)
10 Mar 79	Danny Lopez W KO 2 Danny Castanon, *Salt Lake C, USA* (WBC)
3 Apr 79	Eusebio Pedroza W RSC 11 Hector Carrasquilla, *Panama C, Panama* (WBA)
17 Jun 79	Danny Lopez W KO 15 Mike Ayala, *San Antonio, USA* (WBC)
21 Jul 79	Eusebio Pedroza W RSC 12 Ruben Olivares, *Houston, USA* (WBA)
25 Sep 79	Danny Lopez W RSC 3 Jose Caba, *Los Angeles, USA* (WBC)
17 Nov 79	Eusebio Pedroza W RSC 11 Johnny Aba, *Port Moresby, P N Guinea* (WBA)

Right: Steve Cruz gets a right to Barry McGuigan on the way to taking his world featherweight title in Las Vegas in 1986.

DATE	
22 Jan 80	Eusebio Pedroza W PTS 15 Spider Nemoto, *Tokyo, Japan* (WBA)
2 Feb 80	Salvador Sanchez W RSC 13 Danny Lopez, *Phoenix, USA* (WBC)
29 Mar 80	Eusebio Pedroza W KO 9 Juan Malvarez, *Panama C, Panama* (WBA)
12 Apr 80	Salvador Sanchez W PTS 15 Ruben Castillo, *Tucson, USA* (WBC)
21 Jun 80	Salvador Sanchez W RSC 14 Danny Lopez, *Las Vegas, USA* (WBC)
20 Jul 80	Eusebio Pedroza W KO 9 Sa-Wang Kim, *Seoul, S Korea* (WBA)
13 Sep 80	Salvador Sanchez W PTS 15 Pat Ford, *San Antonio, USA* (WBC)
4 Oct 80	Eusebio Pedroza W PTS 15 Rocky Lockridge, *McAfee, USA* (WBA)
13 Dec 80	Salvador Sanchez W PTS 15 Juan Laporte, *El Paso, USA* (WBC)
14 Feb 81	Eusebio Pedroza W KO 13 Pat Ford, *Panama C, Panama* (WBA)
22 Mar 81	Salvador Sanchez W RSC 10 Roberto Castanon, *Las Vegas* (WBC)
1 Aug 81	Eusebio Pedroza W KO 7 Carlos Pinango, *Caracas, Venezuela* (WBA)
21 Aug 81	Salvador Sanchez W RSC 8 Wilfredo Gomez, *Las Vegas, USA* (WBC)
5 Dec 81	Eusebio Pedroza W KO 5 Bashew Sibaca, *Panama C, Panama* (WBA)
12 Dec 81	Salvador Sanchez W PTS 15 Pat Cowdell, *Houston, USA* (WBC)
24 Jan 82	Eusebio Pedroza W PTS 15 Juan Laporte, *Atlantic C, USA* (WBA)
8 May 82	Salvador Sanchez W PTS 15 Rocky Garcia, *Dallas, USA* (WBC)
21 Jul 82	Salvador Sanchez W RSC 15 Azumah Nelson, *New York C, USA* (WBC)
	Salvador Sanchez was killed in an accident while still champion
15 Sep 82	Juan Laporte W RTD 10 Mario Miranda, *New York C, USA* (WBC)
16 Oct 82	Eusebio Pedroza DREW 15 Bernard Taylor, *Charlotte, USA* (WBA)
20 Feb 83	Juan Laporte W PTS 12 Ruben Castillo, *San Juan, Puerto Rico* (WBC)
24 Apr 83	Eusebio Pedroza W PTS 15 Rocky Lockridge, *Liguma, Italy* (WBA)
25 Jun 83	Juan Laporte W PTS 12 Johnny de la Rosa, *San Juan, Puerto Rico* (WBC)
22 Oct 83	Eusebio Pedroza W PTS 15 Jose Caba, *St Vincent, West Indies* (WBA)
4 Mar 84	Min-Keun Oh W KO 2 Joko Arter, *Seoul, S Korea* (IBF)
31 Mar 84	Wilfredo Gomez W PTS 12 Juan Laporte, *San Juan, Puerto Rico* (WBC)
27 May 84	Eusebio Pedroza W PTS 15 Angel Mayor, *Maracaibo, Venezuela* (WBA)
10 Jul 84	Min-Keun Oh W PTS 5 Kelvin Lampkin, *Seoul, S Korea* (IBF)
8 Dec 84	Azumah Nelson W RSC 11 Wilfredo Gomez, *San Juan, Puerto Rico* (WBC)

DATE	
2 Feb 85	Eusebio Pedroza W PTS 15 Jorge Lujan, *Panama C, Panama* (WBA)
7 Apr 85	Min-Keun Oh W PTS 15 Irving Mitchell, *Pusan, S Korea* (IBF)
8 Jun 85	Barry McGuigan W PTS 15 Eusebio Pedroza, *London, England* (WBA)
6 Sep 85	Azumah Nelson W KO 5 Juvenal Ordenes, *Miami, USA* (WBC)
28 Sep 85	Barry McGuigan W RTD 8 Bernard Taylor, *Belfast, Ireland* (WBA)
12 Oct 85	Azumah Nelson W KO 1 Pat Cowdell, *Birmingham, England* (WBC)
29 Nov 85	Ki-Yung Chung W RSC 15 Min-Keun Oh, *Chonju, S Korea* (IBF)
15 Feb 86	Barry McGuigan W RSC 14 Danilo Cabrera, *Dublin, Ireland* (WBA)
16 Feb 86	Ki-Yung Chung W RTD 6 Tyrone Jackson, *Ulsan, S Korea* (IBF)
25 Feb 86	Azumah Nelson W PTS 12 Marcos Villasana, *Los Angeles, USA* (WBC)
18 May 86	Ki-Yung Chung W PTS 15 Richard Savage, *Taegu, S Korea* (IBF)
22 Jun 86	Azumah Nelson W RSC 10 Danilo Cabrera, *San Juan, Puerto Rico* (WBC)
23 Jun 86	Steve Cruz W PTS 15 Barry McGuigan, *Las Vegas, USA* (WBA)
30 Aug 86	Antonio Rivera W RTD 10 Ki-Yung Chung, *Osan, S Korea* (IBF)
6 Mar 87	Antonio Esparragoza W RSC 12 Steve Cruz, *Fort Worth, USA* (WBA)
7 Mar 87	Azumah Nelson W KO 6 Mauro Gutierrez, *Las Vegas, USA* (WBC)
26 Jul 87	Antonio Esparragoza W KO 10 Pascual Aranda, *Houston, USA* (WBA)
29 Aug 87	Azumah Nelson W PTS 12 Marcos Villasana, *Los Angeles, USA* (WBC)
	Azumah Nelson relinquished title to campaign as a junior lightweight
23 Jan 88	Calvin Grove W RSC 4 Antonio Rivera, *Gamaches, France* (IBF)
7 Mar 88	Jeff Fenech W RSC 10 Victor Callejas, *Sydney, Australia* (WBC)
17 May 88	Calvin Grove W PTS 15 Myron Taylor, *Atlantic City, USA* (IBF)
23 Jun 88	Antonio Esparragoza DREW 12 Marcos Villasana, *Los Angeles, USA* (WBA)
4 Aug 88	Jorge Paez W PTS 15 Calvin Grove, *Mexicali, Mexico* (IBF)
12 Aug 88	Jeff Fenech W RSC 5 Tyrone Daniels, *Melbourne, Australia* (WBC)
5 Nov 88	Antonio Esparragoza W KO 8 Jose Marmolejo, *Masala, Italy* (WBA)

LIGHT-FEATHERWEIGHT

(*Current weight limit:* 122lb/55.3kg. The WBA and IBF call this class 'Junior Featherweight', and the WBC call it 'Super-bantamweight')

DATE	
21 Sep 22	Jack Kid Wolfe W PTS 15 Joe Lynch, *New York C, USA* (NY)
	Jack Kid Wolfe ceased to be recognized by NY (overweight for defence against Carl Duane — title fell into disuse)
3 Apr 76	Rigoberto Riasco W RTD 8 Waruinge Nakayama, *Panama C, Panama* (WBC)
12 Jun 76	Rigoberto Riasco W KO 10 Livio Nolasco, *Panama C, Panama* (WBC)
1 Aug 76	Rigoberto Riasco W PTS 15 Dong-Kyun Yum, *Pusan, S Korea* (WBC)
10 Oct 76	Royal Kobayashi W RSC 8 Rigoberto Riasco, *Tokyo, Japan* (WBC)
24 Nov 76	Dong-Kyun Yum W PTS 15 Royal Kobayashi, *Seoul, S Korea* (WBC)
13 Feb 77	Dong-Kyun Yum W PTS 15 Jose Cervantes, *Seoul, S Korea* (WBC)
21 May 77	Wilfredo Gomez W KO 12 Dong-Kyun Yum, *San Juan, Puerto Rico* (WBC)
11 Jul 77	Wilfredo Gomez W KO 5 Raol Tirado, *San Juan, Puerto Rico* (WBC)
26 Nov 77	Soo-Hwan Hong W KO 3 Hector Carrasquilla, *Panama C, Panama* (WBA)
19 Jan 78	Wilfredo Gomez W KO 3 Royal Kobayashi, *Kitakyushu, Japan* (WBC)
1 Feb 78	Soo-Hwan Hong W PTS 15 Yu Kasahara, *Tokyo, Japan* (WBA)
8 Apr 78	Wilfredo Gomez W RSC 7 Juan Antonio Lopez, *Bayamon, Puerto Rico* (WBC)
6 May 78	Ricardo Cardona W RSC 12 Soo-Hwan Hong, *Seoul, S Korea* (WBA)
2 Jun 78	Wilfredo Gomez W RSC 3 Sakad Petchyindee, *Korat, Thailand* (WBC)
2 Sep 78	Ricardo Cardona W PTS 15 Ruben Valdez, *Cartagena, Colombia* (WBA)
9 Sep 78	Wilfredo Gomez W RSC 13 Leonardo Cruz, *San Juan, Puerto Rico* (WBC)
28 Oct 78	Wilfredo Gomez W RSC 5 Carlos Zarate, *San Juan, Puerto Rico* (WBC)
12 Nov 78	Ricardo Cardona W PTS 15 Soon-Hyun Chung, *Seoul, S Korea* (WBA)
9 Mar 79	Wilfredo Gomez W RSC 5 Nestor Jimenez, *New York C, USA* (WBC)
16 Jun 79	Wilfredo Gomez W RSC 5 Jesus Hernandez, *San Juan, Puerto Rico* (WBC)
23 Jun 79	Ricardo Cardona W PTS 15 Soon-Hyun Chung, *Seoul, S Korea* (WBA)
6 Sep 79	Ricardo Cardona W PTS 15 Yukio Segawa, *Hachinhoe, Japan* (WBA)
28 Sep 79	Wilfredo Gomez W RSC 10 Carlos Mendoza, *Las Vegas, USA* (WBC)

DATE	
26 Oct 79	Wilfredo Gomez W RSC 5 Nicky Perez, *New York C, USA* (WBC)
15 Dec 79	Ricardo Cardona W PTS 15 Sergio Palma, *Barranquilla, Colombia* (WBA)
3 Feb 80	Wilfredo Gomez W RTD 6 Ruben Valdez, *Las Vegas, USA* (WBC)
4 May 80	Leo Randolph W RSC 15 Ricardo Cardona, *Seattle, USA* (WBA)
9 Aug 80	Sergio Palma W KO 6 Leo Randolph, *Washington, USA* (WBA)
22 Aug 80	Wilfredo Gomez W RSC 5 Derrick Holmes, *Las Vegas, USA* (WBC)
8 Nov 80	Sergio Palma W RSC 9 Ulisses Morales, *Buenos Aires, Argentine* (WBA)
13 Dec 80	Wilfredo Gomez W KO 3 Jose Cervantes, *Miami, USA* (WBC)
4 Apr 81	Sergio Palma W PTS 15 Leonardo Cruz, *Buenos Aires, Argentine* (WBA)
15 Aug 81	Sergio Palma W RSC 12 Ricardo Cardona, *Buenos Aires, Argentine* (WBA)
3 Oct 81	Sergio Palma W PTS 15 Vichit Muangroi-Et, *Buenos Aires, Argentine* (WBA)
13 Jan 82	Sergio Palma W PTS 15 Jorge Lujan, *Cordoba, Argentine* (WBA)
27 Mar 82	Wilfredo Gomez W RSC 6 Juan Meza, *Atlantic C, USA* (WBC)
11 Jun 82	Wilfredo Gomez W KO 10 Juan Antonio Lopez, *Las Vegas, USA* (WBC)
12 Jun 82	Leonardo Cruz W PTS 15 Sergio Palma, *Miami, USA* (WBA)
18 Aug 82	Wilfredo Gomez W RTD 7 Roberto Rubaldino, *San Juan, Puerto Rico* (WBC)
13 Nov 82	Leonardo Cruz W KO 8 Benito Badilla, *San Juan, Puerto Rico* (WBA)
3 Dec 82	Wilfredo Gomez W RSC 14 Lupe Pintor, *New Orleans, USA* (WBC)
	Wilfredo Gomez relinquished title to campaign as a featherweight
16 Mar 83	Leonardo Cruz W PTS 15 Soon-Hyun Chung, *San Juan, Puerto Rico* (WBA)
15 Jun 83	Jaime Garza W RSC 2 Bobby Berna, *Los Angeles, USA* (WBC)
26 Aug 83	Leonardo Cruz W PTS 15 Cleo Garcia, *St Domingo, Dominican Republic* (WBA)
4 Dec 83	Bobby Berna W RTD 11 Seung-In Suh, *Seoul, S Korea* (IBF)
22 Feb 84	Loris Stecca W RSC 12 Leonardo Cruz, *Milan, Italy* (WBA)
15 Apr 84	Seung-In Suh W KO 10 Bobby Berna, *Seoul, S Korea* (IBF)
26 May 84	Jaime Garza W KO 3 Felipe Orozco, *Miami, USA* (WBC)
26 May 84	Victor Callejas W RSC 8 Loris Stecca, *Guaynabo, Puerto Rico* (WBA)
8 Jul 84	Seung-In Suh W KO 4 Cleo Garcia, *Seoul, S Korea* (IBF)
3 Nov 84	Juan Meza W KO 1 Jaime Garza, *Kingston NY, USA* (WBC)
3 Jan 85	Ji-Won Kim W KO 10 Seung-In Suh, *Seoul, S Korea* (IBF)
2 Feb 85	Victor Callejas W PTS 15 Seung-Hoon Lee, *San Juan, Puerto Rico* (WBA)
30 Mar 85	Ji-Won Kim W PTS 15 Ruben Palacios, *Suwon, S Korea* (IBF)
19 Apr 85	Juan Meza W RSC 6 Mike Ayala, *Los Angeles, USA* (WBC)
28 Jun 85	Ji-Won Kim W KO 4 Bobby Berna, *Pusan, S Korea* (IBF)
18 Aug 83	Lupe Pintor W PTS 12 Juan Meza, *Mexico C, Mexico* (WBC)
9 Oct 85	Ji-Won Kim W KO 1 Seung-In Suh, *Seoul, S Korea* (IBF)
8 Nov 85	Victor Callejas W RTD 6 Loris Stecca, *Rimini, Italy* (WBA)
	Victor Callejas forfeited WBA recognition (failure to defend against Louie Espinosa)
18 Jan 86	Samart Payakarun W KO 5 Lupe Pintor, *Bangkok, Thailand* (WBC)

***Below:** Wilfredo Gomez, facing camera, successfully defending his world title against Juan Antonio Lopez in 1978.*

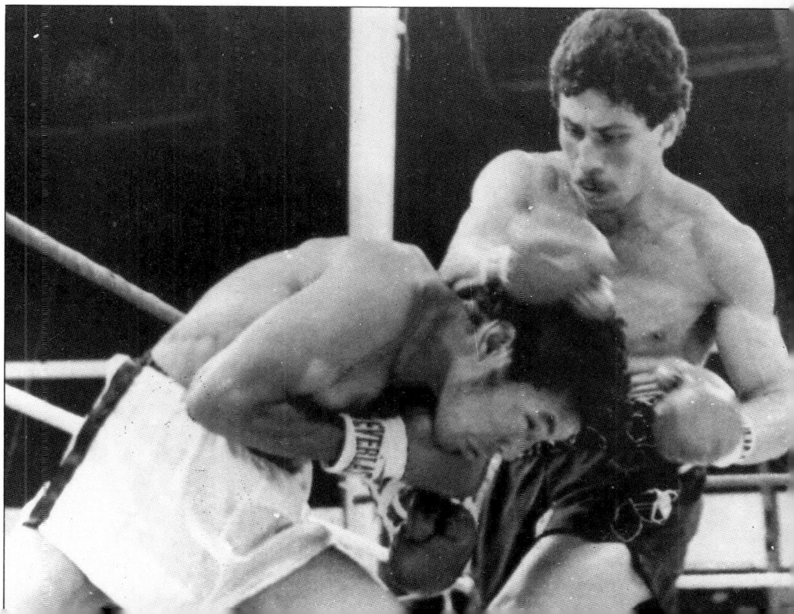

DATE	
1 Jun 86	Ji-Won Kim W KO 2 Rudy Casicas, *Inchon, S Korea* (IBF) *Ji-Won Kim relinquished title (retired)*
10 Dec 86	Samart Payakarun W KO 12 Juan Meza, *Bangkok, Thailand* (WBC)
16 Jan 87	Louie Espinosa W RSC 4 Tommy Valoy, *Phoenix, USA* (WBA)
18 Jan 87	Seung-Hoon Lee W KO 9 Prayoonsak Muangsurin, *Pohang, S Korea* (IBF)
5 Apr 87	Seung-Hoon Lee W KO 10 Jorge Urbina Diaz, *Seoul, S Korea* (IBF)
8 May 87	Jeff Fenech W RSC 4 Samart Payakarun, *Sydney, Australia* (WBC)
10 Jul 87	Jeff Fenech W RTD 5 Greg Richardson, *Sydney, Australia* (WBC)
15 Jul 87	Louie Espinosa W RSC 15 Manuel Vilchez, *Phoenix, USA* (WBA)
19 Jul 87	Seung-Hoon Lee W KO 5 Lion Collins, *Seoul, S Korea* (IBF)
15 Aug 87	Louie Espinosa W KO 9 Mike Ayala, *San Antonio, USA* (WBA)
16 Oct 87	Jeff Fenech W TD 4 Carlos Zarate, *Sydney, Australia* (WBC) *Fenech relinquished title to campaign as a featherweight*
28 Nov 87	Juan Gervacio W PTS 12 Louie Espinosa, *San Juan, Puerto Rico* (WBA)
27 Dec 87	Seung-Hoon Lee W PTS 15 Jose Sanabria, *Pohang, S Korea* (IBF) *Seung-Hoon Lee relinquished title to challenge Zaragoza for the WBC title*
27 Feb 88	Bernardo Pinango W PTS 12 Juan Gervacio, *San Juan, Puerto Rico* (WBA)
29 Feb 88	Daniel Zaragoza W RSC 10 Carlos Zarate, *Los Angeles, USA* (WBC)
21 May 88	Jose Sanabria W KO 5 Moises Fuentes, *Bucaramanga, Colombia* (IBF)
28 May 88	Juan Jose Estrada W PTS 12 Bernardo Pinango, *Tijuana, Mexico* (WBA)
29 May 88	Daniel Zaragoza DREW 12 Seung-Hoon Lee, *Youshan, S Korea* (WBC)
21 Aug 88	Jose Sanabria W PTS 12 Vicenzo Belcastro, *Sicily, Italy* (IBF)
26 Sep 88	Jose Sanabria W RSC 10 Fabrice Benichou, *Nogent-sur-Marne, France* (IBF)
15 Oct 88	Juan J. Estrada W RSC 11 Takuya Muguruma, *Moriguchi, Japan* (WBA)
11 Nov 88	Jose Sanabria W RSC 6 Thierry Jacob, *Gravelines, France* (IBF)

BANTAMWEIGHT

(*Current weight limit:* 118lb/53.5kg)

DATE	
27 Jun 90	George Dixon W RTD 18 Nunc Wallace, *London, England*
23 Oct 90	George Dixon W RSC 40 Johnny Murphy, *Providence, USA* *Dixon relinquished title to campaign as a featherweight*
9 May 92	Billy Plimmer W PTS 10 Tommy Kelly, *New York C, USA*
28 Dec 92	Billy Plimmer W KO 8 Joe McGrath, *New York C, USA*
15 Sep 94	Jimmy Barry W KO 28 Casper Leon, *Lamont, USA* (USA)
24 Sep 94	Billy Plimmer DREW 25 Johnny Murphy, *New Orleans, USA*
26 Nov 94	Billy Plimmer W KO 3 Charley Kelly, *New York C, USA*
28 May 95	Billy Plimmer W KO 7 George Corfield, *London, England*
25 Nov 95	Pedlar Palmer W DIS 14 Billy Plimmer, *London, England*
18 Oct 97	Pedlar Palmer W PTS 20 Dave Sullivan, *London, England*
6 Dec 97	Jimmy Barry W KO 20 Walter Croot, *London, England* (USA)
30 May 98	Jimmy Barry DREW Casper Leon, *New York C, USA* (USA) *Jimmy Barry relinquished US claim (retired)*
12 Dec 98	Pedlar Palmer W RSC 17 Billy Plimmer, *London, England*
17 Apr 99	Pedlar Palmer W RSC 3 Billy Rotchford, *London, England*
22 Sep 99	Terry McGovern W KO 1 Pedlar Palmer, *Tuckahoe, USA*
22 Dec 99	Terry McGovern W KO 2 Harry Forbes, *New York C, USA* *Terry McGovern relinquished title to campaign as a featherweight*
18 Mar 01	Harry Harris W PTS 20 Pedlar Palmer, *London, England* *Harry Harris relinquished title to campaign as a featherweight*
11 Nov 01	Harry Forbes W KO 2 Dan Dougherty, *St Louis, USA*
23 Jan 02	Harry Forbes W KO 4 Dan Dougherty, *St Louis, USA*
27 Feb 02	Harry Forbes W PTS 15 Tommy Feltz, *St Louis, USA*
1 May 02	Harry Forbes DREW 20 Johnny Reagan, *St Louis, USA*
23 Dec 02	Harry Forbes W RSC 7 Frankie Neil, *Oakland, USA*
27 Feb 03	Harry Forbes W PTS 10 Andrew Tokell, *Detroit, USA*
13 Aug 03	Frankie Neil W KO 2 Harry Forbes, *San Francisco, USA*
4 Sep 03	Frankie Neil W KO 15 Billy de Coursey, *Los Angeles, USA*

DATE	
16 Oct 03	Frankie Neil DREW 20 Johnny Reagan, *Los Angeles, USA*
17 Jun 04	Frankie Neil W KO 3 Harry Forbes, *Chicago, USA*
17 Oct 04	Joe Bowker W PTS 20 Frankie Neil, *London, England*
29 May 05	Joe Bowker W PTS 20 Pinky Evans, *London, England* *Joe Bowker relinquished title to campaign as a featherweight*
20 Oct 05	Jimmy Walsh W PTS 15 Digger Stanley, *Chelsea, Mass, USA* *Jimmy Walsh relinquished title to campaign as a featherweight*
22 Apr 07	Owen Moran W PTS 20 Al Delmont, *London, England* (GB) *Owen Moran ceased to be recognized by GB (unable to make the weight)*
8 Jan 08	Johnny Coulon W PTS 10 Kid Murphy, *Peoria, USA* (USA)
29 Jan 08	Johnny Coulon W PTS 10 Kid Murphy, *Peoria, USA* (USA)
10 Feb 08	Johnny Coulon W KO 9 Cooney Kelly, *Peoria, USA* (USA)
11 Feb 09	Johnny Coulon W RTD 5 Kid Murphy, *New York C, USA* (USA)
30 Jan 10	Johnny Coulon W KO 9 Earl Denning, *New Orleans, USA* (USA)
19 Feb 10	Johnny Coulon W PTS 10 Jim Kendrick, *New Orleans, USA* (USA)
6 Mar 10	Johnny Coulon W KO 19 Jim Kendrick, *New Orleans, USA* (USA)
17 Oct 10	Digger Stanley W KO 8 Joe Bowker, *London, England* (GB)
5 Dec 10	Digger Stanley W PTS 20 Johnny Coulon, *London, England* (GB)
19 Dec 10	Johnny Coulon NC 3 Earl Denning, *Memphis, USA* (USA)
26 Feb 11	Johnny Coulon W PTS 20 Frankie Conley, *New Orleans, USA* (USA)
14 Sep 11	Digger Stanley W PTS 20 Ike Bradley, *Liverpool, England* (GB)
3 Feb 12	Johnny Coulon W PTS 20 Frankie Conley, *Los Angeles, USA* (USA)
18 Feb 12	Johnny Coulon W PTS 20 Frankie Burns, *New Orleans, USA* (USA)
22 Apr 12	Digger Stanley W PTS 20 Charles Ledoux, *London, England* (GB/IBU)
23 Jun 12	Charles Ledoux W KO 7 Digger Stanley, *Dieppe, France* (GB/IBU)
24 Jun 13	Eddie Campi W PTS 20 Charles Ledoux, *Los Angeles, USA* (GB/IBU)
31 Jan 14	Kid Williams W KO 12 Eddie Campi, *Los Angeles, USA* (GB/IBU)
9 Jun 14	Kid Williams W KO 3 Johnny Coulon, *Los Angeles, USA*
28 Sep 14	Kid Williams W KO 4 Kid Herman, *Philadelphia, USA*
6 Dec 15	Kid Williams DREW 20 Frankie Burns, *New Orleans, USA*
7 Feb 16	Kid Williams DREW 20 Pete Herman, *New Orleans, USA*
9 Jan 17	Pete Herman W PTS 20 Kid Williams, *New Orleans, USA*
5 Nov 17	Pete Herman W PTS 20 Frankie Burns, *New Orleans, USA*
22 Dec 20	Joe Lynch W PTS 15 Pete Herman, *New York C, USA*
25 Jul 21	Pete Herman W PTS 15 Joe Lynch, *New York C, USA*
23 Sep 21	Johnny Buff W PTS 15 Pete Herman, *New York C, USA*
10 Nov 21	Johnny Buff W PTS 15 Jackie Sharkey, *New York C, USA*
10 Jul 22	Joe Lynch W RTD 14 Johnny Buff, *New York C, USA*
22 Dec 22	Joe Lynch W PTS 15 Midget Smith, *New York C, USA* *Joe Lynch forfeited NY recognition (withdrew from a scheduled defence against Joe Burman)*
10 Oct 23	Abe Goldstein W PTS 12 Joe Burman, *New York C, USA* (NY)
21 Mar 24	Abe Goldstein W PTS 15 Joe Lynch, *New York C, USA*
16 July 24	Abe Goldstein W PTS 15 Charles Ledoux, *New York C, USA*
8 Sep 24	Abe Goldstein W PTS 15 Tommy Ryan, *New York C, USA*
19 Dec 24	Eddie Martin W PTS 15 Abe Goldstein, *New York C, USA*
20 Mar 25	Charlie Rosenberg W PTS 15 Eddie Martin, *New York C, USA*
23 Jul 25	Charlie Rosenberg W KO 4 Eddie Shea, *New York C, USA*
2 Mar 26	Charlie Rosenberg W PTS 10 George Butch, *St Louis, USA* *Charlie Rosenberg forfeited title (overweight for defence against Bushy Graham)*
26 Mar 27	Bud Taylor DREW 10 Tony Canzoneri, *Chicago, USA* (NBA)
5 May 27	Teddy Baldock W PTS 15 Archie Bell, *London, England* (GB)
24 Jun 27	Bud Taylor W PTS 10 Tony Canzoneri, *Chicago, USA* (NBA) *Bud Taylor relinquished title (unable to make weight)*
6 Oct 27	Willie Smith W PTS 15 Teddy Baldock, *London, England* (GB) *Willie Smith ceased to be recognized in GB (inactivity)*
23 May 28	Bushy Graham W PTS 15 Izzy Schwartz, *New York C, USA* (NY) *Bushy Graham relinquished title (unable to make weight)*
18 Jun 29	Al Brown W PTS 15 Vidal Gregorio, *New York C, USA* (NY)
28 Aug 29	Al Brown W PTS 10 Knud Larsen, *Copenhagen, Denmark* (NY/IBU)
8 Feb 30	Al Brown W DIS 4 Johnny Erickson, *New York C, USA* (NY/IBU)
4 Oct 30	Al Brown W PTS 15 Eugene Huat, *Paris, France* (NY/IBU)
11 Feb 31	Al Brown W PTS 10 Nick Bensa, *Paris, France* (NY/IBU)
20 May 31	Pete Sanstol W PTS 10 Archie Bell, *Montreal, Canada* (USA)
25 Aug 31	Al Brown W PTS 15 Pete Sanstol, *Montreal, Canada*
27 Oct 31	Al Brown W PTS 15 Eugene Huat, *Montreal, Canada*
10 Jul 32	Al Brown W PTS 15 Kid Francis, *Marseilles, France*
19 Sep 32	Al Brown W KO 1 Emile Pladner, *Toronto, Canada*
18 Mar 33	Al Brown W PTS 12 Dom Bernasconi, *Milan, Italy*
3 Jul 33	Al Brown W PTS 15 Johnny King, *Manchester, England*

DATE	
19 Feb 34	Al Brown W PTS 15 Young Perez, *Paris, France*
	Al Brown forfeited NBA recognition (failure to defend against Baby Casanova)
26 Jun 34	Sixto Escobar W KO 9 Baby Casanova, *Montreal, Canada* (NBA)
8 Aug 34	Sixto Escobar W PTS 15 Eugene Huat, *Montreal, Canada* (NBA)
1 Nov 34	Al Brown W KO 10 Young Perez, *Tunis, Tunisia* (NY/IBU)
1 Jun 35	Baltazar Sangchilli W PTS 15 Al Brown, *Valencia, Spain* (NY/IBU)
26 Aug 35	Lou Salica W PTS 15 Sixto Escobar, *New York C, USA* (NBA)
15 Nov 35	Sixto Escobar W PTS 15 Lou Salica, *New York C, USA* (NBA)
29 Jun 36	Tony Marino W KO 14 Baltazar Sangchilli, *New York C, USA* (NY/IBU)
31 Aug 36	Sixto Escobar W RSC 13 Tony Marino, *New York C, USA*
13 Oct 36	Sixto Escobar W KO 1 Carlos Quintana, *New York C, USA*
21 Feb 37	Sixto Escobar W PTS 15 Lou Salica, *San Juan, Puerto Rico*
23 Sep 37	Harry Jeffra W PTS 15 Sixto Escobar, *New York C, USA*
20 Feb 38	Sixto Escobar W PTS 15 Harry Jeffra, *San Juan, Puerto Rico*
2 Apr 39	Sixto Escobar W PTS 15 Kayo Morgan, *San Juan, Puerto Rico*
	Sixto Escobar relinquished title (unable to make weight). George Pace was named as champion by the NBA
4 Mar 40	George Pace DREW 15 Lou Salica, *Toronto, Canada*
	Pace retained NBA title
24 Sep 40	Lou Salica W PTS 15 George Pace, *New York C, USA*
13 Jan 41	Lou Salica W PTS 15 Tommy Forte, *Philadelphia, USA*

DATE	
25 Apr 41	Lou Salica W PTS 15 Lou Transparenti, *Baltimore, USA*
16 Jun 41	Lou Salica W PTS 15 Tommy Forte, *Philadelphia, USA*
2 Jan 42	Manuel Ortiz W PTS 10 Tony Olivera, *Oakland, USA* (CALIF)
7 Aug 42	Manuel Ortiz W PTS 12 Lou Salica, *Los Angeles, USA*
1 Jan 43	Manuel Ortiz W PTS 10 Kenny Lindsay, *Portland, USA*
27 Jan 43	Manuel Ortiz W RSC 10 George Freitas, *Oakland USA*
10 Mar 43	Manuel Ortiz W RSC 11 Lou Salica, *Oakland, USA*
28 Apr 43	Manuel Ortiz W KO 6 Lupe Cordoza, *Fort Worth, USA*
25 May 43	Manuel Ortiz W PTS 15 Joe Robleto, *Los Angeles, USA*
12 Jul 43	Manuel Ortiz W KO 7 Joe Robleto, *Seattle, USA*
1 Oct 43	Manuel Ortiz W KO 4 Leonardo Lopez, *Los Angeles, USA*
23 Nov 43	Manuel Ortiz W PTS 15 Benny Goldberg, *Los Angeles, USA*
14 Mar 44	Manuel Ortiz W PTS 15 Ernesto Aguilar, *Los Angeles, USA*
4 Apr 44	Manuel Ortiz W PTS 15 Tony Olivera, *Los Angeles, USA*
12 Sep 44	Manuel Ortiz W KO 4 Luis Castillo, *Los Angeles, USA*
14 Nov 44	Manuel Ortiz W RSC 9 Luis Castillo, *Los Angeles, USA*
25 Feb 46	Manuel Ortiz W KO 13 Luis Castillo, *San Francisco, USA*
25 May 46	Manuel Ortiz W KO 5 Kenny Lindsay, *Los Angeles, USA*
10 Jun 46	Manuel Ortiz W KO 11 Jackie Jurich, *San Francisco, USA*
6 Jan 47	Harold Dade W PTS 15 Manuel Ortiz, *San Francisco, USA*
11 Mar 47	Manuel Ortiz W PTS 15 Harold Dade, *Los Angeles, USA*
30 May 47	Manuel Ortiz W PTS 15 Kui Kong Young, *Honolulu, Hawaii*
20 Dec 47	Manuel Ortiz W PTS 15 Tirso del Rosario, *Manila, Philippines*

Left: *Baltazar Sangchili (right) was the man who finally took Panama Al Brown's title after a reign of six years. The height of Brown is well shown in this picture.*

DATE	
4 Jul 48	Manuel Ortiz W RSC 8 Memo Valero, *Mexicali, Mexico*
1 Mar 49	Manuel Ortiz W PTS 15 Dado Marino, *Honolulu, Hawaii*
31 May 50	Vic Toweel W PTS 15 Manuel Ortiz, *Johannesburg, S Africa*
2 Dec 50	Vic Toweel W RTD 10 Danny O'Sullivan, *Johannesburg, S Africa*
17 Nov 51	Vic Toweel W PTS 15 Luis Romero, *Johannesburg, S Africa*
26 Jan 52	Vic Toweel W PTS 15 Peter Keenan, *Johannesburg, S Africa*
15 Nov 52	Jimmy Carruthers W KO 1 Vic Toweel, *Johannesburg, S Africa*
21 Mar 53	Jimmy Carruthers W KO 10 Vic Toweel *Johannesburg, S Africa*
13 Nov 53	Jimmy Carruthers W PTS 15 Pappy Gault, *Sydney, Australia*
2 May 54	Jimmy Carruthers W PTS 12 Chamrern Songkitrat, *Bangkok, Thailand*
	Jimmy Carruthers relinquished title (retired)
19 Aug 54	Robert Cohen W PTS 15 Chamrern Songkitrat, *Bangkok, Thailand*
	Robert Cohen forfeited WBA recognition (failure to defend against Raton Macias)
9 Mar 55	Raton Macias W RSC 11 Chamrern Songkitrat, *San Francisco, USA* (NBA)
3 Sep 55	Robert Cohen DREW 15 Willie Toweel, *Johannesburg, S Africa* (NY/EBU)
25 Mar 56	Raton Macias W KO 10 Leo Espinosa, *Mexico C, Mexico* (NBA)
29 Jun 56	Mario D'Agata W RTD 6 Robert Cohen, *Rome, Italy* (NY/EBU)
1 Apr 57	Alphonse Halimi W PTS 15 Mario D'Agata, *Paris, France* (NY/EBU)
15 Jun 57	Raton Macias W RSC 11 Dommy Ursua, *San Francisco, USA* (NBA)
6 Nov 57	Alphonse Halimi W PTS 15 Raton Macias, *Los Angeles, USA*
8 Jul 59	Joe Becerra W KO 8 Alphonse Halimi, *Los Angeles, USA*
4 Feb 60	Joe Becerra W KO 9 Alphonse Halimi, *Los Angeles, USA*
23 May 60	Joe Becerra W PTS 15 Kenji Yonekura, *Tokyo, Japan*
	Joe Becerra relinquished title (retired)
25 Oct 60	Alphonse Halimi W PTS 15 Freddie Gilroy, *Wembley, England* (EBU)
18 Nov 60	Eder Jofre W KO 6 Eloy Sanchez, *Los Angeles, USA* (NBA)
25 Mar 61	Eder Jofre W RTD 9 Piero Rollo, *Rio de Janeiro, Brazil* (NBA)
30 May 61	Johnny Caldwell W PTS 15 Alphonse Halimi, *Wembley, England* (EBU)
19 Aug 61	Eder Jofre W RSC 7 Ramon Arias, *Caracas, Venezuela* (NBA)
31 Oct 61	Johnny Caldwell W PTS 15 Alphonse Halimi, *Wembley, England* (EBU)
18 Jun 62	Eder Jofre W RTD 10 Johnny Caldwell, *São Paulo, Brazil*
4 May 62	Eder Jofre W RSC 10 Herman Marquez, *San Francisco, USA*
11 Sep 62	Eder Jofre W KO 6 Joe Medel, *São Paulo, Brazil*
4 Apr 63	Eder Jofre W KO 3 Katsutoshi Aoki, *Tokyo, Japan*
18 May 63	Eder Jofre W RTD 11 Johnny Jamito, *Quezon C, Philippines*
27 Nov 64	Eder Jofre W KO 7 Bernardo Caraballo, *Bogota, Colombia*
17 May 65	Fighting Harada W PTS 15 Eder Jofre, *Nagoya, Japan*
30 Nov 65	Fighting Harada W PTS 15 Alan Rudkin, *Tokyo, Japan*
1 Jun 66	Fighting Harada W PTS 15 Eder Jofre, *Tokyo, Japan*
3 Jan 67	Fighting Harada W PTS 15 Joe Medel, *Nagoya, Japan*
4 Jul 67	Fighting Harada W PTS 15 Bernardo Caraballo, *Tokyo, Japan*
26 Feb 68	Lionel Rose W PTS 15 Fighting Harada, *Tokyo, Japan*
2 Jul 68	Lionel Rose W PTS 15 Takao Sakurai, *Tokyo, Japan*
6 Dec 68	Lionel Rose W PTS 15 Chucho Castillo, *Los Angeles, USA*
8 Mar 69	Lionel Rose W PTS 15 Alan Rudkin, *Melbourne, Australia*
22 Aug 69	Ruben Olivares W KO 5 Lionel Rose, *Los Angeles, USA*
12 Dec 69	Ruben Olivares W RSC 2 Alan Rudkin, *Los Angeles, USA*
18 Apr 70	Ruben Olivares W PTS 15 Chuchu Castillo, *Los Angeles, USA*
16 Oct 70	Chuchu Castillo W RSC 14 Ruben Olivares, *Los Angeles, USA*
3 Apr 71	Ruben Olivares W PTS 15 Chuchu Castillo, *Los Angeles, USA*
25 Oct 71	Ruben Olivares W RSC 14 Katsutoshi Kanazawa, *Nagoya, Japan*
14 Dec 71	Ruben Olivares W RSC 11 Jesus Pimental, *Los Angeles, USA*
19 Mar 72	Rafael Herrera W KO 8 Ruben Olivares, *Mexico C, Mexico*
30 Jul 72	Enrique Pinder W PTS 15 Rafael Herrera, *Panama C, Panama*
	Enrique Pinder forfeited WBC recognition (failure to defend against Rodolfo Martinez)
20 Jan 73	Romeo Anaya W KO 3 Enrique Pinder, *Panama C, Panama* (WBA)
15 Apr 73	Rafael Herrera W RSC 12 Rodolfo Martinez, *Monterrey, Mexico* (WBC)
28 Apr 73	Romeo Anaya W PTS 15 Rogelio Lara, *Los Angeles, USA* (WBA)
18 Aug 73	Romeo Anaya W KO 3 Enrique Pinder, *Los Angeles, USA* (WBA)
13 Oct 73	Rafael Herrera W PTS 15 Venice Borkorsor, *Los Angeles, USA* (WBC)
3 Nov 73	Arnold Taylor W KO 14 Romeo Anaya, *Johannesburg, S Africa* (WBA)
25 May 74	Rafael Herrera W KO 6 Romeo Anaya, *Mexico C, Mexico* (WBC)
3 Jul 74	Soo-Hwan Hong W PTS 15 Arnold Taylor, *Durban, S Africa* (WBA)
7 Dec 74	Rodolfo Martinez W RSC 4 Rafael Herrera, *Merida, Mexico* (WBC)

DATE	
28 Dec 74	Soo-Hwan Hong W PTS 15 Fernando Canabela, *Seoul, S Korea* (WBA)
14 Mar 75	Alfonso Zamora W KO 4 Soo-Hwan Hong, *Los Angeles, USA* (WBA)
31 May 75	Rodolfo Martinez W RSC 7 Nestor Jiminez, *Bogota, Colombia* (WBC)
30 Aug 75	Alfonso Zamora W KO 4 Thanomjit Sukhothai, *Los Angeles, USA* (WBA)
8 Oct 75	Rodolfo Martinez W PTS 15 Hisami Numata, *Sendai, Japan* (WBC)
6 Dec 75	Alfonso Zamora W KO 2 Socrates Batoto, *Mexico C, Mexico* (WBA)
30 Jan 76	Rodolfo Martinez W PTS 15 Venice Borkorsor, *Bangkok, Thailand* (WBC)
3 Apr 76	Alfonso Zamora W KO 2 Eusebio Pedroza, *Mexicali, Mexico* (WBA)
8 May 76	Carlos Zarate W KO 9 Rudolfo Martinez, *Los Angeles, USA* (WBC)
10 Jul 76	Alfonso Zamora W KO 3 Gilberto Illueca, *Juarez, Mexico* (WBA)
28 Aug 76	Carlos Zarate W RSC 12 Paul Ferreri, *Los Angeles, USA* (WBC)
16 Oct 76	Alfonso Zamora W RSC 12 Soo-Hwan Hong, *Inchon, S Korea* (WBA)
13 Nov 76	Carlos Zarate W KO 4 Waruinge Nakayama, *Culiacan, Mexico* (WBC)
5 Feb 77	Carlos Zarate W RSC 3 Fernando Cabanela, *Mexico C, Mexico* (WBC)
29 Oct 77	Carlos Zarate W RSC 6 Danilio Batista, *Los Angeles, USA* (WBC)
19 Nov 77	Jorge Lujan W KO 10 Alfonso Zamora, *Los Angeles, USA* (WBA)
2 Dec 77	Carlos Zarate W RSC 5 Juan Francisco Rodriguez, *Madrid, Spain* (WBC)
25 Feb 78	Carlos Zarate W RSC 8 Albert Davila, *Los Angeles, USA* (WBC)

Left: World bantamweight champion Masahiko 'Fighting' Harada after his successful defence against Alan Rudkin in Tokyo in 1965.

DATE	
18 Mar 78	Jorge Lujan W RTD 11 Roberto Rubaldino, *San Antonio, USA* (WBA)
22 Apr 78	Carlos Zarate W RSC 13 Andres Hernandez, *San Juan, Puerto Rico* (WBC)
9 Jun 78	Carlos Zarate W KO 4 Emilio Hernandez, *Las Vegas, USA* (WBC)
15 Sep 78	Jorge Lujan W PTS 15 Albert Davila, *New Orleans* (WBA)
10 Mar 79	Carlos Zarate W KO 3 Mensah Kpalongo, *Los Angeles, USA* (WBC)
8 Apr 79	Jorge Lujan W RSC 15 Cleo Garcia, *Las Vegas, USA* (WBA)
2 Jun 79	Lupe Pintor W PTS 15 Carlos Zarate, *Las Vegas, USA* (WBC)
6 Oct 79	Jorge Lujan W KO 15 Roberto Rubaldino, *McAllen, USA* (WBA)
9 Feb 80	Lupe Pintor W RSC 12 Alberto Sandoval, *Los Angeles, USA* (WBC)
2 Apr 80	Jorge Lujan W RSC 9 Shuichi Isogami, *Tokyo, Japan* (WBA)
11 Jun 80	Lupe Pintor DREW 15 Eijiro Murata, *Tokyo, Japan* (WBC)
29 Aug 80	Julian Solis W PTS 15 Jorge Lujan, *Miami, USA* (WBA)
19 Sep 80	Lupe Pintor W KO 12 Johnny Owen, *Los Angeles, USA* (WBC)
14 Nov 80	Jeff Chandler W RSC 14 Julian Solis, *Miami, USA* (WBA)
19 Dec 80	Lupe Pintor W PTS 15 Albert Davila, *Las Vegas, USA* (WBC)
31 Jan 81	Jeff Chandler W PTS 15 Jorge Lujan, *Philadelphia, USA* (WBA)
22 Feb 81	Lupe Pintor W PTS 15 Jose Uziga, *Houston, USA* (WBC)
5 Apr 81	Jeff Chandler DREW 15 Eijiro Murata, *Tokyo, Japan* (WBA)
25 Jul 81	Jeff Chandler W KO 7 Julian Solis, *Atlantic C, USA* (WBA)
26 Jul 81	Lupe Pintor W RSC 8 Jovito Rengifo, *Las Vegas, USA* (WBC)
22 Sep 81	Lupe Pintor W KO 15 Hurricane Teru, *Nagoya, Japan* (WBC)
10 Dec 81	Jeff Chandler W RSC 13 Eijiro Murata, *Atlantic C, USA* (WBA)
27 Mar 82	Jeff Chandler W RSC 6 Johnny Carter, *Philadelphia, USA* (WBA)
3 Jun 82	Lupe Pintor W RSC 11 Seung-Hoon Lee, *Los Angeles, USA* (WBC) *Lupe Pintor forfeited WBC recognition (unable to defend due to a motorcycle accident)*
27 Oct 82	Jeff Chandler W RSC 9 Miguel Iriarle, *Atlantic C, USA* (WBA)
13 Mar 83	Jeff Chandler W PTS 15 Gaby Canizales, *Atlantic C, USA* (WBA)
1 Sep 83	Albert Davila W KO 12 Kiko Bejines, *Los Angeles, USA* (WBC)
11 Sep 83	Jeff Chandler W RSC 10 Eijiro Murata, *Tokyo, Japan* (WBA)
17 Dec 82	Jeff Chandler W RSC 7 Oscar Muniz, *Atlantic C, USA* (WBA)
7 Apr 84	Richard Sandoval W RSC 15 Jeff Chandler, *Atlantic C, USA* (WBA)
16 Apr 84	Satoshi Shingaki W RSC 8 Elmer Magallano, *Kawashiwara, Japan* (IBF)
26 May 84	Albert Davila W RSC 11 Enrique Sanchez, *Miami, USA* (WBC) *Albert Davila relinquished title (back injury)*
4 Aug 84	Satoshi Shingaki W PTS 15 Joves de la Puz, *Naha C, Japan* (IBF)
22 Sep 84	Richard Sandoval W PTS 15 Edgar Roman, *Monte Carlo* (WBA)
15 Dec 84	Richard Sandoval W RSC 8 Cardenio Ulloa, *Miami, USA* (WBA)
26 Apr 85	Jeff Fenech W RSC 9 Satoshi Shingaki, *Sydney, Australia* (IBF)
4 May 85	Daniel Zaragoza W DIS 7 Fred Jackson, *Aruba, DWI* (WBC)
9 Aug 85	Miguel Lora W PTS 12 Daniel Zaragoza, *Miami, USA* (WBC)
23 Aug 85	Jeff Fenech W KO 3 Satoshi Shingaki, *Sydney, Australia* (IBF)
2 Dec 85	Jeff Fenech W PTS 15 Jerome Coffee, *Sydney, Australia* (IBF)
8 Feb 86	Miguel Lora W PTS 12 Wilfredo Vasquez, *Miami, USA* (WBC)
10 Mar 86	Gaby Canizales W RSC 7 Richard Sandoval, *Las Vegas, USA* (WBA)
4 Jun 86	Bernardo Pinango W PTS 15 Gaby Canizales, *E Rutherford, USA* (WBA)
18 Jul 86	Jeff Fenech W RSC 14 Steve McCrory, *Sydney, Australia* (IBF) *Jeff Fenech relinquished title to campaign as a light-featherweight*
23 Aug 86	Miguel Lora W RSC 6 Enrique Sanchez, *Miami, USA* (WBC)
4 Oct 86	Bernardo Pinango W RSC 10 Ciro de Leva, *Turin, Italy* (WBA)
15 Nov 86	Miguel Lora W PTS 12 Albert Davila, *Barranquilla, Colombia* (WBC)
22 Nov 86	Bernardo Pinango W RSC 15 Simon Skosana, *Johannesburg, S Africa* (WBA)
3 Feb 87	Bernardo Pinango W PTS 15 Frankie Duarte, *Los Angeles, USA* (WBA) *Bernardo Pinango relinquished title to campaign as a light-featherweight*
29 Mar 87	Takuya Muguruma W KO 5 Azael Moran, *Moriguchi, Japan* (WBA)
15 May 87	Kelvin Seabrooks W KO 5 Miguel Maturana, *Cartagena, Columbia* (IBF)
24 May 87	Chan-Yung Park W RSC 11 Takuya Muguruma, *Moriguchi, Japan* (WBA)
4 Jul 87	Kelvin Seabrooks NC 9 Thierry Jacob, *Calais, France* (IBF)
25 Jul 87	Miguel Lora W RSC 4 Antonio Avelar, *Miami, USA* (WBC)
4 Oct 87	Wilfredo Vasquez W RSC 10 Chan-Yung Park, *Seoul, S Korea* (WBA)

DATE	
13 Nov 87	Kelvin Seabrooks W RSC 4 Ernie Cataluna, *San Cataldo* (IBF)
27 Nov 87	Miguel Lora W PTS 12 Ray Minus, *Miami, USA* (WBC)
17 Jan 88	Wilfredo Vasquez DREW 12 Takuya Muguruma, *Osaka, Japan* (WBA)
6 Feb 88	Kelvin Seabrooks W RSC 2 Fernando Beltran, *Paris, France* (IBF)
30 Apr 88	Miguel Lora W PTS 12 Lucio Lopez, *Cartagena, Colombia* (WBC)
9 May 88	Kaokor Galaxy W PTS 12 Wilfredo Vasquez, *Bangkok, Thailand* (WBA)
9 Jul 88	Orlando Canizales W RSC 15 Kelvin Seabrooks, *Atlantic C, USA* (IBF)
1 Aug 88	Miguel Lora W PTS 12 Albert Davila, *Inglewood, USA* (WBC)
14 Aug 88	Sang-Kil Moon W TD 5 Kaokor Galaxy, *Seoul, S Korea* (WBA)
29 Oct 88	Raul Perez W PTS 12 Miguel Lora, *Las Vegas, USA* (WBC)

LIGHT-BANTAMWEIGHT

(*Current weight limit:* 115lb/52.2kg. The WBA and IBF call the class 'Junior Bantamweight', the WBC calls the class 'Super-flyweight)

DATE	
2 Feb 80	Rafael Orono W PTS 15 Seung-Hoon Lee, *Caracas, Venezuela* (WBC)
14 Apr 80	Rafael Orono W PTS 15 Ramon Soria, *Caracas, Venezuela* (WBC)
28 Jul 80	Rafael Orono DREW 15 Willie Jense, *Caracas, Venezuela* (WBC)
15 Sep 80	Rafael Orono W RSC 3 Jovito Rengifo, *Barquisimeto, Venezuela* (WBC)
24 Jan 81	Chul-Ho Kim W KO 9 Rafael Orono, *San Christobal, Venezuela* (WBC)
22 Apr 81	Chul-Ho Kim W PTS 15 Jiro Watanabe, *Seoul, S Korea* (WBC)
29 Jul 81	Chul-Ho Kim W KO 13 Willie Jensen, *Pusan, S Korea* (WBC)
12 Sep 81	Gustavo Ballas W RSC 8 Sok-Chul Baek, *Buenos Aires, Argentine* (WBA)
18 Nov 81	Chul-Ho Kim W RSC 9 Jackal Maruyama, *Pusan, S Korea* (WBC)
5 Dec 81	Rafael Pedroza W PTS 15 Gustavo Ballas, *Panama C, Panama* (WBA)
10 Feb 82	Chul-Ho Kim W KO 8 Koki Ishii, *Taegu, S Korea* (WBC)
8 Apr 82	Jiro Watanabe W PTS 15 Rafael Pedroza, *Osaka, Japan* (WBA)
4 Jul 82	Chul-Ho Kim DREW 15 Raul Valdez, *Daejon, S Korea* (WBC)
29 Jul 82	Jiro Watanabe W RSC 9 Gustavo Ballas, *Osaka, Japan* (WBA)
11 Nov 82	Jiro Watanabe W RTD 12 Shoji Oguma, *Hamamatsu, Japan* (WBA)
28 Nov 82	Rafael Orono W KO 6 Chul-Ho Kim, *Seoul, S Korea* (WBC)
31 Jan 83	Rafael Orono W KO 4 Pedro Romero, *Caracas, Venezuela* (WBC)
24 Feb 83	Jiro Watanabe W KO 8 Luis Ibanez, *Tsu C, Japan* (WBA)
9 May 83	Rafael Orono W PTS 12 Raul Valdez, *Caracas, Venezuela* (WBC)
23 Jun 83	Jiro Watanabe W PTS 15 Roberto Ramirez, *Sendai, Japan* (WBA)
6 Oct 83	Jiro Watanabe W RTD 11 Soon-Chun Kwon, *Osaka, Japan* (WBA)
29 Oct 83	Rafael Orono W RSC 5 Orlando Maldonado, *Caracas, Venezuela* (WBC)
27 Nov 83	Payao Poontarat W PTS 12 Rafael Orono, *Pattaya, Thailand* (WBC)
10 Dec 83	Joo-Do Chun W KO 5 Ken Kasugai, *Osaka, Japan* (IBF)
28 Jan 84	Joo-Do Chun W KO 12 Prayoonsak Muangsurin, *Seoul, S Korea* (IBF)

DATE	
15 Mar 84	Jiro Watanabe W RSC 15 Celso Chavez, *Osaka, Japan* (WBA)
	Jiro Watanabe forfeited WBA recognition (failure to defend against Kaosai Galaxy)
17 Mar 84	Joo-Do Chun W KO 1 Diego de Villa, *Kwangju, S Korea* (IBF)
28 Mar 84	Payao Poontarat W RSC 10 Guty Espadas, *Bangkok, Thailand* (WBC)
26 May 84	Joo-Do Chun W RSC 6 Felix Marques, *Wonju, S Korea* (IBF)
5 Jul 84	Jiro Watanabe W PTS 12 Payao Poontarat, *Osaka, Japan* (WBC)
20 Jul 84	Joo-Do Chun W KO 7 William Develos, *Pusan, S Korea* (IBF)
21 Nov 84	Kaosai Galaxy W KO 6 Eusebio Espinal, *Bangkok, Thailand* (WBA)
29 Nov 84	Jiro Watanabe W RSC 11 Payao Poontarat, *Kumamoto, Japan* (WBC)
6 Jan 85	Joo-Do Chun W KO 15 Kwang-Gu Park, *Ulsan, S Korea* (IBF)
6 Mar 85	Kaosai Galaxy W KO 7 Dong-Chun Lee, *Bangkok, Thailand* (WBA)
3 May 85	Elly Pical W RSC 8 Joo-Do Chun, *Jakarta, Indonesia* (IBF)
9 May 85	Jiro Watanabe W PTS 12 Julio Solano, *Tokyo, Japan* (WBC)
17 Jul 85	Kaosai Galaxy W RSC 5 Rafael Orono, *Bangkok, Thailand* (WBA)
25 Aug 85	Elly Pical W RSC 3 Wayne Mulholland, *Jakarta, Indonesia* (IBF)
17 Sep 85	Jiro Watanabe W RSC 7 Katsuo Katsuma, *Osaka, Japan* (WBC)
13 Dec 85	Jiro Watanabe W KO 5 Yun-Sok Hwang, *Taegu, S Korea* (WBC)
23 Dec 85	Kaosai Galaxy W RSC 2 Edgar Monserrat, *Bangkok, Thailand* (WBA)
15 Feb 86	Cesar Polanco W PTS 15 Elly Pical, *Jakarta, Indonesia* (IBF)
30 Mar 86	Gilberto Roman W PTS 12 Jiro Watanabe, *Osaka, Japan* (WBC)
15 May 86	Gilberto Roman W PTS 12 Edgar Monserrat, *Paris, France* (WBC)
5 Jul 86	Elly Pical W KO 3 Cesar Polanco, *Jakarta, Indonesia* (IBF)
18 Jul 86	Gilberto Roman W PTS 12 Ruben Condori, *Salta, Argentine* (WBC)
30 Aug 86	Gilberto Roman DREW 12 Santos Laciar, *Cordoba, Argentine* (WBC)
1 Nov 86	Kaosai Galaxy W KO 5 Israel Contreras, *Curacao, DWI* (WBA)
3 Dec 86	Elly Pical W KO 10 Dong-Chun Lee, *Jakarta, Indonesia* (IBF)
	Elly Pical relinquished IBF title to challenge for WBA title
15 Dec 86	Gilberto Roman W PTS 12 Kongtorance Payakarun, *Bangkok, Thailand* (WBC)
31 Jan 87	Gilberto Roman W RSC 9 Antoine Montero, *Montpelier, France* (WBC)
28 Feb 87	Kaosai Galaxy W KO 14 Elly Pical, *Jakarta, Indonesia* (WBA)
19 Mar 87	Gilberto Roman W PTS 12 Frank Cedeno, *Mexicali, Mexico* (WBC)
16 May 87	Santos Laciar W RSC 11 Gilberto Roman, *Reims, France* (WBC)
17 May 87	Tae-Il-Chang W PTS 15 Soon-Chun Kwon, *Pusan, S Korea* (IBF)
8 Aug 87	Jesus Rojas W PTS 12 Santos Laciar, *Miami, USA* (WBC)
12 Oct 87	Kaosai Galaxy W RSC 3 Byong-Kwan Chung, *Bangkok, Thailand* (WBA)
17 Oct 87	Elly Pical W PTS 15 Tae-Il Chang, *Jakarta, Indonesia* (IBF)
24 Oct 87	Jesus Rojas W RSC 4 Gustavo Ballas, *Miami, USA* (WBC)
26 Jan 88	Kaosai Galaxy W PTS 12 Kongtorance Payakarun, *Bangkok, Thailand* (WBA)
20 Feb 88	Elly Pical W PTS 15 Raul Diaz, *Pontianak, Borneo* (IBF)
8 Apr 88	Gilberto Roman W PTS 12 Jesus Rojas, *Miami, USA* (WBC)
9 Jul 88	Gilberto Roman W RSF 5 Yoshiyuki Uchida, *Kawagoe, Japan* (WBC)
1 Sep 88	Elly Pical W PTS 12 Chang-Ki Kim, *Urubaya* (IBF)
14 Oct 88	Kaosai Galaxy W KO 8 Chang-Ho Choi, *Seoul, S Korea* (WBA)
7 Nov 88	Gilberto Roman W PTS 12 Jesus Rojas, *Las Vegas, USA (WBC)*

FLYWEIGHT

***(Current weight limit:* 112lb/50.8kg)**

DATE	
11 Apr 13	Sid Smith W PTS 20 Eugene Criqui, *Paris, France*
	Sid Smith relinquished title after being beaten in catchweights match by Bill Ladbury
26 Jan 14	Percy Jones W PTS 20 Bill Ladbury, *London, England*
26 Mar 14	Percy Jones W PTS 20 Eugene Criqui, *Liverpool, England*
	Percy Jones forfeited title (overweight for defence against Joe Symonds)
18 Oct 15	Joe Symonds W RSC 16 Tancy Lee, *London, England*
14 Feb 16	Jimmy Wilde W RSC 12 Joe Symonds, *London, England*
24 Apr 16	Jimmy Wilde W RTD 11 Johnny Rosner, *Liverpool, England*
26 Jun 16	Jimmy Wilde W RSC 11 Tancy Lee, *London, England*
31 Jul 16	Jimmy Wilde W KO 10 Johnny Hughes, *London, England*
18 Dec 16	Jimmy Wilde W KO 11 Young Zulu Kid, *London, England*
12 Mar 17	Jimmy Wilde W RTD 4 George Clark, *London, England*
18 Jun 23	Pancho Villa W KO 7 Jimmy Wilde, *New York C, USA*
13 Oct 23	Pancho Villa W PTS 15 Benny Schwartz, *Baltimore, USA*
8 Feb 24	Pancho Villa W PTS 15 Georgie Marks, *New York C, USA*
30 May 24	Pancho Villa W PTS 15 Frankie Ash, *New York C, USA*
1 May 25	Pancho Villa W PTS 15 Clever Sencio, *Manila, Philippines*
	Pancho Villa died while still champion
22 Aug 25	Fidel La Barba W PTS 10 Frankie Genaro, *Los Angeles, USA* (USA)
8 Jul 26	Fidel La Barba W PTS 10 Georgie Rivers, *Los Angeles, USA* (USA)
21 Jan 27	Fidel La Barba W PTS 12 Elky Clark, *New York C, USA*
	Fidel La Barba relinquished title (entered university)
28 Nov 27	Frenchy Belanger W PTS 10 Frankie Genaro, *Toronto, Canada* (NBA)
16 Dec 27	Izzy Schwartz W PTS 15 Newsboy Brown, *New York C, USA* (NY)
19 Dec 27	Frenchy Belanger W PTS 12 Ernie Jarvis, *Toronto, Canada* (NBA)
3 Jan 28	Newsboy Brown W PTS 10 Johnny McCoy, *Los Angeles, USA* (CALIF)
6 Feb 28	Frankie Genaro W PTS 10 Frenchy Belanger, *Toronto, Canada* (NBA)
9 Apr 28	Izzy Schwartz W PTS 15 Routier Parra, *New York C, USA* (NY)
20 Jul 28	Izzy Schwartz W DIS 4 Frisco Grande, *New York C, USA* (NY)
3 Aug 28	Izzy Schwartz W KO 4 Little Jeff Smith, *New York C, USA* (NY)
29 Aug 28	Johnny Hill W PTS 15 Newsboy Brown, *London, England* (GB/CALIF)
	Johnny Hill ceased to be recognized by the GB-Californian authorities (this followed a defeat by Emile Pladner in a non-title bout, February, 1929)
2 Mar 29	Emile Pladner W KO 1 Frankie Genaro, *Paris, France* (NBA/IBU)
12 Mar 29	Izzy Schwartz W PTS 12 Frenchy Belanger, *Toronto, Canada* (NY)
18 Apr 29	Frankie Genaro W DIS 5 Emile Pladner, *Paris, France* (NBA/IBU)
22 Aug 29	Willie la Morte W PTS 15 Izzy Schwartz, *Newark, USA* (NY)
	Willie la Morte did not gain New York recognition. New York instituted an eliminating tournament
17 Oct 29	Frankie Genaro W PTS 15 Ernie Jarvis, *London, England* (NBA/IBU)
18 Jan 30	Frankie Genaro W RTD 12 Yvon Trevidic, *Paris, France* (NBA/IBU)
21 Mar 30	Midget Wolgast W PTS 15 Black Bill, *New York C, USA* (NY)
16 May 30	Midget Wolgast W KO 6 Willie la Morte, *New York C, USA* (NY)
10 Jun 30	Frankie Genaro W PTS 10 Frenchy Belanger, *Toronto, Canada* (NBA/IBU)
6 Aug 30	Frankie Genaro W PTS 10 Willie la Morte, *Newark, USA* (NBA/IBU)
26 Dec 30	Frankie Genaro DREW 15 Midget Wolgast, *New York C, USA*
25 Mar 31	Frankie Genaro DREW 15 Victor Ferrand, *Madrid, Spain* (NBA/IBU)
13 Jul 31	Midget Wolgast W PTS 15 Ruby Bradley, *New York C, USA* (NY)
30 Jul 31	Frankie Genaro W KO 6 Jackie Harmon, *Waterbury, USA* (NBA/IBU)
3 Oct 31	Frankie Genaro W PTS 15 Valentin Angelmann, *Paris, France* (NBA/IBU)
27 Oct 31	Young Perez W KO 2 Frankie Genaro, *Paris, France* (NBA/IBU)
31 Oct 32	Jackie Brown W RSC 13 Young Perez, *Manchester, England* (NBA/IBU)
12 Jun 33	Jackie Brown W PTS 15 Valentin Angelmann, *London, England* (NBA/IBU)
11 Sep 33	Jackie Brown W PTS 15 Valentin Angelmann, *Manchester, England* (NBA/IBU)
11 Dec 33	Jackie Brown W PTS 15 Ginger Foran, *Manchester, England* (NBA/IBU)
18 Jun 34	Jackie Brown DREW 15 Valentin Angelmann, *Manchester, England* (NBA/IBU)
	Jackie Brown forfeited IBU recognition (failure to defend against Valentin Angelmann)

***Above:** Pascual Perez (on the right) gets inside a left lead from challenger Yoshio Shirai in Tokyo in May 1955. Perez knocked out Shirai in the fifth to keep the title he took from him six months earlier.*

DATE	
9 Sep 35	Benny Lynch W RTD 2 Jackie Brown, *Manchester, England* (NBA)
16 Sep 35	Small Montana W PTS 10 Midget Wolgast, *Oakland, USA* (NY/CALIF)
6 Jan 36	Valentin Angelmann W RTD 5 Kid David, *Paris, France* (IBU)
16 Sep 36	Benny Lynch W KO 8 Pat Palmer, *Glasgow, Scotland* (NBA)
12 Dec 36	Valentin Angelmann W PTS 15 Ernst Weiss, *Paris, France* (IBU) *Valentin Angelmann ceased to be recognized by the IBU after defeats in non-title bouts*
19 Jan 37	Benny Lynch W PTS 15 Small Montana, *Wembley, England*
13 Oct 37	Benny Lynch W KO 13 Peter Kane, *Glasgow, Scotland* *Benny Lynch forfeited title (overweight for scheduled defence against Jackie Jurich)*
22 Sep 38	Peter Kane W PTS 15 Jackie Jurich, *Liverpool, England*
19 Jun 43	Jackie Paterson W KO 1 Peter Kane, *Glasgow, Scotland*
10 Jul 46	Jackie Paterson W PTS 15 Joe Curran, *Glasgow, Scotland* *Jackie Paterson forfeited title (overweight for scheduled defence against Dado Marino)*
20 Oct 47	Rinty Monaghan W PTS 15 Dado Marino, *London, England* (NBA)
23 Mar 48	Rinty Monaghan W KO 7 Jackie Paterson, *Belfast, Ireland*
5 Apr 49	Rinty Monaghan W PTS 15 Maurice Sandeyron, *Belfast, Ireland*
30 Sep 49	Rinty Monaghan DREW 15 Terry Allen, *Belfast, Ireland* *Rinty Monaghan relinquished title (retired)*
25 Apr 50	Terry Allen W PTS 15 Honore Pratesi, *London, England*
1 Aug 50	Dado Marino W PTS 15 Terry Allen, *Honolulu, Hawaii*
1 Nov 51	Dado Marino W PTS 15 Terry Allen, *Honolulu, Hawaii*
19 May 52	Yoshio Shirai W PTS 15 Dado Marino, *Tokyo, Japan*
15 Nov 52	Yoshio Shirai W PTS 15 Dado Marino, *Tokyo, Japan*
18 May 53	Yoshio Shirai W PTS 15 Tanny Campo, *Tokyo, Japan*
27 Oct 53	Yoshio Shirai W PTS 15 Terry Allen, *Tokyo, Japan*
23 May 54	Yoshio Shirai W PTS 15 Leo Espinosa, *Tokyo, Japan*
26 Nov 54	Pascual Perez W PTS 15 Yoshio Shirai, *Tokyo, Japan*
30 May 55	Pascual Perez W KO 5 Yoshio Shirai, *Tokyo, Japan*
11 Jan 56	Pascual Perez W PTS 15 Leo Espinosa, *Buenos Aires, Argentine*
30 Jun 56	Pascual Perez W RTD 11 Oscar Suarez, *Montevideo, Uruguay*
30 Mar 57	Pascual Perez W KO 1 Dai Dower, *Buenos Aires, Argentine*
7 Dec 57	Pascual Perez W KO 3 Young Martin, *Buenos Aires, Argentine*
19 Apr 58	Pascual Perez W PTS 15 Ramon Arias, *Caracas, Venezuela*
15 Dec 58	Pascual Perez W PTS 15 Dommy Ursua, *Manila, Philippines*

DATE	
10 Aug 59	Pascual Perez W PTS 15 Kenji Yonekura, *Tokyo, Japan*
5 Nov 59	Pascual Perez W KO 13 Sadao Yaoita, *Osaka, Japan*
16 Apr 60	Pone Kingpetch W PTS 15 Pascual Perez, *Bangkok, Thailand*
22 Sep 60	Pone Kingpetch W RSC 8 Pascual Perez, *Los Angeles, USA*
27 Jun 61	Pone Kingpetch W PTS 15 Mitsunori Seki, *Tokyo, Japan*
30 May 62	Pone Kingpetch W PTS 15 Kyo Noguchi, *Tokyo, Japan*
10 Oct 62	Fighting Harada W KO 11 Pone Kingpetch, *Tokyo, Japan*
12 Jan 63	Pone Kingpetch W PTS 15 Fighting Harada, *Tokyo, Japan*
18 Sep 63	Hiroyuki Ebihara W KO 1 Pone Kingpetch, *Tokyo, Japan*
23 Jan 64	Pone Kingpetch W PTS 15 Hiroyuki Ebihara, *Bangkok, Thailand*
23 Apr 65	Salvatore Burruni W PTS 15 Pone Kingpetch, *Rome, Italy* *Salvatore Burruni forfeited WBA recognition (failure to defend against Horacio Accavallo)*
2 Dec 65	Salvatore Burruni W KO 13 Rocky Gattellari, *Sydney, Australia* (WBC)
1 Mar 66	Horacio Accavallo W PTS 15 Katsuyoshi Takayama, *Tokyo, Japan* (WBA)
14 Jun 66	Walter McGowan W PTS 15 Salvatore Burruni, *Wembley, England* (WBC)
15 Jul 66	Horacio Accavallo W PTS 15 Hiroyuki Ebihara, *Buenos Aires, Argentine* (WBA)
10 Dec 66	Horacio Accavallo W PTS 15 Efren Torres, *Buenos Aires, Argentine* (WBA)
30 Dec 66	Chartchai Chionoi W RSC 9 Walter McGowan, *Bangkok, Thailand* (WBC)
26 Jul 67	Chartchai Chionoi W KO 3 Puntip Keosuriya, *Bangkok, Thailand* (WBC)
13 Aug 67	Horacio Accavallo W PTS 15 Hiroyuki Ebihara, *Buenos Aires, Argentine* (WBA) *Horacio Accavallo relinquished WBA version of title (retired)*
19 Sep 67	Chartchai Chionoi W RSC 7 Walter McGowan, *Wembley, England* (WBC)
28 Jan 68	Chartchai Chionoi W RSC 13 Efren Torres, *Mexico C, Mexico* (WBC)
10 Nov 68	Chartchai Chionoi W PTS 15 Bernabe Villacampo, *Bangkok, Thailand* (WBC)
23 Feb 69	Efren Torres W RSC 8 Chartchai Chionoi, *Mexico C, Mexico* (WBC)
30 Mar 69	Hiroyuki Ebihara W PTS 15 Jose Severino, *Sapporo, Japan* (WBA)

DATE	
19 Oct 69	Bernabe Villacampo W PTS 15 Hiroyuki Ebihara, *Tokyo, Japan* (WBA)
28 Nov 69	Efren Torres W PTS 15 Susumu Hanagata, *Guadalajara, Mexico* (WBC)
20 Mar 70	Chartchai Chionoi W PTS 15 Efren Torres, *Bangkok, Thailand* (WBC)
6 Apr 70	Berkrerk Chartvanchai W PTS 15 Bernabe Villacampo, *Bangkok, Thailand* (WBA)
21 Oct 70	Masao Ohba W RSC 13 Berkrerk Chartvanchai, *Tokyo, Japan* (WBA)
7 Dec 70	Erbito Salavarria W RSC 2 Chartchai Chionoi, *Bangkok, Thailand* (WBC)
1 Apr 71	Masao Ohba W PTS 15 Betulio Gonzalez, *Tokyo, Japan* (WBA)
30 Apr 71	Erbito Salavarria W PTS 15 Susumu Hanagata, *Manila, Philippines* (WBC)
23 Oct 71	Masao Ohba W PTS 15 Fernando Cabanela, *Tokyo, Japan* (WBA)
20 Nov 71	Erbito Salavarria DREW 15 Betulio Gonzalez, *Caracas, Venezuela* (WBC)
	Erbito Salavarria forfeited WBC recognition (allegedly used an illegal stimulant)
4 Mar 72	Masao Ohba W PTS 15 Susumu Hanagata, *Tokyo, Japan* (WBA)
3 Jun 72	Betulio Gonzalez W KO 4 Socrates Batoto, *Caracas, Venezuela* (WBC)
20 Jun 72	Masao Ohba W KO 5 Orlando Amores, *Tokyo, Japan* (WBA)
29 Sep 72	Venice Borkorsor W RTD 10 Betulio Gonzalez, *Bangkok, Thailand* (WBC)
2 Jan 73	Masao Ohba W RSC 12 Chartchai Chionoi, *Tokyo, Japan* (WBA)
	Masao Ohba was killed in a road accident while still champion
9 Feb 73	Venice Borkorsor W PTS 15 Erbito Salavarria, *Bangkok, Thailand* (WBC)
	Venice Borkorsor relinquished title to campaign as a bantamweight
17 May 73	Chartchai Chionoi W RSC 4 Fritz Chervet, *Bangkok, Thailand* (WBA)
4 Aug 73	Betulio Gonzalez W PTS 15 Miguel Canto, *Caracas, Venezuela* (WBC)
27 Oct 73	Chartchai Chionoi W PTS 15 Susumu Hanagata, *Bangkok, Thailand* (WBA)
17 Nov 73	Betulio Gonzalez W RSC 11 Alberto Morales, *Caracas, Venezuela* (WBC)
27 Apr 74	Chartchai Chionoi W PTS 15 Fritz Chervet, *Zurich, Switzerland* (WBA)
20 Jul 74	Betulio Gonzalez W RSC 10 Franco Udella, *Sabbiadoro, Italy* (WBC)
1 Oct 74	Shoji Oguma W PTS 15 Betulio Gonzalez, *Tokyo, Japan* (WBC)
18 Oct 74	Susumu Hanagata W RSC 6 Chartchai Chionoi, *Yokohama, Japan* (WBA)
	Chionoi forfeited title (overweight) and the title awarded to Hanagata
8 Jan 75	Miguel Canto W PTS 15 Shoji Oguma, *Sendai, Japan* (WBC)
1 Apr 75	Erbito Salavarria W PTS 15 Susumu Hanagata, *Toyama, Japan* (WBA)
24 May 75	Miguel Canto W PTS 15 Betulio Gonzalez, *Monterrey, Mexico* (WBC)
23 Aug 75	Miguel Canto W RSC 11 Jiro Takada, *Merida, Mexico* (WBC)
7 Nov 75	Erbito Salavarria W PTS 15 Susumu Hanagata, *Yokohama, Japan* (WBA)
13 Dec 75	Miguel Canto W PTS 15 Ignacio Espinal, *Merida, Mexico* (WBC)
27 Feb 76	Alfonso Lopez W RSC 15 Erbito Salavarria, *Manila, Philippines* (WBA)
21 Apr 76	Alfonso Lopez W PTS 15 Shoji Oguma, *Tokyo, Japan* (WBA)
15 May 76	Miguel Canto W PTS 15 Susumu Hanagata, *Merida, Mexico* (WBC)
2 Oct 76	Guty Espadas W RSC 13 Alfonso Lopez, *Los Angeles, USA* (WBA)
3 Oct 76	Miguel Canto W PTS 15 Betulio Gonzalez, *Caracas, Venezuela* (WBC)
19 Nov 76	Miguel Canto W PTS 15 Orlando Javierta, *Los Angeles, USA* (WBC)
1 Jan 77	Guty Espadas W RTD 7 Jiro Takada, *Tokyo, Japan* (WBA)
24 Apr 77	Miguel Canto W PTS 15 Reyes Arnal, *Caracas, Venezuela* (WBC)
30 Apr 77	Guty Espadas W RSC 13 Alfonso Lopez, *Merida, Mexico* (WBA)
15 Jun 77	Miguel Canto W PTS 15 Kimio Furesawa, *Tokyo, Japan* (WBC)
17 Sep 77	Miguel Canto W PTS 15 Martin Vargas, *Merida, Mexico* (WBC)
19 Nov 77	Guty Espadas W KO 8 Alex Santana, *Los Angeles USA* (WBA)
30 Nov 77	Miguel Canto W PTS 15 Martin Vargas, *Santiago, Chile* (WBC)
2 Jan 78	Guty Espadas W RSC 7 Kimio Furesawa, *Tokyo, Japan* (WBA)
4 Jan 78	Miguel Canto W PTS 15 Shoji Oguma, *Tokyo, Japan* (WBC)
18 Apr 78	Miguel Canto W PTS 15 Shoji Oguma, *Tokyo, Japan* (WBC)
13 Aug 78	Betulio Gonzalez W PTS 15 Guty Espadas, *Maracay, Venezuela* (WBA)
4 Nov 78	Betulio Gónzalez W RSC 12 Martin Vargas, *Maracay, Venezuela* (WBA)
20 Nov 78	Miguel Canto W PTS 15 Tacomron Vibonchai, *Houston, USA* (WBC)
29 Jan 79	Betulio Gonzalez DREW 15 Shoji Oguma, *Hamamatsu, Japan* (WBA)
10 Feb 79	Miguel Canto W PTS 15 Antonio Avelar, *Merida, Mexico* (WBC)
18 Mar 79	Chan-He Park W PTS 15 Miguel Canto, *Pusan, S Korea* (WBC)
19 May 79	Chan-He Park W PTS 15 Tsutomo Igarashi, *Seoul, S Korea* (WBC)
6 Jul 79	Betulio Gonzalez W KO 12 Shoji Oguma, *Utsunomiya, Japan* (WBA)
9 Sep 79	Chan-He Park DREW 15 Miguel Canto, *Seoul, S Korea* (WBC)
16 Nov 79	Luis Ibarra W PTS 15 Betulio Gonzalez, *Maracay, Venezuela* (WBA)
16 Dec 79	Chan-He Park W KO 2 Guty Espadas, *Pusan, S Korea* (WBC)
9 Feb 80	Chan-He Park W PTS 15 Arnel Arrozal, *Seoul, S Korea* (WBC)
16 Feb 80	Tae-Shik Kim W KO 2 Luis Ibarra, *Seoul, S Korea* (WBA)
13 Apr 80	Chan-He Park W PTS 15 Alberto Morales, *Taegu, S Korea* (WBC)
18 May 80	Shoji Oguma W KO 9 Chan-He Park, *Seoul, S Korea* (WBC)
29 Jun 80	Tae-Shik Kim W PTS 15 Arnel Arrozal, *Seoul, S Korea* (WBA)
28 Jul 80	Shoji Oguma W PTS 15 Sung-Jun Kim, *Tokyo, Japan* (WBC)
18 Oct 80	Shoji Oguma W PTS 15 Chan-He Park, *Sendai, Japan* (WBC)
13 Dec 80	Peter Mathebula W PTS 15 Tae-Shik Kim, *Los Angeles, USA* (WBA)
3 Feb 81	Shoji Oguma W PTS 15 Chan-He Park, *Tokyo, Japan* (WBC)
28 Mar 81	Santos Laciar W RSC 7 Peter Mathebula, *Orlando, Soweto* (WBA)
12 May 81	Antonio Avelar W KO 7 Shoji Oguma, *Mito C, Japan* (WBC)
6 Jun 81	Luis Ibarra W PTS 15 Santos Laciar, *Buenos Aires, Argentine* (WBA)
30 Aug 81	Antonio Avelar W KO 2 Tae-Shik Kim, *Seoul, S Korea* (WBC)
26 Sep 81	Juan Herrera W KO 11 Luis Ibarra, *Merida, Mexico* (WBA)
26 Dec 81	Juan Herrera W RSC 7 Betulio Gonzalez, *Merida, Mexico* (WBA)
20 Mar 82	Prudencio Cardona W KO 1 Antonio Avelar, *Tampico, Mexico* (WBC)
1 May 82	Santos Laciar W RSC 13 Juan Herrera, *Merida, Mexico* (WBA)
24 Jul 82	Freddie Castillo W PTS 15 Prudencio Cardona, *Merida, Mexico* (WBC)
14 Aug 82	Santos Laciar W PTS 15 Betulio Gonzalez, *Maracaibo, Venezuela* (WBA)
5 Nov 82	Santos Laciar W RSC 13 Steve Muchoki, *Copenhagen, Denmark* (WBA)
6 Nov 82	Eleonicio Mercedes W PTS 15 Freddie Castillo, *Los Angeles, USA* (WBC)
4 Mar 83	Santos Laciar W KO 9 Ramon Neri, *Cordoba, Argentine* (WBA)
15 Mar 83	Charlie Magri W RSC 7 Eleoncio Mercedes, *Wembley, England* (WBC)
5 May 83	Santos Laciar W RSC 2 Shuichi Hozumi, *Shizuoka, Japan* (WBA)
17 Jul 83	Santos Laciar W KO 1 Hi-Sup-Shin, *Cheju, S Korea* (WBA)
27 Sep 83	Frank Cedeno W RSC 6 Charlie Magri, *Wembley, England* (WBC)
24 Dec 83	Soon-Chun Kwon W KO 5 Rene Busayong, *Seoul, S Korea* (IBF)
18 Jan 84	Koji Kobayashi W RSC 2 Frank Cedeno, *Tokyo, Japan* (WBC)
28 Jan 84	Santos Laciar W PTS 15 Juan Herrera, *Marsala, Italy* (WBA)
25 Feb 84	Soon-Chun Kwon W KO 12 Roger Castillo, *Seoul, S Korea* (IBF)
9 Apr 84	Gabriel Bernal W KO 2 Koji Kobayashi, *Tokyo, Japan* (WBC)
19 May 84	Soon-Chun Kwon W PTS 15 Ian Clyde, *Daejon, S Korea* (IBF)
1 Jun 84	Gabriel Bernal W RSC 11 Antoine Montero, *Nimes, France* (WBC)
7 Sep 84	Soon-Chun Kwon NC 12 Joaquin Caraballo, *Chungju, S Korea* (IBF)
15 Sep 84	Santos Laciar W KO 10 Prudencio Cardona, *Cordoba, Argentine* (WBA)
8 Oct 84	Sot Chitalada W PTS 12 Gabriel Bernal, *Bangkok, Thailand* (WBC)
8 Dec 84	Santos Laciar W PTS 15 Hilario Zapata, *Buenos Aires, Argentine* (WBA)
25 Jan 85	Soon-Chun Kwon DREW 15 Chong-Kwan Chung, *Daejon, S Korea* (IBF)
20 Feb 85	Sot Chitalada W RTD 4 Charlie Magri, *London, England* (WBC)
14 Apr 85	Soon-Chun Kwon W KO 3 Shinobu Kawashima, *Pohang, S Korea* (IBF)
6 May 85	Santos Laciar W PTS 15 Antoine Montero, *Grenoble, France* (WBA)
	Santos Laciar relinquished title to campaign as a light-bantamweight
22 Jun 85	Sot Chitalada DREW 12 Gabriel Bernal, *Bangkok, Thailand* (WBC)
17 Jul 85	Soon-Chun Kwon DREW 15 Chong-Kwan Chung, *Masan, S Korea* (IBF)
5 Oct 85	Hilario Zapata W PTS 15 Alonzo Gonzales, *Panama C, Panama* (WBA)
20 Dec 85	Chong-Kwan Chung W RSC 4 Soon-Chun Kwon, *Taegu, S Korea* (IBF)
31 Jan 86	Hilario Zapata W PTS 15 Javier Lucas, *Panama C, Panama* (WBA)
22 Feb 86	Sot Chitalada W PTS 12 Freddie Castillo, *Kuwait* (WBC)
7 Apr 86	Hilario Zapata W PTS 15 Suichi Hozumi, *Nirasaki, Japan* (WBA)

DATE

27 Apr 86 Bi-Won Chung W PTS 15 Chong-Kwan Chung, *Pusan, S Korea* (IBF)
5 Jul 86 Hilario Zapata W PTS 15 Dodie Penalosa, *Manila, Philippines* (WBA)
2 Aug 86 Hi-Sup Shin W RSC 15 Bi-Won Chung, *Inchon, S Korea* (IBF)
13 Sep 86 Hilario Zapata W PTS 15 Alberto Castro, *Panama C, Panama* (WBA)
22 Nov 86 Hi-Sup Shin W RSC 13 Henry Brent, *Chunchon, S Korea* (IBF)
6 Dec 86 Hilario Zapata W PTS 15 Claudemir Dias, *Salvador, Brazil* (WBA)
10 Dec 86 Sot Chitalada W PTS 12 Gabriel Bernal, *Bangkok, Thailand* (WBC)
13 Feb 87 Fidel Bassa W PTS 15 Hilario Zapata, *Barranquilla, Colombia* (WBA)
22 Feb 87 Dodie Penalosa W KO 5 Hi-Sup Shin, *Inchon, S Korea* (IBF)
25 Apr 87 Fidel Bassa W KO 13 Dave McAuley, *Belfast, Ireland* (WBA)
15 Aug 87 Fidel Bassa DREW 15 Hilario Zapata, *Panama City, Panama* (WBA)
5 Sep 87 Chang-Ho Choi W KO 11 Dodie Penalosa, *Manila, Philippines* (IBF)
5 Sep 87 Sot Chitalada W KO 4 Rae-Ki Ahn, *Bangkok, Thailand* (WBC)
18 Dec 87 Fidel Bassa W PTS 12 Felix Marty, *Cartagena, Colombia* (WBA)
16 Jan 88 Rolando Bohol W PTS 15 Chang-Ho Choi, *Manila, Philippines* (IBF)
31 Jan 88 Sot Chitalada W RSC 7 Hideaki Kamishiro, *Osaka, Japan* (WBC)
26 Mar 88 Fidel Bassa W PTS 12 Dave McAuley, *Belfast, N Ireland* (WBA)
6 May 88 Rolando Bohol W PTS 15 Cho-Woon Park, *Manila, Philippines* (IBF)
24 Jul 88 Yong-Kang Kim W PTS 12 Sot Chitalada, *Pohang, S Korea* (WBC)
2 Oct 88 Fidel Bassa W PTS 12 Ray Medel, *San Antonio, USA (WBA)*
5 Oct 88 Duke McKenzie W KO 11 Rolando Bohol, *Wembley, England* (IBF)

LIGHT-FLYWEIGHT

(*Current weight limit:* 108lb/49kg. The WBA and IBF call this class 'Junior Flyweight' and the WBC call the class 'Light-flyweight')

DATE

4 Apr 75 Franco Udella W DIS 12 Valentin Martinez, *Milan, Italy* (WBC)
Franco Udella forfeited WBC recognition (failure to defend against Rafael Lovera)
23 Aug 75 Jaime Rios W PTS 15 Rigoberto Marcano, *Panama C, Panama* (WBA)
13 Sep 75 Luis Estaba W KO 4 Rafael Lovera, *Caracas, Venezuela* (WBC)
17 Dec 75 Luis Estaba W RSC 10 Takenobu Shimabakuro, *Okinawa, Japan* (WBC)
3 Jan 76 Jaime Rios W PTS 15 Kazunori Tenryu, *Kagoshima, Japan* (WBA)
14 Feb 76 Luis Estaba W PTS 15 Leo Palacios, *Caracas, Venezuela* (WBC)
2 May 76 Luis Estaba W PTS 15 Juan Alvarez, *Caracas, Venezuela* (WBC)
1 Jul 76 Juan Guzman W PTS 15 Jaime Rios, *St Domingo, Dominican Republic* (WBA)
17 Jul 76 Luis Estaba W KO 3 Franco Udella, *Maracay, Venezuela* (WBC)
26 Sep 76 Luis Estaba W RTD 10 Rodolfo Rodriguez, *Caracas, Venezuela* (WBC)
10 Oct 76 Yoko Gushiken W KO 7 Juan Guzman, *Kofu, Japan* (WBA)
21 Nov 76 Luis Estaba W RSC 10 Valentin Martinez, *Caracas, Venezuela* (WBC)
30 Jan 77 Yoko Gushiken W PTS 15 Jaime Rios, *Tokyo, Japan* (WBA)
15 May 77 Luis Estaba W PTS 15 Rafael Pedroza, *Caracas, Venezuela* (WBC)
22 May 77 Yoko Gushiken W PTS 15 Rigoberto Marcano, *Sapporo, Japan* (WBA)
17 Jul 77 Luis Estaba W PTS 15 Ricardo Estupinan, *Cruz, Venezuela* (WBC)
21 Aug 77 Luis Estaba W RSC 11 Juan Alvarez, *Cruz, Venezuela* (WBC)
18 Sep 77 Luis Estaba W KO 15 Orlando Hernandez, *Caracas, Venezuela* (WBC)
9 Oct 77 Yoko Gushiken W RSC 4 Montsayarm Mahachai, *Oita, Japan* (WBA)

DATE

30 Oct 77 Luis Estaba W PTS 15 Sor Vorasingh, *Caracas, Venezuela* (WBC)
29 Jan 78 Yoko Gushiken W RSC 14 Aniceto Vargas, *Nagoya, Japan* (WBA)
19 Feb 78 Freddie Castillo W RSC 14 Luis Estaba, *Caracas, Venezuela* (WBC)
6 May 78 Sor Vorasingh W PTS 15 Freddie Castillo, *Bangkok, Thailand* (WBC)
7 May 78 Yoko Gushiken W RSC 13 Jaime Rios, *Hiroshima, Japan* (WBA)
29 Jul 78 Sor Vorasingh W RTD 5 Luis Estaba, *Caracas, Venezuela* (WBC)
30 Sep 78 Sung-Jun Kim W KO 3 Sor Vorasingh, *Seoul, S Korea* (WBC)
15 Oct 78 Yoko Gushiken W KO 5 Sang-Il Chung, *Tokyo, Japan* (WBA)
7 Jan 79 Yoko Gushiken W KO 7 Rigoberto Marcano, *Kawasaki, Japan* (WBA)
31 Mar 79 Sung-Jun Kim DREW 15 Hector Melendez, *Seoul, S Korea* (WBC)
8 Apr 79 Yoko Gushiken W RSC 7 Alfonso Lopez, *Tokyo, Japan* (WBA)
28 Jul 79 Sung-Jun Kim W PTS 15 Stony Carupo, *Seoul, S Korea* (WBC)
29 Jul 79 Yoko Gushiken W PTS 15 Rafael Pedroza, *Kitakyushi, Japan* (WBA)
21 Oct 79 Sung-Jun Kim W PTS 15 Hector Melendez, *Seoul, S Korea* (WBC)
28 Oct 79 Yoko Gushiken W RSC 7 Tito Abella, *Tokyo, Japan* (WBA)
3 Jan 80 Shigeo Nakajima W PTS 15 Sung-Jun Kim, *Tokyo, Japan* (WBC)
27 Jan 80 Yoko Gushiken W PTS 15 Yong-Hyun Kim, *Osaka, Japan* (WBA)
24 Mar 80 Hilario Zapata W PTS 15 Shigeo Nakajima, *Tokyo, Japan* (WBC)
1 Jun 80 Yoko Gushiken W RSC 8 Martin Vargas, *Kochi C, Japan* (WBA)
7 Jun 80 Hilario Zapata W PTS 15 Chi-Bok Kim, *Seoul. S Korea* (WBC)
4 Aug 80 Hilario Zapata W PTS 15 Hector Melendez, *Caracas, Venezuela* (WBC)
17 Sep 80 Hilario Zapata W RSC 11 Shigeo Nakajima, *Gufi, Japan* (WBC)
12 Oct 80 Yoko Gushiken W PTS 15 Pedro Flores, *Kanazawa, Japan* (WBA)
1 Dec 80 Hilario Zapata W PTS 15 Reynaldo Becerra, *Caracas, Venezuela* (WBC)
8 Feb 81 Hilario Zapata W RSC 13 Joey Olivo, *Panama C, Panama* (WBC)
8 Mar 81 Pedro Flores W RTD 12 Yoko Gushiken, *Gushikawa, Japan* (WBA)
24 Apr 81 Hilario Zapata W PTS 15 Rudy Crawford, *San Francisco, USA* (WBC)
19 Jul 81 Hwan-Jin Kim W RSC 13 Pedro Flores, *Taegu, S Korea* (WBA)
15 Aug 81 Hilario Zapata W PTS 15 German Torres, *Panama C, Panama* (WBC)
11 Oct 81 Hwan-Jin Kim W PTS 15 Alfonso Lopez, *Daejon, S Korea* (WBA)
6 Nov 81 Hilario Zapata W RSC 10 Sor Vorasingh, *Korat, Thailand* (WBC)
16 Dec 81 Katsuo Tokashiki W PTS 15 Hwan-Jin Kim, *Sendai, Japan* (WBA)
6 Feb 82 Amado Ursua W KO 2 Hilario Zapata, *Panama C, Panama* (WBC)
4 Apr 82 Katsuo Tokashiki W PTS 15 Lupe Madera, *Sendai, Japan* (WBA)
13 Apr 82 Tadashi Tomori W PTS 15 Amado Ursua, *Tokyo, Japan* (WBC)
7 Jul 82 Katsuo Tokashiki W KO 8 Masahara Inami, *Tokyo, Japan* (WBA)
20 Jul 82 Hilario Zapata W PTS 15 Tadashi Tomori, *Kanazawa, Japan* (WBC)
18 Sep 82 Hilario Zapata W PTS 15 Jung-Koo Chang, *Chonju, S Korea* (WBC)
10 Oct 82 Katsuo Tokashiki W PTS 15 Sung-Nam Kim, *Tokyo, Japan* (WBA)
30 Nov 82 Hilario Zapata W RSC 8 Tadashi Tomori, *Tokyo, Japan* (WBC)
9 Jan 83 Katsuo Tokashiki W PTS 15 Hwan-Jin Kim, *Kyoto, Japan* (WBA)
26 Mar 83 Jung-Koo Chang W RSC 3 Hilario Zapata, *Daejon, S Korea* (WBC)
10 Apr 83 Katsuo Tokashiki DREW 15 Lupe Madera, *Tokyo, Japan* (WBA)
11 Jun 83 Jung-Koo Chang W RSC 2 Masaharu Iha, *Taegu, S Korea* (WBC)
10 Jul 83 Lupe Madera W RSC 4 Katsuo Tokashiki, *Tokyo, Japan* (WBA)
10 Sep 83 Jung-Koo Chang W PTS 12 German Torres, *Daejon, S Korea* (WBC)
23 Oct 83 Lupe Madera W PTS 12 Katsuo Tokashiki, *Sapporo, Japan* (WBA)
10 Dec 83 Dodie Penalosa W RSC 11 Satoshi Shingaki, *Osaka, Japan* (IBF)
31 Mar 84 Jung-Koo Chang W PTS 12 Sot Chitalada, *Pusan, S Korea* (WBC)
13 May 84 Dodie Penalosa W RSC 9 Jae-Hong Kim, *Seoul, S Korea* (IBF)
19 May 84 Francisco Quiroz W KO 9 Lupe Madera, *Maracaibo, Venezuela* (WBA)
18 Aug 84 Jung-Koo Chang W RSC 9 Katsuo Tokashiki. *Pohang S Korea* (WBC)
18 Aug 84 Francisco Quiroz W KO 2 Victor Sierra, *Panama C, Panama* (WBA)
16 Nov 84 Dodie Penalosa W PTS 15 Jum-Hwan Choi, *Manila, Philippines* (IBF)
15 Dec 84 Jung-Koo Chang W PTS 12 Tadashi Kuramochi, *Pusan, S Korea* (WBC)
29 Mar 85 Joey Olivo W PTS 15 Francisco Quiroz, *Miami, USA* (WBA)
27 Apr 85 Jung-Koo Chang W PTS 12 German Torres, *Ulsan, S Korea* (WBC)
28 Jul 85 Joey Olivo W PTS 15 Moon-Jin Choi, *Seoul, S Korea* (WBA)
3 Aug 85 Jung-Koo Chang W PTS 15 Francisco Montiel, *Seoul, S Korea* (WBC)
12 Oct 85 Dodie Penalosa W KO 3 Yani Hagler, *Jakarta, Indonesia* (IBF)
Dodie Penalosa relinquished title to campaign as a flyweight
10 Nov 85 Jung-Koo Chang W PTS 12 Jorge Cano, *Daejon, S Korea* (WBC)
8 Dec 85 Myung-Woo Yuh W PTS 15 Joey Olivo, *Seoul, S Korea* (WBA)

DATE	
9 Mar 86	Myung-Woo Yuh W PTS 15 Jose de Jesus, *Suwon, S Korea* (WBA)
13 Apr 86	Jung-Koo Chang W PTS 12 German Torres, *Kwangju, S Korea* (WBC)
14 Jun 86	Myung-Woo Yuh W RSC 12 Tomohiro Kiyuna, *Inchon, S Korea* (WBA)
13 Sep 86	Jung-Koo Chang W PTS 12 Francisco Montiel, *Seoul, S Korea* (WBC)
30 Nov 86	Myung-Woo Yuh W PTS 15 Mario de Marco, *Seoul, S Korea* (WBA)
7 Dec 86	Jum-Hwan Choi W PTS 15 Cho-Woon Park, *Pusan, S Korea* (IBF)
14 Dec 86	Jung-Koo Chang W RSC 5 Hideyuki Ohashi, *Inchon, S Korea* (WBC)
1 Mar 86	Myung-Woo Yuh W RSC 1 Eduardo Tunon, *Seoul, S Korea* (WBA)
29 Mar 87	Jum-Hwan Choi W PTS 15 Tacy Macalos, *Seoul, S Korea* (IBF)
19 Apr 87	Jung-Koo Chang W RSC 6 Efren Pinto, *Seoul, S Korea* (WBC)
5 Jul 87	Jum-Hwan Choi W RSC 4 Toshiko Matsuta, *Seoul, S Korea* (IBF)
9 Aug 87	Jum-Hwan Choi W RSC 3 Azadin Anhar, *Jakarta, Indonesia* (IBF)
20 Sep 87	Myung-Woo Yuh W KO 8 Rodolfo Blanco, *Inchoh, S Korea* (WBA)
13 Dec 87	Jung-Koo Chang W PTS 12 Isidro Perez, *Seoul, S Korea* (WBC)
7 Feb 88	Myung-Woo Yuh W PTS 12 Wilibaldo Salazar, *Seoul, S Korea* (WBA)
12 Jun 88	Myung-Woo Yuh W PTS 12 Jose de Jesus, *Seoul, S Korea* (WBA)
27 Jun 88	Jung-Koo Chang W RSC 8 Hideyuki Ohashi, *Tokyo, Japan* (WBC)
28 Aug 88	Myung-Woo Yuh W KO 6 Putt Ohyuthanakorn, *Pusan, S Korea* (WBA)
5 Nov 88	Jum-Hwan Choi W PTS 12 Tacy Macalos, *Manila, Philippines* (IBF)
6 Nov 88	Myung-Woo Yuh W KO 7 Bahar Udin, *Seoul, S Korea* (WBA)

MINI-FLYWEIGHT

(*Current weight limit:* 105lb/47.6kg. The WBA and IBF call the class 'Mini-flyweight', and the WBC calls the class 'Strawweight')

DATE	
18 Oct 87	Hiroki Ioka W PTS 12 Mai Thomburifarm, *Osaka, Japan* (WBC)
31 Jan 88	Hiroki Ioka W RSC 12 Kyung-Yung Lee, *Osaka, Japan* (WBC)
10 Jan 88	Louis Gamez W PTS 12 Bung-Jung Kim, *Pusan, S Korea* (WBA)
24 Mar 88	Samuth Sithnarvelpol W TD 11 Pretty Boy Lucas, *Bangkok, Thailand* (IBF)
29 Apr 88	Louis Gamez W RSC 3 Kenji Yokozawa, *Tokyo, Japan* (WBA)
5 Jun 88	Hiroki Ioka DREW 12 Napa Kiatwanchai, *Osaka, Japan* (WBC)
29 Aug 88	Samuth Sithnarvelpol W PTS 15 In-Kyu Hwang, *Bangkok, Thailand* (IBF)
13 Nov 88	Napa Kiatwanchai W PTS 12 Hiroki Ioka, *Osaka, Japan* (WBC)

BIBLIOGRAPHY

The author acknowledges and recommends the following books which were of assistance in compiling the current volume:

Andre, Sam and Fleischer, Nat: *A Pictorial History of Boxing* Hamlyn Publishing Group Ltd, London, 1987 edition

Egan, Pierce: *Boxiana*, Facsimile of 1812 Edition, Vince Harvey Publishing, Leicester, 1971

Golesworthy, Maurice: *Encyclopedia of Boxing*, Robert Hale, London, eighth edition 1988

Grombach, John V.: *The Saga of the Fist*, A.S. Barnes & Co, South Brunswick and New York; Thomas Yoseloff Ltd, London, 1977

Heller, Peter: *In This Corner!*, Simon and Schuster Inc, New York, 1973

Hugman, Barry J.: *Frank Warren's International Boxing Year*, Macdonald/Queen Anne Press, London, 1988 edition

Hugman, Barry J.: *British Boxing Yearbook*, Macdonald/Queen Anne Press, London, various editions

Johnson, Dick: *Bare Fist Fighters of the 18th and 19th Century*, The Book Guild Ltd, Sussex, 1987

Menke, Frank F.: *The Encyclopedia of Sports*, A.S. Barnes & Co, South Brunswick and New York; Thomas Yoseloff Ltd, London, 5th edition 1975

Morrison, Ian: *Boxing — The Records*, Guinness Superlatives Ltd, Enfield, Middlesex, 1986

Mullan, Harry: *The Illustrated History of Boxing*, Hamlyn Publishing Group Ltd, London, 1987

Odd, Gilbert: *Boxing — Cruisers to Mighty Atoms*, Pelham Books Ltd, London, 1974

Odd, Gilbert: *Boxing — The Inside Story*, Hamlyn Publishing Group Ltd, London, 1978

Odd, Gilbert: *Encyclopedia of Boxing*, Hamlyn Publishing Group Ltd, London, 1983

Odd, Gilbert: *Kings of the Ring*, Newnes Books, Feltham, Middlesex, 1985

Skehan, Everett M.: *Rocky Marciano*, Robson Books Ltd, London, 1977

Sugar, Bert Randolph: *The Great Fights*, Windward (W.H. Smith and Son Ltd), London, 1981

In addition the weekly magazine *Boxing News* (London) and the monthly *The Ring* (New York) have been invaluable with their reports and results.

Personal thanks are due to boxing statistician Barry Hugman for help with boxing records.

Index

Page numbers in *italics* refer to illustration captions.
Those in **bold** refer to main entries.
Please note that the Records chapter has not been included in the index.

A

Aaron, Barney 130
Abrams, Georgie 96–7
Accavallo, Horacio 167
Aceves, Mauricio 127
Adigue, Pedro 125–6
Albarado, Oscar 'Shotgun' 109
Ali, Muhammad 29, *61*, **61–9**, *64–5*, *67*, *69*, *70*, 70–1, 85, **174**, *174*, *209*, **216**, *216*
Allen, Terry 166
Allen, Tom 25, 30
Alli, Terence 136
Ambers, Lon 117, 132
Ambrose, John 22
America, prize fighting in 21–3
Anaya, Romeo 158–9
Anderson, Ray 85
Andries, Dennis 87–9, *87–8*, 108
Angelmann, Valentin 165–6
Angotti, Sammy 132–3, 145
Anthony, Tony 84
Antuofermo, Vito 104–5
Apostoli, Fred 96
Aquino, Lupe 111
Aranda, Pascual 149
Archer, Joey 101
Archibald, Joey 145
Arguello, Alexis 126, 129, 136, 138–9, 147, 150, **174**
Arizmendi, Baby, 117, 144
Armstrong, Bob 33
Armstrong, Henry 96, **117**, *117*, 144–5, **175**
Arredondo, Rene 127
Arredondo, Ricardo 138
Arroyo, Harry 136
Attell, Abe 142–3, 141

B

Backus, Billy 120–1
Baek, In-Chul 111, 161
Baer, Buddy 47–8
Baer, Max 43–4, *44*, 46, 48, **175**
Baez, Pablo 122
Bain, Abe 82
Bainge, Bill 21
Baird, Doyle 85
Baker, Mike 110
Baldock, Terry 156–7
Baldwin, Caleb 16, 92, 130
Ballerino, Mike 138
Bantamweights 154 *et seq*
Barclay, Captain 17
Bare-knuckle fighting, end of 27
Barkley, Iran 107–8
Barnes, George 118
Barth, Carmen 91, 96
Bartholomew, Jack 16
Bartolo, Sal 145
Basilio, Carmen 99–101, *100*, 118, **215**
Basora, Jose 98
Bass, Benny 138, 144
Bassa, Fidel 169–70
Bassett, Percy 146
Bassey, Hogan Kid 146
Battaglia, Frank 96
Battalino, Christopher 'Battling' 144
Belanger, Albert 'Frenchy' 165
Belcastro, Vicenzo 151
Belcher, Jem 16–17, **176**
Beltran, Fernando 160
Bell, Archie 156
Bell, Tommy 118
Belloise, Mike 144–5
Belloise, Steve 96
Benitez, Wilfred 110–11, 121, **125–6**, **176**
Bennett, Lonnie 86
Benton, Bernard 76
Benvenuti, Nino 101–2, 109, **176**
Berbick, Trevor 71–3
Berg, Jack 'Kid' 124, 132, **177**, *177*
Berlenbach, Paul 81–2, 102
Bernal, Gabriel 168
Bernstein, Jack 137
Bershore, Freddie 50
Berua, Bobby 151
Blocker, Maurice *113*, 123
Bogan, Fred 142
Bogs, Tom 102
Bold Bendigo **19–20**, *19*, **176**
Bonavena, Oscar 64–5
Bonds, Larry 122
Boone, John 13
Borkorsov, Venice 158, 167–8
Bossi, Carmelo 109
Boza-Edwards, Cornelius 136, 139
Boulware, Vince 89
Bouttier, Jean-Claude 102–3, *103*
Bowdry, Jesse 84
Bowker, Joe 154
Bowler, James 24
Braddock, James J. 44–6, 82, **177**
Brady, William A. 31, 33
Brain, Benjamin 13–14
Bramble, Livingstone 136
Bratton, Johnny 118
Braxton, David 111
Braxton, Dwight 87
Brazier, Harold 127
Breland, Mark 123
Brennan, Bill 39
Briscoe, Benny 102, 104
Britt, Jimmy 130
Britton, Jack 16, 115, 124, **177**
Bronson, Ray 114
Broome, Harry 20
Broughton, Jack 10, *11*, 12, **177**
Rules 11, *12*
Brouillard, Lou 95, 116
Brown, Charlie 'Choo Choo' 136
Brown, Charlie 'White Lightening' 136
Brown, Jacko 165
Brown, Joe 127, 133
Brown, Newsboy 165
Brown, Panama Al 153, 156, *157*, **177**
Brown, Simon 123
Bruno, Frank 72
Buchanan, Ken 129, 134–5, *135*
Buckhorse, The Noted 10
Bugner, Joe 66–7, *69*, 71
Bumphus, Johnny 123, 126
Burge, Dick 130
Burke, James 18–20, 22
Burman, Joe 155
Burnett, Jesse 76, 86
Burns, Frankie 155
Burns, Tommy *34*, **34–5**, 80, **178**
Burrows, Bill 17
Burruni, Salvadore 167
Byrne, Simon 18–19

C

Caestus 8–9
Caldwell, Johnnie 158–9
Callahan, Andy 95
Callahan, Jack 111
Callahan, Mushy 124
Callejas, Victor 149–50
Callura, Jackie 145
Camacho, Hector 'Macho' 129, 136, *137*, 139
Camel, Marvin 76
Campbell, Frankie 43
Candel, Carmelo 95
Canizales, Gaby 159
Canizales, Orlando 160
Cannon, Tom 18
Canto, Miguel 168
Canzoneri, Tony 124–5, 129, 132, 144, 156, **178**
Caramanolis, Richard 88
Cardona, Prudencio 168
Cardona, Ricardo 150
Carmona, Chango 135
Carnera, Primo **43**, *42–3*, 173, **178**
Carney, Jem 130
Carpentier, Georges 29, 37, 39, *39*, 81, *81–2*, **178**, *179*
Carrasco, Pedro 134–5
Carrasquilla, Hector 150
Carroll, Hal 85
Carter, Jack 18
Carter, Jimmy 133
Carruthers, Jimmy 153, 156–7
Castellini, Miguel 110
Castillo, Freddie 168, 171
Castillo, Jesus 'Chuchu' 158
Cataluna, Ernie 160
Caunt, Ben 19–20, 22, 92
Cerdan, Marcel 91, **97–8**, **179**
Cervantes, Antonio 125–6
Chacon, Bobby 136, 139, 148
Chambers, Arthur 130
Chandler, Jeff 159
Chandler, Tom 92
Chaney, George 'KO' 137
Charles, Ezzard 49–53, *53*, 83, **179**
Charles, Ralph 120
Charnley, Dave 133
Chavez, Julio Cesar 137, 139, **180**
Chervet, Fritz 168
Chionoi, Chartchai 163, 167–8
Chip, George 93–4
Chitalada, Sot 163, 168
Chocolate, Kid 124, 132, 138, 144, **180**
Choi, Chang-Ho 170–1
Choynski, Joe 31
Chuvalo, George *62*, 62–5
Ciambra, Joey 109
Clark, Elky 165
Clark, Scott 121
Clay, Cassius *29*, *59–60*, **59–65**
see also Ali, Muhammad
Clay, Von 84
Cobb, Tex 71
Coburn, Joe 24–5
Cochrane, Freddie 'Red' 118
Cockell, Don *49*, 53
Coetzee, Gerrie 70–1
Coggi, Juan 126
Cohen, Max 104
Cohen, Robert 158
Cokes, Curtis 120
Collins, Joe 102
Collyer, Sam 130
Colton, Eddie 85
Coming up to scratch 10
Conlon, Johnny 154–5
Conn, Billy 48, 79, 83, **180**
Conn, Joe 164
Conteh, John, 3, 85–6, *86*, **181**
Cooney, Gerry *70*, 71
Cooper, Henry 55, 59, 63
Coopman, Jean-Pierre 68
Corbett, James J. 29, *30*, 30–4, 80, 82, *180*, **181**, **210**
Corbett, Young II 142, *147*
Corbett, Young III 96, 116
Corcoran, Peter 13
Corelli, Frankie 145
Costello, Bill 127
'Country McCluskey' 22
Courtney, Peter 32
Cowdell, Pat 148–9
Creedon, Dan 92
Crawley, Peter 18
Crawley, Tyrone 136
Cribb, Tom 16–18, **181**, *181*
Criqui, Eugene 143–4, 164
Croot, Walter 154
Crous, Piet 76
Crowley, Dave 144
Cruz, Leonardo 150
Cruz, Paul 147
Cruz, Roberto 125
Cruz, Steve *143*, 149
Cuello, Miguel 86
Curran, Joe 166
Curry, Bruce 126
Curry, Don 108, 111, 122–3
Curtis, Dick 130
Curto, Vinnie 89
Czyz, Bobby 87–8

D

d'Agata, Mario 158
d'Amato, Cus 54, 58, 85
Dade, Harold 156
Dagge, Eckhard 110
Daniels, Terry 65
Darcy, Les 91, 94, 115, **181**
Darts, Bill 13
Dauthuille, Laurent 98, **214**
Davila, Albert 160
Davis, Bill 24–5
Davis, Eddie 87–8
Davis, Howard 127, 136
Davis, Johnny 87
Davis, Kid 166
Davis, Teddy 'Red Top' 146
Day, Davey, 132
de Jesus, Esteban 135
de la Rosa, Johnny 139
de Leon, Carlos 76–7
de Marco, Tony 118
de Marco, Paddy 133
de Oliveira, Miguel 109
de Paula, Frankie 85
del Papa, Piero 85
Delaney, Jack 81–2, 102
Demont, Al 154
Dempsey, Jack 29, *38–9*, **38–41**, *41*, **182**, **212**
Dempsey, Jack 'Nonpareil' 32, 91–2, 132, **182**
Devlin, Chuck 95
Diamond, Al 95
Diaz, Elió 122
Diaz, Paul 161
Dillon, Jack 80, 93
Dixon, George 141–2, 154, **182**
Dokes, Michael 70–1
Donovan, Professor Mike 92
Dougherty, Dan 154
Douglas, James 74
Douglas, John Sholto, Marquess of Queensbury 25–6
Dower, Dai 166
Downes, Terry *49*, 84, 101
Downey, Bryan 94
Doyle, Jimmy 118

Driscoll, 'Peerless' Jim 141, 143, **183**
Duane, Carl 150
Duffy, Paddy 114
Duke of Cumberland 12–13
Dundee, Angelo 59
Dundee, Joe 95, 116
Dundee, Johnny 137–8, 143–4
Dundee, Vince 95, 116
Dunn, Richard 68
Dupas, Ralph 109, 133
Dupree, Jimmy 85
Duran, Jose 109
Duran, Roberto 105, 110–11, 121, *129*, 129, 134–5, *135*, **183**, *183*
Durelle, Yvon *84*, 84, **216**
Dutch Sam the Terrible Jew 16
Dykes, Bobby 118

E

Ebihara, Hiroyuki 167
Echegaray, Victor 138
Edwards, Billy 114, 130
Edwards, Willie 88
Elias, Samuel 16, 130
Elizondo, Roberto 136
Elliott, Jimmy 25
Ellis, Jimmy 64–5, 68
Ellis, Lester 139
Elorde, Gabriel 'Flash' 134, 138, 146, **184**
England, revival of boxing in 8–10
Erne, Frank 130
Ertle, Johnny 'Kowpie' 155
Escalera, Alberto 138–9
Escobar, Sixto 156
Espada, Angel 121
Espadas, Gustavo 'Guty' 168
Espana, Ernesto 135–6
Esparragoza, Antonio 149
Espinal, Eusebio 161
Espinosa, Louis 150–1
Estaba, Louis 171
Estrada, Juan Jose 151
Evangelista, Alfredo 68–9
Everett, Tyrone 139

F

Famechon, Ray 146–7
Fancy, The 10
Farr, Tommy 46, *46*
Fasari, Charlie 118
Fearns, Duggan 13
Fearby, Jack 16
Feldman, Lew 144
Fenech, Jeff 149, 151, 160, **184**, *184*
Ferns, Rube 114
Fernandez, Florentino 101
Fernandez, Jorge 119
Fernandez, Perico 126
Ferrand, Victor 165
Fields, Jackie 116
Figg, James 7, 10, *11*, **184**
Finnegan, Chris 85
Finnegan, Honeyboy 144
'First Knight of the Cleaver' 12
Fist-fighting 9
Fitzsimmons, Bob 24, *32–3*, 32–4, 80, 91–2, **184**, **210**
Fleischer, Nat 62
Flores, Jose Maria 77
Flores, Pedro 171
Flowers, Tiger **94**, *95*
Flynn, Jim 35, 37
Fogarty, Jack 92
Folley, Zora 57, 63
Foord, Ben 46
Forbes, Harry 142, 154
Foreman, George 66–7, *67*, **185**
Foster, Bob 65, 79, 85, **185**, *185*
Foure, Pierre 85–6
Fourie, Mike 85
Fox, Blackjack Billy 83
Fox, Richard Kyle *26*
Fox, Tiger Jack 83
Frank, Scott 71
Franklin, Matt 86
Fratto, Rocky 110
Frawley Law 38, 94
Frazer, Alfonso 125
Frazier, Joe 63–6, *64–5*, 68, 85, 102, **186**, *186*, *209*, **216**, *216*
Frazier, Marvis 71
Freeman, Charles 20
Freeman, Tommy 116
Frias, Arturo 136
Frush, Danny 143
Fujii, Paul 125
Fuller, William 22
Fulljames, George 92
Fullmer, Don 102
Fullmer, Gene 99–101
Furlano, Nicky 126
Furr, Phil 117

G

Gainer, Al 83
Gains, Larry 43
Galandez, Victor 86
Galaxy, Kaokor 160–1
Galaxy, Kaosai 160–1
Galento, 'Two-Ton' Tony 47, *47*
Gallardo, Jesus 89
Gamble, Andrew 16
Gamez, Leo 171
Gans, Joe 129–30, *131*, **186**, **211**
Garcia, Ceferino 96, 117
Gardner, George 80
Gardner, Jimmy 114
Gardner, Tony 109
Garza, Jaime 151
Gavilan, Kid 118
Gaymon, Dorsey 76
Genaro, Frankie 163, 165
Gibbons, Tommy 39
Gilroy, Freddie 158
Giminez, Carlos 126
Glover, Mike 115
Godfrey, Captain 10
Goldman, Charley 51
Goldstein, Abe 155–6
Gomes, Harold 138
Gomez, Antonio 147
Gomez, Wilfredo 139, 148–50, *151*, 158, **186**
Gonzales, Alonzo 169
Gonzalez, Betulio 167–9, 171
Gonzales, Rodolfo 127, 135
Gonzalez, Manuel 110
Goodrich, Jimmy 132
Goodwin, Bob 82
Goss, Joe 24–5, *25*, 30
Graham, Billy 118
Graham, Bushy 156
Grande, Frisco 165
Gray, Clyde 120–1
Graziano, Rocky 91, **96–7**, *97*, 99, 118, **187**, **213**
'Great Gun of Windsor, The' 18
Greb, Harry 91, **94**, *95*, 116, **187**, *187*
Green, Dave 'Boy' 121
Green, George 92, 114
Green, Harold 97
Greer, Michael 77
Greek Boxing 7, 8
Gregorio, Vidal 156
Gregory, Eddie 86
Gregson, Bob *16*, 16–17
Gretting, Bill 10
Griffith, Emile 101–2, 110, 119–20, *119*, **187**
Griffo, Young 142
Grove, Calvin 149
Guest, Milton 122
Gully, John *16*, 16
Gumbs, Roy 89

H

Hagan, Jack 80
Hagler, 'Marvelous' Marvin 89, 91, *91*, **104–7**, 105, *106*, **188**, *188*, **217**
Halima, Alphonse 158
Hamada, Tsuyoshi 127
Hamsho, Mustafo 105
Harada, Masahiko 'Fighting' 147, 153, 158, 166, **188**
Hargrove, Earl 111
Harrington, Stan 109
Harris, Dooney 92
Harris, Harry 154
Harris, Roy 54
Hart, Marvin 34, 80
Harvey, Len 82–3, 95, **188**
Hatcher, Gene 'Mad Dog' 123, 126
Haugen, Greg 136
Hawkins, Dal 142
Hayman, Alfonso 121
Hearns, Thomas 88, *89*, *91*, 91, 106, *106*, **108**, 111, 121, 122, *122*, **188**, *189*
Heenan, John C, 21, 23, *23*, 24, **210**
Heeney, Tom 41
Herman, Pete 155, 164
Hernandez, Carlos 125
Hernandez, José 109
Hernandez, Lionel 138–9
Herrera, Antonio 147
Herrera, Carlos 110
Herrera, Juan 169
Herrera, Rafael 158
Hicken, Abe 130
Hickman, Tom 17–18
Hicks, Tommy 85
Higgins, Enrique 147
Hill, Johnny 165
Hill, Virgil 88
Hilton, Matthew 111
Hines, Robert 111
Hinton, Gary 127
Hogarth, William 10
Holberg, Waldemar 114–15
Holmes, Larry 68–72, *70*, 74–5, 87, *173*, **189**, *189*
Holmes, Lindell 89
Holtzer, Maurice 145
Holyfield, Evander 76–7, *77*, **190**
Honeyghan, Lloyd *113*, 122–3, *123*, **190**, *190*
Hong, Soo-Hwan 150, 159
Hoon-Lee, Seung 151
Hooper, Bill 13–14
Hope, Maurice 104, 110, *110*
Horton, Dick 17
Horton Law, repeal of 80
Houseman, Lou 80
Hudkins, Ace 94
Hudson, Joshua 18
Hughes, Johnny 164
Humez, Charles 99
Humphries, Richard *14*, 14
Hurst, Sam 23–4
Hutchings, Fred 111
Hutchins, Len 86
Hyer, Jacob 21
Hyer, Tom 22

I

Ibarra, Luis 168
Inoki, Antonio 68
IBF, formation of 71
Ioka, Hiroki 171
Ishimatsu, Guts 134–5
Ivy, Bobby 'Poison' 145

J

Jack, Beau 132–3, *133*
Jackson, Fred 160
Jackson, John **15–16**, *15*, **190**, *192*
Jackson, Julian 111
Jackson, Peter *31*, 33
Jackson, Tommy 'Hurricane' 54
Jacob, Thierry 160
Jacobs, Joe 44
Jacobs, Mike 44–9
Jadick, Johnny 124
Jaks, Vilda 95
Jeby, Ben 95
Jeffra, Harry 145, 156
Jeffries, James J. *33*, 33–4, 36–7, *37*, **191**, *191*, **211**
Jofre, Eder 147–8, 153, 158–9, **191**
Johansson, Ingemar *55*, 55–6, **191**
Johnson, Fred 142
Johnson, Harold 84
Johnson, Jack 29, 34–5, *35–7*, **36–8**, 93, **211**
Johnson, Jim 37
Johnson, Marvin 86
Johnson, Tom 13–14
Johnson, Vonzell 87
Jones, Aaron 20–1
Jones, Colin 122
Jones, Doug 59, 63, 84
Jones, Eddie 85
Jones, Gorilla 95–6
Jones, Leroy 70
Jones, Paddington 16
Jones, Percy 164
Jones, Ralph 'Tiger' 99
Jordan, Ben 142
Jordan, Don **118–19**
Jorgensen, Paul 138
Joseph, Young 115
Joyce, Willie 124
Juchau, Tom 13
Jurich, Jackie 166

K

Kacar, Slobodan 87
Kalambay, Sumba 107–8
Kalule, Ayub 110–11, 122
Kameda, Akio 127
Kane, Peter 166
Kansas, Rocky 132
Kaplan, Louis 'Kid' 144
Kates, Richie 86
Kearns, Jack 'Doc' 38
Kelly, Brian 85
Kelly, Hugo 80
Kelly, John 92
Kelly, Tommy 154
Kendall, Andy 85
Kenty, Hilmer 135
Ketchel, Stanley 36, 91, 93, *93*, 114, **192**
Kid, Dixie 114
Kilbane, Johnny 141, 143
Kilrain, Jake 26–7, *27*, 30–1
King, Don 72
King, Mick 94
King, Tom 24
Kingpetch, Pone 163, 166–7
Klaus, Frank 93–4
Klick, Frankie 138, 144
Kotey, David 148
Kramer, Danny 144
Krieger, Solly 96
Kwon, Soon-Chun 161, 170

L

LaBarba, Fidel 144, 163, 165
La Blanche, George 92
Labrowitz, Barney 80–1
Laciar, Santos 161, 163, 169
Ladbury, Bill 164
Laguna, Ismael 133
Lalonde, Don 88
La Morte, Willie 165
LaMotta, Jake 83, 91, **97–8**, **193**, **214**
Lane, Kenny 124, 133
Langan, Jack 18
Langford, Sam 35
Langham, Nat 92
Language, additions to 9
Larkin, Tippy 124, 132
La Rocca, Mino 122
Larson, Knud 156
LaStarza, Roland 51–2
Lastra, Cecilio 147–8
Latzo, Pete 82, 116
Lavigne, George 'Kid' 114, 130
Layne, Alfredo 139
Lazzaro, Vincent 95
Ledoux, Charles 154
Ledoux, Scott 70
Lee, Glen 96
Lee, Seung-Hoon 160–1
Lee, Tancy 164
Lee, William 'Caveman' 105
Legra, Jose 147
Lemos, Richie 145
Leon, Caspar 154
Leonard, Benny 115, 129, 132, **193**
Leonard, Sugar Ray 88, **106–7**, *107–8*, 110, 121–2, *122*, **193**, *193*, **217**
Lesnevich, Gus *49*, 50, 83
Levinsky, Battling 80–1
Lewis, Harry 115
Lewis, Hedgemon 120
Lewis, John Henry 82–3
Lewis, Ted 'Kid' *81*, *115*, **115**, **194**
Lewis, Willie 115
Licata, Tony 104
Limon, Rafael 139
Liotta, Leonard 118
Liston, Sonny *29*, *58*, **57–60**, 62, 76, **194**, *194*
Little, Freddie 109
Loche, Nicolino 125
Lockridge, Rocky 139, 149
Logart, Isaac 118
Lomsky, Leo 82
London, Brian 54–5, 63
Lonsdale, Lord 124
Lopez, Alfonso 168
Lopez, Danny 'Red' 148, *148*
Lopez, Ernie 120
Lopez, Tony 139
Lopez, Yacqui 76, 86–7
Lopopolo, Sandro 125
Lora, Miguel 153, 160, *160*
Loughran, Tommy 79, 82, **195**
Louis, Joe **44–50**, **45**, 51, 83, **195**, *195*
Louis, Young Joe 76
Lucas, Pretty Boy 171
Lujan, Jorga 159
Lyle, Ron 67–8
Lynch, Benny 163, *165*, 165–6, **196**, *196*
Lynch, Joe 150, 155, *155*, 164
Lyons, Tom 13

M

McAuley, Dave 'Boy' 169–70, *169–70*
McAuliffe, Jack 130
McAvoy, Jock 82–3, 95
McCaffrey, Dominic 30
McCallum, Mike 108, **111**
McCarthy, Billy 92
McCarthy, Cal 142
McCoole, Mick 24–5
McCormick, Tom 115
McCoy, Al 94
McCoy, Johnny 165
McCoy, Kid 80, 92, 114
McCrory, Milton 111, 122
MacDonald, Jim 88
MacDonald, Rod 76
McFarland, Packy 132
McGirt, James 127
McGoorty, Eddie 94
McGovern, Terry 142, *143*, 154, 197
McGowan, Walter 167
McGuigan, Barry *143*, 149
McIntosh, Hugh D. 35
McKay, Sandy 19
McKeever, Charley 114
McKenzie, Duke *163*, 170
McLagen, Victor 36
McLarnin, Jimmy 116–17, 124, *125*, 132, 165, **197**
McNeeley, Ted 56
McTigue, Mick 81–2
McVey, Sam 35
Mace, Jem 24, 24–5, 30, **196**
Machin, Eddie 62
Mack, Marvin 89
Macone, Harry 18
Madden, Owney 43
Maddox, George 16
Madera, Lupe 171
Magri, Charlie *163*, 168
Maher, Peter 32
Maier, Dave 82
Malone, Jock 94
Mamakos, Steve 96
Mamby, Saoul 126
Mancini, Ray 136
Mandell, Sammy 132
Manly, Joe 127
Mann, Nathan 46
Manning, Percy 120
Mantell, Frank 93
Marcano, Alfredo 138, 148
Marciano, Rocky **51–4**, *53*, 84, **196**, *196*, **214**, *215*
Marino, Dado 166
Marino, Tony 156
Marsh, Terry 127, *127*
Martelli, Mauro 123
Martin, Eddie 156
Martin, Jerry 87
Martin, Leotis 64
Martinez, Emilio 83
Martinez, Hilario 116
Martinez, Mario 142
Martinez, Rodolfo 158
Martinez, Valentin 171
Martinez, Vince 118
Mathebula, Peter 169
Mathieson, Johnny 115
Mathis, Buster 65, 102
Matthews, Harry 51, 53
Matthews, Matty 114
Mattioli, Rocky 110, *110*
Maturana, Miguel 160
Mauriello, Tami 48, 83
Maxim, Joey 49–51, 54, 83–4, 99
Mayweather, Roger 127, 139
Medal, Mark 111
Meggs, George 13
Mehegan, Hughie 132
Mellody, Billy 'Honey' 113–15
Mendes, Ramon 104
Mendoza, Daniel **14–15**, *14*
Menetrey, Roger 120
Mercedes, Eloncio 168
Meza, Juan 'Kid' 151
Michael, Barry 139
Mildenberger, Karl 63–4
Miller, Freddie 144
Milligan, Tommy 94
Mills, Freddie 83, **197**
Millson, George 13
Minter, Alan *104*, 105
Miranda, Mario 148
Miske, Billy 38
Mitchell, Brian 139
Mitchell, Charlie 26, 30, 32
Mitchell, Myron 'Pinkie' 124
Mitchell, Ritchie 132
Mitri, Tiberio 98
Mohatar, Mimoun 121
Molina, Juan 139
Molinares, Tomas 123
Molyneaux, Tom 7, *17*, 21
Monaghan, Rinty *49*, 166
Monson, Carlos 91, **102–4**, *103*
Montana, Small *165*, 166
Montano, Tony 109
Montgomery, Bob 133, *133*
Monzon, Carlos 120, 197
Moore, Archie 49, 53–4, 59, 79–80, **84**, *84*, 99, **198**, 216
Moore, Davey 110–11, 146
Moore, Pal 164
Moran, Azael 159
Moran, Frank 37–8
Moran, Owen 131, 143, 154
Moreno, Ricardo 146
Morgan, Tod 138
Morrissey, John 22–3
Moyer, Denny 102, 109, 119
Mugabi, John 'The Beast' 106, 111
Muguruma, Takuya 159
Muhammad, Matthew Saad 86–7
Muhammad, Mustapha 86–7
Muhammed, Prince 87
Mundine, Tony 104
Muniz, Armando 120–1
Munroe, Jack 34
Murata, Eijiro 159
Murphy, Billy 142
Murphy, Bob 83
Murphy, Frank 142
Murphy, Johnny 154
Murphy, Kid 154
Murphy, Lee Roy 76

N

Nakayama, Waruinge 150
'Napoleon of the Ring' 21
Napoles, Jose 103, 120, *120*, **198**
NBA, formation of 49, 61
Navarro, Ruben 134, 138
Nazario, Juan 137
Neat, Bill 17–18
Needham, Danny 114
Neil, Frankie 154
Nelson, Azumah 139, 141, 148–9
Nelson, Battling 129, 131, *131*, 211
Neusel, Walter 46
Nicholls, George 16, 82
'No Decision' bouts 38
Noel, Claude 135–6
Norris, James D. 49
Norton, Ken 66, 68
Nova, Lou 48
Nunn, Michael 'Second To' 108

O

O'Brien, Philadelphia Jack 35, 80, 92–3
O'Connell, Paddy 19
O'Donnell, Steve 32–3
O'Dowd, Mike 94
O'Grady, Sean 135–6
O'Keefe, Pat 93
O'Kelly, Captain Dennis 13
O'Rourke, Samuel 19, 22
Obed, Elisha 109–10
Obelmejias, Fuljencio 89, 105
Ocasio, Osvaldo 69, 76–7
Ohba, Masao 167–8
Olajide, Michael 107
Olin, Bob 82–3
Oliva, Patrizio 126
Olivares, Ruben 147–8, 153, 158, **198**
Oliver, Tom 18
Olivo, Joey 171
Olsen, Carl 'Bobo' 84, 98–9
Oma, Lee 50
Orme, Harry 20, 92
Orono, Rafael 160–1
Orozio, Felipe 151
Ortega, Gasper 118
Ortega, Rafael 147
Ortiz, Carlos 124, 133–4, **198**
Ortiz, Manuel 153, 156, 166, 198
Otti, Emanuel 89
Overlin, Ken 96
Owen, Johnny 158–9
Ozaki, Fujio 123

P

Pace, George 156
Paddock, Tom 20, 23
Paez, Jorge 149
Page, Greg 71
Painter, Ned 18
Palacios, Jose 121
Palma, Sergio 150
Palmer, Thomas 'Pedlar' 154
Palomino, Carlos 120
Papke, Billy 91, *93*, 93
Papp, Laszlo 85
Paret, Benny 'Kid' 101, 119, *119*
Park, Chan-He 168
Park, Cho-Woon 170–1
Park, Chong-Pal 89
Parkey, Rickey 76
Parlov, Mate 86
Pasireron, Polly 89
Paster, Bob 48
Pastrano, Willie 84
Paterson, Jackie 166
Patterson, Floyd **54–8**, *55*, *57*, *61*, 61–2, 64–5, **199**, *199*
Paul, Jimmy 136
Paul, Melvin 136
Paul, Tommy **144**
Pazienza, Vinny 127, 136
Pearce, Henry 16
Pedroza, Eusebio 141, 148–9, *149*, 159, **199**
Pedroza, Rafael 161
Pelkey, Arthur 37
Pender, Paul 100–1
Penalosa, Dodie 170–1
Pep, Willie 141, 145–6, *145*, **200**
Perez, Pascual 163, 166, **200**
Perez, Victor 'Young' 165
Perkins, Eddie 124–5
Perrata, Gregario 84
Perrin, Jimmy 145
Perrins, Isaac 13
Perry, William 20–1
Petrolle, Billy 132
Phal, Louis 81, *82*
Phelps, Bill 19
Piaskowy, Gerhard 109
Pilleteri, Antonio 124
Pinango, Bernardo 151, 159
Pinder, Enrique 158–9
Pintor, Lupe 150–1, *151*, 158–9
Pipes, Tom 10
Pitalua, Alfredo 135
Pladner, Emile 165
Plimmer, Billy 154
Pompey, Yolande 84
Poulson, Harry 20

Pratesi, Honore 166
Primera, Luis 122
Pryor, Aaron 126, **200**

Q

Qawi, Dwight Muhammad 76–7, *77*, 87
Quarry, Jerry 64–5, 68
Queensbury Rules 7, 25–6

R

Ramirez, Jose Luis 136–7
Ramos, Ultimo 'Sugar' 134, 146
Randall, Jack 92, 130
Randolph, Leo 150
Ranzany, Pete 121
Ratcliff, Alfonso 76
Reagan, Johnny 92, 142
Reyes, Antonio 127
Richmond, Bill 16–17, 21
Richardson, Greg 151
Rickard, Tex 38–41, 102, 130, *131*
Risko, Babe 95–6
Risko, Johnny 41
Ritchie, Willie 129, 131–2
Rivera, Antonio 149
Rivers, Joe 131–2, 212
Roach, Lavern 97
Robertson, Floyd 146
Robinson, Sen 110
Robinson, Sugar Ray 83, 91, *98*, **98–100**, *100*, 108, 118, **200**, *201*, **215**
Robles, Rudy 104
Rodak, Leo 145
Rodriguez, Edouardo 122
Rodriguez, Lucien 71
Rodriguez, Luis 102, 119–20
Rojas, Jesus 161
Rojas, Paul 147
Roldan, Juan 106, 108
Romero, Orlando 136
Rondon, Vincente 85
Rooke, George 92
Root, Jack 34, 80
Rosario, Edwin 136–7, *137*
Rose, Lionel 158
Rosenberg, Charlie 'Phil' 156
Rosenberg, Dave 94
Rosenbloom, Maxie 82
Rosi, Gianfranco 111
Rosner, Johnny 164
Ross, Barney 96, 117, 124, 132, 201
Ross, Hugh 94
Rossman, Mike 86
Rottoli, Angelo 77
Rouse, Roger 85
Routis, Andre 144
Ruffin, Bobby 145
Ruhlin, Gus 33–4
Ruthaly, Janos 80
Ryan, Paddy 25, *25*
Ryan, Tommy 30, 80, 92–3, 114, **201**

S

Saddler, Sandy 138, 141, 145–6, *145*, **201**
Saijyo, Shozo 147
Salas, Lauro 133, 138
Salavarria, Erbito 167–8
Saldano, Horacio 120
Saldivar, Vicente 141, 146, *146*, **202**
Salica, Lou 156
Sanabria, Jose 151
Sanchez, Clemente 147
Sanchez, Elroy 158
Sanchez, Salvador 141, 148, *148*, 150, 202
Sanders, Ed 55
Sandeyrou, Maurice 166
Sandoval, Richard 159
Sanstol, Pete 156
Santana, Miguel 136
Santos, Carlos 111
Santry, Eddie 142
Sarron, Petey 144
Savold, Lee 49–51
Saxton, Johnny 118
Sayers, Tom **21**, *21*, 23, *23*, 92, **202**, **210**
Schmeling, Max 41–7, *42*, *45*, 116, **202**
Schwarz, Izzy 156, 165
Scott, Fraser 102
Scott, 'Phainting' Phil 42
Seabrooke, Kelvin 160
Sears, David 87–8
Sekorski, Rod 76
Sequenan, Rod 139
Serrano, Sam 138–9
Shaaf, Eddie 43
Shank, Reuben 97
Sharkey, Jack 41–4, 82, 202
Sharkey, Tom 33
Shavers, Earnie 68–9
Shibata, Kuniaki 138, 147
Shields, Randy 121–2
Shingaki, Satoshi 160, 171
Shipes, Charlie 120
Sibson, Tony 88, *88*, 105, *108*, 108
Siki, Battling 81, *82*
Simon, Abe 47–8
Sims, Robbie 108
Singer, Al 132
Slack, Jack 12–13
Skouma, Said 111
Slattery, Jimmy 81–2
Slaughter, Sammy 95
Slavin, Frank 27, 30
Smith, Gunboat 37
Smith, James 'Bonecrusher' 72–4
Smith, Jeff 94
Smith, Jem 26–7, 30
Smith, John (Noted Buckhorse) 10
Smith, Kosie 86
Smith, Lonnie 127
Smith, Midget 155
Smith, Mysterious Billy 114, 203
Smith, Wallace 'Bud' 133
Smith, Willie 156
Snipes, Renaldo 71
Solis, Julian 159
Solomons, Jack *49*, 49
Soose, Billy 96
Sorimachi, Ryu 109, 121
Spinks, Leon 68, *69*, 71–2, 76, **203**, *203*
Spinks, Michael 29, 73, 75, *75*, 79, **87**, **203**
Spring, Tom 18
Squires, Bill 35
Stacey, John H. 120, *120*
Stafford, Roger 122
Stander, Ron 65
Stanley, George 'Digger' 154
Starling, Marlon 122–3
Stecca, Louis 150
Steele, Freddie 95–6
Stephens, Randy 76
Stevens, Bill 13
Stevenson, George 10
Stewart, Leslie 87–8
Stillman, Abe 82
Stribling, Young 81
Sullivan, Dave 142
Sullivan, Jack 93
Sullivan, Jim 93
Sullivan, John L. 7, 25–7, *26–7*, 30–2, 102, **204**
Sullivan, Mike 93, 114
Sullivan, Steve 'Kid' 138
Sullivan, Tommy 143
Sutherland, Murray 87, 89
Swift, Owen 19
Symonds, Joe 164

T

Takayama, Katsuyoshi 167
Tangstad, Steffan 73
Tarleton, Nel 144
Tate, John 69–70
Tate, Frank 107–8
Taylor, Arnold 159
Taylor, Bernard 149
Taylor, Charles 'Bud' 156
Taylor, George 10
Taylor, Meldrick 127
Tendler, Lew 132
Terranova, Phil 145
Terrell, Ernie 62–4
Tessman, Mark 85
Thil, Marcel 95–6
Thomas, Duane 111
Thomas, Harry 46
Thomas, Joe 95
Thomas, Pinklon 71–2, 74, 76
Thomas, Tiger 95
Thompson, William **19**, *19*, **176**
Thompson, Young Jack 116
Thornton, Wayne 85
Tiger, Dick 85, 101, **204**
Tillis, James 'Quick' 70, *77*
Torres, Battling 124–5
Torres, Elfren 167
Torres, Jose 85
Toweel, Vic 156–7
Toweel, Willie 158
Traversaro, Aldo 86
Trice, Tyrone 123
Tubbs, Tony 72, 75
Tucker, Tony 74
Tunney, Gene *40–1*, 40–1, 95, **204**, **212**
Turpin, Randolph *49*, 91, *98*, **98–9**, **204**
Tyson, Mike 29, **72–5**, *73*, *74*, 79, *173*, 205, *205*

U

Udella, Franco 170–1
Uehara, Flipper 147–8
Ursua, Amado 171
Uzcudun, Paolino 41, 43

Acknowledgements

Action Images: 77(b), 106(l), 112/13, 126/7, 128/9, 137(t). Allsport/Roger Gould (Australia): 152/3. Allsport (U.K.) Ltd: 4, 59, 70(l), 73, 74, 77(t), 78/9, 86, 87, 88, 90/1, 104, 105, 106(r), 107, 108, 122, 123, 137(b), 140/1, 162/3, 183, 184, 188, 189(t), 190, 193, 205, 218/19, 222, 232, 242. Associated Press: 120/1, 134, 135, 151, 157, 160/1, 164/5, 208/9, 229, 231, 236, 243. Colorsport: 68(tl,b), 70(r), 75, 172/3, 174, 185, 186, 189(b), 203, 220, 237. Mary Evans Picture Library: 8, 9, 12, 22. Michael Holford: 6/7. Hulton Deutsch Collection: 15, 60, 98/9, 103, 116, 143 Bettman Archive, 194, 207, 213, 245, 246, 249. Peter Newark's Historical Pictures: 11, 14, 16, 17, 18, 19, 21, 23, 24, 25, 26(tl,tr), 27, 30, 31, 32, 33, 34, 35, 36, 37, 38, 39, 40, 41, 42, 43, 44, 45, 46, 47, 48/9, 50, 51, 53, 58, 61, 62/3, 64, 65, 66/7, 68(tr), 81, 82, 84/5, 93, 95, 97, 100, 115, 117, 125, 130(l,r), 133, 145, 167, 177, 179, 180, 181, 182, 187, 191, 192, 195, 196(l,r), 199, 201, 206, 210, 214/15, 215, 226, 234/5, 240. Pacemaker Press International Ltd: 168/9, 170. Popperfoto: 28/9, 55, 57, 89, 146/7, 148, 155, 159, 216/17. Sporting Pictures (UK) Ltd: 110. Topham Picture Library: 119, 149, 228.

V

Vaca, Jorge 123
Valdez, Rodrigo 103–4
Valentino, Pat 50
Velasquez, Ramon 134
Valoy, Tommy 150
Vasquez, Wilfredo 160, *160*
Villa, Pancho 163–5, **206**
Villaflor, Ben 138–9
Volbrecht, Harold 121, 123

W

Wajima, Koichi 109–10
Walcott, Jersey Joe 48–52, *51*, 62, 114, 130, 206, *206*, **214**, *214–15*
Walker, Mickey 82, 89, 91, 94–5, **115–16**, *116*, **206**
Wallace, Nunc 154
Walsh, Andy 114
Walsh, Jimmy 154
Ward, Bill 15
Ward, Jem 18, 20
Warren, Frankie 127
Watson, Seaman Tommy 144
Watson, William 31
Watt, Jim 129, 135–6, *137*
Weaver, Mike 69–72
Webb, Spider 100
Wells, Matt 115
Welsh, Freddy 129, 132, 206
Wepner, Chuck 67
West, Tommy 93, 114
Weston, Harold 121
Whitaker, Bob 10
Whitaker, Pernell 137
White, Charley 132
White, Slugger 133
Whitfield, Ted 120
Wilde, Jimmy 155, *155*, 163–5, *167*, **207**
Willard, Jess *38*, 38
Williams, Carl 72
Williams, Cleveland 63
Williams, Ike 124, 133
Williams, Kid 154–5
Williams, 'Prince' Charles 88
Williams, Tom 114
Williamson, J.B. 87
Willis, John 23
Wills, Harry 40
Wilson, Joe 164
Wilson, Johnny 94
Wilson, Tug 102
Winstone, Howard 146, *146*
Winter, Tom 18
Witherspoon, Tim 71–3, 76
Wolfe, Jack 'Kid' 150
Wolgast, Ad 129, 131, 212
Wolgast, Midget 165–6
Woodcock, Bruce 49–50
WBA, coming into existence 61, 103
WBC, creation of 61, 103
Wright, Albert 'Chalky' 145

Y

Yamabe, Buzzsaw 138–9
Yankee Sullivan 22–3
Yarosz, Teddy 95
Young, David 156
Young, Jimmy 68
Young, Paddy 99

Z

Zale, Tony 91, 96, **96–7**, *97*, **207**, *207*, 213, *213*
Zapata, Hilario 169–70
Zaragoza, Daniel 151, 160
Zarate, Carlos 150–1, 158
Zivic, Fritzie 117–18